Fodor's

MOROCCO

WELCOME TO MOROCCO

For centuries, Morocco has inspired travelers with its colorful energy, fascinating history, and dazzling combination of Arab, European, and African influence. From vibrant and bustling medinas to the sparse but breathtaking Sahara, the country packs a remarkable variety of adventures into its corner of North Africa. Surfers catch waves at windswept Atlantic coast beaches and hikers trek the scenic Atlas Mountains. Kasbahs and mosques offer a glimpse of a more mystical time, while hip cafés and high-design riads reflect Moroccans' modern, cosmopolitan side.

TOP REASONS TO GO

★ **Exotic Cities:** Sultry Marrakesh, market-filled Fez, historic Rabat.

★ **History:** Ancient ruins, mosques, and Berber villages invite discovery.

★ **Beaches:** From Agadir to Essaouira, surfing and sunbathing abound.

★ **Souks:** Traditional crafts, leather, rugs, and more are for sale in bright markets.

★ **Food and Drink:** Stewed tagines, saffron couscous, smoked zaalouk, mint tea.

★ **Trekking:** The rugged High Atlas and vast Sahara await exploration by camel or on foot.

Fodor's MOROCCO

Publisher: Amanda D'Acierno, *Senior Vice President*

Editorial: Arabella Bowen, *Editor in Chief*; Linda Cabasin, *Editorial Director*

Design: Tina Malaney, *Associate Art Director*; Chie Ushio, *Senior Designer*; Ann McBride, *Production Designer*

Photography: Jennifer Arnow, *Senior Photo Editor*; Jennifer Romains, *Photo Researcher*

Production: Linda Schmidt, *Managing Editor*; Evangelos Vasilakis, *Associate Managing Editor*; Angela L. McLean, *Senior Production Manager*

Maps: Rebecca Baer, *Senior Map Editor*; David Lindroth, Mark Stroud (Moon Street Cartography) *Cartographers*

Sales: Jacqueline Lebow, *Sales Director*

Marketing & Publicity: Heather Dalton, *Marketing Director*; Katherine Punia, *Publicity Director*

Business & Operations: Susan Livingston, *Vice President, Strategic Business Planning*; Sue Daulton, *Vice President, Operations*

Fodors.com: Megan Bell, *Executive Director, Revenue & Business Development*; Yasmin Marinaro, *Senior Director, Marketing & Partnerships*

Copyright © 2015 by Fodor's Travel, a division of Random House LLC

Writers: Rachel Blech, Olivia Gunning Bennani, Sarah Gilbert, Safia Shah, Lynn Sheppard, Joe Worthington

Lead Editor: Amanda Sadlowski

Editors: Mike Dunphy, Denise Leto, Sue MacCallum-Whitcomb
Production Editor: Jennifer DePrima

6th Edition

ISBN 978-1-101-87800-2

ISSN 1527-4829

All details in this book are based on information supplied to us at press time. Always confirm information when it matters, especially if you're making a detour to visit a specific place. Fodor's expressly disclaims any liability, loss, or risk, personal or otherwise, that is incurred as a consequence of the use of any of the contents of this book.

SPECIAL SALES

This book is available at special discounts for bulk purchases for sales promotions or premiums. For more information, e-mail specialmarkets@penguinrandomhouse.com

PRINTED IN THE UNITED STATES OF AMERICA

10 9 8 7 6 5 4 3 2 1

CONTENTS

ABOUT
THIS GUIDE

Fodor's Recommendations

Everything in this guide is worth doing—we don't cover what isn't—but exceptional sights, hotels, and restaurants are recognized with additional accolades. Fodor'sChoice★ indicates our top recommendations; and **Best Bets** call attention to notable hotels and restaurants in various categories. Care to nominate a new place? Visit Fodors.com/contact-us.

Trip Costs

We list prices wherever possible to help you budget well. Hotel and restaurant price categories from $ to $$$$ are noted alongside each recommendation. For hotels, we include the lowest cost of a standard double room in high season. For restaurants, we cite the average price of a main course at dinner or, if dinner isn't served, at lunch. For attractions, we always list adult admission fees; discounts are usually available for children, students, and senior citizens.

Hotels

Our local writers vet every hotel to recommend the best overnights in each price category, from budget to expensive. Unless otherwise specified, you can expect private bath, phone, and TV in your room. For expanded hotel reviews, facilities, and deals visit Fodors.com.

Top Picks	Hotels &
★ Fodor'sChoice	Restaurants
	Hotel
Listings	Number of rooms
⊠ Address	❍1 Meal plans
⊠ Branch address	✕ Restaurant
☎ Telephone	Reservations
🖷 Fax	Dress code
⊕ Website	No credit cards
✑ E-mail	$ Price
Admission fee	**Other**
⊙ Open/closed times	⇨ See also
Ⓜ Subway	☞ Take note
⊹ Directions or Map coordinates	Golf facilities

Restaurants

Unless we state otherwise, restaurants are open for lunch and dinner daily. We mention dress code only when there's a specific requirement and reservations only when they're essential or not accepted. To make restaurant reservations, visit Fodors.com.

Credit Cards

The hotels and restaurants in this guide typically accept credit cards. If not, we'll say so.

EUGENE FODOR

Hungarian-born Eugene Fodor (1905–91) began his travel career as an interpreter on a French cruise ship. The experience inspired him to write *On the Continent* (1936), the first guidebook to receive annual updates and discuss a country's way of life as well as its sights. Fodor later joined the U.S. Army and worked for the OSS in World War II. After the war, he kept up his intelligence work while expanding his guidebook series. During the Cold War, many guides were written by fellow agents who understood the value of insider information. Today's guides continue Fodor's legacy by providing travelers with timely coverage, insider tips, and cultural context.

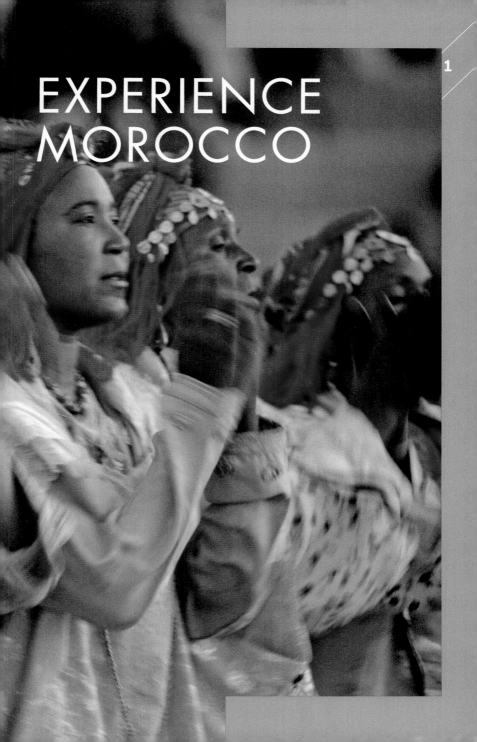

EXPERIENCE
MOROCCO

WHAT'S WHERE

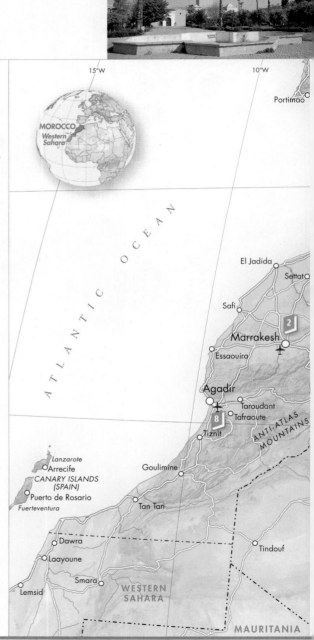

Numbers refer to chapters.

2 Marrakesh. Marrakesh is the turning point between Morocco's north and south, Arab and Berber, big city and small town. If you see only one city in Morocco, make it Marrakesh.

3 Tangier and the Mediterranean. Many of Morocco's most dramatic social and economic contrasts are immediately and painfully evident in Tangier and vicinity. Both the mountain stronghold at Chefchaouen and the coastal city of Tetouan are also worth visiting.

4 Rabat and Casablanca. Morocco's economic capital, Casablanca, and political capital, Rabat, are the country's most Europeanized cities. Meanwhile, the Atlantic beaches offer miles and miles of wild surf, sand, and sea.

5 Fez and the Middle Atlas. The Arab-Islamic and Berber chapters in Morocco's history are most evident in the cities of Fez and Meknès. Side trips to the Roman ruins at Volubilis and the holy town of Moulay Idriss are musts, while the Middle Atlas is an underrated mountain range of great natural beauty.

6 The High Atlas. Although parts of the High Atlas can be mobbed with hikers at

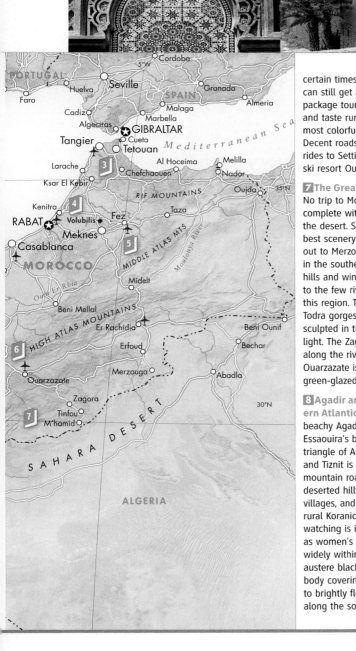

certain times of year, you can still get away from the package tours on foot or mule and taste rural Morocco at its most colorful and hospitable. Decent roads offer pleasant rides to Setti Fatma and the ski resort Oukaïmeden.

7 The Great Oasis Valleys. No trip to Morocco is complete without a taste of the desert. Some of Morocco's best scenery is on the way out to Merzouga or M'Hamid in the southeast, where arid hills and winding oases cling to the few rivers that sustain this region. The Dadès and Todra gorges seem impossibly sculpted in the late afternoon light. The Zagora Valley along the river Drâa south of Ouarzazate is known for its green-glazed pottery.

8 Agadir and the Southern Atlantic Coast. Busy, beachy Agadir contrasts with Essaouira's breezy grace. The triangle of Agadir, Tafraoute, and Tiznit is formed by curvy mountain roads studded with deserted hilltop kasbahs, villages, and centuries-old rural Koranic schools. People-watching is interesting here, as women's wraps vary widely within the region, from austere black or navy full-body coverings in Taroudant to brightly flowered garments along the southern coast.

MOROCCO TODAY

Politics

Following the fall of regimes in Tunisia, Libya, Egypt, and Yemen, and major unrest in neighboring Algeria, the world's gaze shifted nervously to Morocco. Widely regarded as the most moderate and stable of North African nations, the kingdom acted fast to appease dissenters. Although a cautious modernizer in the past, King Mohammed VI, who had already introduced some economic and social liberalization, revised the constitution in 2011 in response to "Arab Spring" protests and appointed a new government in January 2012. His ability to calm his populace, most of whom remember the far fiercer reign of his father, Hassan II, ensured the stability of his kingdom and won him the trust of Western nations. Encouraged by Mohammed VI's popularity with his people and his crackdown on suspected Islamic militants after deadly suicide bombings in Casablanca in 2003, Washington granted Morocco the status of non-NATO ally.

Despite the close proximity of the kingdom to Europe (it almost touches Spain in its north and was once ruled by France), Morocco remains friendly with the continent, but staunchly independent. Long-term efforts by the UN have tried to end the political deadlock that continues in the Western Sahara, which Morocco seized after Mauritania and Spain withdrew in 1970s, with little success.

Economy

Morocco is lucky to enjoy a vibrant and expanding tourist trade; a good annual supply of exports in the form of handicrafts, fruits, vegetables, nuts, and oils; and an economy that has so far resisted the prolonged recession experienced by its European neighbors. As with other African countries, the kingdom's principal wealth comes from natural resources, with Morocco's key raw material being phosphate (used in pesticides, animal feed, and fertilizers). The Moroccan economy remained resilient in 2013, with a growth rate of 4.7%, bolstered by political and social stability. Despite these factors, the country has found it increasingly hard to tackle youth unemployment, which stood around 19% in 2013 and continues to cause concern, due to the vulnerability of the nation's young men to radicalization. In a bid to disperse dissent, there has been a push in recent years to clear the shantytowns common in the major cities and move squatters into specially constructed concrete residences out of town.

Women's Rights

In recent years, King Mohammed VI has had to balance the demands of feminist organizations, calling for an expansion of women's rights, with resistance from the country's Islamic political parties, who fiercely oppose change. A decade ago, Morocco made sweeping reforms to its family-law code, the Moudawana, creating one of the most progressive family codes in the Arab world. The new Moudawana gives women significantly more rights and protections. They now have the right to request a divorce, the legal age of marriage has leapt from 15 to 18, and polygamy is now severely restricted. Women also now have the right to child support and shared custody. Three years ago, the country passed a new constitution guaranteeing gender equality. That said, incongruities concerning women's rights remain, with inheritance laws still strongly in favor of male heirs (they receive double that received by women). Meanwhile, inequality in pay remains the norm, and judges are not averse to finding ways around the new laws (there are reports that courts are granting permission for the marriage of minors in 90% of the cases appearing before them).

Religion

An estimated 99% of Moroccans are Muslim, with the king being able to trace his lineage to the Prophet Mohammed. The second religion is Christianity, which predates Islam; Moroccans are, on the whole, tolerant of other people's beliefs. As in most Islamic countries, a faith of any sort is easier to understand than no faith at all. Prayers are said five times a day, with men tending to gather in mosques upon hearing the call to prayer. It is common to see men praying elsewhere, such as by the side of the road, in fields, or even corners of the office. Women tend to pray only in the home and seldom stop work to pray in public throughout the day. It is considered highly impolite to interrupt a person who is praying and advisable not to cross in front of them. Fasting takes place during the holy month of Ramadan, which falls in the ninth month of the lunar cycle, and it is the desire of all Muslims to make the pilgrimage, or Hajj, to Mecca at least once.

Despite a close regard for Islam, Moroccans tend to interpret its laws in a less conservative way than many Muslim lands. Travelers familiar with other Islamic nations, such as Pakistan or Saudi Arabia, may be surprised by the fact that modesty in women's dress emphasizes covering the skin rather than disguising the female form. It is not uncommon to see young girls wearing skin-tight jeans with long-sleeve T-shirts and headscarves, rather than the voluminous coverings commonly seen in other Muslim regions. Female visitors find it useful to carry a long scarf or sarong to cover their shoulders or hair upon occasion. There are times when bare arms and low necklines attract unwelcome attention. Similarly, beachwear, shorts, and skirts above the knee are best restricted to the beach. Men are not expected to wear shorts in formal or mixed company and should never go bare-chested anywhere but the beach.

Music

Music is integral to daily and ritual life in Morocco, both for enjoyment and as social commentary. It emanates from homes, stores, markets, and public squares everywhere. *Joujouka* music is perhaps the best known, but every region has its own sound. In the Rif you hear men singing poetry accompanied by guitar and high-pitched women's choruses; in Casablanca, *rai* (opinion) music, born of social protest, keeps young men company on the streets; cobblers in the Meknès medina may work to the sound of violin-based Andalusian classical music or the more folksy Arabic *melhoum,* or "sung poetry." You know you've reached the south when you hear the banjo strum of Marrakesh's roving storytellers. *Gnaoua* music is best known for its use in trance rituals but has become a popular form of street entertainment; the performers' brass *qraqeb* hand cymbals and cowrie-shell-adorned hats betray the music's sub-Saharan origins. This rich culture of sound has been modernized in recent years with fusions of Western-influenced pop music and traditional Moroccan beats. Morocco's music festivals are growing every year in size, quality, and recognition.

MOROCCO PLANNER

Safety

Despite neighboring regime changes, Morocco continues to be a safe and popular tourist destination for international travelers. Throughout the country, modern tourist facilities and transportation are widely available. Though pickpockets are problematic in bustling public areas, souks, and beaches, violent crime is relatively rare in Morocco. Female visitors, especially those traveling alone, may face irritating harassment and unwanted attention from vendors and local men, though it's rarely dangerous. It's best to avoid eye contact, ignore the pestering, and walk away briskly, as you would anywhere in the world. Traveling to remote regions of the country poses no particular safety risks; however, it's best with a qualified guide. Unfortunately, at this writing, the potential for terrorist violence—particularly against U.S. interests and citizens—remains elevated.

When to Go

The best times to go to Morocco are spring and fall, specifically March, April, and October. Spring is ideal—the sky is a beautiful deep blue, washed clear by the winter rain, and wildflowers blanket the landscape. Winter is the best time to see the desert and most of the south; summer is best for exploring the High Atlas. If you like a hot sun, come in July, August, or early September. The period between late September and December is pleasant, with cool evenings. January, February, and March are changeable and sometimes chilly or rainy.

The Atlantic and Mediterranean coastal resorts are crowded during summer for school vacation, so it's best to see the coast another time; June is still warm, and the beaches are much less crowded.

Ramadan is not usually a huge impediment to travel by non-Muslims. However, during this month-long fast all cafés and nearly all restaurants are closed during the day, and the pace of work is reduced. Dates for Ramadan vary annually.

Climate

Morocco enjoys a Mediterranean climate. Inland temperatures are high in summer—sometimes in excess of 104°F (40°C)—and cool in winter. The coastal regions have a more temperate climate, warmer in winter and less brutally hot in summer. Rain falls mainly in winter, from October through March, often with more in November and March. Northern Morocco, especially the Rif Mountains, gets more rain than the south.

Because of these climate variations throughout Morocco, be sure to consult the appropriate chapters for details on each region you plan to visit.

Getting Here

Edged by the Atlantic and the Mediterranean and bordering Algeria to its east, Morocco is most accessible by air or ferry from Spain or Gibraltar. Tourism, world trade, and generally amicable international relations ensure the kingdom is well served by major international airlines and its own national carrier, Royal Air Maroc (RAM). Major points of entry are Tangier port and airport to the north, Casablanca (as the business hub, commands the best international flights), Rabat (despite being the capital is less well connected than Casablanca), Marrakesh and Fez (by far the most popular tourist destinations), and Agadir, the country's popular, southern beach destination. In addition to direct flights, a significant number of tourists reach the country via cruise ship, often as part of a multicountry excursion. Despite sometimes-rough terrain, travelers are not short of transportation options via which to explore the country.

Getting Around

Road conditions are acceptable in Morocco, certainly around the major cities, although driving practices leave much to be desired. The country's transportation infrastructure has grown significantly in recent years and continues to expand. New highways connect many major cities, making it easier for travelers to get from one place to another. Traveling by road between Casablanca and Marrakesh, Tangier, or Agadir is now easy, reliable, and quick. Morocco's first tramway is up and running in Rabat, connecting the country's capital to its sister city, Salé, and helping ease congestion between and within the two. Casablanca has also constructed a tramway. Despite the trams, the nation's cities and villages remain heavily reliant on buses, local taxis, and trains. Rural areas are reasonably well served by Mercedes taxis and coaches, although it is common to see farmers ride all manner of donkey- and mule-pulled carts into town on market day. Also vying for road space are scooters favored by tradesmen, powerful motorbikes, and an assortment of cars, 4x4s, and buses. The rail network is extensive, linking Tangier, Fez, Rabat, Casablanca, Marrakesh, and Agadir. Car-rental companies are becoming more common and reliable, with the best operators available at Casablanca's Mohammed VI airport.

Islam in Morocco

Although deeply committed to Islam, Moroccans are on the whole content to view their faith as a personal contract with their god. Each year, the holy month of Ramadan unites the nation, with many Moroccans living abroad returning to the country in order to observe the fast with their families. During Ramadan, the day is reversed, with only basic jobs getting done during daylight, and meals, and even business activities, moved to the hours between dusk and dawn. Although not always possible, it is generally considered good manners to avoid smoking, eating, and drinking in front of Muslims who are fasting.

QUINTESSENTIAL MOROCCO

Mint Tea

Moroccan mint tea, or *atai* as it is commonly known, plays a vital role in Moroccan culture. Although packed with antioxidants, this green tea blended with mint leaves is the drink of hospitality rather than of health. In a country where women most commonly prepare refreshments in the home, Atai is traditionally a man's affair. Ritually mixed and presented to guests as an ice-breaker, its preparation is considered something of an art form and is relatively complex compared to tea-brewing methods elsewhere. Eye-flickeringly sweet (around five teaspoons of sugar are used per teaspoon of tea) the beverage is poured from a height of around half a meter, resulting in a foamy head and an aerated and aromatic golden liquid. The longer the tea steeps in the pot the stronger it becomes, hence the popular saying: the first glass is as gentle as life, the second glass as strong as love, the third glass as bitter as death.

No social meeting is complete without a minimum of three glasses; the mild digestive is considered so fundamental to almost all daily interactions that it is laughingly referred to as "Berber whiskey." If you are lucky enough to be invited into a Moroccan home, expect to liberally partake of this symbol of friendship; to refuse is viewed as a virtual declaration of hostility. What is more, no business transaction is clinched without the brew, as becomes immediately apparent when haggling in the souks.

The Outdoors

Blessed with endless beaches, mountains, deserts, and plains that stretch as far as the eye can see, Morocco offers travelers multiple chances to embrace the great outdoors. The mainly temperate climate and relatively easy escape from its various urban sprawls make this a country waiting to be

A good start to learning Moroccan culture is to embrace some of the ongoing rituals of daily life. These are a few highlights—customs and sites you can experience with relative ease.

discovered. Whether you hike in the Atlas and climb its snowy peaks, play golf, kite surf on the turbulent waters of the Atlantic, hot-air balloon across desert sands, or ramble by the many waterfalls (look out for native Barbary apes), you are likely to be impressed by the timeless beauty of the landscape. Your journey into these areas of outstanding beauty will not be a lonely one: along the way life is played out in the open, whether goats leisurely chewing at argan trees, hunched countrywomen peacefully herding their cows towards a succulent hibiscus hedging, or small boys playing football around the steep blind bends of the mountain passes. Outdoor excursions are generally easy to organize through a local guide or your hotel.

Markets

Never underestimate what you might find in the souk. From Art Deco gems in Marrakesh's collectibles market to a 1950s food processor in Casablanca's junk market, a fascinating array of items washes up in these bastions of the unexpected. Weekly markets, to which farmers and their families flock, are awash with livestock, fruits, vegetables, spices, and nuts, as well as scented oils, repurposed paint-can buckets, and all manner of animal feed. Next to the baked-clay crockery and fluorescent-pink-and-green popcorn, the apothecary stalls dispense dried chameleons, split rocks with fossils inside, and fragments of meteorite. Look more closely and you might be lucky enough to spot some antique Berber jewelry or a highly collectible white-and-silver wedding blanket. Moroccan markets, souks, and bazaars buzz with life.

MOROCCO
TOP ATTRACTIONS

Ben Youssef Medersa, Marrakesh
(A) The Saadian sultan Abdallah al-Ghallib rebuilt this 9th-century madrassa as the largest Koranic school to rival Imam Fassi's madrassa in Fez. The visual impact is evident in the expansive main courtyard and exquisite tile mosaics. It's one of the best-preserved historic sites in Marrakesh.

Cascades d'Ouzoud, Central High Atlas Mountains
(B) Some 40 miles southwest of Bin el Ouidane, the majestic succession of waterfalls plunging into the canyon of Wadi el-Abid 330 feet below is a natural wonder not to be missed.

Djemâa el Fna and Souks, Marrakesh
Haggle for handmade rugs, leather, silver, and pottery still crafted in ancient artisan workshops. Feast on succulent lamb kebabs, chicken tagine, pigeon pastilla, and vegetable couscous. Sip mint tea. Wend your way through the narrow labyrinth of medina passages and squares.

This must-do experience thrills, entertains, and sometimes overwhelms even the most seasoned traveler.

Erg Chebbi and Erg Chigaga Sand Dunes, near Merzouga
(C) For a once-in-a-lifetime experience, escape into the world of the Berber nomads and explore these windswept Saharan dunes stretching 19 miles and rising to 820 feet.

Essaouira, the Fortified Coastal Town
(D) The rough Atlantic waves pounding against the rocky shoreline add drama to this romantic fortressed fishing village designated a UNESCO World Heritage Site. Stroll along the cannon-lined *sqalas* (sea bastions) toward the ramparts that lead to the picturesque port and medina.

Fez el-Bali (Old City), Fez
(E) Step into a time warp in this 9th-century medina, the world's most active medieval city. With culturally important fondouks, riads, medersas, mosques, and

palaces dating back 1,000 years filling the 9,500 alleyways, it's no surprise Fez el-Bali is a UNESCO World Heritage Site.

Hassan II Mosque, Casablanca

(F) One of the largest mosques in the world covers almost a million square feet and holds up to 25,000 people. Two-thirds of the building is over the sea, where the minaret's light beacon shines 20 miles towards Mecca. It ranks as the country's most exceptional representation of Moroccan artistry for its ornate carved stucco, *zellij* tile work (a type of mosaic), and onyx-and-marble details.

Koutoubia Minaret, Marrakesh

(G) Rising 300 feet, the iconic carved-stone-and-green-tile tower is the architectural centerpiece of the Almohad dynasty. One of the largest mosques of the Western Muslim world, the Koutoubia is off-limits to non-Muslims; its minaret, however, serves as a major orientation point for everyone in the city and captures the collective ear when the imam delivers the daily call to prayer.

Valley of the Kasbahs, near Ouarzazate

(H) Secret gorges. Breathtaking canyons. Spectacular rock formations. In the High Atlas, the stunning Dadès Valley is a mystical region dotted with palm trees and sandstone kasbahs that rise from the barren landscape. To start the magical journey, head to the Aït Ben Haddou, a UNESCO World Heritage Site featured in blockbuster films and only a short distance from the oasis town of Ouarzazate.

TOP EXPERIENCES

Trek the mountains of the High Atlas.
For spectacular vistas and fresh air, the High Atlas is a perfect getaway from the hustle and bustle of urban Morocco. North Africa's tallest peak, Djebel Toubkal, rises to nearly 14,000 feet and is only a two-day climb, best done in late summer. Amateur hikers, with guides, follow less strenuous but equally rewarding routes through rural Berber villages and rocky paths. Head to the Ourika Valley for a variety of outdoor adventure—it's a justifiably popular region to hang glide, ski, or ride mules to hidden waterfalls and tranquil hilltop gardens. The popularity of such outdoor pursuits has really escalated in Morocco in recent years, with world-class operators such as Epic Running offering memorable training camps and excursions.

Support local women by buying direct.
Support female independence with a visit to a fair-trade training center such as the Flying Camel Women's Workshop in the Khouribga–Oued Zem region. Here you can tour the production workshop, see women learning vital new skills, and contribute to their artisan cooperative by buying handmade gifts from their small boutique.

Visit the dye pits of Fez.
Snatch up a generous sprig of mint and courage and make your way to the centuries-old dye pits of the ancient city of Fez. Amid the stench and color you are able to see hides curing in the sun and marvel at the rainbow of hues occupying the vats beneath the terraced rows. This is the place to find beautiful leather wares, from slippers and belts to poufs.

Appreciate Koranic scholarship in a historic medersa.
A quiet spot in front of the central marble ablutions pool is the perfect place to view several masterpieces of Islamic architecture. Look for intricate zellij tile work along arched corridors, ornate wood carvings in domed ceilings, sculpted stone friezes bearing symbolic Arabic calligraphy, and beautifully detailed stained-glass windows in prayer halls and reflection rooms in these culturally rich buildings.

Eat like a local.
Take a break from the predictability of restaurant food and eat on the hoof. Getting hungry in one of the country's major cities? Why not visit the food market, grab some meat or fish, and seek out one of the many local cafés competing to cook it for you? After a few minutes, and fewer dirhams, you have a feast consisting of your now-cooked foods, plus salads, bread, and tongue-tingling soda. Move a step closer to living like a local and invest in a *tanjia* clay pot. Take this to the food market, present it to the butcher, and he'll wordlessly fill it with meat, followed by a handful of spices and vegetables. All you have to do is locate the nearest wood-fired public bath and hand the pot to the furnace stoker, where he'll place it in the embers used to heat the water. Return for a few hours later to find your fragrant meal bubbling, succulent, and ready to melt in your mouth. Want delicious authentic meat dishes but don't want to buy your own ingredients? Head for the nearest gas station, where chances are you'll find a butcher's shop on its forecourt, and beside it an unassuming café that makes the best meat skewers, cutlets, and stews for miles around.

Listen and learn at a local festival.

One of the best ways to experience the rich heritage is to participate in a local event. Head to Kelaâ M'Gouna in the Dadès Valley in May; it's home to the country's largest rosewater distillery plant. Each spring, the small oasis village celebrates the flower harvest. In early June, enjoy the chants, lyricism, and intellectual fervor of international musicians, Sufi scholars, and social activists at the World Sacred Music Festival in Fez. In late June, the traditions of Gnaoua music, a blend of African and Berber song and dance, are celebrated in the seaside resort village of Essaouira. Experience the Imilchil Berber marriage feast in autumn. In December, the Marrakech International Film Festival is the hottest spot for international celebrity sightings. The all-important Eid al-Fitr (Feast of the Fast Breaking) showcases Moroccan tradition with three days of joyous celebration at the end of Ramadan.

Pamper yourself in a hammam.

Getting scrubbed and steamed at a local *hammam* does wonders for the weary. Whether you choose a communal public bath or private room in an upscale riad, this traditional therapy of brisk exfoliation and bathing using natural cleansers has promoted physical and mental hygiene and restoration for centuries. Public hammams are clean and inexpensive. Le Royal Mansour and the Astana Spa in Marrakesh are exceptionally luxurious spots to experience this special cultural ritual. If you do opt for the public baths, rather than the private luxury option, be advised that scrubbing can prove abrasive and often rather intimate.

Relax in a riad.

Spend a night in mosaic splendor in your choice of countless *riads*. Forgo a hotel room and head for a room with authentic charm in one of these hidden gems, most often found in a city's medina. There isn't necessarily air-conditioning, the pool might only be the size of a bathtub, and breakfast most likely is served on the roof, but you'll experience the magic of bygone Morocco, complete with fretwork screens, sumptuous upholsteries, and cool tiled floors.

Soothe the eyes in the blue-washed town of Chefchaouen.

Founded in the 15th century by Spanish exiles, the village of Chefchaouen, in the foothills of the Rif Mountains, is widely considered to be one of Morocco's most picturesque places. Relax beneath verdant shade trees on the cobblestoned Plaza Uta el-Hamman. Ride a camel to the dunes of the Sahara. Wander the steep Andalusian passageways, where buildings bathed in cobalt and indigo hues blend with terracotta-tiled roofs, pink-scarved women, violet blossoms, and ocher-and-poppy-red wool carpets to create a vibrant canvas of color. Ride a camel to the dunes of the Sahara. For an unforgettable adventure, mount a dromedary camel to explore the undulating orange dunes and abandoned kasbahs of the desert, a magical region immortalized in film and fiction. Select an overnight tour to stay in a Bedouin tent in the Erg Chebbi or Erg Chigaga desert wilderness.

IF YOU LIKE

Beaches

With coasts on both the Mediterranean Sea and the Atlantic Ocean, Morocco has hundreds of miles of sandy beaches, many of which remain unspoiled and undeveloped. Dangerous currents and national park preservation explain why some beaches are unused, and litter can be a problem, but nevertheless, gems abound. Surfing the choppy waters of the Atlantic has become a popular pastime for tourists and Moroccans alike, with many top-notch surf schools popping up along the best stretches. The port towns of Essaouira, Sidi Ifni, Asilah, and Al Hoceima make peaceful, low-key coastal getaways.

Those familiar with tourist beaches in other countries may be struck by the modesty on Morocco's public sands. Female holidaymakers wishing to bare more than their arms and legs may feel more comfortable at a private beach attached to a coastal hotel or restaurant rather than a public beach.

■ **Agadir.** Agadir is a major destination for the high-density, European-package-tour, tanning crowd. For families looking for safe beaches and bathing with plenty of activities for the young, this is the spot.

■ **Oualidia.** Popular with surfers and windsurfers, this is an important beach destination just 90 minutes southwest of Casablanca.

■ **Plage Robinson.** Just west of Tangier, this much-visited beach offers sun and sand; the Caves of Hercules, where mythology has Hercules resting up after separating Africa from Europe; and a lively café-and-restaurant scene.

■ **Sidi Ifni and Essaouira.** The strongest windsurfing breezes in all of Africa blow across the burgundy rock formations and waters of Sidi Ifni and Essaouira.

People-Watching

Morocco is a visual spectacle in every sense, and without a doubt, the human fauna are the runaway stars of the show. French painters such as Delacroix and Matisse and the great Spanish colorist Marià Fortuny all found the souks, fondouks, and street scenes of Marrakesh, Fez, and Tangier irresistible. Today's visitors to this eye-popping North African brouhaha are well advised to simply pull up a chair and take in some of the most exotic natural street theater in the world.

■ **Djemâa el Fna, Marrakesh.** This cacophonous market square is unlike anything else on earth. Settle into a rooftop café for an unobstructed view of the acrobats, storytellers, musicians, dancers, fortune-tellers, juice carts, and general organized chaos.

■ **Fez el-Bali.** The to-and-fro pulsation of Fez's medina makes it the perfect place to watch Moroccans doing what Moroccans do. Great spots include the cafés around Bab Boujeloud and Bab Ftouh, though the latter is much less amenable to travelers.

■ **Place Moulay Hassan, Essaouira.** Locals, temporary locals, and fishermen are all welcome to linger in this laid-back plaza and watch the world go by from an outdoor café. Try a cup of *louiza*—warm milk with fresh verbena leaves.

■ **Grand Socco, Tangier.** Every conceivable manifestation of Old Testament–looking humanity seems to have found its way to Tangier's Grand Socco from the Rif Mountains and the interior. A stroll down rue de la Liberté into the food souk puts you in the middle of it all.

The Outdoors

Spectacular landscapes make Morocco a destination for nature lovers. It is also a haven for birds, playing host to almost 500 species. If you are lucky you may see nesting storks, wintering flamingos, perhaps even a rare slender-billed curlew or marsh owl. Some of the best scenery is found in the mountains, where Berber hospitality makes hiking an unforgettable experience. Rock climbing is possible in the Todra and Dadès gorges on and the peaks outside Chefchaouen. Oukaïmeden has facilities for skiing, and a few other liftless runs await the more athletic. Golf is available in Rabat, Casablanca, Marrakesh, and Agadir, and new luxury courses are springing up at a surprising rate.

■ **High Atlas.** People come from around the world to trek in these mountains, drawn by the rugged scenery, bracing air, and rural Berber (Imazighen) culture. Hiking is easily combined with mule riding, trout fishing, and vertiginous alpine drives.

■ **Merzouga dunes.** Southeast of Erfoud, beyond Morocco's great oasis valleys, these waves of sand mark the beginning of the Sahara. Brilliantly orange in the late afternoon sun, they are gloriously desolate at sunrise.

■ **Palm groves and villages, Tafraoute.** A striking tropical contrast to the barren Anti-Atlas Mountains and agricultural plains farther north, the oases are scattered with massive, pink cement houses built by wealthy urban merchants native to this area.

Architecture

Refined Islamic architecture graces the imperial cities of Fez, Meknès, Marrakesh, and Rabat. Mosques and *medersas* (schools of Koranic studies) dating from the Middle Ages, as well as 19th-century palaces, are decorated with colorful geometric tiles, bands of Koranic verses in marble or plaster, stalactite crevices, and carved wooden ceilings. Built by Morocco's Jews, the Mellahs, with their glass-walled balconies, contrast with the Islamic emphasis on turning inward. French colonial architecture prevails in the Art Deco and neo-Mauresque streets of Casablanca's Quartier des Habous. Outside these strongholds of Arab influence are the *pisé* (rammed earth) kasbahs in the Ouarzazate–Er-Rachidia region, where structures built with local mud and clay range from deep pink to burgundy to shades of brown.

■ **Aït Ben Haddou, near Ouarzazate.** Strewn across a hillside, the red-pisé towers of this village fortress resemble a melting sand castle. Crenellated and topped with blocky towers, it's one of the most sumptuous sights in the Atlas Mountains.

■ **La Bahia Palace, Marrakesh.** Built as a harem, and interspersed with cypress-filled courtyards, La Bahia has the key Moroccan architectural elements—light, symmetry, decoration, and water.

■ **Bou Inania medersa, Fez.** The most celebrated of the Kairaouine University's 14th-century residential colleges, Bou Inania has a roof of green tiles, a ceiling of carved cedar, stalactites of white marble, and ribbons of Arabic inscription.

FLAVORS OF MOROCCO

Close your eyes, inhale, and breathe the spices of North Africa. Situated on ancient trade routes, the kingdom benefits from a vibrant import trade from all corners of the world and an agreeable climate. Despite the summer heat, the fertile red earth, expansive coasts, and cooler mountains produce a bountiful harvest from field, orchard, and ocean. Arab, African, Persian, and French influences fuse with ancient Berber culinary skills in the kitchen.

Drinks

Mint tea is at the very heart of Moroccan cuisine and culture. Whether in cosmopolitan Casablanca or a rural Berber village in the Atlas Mountains, there is one universal truth: *thé* is served. Recipes vary from region to region—and even from family to family—but all contain a mix of green tea, fresh mint leaves, and sugar. **Coffee** is served black (*café noir*), with a little milk (*café crème*), or half milk–half coffee (*nuss nuss* in the Moroccan dialect). **Orange juice,** freshly squeezed, is abundantly available in cafés and restaurants.

Bread

There is no foodstuff more important to this nation than bread. Seen as God-given, bread is used for mopping up the juices of thick stews, or in place of a fork, in a country where food is traditionally eaten with the fingers. Due to its cultural and religious significance, bread is never placed directly on the ground or thrown away, and it is common to see great piles of stale crusts drying in public areas, ready for collection by the poor or those wanting to feed animals. Bread comes in a variety of shapes and sizes, from the crumbly *harcha* (a popular, yellow, semolina-rich teatime snack) to the easy-to-eat, puffy *batbout,* which resembles

a pitta pocket and is best stuffed with fish, salad, or meat. The daily bread of the nation is *khobz,* which is a common round loaf of whole-meal or white flour.

Seasonings

Several notable spices and herbs are common in Moroccan cuisine: cumin, paprika, garlic, salt, pepper, ginger, cinnamon, coriander, saffron, turmeric, sesame seeds, fresh parsley, cilantro, *harissa* (red-chili-and-garlic paste), olive oil, and olives. Preserved lemons are another key ingredient in many tagine recipes and some salads. It is common to find cumin on the table in place of salt and pepper as a seasoning.

Breakfast

With Muslims rising at dawn to pray, breakfast is an important and often hearty meal, consisting of a variety of dishes and beverages. There's mint tea and freshly squeezed orange juice, bread, olive oil, honey, nuts, and omelets fried with preserved meat (*khlea*). There are the usual French croissants, *pain au chocolat,* and crêpes, plus two delicious traditional Moroccan alternatives. The first is *msemn,* a layered pastry–pancake oozing melted butter and honey. The second is a small holed pancake called a *baghir* that is similar to a drop scone or crumpet. This is equally delicious eaten with honey or jam.

Moroccan Salads

No meal is complete in Morocco without a salad (*salade marocaine*), a simple dish of chopped tomatoes, parsley, and onion, quite often brought to the table whether ordered or not. Dressed with a dash of lemon juice and good amount of olive oil, this tangy, refreshing salad goes well with all manner of main courses. Other popular salads to try are eggplant pureed with

yogurt and spices, and roasted bell peppers marinated with garlic.

Tagines

A *tagine* is the name for both the stew served in most Moroccan homes at lunch and dinner and the name of the traditional clay pot with a tall, cone-shaped lid in which it is generally cooked. Moroccan tagines use chicken, beef, or lamb as the base along with vegetables like carrots, peas, green beans, and a variety of other ingredients, including chickpeas, olives, apricots, prunes, and nuts. Typical tagines are chicken and preserved lemon, lentils with meat and prunes, chicken and almonds, and *kefta* (ground meat) and egg.

Couscous

Couscous is probably the most famous Moroccan dish, combining tiny balls of steamed wheat pasta with a meat-and-vegetable stew poured on top. The meat base for the stew can be chicken, beef, or lamb, and vegetables usually include a combination of turnip, carrot, sweet potato, pumpkin, and zucchini, with chickpeas and raisins sprinkled throughout. Couscous is typically a Friday-lunch meal but is served at other times as well.

Pastilla

Pastilla is an elaborate meat pie combining sweet and salty flavors. Traditionally filled with pigeon, it is often prepared with shredded chicken. The meat is slow-cooked with spices and then combined with cinnamon, ground almonds, and crisp, thin layers of a phyllo-like dough. Pastilla is reserved for special occasions due to the complexity of its preparation. In urban areas, it is common to find a phyllo chef hard at work preparing the sheets for sale to women without the space, time, or skill to prepare the pastry at home.

Vegetarians

Since meat is expensive and considered a luxury for many Moroccans, it is not eaten in the home every day. That said, the idea of vegetarianism is foreign to the culture, as eating meat is seen as being preferable to going without. Vegetarians should be wary of "vegetarian" dishes on the menu, since to the majority of Moroccans "meat" refers to red meat rather than to poultry or fish. With chicken sometimes viewed as a nonmeat option, salads, bread, and eggs offer more reliable alternatives.

Dessert

After a meal, Moroccan desserts are often limited to fresh seasonal fruit. Many types of Moroccan pastries and cookies exist, almost always made with almond paste. These pastries are often reserved for special occasions or served to guests with afternoon tea. One common pastry is *kaab el-ghzal* ("gazelle's horns"), which is filled with almond paste and topped with sugar.

Prohibited Items

Both pork and alcohol are forbidden by Islam. Pork is difficult to find in the country except in larger cities with upscale markets and hotels catering to foreigners. Alcohol is drunk (discreetly) by men all over the country and sold openly in hotels catering to foreigners. Both beer and wine are produced domestically.

KIDS AND FAMILIES

Traveling in Morocco with children is great fun, especially since Moroccans adore kids. Locals usually warm to and greet travelers with kids more enthusiastically than they would the average tourist. However, at the same time, expect a few practical challenges along the way.

Choosing a Place to Stay

Choosing the right place depends largely on the ages of your children, type of holiday you want, regions you wish to visit, and your budget.

For a beach-based holiday with on-site kid's activities, a modern resort destination like Agadir is ideal. Here there is **Club Med** or **ClubHotel Riu Tikida Dunas.** Farther up the coast, the beach at Essaouira offers lots of water sports, and **Sofitel** has a private beach and a pool. There is a pretty coastal lagoon resort at Oualidia too—popular with Moroccan vacationers—and hotel **La Sultana Oualidia** is luxurious.

For rural-based activity holidays and trekking, most places are fairly simple mountain *gîtes* (self-catering apartments or homes), *auberges* (hostels), and *maisons d'hôtes* (essentially bed-and-breakfasts based in private homes). For top-notch deluxe accommodation accessible by road try **Kasbah Tamadot** in Asni near Mt. Toubkal National Park, or **La Pause Marrakech,** a deluxe desert-style camp near Marrakesh with outdoor activities including donkey and camel rides. The **Xaluca** group of hotels also has family-friendly five-star hotels convenient for hiking trips to the Dadès Gorge and Sahara desert in Erfoud and Merzouga.

Cities such as Fez, Meknès, and Marrakesh have the widest variety of accommodations. Although a traditional Moroccan riad or riad-style boutique hotel offers atmosphere in the old medinas, it may be a less attractive option for families with younger kids. You may prefer a more modern hotel, but realize that not all have elevators, even newer ones. If you don't fancy a hotel in the new town, and a riad doesn't suit you, consider renting a villa or apartment, some of which provide a maid, cook, and babysitting services.

Top Experiences for Families

Morocco does not have many ready-made attractions such as zoos or theme parks, but if you like spectacular natural beauty, your family will be well served.

Sahara Desert. You can see the desert by foot, camel, or four-wheel-drive vehicle on short, hour-long rides into the dunes or on full-day treks through an oasis. You can also pack for a multiday trip deep into the Sahara with a nomad guide. Visit Erg Chebbi or Erg Chigaga to climb the highest sand dunes in Morocco, and then glide down on a sand board. Many hotels have their own desert camps, and there are countless agencies in Marrakesh, Ouarzazate, Zagora, Merzouga, and M'Hamid which can fix you up.

Water Sports and Beaches. Agadir has a large concentration of all-inclusive resorts, though few people would go all the way to Morocco for a beach vacation. Families with older children and teenagers should check out the coast between Sidi Ifni and Essaouira for some of the best spots for **kite-surfing, windsurfing,** and **surf schools.** In Marrakesh, **Oasiria** has two pools, waterslides, gardens, and restaurants for hungry kids and parents.

Mountain Trips. Mule trekking or hiking in the **High Atlas Mountains** near Mt. Toubkal is easily achievable for younger children, while toddlers can hop up in front of mom or dad on a mule. Families with younger kids can stay in one place and take day

hikes; if you have older children, you can travel with a guide, staying in simple mountain gîtes as you pass through neighboring valleys—or even attempt the summit. In the foothills of the High Atlas Mountains near Marrakesh, **Terres d'Amanar** is an outdoor activity center with archery, climbing, zip lines, and crafts workshops. Near the **Dadès Gorge**, with the help of a local guide, you can visit nomad families living in caves and old salt mines.

Film Studios. The **Atlas Film Studios** in Ouarzazate makes for an interesting visit if you're heading south. You can walk through some of the film sets used in major movies such as *Kundun, Kingdom of Heaven*, and *The Mummy*.

Markets and Bazaars. The ancient medieval medinas of Fez and Marrakesh are full of exotic delights—the intricate architecture of imperial palaces and mosques, colorful chaos of the souks, intoxicating smell of sizzling street food, and labyrinthine alleyways where tourists, shoppers, and traders intertwine. In Marrakesh, the bustling main square, **place Djemâa el Fna**, fascinates children and adults alike with its daily cornucopia of musicians, snake charmers, henna artists, storytellers, and acrobats. At night, it is transformed into the biggest outdoor barbecue in the world.

History. Explore one of Morocco's most famous historic sights, the ruined Roman city of **Volubilis** near Meknès, and the **Rabat Archaeological Museum**, which houses many relics from this site. In the Valley of a Thousand Kasbahs, along the Drâa and Dadès valleys, be sure to see the kasbahs of **Telouet, Aït Ben Haddou**, and **Taourirt**. The museum at **Ksar Tissergate** near Zagora is also well worth visiting.

Wildlife. Walk in the beautiful cedar forests near **Azrou** and visit an 800-year-old tree as Barbary apes swoop overhead.

Classes. Learning to shop for vegetables in the souks and cook your own tagine is a great family activity. Cooking classes at **Souk Cuisine** in Marrakesh and **Café Clock** in Fez are good starting points.

Practical Considerations

Baby Care. There are almost no public baby-changing facilities anywhere in Morocco. You can buy disposable diapers in city chain supermarkets such as Aswak Assalam, Marjane, and Acima. In rural areas you may struggle to find them, so stock up if touring. The same goes for baby formula, though any café or restaurant is happy to boil you water for mixing. Breast-feeding should be done discreetly and away from public view.

Traveling with Smaller Kids. Most car-rental agencies and tourist transport providers are able to supply a child seat (but check in advance). In taxis and buses there is rarely even a seat belt. If a child is small enough to sit on your lap, he or she usually travels for free on buses and taxis.

Walking. Sidewalks are rare, or else broken and narrow, which makes pushing a stroller difficult. It's easier to hook up a baby knapsack or carry small children.

Sun Care. Children are very prone to sunburn, dehydration, and sunstroke, so always have plenty of drinking water, strong sunscreen, sunhats, and T-shirts for covering up.

RECOMMENDED TOUR OPERATORS

Tour operators tend to fall into two major groups: those organized in advance—most often via the Internet—and those engaged on the ground. Morocco's infrastructure has improved in recent years, making traveling around the country by train or even by car easier. But there are two areas where it may be more helpful to have a local guide, even if you don't choose to do a fully guided trip to Morocco. Despite some development in rural Morocco's infrastructure, the High Atlas remains relatively undiscovered: hence its unspoiled charm. In order to reap the rewards of such an area, suitable transport (whether organized in advance or upon arrival in the region) and an experienced driver are keys to a successful trip. The same is said for the desert, where arranging camels, four-wheel-drive transportation, and tented camps is best done through a well-connected local guide.

For both the High Atlas and Sahara regions, local guides are easily found in Marrakesh or, for the High Atlas, in the small hill stations, most notably Imlil. A homegrown guide personalizes your traveling experience, often suggesting unknown restaurants and small riads, or organizing (with your permission) a visit to his or her own home. The plus side here is the authentic cultural experience; the downside may be a lack of reliability, possibly poor vehicle maintenance, and limited English. All the good hotels in Marrakesh can make these arrangements, even with little prior notice. Prices vary greatly, but you should expect to pay around $150 a day for a vehicle and driver-guide (and you should tip around $10 per day). If recruiting locally, expect to pay in dirhams—in cash, rather than credit card. If making these arrangements in advance, check how experienced a tour operator or guide is. The reader forums on Fodors.com are a useful source of feedback and control.

You tend to get what you pay for in Morocco, and almost anything is possible, with operators capable of arranging all manner of tours. High-end travel, for example, might include air-conditioned luxury transport, five-star accommodations, spa treatments, and lavish meals. Another option might be experience-based: with quad biking, ballooning, cooking classes, a trip to a local *moussem* (festival), or skiing in Oukaïmeden. Very popular these days are ecotours, which typically arrange stays in unspoiled Berber hamlets or eco-lodges; visit local cooperatives, such as the salt pans and potteries; and shower under breathtaking waterfalls.

Luxury Tours

Abercrombie and Kent. Pioneers for years in the luxury travel market, this hugely respected outfitter offers a number of tailor-made, high-end packages to Morocco. ☎ 800/554–7016 ⊕ *www.abercrombiekent.com* ✉ *From $845.*

Kensington Tours. *National Geographic Traveler* award winner for 2014, this high-end company vows to delve deeper into the real Morocco, without compromising on comfort or quality. Devised to deliver trips that involve more personal discovery than prepackaged adventure, these travels are inspired by the intrepid explorer and Royal Geographic Society Fellow Jeff Willner. ☎ 888/903–2001 ⊕ www.kensingtontours.com ✉ *From $1,729.*

Experiential Tours

Blue Men of Morocco. This American-owned company organizes ecotours of Morocco. Founder Elena Hall lives in Spain and puts

together itineraries for travelers wishing to engage in low-impact voyages, such as simple Sahara stays and camel excursions. Guides are locally recruited, and many of the profits are funneled back into local communities. ☎ *952/463–387 in Spain* ⊕ *www.bluemenofmorocco.com* ✉ *From $650.*

Epic Running. A fresh concept in ecotourism, this young but already well-respected company runs tours and training camps for runners of all fitness levels. Low-impact explorations into some of Morocco's most beautiful and hospitable areas are promised, along with experiences go leave you toned, refreshed, and in tune with your surroundings. Travelers relax after activities in comfortable surroundings at which a team of physio and holistic health practitioners are on hand. ☎ *771/440–2519* ⊕ *www.epicrunning. co.uk* ✉ *From $2,545.*

Plan-it Fez. Plan-It Fez promises a new world of sensory experiences in the old world of Fez. Hugely experienced company founders (Australian Michele Reeves and Briton Gail Leonard) are passionate about sharing their discoveries in and around this ancient city and Morocco-wide. They create experiences that let you taste, smell, feel, and hear Morocco rather than merely seeing it. Immensely popular are their culinary adventures which incorporate tastings, cooking classes, and supplier tours. ☎ *0535/63–87–08* ⊕ *www. plan-it-fez.com* ✉ *From $100.*

High Atlas Tours

Moroccan Mountain Guides. This team of young, passionate Berber and Spanish guides specialize in the High Atlas. The crew is adept at finding hotels with a family atmosphere and offering cultural tours in remote areas. There's a strong slant to ecotours, including mountain biking, Toubkal ascents, and bivouacs. English, Spanish, French, Arabic, and Berber speakers are available. ☎ *0657/71–10–53 in Morocco* ⊕ *www. moroccomountainguides.co.uk* ✉ *From $120.*

Xaluca Tours. This company based in the Atlas runs an impressive list of life-changing experiences in tour form including desert treks along nomad trails by camel and 4x4. ☎ *0535/57–84–50 in Morocco* ⊕ *www.xaluca.com* ✉ *From $1,250.*

Sahara Tours

Desert Majesty. Based in Ouarzazate, this company offers budget 4x4 tours using local drivers who know the region inside and out. One of their tours visits rock-carvings at Tinzouline and Tata in southern Morocco. ⊕ *www.desertmajesty.com* ✉ *From $200.*

Sahara Expeditions. This no-frills operation offers group desert excursions for one to three nights with guaranteed daily departures from Marrakesh. ⊕ *www. saharaexpe.ma* ✉ *From 200 DH.*

RENTING A RIAD

Only once you venture forth into the ancient higgledy-piggledy medinas of Fez, Meknès, Marrakesh, or Essaouira do you find a truly authentic Moroccan riad, and even then you could still walk past it, blissfully unaware.

What is a riad?

These beautiful, cloistered dwellings are usually tucked away discreetly behind heavy wooden doors set into high, featureless walls on blind alleys, called *derbs*. Traditional riad-style houses were (and still are) the domain of wealthier families and pass down from one generation to the next. They contain many of the same decorative and structural elements as their more palatial counterparts, including hand-cut, colorful tiles (zellij), silky *tadelakt* walls of finely pressed and waxed plaster, painted cedarwood ceilings, arched colonnades, living rooms on the ground floor, and sleeping quarters on the upper floors. At the center of a riad is an ornamental garden with a central fountain or water feature and rooms that peer inward through windows of wrought iron or wooden latticework.

In more recent times, with changing fashions and the development of modern *nouvelle villes* by colonial rulers, many Moroccans relinquished their old houses for more comfortable dwellings with 20th-century sanitation and modern household amenities. However, the faded charm and beauty of these traditional structures have captured the imagination of foreign investors, who often snap them up as holiday retreats; many have been restored lovingly to their former glory with sumptuous attention to detail and the addition of state-of-the art facilities. Now, hundreds of riads offer boutique accommodations in Morocco's older cities, usually with about three to six bedrooms over two levels.

Why rent a riad?

Renting a riad in one of Morocco's medieval towns is a superb alternative to the often-charmless option of larger hotels in the modern districts. Most riads are rented on a per-room, per-night basis, and public areas are shared with other tourists. However, nearly all riads offer their entire accommodation at a reduced rate for exclusive rental if booked far enough in advance (perhaps six months to one year ahead). For large families and groups of friends, taking on an entire riad gives an authentic and colorful taste of traditional Moroccan life. Noise easily carries in a riad, due to its enclosed nature, so renting the entire premises gives more freedom to party well after bedtime.

What is included?

Riads that operate year-round as guesthouses have an on-site manager who attends to daily housekeeping and security and performs concierge services. Of course, some people want complete privacy, so ask if the manager is on duty during your stay. Quoted prices usually include daily cleaning, breakfast, bed linen and towels, Wi-Fi, satellite TV, a DVD player, hair dryers, and access to the kitchen for cooking your own meals. Ask at the time of booking if there's an extra charge for electricity or firewood. Additional meals, private transport, guides, special activities, and excursions can normally be arranged for an additional cost.

How much does it cost?

Riads come in all sizes and levels of luxury, so prices range anywhere from 300 DH to 3,000 DH per room per night. A midrange, well-equipped, and stylishly furnished riad costs approximately 700

to 1,000 DH per night per room; for a typical riad with four bedrooms, expect to pay around 2,500 DH to 3,500 DH per night, including a discount for stays of more than one night. For deluxe riads or villas in the outlying Palmery area of Marrakesh, the sky is the limit for nightly rental prices.

What about location?

Riads are usually tucked away into side streets just wide enough for a donkey cart and buzzing mopeds. Check how far the riad is from the main tourist areas and souks. Check if the neighborhood is safe, well-lighted, and has a taxi stand or parking lot within easy walking distance. Moroccan medinas can be hazardous after dark because sidewalks are poorly maintained, and tourists can get hassled by beggars.

How many rooms/beds do you need?

Riad bedrooms are often narrow, so double beds are most common. Ask in advance if you need twin-bed rooms, extra single beds, or cribs.

Do you need a pool?

Most riads have some kind of water feature within the patio or perhaps on the roof terrace; however, a "pool" is usually little more than a plunge pool. If you want to swim, you might prefer a hotel. Or you could really splurge by renting a private pavilion within the grounds of a villa in the Palmery area of Marrakesh.

What time of year are you visiting?

Moroccan winters can be bitterly cold and wet, so check that rooms are heated and that cost of heating is included. If there are open fires, ask who supplies the firewood and sets the fire for you. By contrast, the summers can be ferociously hot, so check that there is air-conditioning and that it is included in the rental price.

How old are the members of your party?

Most riads have three levels, with access to most of the upper bedrooms via narrow and winding tiled staircases. If you have small children or members of your party with restricted mobility, a riad may not be the best choice. Also, be sure to check with the owner to ensure the riad allows children.

How do you find a riad to rent?

A simple Internet search turns up dozens of riads, and if booking far ahead, you should be able to rent a full riad. If you do not speak French, search for a riad with English-speaking management—one simple indicator is if the website is written in good English. Good sources for privately owned riads that can be rented directly from the owner include ⊕ *www.ownersdirect.co.uk* and ⊕ *www.vacationrentalpeople.com*. There are also agencies such as ⊕ *www.riadsmorocco.com,* which represent various properties. Finally, for the high end of the market, companies such as ⊕ *www.boutiquesouk.com* and ⊕ *www.fesmedina.com* organize stays at premier properties with full concierge service.

BOOKS AND MOVIES

One of the best ways to get into the travel spirit for any country is to read a book or watch a film set there. Here are some mood-setting recommendations.

RECOMMENDED READING

Books on Morocco written by foreign authors abound and provide a great way to learn about the country's culture and traditions before you travel there.

Paul Bowles

The late American expatriate writer, who lived for many years in Tangier, is among the most well-known. Although Bowles's most famous novel, *The Sheltering Sky,* purports to take place in Algeria, the tale of a doomed triangle of young Americans adrift in North Africa is quintessentially Moroccan in tone and content. *The Spider's House* is a superb historical novel and portrait of Fez at the end of the French protectorate. The most comprehensive collection of Bowles's short stories is the *Collected Stories 1939–76,* a series of musings and accounts of daily events that Bowles effortlessly (or so it seems) elevates to the level of artistic essays. All of Bowles's nonfiction is notable, but *Their Heads Are Green and Their Hands Are Blue* is the most revealing and informative on Morocco.

Tahir Shah

For an amusing and eye-opening journey into the hidden underbelly of Casablanca, Tahir Shah's *Casablanca Blues* is recommended. The novel builds on Shah's earlier books (especially *The Caliph's House* and *In Arabian Nights*), informing through twists and turns on Moroccan culture, superstitions, etiquette, and the kingdom's rich folklore. The popularity of this latest work comes as no surprise to readers of the author's previous books on this region, which humorously describe his restoration of a crumbling mansion in the middle of a Casablanca slum and detail the art of storytelling. Dar Khalifa, the house in question, remains to this day, despite an intensive beautification project raging around its charming old walls. As in his previous two books on Morocco, Shah's writing is packed with personal accounts, anecdotes, and insights.

Richard Hamilton

The Last Storytellers is essential reading for visitors to Marrakesh, and makes a perfect holiday companion. This collection of traditional tales from the city, complete with a historical introduction, helps travelers understand its culture and mystery. Marrakesh has been central to Morocco's ancient storytelling tradition for nearly a thousand years. Storytellers have gathered in the legendary square of the city, to recount ancient folktales and fables to rapt audiences since its foundation in the 11th century. But this unique chain of oral wisdom, once passed seamlessly from generation to generation, is now on the brink of extinction. Hamilton witnesses, firsthand, the death throes of this rich and captivating tradition and, in the labyrinth of the medina, tracks down the last few remaining storytellers, recording these precious tales for posterity and enjoyment.

Travel Literature

Highlights include *The Voices of Marrakesh,* by Elias Canetti; *Tangier: City of the Dream,* by Iain Finlayson; and *A Year in Marrakesh,* by Peter Mayne. Among turn-of-the-20th-century accounts, French novelist Pierre Loti's *Au Maroc* is a classic. Charles de Foucauld, a French nobleman, army officer, and missionary, chronicled his time in Morocco in *Reconnaissance*

au Maroc. For more historical and ethnographical accounts, find Edith Wharton's 1920 *In Morocco*; Antoine de Saint-Exupéry's *Wind, Sand and Stars*; and Walter Harris's 1921 *Morocco That Was*. *Zohra's Ladder & Other Moroccan Tales*, by Pamela Windo, is a collection of stories that took place during the author's seven years living in Morocco; Windo depicts both the stunning landscapes of the country and genuine connections she made with the people. The book makes a good companion to a guidebook when traveling to Morocco.

Food

Paula Wolfert's *Couscous and Other Good Food from Morocco* is excellent for its fabulous recipes, photographs, and background on the Moroccan social context. Kitty Morse, born in Casablanca to a French mother and British father, is the author of five cookbooks on the cuisine of Morocco and North Africa, including *Cooking at the Kasbah: Recipes from my Moroccan Kitchen* and *The Scent of Orange Blossoms*. *Clock Book: Recipes from a Modern Moroccan Kitchen,* by food critic and travel writer Tara Stevens, provides new twists on traditional Moroccan dishes.

FILMS

More and more often, films from Moroccan directors are both entertaining and shed light on Moroccan culture, but they may be difficult to find on DVD.

Horses of God is a highly controversial but beautifully shot drama set in the shantytowns of Casablanca and based on the 2003 terrorist attacks across the city. The 2012 film focuses on young men and their radicalization once faced with poverty, corruption, violence, and mental illness.

It is a troubling portrayal of youth without hope or regard for others; one that has been labeled as "brutal" by its critics, both at home and abroad. The work is sometimes cited as a warning to the country's policymakers, who are keenly aware of the need to raise the standard of living among the poor and disenfranchised. Moroccan Arabic with French subtitles.

Marock, a 2005 film (in French) by female director Laïla Marrakchi, was highly controversial, exploring the romantic relationship between two teenagers, one Muslim and one Jewish. In addition to the interreligious theme, the movie shows viewers the contrast between rich and poor and how the two worlds meet continuously yet stay forever separate.

Of the many Western films set in Morocco, and no doubt the most famous, is the 1942 classic *Casablanca*.

Hideous Kinky, the 1998 adaptation of the novel by the same name, tells the story of an adventurous young mother who moves to Marrakesh in the 1960s.

The Sheltering Sky, Bernardo Bertolucci's 1990 interpretation of Paul Bowles's 1949 novel, is a dark, romantic comedy with stunning images of North Africa.

One story line in Alejandro González Iñárritu's 2006 *Babel,* featuring Brad Pitt and Cate Blanchett, takes place in the High Atlas Mountains.

Morocco has a vibrant film studio, and a great many films that do not take place in Morocco were nonetheless shot there, most notably *Othello, Lawrence of Arabia, The Last Temptation of Christ, Kundun, Gladiator, Black Hawk Down, Alexander, Body of Lies, Green Zone, The Bourne Ultimatum,* and *Hanna.*

GREAT ITINERARIES

THE IMPERIAL CITIES: THE CLASSIC TOUR OF MOROCCO

For longer stays in Morocco, tailor your tour around more exhaustive exploring of regions and adventurous diversions. If time is limited, focus on the major experiences and sights. This weeklong holiday gives you enough time to sample the best of Morocco. Remember to add a day on each end for travel time (a direct flight from New York to Casablanca takes approximately eight hours), and pace yourself to see the most important places.

Day 1: Arrival in Casablanca

Flights generally arrive in Casablanca in the early morning. The city doesn't have that many sights and only requires a few hours to see them all. As your starting point, visit the **Hassan II Mosque** and the Mohammed V Square in the **Habous Quarter** designed in French colonial, Art Deco style. You're going to be exhausted anyway after a transatlantic flight, so spend your first night in Casablanca; however, if you want to make an early start in the morning, travel one hour along the coast to Rabat.

Day 2: Rabat

Explore the capital city of Rabat. The best sites in the city are the **Hassan Tower** and **Mohammed V Mausoleum, Chellah Gardens and Necropolis,** and **Oudayas Kasbah** overlooking the Atlantic Ocean. In the late afternoon, drive to Meknès to spend the night.

Day 3: Meknès & Volubilis

Begin your tour by passing the **Bab Mansour** and visiting the holy **Mausoleum of Moulay Ismail,** which is open to non-Muslims. Walk towards the lively place el-Hedime, which leads towards the medina. Tour the open bazaars of the medina streets; enjoy an inexpensive classic Moroccan lunch; and visit the food souk near the row of pottery stands. The **Museum of Moroccan Art** in the 19th-century Dar Jamai palace and **Heri el Souani** (Royal Granaries) are recommended stops. In the afternoon, drive 30 minutes to the ancient Roman archeological ruins of **Volubilis.** When you approach, the Triumphal Arch rises in the open field. Count on 90 minutes for a thorough visit. The Tangier Gate, House of Orpheus, House of Columns, and House of Ephebus are must-sees. You can spend the night at Volubilis or head back to Meknès.

Days 4 and 5: Fez

Try to arrive in Fez as early as possible so you can spend two full days exploring everything the **Fez el-Bali, Fez el-Djedid,** and **Ville Nouvelle** have to offer: medieval monuments, artisan workshops, public squares, ancient tombs, cultural museums, chaotic souks, atmospheric cafés, and palatial gardens. The blue-tiled gate of **Bab Boujeloud** is the gateway to the main alley of Talaa Kebira. The most important sites include the **Bou Inania medersa, Attarine madrassa, Mausoleum of Zaouia Moulay Idriss II,** and **Karaouine Mosque and University** (the latter generally considered the oldest academic institution in the world). Visit the restored **Nejjarine fondouk** for the best examples of woodworking craftsmanship. Watch the full fabrication process of the leather tanneries from a rooftop terrace. Shop for the famous blue-and-white Fassi pottery. If time permits, see arts and crafts (including a must-see collection of astrolabes) at the **Dar Batha Museum** housed in a beautiful, 19th-century, Hispano-Moorish palace. Discover the area of the **Royal Palace** (Dar el-Makhzen) that leads to the active Mellah quarter beyond the

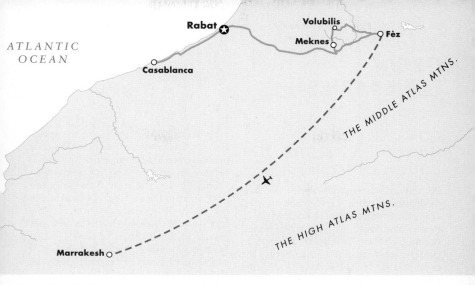

Fez el-Djedid. Watch the sunset over the entire medina from the **Merenid tombs** or **Musée des Armes** atop the hills of the Borj Nord or from the **Borj Sud**, south of the walled city. Indulge in an authentic Fassi dinner in a riad courtyard. Spend two nights here.

Days 6 and 7: Marrakesh

The quickest way to travel the 398-km (242-mile) distance between Fez and Marrakesh is by plane; but be warned, most flights stop off in Casablanca. After dropping your bags at your hotel in Marrakesh, hit the ground running. The best place to start is the famed **Djemâa el Fna**, the perfect gateway into the labyrinth of medina streets filled with hundreds of souks, including the **Souk des Teinturiers** for leather, **Souk Addadine** for metalwork, and **Souk Zarbia**, the main carpet market. The **Ali ben Youssef Medersa, Dar Si Saïd** museum, **Palais Bahia**, and **Koutoubia Mosque** are important sites (though non-Muslims cannot enter the mosque). Walk south of the Palais Bahia to explore the bustling streets of the Mellah, the former Jewish quarter and largest in Morocco. In the evening, splurge on a Moroccan feast, or head to the open grills in back on the busy main square. On your second day in Marrakesh, take a petit taxi for a relaxing

TIPS

■ The only mosque in Morocco non-Muslims can enter is the Hassan II Mosque in Casablanca. Visits are allowed only between prayer times (with official on-site guides) at 10 am, 11 am, and 2 pm.

■ During Ramadan, check for special hours; while many sites are open on holy days, some local restaurants and cafés close for the day or entire month.

■ Make your visit more special by attending an annual outdoor event, such as the World Sacred Music Festival held in Fez or the Marrakesh Popular Arts Festival, which hosts traditional musicians and dancers from all over Morocco.

promenade through the **Ville Nouvelle** and lush **Majorelle Gardens and Museum,** where you can do some bird-watching and see an extraordinary collection of Islamic ceramics, textiles, jewelry, and art. After, head back towards the medina and visit the 16th-century **Saadian Tombs** for one of the country's finest representations of Islamic architecture. Plan a relaxing hammam treatment to rejuvenate after a week of touring.

GREAT ITINERARIES

COASTAL AND INLAND OASES: THE SOUTHERN TOUR

For those who want to escape the bustling medinas and touristy feel of the imperial cities, the Southern Atlantic coastline is the perfect alternative, with miles of deserted beaches, enchanting seaside villages, and colorful exotic landscapes to enrich the mind and spirit. The scenery is stunning and varied with rocky wilderness, vast seascapes, and fertile plains. Much of the area (except for Agadir) remains pristine and gets relatively few visitors. Swim, surf, sunbathe, bird-watch, and breathe in fresh ocean air. Laid-back towns, surfer havens, coastal resorts, and unexpected oases offer a holistic way to learn about local culture, food, language, and history.

Day 1: Marrakesh

Fly directly to Marrakesh Menara International Airport. Rent a car in the airport terminal, and check in to a hotel in Guéliz. Take a taxi to enjoy a delectable Moroccan dinner and experience the exotic activity of the **Djemâa el Fna**, the city's main square. Don't miss the city's excellent nightlife, with live street entertainment, local clubs, bars, and theater performances showcasing the fusion of Berber, Arab, African, and Andalusian influences in music and dance.

Day 2: Essaouira

Rise early to drive west towards the relaxing, picturesque port city of Essaouira. After you check in to your hotel, take a walking tour of the harbor and town of whitewashed houses. Have lunch near the shore. Don't miss the fresh charcoal-grilled sardines and shrimp in seaside food stalls. The town is a hub for contemporary Moroccan artists—check out art galleries showcasing Gnaoua expressionism. Shop the colorful pedestrian-only medina streets for ceramics, thuya wood, *babouches* (leather slippers), and woven fabrics. Watch the sunset on the ocean horizon atop the ramparts of the **kasbah**. For the best panoramic view, access the fortress at **Skala de la Ville**, the cliffside sea bastion lined with brass cannons. Dine on fresh local seafood at a casual open grill or in one of many restaurants along the shore.

Day 3: Agadir

Head south to Agadir, stopping off for magnificent sea views on the undisturbed sand dunes of Morocco's most beautiful beaches. **Sidi Kaouki, Tafelney, Bhibeh,** and **Moulay Bouzerktoun** are the most well-known beaches to sunbathe and dip your toes into the Atlantic waters. **Taghazoute** attracts windsurfers and offers brisk ocean breezes. When you finally arrive in Agadir, visit the **kasbah** and **fish stalls** by the harbor. Enjoy dinner and one night here.

Day 4: Tiznit

Continue your journey to Tiznit, famous for its silver and wool blankets. Stay one night in Tiznit to experience local Berber living and hit its wonderful market, especially if you are looking for jewelry.

Day 5: Tafraoute

On Day 5, discover the natural beauty of the Anti-Atlas region, passing palm groves, almond orchards, rocky landscapes, fertile valleys, and fortified towns. Pass through the small villages **Igherm** and **Oumnast** before enjoying the exotic beauty of Tafraoute. Explore the **Amen Valley** region, then return to town in the late afternoon. Spend the night at the Hotel Kerdous, overlooking a dramatic valley on the road to Tiznit.

ATLANTIC
OCEAN

Essaouira ○ — Marrakesh ●
Taroudant ○ ◆ Kasbah de Frieja
Agadir ○
Igherm ○
THE ANTI-ATLAS MTNS.
Tiznit ○ — Tafraoute ○

Day 6: Taroudant

Take a relaxing drive towards Taroudant. The atmosphere is very low-key. Walk around the open markets and historic ramparts. The red-ocher-walled city is well known for handcrafted silver items and aromatic spices. There are two main souks in the village. In the medina, don't miss the jewelry souk, fish market, kasbah, and pretty gardens. Listen for Tashelheit, the Berber dialect of the southern Souss region. On Sunday, locals from surrounding areas sell produce, livestock, and various wares near the main gate. A short loop drive east, about 10 km (6 miles) from Taroudant, takes you through the fertile Souss valley plains and barren terrain leading towards the ruins of the Kasbah de Frieja. Spend the night in Taroudant.

Day 7: Return to Marrakesh

Count on a few hours to return to your starting point. If you plan to depart on the same day, head straight to the Menara airport. If you decide to stay one more evening, head back to the famed Djemâa el Fna, and shop for last-minute souvenirs in the **Souk des Teinturiers** for leather, **Souk Addadine** for metalwork, and **Souk Zarbia** for carpets. The **Ali ben Youssef Medersa**, **Dar Si Saïd** museum, **Palais Bahia**, and

TIPS

■ Go off the beaten track—head to coastal destinations of Oualidia and Mirleft, a small village fast becoming a trendy spot for surfers and sun worshippers.

■ For an outdoor adventure, arrange a horse ride on the beach or rent ATVs through several stables or quad-trek companies.

■ To avoid serious problems, buy and carry a supply of bottled water to beat the heat on beaches and while walking through the villages and open terrain of the Anti-Atlas. Bring sunscreen. Both are difficult to find on the road.

■ Carry an Arabic phrase book. English is not widely spoken in rural regions.

Saadian Tombs are important sites. If time and energy permit, walk south of the Palais Bahia to explore the bustling streets of the Mellah, the largest former Jewish quarter in Morocco. Another option is to book a hammam treatment in your hotel for a final hedonistic treat.

GREAT ITINERARIES

QUINTESSENTIAL MOROCCO: THE GRAND TOUR

In two weeks you can experience most of Morocco: coastal havens on the Atlantic coast, the High Atlas Mountains, pre-Saharan palmeries, Berber and Moorish architecture, rural hillside towns, and exquisite imperial cities.

Days 1 and 2: Tangier, Tetouan, and Chefchaouen

The best way to enjoy Tangier is by taking a walking tour along the beachfront. Enter the medina and see the **Grand Mosque** and large market at the **Grand Socco.** Head to the north side of the mosque to enter the beautiful **Mendoubia Gardens** before meandering through the smaller alleyways to the **Petit Socco.** From here, reach the 15th-century **kasbah** and sultanate palace of **Dar el-Kakhzen,** which houses the **Museum of Moroccan Arts** and **Museum of Antiquities.** Visit the historic **American Legation Cultural Center and Museum** commemorating the first diplomatic relations between the United States and Morocco. Enjoy a leisurely dinner by the water. On Day 2, pick up a rental car and drive southeast through the Rif Mountains to visit the Berber village of **Tetouan,** the historic town and UNESCO World Heritage Site dating from the 8th century. Continue onto the stunning blue-washed hillside city of **Chefchaouen;** stay in Lina Ryad and Spa, which is nestled in the heart of the medina.

Day 3: Meknès and Volubilis

Start early on Day 3. Drive through **Ouazzane** en route to Fez, stopping off at the Roman ruins of **Volubilis.** Spend at least 90 minutes walking the grounds. The Tangier Gate, Diana and the Bathing Nymphs mosaic, House of Orpheus, House of Columns, and House of Ephebus are must-sees. Then continue onto Meknès, arriving by midday. Pass the **Bab Mansour** and visit the holy **Mausoleum of Moulay Ismail,** which is open to non-Muslims. Walk toward the lively place el-Hedime, which leads into the medina. Tour the open bazaars of the medina streets and have some lunch. Near the row of pottery stands, visit the food souk. The **Museum of Moroccan Art** in the 19th-century Dar Jamai palace and **Heri el-Souani** (Royal Granaries) are recommended stops. Late in the afternoon, get back in the car and continue to Fez, arriving by nightfall, and splurge on a sumptuous Fassi meal.

Days 4 and 5: Fez and the Middle/High Atlas

Spend Day 4 and the morning of Day 5 exploring the Fez **medina,** absorbing the view from one of many rooftop terraces overlooking this ancient labyrinth or atop the hill of the **Musée des Armes** for an incredible panorama of the whole city. Tour the Fez el-Bali and Fez el-Djedid. Don't miss the blue-tiled gate of **Bab Boujeloud, Bou Inania medersa, Attarine madrassa, Zaouia Moulay Idriss II, Nejjarine fondouk,** and **Karaouine Mosque and University.** Visit the tanneries to find leather bargains, and explore the souks for famous blue-and-white Fassi pottery and carved thuya wood. On the afternoon of Day 5 head south through olive groves and small villages before reaching the indigenous macaques playing in their natural habitat of the serene **Azrou Cedar Forest** en route to **Erfoud,** where you can spend the night.

Days 6 and 7: Merzouga Dunes and Ouarzazate

Rise very early on Day 6 to catch the sunrise over the **Merzouga dunes,** and then get on the road to **Tinerhir.** Visit the

spectacular **Todra Gorge** and stay overnight in this pastoral region. On Day 7 explore the rugged landscape on the **kasbah** route in the Dadès Valley, passing stunning cliffs and canyons on the road to **Ouarzazate**. Treat yourself to a night at the wow-factor Hotel Sultana, where you can star-gaze surrounded by flickering lanterns.

Days 8–11: Marrakesh and Essaouira

Devote Day 8 to drive the Tizi-n-Tichka pass to Marrakesh, stopping off at the *ksour* (fortified villages) of **Aït Ben Haddou** and **Telouet**. Settle into a Marrakesh hotel by nightfall, and spend days 9 and 10 storming the medina, architectural monuments, and **Djemâa el Fna**. On Day 11, escape the crowds and head west to the calm coastal town of **Essaouira** for a relaxing afternoon and evening by the Atlantic shores.

Days 12–14: Safi, Casablanca, and Rabat

Day 12 takes you north along the coast to **El Oualidia**, where you should try some of the famous oysters, then on to the Portuguese port town of **El Jadida**. Spend the night here at the charming Hotel L'Iglesia. On Day 13, check out the stunning oceanside **Hassan II Mosque** in Casablanca before heading up to Rabat for your last day.

TIPS

■ If you'd rather stick mainly to the four imperial cities, take the train instead of a rental car. It's inexpensive, reliable, and fast.

■ A car is the best and sometimes only way to reach Morocco's mountainous area, small coastal villages, and rural regions, where roads are often rough and dirt.

■ Avoid driving at night. Roads are not well lighted, if at all.

■ Consider an adventure tour like camel riding in the Sahara, white-water rafting on the Ahansal River, or hot-air ballooning over the Ourika Valley.

■ Avoid faux guides and unlicensed tour drivers.

Wander through Rabat's **rue des Consuls** for last-minute purchases on your way to the 12th-century **Kasbah des Oudayas**, savoring your final taste of imperial Morocco. Casablanca is about an hour by train.

THE DYNASTIES OF MOROCCO

For centuries, Morocco, whose essence lies in a culturally rich mosaic of Arabic, European, and African influences, has lured and intrigued foreigners. With a complex and tumultuous history dating back more than 5,000 years, Morocco today is as unique and exotic as the diverse ethnic civilizations that have shaped everything here from language, music, art, and architecture to politics, education, and the economy. *by Victoria Tang*

At the crossroads between East and West, Africa and Europe, Morocco has attracted invading conquerors seeking a strategic foothold in fertile valleys, desert oases, and coveted coastal outposts on the Atlantic and Mediterranean. Excavations from the 12th century BC show the remains of Phoenician settlements in ancient times. It was not until the 7th century, when Arabian crusaders introduced Islam, that the Moroccan political landscape became more spectacular, often extreme, with radical religious reformers found-ing Muslim kingdoms in the midst of Christian encroachments and nomadic Berber tribal rule. Rural Berber tribes engaged in lawless conflict, battling it out with bloody family feuds in the harsh Sahara and unforgiving cliffs of the Atlas mountains. Successive invasions by Arab, French, and Spanish civilizations ensued, but the indigenous Berbers survived, remaining an integral component of today's Morocco. European colonization ultimately gave way to Morocco's independent state and a centralized constitutional government, still ruled today by sultan monarchs, descended from the Alaouite Dynasty.

(left) Casablanca's Hassan II Mosque (top) Tomb of Moulay Ismail, Méknes

(left) A mosaic in the Roman ruins at Volubilis (above) an aerial view of the city of Moulay Idriss (right) a Roman coin excavated near Essaouira, on Morocco's Atlantic coast

Predynastic Morocco

1200 BC – AD 700

As Phoenician trading settlements expanded along the Mediterranean, the Romans also began to spread west through North Africa, declaring Volubilis its capital, whose ruins stand outside of Meknès. Along Morocco's coasts, Portuguese incursions left ramparts surrounding Essaouira and El Jadida. The first Arab invasions occurred circa AD 682, collapsing the Roman Empire. The indigenous Imazighen Berbers embraced Islamic conquests, paving the way for the emergence of dynastic kingdoms.

- Lixus (⇨ Ch. 3)
- Volubilis (⇨ Ch. 5)
- Essaouira (⇨ Ch. 8)

Idrissid Dynasty

788 – 1000

Under the regime of Oqba Ibn Nafi, Arabs spread the religion of Islam and its holy language, Arabic, both of which took hold (to varying degrees) throughout Morocco. In 788, exiled from Baghdad, Moulay Idriss I established the first Islamic and Arab dynasty that lasted almost 200 years. He set out to transform the village of Fez into the principal city of western Morocco. In 807, Idriss II, his son, founded Fez el-Bali (literally, Fez the Old) as the new intellectual capital in the Fez River's fertile basin—the Oued Fez, also known as Oued el-Yawahir, the River of Pearls. Attracted by its importance, Andalusian and Tunisian Muslims arrived and established one of the most significant places of learning during its time—the Kairaouine University. The Fez medina is divided into two quarters on either side of the Fez River. The Andalusian Quarter originally housed refugees from Moorish Spain, who had begun to flee the *Reconquista* (the Christian re-conquest of Spain); the Kairaouine Quarter originally housed refugees from the Kairaouine. By the 10th and 11th centuries, the Bedouin tribe known as the Benu Hilal descended upon rural regions, destroying farmlands and villages.

- Kairaouine University (Fez, ⇨ Ch. 5)
- Moulay Idriss Mausoleum (Fez, ⇨ Ch. 5)

IN FOCUS THE DYNASTIES OF MOROCCO

(top left) Aït Ben Hadou, a ksar near Ouarzazate (near right) the entrance gates to Chellah, Rabat (far right) the towering minaret for the Koutoubia Mosque in Marrakesh

Almoravid Dynasty
1060–1150

From the south, one of the major Berber tribes emerged to create the Almoravid Dynasty, which led conquests to control desert trade routes to the north. By 1062, the Almoravids controlled what is now Morocco, Western Sahara, and Mauritania. Youssef ibh Tashfin established Marrakesh as his capital, building fortressed walls and underground irrigation channels, and conquered Tiemcen—what is today Algeria. He eventually extended his kingdom north into Spain by 1090.

■ Ben Youssef Medersa (Marrakesh, ⇨ Ch. 2)
■ Aït Benhaddou (⇨ Ch. 7)

Almohad Dynasty
1150–1248

The Almohad Dynasty, started by radical reformer Ibn Toumert (the Torch) in the High Atlas village of Tinmal, gave rise to an empire stretching across Spain, Tunisia, and Algeria. The Almohads built the current capital of Rabat and its famous landmarks, Marrakesh's iconic Koutoubia mosque, and the Giraldi Tower in Seville. After 100 years of rule, the Almohad empire collapsed because of civil warfare, causing Berbers to return to local tribes.

■ Koutoubia Mosque (Marrakesh, ⇨ Ch. 2)
■ Hassan Tower (Rabat, ⇨ Ch. 4)

The Merinid Dynasty
1248–1465

The nomadic Ben Merin Berber tribe from the Sahara established the Merinid Dynasty, pushing westward into northeastern Morocco and ousting the Almohads, who were once their masters. As Merinid tribesmen waged holy wars, they seized control of the Fez el-Jdid, constructing numerous Islamic mosques and madrassas (colleges). Jewish and Muslim refugees arrived fleeing the Spanish Inquisition, while invasions from Portugal and Spain captured coastal cities.

■ Bou Inania (Fez, ⇨ Ch. 5)
■ Chella necropolis (Rabat, ⇨ Ch. 4)

(far left) Asilah, a city in northern Morocco (near left) the Saadian Tombs in the Marrakesh medina (above) the fortified walls of Taroudant

The Wattisid Dynasty
1465 – 1554

Facing mounting territorial occupation by the Portuguese in what are now Tangier, Essaouira, and Agadir, the Merinids lost control to the Wattisids, who recruited high-ranking Muslim chiefs (viziers) to assume powers of the sultanate. The Wattisids reigned between 1472 and 1554 from Fez, relinquishing rule because of Moorish conquests on the Moroccan side of the Straits of Gibraltar. By 1492, Muslims had lost control of Spain and sought refuge back in the Maghreb.

■ Dar el Makhzen (Fez, ⇨ Ch. 5)
■ Asilah (⇨ Ch. 3)

The Saadian Dynasty
1554 – 1669

As the first Arab kingdom since the Idrissids, the Saadian Dynasty drove out the Christians. Lacking any loyalty to Berber tribes, they also proclaimed their superiority as direct descendants of the prophet Mohammed. The Saadi family originally settled in the Drâa Valley near Zagora in the 12th century and later in the Sous near Taroudant, which became the Saadian capital until they declared Marrakesh their sultanate in 1524. The greatest of the eleven Saadian sultans, Ahmed el Mansour, reigned for more than 25 years, building ties with England's monarchy as well as Spain.

He commanded an army to conquer the West African Songhai empire and led a gold rush on the Niger River. His impact on Morocco as "The Victorious" ended when he died in 1603, leaving his vast kingdom to his sons, who continued to reign for the next 60 years in both Marrakesh and Souss but failed to keep order and peace. General anarchy swept the country as Jewish and Muslim refugees from Catholic Spain arrived on chaotic shores while bands of pirates (the notorious Barbary pirates) sailed from Rabat and Salé.

■ Saadian Tombs (Marrakesh, ⇨ Ch. 2)
■ Taroudannt (⇨ Ch. 8)
■ Salé (⇨ Ch. 4)

Moulay Rashid captures Marrakesh from Saadiens	Morocco signs a treaty with Spain	Morocco becomes a French protectorate	Moroccan independence
1700	**1800**	**1900**	**2000**

1

IN FOCUS THE DYNASTIES OF MOROCCO

(far left) Moulay Ismail, who united and liberated Morocco from European powers in 1672 (near left) the gardens of the Museum of Moroccan Arts, Fez (bottom right) Tangier's waterfront promenade

The Alaouite Dynasty

1669 – 1894

The Alaouite Dynasty, founded by Moulay Rashid, captured Marrakesh in 1669. By 1672, the ruler Moulay Ismail seized Meknès, launching years of brutal holy wars while effectively liberating the country from European powers and laying the foundation for European trade relations. In 1767, Morocco signed a peace treaty with Spain and a trading agreement with France. In 1787, a U.S. peace treaty was signed. But the 19th century saw losses of territory to France.

■ Moulay Ismail Mausoleum (Meknès, ⇨ Ch. 5)
■ Dar Batha Museum (Fez, ⇨ Ch. 5)

European Conquest

1906 – 1956

By 1906, the majority of Africa was under European rule. Moulay el Hassan was the last of the pre-colonial sultans. After his son Abd el Aziz took over, Morocco, though still independent, was on the verge of bankruptcy after years of borrowing from European powers, in particular France. The Treaty of Fez in 1912 distributed Morocco's regions between Spain and (mostly) France, declaring the country as a French protectorate with Rabat as its capital. It was during this time that the Glaoui, who controlled one of the High Atlas passes from their kasbah at Telouet, became

allies with the French. Uprisings took place in the 1920s, and by the 1930s and 1940s, violent protests across the country heightened as the independence movement of the Istiqlal Party gained strength in Fez. Writers including Paul Bowles settled in Tangier, an international zone since 1923, and began an artistic counter-culture there. By 1955, the situation had reached a boiling point; France granted Morocco independence in 1956.

■ El Bahia Palace (Marrakesh, ⇨ Ch. 2)
■ Glaoui Kasbah (Telouet, ⇨ Ch6)
■ Tangier (⇨ Ch. 3)

(above) The Mohammed V
Mausoleum, Rabat (right)
Agadir's popular beachfront

Return of the Alaouite Dynasty

1956 – 1961

In 1956, Mohammed V returned from exile to regain the Moroccan throne. The Glaoui-French alliance was broken, and the Glaoui Dynasty went into an immediate decline. When Mohammed V died unexpectedly in 1961, his son, Hassan II, inherited the responsibility to continue social and political reforms, building up the country and maintaining his position as the country's spiritual leader. Hassan II was instrumental during the 1970s and 1980s in developing foreign relations between North Africa and the world.

■ Mohammed V Mausoleum (Rabat) (⇨ Ch. 4)

A New Morocco

1961 – 1987

The ascension of King Hassan II reflected the dynamic yet insecure spirit of a country in transition. Radical left-wing supporters emerged as serious threats to the monarchy. The Socialist Union of Popular Forces campaigned for radical reforms, a view shared by newly-independent Algeria, which briefly engaged in a territorial war with Morocco over disputed frontiers. Militants tried but failed to assassinate King Hassan II five times between 1963 and 1977. Rioting leftists took to the streets in violent protest against what they considered autocratic, absolute rule. At the same time, beach resorts were being built in Agadir in the 1970s and early 1980s, creating an influx of European beach-goers.

The desolate Western Sahara region in the deep south became one of Africa's most controversial and longest-running territorial conflicts beginning with the Green March of 1975, when Morocco exerted its control over the territory. The area remained a powder keg for explosive behavior throughout the 1980s, as stakes remain high to own the area's valuable natural resources, including phosphate deposits, fish reserves, and oil.

■ Agadir (⇨ Ch. 8)

| On Nov. 6, Hassan II orders "Green March" into Western Sahara | Mohammed VI becomes King | New family code gives women more power | Political reforms after "Arab Spring" uprisings |

| **1980** | **2000** | **2010** | **2020** |

1

IN FOCUS THE DYNASTIES OF MOROCCO

(above) Moroccan women can be both modern and traditional (right) Quartier des Habous, Casablanca

The Progressive Years
1987 – 1999

Morocco granted more local control and even elected a house of representatives. Infrastructure began to improve. The Casablanca Stock Exchange installed an electronic trading system in the early 1990s. A busy film economy, which had begun in the early 1960s, began to develop in Ouarzazate. With the death of King Hassan II in 1999, his son, Mohammed Ben al Hassan, was immediately enthroned as Mohammed VI at the age of 36 in a peaceful transition.

- Atlas Studios (Ouarzazate, ⇨ Ch7)
- Hassan II Mosque (Casablanca, ⇨ Ch. 4)

Modern Morocco
1999 – 2011

When King Mohammed VI married engineer Salma Bennani in 2002, she became the first wife of a Moroccan ruler to be publicly acknowledged and given a royal title. Women's rights have since improved. The minimum age for matrimony has risen to 18, and women have more freedom of choice in marriage and divorce. Women have also won seats in parliamentary elections. Terrorist bombings in 2003 and 2011 have raised fears of radical Islamic extremists, but King Mohammed VI has tried to expand constitutional reforms to create more freedom and limit the powers of the monarchy. Morocco has sought membership in the European Union, but the stalemate in Western Sahara remains unresolved, something that has hindered the region's stability and prosperity. The king continues to implement reforms and retain the affection of his people despite the 2011 Arab Spring, which toppled the more oppressive regimes of Morocco's neighbors. Mohammad VI has also adopted a moderate role in the government, which is seen as key to centering hardline Islamic preachers who are widely regarded as responsible for the radicalization of young men in Morocco, the Maghreb, and the Middle East.

FAQS

What currency does Morocco use? How can I exchange money?

The Moroccan currency is the dirham, denoted by DH or MAD. There are 100 centimes to one dirham. Denominations of 200, 100, 50, 25, and 20 DH are in circulation, with more than one style of note currently available. Coins are available in denominations of 10, 5, 2 and 1 DH, or 50, 20, 10 and 5 centimes.

Is Morocco cheap?

As a general rule, life in Morocco costs between one- and two-thirds less than life in a developed Western nation. That said, certain items are expensive, including meat, imported goods, and luxury items such as electronic equipment and cars. Public transport is very reasonable and the prices of public staples such as bread, bottled cooking gas, and flour are government-controlled.

Is the water safe to drink?

Though Moroccan tap water is relatively safe, tourists should still drink bottled or boiled water and avoid drinking from public fountains. Resist the temptation to add ice to room-temperature beverages. Brushing your teeth with tap water is usually okay.

How conservatively should I dress?

In larger cities, Morocco continues to be at the crossroads of traditional and modern culture and still tolerant of foreign influences. As a visitor, it's best to respect the locals with proper attire. Men should wear short- or long-sleeved shirts with long pants. Women should always cover their legs and shoulders. Very short skirts, shorts, and tank tops offend Moroccans, especially in smaller villages. Beachwear is strictly for the beach or private pools.

Do I need to speak Arabic?

Basic knowledge of Arabic and French phrases goes far, since these are Morocco's official languages. Many locals speak a Moroccan Arabic dialect with rural Berber roots, while English is heard more often in shops, hotels, and restaurants in larger towns.

Is it possible to drink wine, beer, or alcohol here?

Although alcohol is forbidden by Islam, it is readily available in restaurants, bars, and hotels classified with three stars or more. Supermarkets also sell wine and spirits to foreigners with proper identification, except during the holy days of Ramadan.

How much should I tip?

Tipping between 10% and 15% is customary. Keep on hand small bills and coins for attendants, taxi drivers, and servers. Guides expect about 100 DH per each hour hired. If someone helps you find your way back to your hotel, a tip of 10 DH should be offered.

Do I need a visa or vaccinations?

Americans on a typical vacation do not require visas, though everyone must carry a valid passport. There are no mandatory vaccinations.

Can I use my cell phone and laptop in Morocco?

As long as international roaming is enabled on your quad-band GSM mobile phone, you should be able to make and receive calls, but you may incur a hefty surcharge for this service; data roaming is particularly expensive. If you want to use a Moroccan prepaid SIM card, ask your service provider to unlock your phone. Laptops work with a European French plug adapter. Wi-Fi is widely available, especially in hotels and cafés.

MARRAKESH

WELCOME TO MARRAKESH

TOP REASONS TO GO

★ **Djemâa el Fna:** Wander amid the sizzle and smoke of the world's most exuberant marketplace.

★ **Souk shopping:** Lose yourself (literally) in the alluring lanes of the bazaars of the souk and the city.

★ **Authentic accommodations:** Stay in a riad and sip mint tea in the airy confines of your bougainvillea-filled courtyard haven.

★ **Historic sights:** Step back in time to the elaborate tombs and palaces of the Saadian sultans, and the calm and beauty of the intricate medersa.

★ **Dance till dawn:** From intimate clubs with belly dancers and hookah pipes to full-on techno raves with international DJs, Marrakesh is the hedonistic capital of Morocco.

1 Medina. The old walled city contains the bulk of the attractions, the *souks*, and *riads*. It's a warren of narrow *derbs*, where it's easy to get lost.

2 Guéliz. Northwest of the medina, Guéliz is the modern administrative center, home to the tourist information office, numerous tour agencies, fashionable boutiques, art galleries, cafés, and restaurants; avenue Mohammed V runs down its spine.

3 Hivernage. Southwest of the ramparts, south of avenues Hassan II and Mohammed V, Hivernage is populated largely with upmarket hotels and nightclubs. Its long, tree-lined boulevards stretch out to the Agdal and Menara gardens.

4 TO PALMERY
(SEE INSET AT RIGHT)

Majorelle Garden

Blvd. de Safi

Blvd. Allalel Fassi

GUÉLIZ **2**

Ave. Mohammed V

Ave. Moulay Abdallah

Rue de la Doukala

VILLE NOUVELLE

Ave. Hassan II

Rue Cadi Ayad

Place du 16 November

Rue des Nations Unies

Place de la Liberté

El Harti Gardens

Moulay El Hassan

Ave. Mohammed V

Ave.

Ave. Monturi

Rue Harel Ibrahim

Rue Echouada

Blvd. Ezzamour

Rue Abou-El Abbas Sti

Jardins de la Koutou

HIVERNAGE **3**

Ave. Bab Jdia

Ave. de la Ménara

Place de la Jeunesse

Ave. Gmassa

Route du Barrage

0 ————— 1 miles
0 ————— 1 kilometers

2

1 MEDINA

Douar Ouled Messaoud

The Palmery

Zone Residentielle

Guéliz
Train Station

Medina

Hivernage
Ménara Garden

Agdal Garden

Blvd. 11 Janvier

Rte. de Casablanca

Ave. Abdelkrim, al Karib

Rte. de Safi

Ave. Mohammed VI

Ave. Gnassa

Rte. de Fes

Rte. des Remparts

Route de Remparts

SOUKS

Place Rahba Kedima

Place Bab Fteuh

Place Djemâa el Fna

Rue Dar El Bacha

Rue Sidi El Yumami

Rue Sidi Boulabada

Ave. Ba Ahmed

Rue Moulay Ismail

Rue Bien Marine

Rue Riad Zitoun El Jedid

Rue Oukassi Bou Mrikaa

Rue Arset El Maach

Route d'Ourika

MELLAH

KASBAH

Route de Remparts

Ave. Al Madrasse

Ave. Al Mssalla

Ave. Tassitante

Agdal Garden

Per Fatima Zohra

0   1.5 mi
0   1.5 km

4 The Palmery. The
Palmery is a 30,000-acre
oasis, 7 km (4½ miles) north
of the medina between
the roads to Casablanca
and Fez. Once a series of
date plantations, it's now
a hideaway for the rich
and famous, with a crop of
luxury hotels and secluded
villas springing up among
the palms.

GETTING ORIENTED

Negotiating the twisting and
turning alleys deep in the
medina is a voyage in itself.
If you don't hire a guide,
keep a guidebook or at least
a map with you at all times;
comfortable, flat shoes and
a sense of humor will also
help. The medina, although
not quite as enclosed and
intense as the one in Fez,
takes some patience—street
names are often signposted
only in Arabic, if at all. A
small street is called a *rue*
in French or a *zencat* in
Arabic; an even smaller alley
is called a *derb*. Guéliz,
in comparison, is easy to
navigate. The wide streets
are signposted in French
and lined with orange and
jacaranda trees, office buildings, modern stores, and a
plethora of sidewalk cafés.

Updated by
Rachel Blech

Marrakesh is Morocco's most intoxicating city. Ever since Morocco's "Jewel of the South" became a trading and resting place on the ancient caravan routes from Timbuktu, the city has barely paused for breath.

Lying low and dominating the Haouz Plain at the foot of the snow-capped High Atlas Mountains (a marvelous sight on a sunny day), the city was stubbornly defended against marauding tribes by successive sultans. They maintained their powerful dynasties and surveyed their fertile lands from the Menara Garden's tranquil olive groves and lagoon, and the Agdal Gardens' vast orchards. Today, exploring the city has never been easier. A crackdown on hustlers who hassle and an undercover Tourist Police mean that you're freer than ever before to wander and wonder.

The medina is Marrakesh's miracle—a happy clash of old and new, in turn beguiling and confusing. Virtually unchanged since the Middle Ages, Marrakesh's solid, salmon-pink ramparts encircle and protect its mysterious labyrinthine medina, hiding palaces, mansions, and bazaars. Pedestrians struggle to find their balance on the tiny cobbled lanes among an endless run of mopeds, donkey carts, and wheelbarrows selling a mixture of sticky sweets and saucepans. But pick up your jaw, take your time, and take it all in, stewing in the Rose City like a mint leaf in a pewter teapot.

PLANNING

WHEN TO GO

Marrakesh can get surprisingly cold in the winter and after the sun goes down. Although the sun shines almost year-round, the best time to visit is in spring, when the surrounding hills and valleys are an explosion of colorful flowers, and fall, when the temperature is comfortable enough to warrant sunbathing. The only exception in that period is during Easter week, which brings crowds. July and August can be unbearably hot, with daytime temperatures regularly over 100°F. Christmas and New Year is peak season and the city fills to bursting, with hotels and riads booked up months in advance.

PLANNING YOUR TIME

To get a true feel for the charm and chaos of Marrakesh, a stay of at least five full days is recommended. Deciding exactly where to stay depends largely on personal taste and budget. Inside the ancient walled

medina, cozied up in a traditional riad, you'll never be far from the souks and historic sights. Most are reached on foot through a muddle of alleys with a taxi stand usually no more than a short walk from the front door. Small taxis and horse-drawn carriages can navigate to other points in the medina or into the *nouvelle ville* neighborhood. Families may prefer to opt for modern hotels in **Hivernage** or **Guéliz** where the vibe is more European. The streets here are safe (though the paving often broken and hazardous) and taxis are plentiful for the short hop to the medina. Farther afield is the luscious **Palmery,** oozing exclusivity and offering boutique hotels for idyllic days of total relaxation to a sound track of birdsong. The drawback here is that transport into town gets costly, at around 150 DH for a taxi each way.

GETTING HERE AND AROUND

AIR TRAVEL

Menara Airport in Marrakesh receives domestic flights from Casablanca and direct international flights from the United Kingdom, Ireland, and Scandinavia. Flights from the United States, Canada, Brazil, and the Middle East pass through Casablanca. The trip from the airport to town is only 15 minutes by car, taxi, or bus. Public Bus No. 19 departs the airport every 30 minutes from 6:30 am to 9:30 pm daily. It stops at the place Djemâa el Fna and continues through to Guéliz, serving most of the main hotels along avenues Mohammed V and Mohammed VI (cost 30 DH). The standard charge for a run into the medina in petits taxis starts at about 80 DH during the daytime and 120 DH after 8 pm, but you will have to negotiate. Grand taxis cost 100 DH to 150 DH during the day, 150 DH to 200 DH after 8 pm.

BUS TRAVEL

Intercity buses all leave from Marrakesh. Use the *gare routière* at Bab Doukkala for national public buses, or the Supratours or Compagnie du Transports au Maroc (CTM) bus stations in Guéliz. Buses arrive at the gare routière from Casablanca, Rabat, Fez, Agadir, Ouarzazate, and other cities. CTM and Supratours buses have their own terminals, but also stop at the gare routière. They are quicker, safer, and more comfortable than public buses to most key destinations. Supratours, which has its office next door to the train station on avenue Hassan II, links up with Morocco's train network, with bus routes to destinations south and west of Marrakesh.

Within Marrakesh, the public Alsa City Bus runs all over town; fares are a standard 4 DH.

Bus Contacts ALSA City Bus ☎ *0524/33–52–70* ⊕ *www.alsa.ma.* **Compagnie de Transports au Maroc (CTM).** ✉ *Gare Routière, Bab Doukkala* ☎ *0522/54–10–10* ⊕ *www.ctm.ma* ✉ *Rue Abou Bakr Seddiq, near Theatre Royal, Guéliz* ☎ *0522/54–10–10* ⊕ *www.ctm.ma.* **Supratours** ✉ *Av. Hassan II, near train station, Guéliz* ☎ *0890/20–30–40* ⊕ *www.oncf.ma.*

CALÈCHE TRAVEL

Calèches are green, canopied, horse-drawn carriages that hold four to five people. Even if they do scream "tourist," they're a great way to reach your evening meal, and children love riding up front beside the driver. They're also picture-perfect for trips out to enjoy the Majorelle,

Menara, and Agdal gardens. You should always agree on a price beforehand, but keep in mind that rides generally cost a minimum of 150 DH per hour; trips to the Palmery might cost 500 DH, and round-trip excursions (circling the ramparts, say) might cost 300 DH. There are two main pickup stops: one is in the medina, along the left side of the street stretching from the Djemâa el Fna to the Koutoubia Mosque; the other is in Guéliz, just south of the place de la Liberté and west of Bab Nkob. You can also try flagging one down.

CAR TRAVEL

Marrakesh is in Morocco's center, so it connects well by road with all other major destinations. Most of these roads are good, two-lane highways with hard, sandy shoulders for passing. There is a new freeway connecting Marrakesh to Casablanca in the north and Agadir to the southwest.

Within the Marrakesh medina, driving is not recommended. Cars can pass through some of the medina's narrow alleys, but not all, and unless you know the lay of the land you risk getting stuck and being hard-pressed to perform a U-turn. Outside the medina, in the nouvelle ville and suburbs, traffic is frenetic and locals freely admit that stoplights and lane markings are purely decorative and rarely observed. It can be hazardous to drive here as well.

Rental Cars Amsterdam Cars ⊠ *No. B, 112, av. Mohammed V, Guéliz* ☎ *0611/71–70–60, 0662/20–00–21* ⊕ *www.amsterdamcar.com.* **Avis** ⊠ *Marrakech Menara Airport, Hivernage* ☎ *0524/43–31–69* ⊕ *www.avis. com.* **Europcar** ⊠ *63, bd. Zerktouni, in the Afriqui gas station forecourt, Guéliz* ☎ *0524/43–12–28* ⊕ *www.europcar.com.* **Hertz** ⊠ *154, av. Mohammed V, Guéliz* ☎ *0524/43–99–84* ⊕ *www.hertz.ma.* **Label Voiture** ⊠ *No. 20, Immeuble 90, bd. Zerktouni, 1st fl., Guéliz* ☎ *0524/42–15–19* ⊕ *www.labelvoiture.com.* **Medloc** ⊠ *No. 3, 75, rue Ibn Aicha, 1st fl., Guéliz* ☎ *0524/43–57–57* ⊕ *www.medloc-maroc.com.*

TAXI TRAVEL

Petits taxis in Marrakesh are small, beige, metered cabs permitted to transport three passengers. A petit taxi ride from one end of Marrakesh to the other should cost around 20 DH (50% extra from 8 pm to 6 am). Taxi Vert is a new dial-a-cab service that allows you to preorder a petit taxi for a specific pickup for 15 DH on top of the metered charge, very useful for late at night. *Grands taxis* are the ubiquitous, old four-door Mercedes and have two uses. Most often they simply take a load of up to six passengers on short hauls to suburbs and nearby towns, forming a reliable, inexpensive network throughout each region of Morocco. They can also be chartered for private hire for excursions and airport transfers.

Taxi Contacts Taxi Vert ☎ *0524/40–94–94.*

TRAIN TRAVEL

Marrakesh is connected by good train service to Tangier, Rabat, Casablanca, and Fez. The train station is located on avenue Mohammed VI at the junction with avenue Hassan II in Guéliz and is Morocco's main southern terminus. Advance reservations can be made for first class only. Per day there are six trains to Tangier, eight to Fez, and nine to Casablanca.

Train Contact ONCF ✉ *Av. Mohammed VI, at av. Hassan II, Guéliz* ☎ *0890/20–30–40* ⊕ *www.oncf.ma.*

GUIDES AND TOURS

Guides can be helpful when navigating the medina's serpentine streets. They can point out little-known landmarks and help you understand the city's complicated history. You are best off booking a licensed guide through a tour company, and your hotel's staff will be able to suggest one to suit your interests. Although guides can be very knowledgeable about the city, don't rely on them for shopping. Store owners will inflate prices in order to give the guides kickbacks. The going rate for a city guide is 300 DH for a half day, 500 DH for a full day.

The Conseil Regional du Tourisme office near the Koutoubia Mosque has maps, brochures, and general tourist information for Marrakesh and the surrounding area.

TOUR COMPANIES AND GUIDES

Conseil Régional du Tourisme. The tourist office near the Koutoubia Mosque has maps, brochures, and general tourist information for Marrakesh and the surrounding area. ✉ *Pl. Ibn Youssef Tachfine, off av. Hommane el Fatouakia, Medina* ☎ *0524/38–52–61* ⊙ *Oct.–Apr., weekdays 8:30–noon and 3–6:30; May–Sept., weekdays 9–3.*

Legendes Evasions. This highly respected local agency runs chauffeured vehicle tours to some of the Berber villages around Marrakesh. Day trips start at around 2,200 DH for up to four people per car. ✉ *Galerie Elite, 212, av. Mohammed V, 1st fl., Guéliz* ☎ *0524/33–24–83* ⊕ *www.legendesevasions.com.*

Mohammed Lahcen. If you want a top-notch private guide for Marrakesh, you can't beat English-speaking Mohammed Lahcen. The going rate for a city guide is 300 DH for a half day, 600 DH for a full day. ☎ *0661/20–06–39* ✍ *bab_adrar@hotmail.com.*

Office National Marocain du Tourisme ✉ *Pl. Abdel Moumen Ben Ali, av. Mohammed V and rue Yougoslavie, opposite Les Negoçiants café, Guéliz* ☎ *0524/43–61–31* ⊙ *Weekdays 8:30–4:30.*

Sahara Expedition. This budget agency runs daily group excursions and tours throughout the region, including Ourika Valley and Essaouira. Three-day sprints via minibus to the Sahara desert at Merzouga start from 1,000 DH per person with very basic hotels. ✉ *22, bd. Mohammed Zerktouni, Guéliz* ☎ *0524/42–97–47* ⊕ *www.saharaexpe.ma.*

Said el-Fagousse. The amiable Said el-Fagousse has encyclopedic knowledge of Marrakesh's secret treasures and Moroccan history. Originating from the desert village of M'Haimd el Ghizalne, he is a qualified guide for both city and nationwide destinations. His rates are 400 DH for a half day, 700 DH for a full day. ☎ *0662/02–47–04* ✍ *moroccotourguide@gmail.com.*

SheherazadVentures. This Marrakesh-based English-Moroccan company organizes private tailored tours with a cultural focus. They're specialists in Sahara experiences (think 4x4s and camel trekking), active day excursions from Marrakesh, and national tours. Rates start around 1,000 DH per day depending on group size, accommodation, and length of tour. ✉ *No. 55, Residence Ali (C), av. Mohammed VI, near Café Cesar, Guéliz* ☎ *0615/64–79–18* ⊕ *www.sheherazadventures. com.*

SAFETY

Like other Moroccan cities, Marrakesh is quite safe. While women—particularly those traveling alone or in pairs—are likely to suffer from catcalls and whistles, there is generally little physical risk. The city does have its fair share of pickpockets, especially in markets and other crowded areas; handbags should be

> **BEST MARRAKESH MAP**
>
> An accurate map is key to finding your way around Marrakesh. The best pocket map is "Marrak'Chic Shopping Map," which marks out different areas of the souks as well as key landmarks, restaurants, and hotels. It also extends into Guéliz and Hivernage. Pick one up at a newsstand or bookstore for 15 DH. An excellent large-scale map of the medina published by MedinaCarte.com plots every convoluted twist and turn. It's available at bookstores or online and costs 100 DH.

zippered and held beneath an arm, and wallets placed in front pockets. The old city shuts down relatively early, so don't wander its dark alleys late at night. The Moroccan Tourist Police take their jobs very seriously, so don't hesitate to call on them. They operate undercover so are hard to identify, but in the medina they are never far away; ask any guide or shopkeeper to alert them if you are in trouble. Their office is on the northern side of the place Djemâa el Fna.

Brigade Touristique (Tourist Police) ✉ *Pl. Djemâa el Fna* ☎ *0524/38–46–01.*

EXPLORING MARRAKESH

Most of the medina is navigable only on foot, and you may opt to engage one of the official city guides to steer you through the maze. Qualified guides can be worth their weight in gold as they shield you from overzealous merchants and share the city's colorful history, but some push their clients towards shopping to earn a handsome commission. Make it clear at the outset if you want to shop. The going rate for a city guide is 300 DH for a half day, 600 DH for a full day. Many apps for unguided walking tours are available online, for example at ⊕ *www. gpsmycity.com*; if you go this route, keep an eye on your phone and bag.

Most of the medina's monuments charge an entry fee of 10 DH to 50 DH and have permanent but unsalaried on-site guides; if you use one, tip him about 30 DH to 50 DH.

MEDINA

If you can see the ramparts, you're either just inside or just outside the medina. In some respects not much has changed here since the Middle Ages. The medina is still a warren of narrow cobblestone streets lined with thick-walled, interlocked houses; designed to confuse invaders, the layout now serves much the same purpose for visitors. Donkeys and mules still deliver produce, wood, and wool to their destinations, and age-old crafts workshops still flourish as retail endeavors.

TOP ATTRACTIONS

Fodor'sChoice ★ **Ali ben Youssef Medersa.** If you want a little breath taken out of you, don't pass up the chance to see this extraordinarily well-preserved 16th-century Koranic school, North Africa's largest such institution. The delicate intricacy of the *gibs* (stucco plasterwork), carved cedar, and *zellij* (mosaic) on display in the central courtyard makes the building seem to loom taller than it really does. As many as 900 students from Muslim countries all over the world once studied here, and arranged around the courtyard are their former sleeping quarters—a network of tiny upper-level rooms that resemble monks' cells. The building was erected in the 14th century by the Merenids in a somewhat different style from that of other medersas; later, in the 16th century, Sultan Abdullah el Ghallib rebuilt it almost completely, adding the Andalusian details. The large main courtyard, framed by two columned arcades, opens into a prayer hall elaborately decorated with rare palm motifs as well as the more-customary Islamic calligraphy. The medersa also contains a small mosque. ⊠ *Just off rue Souk el Khemis, Medina* ☎ *0524/44–18–93* 🖾 *50 DH for medersa, 60 DH combination ticket with Musée de Marrakech* ۞ *Daily 9–6.*

Dar Si Saïd. This 19th-century palace is now a museum with an excellent collection of antique Moroccan crafts including pottery from Safi and Tamegroute, jewelry, daggers, kaftans, carpets, and leatherwork. The palace's courtyard is filled with flowers and cypress trees, and furnished with a gazebo and fountain. The most extraordinary salon is upstairs; it's a somber room decorated with gibs cornices, zellij walls, and an amazing carved-cedar ceiling painted in the *zouak* style (bright colors in intricate patterns). Look for the prize exhibit, a marble basin with an inscription indicating its 10th-century Córdoban origin. The basin, which is sometimes on loan to other museums, was once given pride of place in the Ali ben Youssef Mosque in the north of the souk. It was brought to Morocco by the Almoravid sultan in spite of its decorative eagles and griffins, which defy the Koran's prohibition of artistic representations of living things. Guides are available on-site. ⊠ *Riad Zitoune El Jdid, Derb Si Saïd, Medina* ☎ *0524/38–95–64* 🖾 *20 DH* ۞ *Wed.–Mon. 9–5.*

Fodor'sChoice ★ **Djemâa el Fna.** The carnivalesque open square right at the center of the medina is Marrakesh's heartbeat and a UNESCO World Heritage Site. This centuries-old square was once a meeting point for regional farmers and tradesmen, storytellers and healers; today it's surrounded by bazaars, mosques, and terraced cafés with perfect balcony views over the action. Transvestite dancers bat their eyelashes; cobras sway to the tones of snake charmers; henna women make their swirling marks on your hands; fortune-tellers reveal mottled futures; apothecaries offer bright-powder potions and spices; bush dentists with Berber molars piled high on tables extract teeth; and, best of all, men tell stories to each other the old way, on a magic carpet around a gas lamp.

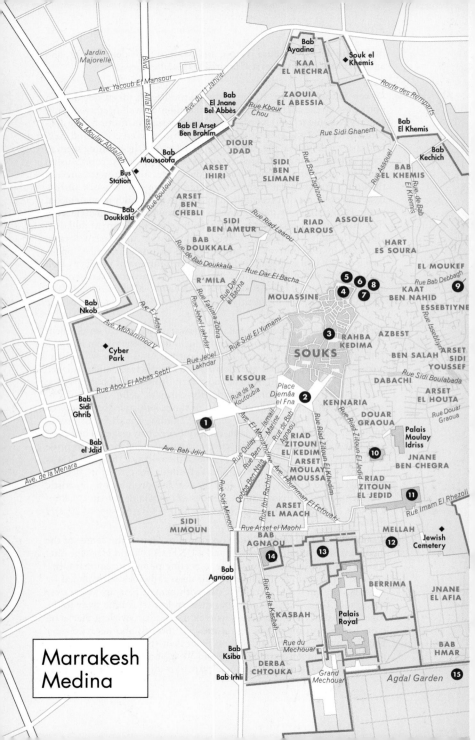

Marrakesh Medina

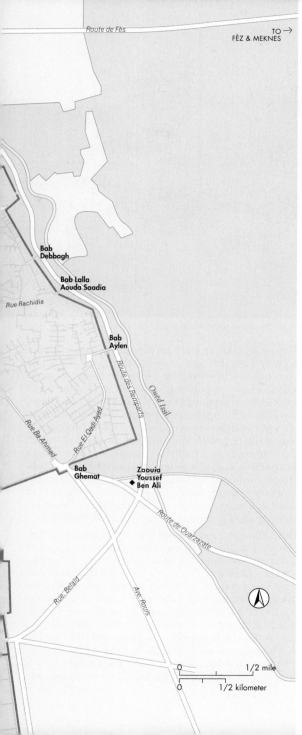

Route de Fès

TO →
FÈZ & MEKNES

Bab
Debbagh

Bab Lalla
Aouda Saadia

Rue Rachidia

Bab
Aylen

Route des Remparts

Oued Issil

Rue Ba Ahmad

Rue El Qadi Ayad

Bab
Ghemat

Zaouia
Youssef
Ben Ali

Route de Ouarzazate

Rue Belaïd

Ave. Roufis

0   1/2 mile

0   1/2 kilometer

The El Badi Palace, built by the Saadian sultans, is one of the largest structures in Marrakesh's medina.

All day (and night) long you can get fresh orange or grapefruit juice from the green gypsy carts that line up round the square, for about 4 DH a glass. You can also buy a shot of cool water from one of the roving water sellers, whose eye-popping costumes carry leather water pouches and polished-brass drinking bowls. Or snack on sweet dates, apricots, bananas, almonds, sugar-coated peanuts, and walnuts from the dried fruit–and–nut stalls in the northwest corner. Meat and vegetable grills cook into the night, when Marrakshis come out to eat, meet, and be entertained. It might be a fun bazaar today, but once upon a time the Djemâa's purpose was more gruesome; it accommodated public viewings of the severed heads of sinners, criminals, and Christians. *Djemâa* actually means "meeting place" and *el Fna* means "the end" or "death," so as a whole it means something along the lines of "assembly of death" or "meeting place at the end of the world." ✉ *Medina*.

El Badi Palace. This 16th-century palace was once a playground for Saadian princes and visiting diplomats—a mammoth showpiece for opulent entertaining. Today it's a romantic set of sandstone ruins, policed by nesting storks. Sultan Ahmed el Mansour's lavish creation was ransacked by Moulay Ismail in the 17th century to help him complete his own palace at Meknès. But it's not hard to see why the palace, whose name translates as "The Marvel," was once among the world's most impressive monuments. A huge swimming pool in the center (still there today, but empty) is flanked by four others, along with four sunken orange orchards. The main hall was named the Koubba el Khamsiniyya, referring to its 50 grand marble columns. Along the southern wall is a series of underground corridors and dungeons. It's a vast, calm, and mystical place. Also on display is a collection of goods from the Minbar (pulpit from which the Imam gives services) of the Koutoubia Mosque. If you use an on-site guide (otherwise unpaid), who can bring the place to life, you should also tip 30 DH to 50 DH. ■ TIP→ **The palace is currently hosting the Marrakech Museum for Photography and Visual Arts until its modernist complex, designed by David Chipperfield, is completed in 2016 at a site near the Menara Gardens.** ⊠ *Enter ramparts and enormous gateway near pl. des Ferblantiers, Kasbah* ☎ *0524/37–81–63* 🖾 *10 DH for palace, 20 DH for palace and Koutoubia Mosque Minbar* ☉ *Daily 9–5:45.*

Fodor's Choice
★

Koutoubia Mosque. Yacoub el Mansour built Marrakesh's towering Moorish mosque on the site of the original 11th-century Almoravid mosque. Dating from the early 12th century, it became a model for the Hassan Tower in Rabat and La Giralda in Seville. The mosque takes its name from the Arabic word for book, *koutoub,* because there was once a large booksellers' market nearby. The minaret is topped by three golden orbs, which, according to one local legend, were offered by the mother of the Saadian sultan Ahmed el Mansour Edhabi in penance for fasting days she missed during Ramadan. The mosque has a large plaza, walkways, and gardens, as well as floodlights to illuminate its curved windows, a band of ceramic inlay, pointed *merlons* (ornamental edgings), and various decorative arches. Although non-Muslims may not enter, anyone within earshot will be moved by the power of the evening muezzin call. ⊠ *South end of av. Mohammed V, Medina.*

Fodor's Choice
★

La Bahia Palace. This 19th-century palace, once home to a harem, is a marvelous display of painted wood, ceramics, and symmetrical gardens. Built by Sultan Moulay el Hassan I's notorious Grand Vizier Bou Ahmed, the palace was ransacked on Bou Ahmed's death, but you can still experience its layout and get a sense of its former beauty. Don't forget to look up at smooth arches, carved-cedar ceilings, *tadlak* (shiny marble) finishes, gibs cornices, and zouak painted ceilings. Fancy a room? Each one varies in size according to the importance of each wife or concubine. The entire palace is sometimes closed when the royal family is in town, since their entourage often stays here. If you use an on-site guide, you should also tip 30 DH to 50 DH. ⊠ *Rue Riad Zitoun el Jdid, near pl. des Ferblantiers, Medina* 🖾 *10 DH* ☉ *Daily 9–5.*

Les Terrasses de l'Alhambra. In Djemâa el Fna's northeastern corner, this is the classiest option, with decent pizza and pasta and warm wood panels. It's tucked away at the edge of the square, but still has lovely views. Bag a seat on the top terrace. No credit cards are accepted and no alcohol served. ⊠ *Pl. Djemâa el Fna, opposite Café de France, Medina* ☎ *0524/42–75–70.*

Fodor's Choice
★

Musée de Marrakech. The main reason to come to this small but perfectly formed museum next door to the Ali ben Youssef Medersa is not the exhibitions, but rather the stunning central atrium, a tiled courtyard containing a huge lamp shade that resembles a UFO descending. Set within the restored 19th-century Menebhi Palace, this is a perfect place to relax while enjoying Moroccan architecture and gentle music piped through speakers. The temporary exhibitions in the courtyard are often of beautiful artifacts and paintings (some for sale), but they're poorly displayed and lack English translations. The museum also has a good bookstore and a café. ■TIP→ **The restrooms are spotless and worth the admission price if you find yourself far from your hotel.** ⊠ *Pl. ben Youssef, Medina* ☎ *0524/44–18–93* ⊕ *www.museedemarrakech. ma* ⊡ *50 DH for museum, 60 DH combination ticket with Ali ben Youssef Medersa* ⊙ *Daily 9–6.*

Saadian Tombs. This small, beautiful 16th-century burial ground is the permanent resting place of 166 Saadians, including its creator, Sultan Ahmed el Mansour, the "Golden One." True to his name, he did it in style—even those not in the lavish mausoleum have their own colorful zellij graves, laid out for all to see, among the palm trees and flowers. Because the infamous Moulay Ismail chose not to destroy them (he was apparently superstitious about plundering the dead), these tombs are one of the few Saadian relics left. He simply sealed them up, leaving only a small section open for use. The complex was rediscovered only in 1917 by General Hubert Lyautey during the French protectorate. Passionate about every aspect of Morocco's history, the general undertook the restoration of the tombs.

The central mausoleum, the **Hall of Twelve Columns,** contains the tombs of Ahmed el Mansour and his family. It's dark, lavish, and ornate, with a huge vaulted roof, carved cedar doors and *moucharabia* (carved wooden screens traditionally used to separate the sexes), and gray Italian marble columns. In a smaller inner mausoleum, on the site of an earlier structure containing the decapitated body of the Saadian dynasty's founder, Mohammed esh Sheikh, is the tomb of El Mansour's mother. ■TIP→ **Get here either early or late to avoid the crowds and to see the monuments swathed in soft golden sunlight.** If you use one of the on-site guides (who are unpaid), you should tip 30 DH to 50 DH. ⊠ *Rue de la Kasbah, across small square from mosque* ⊡ *10 DH* ⊙ *Daily 9–5:45.*

Fodor's Choice
★

Souks. The vast labyrinth of narrow streets and derbs at the center of the medina is the souk—Marrakesh's marketplace and a wonder of arts, crafts, and workshops. Every step brings you face-to-face with the colorful handicrafts and bazaars for which Marrakesh is famous. In the past, every craft had a special zone within the market—a souk within the souk. Today savvy vendors have pushed south to tap trading opportunities as early as possible, and few of the original sections remain. Look for incongruities born of the modern era. Beside handcrafted wooden pots for kohl eye makeup are modern perfume stores; where there is a world of hand-sewn djellabas at one turn, you'll find soccer jerseys after the next; fake Gucci caps sit beside handmade Berber carpets, their age-old tassels fluttering in the breeze.

■TIP→ **As you wander through the souk, take note of landmarks so you can return to a particular bazaar without too much trouble. Once the bazaars' shutters are closed, they're often unrecognizable.** The farther north you go the more the lanes twist, turn, and entwine. Should you have to retrace your steps, a compass comes in handy, as does a mental count of how many left or right turns you've taken since you left the main drag. But mostly you'll rely on people in the souk to point the way. If you ask a shopkeeper rather than a loitering local, you'll be less likely to be "guided." ⊠ *North of pl. Djemaâ el Fna, Medina.*

NEED A BREAK?

Chez Lamine Hadj Mustapha. Although the row of severed lambs' heads out front may not be everyone's idea of culinary heaven, Marrakshis love Chez Lamine Hadj Mustapha, and you'd be missing out not to try it. English TV chef Jamie Oliver chose this spit-and-sawdust street restaurant in a filming trip for a gutsy example of Moroccan roast lamb specialty, *mechoui*—and it's not every day you walk past a whole lamb being cooked. Follow a tiny street that leads off the Djemâa el Fna (to the left of Les Terrasses de l'Alhambra) and you'll see exactly that. Ask to see the oven—a hole in the ground where the entire animal is cooked over hot wood ash. The meat is then hauled up and cut in front of you, served with bread for a cheap 20 DH sandwich, or for larger amounts at 140 DH per kilogram. If you're nervous, ask for a small taste first. However much you have, sprinkle the meat with a delicious cumin-and-salt spice mix and wash it all down with mint tea. Get there before noon. Cash only. ⊠ *18–26, Souk Ablouh, Medina* ☎ *0661/39–84–28.*

WORTH NOTING

Agdal Garden. Some say dull scrub; others, pinnacle of romance. Stretching a full 3 km (2 miles) south of the Royal Palace, the Jardin de l'Aguedal comprises vast orchards, a large lagoon, and other small pools, all fed by an impressive, ancient system of underground irrigation channels from the Ourika Valley in the High Atlas. The entire garden is surrounded by high *pisé* (a mixture of mud and clay) walls, and the olive, fig, citrus, pomegranate, and apricot orchards are still in their original raised-plot form. The largest lagoon, the grandiose Tank of Health, is said to be the 12th-century creation of an Almohad prince, but, as with most Moroccan historic sites, the Agdal was consecutively abandoned and rebuilt—the latest resurrection dates from the 19th century. Until the French protectorate's advent, it was the sultans' retreat of choice for lavish picnics and boating parties. ■ TIP→ If you're here on a clear day, don't miss the magic and majesty of a 180-degree turn, from facing the Koutoubia Mosque (northwest) to facing the Atlas Mountains (southeast). ⊠ *Medina ⊹ Approach via Méchouar; or from outside the ramparts, walk left on rte. d'Agdal and the main garden entrance will be on your right* ☉ *Fri. and Sun. 9–6.*

Ali ben Youssef Mosque. After the Koutoubia, this is the medina's largest mosque and Marrakesh's oldest. The building was first constructed in the second half of the 12th century by the Almoravid sultan Ali ben Youssef, around the time of the Qoubba Almoravid. In succeeding centuries it was destroyed and rebuilt several times by the Almohads and the Saadians, who changed its size and architecture accordingly; it was last overhauled in the 19th century, in the then-popular Merenid style. Non-Muslims may not enter. ⊠ *Just off rue Souk el Khemis, rue Assouel, next to Ali ben Youssef Medersa, Medina.*

Maison de la Photographie. A new addition to the Marrakech cultural scene, this restored riad houses a special collection of original black-and-white photos depicting life in Moroccan communities between 1862 and 1950. There is also a very pleasant roof terrace café. You can find the Maison de la Photographie just behind the Ali ben Youssef Medersa. ⊠ *Rue Ahel Fes, Medina* 📞 *0524/38–57–21* ⊕ *www. maisondelaphotographie.ma* 💰 *40 DH* 🕐 *Daily 9:30–7.*

Mellah. As in other Moroccan cities, the Mellah is the old Jewish quarter, once a small, walled-off city within the city. Although it was once home to a thriving community of native and Spanish Jews, along with rabbinical schools and scholars, today it's home to only a few Jewish inhabitants. You can visit the remains of a couple of synagogues with the help of an official guide, or local kids will be happy to point the way in return for a few dirhams. The Lazama Synagogue is open daily and is still used for weddings and bar mitzvahs of foreign visitors. It has a pretty, blue-tile inner courtyard. The Mellah gets its name from the Arabic word for salt, and some say that the Jewish residents who lived here acquired their wealth through the salt trade. ⊠ *Medina.*

Qoubba Almoravid. This is the city's oldest monument and the only intact example of Almoravid architecture in all of Morocco (the few other ruins include some walls here in Marrakesh and a minaret in El Jadida). Dating from the 12th century, this masterpiece of mechanical water-works somehow escaped destruction by the Almohads. It was once used for ablutions before prayer in the next-door Ali ben Youssef Mosque (relying on the revolutionary hydraulics of *khatteras*, drainage systems dug down into the water table), and also had a system of toilets, showers, and faucets for drinking water. It was only excavated from the rubble of the original Ali ben Youssef Mosque and Medersa in 1948. ■ TIP→ The monument is in an advanced state of disrepair and in 2014 was closed to the public for safety reasons. You can view it from the exterior perimeter. ⊠ *Pl. Ben Youssef, Medina.*

Ramparts. The medina's amazingly well-preserved walls measure about 33 feet high and 7 feet thick, and are 15 km (9 miles) in circumference. The walls are fashioned from local reddish clay laid in huge blocks. The holes that are visible on the exterior surface are typical of this style of construction, marking where wooden scaffold supports have been inserted as each level is added. Until the early 20th century, before the French protectorate, the gates were closed at night to prevent anyone who didn't live in Marrakesh from entering. Eight of the 14 original *babs* (arched entry gates) leading in and out of the medina are still in use. Bab Agnaou, in the Kasbah, is the loveliest and best preserved of the arches. ■ TIP→ The best time to visit the walls is just before sunset, when the swallows that nest in the ramparts' holes come out to take their evening meal. A leisurely calèche drive around the perimeter takes about an hour.

Tanneries. For a whiff of Marrakesh life the old way, the tanneries are a real eye-waterer, not least because of the smell of acrid pigeon excrement, which provides the ammonia that is vital to the tanning process. Six hundred skins sit in a vat at any one time, resting there for up to

2

two months amid constant soaping, scrubbing, and polishing to get the leather strong, supple, clean, and ready for use. Goat and sheep skins are popular among Berbers, while Arabs prefer camels and cows and tend to use more machine processes and chemical agents. Once the hides have been stripped of fur, washed, and made supple through this six-week process, the final stage involves soaking and rubbing in a mix of ground mimosa bark and water, which eventually turns the grayish-green hides into the natural reddish-brown or "tan" shade that we always expect in our natural leather goods. The tanned skins are dried in the sun and then sold directly to the artisans near Ali ben Youssef Mosque. Additional color dyeing takes place after the skins have been purchased by the artisans in another part of the souk.

Thirteen tanneries, mixing both Berber and Arab elements, are still in operation in the Bab Debbagh area in the northeast of the medina. Simply turn up rue de Bab Debbagh and look for the tannery signs above several open doorways to both the right and left of the street. To visit one of them, just pop in and the local manager will offer you mint leaves to cover the smell, explain the process, and guide you around the vats of dyes. In return he'll hope for a healthy tip to share with his workers; this is a dying art in a poor dyeing area, so the more you can tip, the better.

■TIP→ **Finding avenue Bab Debbagh can be frustrating; it's easier to approach via taxi from outside the ramparts and be dropped off at Bab Debbagh, or to ask an official guide to include the visit as part of a set itinerary. Once in the vicinity, you'll be inundated with offers from would-be guides who will then ask for money; solo travelers and women should exercise caution.** ⊠ *Av. Bab Debbagh, Medina.*

GUÉLIZ AND HIVERNAGE

In addition to office buildings, contemporary shops, and malls—none of which may exceed the nearest mosque's height—Guéliz has plenty of sidewalk cafés, international restaurants, art galleries, upscale boutiques, and antiques stores. Connecting the two sectors, between avenues Mohammed VI and Hassan II, are the delightful public Harti Gardens. Hivernage is a leafy suburb by comparison, with olive trees, roses, and orange trees lining its boulevards. It's the most expensive urban residential district in the city, with gated private residences interspersed with smart hotels, casinos, nightclubs, restaurants, and chic cafés.

TOP ATTRACTIONS

Fodor's Choice
★

Majorelle Garden. The Jardin Majorelle was created by the French painter Louis Majorelle, who lived in Marrakesh between 1922 and 1962. It then passed into the hands of another Marrakesh lover, the late fashion designer Yves Saint Laurent. If you've just come from the desert, it's a sight for sore eyes, with green bamboo thickets, lily ponds, and an electric-blue gazebo. There's also a villa housing a fascinating Berber Museum with regular exhibitions, a museum shop, and a delightful café. ■TIP→ **Try to visit in the early morning before the tour groups—you'll hear the chirruping of sparrows rather than the chatter of humans.** ⊠ *Av. Yacoub el Mansour, main entrance on rue Yves St. Laurent,*

Guéliz ☎ *0524/31–30–47* ⊕ *www.jardinmajorelle.com* 🖃 *Garden 50 DH, museum 25 DH* ☉ *Daily 8–6:30.*

WORTH NOTING

Marché Central. The once-thriving Central Market in Guéliz was moved from its old home on avenue Mohammed V to make way for the luxury Carré Eden shopping mall, which opened in 2014. The market can now be found on rue Ibn Toumert, close to the Gendarmerie Royale and behind Marrakech Plaza. It's much more low-key, but still a favorite place for locals and expats to shop for meat (including horse meat), fresh fish, and cut flowers. There are also a few small crafts shops. ✉ *Rue Ibn Toumert, opposite the Gendarmerie Royale, Guéliz.*

Menara Garden. The Menara's lagoon and villa-style pavilion are ensconced in an immense royal olive grove, where pruners and pickers putter and local women fetch water from the nearby stream, said to give *baraka* (good luck). A popular rendezvous for Marrakshis, the garden is a peaceful retreat. The elegant pavilion—or *minzah,* meaning "beautiful view"—was created in the early 19th century by Sultan Abd er Rahman, but it's believed to occupy the site of a 16th-century Saadian structure. In winter and spring snowcapped Atlas peaks in the background appear closer than they are; and, if you are lucky, you might see green or black olives gathered from the trees from October through January. Moroccan families swarm here during the holidays to picnic in the olive groves. Children can throw chunks of bread to the huge carp in the pool or ride camels outside the garden gate. ✉ *Hivernage* ✛ *From Bab el Djedid, the garden is about 2 km (1⅓ miles) down av. de la Menara* ☉ *Daily 8–6.*

THE PALMERY

The expanse of palm groves to the north of the medina is dubbed the "Beverley Hills" of Marrakesh, a place of manicured golf courses, private villas hidden behind high walls, upmarket resort hotels, and luxurious secret gardens. Though there are no real tourist attractions here, the area is well worth visiting for its handful of notable restaurants and dinner-cabaret venues and the recently opened Museum of the Palmery, showcasing contemporary Moroccan art.

Fodor's Choice ★ **Museum of the Palmery.** Signposted on the route de Fès as you head out to the Palmery, this cultural oasis is well worth a detour. Marrakesh-born Abderrazzak Benchaabane—ethnobotanist, perfume maker, garden designer, and local legend—has created an enchanting walled garden and, within it, a contemporary art museum. The garden adjoins his home and exhibits his own collection of contemporary Moroccan art, paintings, and sculptures. Benchaabane was responsible for the restoration of the Majorelle Gardens at the request of Yves Saint Laurent in 1998, and the garden designs here clearly reflect his passion for creating beautiful natural spaces. The indoor gallery and arcades open out to a water garden with pergolas and pavilions, an Andalusian garden, rose beds, and cactus gardens. ✉ *Dar Tounssi, rte. de Fès, Palmery* ☎ *0661/09–53–52* 🖃 *40 DH* ☉ *Daily 8–6.*

The Majorelle Gardens were most famously owned by the French designer Yves Saint Laurent.

WHERE TO EAT

Marrakesh has arguably the best selection of restaurants in Morocco; as a group they serve equal parts Moroccan and international cuisine. Restaurant dining, however, is a relatively new phenomenon for Moroccans, who see eating out as somewhat of a shame on the household. The younger generation has embraced the trendy cafés and restaurants of Guéliz and Hivernage, but as for the older generation, even the wealthiest Marrakshis would prefer to invite friends over to sample home cooking than to go out for the evening. To get an idea (albeit a rather expensive one) of traditional yet sumptuous Moroccan entertaining, treat yourself to an evening at one of Marrakesh's popular riad gastronomique restaurants in the medina.

You can also eat well at inexpensive sidewalk cafés in both the medina and Guéliz. Here, don't miss out on a famous local dish called *tanjia,* made popular by workers who slow-cook lamb or beef in an earthenware pot left in hot ashes for the whole day.

Most restaurants in Marrakesh tend to fall into two categories. They're either fashionable, flashy affairs, mostly in Guéliz and the outlying areas of Marrakesh, which serve à la carte European and Moroccan cuisine, or they're more traditional places, often tucked inconspicuously into riads and old palaces in the medina. Both types can be fairly pricey, and, to avoid disappointment, are best booked in advance. They also tend to open quite late, usually not before 7:30 in Guéliz and 8 in the medina, although most people don't sit down to eat until 9 or 9:30. In recent years a third dining category, the dinner-cabaret, has become a popular format, attracting tourists, expats, and well-heeled Moroccans for their entertainment value, if not necessarily for their cuisine.

There's no set system for tipping. Your check will indicate that service has been included in the charge; if not, tip 10% or 15% for excellent service.

Restaurants are listed alphabetically within neighborhood. Use the coordinate (✛ D2) at the end of each listing to locate a site on the Where to Eat and Stay in the Medina map.

WHAT IT COSTS IN DIRHAMS			
$	$$	$$$	$$$$
under 80 DH	80 DH–150 DH	151 DH–300 DH	over 300 DH

Restaurant prices are the average cost of a main course at dinner, or if dinner is not served, at lunch.

COOKING SCHOOLS

With so many chic riads serving up a culinary storm, it's no surprise that cooking schools in Marrakesh have taken off in recent years. Tagines, couscous, and briouates are all on the menu for the Maghrebian master chef in the making. Many hotels now arrange their own cooking classes in-house too.

Café Clock Marrakech. The all-day course starts with a shopping trip to the local market before returning to the kitchen on the terrace of Café Clock in the Kasbah neighborhood. The group chooses from a menu of tagines or couscous, cooked salads, harira soup, Moroccan pastries, dessert, and flat breads. Sometimes the day involves visiting a local community oven to bake bread. Classes are 600 DH per person (cash only) and must be reserved in advance. ⊠ *224, Derb Chtouka, Kasbah* ☎ *0524/37–83–67* ⊕ *www.cafeclock.com.*

Jnane Tamsna. Cooking classes and holiday courses are offered upon request in the charming cottage compound with a thriving organic garden in the middle of the Palmery. An English-speaking chef gives instruction in the preparation of exquisite Moroccan recipes that are easy to replicate back home. Classes are 550 DH per person (minimum four people). ⊠ *Douar Abiad, Circuit de la Palmeraie, Palmery* ☎ *0524/32–84–84* ⊕ *www.jnane.com.*

La Maison Arabe. Originally a fine Moroccan restaurant run by two revered French ladies in 1946—frequented by the pasha and visiting royals and a favorite of Sir Winston Churchill—La Maison Arabe is now a luxury boutique hotel. It continues to enjoy a reputation for great Moroccan cuisine, and was in fact one of the first establishments in Marrakesh to offer cooking courses. Nowadays the classes are open to guests and nonguests in groups of up to eight people at a time, instructed by a *mada* (female head cook). Courses are run daily in the upstairs modern kitchen with a translator on hand (Arabic, English, French). Participants learn about the key spices and how to prepare signature Moroccan dishes such as tagines, couscous, pastilla, pastries, and Moroccan cooked salads. The class is about four hours long, and at the end you eat the meal you have prepared. ✉ *1, Derb Assehbe, Bab Doukkala, Medina* ☎ *0524/38–70–10* 🌐 *www.lamaisonarabe.com.*

FAMILY **Souk Cuisine.** The very popular daylong cooking classes run by Dutch cook Gemma van de Burgt will have you mastering the art of tagine preparation before you know it. Classes meet at Café de France to shop for spices and ingredients in the medina, then prepare a meal together. The price (500 DH; cash only) includes recipes to take home, lunch, and a glass of wine. Children eight years and up are welcome, too. ✉ *46/47, Derb Moulay Abdelkader, Derb Dabachi, Medina* ☎ *0524/80–49–55* 🌐 *www.soukcuisine.com.*

2

MEDINA

$$$$ MOROCCAN 🍴 **Al Baraka.** It's easy to fancy yourself one of Morocco's 19th-century elite in this grand, white-tile riad, once home to the pasha. Set menus for different budgets feature traditional *briouates* (spicy dumplings) as well as tagines and couscous. It's geared to tourists, and the food is less impressive than the surroundings. You have the choice of dining on brocade divans in the salon or in the enormous courtyard filled with orange trees, musicians, and the odd belly dancer. [$] *Average main: 320DH* ✉ *1, Djemâa el Fna, next to Commissariat de Police, Medina* ☎ *0524/44–23–41* 🌐 *www.albaraka-marrakech.com* ✥ *E3.*

$$ ITALIAN 🍴 **Café Arabe.** This three-story restaurant in the heart of the medina is a happening place by day and by night, serving both Moroccan and Italian food. Homemade pastas are on offer at this Italian-owned place, but main courses also include grilled swordfish, lamb, and beef. The lantern-lighted terrace, complete with a trickling fountain, is a good place to stop for drinks. [$] *Average main: 150DH* ✉ *184, rue el Mouassine, Medina* ☎ *0524/42–97–28* 🌐 *www.cafearabe.com* ✥ *E2.*

$ MOROCCAN FAMILY 🍴 **Café Clock Marrakech.** Mike Richardson brings his hugely successful cross-cultural café project, first established in Fez, to a second home in the Kasbah area of Marrakesh. Enthusiastic staff serve modern Moroccan plates including camel burgers, salads (the one with grilled chicken, blue cheese, figs, and honey is recommended), veggie platters, and homemade ice cream. Along with this is a menu of cultural activities: exhibitions, live traditional music, local bands, belly-dance lessons, cooking classes, and film screenings. Do not miss the *al halqa* (storytellers' circle) on Thursday night, when the ancient tradition of the place Djemâa el Fna is performed in *darija* (the local Moroccan Arabic dialect) by el Haj, a veteran storyteller, and then reinterpreted in English by Moroccan storytellers-in-training. No alcohol is served, and it's cash only. [$] *Average main: 60DH* ✉ *224, Derb Chtouka, Kasbah* ☎ *0524/37–83–67* 🌐 *www.cafeclock.com* 💳 *No credit cards* ✥ *D6.*

$ CAFÉ 🍴 **Café des Épices.** In the medina's "spice square," this little café has set a trend in recent years, and copycat cafés have sprung up with woven stools and low wooden tables. The original teeters over three levels and has a great rooftop view over the veiled women selling basketware and woolly hats below. Suitably enough, it offers spiced tea and cinnamon coffee along with a good complement of juices and light snacks. The same owner also runs Le Jardin, a small restaurant tucked into a courtyard in the north of the souks. [$] *Average main: 60DH* ✉ *75, Rahba Lakdima, Medina* ☎ *0524/39–17–70* 🌐 *www.cafedesepices.net* ✥ *F2.*

$ MOROCCAN

🍴 **Chez el Bahia.** It won't win prizes for design, but this cheap joint is perfect for a lunchtime or evening pit stop. Locals and visitors alike frequent this friendly and atmospheric canteen just on the right before the road opens into Djemâa el Fna. Tagine pots stand two rows deep on the street stall outside, and a barbecue sizzles away. If you place your order in advance there are much more interesting specialties available, including spiced aubergine tagine and pastillas. It's cash only. [$] *Average main: 55DH* ✉ *Riad Zitoune el Kdim, 206, Medina* 💳 *No credit cards* ✥ *F4.*

$$$$ MOROCCAN Fodor's Choice ★

🍴 **Dar Marjana.** If you can only visit one of Marrakesh's traditional riad restaurants, make it this one. Cocktails featuring *mahia*—fig liqueur—are served on low-slung tables around a delightful courtyard. Then you move to salons (ask for the larger minzah) to recline on brocade divans and enjoy wave after wave of classic Moroccan cuisine. The couscous is impossibly fluffy, and if the lamb tagine came off the bone any easier it would be floating. To round this off, a troupe of lively Gnaoua musicians brings you to your senses before a belly dancer brings you to your feet. The fixed price includes an aperitif, wine with the meal, and an after-dinner drink. [$] *Average main: 700DH* ✉ *15, Derb Sidi Tair, Bab Doukkala, opposite Dar el Basha, Medina* ☎ *0524/38–51–10* 🌐 *www.darmarjana.com* ✍ *Reservations essential* ⏲ *Closed Tues. and Ramadan. No lunch* ✥ *D1.*

$$$$ MOROCCAN

🍴 **Dar Moha.** This isn't the most stylish riad, but it has an established reputation for its fixed dinner menu of *nouvelle cuisine marocaine*. Delicious adaptations of traditional dishes include a tiny melt-in-your-mouth *pastilla* (sweet pigeon pie) filled with a vegetable puree, and strawberries wrapped in wafer-thin pastry and rolled in ground almonds. Steer clear of the poky salons; head instead for the outside tables arranged around a small pool and shaded by lush banana palms. Andalusian lutes and Gnaoua music accompany dinner. Lunch is à la carte. [$] *Average main: 530DH* ✉ *81, rue Dar el Bacha, Medina* ☎ *0524/38–64–00* 🌐 *www.darmoha.ma* ✍ *Reservations essential* ✥ *D1.*

$$$$ MOROCCAN

🍴 **Dar Yacout.** The palatial Yacout is in a house designed as a *One Thousand and One Nights* restaurant and, as it's one of Marrakesh's luxurious five-course *gastronomique* experiences, you need to be seriously hungry to make the most of it. Its location deep in the medina only adds to its mystery. Aperitifs are taken on the rooftop to the haunting chants of a Gnaoua musician. A traditional Moroccan feast is served in several different settings: beside the pool on the lantern-festooned terrace; in a vaulted upstairs room; in an intimate glass-walled salon; or in the lush, cushion-filled main salon. Courteous, discreet waiters in white djellabas and red fezzes scurry about to fulfill your every need. This is an exotic experience in a magical setting, but the standard of food has declined in recent years, so this is no longer the best value. [$] *Average main: 700DH* ✉ *79, Sidi Ahmed Soussi, Bab Doukkala* ☎ *0524/38–29–29* 🌐 *www.yacout.ma* ✍ *Reservations essential* ⏲ *Closed Mon. No lunch* ✥ *D1.*

$ VEGETARIAN

🍴 **Earth Café.** Tired of tagines? Vegetarians and vegans may feel unloved in Marrakesh until they get to Earth Café, where they rule the roost.

This wholesome little eatery is tucked into a side alley near the main square. As you walk through to the seating areas out back you'll be tempted by the aromas swirling up from the open kitchen. Up the winding narrow stairs are cushioned seating alcoves (looking a bit scruffy these days) with orange-painted walls and a balcony hung with tropical plants. A beetroot, ginger, and orange juice cocktail will perk you up, or try the generous portions of mains such as pastry-wrapped goat cheese, pumpkin, spinach, and apple. The only downside is that there are no windows or open terrace, and as such it gets hot and a bit claustrophobic. No alcohol is served, and it's cash only. $ *Average main: 70DH* ⊠ *2, Derb Zouak, off Riad Zitoune Lkdim, Medina* 🕾 *0661/28–94–02* ⊕ *www.earthcafemarrakech.com* ▭ *No credit cards* ⊹ *F5.*

$
MOROCCAN
✕ **Haj Brik.** In a row of grill cafés on a narrow side street running south off Djemâa el Fna, Haj Brik is one of the best. Everything is prepared so well that it has been in business longer than most. The menu focuses on grilled lamb chops, merguez, kefta, and kidneys, each served with bread, olives, tomato salad, and hot sauce. Everything cooks on an indoor grill at the front of the shop, sending billowing smoke and smells over the diners. Cash only. $ *Average main: 40DH* ⊠ *39, rue Bani Marine, through arch just left of post office in Djemâa el Fna, Medina* ▭ *No credit cards* ⊹ *E4.*

$$
INTERNATIONAL
FAMILY
✕ **La Terrasse des Épices.** Hidden on a rooftop deep within the northern quarter of the souks, this all-day restaurant is a popular spot for expats, tourists, and trendy locals. The menu mixes Moroccan and international cuisine from fish tagine and *tanjia* (beef or lamb cooked slowly for several hours over charcoal in an earthenware jug) to pasta dishes, goat cheese salad, and tenderloin steaks. The contemporary variations on a Moroccan theme extend also to the decor—intimate cushioned booths are lit by woven lamp shades and decorated with modern artwork. It's a good place for families who want a little space out of the mayhem of the souks where tired kids can sprawl on the seating. Spiced teas and coffees are served too—hence the name. No alcohol is served. $ *Average main: 120DH* ⊠ *15, souk Cherifia, Sidi Abdelaziz, Medina* 🕾 *0524/37–59–04* ⊕ *www.terrassedesepices.com* ⊗ *Closed during Ramadan* ⊹ *F1.*

$$$
MOROCCAN
✕ **Le Foundouk.** This French-run place hidden at the souk's northern tip is regularly booked with upscale tourists and expats, and is well suited for an intimate evening for two. The sunny rooftop garden is a good lunch or afternoon tea spot. A smaller terrace adorned with statues and masks from West Africa rounds out the dining-room options. Chic à la carte dishes include foie gras and fig tagine; for a lighter snack at lunchtime try an eggplant mille-feuille with mozzarella. The ground-floor bar is also open to nondiners. $ *Average main: 170DH* ⊠ *55, Souk Hal Fassi, Kat Bennahid, near the Ali ben Youssef Medersa, Medina* 🕾 *0524/37–81–90* ⊕ *www.foundouk.com* ⬡ *Reservations essential* ⊗ *Closed Mon.* ⊹ *G1.*

$$
INTERNATIONAL
Fodor'sChoice
★
✕ **Le Jardin.** Building on the success of his Café des Épices, young Moroccan entrepreneur Kamal Laftimi has sprouted another high-quality culinary pit stop in the heart of the souks. Fresh local produce is displayed

at the entrance, the central courtyard is tiled in green with banana trees shading the tables, and a chill vibe pervades the air. Innovative dishes such as mango and cucumber salad or duck with caramelized figs are served for lunch and dinner. ■ TIP→ This is one of the few places in the souks that serves wine and beer and has plenty of options for vegetarians. $ *Average main: 120DH* ⊠ *32, Souk el Jeld, Sidi Abdelaziz, Medina* ☎ *0524/37–82–95* ⊕ *www.lejardin.ma* ✛ *F1.*

$$
MOROCCAN

✕ **Le Marrakchi.** With zellij walls, painted cedar ceilings, and white-tile floors, this old palace serves up good Moroccan cuisine with modern flair—and a floor show with belly dancers thrown in (nightly around 9 pm). You can choose from the à la carte menu or one of the set menus, which begin at 280 DH. Reserve in advance for a table on the top floor with a panoramic view of the square. Service can be surly, and prices are rather high. $ *Average main: 150DH* ⊠ *52, rue des Banques, just off Djemâa el Fna, Medina* ☎ *0524/44–33–77* ⊕ *www. lemarrakchi.com* ✛ *F3.*

$$$
MOROCCAN

✕ **Le Tanjia.** This stylish restaurant is a good bet for a special night out with traditional Moroccan cuisine, Oriental live music, and slick service. The three-tiered restaurant is centered around a rose-filled fountain of the inner patio. By day, you can take a lunch of Moroccan salads on the covered terrace overlooking a busy souk. By night, enjoy dinner and a glass of wine while marveling at the shimmying of belly dancers. Tanjia is a traditional, slow-cooked meat dish specific to Marrakesh, and it is served here with aplomb. $ *Average main: 160DH* ⊠ *14, Derb J'did, next to pl. des Ferblantiers, Medina* ☎ *0524/38–38–36* ✛ *G6.*

$$$$
MOROCCAN

✕ **Le Tobsil.** The name may be Arabic for "dish," but get ready for several, a procession of flavors served in crescendo at this fine-dining restaurant. The traditional Moroccan fixed menu, featuring not one but two tagines (first poultry, then lamb), couscous, starter, and dessert, is wheeled out in serious style. Dine among lanterns and petals in the intimate yellow-ocher courtyard of this small riad hidden just inside Bab L'Ksour. It's stylish and friendly, and the cuisine is very good. A fixed-price menu includes four courses and drinks. $ *Average main: 650DH* ⊠ *22, Derb Abdellah ben Hessaien, R'mila Bab L'Ksour, Medina* ☎ *0524/44–15–23* ⌒ *Reservations essential* ☉ *Closed Tues., and July and Aug. No lunch* ✛ *D3.*

$
MOROCCAN

✕ **Restaurant el Bahja.** This small, tiled medina café is a popular budget choice serving beef and chicken tagines and, in winter, *loubia* (bean stew) or spicy lentils in addition to standard grill fare. Cash only. $ *Average main: 40DH* ⊠ *41, rue Bani Marine, Medina* ☎ *0524/44–03–43* ⊟ *No credit cards* ☉ *Closed during Ramadan* ✛ *E4.*

$
MOROCCAN

✕ **Restaurant Tiznit.** Climb the narrow tiled stairway into this tiny little restaurant right at the edge of the Djemâa el Fna square and you can find simple, delicious food, most notably the rabbit tagine cooked with raisins. Squeeze yourself into the table at the back by the window and you get one of the best sunset views across the buzzing square below and to the Koutoubia beyond. Cash only, and no alcohol is served. $ *Average main: 50DH* ⊠ *28, Souk el Kessabine, just past Café France, Medina* ☎ *0524/42–72–04* ⊟ *No credit cards* ☉ *Closed during Ramadan* ✛ *F3.*

Dar Marjana is the best of Marrakesh's riad-style restaurants.

$$$ JAPANESE Fodor's Choice ★ 🍴 **Zourouni.** The best-kept secret in the medina is this private restaurant within a family home, serving excellent Japanese food with fresh, locally sourced ingredients. Reservations are required 24 hours in advance as the food is bought in specially for each booking from local markets. The Belgian-Japanese couple who live here open their splendid riad home and serve a set menu including sushi, sashimi, ginger-spiced eggplant, miso soup, and other delicate dishes, which vary according to what owner Yumiko can find in the souk early on the same morning. You'll find delightful décor, antique mirrors, candelabras, and purple velvet seating for a maximum of a dozen people. It's BYO wine or beer and cash only. [$] *Average main: 250DH* ✉ *14, Derb Jdid, Riad Zitoune Lkdim, Medina* ☎ *0666/74–67–28* ✍ *Reservations essential* 💳 *No credit cards* 🕒 *Closed Mon. and Fri., and July and Aug. No lunch* ✥ *F5.*

GUÉLIZ

Marrakesh's restaurant scene changes faster than a belly dancer at quitting time, and today's hot tagine can quickly become tomorrow's soggy couscous. This is especially true in trendy, finicky Guéliz. Some of the most celebrated restaurants have built their reputations around stunning décor rather than stunning food, but they're still worth going to as long as you know this. Sound out local opinion, and don't be afraid to take a chance.

$$ MOROCCAN 🍴 **Al Fassia Guéliz.** Serving some of the best à la carte Moroccan food in the city, Al Fassia has a long-standing reputation for high-quality traditional food without any obligation to participate in a five-course gastronomic feast. Run by women, it brings classic cooking to Guéliz

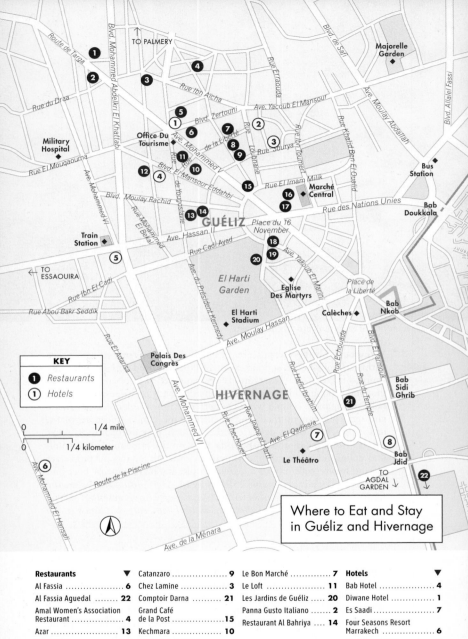

Where to Eat and Stay in Guéliz and Hivernage

with an affordable menu that includes tasty tagines, tender brochettes with saffron rice, couscous topped with caramelized onions, succulent tangia, and sweet-savory pigeon pastilla. The Guéliz restaurant can be noisy and crowded with slow service if there are large party bookings. The owners have opened a second restaurant, Al Fassia Aguedal, a few kilometers out of town, to cope with demand. [$] *Average main: 120DH* ✉ *55, bd. Zerktouni, Guéliz* ☎ *0524/43–40–60* 🌐 *www.alfassia.com* ✍ *Reservations essential* 🕒 *Closed Tues. No lunch.*

$ MOROCCAN FAMILY 🍴 **Amal Women's Association Restaurant.** The name may seem off-putting, but this pretty little restaurant-cum-social-project near the public hospital ticks all the boxes: great food, great prices, great ethics, great service. A nonprofit center established the restaurant to help women from troubled backgrounds learn culinary skills to earn an independent living. The result is this friendly, brightly furnished restaurant and garden terrace, which attracts locals and expats for its excellent Moroccan and international dishes. Try the *seffa au poulet,* a delicious sweet-and-savory dish of chicken with vermicelli and cinnamon. No alcohol, but lots of freshly squeezed juices are served. Cash only. [$] *Average main: 40DH* ✉ *Av. Ben Ahmed and rue Ibn Sina, Guéliz* ☎ *0524/44–68–96* 💳 *No credit cards* 🕒 *No dinner.*

$$$ LEBANESE 🍴 **Azar.** Comprising both a restaurant and a nightclub, Azar exudes contemporary Oriental charm both through its Lebanese-Moroccan cuisine and its intriguingly modern take on traditional Moroccan design. Intimate enough for a romantic twosome but laid-back enough for casual gatherings, the interiors are bedecked with brass lanterns, leather poufs, and satin cushions intermingled with retro plastic-mold chairs and honeycomb-sculpted plaster walls. The menu offers Lebanese staples such as tabbouleh, falafel, and hummus with marinated grilled meat kebabs and cutlets for main courses. A selection of *mezzé du chef* makes a very enjoyable and affordable light meal for two. The top floor of the restaurant hosts live Oriental music every night in its sultry club and bar. [$] *Average main: 170DH* ✉ *Rue de Yougoslavie, at bd. Hassan II, Guéliz* ☎ *0524/43–09–20* 🌐 *www.azarmarrakech.com* 🕒 *Closed during Ramadan. No lunch.*

$$ ASIAN 🍴 **Bistro Thai.** Thai, Vietnamese, and Japanese offerings are intermingled with Oriental silks and Balinese goddesses adorning the walls in this stylish restaurant, which is geared towards western tastes. Beautifully presented plates of sushi nearly all feature cream cheese, which may horrify the purist and makes the food heavier than it should be. That said, the Vietnamese *bo bun* (beef with peanut sauce) and the seaweed salad are tasty. It's a perfect marriage on the surface, but the quality of food is inconsistent and not classically Thai. **TIP→ The fixed-price lunch menu is a good value at 120 DH.** [$] *Average main: 125DH* ✉ *8, av. Oued el Markhazine, opposite the Royal Tennis Club, Guéliz* ☎ *0524/45–73–11* 🕒 *No lunch Mon.*

$$ BISTRO 🍴 **Brasserie de Flore.** French expat Philippe Duranton's brasserie offers hearty French rustic cuisine—onion soup with toasted gratin topping, bouillabaisse, snails, pork medallions in mustard sauce, and so on. (Ignore the club sandwiches and standard snack menus, which are overpriced and tasteless.) The restaurant has a prime position on the

Marrakesh Plaza in Guéliz, with acres of outdoor seating. Indoors you could imagine yourself in an early-20th-century Paris bistro with padded leather booths, crystal chandeliers, ceiling fans, and art nouveau mirrors painted with Grecian nymphs. Alcohol and cocktails are served in the restaurant, but not on the terrace. [$] *Average main: 150DH* ✉ *Marrakesh Plaza, Pl. du 16 Novembre, Guéliz* ☎ *0524/45–80–00* 🌐 *www.brasseriedeflore.com.*

$$ INTERNATIONAL 🍴 **Café du Livre.** Peruse a quirky collection of secondhand books, participate in the Monday quiz nights, come for dinner, or just have a light lunch of *salade riche* with spiced chickpeas, caramelized onions, beetroot, goat cheese, and grated carrot. Café du Livre has been popular with locals and expats over the past decade and has recently been acquired by an American-Moroccan couple. Apart from ethnic-food nights, there are plenty of vegetarian options and American-style burgers. This upstairs café is tucked behind the Carré Eden shopping mall, just next to the Hotel Toulousaine. There's live music Friday and Saturday, but it can get very smoky. [$] *Average main: 90DH* ✉ *44, rue Tarik ben Ziad, Guéliz* ☎ *0524/44–69–21.*

$$ INTERNATIONAL FAMILY 🍴 **Café 16.** This modern terrace café with lime-green parasols sits at the edge of the Marrakesh Plaza in the heart of Guéliz. At the indoor restaurant you can enjoy a glass of wine or cold beer until 1 am and food until 11 pm. The menu leans toward light bites and lunches—salads, club sandwiches, and hamburgers. The range of salads is imaginative; they're all freshly made, and even the half portion makes a satisfying meal. Main dishes include chicken-coconut curry as well as monkfish tagine. A kids' menu is available, as well as ice cream, pastries, and cakes. [$] *Average main: 130DH* ✉ *Marrakesh Plaza, pl. du 16 Novembre, Guéliz* ☎ *0524/33–96–70* 🌐 *www.16cafe.com.*

$$ ITALIAN 🍴 **Catanzaro.** One of Marrakesh's most popular restaurants for locals and expats, this homey Italian spot offers dining on two floors, brightened by red-chintz tablecloths. The menu has a good selection of Italian salads, pastas, and pizzas at prices that make them a fabulous value. Alcohol is served, and at reasonable prices for this part of town. [$] *Average main: 80DH* ✉ *Rue Tariq Ibn Ziad, Guéliz* ☎ *0524/43–37–31* ✍ *Reservations essential* ⏲ *Closed Sun.*

$ MOROCCAN 🍴 **Chez Lamine.** Slightly more elegant than its hole-in-the-wall branch in the souks, Chez Lamine has a reputation for the best *mechoui* (whole roasted lamb) in town and couscous on Friday. Its streetside tables in Guéliz are regularly filled with Moroccan families. You can choose to sit indoors or outdoors in this popular local eatery at tables made from sewing-machine stands. Apart from mouthwatering tagines, try the restaurant's other specialty, *tangia marrakchia* (lamb cooked very slowly for hours in earthenware jars). No alcohol. [$] *Average main: 60DH* ✉ *Rue Ibn Aicha, opposite Montecristo, Guéliz* ☎ *0524/43–11–64* 💳 *No credit cards* ⏲ *Closed during Ramadan.*

$$$ FRENCH 🍴 **Grand Café de la Poste.** The colonial atmosphere provides a fabulous backdrop for excellent (if pricey) salads, pastas, steaks, and fish specials including oysters from Oualidia. In spring and summer, you can enjoy a cold Casablanca beer on the covered veranda. For an indulgent dessert try the *gâteau chocolat coulant* (a decadent type of chocolate cake).

Arrive early to enjoy free tapas-style appetizers from 6:30 pm to 7:30 pm. $ *Average main: 170DH* ⊠ *Bd. el Mansour Eddahbi at av. Imam Malik, just off av. Mohammed V, Guéliz* ☎ *0524/43–30–38.*

$$ ✕ **Kechmara.** This is one of the trendy places to hang out in the new city,
EUROPEAN with ice-cool midcentury design, contemporary art on display, and some of the best salads in town. Local cognoscenti believe the food could be better—think of it for a lunch drop-in than an all-out dinner option. At night, the interior gets loud and smoky, but the pergola roof-terrace and burger menu make it a suitable early-dinner choice for families with teenagers who want something a little more sophisticated then the fast-food joints down the road. You can always go back in the evening for relaxed drinks at the terrace bar if you like. $ *Average main: 120DH* ⊠ *3, rue de la Liberté, Guéliz* ☎ *0524/42–25–32* ⊕ *www.kechmara. com* ⊙ *Closed Sun.*

$$ ✕ **La Cuisine de Mona.** The big, cheerful personality of Lebanese-born res-
LEBANESE taurateur Mona is evident as you step into this tiny restaurant beyond the fringes of Guéliz. Candy-pink garden tables and lime green walls decorated with fez hats are crammed into every available space including the upstairs mezzanine. The fresh meze platters include hummus, tabbouleh, baba ghanoush, marinated chicken wings, stuffed Lebanese bread, and shawarma; it's good-value food, though drinks are pricey. This eatery is popular with many locals and expats, so book in advance. $ *Average main: 90DH* ⊠ *Residence Mamoune 5, 115b, Quartier el Ghoul, off rte. de Targa, Guéliz* ☎ *0618/13–79–59* ⊕ *www. lacuisinedemona.com* ⊙ *Closed Sun.*

$$$ ✕ **La Trattoria.** Due partly to the pizzazz of its late owner, Giancarlo,
ITALIAN La Trattoria has long held a place among Marrakesh's top restaurants and, unlike others, has kept up a consistently high standard. The current owner, Mohammed Anaflouss, took over in 2000, and with neo-Moorish renovations overseen by Bill Willis, this ornate restaurant still draws a loyal and select clientele. Tapas and predinner drinks can be enjoyed in the lush terrace bar, with jungle foliage in danger of dipping into your aperitif, or you can sit beside the pool and enjoy a good entrecôte or one of the many seafood pastas. $ *Average main: 180DH* ⊠ *179, rue Mohammed el Béqal, Guéliz* ☎ *0524/43–26–41* ⊕ *www. latrattoriamarrakech.com* ⌂ *Reservations essential* ⊙ *No lunch.*

$$ ✕ **L'Annexe.** Bistro meets resto in this popular, affordable French eatery
FRENCH at the edge of Guéliz. The three-course lunch menus are an exceptional value at 120 DH. In true Parisian style, the menu favors carnivores: foie gras, beefsteaks, braised lamb chops, and confit of duck, for example; homey country dishes such as salade Niçoise or Provençal fish soup, as well as tempting grilled swordfish, red mullet, and tuna might please the rest. Choose the upstairs mezzanine dining area for a more intimate atmosphere; the downstairs bistro-style restaurant gets crowded. $ *Average main: 120DH* ⊠ *14, rue Moulay Ali, Guéliz* ☎ *0524/43–40–10* ⊕ *www.lannexemarrakech.com* ⊙ *No lunch Sat.; no dinner Sun.*

$ ✕ **L'Atelier Cuisine.** This bright, cheery little eatery with sidewalk terrace
FRENCH is ideal for late breakfast (it opens at 10 am), brunch, lunch, or an early
FAMILY dinner. Choose from umpteen types of coffees, teas, and infusions, or freshly blended fruit smoothies. The daily menu features hot and cold

The Djemâa el Fna really comes alive at sunset, when its many food vendors open their stalls.

soups, individually cooked casseroles, and oven-baked gratins, as well as fresh garden salads, quiches, vegetable flans, and homemade desserts. It's a great spot for hearty French Provençale cooking, but it closes at 7 pm and does not serve alcohol. [$] *Average main: 60DH* ✉ *8, rue Oued el Makhazine, opposite Harti Gardens, Guéliz* ☎ *0661/94–33–73* 🌐 *www.lesatelierscuisine.com* 🕒 *Closed Sun. No dinner.*

$$$ FRENCH ✕ **Le Bon Marché.** Modern French "bistronomie" is the key ingredient at this stylish restaurant, which has recently proved very popular with locals, expats, and tourists. Aside from the daily lunch and dinner à la carte menus, from time to time there are special theme-menu nights, such as a wine tasting with oysters. Standout main dishes include calamari and chorizo, with squid-ink pasta or sole meunière with almond butter and pureed potato. A daily three-course fixed-price lunch menu runs 110 DH. There's a great wine selection too. [$] *Average main: 180DH* ✉ *34, rue de la Liberté, Guéliz* ☎ *0524/43–31–43.*

$$ INTERNATIONAL ✕ **Le Loft.** This is where expats and many young Marrakshis come for a touch of New York style in a bistro setting. Le Loft is popular for its menu of steaks: filet, entrecôte, and tartare. There are cheeseburgers, giant Caesar salads, pasta dishes, some vegetarian options, and other French bistro fare. Bentwood chairs, cushioned booths, bare brick walls, suspended industrial lighting, and huge pop-art prints give a funky, modern vibe. It can also get very smoky and noisy. The fixed-price lunch menu is a good value at 110 DH. [$] *Average main: 120DH* ✉ *18, rue de la Liberté, Guéliz* ☎ *0524/43–42–16* 🌐 *www.loft-marrakech.com.*

$$ FRENCH FAMILY ✕ **Les Jardins de Guéliz.** Hidden at the edge of the Harti Gardens, this French-owned restaurant is a good value, with an excellent buffet lunch

CLOSE UP

Marrakesh Street Food

Marrakshis have perfected the art of cooked street food, traditionally the province of the working class. There are hundreds of sidewalk grills scattered throughout both the medina and Guéliz. Step up for a tasty, satisfying meal at one of these institutions; it's a priceless experience that costs next to nothing. From midday to midnight, choose from grilled minced beef, sausage, lamb chops, brochettes, Moroccan salads, and french fries, supplemented by bread, olives, and hot sauce. (No credit cards, clearly.)

DJEMÂA EL FNA

For the ultimate grilling experience, there's only one place. By dusk, more than a hundred stalls sizzle and smoke their way through mountains of fresh meat and vegetables. Step up to the stall of your choice and order from the wild array of perfectly done veggies, salads, *kefta* (beef patties), merguez sausages, beef brochettes, couscous, and even french fries. In cooler months or during Ramadan, try a bowl of hearty *harira* (chickpea, lentil, and meat soup) or country eggs in homemade bread. The meal starts with free bread (to weigh down your paper place setting) and a hot dipping sauce called *harissa*. The mint tea at the end should be free, too.

There's little continuity of quality, even at the same stall, so it's luck and instinct all the way for each sitting. However, since leftovers are given to the poor every night, the food is always freshly made. Vendors will do anything to attract your attention, from dragging you to a seat, chasing you down the lanes, and best of all, performing the occasional comic rundown of classic English phrases ("It's bloody marvelous!") with matching Cockney accent. ■TIP➔ **Eat where the Moroccans eat: they know what to order, how much to pay, and they really get into their food.**

OTHER MEDINA GRILLS

If the idea of dining at one of the stalls on the square does not appeal to you, there are a lot of casual grill restaurants either on the square or in the streets immediately surrounding it. We can recommend three in particular that are popular with the locals: Haj Brik, Restaurant Tiznit, and Restaurant El Bahja (➪ *see Medina in Where to Eat).* (Remember that none of these serve alcohol.)

and evening international à la carte menu. Entering the gateway to Les Jardins de Guéliz feels like discovering a secret garden—which in effect it is. Backing directly on to the Harti Gardens, the wooden door in the external wall leads to a mini faux-kasbah restaurant with a light, airy conservatory and pretty gardens—perfect for a family lunch. The midday buffet has lots of vegetarian choices, including tortillas, stuffed vine leaves, cooked salads, and rice and pasta salads; there are fewer veggie choices for dinner. Carnivores can choose from among beef Stroganoff, steaks, lasagna, and also some Moroccan dishes. It's child-friendly, with outdoor tables on a shaded terrace and a couple of turtles patrolling the grounds. $ *Average main: 100DH* ⊠ *Av. Oued el Makhazine, next to Royal Tennis Club, Guéliz* ☎ *0524/42–21–22* ⊗ *Closed Sun. and during Ramadan.*

$
CAFÉ
FAMILY
Fodor's Choice
★

Panna Gusto Italiano. This ice-cream parlor with light snacks is at the very far end of Guéliz, but well worth the journey. The ice cream at this Italian-owned and -managed shop is to die for: possibly the best in Morocco! The ice cream and sorbet is made with all-natural ingredients and no additives, and flavors vary every month. In summer choose from fig, banana, watermelon, peach, even ginger with lavender. In autumn you'll find spiced chocolate, orange with cinnamon, date, and saffron flavors. There's a comfortable outdoor seating area, and the Sunday brunch is a great value at 115 DH per person for a buffet of cold meats, salads, handmade cheeses, and pasta dishes. $ *Average main: 25DH* ⊠ *89, rte. de Targa, at rue du Capitaine Arrigui, Guéliz* 🕾 *0524/43–65–65* ⊕ *www.pannagustoitaliano.com* ☺ *Closed Mon.*

$
SEAFOOD

✕ **Restaurant Al Bahriya.** Cheap and cheerful, this restaurant is possibly the best catch in town. The no-frills Moroccan street restaurant in the heart of Guéliz (near La Grande Poste) is packed at night with locals getting their fishy fix. Choose from the sidewalk display of fresh seafood as you walk in, or simply ask for a mixed plate—sole, calamari, monkfish, prawns—all served with wedges of lime and olives. $ *Average main: 60DH* ⊠ *75 bis, av. Moulay Rachid, Guéliz* 🕾 *0524/84–61–86* ▭ *No credit cards* ☺ *Closed during Ramadan.*

HIVERNAGE

Hivernage is known for its large upmarket chain hotels and some very exclusive apartment buildings. Among them are also a scattering of decent restaurants and cafés—some independent, some located within hotels, and some even attached to the outlying nightclubs. On avenue Mohammed VI (opposite the Palais de Congrès) are a number of pizzerias and a few upscale restaurants. Towards the Guéliz end of avenue Moulay el-Hassan, near the old football stadium, is a cluster of international restaurants.

$$
MOROCCAN

✕ **Al Fassia Aguedal.** The Al Fassia name has become synonymous with fine Moroccan cuisine in Marrakesh, and with tables hard to come by in Guéliz, this branch opened in the boutique Hotel Al Fassia near the Agdal Gardens. The high standards set by the older sister restaurant are in no way undermined, though service can be slow. The atmosphere is elegant though casual, and the restaurant is more spacious and tranquil than its city-center counterpart. On a warm evening a table on the terrace is very romantic. The menu offers the same traditional fare as the Guéliz restaurant, and the chicken tagine with caramelized pumpkin comes highly recommended. $ *Average main: 150DH* ⊠ *Hotel Al Fassia, 9 bis, rte. de Ourika, Zone Touristique de l'Aguedal, Hivernage* 🕾 *0524/38–11–38* ⊕ *www.alfassia-aguedal.com* ⌦ *Reservations essential* ☺ *No lunch.*

$$$
MOROCCAN

✕ **Comptoir Darna.** With dark mahogany beams and panels that give the interior a clubby feel, this restaurant offers traditional Moroccan and European cuisines. It remains a nighttime draw for hip Marrakshis and visitors alike, full of Oriental styling, musicians, belly dancers (starting at 9:45), and an upstairs DJ spinning chilled-out world-music vibes. There's a small dance floor for those who want to swirl to the tunes, but it's the exotic ambience that attracts the crowds, rather than the quality of food. $ *Average main: 200DH* ⊠ *Av. Echouhada, Hivernage* ☏ *0524/43–77–02* ⊕ *www.comptoirmarrakech.com* ☾ *No lunch.*

THE PALMERY

$$$ ✕ **Le Mantra.** Authentic Indian cuisine has finally arrived in Marrakesh, **INDIAN** and in splendid fashion. The Taj Palace Hotel has lavish Oriental styling throughout by American architect Stuart Church. Within the hotel is Le Mantra restaurant, which serves not just classic Indian cuisine, but also Japanese sushi and teriyaki dishes from a show kitchen. There's also a menu for children. Décor is plush and exotic, with purple carpets, Thai silks, bamboo ceilings, and Chinese lanterns. Locals in the know, as well as residents of Taj Palace, come here to get their fix of fenugreek and other spices with a bit more pep than are traditionally found in Morocco. $ *Average main: 250DH* ⊠ *Taj Palace Hotel, Annakhil, Palmery* ☏ *0524/32–77–77* ⊕ *www.tajhotels.com* ⌂ *Reservations essential* ⌂ *Jacket required* ☾ *Closed Sun. No lunch.*

WHERE TO STAY

Marrakesh has exceptional hotels. Five stars are dropped at every turn, the spas are superb, and the loving attention to detail is overwhelming. If, however, you'd prefer not to spend a fortune sleeping in the bed where a movie star once slumbered, solid budget and midrange options abound. They're small, clean, and suitably Moroccan in style to satisfy adventurous penny-pinchers.

To take on the historic heart of Marrakesh and live like a pasha of old, head to one of the medina's riads. Riad restorations, many by ultrafashionable European expats, have taken over the city; you'd trip over them, if only you knew where they were. Anonymous doors in the narrow, twisting derbs of the medina, and especially the souks, transport you to hidden worlds of pleasure. There are cheap ones, expensive ones, chic ones, funky ones, plain ones. Riads normally have around four to six rooms arranged around a courtyard and each room can be rented individually on a nightly basis. For special events and larger gatherings, it's worth considering booking the whole property.

Marrakesh is something of a Shangri-la for designers who, intoxicated by the colors, shapes, and patterns of the city, feel free to indulge themselves in wildly opulent and ambitious designs. Although it isn't all tasteful, much of the décor and style in Marrakesh hotels and riads is fascinating and easy on the eye.

Most of the larger hotels (classified with three, four, or five stars by the Moroccan government) are in Guéliz, Hivernage, and a new zone touristique located beyond the Agdal Gardens heading out of town on the route de Ourika. If you prefer something authentic and inexpensive near the action, choose one of the numerous small and clean hotels in the medina near Djemâa el Fna.

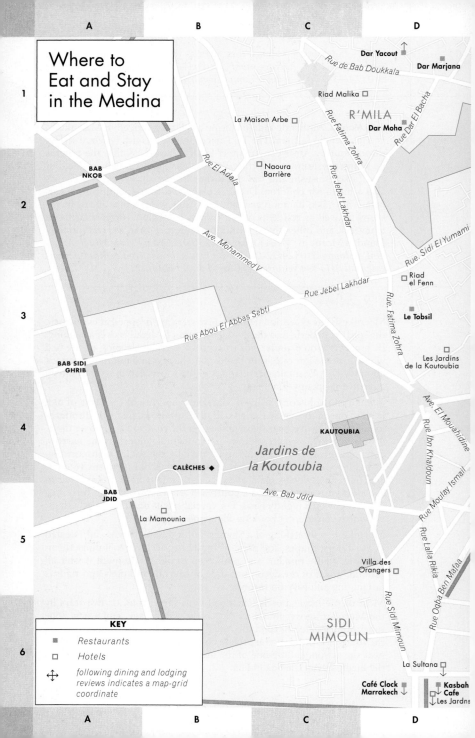

Where to Eat and Stay in the Medina

A

B

C

D

1

Rue de Bab Doukkala

Dar Yacout

Dar Marjana

Riad Malika ☐

R'MILA

La Maison Arbe ☐

Rue Fatima Zohra

Rue Dar El Bacha

Dar Moha

BAB NKOB

Rue El Adala

Naoura ☐
Barrière

Rue Jebel Lakhdar

2

Ave. Mohammed V

Rue Sidi El Yumami

Rue Jebel Lakhdar

Riad ☐
el Fenn

3

Rue Abou El Abbas Sebti

Rue Fatima Zohra

Le Tobsil

BAB SIDI GHRIB

Les Jardins ☐
de la Koutoubia

Ave. El Mouahidine

4

KAUTOUBIA

Rue Ibn Khaldoun

_Jardins de
la Koutoubia_

CALÈCHES ◆

Rue Moulay Ismail

BAB JDID

Ave. Bab Jdid

La Mamounia ☐

Rue Lalla Rikia

5

Villa des ☐
Orangers

Rue Oqba Ben Mafaa

Rue Sidi Mimoun

**SIDI
MIMOUN**

6

La Sultana ☐

KEY

■ _Restaurants_

☐ _Hotels_

↔ _following dining and lodging
reviews indicates a map-grid
coordinate_

Café Clock ↓
Marrakech

■ **Kasbah**
☐ Cafe
↓ Les Jardins

A

B

C

D

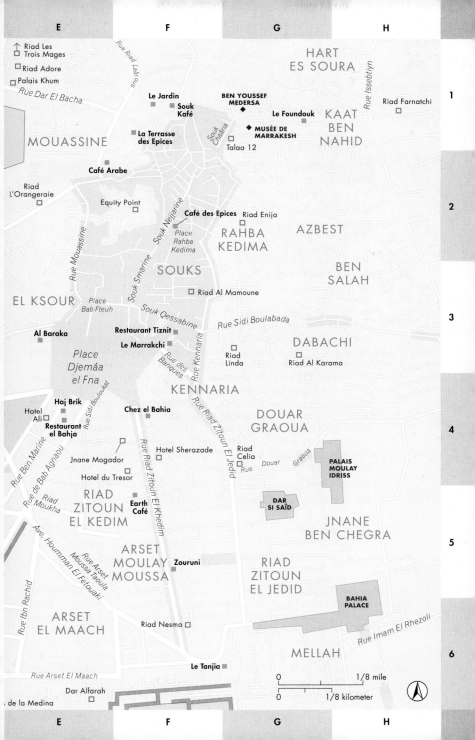

Hotels and riads vary their prices wildly between high and low season. This means that if you time your trip right you can find some great deals. High season runs from October to May, with spikes at Christmas, New Year's, and Easter.

Hotel reviews have been shortened. For full information, visit Fodors.com. Lodgings are listed alphabetically within neighborhood. Use the coordinate (✣ D2) at the end of each listing to locate a site on the Where to Eat and Stay in the Medina map.

WHAT IT COSTS IN DIRHAMS			
$	$$	$$$	$$$$
under 700 DH	700 DH–1,500 DH	1,501 DH–3,500 DH	over 3,500 DH

Hotel prices are the lowest cost of a standard double room in high season.

RENTING A RIAD

Nothing beats taking over a riad for a few days. We mean booking the whole darn thing, not just a room. Commandeering a beautifully restored 16th-century palace isn't cheap, but riads in the medina and small villas in the Palmery are geared for private parties. Their staffs can help organize meal plans, special itineraries, weddings, birthday parties, cooking classes, and activities. There are around 2,000 riads being run as guesthouses in Marrakesh, and most of them will rent the whole property if the reservation is made far enough in advance. Reserve directly with the owner or via an intermediary booking website, or for full luxury concierge service including event planning, catering, activities, and private transport, engage the services of an agency. From trendy and luxurious to homely and traditional, the choices may seem overwhelming, but as long as you find one that appeals to you (not hard!), you're set for an unforgettable experience. In addition to the individual riads listed below, try the following event planners and rental agencies that specialize in Marrakesh riads.

Boutique Souk ☎ *0661/32–44–75* 🌐 *www.boutiquesouk.com.*

Hip Marrakech ✉ *Medina* ☎ *207/570–0336 UK* 🌐 *www.hipmarrakech.com.*

Marrakech Medina ✉ *102, rue Dar el Bacha, Souika Sidi Abd al Aziz, Medina* ☎ *0524/29–07–07* 🌐 *www.marrakech-medina.com.*

MEDINA

$$ B&B/INN 🏨 **Dar Alfarah.** This lovely riad is near the Badi Palace in the Mellah quarter, tucked down a side street that leads to the Kasbah area. **Pros:** good location; plenty of atmosphere. **Cons:** small pool. [$] *Rooms from: 990DH* ✉ *58, Derb Touareg, Ksibat N'Hass, Kasbah* ☎ *0524/38–42–69* 🌐 *www.daralfarah.com* 🛏 *2 rooms, 7 suites* 🍴 *Breakfast* ✣ *E6.*

$ B&B/INN 🏨 **Hotel Ali.** A long-standing favorite among budget travelers and right at the edge of the main square, Hotel Ali's rooms have en-suite baths and air-conditioning, and guests have access to a 24-hour currency-exchange bureau. **Pros:** great place to meet fellow travelers; right on the main square. **Cons:** a little noisy. $ *Rooms from: 400DH* ✉ *Rue Moulay Ismail, 55 yards from Dejmâa el Fna, Medina* ☎ *0524/44–49–79* ⊕ *www.hotel-ali.com* ⤴ *43 rooms, 2 dorms* ▭ *No credit cards* ⃝❘ *Breakfast* ✛ *E4.*

$
B&B/INN
🖼 **Hotel Sherazade.** A series of gorgeous rooftop terraces, stylish tents, and the plant-filled courtyards of two conjoined riads beguile you into thinking this is a much more expensive hotel. **Pros:** good location; restful setting; warm and welcoming. **Cons:** few amenities; not all rooms have private bathrooms. $ *Rooms from: 550DH* ✉ *3, Derb Djemâa, Riad Zitoun Elkedim, Medina* ☎ *0524/42–93–05* ⊕ *www. hotelsherazade.com* ⤴ *23 rooms* ⃝❘ *No meals* ✛ *F4.*

$
B&B/INN
🖼 **Hotel du Tresor.** A haven for artists and design lovers, this beautifully converted hotel near the Djemâa el Fna has been featured in design magazines. **Pros:** fantastic location; top-notch design; helpful management. **Cons:** pool is tiny and overlooked in small courtyard; cash only. $ *Rooms from: 580DH* ✉ *77, Sidi Boulokat, Riad Zitoun Kdim, Medina* ☎ *0524/37–51–13* ⊕ *www.hotel-du-tresor.com* ⤴ *13 rooms, 3 suites* ▭ *No credit cards* ⃝❘ *Breakfast* ✛ *F4.*

$
B&B/INN
🖼 **Jnane Mogador.** This budget riad is a cut above the rest; fountains, tadelakt columns, wood-clad rooms, a rooftop terrace, and cascading plants contribute to an air of elegance. **Pros:** near the main square; very good value. **Cons:** some rooms can be dark; not all rooms have air-conditioning; books up months in advance. $ *Rooms from: 480DH* ✉ *116, Riad Zitoun Kedim, Derb Sidi Bouloukate, Medina* ☎ *0524/42–63–23* ⊕ *www. jnanemogador.com* ⤴ *17 rooms, 1 suite* ⃝❘ *No meals* ✛ *F4.*

$$$
HOTEL
🖼 **La Maison Arabe.** Owner Fabrizio Ruspoli created this small hotel for those craving old-fashioned charm: his hotel artfully blends Moorish and European design, and each of the four courtyards offers grandeur on an intimate scale. **Pros:** lots of little nooks; renowned cooking school. **Cons:** some rooms are small; pool is in the middle of the outdoor restaurant. $ *Rooms from: 2300DH* ✉ *1, Derb Assehbe, Bab Doukkala, Medina* ☎ *0524/38–70–10* ⊕ *www.lamaisonarabe.com* ⤴ *26 rooms, 14 suites* ⃝❘ *Breakfast* ✛ *C1.*

$$$$
HOTEL
Fodor'sChoice
★
🖼 **La Mamounia.** Since 1923, Morocco's most prestigious hotel has achieved legendary status for its opulence, grandeur, celebrity guest list, and hefty price tag. **Pros:** one of the finest hotels in the world; exquisite restaurants. **Cons:** standard rooms are small; ground-floor rooms have no view of garden; exorbitant bar/restaurant prices; slow service. $ *Rooms from: 5600DH* ✉ *Bab Jdid, Medina* ☎ *0524/38–86–00* ⊕ *www.mamounia.com* ⤴ *136 rooms, 71 suites, 3 riads* ⃝❘ *No meals* ✛ *B5.*

$$$
HOTEL
🖼 **La Sultana Marrakech.** There's a certain over-the-top charm to this series of five luxurious riads of palatial proportions, each with a different decorative theme, but compared to other hotels in this same price range it delivers good value and great service. **Pros:** fireplaces in every room; impeccable service. **Cons:** very expensive; small pool; cheapest rooms are small. $ *Rooms from: 3500DH* ✉ *403, rue de la Kasbah, on a tiny alley heading left just behind Saadian tombs, Kasbah* ☎ *0524/38–80–08* ⊕ *www.lasultanamarrakech.com* ⤴ *28 rooms* ☾ *Closed Aug. (usually)* ✛ *D6.*

La Mamounia is one of Morocco's grande dame hotels, not to mention one of the finest luxury hotels in Africa.

$$$ HOTEL 🏨 **Les Jardins de la Koutoubia.** Despite its location on an unprepossessing street, this hotel has a rather grand and opulent interior that cannot fail to impress. **Pros:** central location; great pool areas; wheelchair accessible. **Cons:** expensive; décor is tired. [$] *Rooms from: 2400DH* ✉ *26, rue de la Koutoubia, Medina* ☎ *0524/38–88–00* 🌐 *www.lesjardinsdelakoutoubia.com* 🛏 *72 rooms, 35 suites* 🍴 *Breakfast* ✥ *D3.*

$$$ HOTEL FAMILY 🏨 **Les Jardins de la Medina.** This 18th-century palace once belonging to the cousin of King Hassan II is now a luxurious boutique hotel with lush gardens hidden in the Kasbah area of the medina. **Pros:** fabulous gardens; stylish décor. **Cons:** 15-minute walk to reach main square. [$] *Rooms from: 3200DH* ✉ *21, Derb Chtouka, Kasbah, Medina* ☎ *0524/38–18–51* 🌐 *www.lesjardinsdelamedina.com* 🛏 *36 rooms* 🍴 *Breakfast* ✥ *D6.*

$$$ RESORT FAMILY 🏨 **Naoura Barrière Marrakech.** The first venture onto African soil from this well-respected French luxury hotel chain, the Naoura Barrière is ideally situated on the edge of the medina but an easy walk from the main sights. **Pros:** family-friendly; central location; the private villas are exceptional. **Cons:** noisy pool area; lack of outdoor garden spaces; hotel rooms lack character. [$] *Rooms from: 2800DH* ✉ *Rue Djbel Alakhdar, Bab Doukkala* ☎ *0524/45–90–00* 🌐 *www.naoura-barriere.com* 🛏 *32 rooms, 53 suites, 26 villas* 🍴 *Breakfast* ✥ *C2.*

$$ B&B/INN Fodor's Choice ★ 🏨 **Palais Khum.** This exquisite, Italian-owned boutique riad opened in 2014 just off the Dar el Bacha and features gorgeous interiors that blend European, Italian, and Moroccan influences. **Pros:** fabulous design; quiet location. **Cons:** no outdoor pool. [$] *Rooms from: 1500DH*

✉ 2, Derb el Henaria, off rue Dar el Bacha, Medina ☎ 0524/39–03–89 🌐 www.palaiskhum.com 🛏 3 rooms, 8 suites 🍴 Breakfast ✥ E1.

$$$ B&B/INN 🏨 **Riad Adore.** The jewel in the crown of the English-owned Pure Riads collection, Riad Adore is decorated in cool, pale shades of white, beige, and gray, with tadelakt walls and subtle lighting—an elegant and sophisticated guesthouse close to the main medina action. **Pros:** elegant design; great location. **Cons:** small splash pool; hard to find. [$] *Rooms from: 1800DH* ✉ *97, Derb Tizouagrine, off rue Dar el Bacha, Medina* ☎ *0524/37–77–37* 🌐 *www.riadadore.com* 🛏 *10 rooms, 2 suites* 🍴 *Breakfast* ✥ *E1.*

$ B&B/INN 🏨 **Riad Al Karama.** This inexpensive and delightful riad within easy walking distance of place Djemâa el Fna and the souks has carved deep green doors and scattered, bloodred carpets in the central patio garden, around which are the cozy winter salon and dining room. **Pros:** beautiful style; great personal service. **Cons:** the Cinnamon Room (Chambre Cannelle) is very cramped; minimum three-night stay required in high season (between Christmas and New Year's). [$] *Rooms from: 660DH* ✉ *119, Derb Jdid, off rue Dabachi, Medina* ☎ *0600/01–30–13* 🌐 *www.riadalkarama.com* 🛏 *3 rooms, 1 suite* 🍴 *Breakfast* ✥ *G3.*

$ B&B/INN 🏨 **Riad Al Mamoune.** This French-owned family-run riad is a peaceful, pocket-friendly retreat amid the chaos of the souk; rooms are decorated with Moroccan flair, with tiled cast-iron tables and colorful textiles, and a touch of romance in the first-floor room with a four-poster bed. **Pros:** good prices all year; friendly and informal; interconnecting rooms in the suite ideal for families. **Cons:** hard to find; splash pool is grubby. [$] *Rooms from: 510DH* ✉ *140, Derb Aarjane, Rahba Kédima, east of rue Semarine through Souk aux Épices, then follow signs from Rahba Lakdima, Medina* ☎ *0524/39–19–58* 🌐 *www.riadalmamoune.com* 🛏 *6 rooms, 1 suite* 🍴 *Breakfast* ✥ *F3.*

$ B&B/INN 🏨 **Riad Celia.** This simple riad is a good choice for budget-friendly riad accommodation in one of the most popular neighborhoods in the medina: it may not have all the flourishes of the more luxurious guesthouses, but it still holds true to the traditional values of Moroccan hospitality and good service. **Pros:** great location; helpful staff; lunch and dinner are available by request. **Cons:** can be noisy; cheapest rooms are small. [$] *Rooms from: 500DH* ✉ *1, Douar Graoua, Riad Zitoune Jdid, Medina* ☎ *0524/42–99–84* 🌐 *www.hotelriadcelia.com* 🛏 *12 rooms, 1 suite* 🍴 *Breakfast* ✥ *G4.*

$$$ HOTEL 🏨 **Riad el Fenn.** Vanessa Branson (sister of the British entrepreneur) created this riad "adventure" in 2002, and since then it has been reworked and extended to create a palace of individually conceived rooms designed with a stylish modern aesthetic. **Pros:** dripping with good taste; loads of communal spaces for relaxation; accessible to travelers with disabilities. **Cons:** cheaper courtyard rooms are often fully booked. [$] *Rooms from: 2200DH* ✉ *2, Derb Moulay Abdellah ben Hessaien, Bab Ksour, Medina* ☎ *0524/44–12–10* 🌐 *www.riadelfenn.com* 🛏 *10 rooms, 14 suites* 🍴 *No meals* ✥ *D3.*

$$$ B&B/INN 🏨 **Riad Enija.** Walking through the heavy door that opens into Riad Enija is like stepping into a fairy tale: sculptures, Italian lamps, carved doors, and unique handmade furnishings make this home more of a living

gallery than a guesthouse, and visitors return again and again. **Pros:** high-quality services; unique experience. **Cons:** expensive; no nearby car access. [$] *Rooms from: 2500DH* ✉ *9, Derb Mesfioui, Rahba Lakdima, Medina* ☎ *0524/44–09–26* 🌐 *www.riadenija.com* 🛏 *6 rooms, 9 suites* 🍴 *Breakfast* ✣ *G2.*

$$$$ B&B/INN 🏨 **Riad Farnatchi.** On the souk's northern tip is this lavish, deluxe riad spread across five adjoining properties; hidden among artisans at work are wide white walls with carved stucco, enormous mosaicked suites with marble baths, an overflowing tiled courtyard pool, and elite clientele. **Pros:** excellent service; royal treatment. **Cons:** expensive; edgy neighborhood. [$] *Rooms from: 4350DH* ✉ *2, Derb el Farnatchi, Qa'at Benahid, Medina* ☎ *0524/38–49–10* 🌐 *www.riadfarnatchi.com* 🛏 *9 suites* ⏲ *Closed Aug.* 🍴 *Breakfast* ✣ *H1.*

$ B&B/INN 🏨 **Riad Linda.** A Scottish-owned riad with English-speaking staff onsite, Riad Linda is an unpretentious and welcoming little guesthouse that gives excellent value for the price. **Pros:** excellent value; in the heart of the medina. **Cons:** no pool; far from nearest taxi drop-off point. [$] *Rooms from: 650DH* ✉ *93, Derb Jemaa, Derb Dabbachi, Medina* ☎ *0524/39–09–27* 🌐 *www.riadlinda.com* 🛏 *5 rooms, 1 suite* 🍴 *Breakfast* ✣ *G3.*

$$ B&B/INN Fodor's Choice ★ 🏨 **Riad l'Orangeraie.** With easy access from Bab L'Ksour and just five minutes' walk to Djemâa el Fna, this luxurious riad is a great base for exploring the medina. **Pros:** English-speaking staff; great location. **Cons:** rooms next to the pool can be noisy; 30% surcharge at Christmas and New Year. [$] *Rooms from: 1500DH* ✉ *61, rue Sidi el Yemani, Mouassine, Medina* ☎ *0661/23–87–89* 🌐 *www.riadorangeraie.com* 🛏 *7 rooms, 3 suites* 🍴 *Breakfast* ✣ *E2.*

$$ B&B/INN 🏨 **Riad Les Trois Mages.** Tucked in a derb in the Riad Laarouss neighborhood, Les Trois Mages is a delightful small riad with English-speaking staff and spacious, tastefully furnished rooms. **Pros:** rooftop pool; great service. **Cons:** quite far from the main square. [$] *Rooms from: 1200DH* ✉ *11, Derb Jemaa, off rue el Gza, Riad Laarouss, Medina* ☎ *0524/38–92–97* 🌐 *www.lestroismages.com* 🛏 *6 rooms, 1 suite* 🍴 *Breakfast* ✣ *E1.*

$$ B&B/INN 🏨 **Riad Malika.** The rambling, relaxing Malika was one of the first riads to reinvent itself in the 1990s, and owner Jean-Luc Lemée and his English-speaking wife are full of anecdotes about Morocco. **Pros:** plenty of charm; congenial hosts; unique design; easily accessibly by car. **Cons:** far from main square. [$] *Rooms from: 1100DH* ✉ *29, Arsat Aouzal, Bab Doukkala, Medina* ☎ *0524/38–54–51* 🌐 *www.riadmalika.com* 🛏 *9 rooms, 5 suites* 🍴 *Breakfast* ✣ *D1.*

$ B&B/INN 🏨 **Riad Nesma.** Proof that staying in a beautiful riad with elegant rooms does not have to break the bank, this Moroccan-run guesthouse is a real treasure, newly extended to add a second tier of rooms. **Pros:** excellent value; beautiful rooms. **Cons:** no pool; no ground-floor access. [$] *Rooms from: 650DH* ✉ *128, Riad Zitouen Lakdim, Medina* ☎ *0524/44–44–42* 🌐 *www.riadnesma.com* 🛏 *11 rooms* 🍴 *Breakfast* ✣ *F6.*

$$$ B&B/INN 🏨 **Talaa 12.** This modernist, minimalist riad—almost next door to the Museum of Marrakech in the heart of the medina—has rooms drenched in natural creams and beiges and beds low and draped with just enough

color to make them inviting (though a few more comfy chairs in the bedrooms would not go amiss). **Pros:** central location; elegant design. **Cons:** no pool; expensive. [$] *Rooms from: 2000DH ✉ 12, Talaa ben Youssef, on the way to Ali ben Youssef Medersa, Medina ☎ 0524/42–90–45 🌐 www.talaa12.com ⇆ 4 rooms, 4 suites 🍴 Breakfast ✣ G1.*

$$$$ HOTEL 🏨 **Villa des Orangers.** Formerly the private residence of a Marrakesh judge, this exquisite property has all the understated glamour and class you'd expect from a Relais & Chateaux hotel, with unobtrusive service, libraries to hide away in, and bedrooms with enormous bathrooms. **Pros:** unsurpassed luxury; plenty of privacy. **Cons:** very expensive; wood-paneled rooms rather gloomy. [$] *Rooms from: 4300DH ✉ 6, rue Sidi Mimoun, Medina ☎ 0524/38–46–38 🌐 www.villadesorangers.com ⇆ 21 suites, 6 rooms 🍴 Some meals ✣ D5.*

GUÉLIZ

The hotels in Guéliz mostly cater to package holiday groups, so unless you're with a family in need of a big hotel to drown out the noise you make, they may not appeal to you. They overflow with facilities but lack the character or personal service you find in an old riad. Still, we've found a few that buck the trend and are all in lively, city center locations.

$$ HOTEL 🏨 **Bab Hotel.** This upmarket boutique hotel in the heart of Guéliz is chic and hypermodern in style, with trendy designer furniture, a space-age lounge bar, and minimalist bedrooms furnished in pale shades. **Pros:** funky interior design; great location. **Cons:** small pool; poor breakfast; maintenance issues; slack service. [$] *Rooms from: 1320DH ✉ Rue Mohammed el Beqqal at bd. Mansour Eddahbi, Guéliz ☎ 0524/43–52–50 🌐 www.babhotel-marrakech.com ⇆ 30 rooms, 15 suites 🍴 Breakfast.*

$$ HOTEL 🏨 **Diwane Hotel.** This city-center hotel has a huge, riad-style atrium, giving it some sense of charm along with standard hotel amenities. **Pros:** great location; good-size pool. **Cons:** the bars are shabby and smoky; standard of buffet restaurant is inconsistent. [$] *Rooms from: 928DH ✉ 24, rue de Yougoslavie, corner of av. Mohammed V, Guéliz ☎ 0524/43–22–16 🌐 www.diwane-hotel.com ⇆ 115 rooms, 10 suites 🍴 Breakfast.*

$$ HOTEL 🏨 **Le Caspien Hotel.** A modern three-star hotel with small pool, decent restaurant, bar area, and clean, spacious rooms, Le Caspien is a convenient local base in the heart of Guéliz with some traditional decorative touches such as stucco cornices, carved wooden doors, and *beldi* (a traditional, handmade, mosaic tile) floors. **Pros:** central location; good value for money. **Cons:** Wi-Fi only in common areas, not rooms; hot water not always reliable. [$] *Rooms from: 960DH ✉ 12, rue Loubnane, Guéliz ☎ 0524/42–22–82 🌐 www.lecaspien-hotel.com ⇆ 36 rooms, 2 suites 🍴 Breakfast.*

$$ HOTEL 🏨 **Moroccan House Hotel.** This Morrocan-run hotel has questionable taste in interior décor, but it's a well-priced option with spacious rooms, lots of character, and a friendly atmosphere. **Pros:** authentic Moroccan feel; central location. **Cons:** small pool; tired décor; no bar. [$] *Rooms*

from: 952DH ✉ 3, rue Loubnane, Guéliz ☎ 0524/42–03–05 🌐 www.moroccanhousehotels.com ⇜ 50 rooms, 10 suites 🍽 No meals.

$$ HOTEL **Opera Plaza Hotel.** Next to the train station and opposite the Theatre Royal, this modern four-star hotel makes a convenient base—not the most glamorous location, but taxis are on the doorstep for the short skip to the old medina and it's walking distance to the rest of Guéliz. **Pros:** lovely pool area; central location. **Cons:** lacks charm; long walk to medina; service can be slack. [$] *Rooms from: 1200DH ✉ Av. Mohammed VI and av. Hassan II, Guéliz ☎ 0524/35–15–15 🌐 www.operaplazahotel.com ⇜ 106 rooms, 9 suites 🍽 Breakfast.*

HIVERNAGE

Wide, shaded streets lined with orange and olive trees, and a few secluded villas with palm trees towering above the garden walls create a sense of tranquillity and affluence in this neighborhood just to the west of the ramparts. However, Hivernage also houses a number of large hotels that are ideal for families that want plenty of amenities, exotic garden space, swimming pools, and even wheelchair access. It's a great location not too far from the old medina. After dark, Hivernage is abuzz, as many of the smartest nightclubs are in this area. A calèche ride along the avenues makes for a pleasant afternoon jaunt as part of a city tour.

$$$ HOTEL FAMILY **Es Saadi Gardens & Resort.** The 1950s design of this former casino does little to inspire, but this family-run hotel with every amenity does the job. **Pros:** family-friendly; spacious grounds. **Cons:** dated design; impersonal; expensive. [$] *Rooms from: 2800DH ✉ Rue Ibrahim el Mazini, Hivernage ☎ 0524/44–88–11 🌐 www.essaadi.com ⇜ 140 rooms, 93 suites, 10 villas 🍽 Breakfast.*

$$$$ RENTAL FAMILY **Four Seasons Resort Marrakech.** Opened in 2012, Four Seasons has created a luxurious mini-medina outside the walls of the old city: avenues of palm trees, arcades, and patios connect the low-rise pavilions, all surrounded by acres of exotic gardens, terraces, pools, and fountains. **Pros:** pure luxury; family-friendly. **Cons:** far from medina; hefty price tag on any extras arranged through the hotel. [$] *Rooms from: 6300DH ✉ 1, bd. de la Menara, Hivernage ☎ 0524/35–92–00 🌐 www.fourseasons.com ⇜ 114 rooms, 27 suites 🍽 No meals.*

$$ HOTEL **Hivernage Hotel & Spa.** This recently renovated property nestled among the golden triangle of large hotels has a touch more class than the local giants that cater to a mass market, with great spa facilities, terrific food, and a hipster vibe, but since its acquisition by the Warwick International Hotel chain, it has lost its polish. **Pros:** great food; great location. **Cons:** chain-hotel feel; poor customer service. [$] *Rooms from: 1400DH ✉ Av. Echouhada, at rue des Temples, Hivernage ☎ 0524/42–41–00 🌐 www.hivernage-hotel.com ⇜ 75 rooms, 10 suites 🍽 Breakfast.*

THE PALMERY

Staying in the Palmery is a good choice if you're looking for a relaxing vacation and won't feel guilty about exchanging the medina's action for an idyll in your own private country palace. It's also close

2

to Marrakesh's famous golf courses. The drawback is the 7-km (4½-mile) distance from Marrakesh, which necessitates a car, a taxi, or use of infrequent hotel shuttles.

$$$
HOTEL
Fodor's Choice
★

Dar Zemora. The unpretentious charms of this country villa will ease your guilt about staying in the Palmery and possibly seeing less of Marrakesh. **Pros:** regal views; friendly English-speaking staff. **Cons:** meals are expensive; minimum stay usually required. $ *Rooms from: 2600DH ✉ 72, rue el Aandalib, Ennakhil, just off road to Fez, Palmery ☎ 0524/32–82–00 ⊕ www.darzemora.com ⇥ 7 rooms, 3 suites* ◯| *Breakfast.*

$$$$
RESORT

Hotel Amanjena. Just south of the Palmery, this blend of Moorish and ancient Egyptian architecture, completed in a palette of subtle hues and set in its own grounds away from the city, lives up to its name: a peaceful paradise. **Pros:** stunning architecture; incredible attention to detail. **Cons:** you will need deep pockets to stay here for even a short time; few on-site activities. $ *Rooms from: 8800DH ✉ Old rte. de Ouarzazate, Km 12, Palmery ☎ 0524/39–90–00 ⊕ www.amanresorts. com ⇥ 32 pavilions, 7 villas* ◯| *Breakfast.*

$$$
RESORT
ALL-INCLUSIVE
FAMILY

Hotel Riu Tikida Palmeraie. If you yearn to stay in Marrakesh's exclusive Palmery but haven't the budget for a chic boutique retreat, this all-inclusive resort may just fit the bill; the rooms are spacious, with simple Moroccan styling, standard mod cons, and a terrace or balcony. **Pros:** acres of outdoor space; everything included in one price. **Cons:** minimum three- to five-night stay; buffet selection not kept topped up; crowded with package tours. $ *Rooms from: 1700DH ✉ Km 6, rte. de Fès, Circuit de la Plameraie, Palmery ☎ 0524/32–74–00 ⊕ www.riu. com ⇥ 368 rooms, 20 suites* ◯| *All-inclusive.*

$$$
HOTEL
Fodor's Choice
★

Jnane Tamsna. The word *jnane* means "garden," and this luxury property lives up to its name: modeled in a hacienda style that blends Moroccan with Mexican, the five villas and pavilions that make up this oasis complex are surrounded by palms, olive trees, cactus gardens, herbs, and rose beds. **Pros:** plenty of pampering; charitable projects supported. **Cons:** swimming pools not heated year-round. $ *Rooms from: 2750DH ✉ Douar Abiad, Circuit de la Palmeraie, Palmery ☎ 0524/32–84–84 ⊕ www.jnane.com ⇥ 24 rooms, 2 suites* ◯| *Breakfast.*

$$$$
HOTEL

Ksar Char-Bagh. Rising like a Byzantine, 14th-century kasbah from the Palmery and surrounded by 10 acres of manicured grounds, this Relais & Chateaux hotel is the last word in sumptuous, escape-it-all luxury. **Pros:** beautiful décor; huge heated pool. **Cons:** service sometimes falls short; restaurant is expensive. $ *Rooms from: 4000DH ✉ Djnan Abiad, Circuit de la Palmeraie, Palmery ☎ 0661/91–72–33 ⊕ www. ksarcharbagh.fr ⇥ 13 rooms, 2 suites, 13 apartments ⊙ Closed Aug.* ◯| *Breakfast.*

$$$
HOTEL

Les Deux Tours. The Two Towers enjoys a magnificent garden setting with accommodation in neoclassical villas designed by architect-owner Charles Boccara; rooms and suites are all spread across six individual villas, each with a patio or small pool. **Pros:** huge beds in the expensive suites; pretty pool and gardens. **Cons:** standard rooms cramped and stuffy; décor and upholstery battered and faded; no disabled access. $ *Rooms from: 2250DH ✉ Douar Abiad, Circuit de la Palmeraie,*

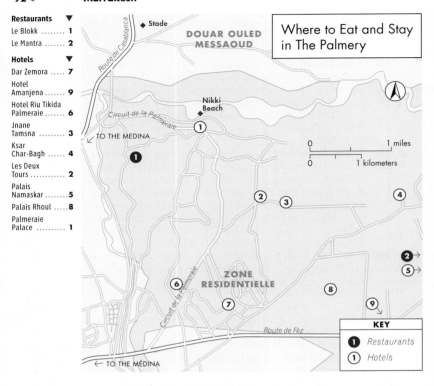

Where to Eat and Stay in The Palmery

Palmery ☎ 0524/32–95–27 ⊕ www.les-deux-tours.com ⟿ 12 rooms, 16 suites, 8 private pool residences ⭗ Breakfast.

$$$$
RESORT
Fodor's Choice
★
🏨 **Palais Namaskar.** You'll feel like incognito royalty at this dreamy resort, opened in 2012 in Marrakech's Palmery suburb, where you can wander through 12 acres of lush gardens and ponds before ducking into your own palace-style accommodations, many with Atlas mountain views. **Pros:** romantic setting; excellent service; pampering spa; luxurious style in spades. **Cons:** 25 minutes from central Marrakesh; five-star prices. ⓢ Rooms from: 4950DH ⊠ Rte. de Bab Atlas, No. 88/69, Province Syba, Palmery ☎ 0524/29–98–00 ⊕ www.palaisnamaskar.com ⟿ 6 rooms, 14 suites, 10 villas, 3 palaces ⭗ Breakfast.

$$$
HOTEL
🏨 **Palais Rhoul.** This flashy, horseshoe-shape mansion is the height of bohemian boutique chic, if a bit Beverley Hills: in a garden of palm trees and flowers, each of the exceedingly large rooms is decorated in an ornate mixture of Moroccan and Art Deco styles. **Pros:** the height of luxury; magnificent spa treatments. **Cons:** restaurant overrated; little English spoken; pool not heated. ⓢ Rooms from: 3200DH ⊠ Rte. de Fès, Circuit de la Palmeraie, Palmery ☎ 0524/32–94–94 ⊕ www.palais-rhoul.com ⟿ 8 rooms, 4 suites, 8 garden tents ⭗ Breakfast.

$$$
RESORT
FAMILY
🏨 **Palmeraie Palace.** Tasteful it isn't, but this giant, gaudy, self-contained bubble in the middle of the Palmery offers every kind of distraction, and plenty to keep children amused. **Pros:** great for golfers; plenty

of pampering; family-friendly. **Cons:** lacks charm; poor customer service. ⓢ *Rooms from: 1650DH* ⊠ *Circuit de la Palmeraie, Palmery* ☎ *0524/33–43–43* ⊕ *www.palmeraieresorts.com* ⇒ *286 rooms, 28 suites* ⊘ *Breakfast.*

NIGHTLIFE

Without doubt, Marrakesh is Morocco's nightlife capital. Options include everything from the free but fascinating goings-on at Djemâa el Fna square to the hedonistic cocktail scene of Hivernage, with its cluster of casinos, cabarets, and nightclubs.

MEDINA

BARS

Alcohol was once frowned-upon in the medina, and while it's still unthinkable to swig liquor on the streets, there are a few good places to go for a drink within the city walls. However, things tend to wind down early in the medina.

Café Arabe. One of the most beautiful settings is Café Arabe, a galleried, bougainvillea-strewn riad with a sleek rooftop bar and two relaxed dining salons. Enjoy cocktails, Moroccan wine, or champagne. The pasta dishes are all homemade, so come for dinner and make an evening of it. ⊠ *184, rue el Mouassine, Medina* ☎ *0524/42–97–28* ⊕ *www. cafearabe.com.*

Kosybar. The Kosybar and restaurant is a long-standing favorite in Marrakesh for a late-night drink in the medina, served with live jazz entertainment every night, and a platter of sushi if you wish. Enjoy classic cocktails on the large roof terrace, which has great views of the storks nesting in the nearby ramparts of the Badii Palace and into the "lantern-making" square (place des Ferblantiers) below. The interior restaurant and bar, with mosaic-tiled floors, wrought-iron balustrades, and fireplaces, are truly cozy. ⊠ *47, pl. des Ferblantiers, Kzadria, Medina* ☎ *0524/38–03–24* ⊕ *www.kosybar.com.*

La Maison Arabe. The intimate surroundings of the jazz bar at hotel La Maison Arabe provide an intimate fireside setting for cocktails and a tasty menu of light savory snacks. A resident pianist tickles the ivories every evening from 7 to 9. ⊠ *1, Derb Assehbe, Bab Doukkala, Medina* ☎ *0524/38–70–10* ⊕ *www.lamaisonarabe.com.*

Le Salama. A stone's throw from the Djemâa el Fna and up a narrow staircase, Le Salama is one of the few places in the medina where you can grab a cold beer or an aperitif without having to eat dinner. Drinks are served either at the bar area in the elegant, colonial-style restaurant or on the top terrace, which has panoramic views across to the Koutoubia. ⊠ *40, rue des Banques, Kennaria, Medina* ☎ *0524/39–13–00* ⊕ *www.lesalama.com.*

Les Jardins de la Koutoubia. The attractive Art Deco stylings and extensive cigar rack of the piano bar at hotel Les Jardins de la Koutoubia are decadent. A pianist plays 7 to midnight. ✉ *26, rue de la Koutoubia, Medina* ☎ *0524/38–88–00* ⊕ *www.lesjardinsdelakoutoubia.com.*

Rock'n'Kech. Reasonably priced drinks make this rooftop bar popular with Moroccans and expats. The décor is kitsch, with fiberglass-molded rocks, dinosaur-egg lamps, and a few sparse plants, but the main attraction is the fabulous uninterrupted view to the Koutoubia. The entrance is through a small door and up several flights of stairs, hidden on a street where artisans are busy stitching tents and awnings. ✉ *Bd. Fatima Zahra, Medina* ☎ *0643/22–14–70.*

CAFÉS

Nowhere is café culture busier than on Djemâa el Fna, where several terraces compete for the award for best view of the square.

Café de France. Just opposite Les Terrasses, Café de France is much past its prime, but as long as you're only interested in a late-night glass of mint tea with a good view, it does the trick. On the ground floor it also has a tiny snack restaurant with bright plastic tables, serving sandwiches and quick bites until closing time. Head to the top floor for a ringside view of the square. ✉ *Pl. Djemâa el Fna, on northeastern corner, Medina* ☎ *0524/44–23–19.*

Grand Balcon du Café Glacier. To catch the sunset and the beginnings of the alluring smoke and sizzle of the grills, the rightly named Grand Balcon du Café Glacier, to the south of the square, is a top choice. It shuts relatively early, though (around 10 pm), and you'll have to compete for elbow room with all the amateur photographers who throng the best spot. Service is slow and soft drinks overpriced—but that's not unexpected for this bird's-eye view. ✉ *Pl. Djemâa el Fna, Medina.*

CASINO

La Grand Casino de La Mamounia. The casino at La Mamounia has a large room for roulette, poker, and blackjack; a slot-machine hall; and is open until 6 am. You'll need to dress up to gain entrance to this exclusive establishment. ✉ *Av. Bab Jdid, Medina* ☎ *0524/44–45–70* ⊕ *www. grandcasinomamounia.com.*

GUÉLIZ

BARS

For evening drinks in elegant surroundings, dress the part and head to one of Marrakesh's prestigious hotels. In Guéliz there are a few other late-night bars with live music scattered in the side streets south of place du 16 Novembre along avenue Mohammed V. Night owls in search of something livelier should head to the trendy hangouts in Guéliz and Hivernage or the cavernous clubs in the new Aguedal Zone Touristique, some 5 km (3 miles) out of town on avenue Mohammed VI.

Djellabar. This old Guéliz building has been artfully converted into one of the hippest late-night bars in town, with a live DJ playing a mix of Western, world, and Oriental tunes. The original mosaic tiling still lines the alcoves, and pop-art paintings line the walls. Trendy but not snobby, the club welcomes all ages and nationalities, expats, locals, and tourists alike. ✉ *2, rue Iman Ibn Hanifa, Guéliz* ☎ *0524/42–12–42* ⊕ *www. djellabarmarrakech.com.*

Sky Bar. For a bird's-eye view of the red city, climb to the Sky Bar at the top of La Renaissance Hotel in Guéliz. Drinks are expensive, but it's a rum with a view that encompasses everything in the city, from the Koutubia Mosque to the High Atlas Mountains in the distance. ✉ *La Renaissance Hotel, Av. Mohammed V, corner of bd. Zerktouni, Guéliz* ☎ *0524/33–77–77* ⊕ *www.renaissance-hotel-marrakech.com.*

NIGHTCLUBS

Montecristo. The Cuban-theme surroundings and sounds of Montecristo, complete with Che Guevara portraits, has caught the imagination of the city's groovers and shakers. You can smoke *sheesha* on the roof terrace, dine downstairs, or dance the night away in the Baoli Club—but be aware of the omnipresent "working girls." ✉ *20, rue Ibn Aicha, Guéliz* ☎ *0524/43–90–31* ⊕ *www.montecristomarrakech.com.*

HIVERNAGE

BARS

Comptoir Darna. A lively crowd gathers regularly in the darkened corners of popular Comptoir Darna to dance to the tunes of the top-floor DJ. ✉ *Av. Echouhada, Hivernage* ☎ *0524/43–77–02* ⊕ *www. comptoirmarrakech.com.*

CASINO

Es Saadi. Apart from La Mamounia, the only casino of note in Marrakesh is the one in the gardens of the Es Saadi hotel, set apart from the main building. The first in town, it has undergone a revamp and contains a mixture of one-armed bandits and tables for roulette and blackjack. There are also regular poker tournaments and poker games every night from 6 pm to 8 am. ✉ *Hotel Es Saadi, rue Ibrahim El Mazini, Hivernage* ☎ *0524/33–74–00* ⊕ *www.essaadi.com.*

DINNER SHOWS

Lotus Club. The cabaret entertainment at Lotus Club is its raison d'être— and clearly built into the prices for drinks and food, which includes Mediterranean, Moroccan, and Japanese dishes. The show, titled "Oh La La!," features a burlesque-style revue of samba, Asian, and Egyptian-inspired vignettes performed by corseted dancers flaunting feather boas, and live music from Moroccan guitar virtuoso Mood. Come around 9 pm to see the show. ✉ *Rue Ahmed Chawki, Hivernage* ☎ *0524/42–17–36* ⊕ *www.lotusclubmarrakech.com.*

NIGHTCLUBS

555 Famous Club. Overtaking Pacha in terms of popularity with the local Moroccan crowd and visitors, the 555 Club opened in 2012 and plays deafening house, R&B, and hip-hop with guest DJs on the weekend. ✉ *Av. Mohammed VI, Aguedal Zone Touristique, Hivernage* ☎ *0678/18–10–85* ⊕ *www.beachclub555.com.*

Le Théâtro. Hip, loud, and gregarious, Le Théâtro draws locals and tourists for its festive vibe. On the menu are house music, hard-core Dutch house, live DJs, candy girls, and circus cabaret acts. ✉ *Hotel Es*

Annual Festivals

Marrakesh's annual folklore festival of Moroccan music, theater, and dance—the **Festival National des Arts Populaires**—draws performers from all over Morocco and may even include an equestrian fantasia event. Held in July on the grounds of El Badi Palace and at the Theatre Royal, this highly worthwhile festival lasts about three days.

The **Marrakesh International Film Festival** is held in early December. Since 2000, this high-profile event has attracted the glitterati of the international movie world for screenings of Moroccan and international films throughout the city. Previous special guests have included Susan Sarandon, Leonardo DiCaprio, Martin Scorsese, and Alan Parker. For more information, the festival has a website: ⊕ en. festivalmarrakech.info.

The brainchild of Vanessa Branson, the **Marrakech Biennale** strives to address social issues using the contemporary arts and features talks, exhibitions, and installations throughout the city by Moroccan and international artists. It usually takes place in March, and the next event is anticipated for 2016. See the website (⊕ www.marrakechbiennale.org) for details of future events.

Aïd el-Arch (Throne Day), the commemoration of the king's coronation, is always on July 30. Parades and fireworks create a festive ruckus, and throngs of people fill the streets to listen and dance to live music. **Aïd el-Seghrir** celebrates the end of Ramadan and is felt largely as a citywide sigh of relief. **Aïd el-Kebir**, the Day of Sacrifice, has a somber tone; approximately 2½ months after the end of Ramadan, Muslims everywhere observe the last ritual of the pilgrimage to Mecca by slaughtering a sheep.

Saadi, rue Ibrahim El Mazini, Hivernage ☎ 0524/44–88–11 ⊕ www. theatromarrakech.com.

Pacha. The supertrendy superclub—a Marrakesh favorite—boasts a reputation as one of the biggest clubs in Africa. There are two restaurants, a swimming pool, bar, boutique, chill-out room with live music, and, of course, a dance floor featuring international guest DJs. It costs 250 DH to walk in the door, and taxis there and back can prove expensive (estimate 150 DH each way). ⊠ Av. Mohammed VI, Zone Touristique Aguedal, Hivernage ⊕ www.pachamarrakech.com.

Fodor'sChoice **Palais Jad Mahal.** One of the hippest nightspots is the Indian-tinged Jad Mahal, with its exorbitantly priced drinks and a lavish belly-dancing display that manages to soothe your empty wallet. The house band plays each evening, and upstairs is the hard-core Silver nightclub for those wanting to stay until dawn. ⊠ 10, rue Fontaine de la Mamounia, Bab Jdid, next to the Sofitel, Hivernage ☎ 0524/43–69–84 ⊕ www. jad-mahal.com.

Silver. After an Oriental-style evening in Jad Mahal, head underground to party until the early hours in the dazzling world of Silver. Pumping techno and acid house, DJs attract a youthful crowd of Moroccans. Jad

Mahal patrons don't have to pay the 200 DH cover. ⊠ *19, rue Haroun Errachi, Hivernage* ☎ *0663/73–15–42* ⊕ *www.silvermarrakech.com.*

SO Night Lounge. A stylish nightspot with contemporary décor and furnishings, attracting an upmarket crowd of tourists, Moroccans, and expats alike, SO has live music and resident DJs, a Moroccan restaurant, licensed bar, chill-out spaces, and a relaxed garden terrace area to enjoy sheesha and alcohol-free cocktails. Sofitel residents and diners at SO Food restaurant avoid the hefty 250 DH cover. ⊠ *Sofitel, rue Haroun Errachid, Hivernage* ☎ *0524/42–56–00.*

PALMERY

DINNER SHOWS

Chez Ali. The long-standing nightly spectacle that takes place at Chez Ali is a Disneyworld-meets-Marrakesh experience, catering to the mass tourism market. After a multicourse dinner of couscous, pastilla, and tagine in breezy tents, the *fantasia* begins in the outdoor arena. Featuring hundreds of performers and dozens of horses, this singing-and-dancing pageant is a celebration of traditional culture. It's all very tacky and you'll feel pressured into tipping the lackluster performers that snag you at every possible opportunity. Taxis will take you there, or your hotel can organize an all-inclusive price that includes round-trip transportation. ⊠ *Circuit Jaafaria, Douar Belguid, Palmery* ☎ *0524/30–77–30* 🍽 *450 DH.*

Fuego Latino. A high-octane performance of samba drummers, musicians, and carnival dancers shimmying their way among the crowd and dancing on the tabletops, Fuego Latino includes an all-you-can-eat extravaganza of grilled meats and fish in the Brazilian *churrascaria* style. You can also enjoy the show from the bar (with hefty drinks prices). The show starts around 9 pm. ⊠ *Palmeraie Palace Hotel, Circuit de la Palmeraie, Palmery* ☎ *0619/27–29–45* ⊕ *www.palmeraiemarrakech. com* ⊗ *Closed during Ramadan.*

Le Blokk. Located in the Palmery, outside of town, Le Blokk is a dinner-cabaret venue well worth the taxi ride. The décor is chic, and dishes like duck with balsamic vinegar and lamb with thyme are reasonably priced. The live music and entertainment, however, takes center stage. Tap your feet while talented singers perform songs from the last 50 years, followed by acrobatic performers who start to twirl from the ceilings around midnight. Top off the night with DJs spinning Oriental and Western dance music until around 1 am. Reservations are a must. ⊠ *Circuit de la Palmeraie, next to Mehdi Palace, Palmery* ☎ *0674/33–43–34* ⊕ *www.leblokk.com* ⊗ *Closed Mon. and during Ramadan.*

SHOPPING

Marrakesh is a shopper's bonanza, full of the very rugs, handicrafts, and clothing you see in the pages of magazines back home. Most bazaars are in the souk, just north of Djemâa el Fna and spread through a seemingly never-ending maze of alleys. Together, they sell almost everything imaginable and are highly competitive. Bargaining here is hard, and you can get up to 80% discounts. So on your first exploration, it's often a better idea to simply wander and take in the atmosphere than to buy. You can check guideline prices in some of the more well-to-do parts of town, which display fixed price tags for every object.

There are a number of crafts and souvenir shops on avenue Mohammed V in Guéliz, as well as some very good Moroccan antiques stores and designer shops that offer a distinctly modern take on Moroccan clothing, footwear, and interior decoration. These allow buyers to browse at their leisure, free of the souk's intense pressures. Many have fixed prices, with only 10% discounts after haggling. Most of these stores are happy to ship your purchases overseas. Bazaars generally open between 8 and 9 am and close between 8 and 9 pm; stores in Guéliz open a bit later and close a bit earlier, some breaking for lunch. Some bazaars in the medina close on Friday, the Muslim holy day. In Guéliz, most shops are closed on Sunday.

OFF THE BEATEN PATH

Away from the medina and beyond Guéliz, the gritty, nontouristy industrial zone of **Sidi Ghanem** has recently become a hot shopping destination, with local designers and artisans setting up workshops and showrooms targeting the wholesale and export market. Riad owners, restaurateurs, hoteliers, expats, and tourists scour the outlets to buy superior-quality, contemporary-style housewares, furnishings, ceramics, fashion, jewelry, and perfumes. About 5 km (3 miles) out of town on the route de Safi, it requires hiring a taxi for a few hours to take you there, wait while you shop, and then bring you back downtown.

BARGAINING

Bargaining is part of the fun of shopping in the medina's souks. Go back and forth with the vendor until you agree on an acceptable price. If you are not sure if the vendor's "lowest price" is really the lowest, slowly leave the store—if the vendor follows you, then you can negotiate further. If bargaining is just not your thing and you don't mind paying a little extra, consider the shops of Guéliz. Although these shops are not as colorful as the souks, a reasonable variety of high-quality goods are on offer.

SHOPPING GUIDES

Many guides have (undeclared) affiliations with certain shops, and taking on a guide may mean you'll be delivered to the boutique of their choice, rather than your own discovery. You should be fine on your own, as long as you keep your eyes peeled for mini-adventures and overly aggressive sellers. Small boutique shopkeepers who can't afford to tip guides will thank you for it.

There are also a few personal shopping guides working in Marrakesh (mostly expats), trying to strike the best deal for the customer and take the pain out of seeking, finding, and haggling for those "must-have" items.

FONDOUKS

If you tire of the haggling in the souk but still want to pick up a bargain, try visiting a *fondouk*. These were originally storehouses, workshops, and inns frequented by merchants and artisans on their journeys across the Sahara (known as *caravanserai* in the Middle East), and are still in use today, particularly by Berber merchants bringing carpets and other goods from surrounding villages; others are staffed by artisans at work on goods destined for the market. They're easily recognized by courtyards full of junk, usually with galleries on upper levels. Fondouks always keep their doors open, so feel free to look around. Because you deal with the artisans directly, there's less of a markup on prices. There are a couple of fondouks on the Dar el Bacha as you head towards the souk, and on rue Bab Taghzout by the fountain known as Shrob ou Shouf ("Drink and Look").

Patrizia Bell-Banner. Personal shopper Patrizia Bell-Banner is an interior decorator living between London and Marrakesh. She knows her way through the best boutiques of the souks and out to the designer show-rooms of the Sidi Ghanem industrial zone, and can point you in the direction of those special items you may be seeking. ☎ *0661/42–43–82* ✍ *patbanner@onesourcehomesearch.com.*

MEDINA

THE SOUKS

From dried fruit to handbags, carpets to candlesticks, the jumbled laby-rinth of merchants and artisan workshops to be found in the souks of the Marrakesh medina is one of the wonders of the city, where all man-ner of curious exotic items can be found. It stretches north from the place Djemâa el Fna to the Ali ben Youssef Medersa. Each souk has a name that defines its specialty and that relates to the crafts guilds that used to control each area.

Heading north from Bab Fteuh square, near the place Djemâa el Fna, the souks are laid out roughly as follows:

Souk Semmarine: textiles and souvenirs; Souk Rahba Kdima: spices, herbs, apothecaries, woolen hats, baskets; Souk el-Kebir: carpets, leather goods, and wood wares; Souk Zarbia: carpets; Souk des Bijoutiers/Souk Tagmoutyime: jewelry; Souk el-Attarine: polished copper and brass and mirrors; Souk des Babouches/Souk Smata: leather slippers; Souk des Teinturiers/Souk Sebbaghine: fabric and wool. Several other souks—including Souk Chouari: wood-carpenters; Souk Haddadine: black-smiths; and Souk Cherratine: leatherworkers—are at the northern end.

Generally, credit cards are not accepted here, except at the more upmar-ket bazaars and shops. Most places are open daily from 9 to 9, though some places close on Friday. A small side market called Souk Cherifia is located at the northern end of the souks beyond Souk Haddadine. The ground floor sells standard touristic items, but go up to the second floor near the entrance to La Terrasse des Épices restaurant and you'll find several fascinating little boutique outlets offering trendy young fashion and housewares designers including Art/C, Sylvie Pissard, and Créazen.

Carpet Souk. The site of the old slave auctions held up until the French occupied the city in 1912, the main carpet souk—called the Souk Zra-bia or Le Criée Berbère—has a flat, shiny floor in the middle of the surrounding boutiques used to roll out the rugs to display to potential buyers. To get there head north on rue Semarine, and just after the Souk el Attarine branches off left, take the next right turn off the street (which is now more properly named rue Souk el-Kebir—the Big Souk Street). The carpet souk can also be reached from a passage in Rahba Qdima's northeast corner (to the right of Le Café des Épices). ⊠ *Rahba Qdima, Medina.*

Leather Souks. At the northeastern edges of the souk (just beyond the northern end of the main rue Souk el-Kebir) are the leatherworkers—busy cutting out templates for babouches, hammering and polishing, and making up bags and satchels from several types of animal skins. Look for signs to the Souk des Sachochiers (bag makers), Souk Chairia, and Souk Cherratine, all leatherworking areas. The tanneries, where the raw hides have been prepared and dyed, are some 20 minutes walk farther northeast from Souk Cherratine along rue Bab Debbagh. Also in the northeast are a range of instruments, especially drums (Souk Moulay) and woven baskets (Souk Serrajine). ⊠ *Rue Souk Chairia, Medina.*

Rue Mouassine. One of the easiest ways to head back to Djemâa el Fna from a day of souk shopping is to find rue Mouassine, the souk's westernmost main north–south artery (the other main artery is rue Souk Semarine, on the eastern side of the souks). Rue Mouassine is quite easy to find, and it's almost impossible to veer away from the correct path once you're on it; the simplest route is to take a counterclockwise loop from behind the Ben Youssef Medersa—when you hit the big mosque, you've hit rue Mouassine. This is heavy souvenir territory, with the whole gamut of goods on display—lanterns, teapots, scarves, babouches, djellabas. It's an easy trip south. ■ TIP→ Look for Fnac Berbère, the Berber bookshop, on the southern section of rue Mouassine (the southern section from the fountain to Bab Fteuh square is sometimes known as rue Fehl Chidmi). It's a good landmark. The street spits you out into the northeast corner of Bab Fteuh square, and from there it's a short hop down to Djemâa el Fna. ⊠ *Medina.*

NEED A BREAK?

Dar Cherifa. Wind down at Dar Cherifa, an airy 16th-century riad turned café turned library turned art gallery. It puts on the occasional cultural evening, including poetry readings, traditional music, and storytelling. It also styles itself as a literary café, so you can take a book on Morocco down from the shelves, sit on the low-slung cushions at the foot of the four pillars, and sip mint tea. Alternatively, peruse the art exhibitions and enjoy a light lunch in the elegant alcoves: magical. ⊠ *8, Derb Cherfa Lakbir, Mouassine, Medina* ☎ *0524/42–64–63* ⊕ *www.darcherifa.com.*

Souk des Babouches. Best approached by taking the main left fork onto Souk el Attarine where it branches off from rue Souk el-Kebir and then continuing north for about 150 yards, the Souk Principal des Babouches—also called Souk Smata—is on the right-hand side and is filled with the pointed leather slippers so beloved of Moroccans. The small doorway opens up to an enormous emporium with examples in every color imaginable.

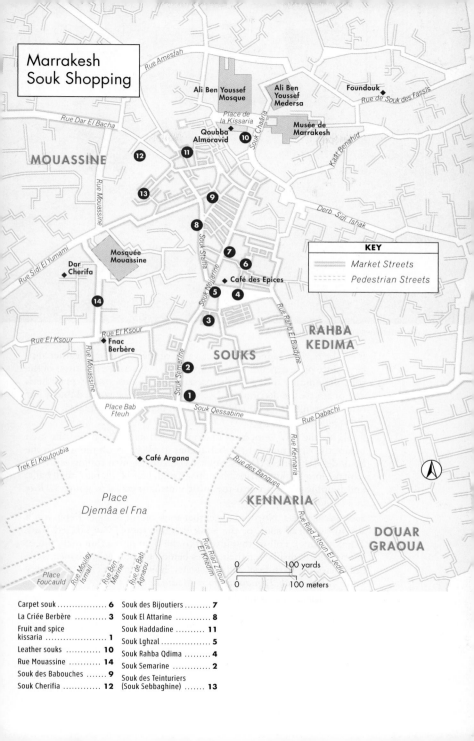

Marrakesh Souk Shopping

KEY

Market Streets

Pedestrian Streets

Ali Ben Youssef Mosque

Ali Ben Youssef Medersa

Foundouk

Rue Amesfah

Rue de Souk des Fassis

Rue Dar El Bacha

Place de la Kissaria

Qoubba Almoravid

Musée de Marrakesh

Souk Chaaria

Kâat Benahid

MOUASSINE

Rue Mouassine

Derb Sidi Ishak

Rue Sidi El Yamani

Mosquée Mouassine

Dar Cherifa

Souk Smarine

Souk Stafia

Café des Epices

RAHBA KEDIMA

Rue Rahb El Bladyne

Rue El Ksour

Rue El Ksour

Fnac Berbère

Rue Mouassine

SOUKS

Souk Semarine

Place Bab Fteuh

Souk Qessabine

Rue Dabachi

Rue Kennaria

Café Argana

Rue des Banques

KENNARIA

Rue Riad Z'itoun El Jedid

DOUAR GRAOUA

Place Djemâa el Fna

Trek El Koutoubia

Rue Moulay Ismail

Rue Ben Marine

Rue de Bab Agnaou

Rue Riad Z'itoun El Khedim

Place Foucauld

| 0 | 100 yards |
| 0 | 100 meters |

Colorful spices are sold in the Marrakesh souks.

It can be hard to judge the proper value of these fairy-tale leather slippers, since price depends on so many things, such as the thickness of the sole, the number of layers, the presence or absence of a stepped heel, and of course the decoration. Use your nose, but be warned that a fair price can range from 60 DH to 400 DH, depending on quality. (⇨ *For more on buying slippers, see Chapter 10.*)

Look for the tiny wool boutique on the left as you come to the arch before the right turn for the babouches market. It's on the way to the Souk des Teinturiers (Dyers' Souk). You can see men rolling out wool to make into fetching striped handbags, and, best of all, into small balls, and looping them up into the most unusual necklaces going. ⊠ *Rue Souk Smata, Medina.*

Souk des Bijoutiers. North of the carpet souk on rue Souk el-Kebir you'll see an overhead sign for the Souk des Bijoutiers (also labeled Souk Tagmoutyime). Follow that just off to the right into a thin mall, full of jewelry stores displaying their wares behind glass. It is by no means the only place in Marrakesh to buy jewelry, however, especially the bulky kind. ⊠ *Rue Souk Tagnaoutuyime, Medina.*

Souk des Teinturiers. Using the Mouassine Mosque as a landmark, keep the Mouassine fountain on your right and continue until the street widens out with shops on either side. At the point where it branches into two alleys running either side of a shop selling handmade lamps and textiles, take an immediate sharp left turn. You can follow that derb and look for the helpfully daubed word "teinturies" in spray paint and then head right. Souk des Teinturiers is also called Souk Sebbaghine. The main square for fabric dyeing is hidden down a little shimmy to the right and then immediately left, but anyone can direct you. Here you'll see men dipping fabrics into vats full of hot dye. Don't forget to look up—there are scarves and trains of wool hanging all over, in individual sets of the same bright colors.

For the best view, head into the dyers' square and ask to be led into the boutique. A dyer can show you the powders that the colors come from. A lovely bit of magic involves the fact that green powder dyes fabric red; red powder dyes things blue; and yellow powder dyes things purple. Head up the steep stairs and onto the roof if you are allowed— a spectacular view of industry unfolds, with headscarves and threads of every color hanging up to dry in separate color blocks all over the rooftops. ⊠ *Rue Souk Sebbaghine, Medina.*

Souk el Attarine. Traditionally the market street for perfumes, essential oils, and spices, Souk el Attarine is one of the main left turns from Souk Semarine (as you head north), leaving the road at a "10 o'clock" angle. If this is as deep as you wish to explore in the souks, then you can make an interesting loop by walking as far as the entrance to the Souk des Babouches (on the right) and then soon after take a turn off left, passing through the wool-dyers' souk and heading to the Mouassine mosque. Turning left after the mosque you head back south eventually, down rue Mouassine to rejoin Bab Fteuh square. ⊠ *Rue Souk el Attarine, Medina.*

Souk Haddadine. From rue Souk el Attarine, follow that main souk street as faithfully as possible and it will take you north, looping clockwise to the east, and through the ironmongers' souk, where you'll see blacksmiths at work, hammering out lanterns and wrought-iron chairs. ⊠ *Medina.*

Souk Lghzal. North of Djemâa el Fna on Souk Semarine, you pass a fairly prominent derb that turns off to the left (rue R'mila Bab Ksour, also called rue el-Ksour). Take the next right turn and wander down a few yards (towards the Spice Square, or Rahba Qdima) and on the right you will find the small square of Souk Lghzal, the Wool Souk. Today women sell secondhand clothes in the square, and the odd djellaba. A real treat can be found in the apothecary stalls leading up to the entrance to the square, and immediately to the right on entering it. There are spices and potions galore, as well as animal skins (zebra, snake, leopard), used by women for magic: mostly in their desire for marriage and pregnancy. ⊠ *La Criée Berbère, Medina.*

Souk Rahba Qdima. Just a quick turn right and then left out of the Souk Lghzal (via rue Souk Semarine) is the large square called Souk Rahba Qdima. Pushier and more mass-market than the spice street, this is the souk's main spice center. There are also lots of woven baskets and hats for sale here. If you are feeling peckish or just tired, pause for a pleasant pit stop at the Café des Épices. ⊠ *Medina.*

Souk Semarine. From Djemâa el Fna take the street just to the left of the Café Argana, which leads into the small Bab Fteuh square, and then keep bearing right. To the left there is a *kissaria* (covered market), with dried fruits, herbs and spices, essential oils, and traditional colored eye kohls. Veer right into the covered market, past a couple of stands selling teapots and mint tea glasses, and take a left onto rue Souk Semarine.

It's signposted and lined with fabrics and inexpensive souvenirs. ⊠ *Rue Souk Semarine, Medina.*

NEED A BREAK? **Souk Kafé.** After a hectic few hours in the souks, sampling potions, tasting tea, haggling prices, and nimbly jumping out of the way of mopeds, the Souk Kafé welcomes the frazzled traveler. Just beyond the Souk Cherifa and Souk Semmarine, you can relax in the stylish lounge of this converted old family house and admire your purchases. Colorful textiles, leather pouffes, African artifacts, and old photos adorn the walls; from the small terrace you can gaze over the surrounding rooftops. The menu offers standard Moroccan dishes, or you can just call in for mint tea, coffee, or a fresh-fruit smoothie. Cash only, and no alcohol is served. $ *Average main: 80DH* ⊠ *11, Derb Souk Jdid, Sidi Abdelaziz, Medina* ☎ *0662/61-02-29* ▤ *No credit cards.*

SPECIALTY STORES

ANTIQUES

ETs. Bouchaib Complexe d'Artisanat. This three-level store is usually either full or empty, depending on whether the latest tour bus has dropped off a load of shoppers. Still, don't let that put you off. Originally a carpet store, it has expanded to a superstore with an escalator to take you inside. Ornate goods range from Jewish-Berber handwritten scrolls to man-size teapots, and each one has an individual price tag. The reliable shipping department wraps fragile items in more rolls of bubble wrap than you thought possible. On large orders, haggle up to 25%. Do not expect original genuine antique pieces. ⊠ *7, Derb Baissi, rue de la Kasbah, Kasbah* ☎ *0524/38-18-53* ⊕ *www.complexeartisanal.com.*

Fodor'sChoice ★ **Khalid Art Gallery.** Popular with the international jet set, the reputable Khalid Art Gallery is a gorgeous riad full to the brim of the most sought-after Moroccan antiques, Jewish-Moroccan treasures, and Berber pieces. Owner Khalid speaks excellent English and is an authority on most of the art coming out of Marrakesh. ⊠ *14, rue Dar el Basha, Mouassine, Medina* ☎ *0524/44-24-10* ☾ *Closed Aug.*

Fodor'sChoice ★ **Le Trésor des Nomades.** The highly respected Le Trésor des Nomades, owned by Mustapha Blaoui, sells antique doors, carpets, Berber jewelry, and all kinds of lamps. It's so well known that there is no sign over the door. ⊠ *142, rue Bab Doukkala, Medina* ☎ *0524/38-52-40.*

Twizra. Prices are high at this general antiques and jewelry store in the Kasbah—so haggle hard! They can (reliably) organize international shipping and also accept credit cards. ⊠ *361, Bab Agnaou, Medina* ☎ *0524/37-65-65.*

ART

Atelier de Marrakech Art et Culture. This art association puts on exhibitions by local artists and showcases artists at work. You'll find them in the arcades surrounding the 16th-century public fountain next to Bab Doukkala mosque; the building that houses the fountain has been transformed into a gallery. Visitors can buy work they like. ⊠ *Fontaine Lalla*

Aouda, rue Bab Doukkala, behind mosque Bab Doukkala, Medina ☎ *0668/32–84–74* ⊗ *Mon.–Sat. 10:30–1:30 and 3:30–7:30.*

Miloud Art Gallery. This shop carries a very nicely curated collection of upscale Moroccan items for the home. Clothing and bags for women are in the back. ✉ *48, Souk Cheratine, Medina* ☎ *0524/42–67–16.*

Ministero del Gusto. For something a bit more cutting edge, Ministero del Gusto combines boutique and gallery and shows off gorgeous items in both. Vintage clothing is also for sale. ✉ *22, Derb Azzouz el Mouassine, off rue Sidi El-Yamami, Medina* ☎ *0524/42–64–55* ⊕ *www. ministerodelgusto.com* ⊗ *Weekdays 10–1:30, and by appt.*

BOOKS

Fnac Berbère. This shop is renowned for its range of books on Berber life and culture. The little *café littéraire* up the stairs immediately to the left of the bookstore also has a small selection of books, though not the same owner. ✉ *Rue Mouassine, Medina.*

Librairie Dar el Bacha. Here you'll find a good selection of guidebooks, maps, cookbooks, art books, novels, and postcards. ✉ *2, rue Dar el Bacha, Medina* ☎ *0524/39–19–73.*

Librarie el Ghazali Ahmed Ben Omar. This shop just off the place Djemâa el Fna has a range of guidebooks, cookbooks, volumes on Moroccan history in English, and maps. ✉ *51, rue Bab Aganou (also known as av. Prince Moulay Rachid), off pl. Djemâa el Fna, Medina* ☎ *0524/44–23–43* ⊗ *Closed Sun.*

CARPETS

Bazaar Jouti. This spacious two-story shop has a wide selection of rugs and carpets and can arrange for shipping on the spot. Mohammed and Karimi both speak good English. ✉ *16–19, souk des Tapis, Rahba Lakdima, Medina* ☎ *0524/44–32–19.*

Palais Saâdiens. This shop has an enormous selection of Berber, Bedouin, and Arab carpets. ✉ *16, rue Moulay Taib, Ksour, Medina* ☎ *0524/44–51–76.*

CLOTHING

Aya's. This shop sells bespoke kaftans and tunics made with the highest quality fabrics—cashmeres, linens, silks—all hand-embroidered. Celebrity clients include Prince, Julia Roberts, and Hugh Jackman. ✉ *11 bis, Derb Jdid, Bab Mellah, near Le Tanjia restaurant, Medina* ☎ *0524/38–34–28* ⊕ *www.ayasmarrakech.com* ⊗ *Closed Sun.*

Maktoub. Easy to find near the Mouassine Fountain, this boutique has a selection of contemporary Moroccan designer accessories and fashion items. It's a pricey collection of designs by Max & Jan, Second Life (recycled designer fabrics), and other up-to-the-minute artisan names. It also now has an outlet for well-heeled, trendy kids just farther along the street. ✉ *128, Mouassine Fontaine, rue Sidi Yemani, Medina* ☎ *0524/37–55–70* ⊕ *www.maxandjan.ma.*

Warda La Mouche. This shop stocks handmade clothing for women in great fabrics and colors with Moroccan design elements. The tunics are especially wearable and figure-flattering. Expect to pay London or New

York prices. Credit cards are accepted. ⊠ *127, rue Kennaria, Medina* 🕾 *0524/38–90–63* ⊘ *Closed Aug.*

CRAFTS

Antiquités du Sahara. Handcrafted jewelry from southern Morocco of Berber, Touareg, and Blue Men traditions is for sale here. ⊠ *176, Rahba Lakdima, next to the carpet market, Medina* 🕾 *0524/44–23–73.*

Ensemble Artisanal. This is a great way to see all the wares of the souk under one hassle-free umbrella. Several boutiques in modern confines display fixed prices (which are high) for handicrafts including babouches, embroidery, lanterns, bags, jewelry, carpets, and paintings. There's even a snack bar. ■TIP➜ **Make a note of prices here and then aim to pay around 25% less in the souks.** ⊠ *Av. Mohammed V, Medina* 🕾 *0524/38–66–74* ⊘ *Closed Sun.*

Wish Wish Art. This emporium of jewelry and furnishings has a variety of beautiful handicrafts, including magnificently inlaid game tables. ⊠ *23, rue el Mouassine, Medina* 🕾 *0524/39–09–90.*

HEALTH AND BEAUTY

Aachab Atlas. This apothecary is stuffed from floor to ceiling with spices, perfumes, and traditional medicines for ailments such as rheumatism and back pain. The helpful staff speak fluent English, and credit cards are accepted. ⊠ *Rue sidi el Yamani, Bab Laksour, Medina* 🕾 *0524/42–67–28.*

GUÉLIZ

ANTIQUES

La Porte d'Orient. This sibling of the medina's Porte d'Or sells Moroccan and Asian antiques. It's geared toward those who prefer to browse before buying. ⊠ *9, bd. Mansour Eddahbi, near Hotel Agdal, Guéliz* 🕾 *0524/43–89–67* ⊘ *Closed Sun.*

L'Orientaliste. This is a charming mixed bag of a place, with old bottles, copper bowls, candlesticks, early 20th-century engravings, Fez pottery, furniture, perfume, and all sorts of antiques. There are two locations on the same street. ⊠ *11 and 15, rue de la Liberté, Guéliz* 🕾 *0524/43–40–74* ⊘ *Closed Sun.*

Marco Polo. In Guéliz for years, Marco Polo sells all kinds of antique Moroccan and Asian furniture as well as other artifacts. You'll find it next to Al Fassia Restaurant. ⊠ *55, bd. Zerktouni, Immeuble Taieb, Guéliz* 🕾 *0524/43–53–55* ⊘ *Closed Sun.*

ART

BCK Gallery. Exhibitions of contemporary art and sculpture from new and emerging Moroccan and international artists are on display here, and Marrakshi trendsetters can be spotted at the gallery openings. ⊠ *Résidence Al Hadika El Koubra, rue Ibnou Aïcha Imm C, Guéliz* 🕾 *0524/44–93–31.*

David Bloch Gallery. This small modern gallery showcases up-and-coming contemporary Moroccan artists. ✉ *8 bis, rue des Vieux Marrakchi, Guéliz* ☎ *0524/45–75–95* ⊕ *www.davidblochgallery.com* ⊙ *Closed Sun.*

Lawrence-Arnott Gallery. This long-established gallery in the city has a treasure trove of individual pieces, sculptures, prints, and paintings for sale. ✉ *Immeuble El Khalil, av. des Nations Unies, opposite Gendarmerie Royale, Guéliz* ☎ *0524/43–04–99* ⊕ *www.lawrence-arnott.com* ⊙ *Closed Sun.*

Matisse Gallery. This gallery has an interesting collection of works by young Moroccan artists, Moroccan masters, and the Orientalists. ✉ *No. 43 Passage Ghandouri, 61, rue de Yougoslavie, Guéliz* ☎ *0524/44–83–26* ⊕ *www.matisseartgallery.com.*

Tindouf Gallery. This gallery houses a permanent exhibit of orientalist paintings, ornate inlaid furniture, and antique ceramics. There is a constantly changing program of exhibitions and works for sale by top-notch Moroccan artists and foreign painters living in the kingdom. ✉ *22, bd. Mohammed VI, Guéliz* ☎ *0524/43–09–08* ⊕ *www.gallerytindouf.com* ⊙ *Closed Sun.*

BOOKS

Librairie Papeterie Ahmed Chatr. Greetings cards, schoolbooks in Arabic and French, and some English-language books—including novels, maps, and coffee-table books on Moroccan culture—are sold here. It also has office stationery supplies and a new outlet just around the corner with a huge range of art materials. ✉ *19–21, av. Mohammed V, Guéliz* ☎ *0524/44–79–97* ⊙ *Closed Sun.*

CLOTHING

Atika Boutique. This boutique is best known for its shoes, especially its soft leather moccasins in every shade of the rainbow. They rarely accept credit cards. ✉ *34, rue de la Liberté, Guéliz* ☎ *0524/43–64–09* ⊙ *Closed Sun.*

Founoon. This is the place for stylish prêt-à-porter clothing, handmade bags, and designer totes from a young Moroccan designer, as well as imported chunky bone bracelets from India and glass, heatproof Moroccan teapots. ✉ *119, rue Mohammed El Bekkal, Guéliz* ☎ *0524/44–88–41* ⊕ *www.founoon.ma* ⊙ *Closed Sun.*

Hadaya. This designer boutique sells T-shirts, sundresses, sandals, handmade shoes, funky bags, and accessories. ✉ *31, rue Majorelle (also known as rue Yves St. Laurent), opposite Majorelle Garden, Guéliz* ☎ *0524/29–28–84.*

Intensite Nomade. Browse chic and rather expensive Moroccan-inspired clothing for men and women, designed by Frédérique Birkemeyer. ✉ *139, av. Mohammed V, Guéliz* ☎ *0524/43–13–33* ⊙ *Closed Sun.*

Michele Baconnier. This boutique sells high-end clothing, jewelry, babouches, and bags that offer a hip twist on contemporary design. ✉ *6, rue des Vieux Marrakchis, Guéliz* ☎ *0524/44–91–78* ⊕ *www.michele-baconnier.net* ⊙ *Closed Sun.*

Place Vendome. Come here to find gorgeous leather goods of much better quality than what is offered in the souks. ⊠ *141, av. Mohammed V, corner of rue de la Liberté, Guéliz* ☎ *0524/43–52–63* ⊘ *Closed Sun.*

CRAFTS

FodorśChoice
★

33 Rue Majorelle. Slap-bang opposite the gates to the Majorelle Garden, this bright and funky new concept store stocks a range of fashions and quirky crafts, jewelry, and souvenirs from hip young Moroccan and European designers all working in and inspired by Marrakesh. ⊠ *33, rue Majorelle (also known as rue Yves St. Laurent), Guéliz* ☎ *0524/31–41–95* ⊕ *www.33ruemajorelle.com.*

Al Badii. Some of the most luxurious riads in town were furnished using artworks, crafts, and antiques from this quiet store. ⊠ *54, bd. Moulay Rachid, Guéliz* ☎ *0524/43–16–93* ⊘ *Closed Sun.*

Bazaar Ben Rahal. No longer in the Medina's Souk des Tapis, but rather in a shop in Guéliz, Bazaar Ben Rahal has a magnificent array of Berber tribal rugs and carpets. Owner Mohamed Taieb Sarmi can also show you more examples from his stockroom upstairs or from his house in Bab Doukkala, where he will painstakingly explain their origins and value. Sarmi sends rugs and carpets anywhere in the world; for packages to the United States, the import tax is paid in Morocco. English is spoken. ⊠ *28, rue de la Liberté, Guéliz* ☎ *0524/43–32–73* ⊘ *Closed Sun.*

TinMel. The gallery TinMel sells artworks, ceramics, antique carpets, and furniture. ⊠ *38, rue Ibn Aisha, Guéliz* ☎ *0524/43–22–71* ⊘ *Closed Sun.*

JEWELRY

Bazar Atlas. Come to browse an enormous selection of jewelry, including the heavy silver *filbules* favored by Berber women to weigh down their dresses; the filbules have become a symbol of the Berber way of life. Owner Said speaks good English and has another store in the medina. ⊠ *129, av. Mohammed V, Guéliz* ☎ *0663/62–01–03* ⊘ *Closed Sun.*

Brins d'Orient. Come here for silver jewelry crafted using traditional Moroccan motifs and designs and semiprecious stones, as well as an unusual modern slant on classic pendants, rings, and necklaces. There is another shop in the medina, just off place Djemâa el Fna and around the corner from Café de France. ⊠ *10, rue Majorelle, Guéliz* ☎ *0524/38–38–80* ⊘ *Closed Sun.*

HAMMAMS

The *hammam* (bath) ritual is part of Moroccan culture. The following public hammams are of an acceptable standard for tourists, but the private hammams and spas are a treat open to all (even nonguests, if in a hotel).

PUBLIC HAMMAMS

Hammam el Basha. As far as public hammams go, this is one of the largest and most accessible (it's 10 minutes north of Djemâa el Fna). Even in its current rundown condition you get a good sense of how impressive this hammam must have been in its heyday. Instead of the typical series of small low rooms, here you bathe in large, white-tiled chambers that give a pleasant sense of space. After your bath, dry and dress in a huge

2

domed hall skirted with inset stone benches. There are segregated hours for men and women. ⊠ *20, rue Fatima Zohra, Medina* ☏ *20 DH* ▭ *No credit cards* ⊙ *Daily: men 7–1 and women 1–9.*

Semlalia Hammam. The oldest public hammam in Guéliz opened in 1965 and is still thriving. For the uninitiated, you can ask for somebody to help you through the process and they'll scrub you down with black soap made from olives. For the basic use of the hammam you'll pay 12 DH; for the use of the hammam, black soap, exfoliation, and a *kaçal* (male or female attendant) to scrub you down, the cost is 100 DH. ⊠ *48, bd. Mohammed El Khattabi Abdelkrim, rte. de Casablanca, Guéliz* ☎ *0661/92–99–25* ☏ *12 DH* ⊙ *Daily 6 am–9 pm.*

PRIVATE HAMMAMS

Hammam de la Rose. As you step into the cool blue relaxation room with subtle lighting and chic décor, you might mistake this city-center hammam for a nightclub; but the gentle music, perfume, and whispering staff are pure spa. The two hammams are steaming hot all day, and a traditional, or *beldi* hammam with exfoliation and spice-infused cleanse costs 250 DH. Massages and other treatments are available too, and a couples' hammam can be booked as well. ⊠ *130, Dar el Bacha, Medina* ☎ *0524/44–47–69* ⊕ *www.hammamdelarose.com* ☏ *From 250 DH.*

Hammam Ziani. Sister to Casablanca's Ziani, this hammam not far from Bahia Palace in the medina is highly recommended. Both men and women are welcome. It's traditional without being in the slightest bit down-at-the-heels. The full hammam and *gommage* (exfoliation) works cost 120 DH, while packages priced between 250 DH and 300 DH include hammam, scrubbing, massage, and an algae wrap. ⊠ *14, Riad Zitoune Jdid, near Bahia Palace, Medina* ☎ *0662/71–55–71* ⊕ *www. hammamziani.ma* ☏ *100 DH* ▭ *No credit cards.*

Les Bains de l'Alhambra. This candlelit marble hammam has sunken baths filled with floating oranges and bath oils and a colonnaded patio for relaxing. Hammam starts at 150 DH for 45 minutes including a foot bath and foot massage. Massages and other beauty treatments are on the menu, too. ⊠ *9, Derb Rahala, Kasbah, Medina* ☎ *0524/38–63–46* ⊕ *www.lesbainsdelalhambra-marrakech.com.*

Les Bains de Marrakech. A temple to exotic beauty treatments and therapies, Les Bains de Marrakech will bathe you in milk with orange water and rose petals, massage you with argan oil, and and rub you down with mint-steamed towels. Reservations are required. ⊠ *2, Derb Sedra, Bab Agnaou, Kasbah* ☎ *0524/38–14–28* ⊕ *www.lesbainsdemarrakech. com* ☏ *170 DH.*

HOTEL HAMMAMS

La Maison Arabe. A morning or afternoon spent in this sumptuous hotel's hammam will make you feel like royalty. The staff may not scrub you quite as hard as you like, but the hammam room is beautiful, and the small pool filled with roses is just for you. It's popular, so reservations are essential. ⊠ *La Maison Arabe, 1, Derb Assehbe, Bab Doukkala, Medina* ☎ *0524/38–70–10* ⊕ *www.lamaisonarabe.com* ☏ *650 DH for hammam and 30-min massage.*

La Mamounia. A day pass to the Mamounia's hammam or spa and swimming pool is an extravagance fit for special celebrations and allows you to spend some downtime at this famously exclusive establishment. The hammam and spa is open by reservation only, required for both hotel guests and nonguests. ⊠ *Av. Bab el Djedid, Medina* ☎ *0524/44–44–09* ⊕ *www.mamounia.com* ✉ *500 DH day pass, 1,000 DH hammam* ⊙ *Weekdays by reservation only.*

La Sultana Marrakech. In the Kasbah district, close to the Royal Palace, the hammam at hotel La Sultana Marrakech offers bath therapy, affusion showers (showers with lukewarm water combined with hand massage), hammam, Jacuzzi, and sauna. ⊠ *403, rue de la Kasbah, Kasbah* ☎ *0524/37–54–64* ⊕ *www.lasultanamarrakech.com* ✉ *400 DH for Royal hammam, 1,100 DH with 50-min massage.*

FAMILY **U Spa Barrière.** Underground at the Naoura Barrière hotel, this state-of-the-art spa offers not just hammams, scrubs, and scented beauty treatments, but a heated hydrotherapy pool with water jets, bubble seats, and a walk-against-the-current area. It's fully accessible to disabled clients and open to nonguests. A basic hammam with body scrub starts at 400 DH for 30 minutes and includes access to the hydro pool. Treatments for children are also available. ⊠ *Naoura Barrière, Rue Djebel Alakhdar, Bab Doukkala, Medina* ☎ *0524/45–90–00* ⊕ *www. lucienbarriere.com* ✉ *400 DH.*

SPORTS AND THE OUTDOORS

With more than 300 days of sunshine a year, Marrakesh residents pretty much live outdoors. Beat the heat in an upscale pool complex or meander through the public gardens. Whatever you do, don't forget the sunscreen for outdoor activities. But also realize that not all activities take place outdoors. Going to a hammam or taking a cooking class can also be rewarding, especially on the more unpredictable winter days.

CAMEL TREKKING

Dunes & Desert Exploration. This reliable outfitter organizes all kinds of adventure activities including 90-minute camel rides in the Palmery. If you don't have time to get to the Sahara to experience the real desert, then a quick jaunt in the Marrakesh oasis is the next best thing. Prices start at 275 DH per person including return transfer from your hotel. ☎ *0524/35–41–47* ⊕ *www.dunesdesert.com.*

CYCLING

Marrakech City Bike Tours. Take a two- or four-hour guided bike tour through the city's old quarters, via the ramparts or out to the Palmery. Prices start at 450 DH per person (two-person minimum). ⊠ *Cyberparc Moulay Abdessalam, av. Mohammed V, Medina* ☎ *0661/24–01–45* ⊕ *www.marrakech-city-bike-tour.com.*

Continued on page 114

HAMMAM RITUAL
SPREADER OF WARMTH

by Victoria Tang

To escape the bustling souks and crowded cities—or simply to recover from hours of trekking and touring—a hammam is the perfect retreat to soothe both your body and soul in a uniquely Moroccan way.

Essential to Moroccan life, hammams are hydrotherapeutic rooms best described as something between a Turkish bath and a Finnish sauna. Like the tagines used to cook the national dish, hammams provide a mixture of baking and steaming. Water pipes run beneath marble-tiled floors, which are heated by wood fires below ground. For public hammams, at least, these fires are the same ones used for the neighborhood's breadbaking ovens, which is why you'll usually find them in the medina of any Moroccan town. Water arrives through taps and creates a constant, light steam before being removed by drains at the center of the room. Although many hammams are old, all public hammams are relatively clean and subject to constant checks.

Walking into a public hammam for the first time can be daunting or disenchanting if you're imagining a luxurious bathing chamber. It isn't a full-service spa—like those now offered in many upscale riads and hotels—but rather a basic, unadorned public bath, with no signs for the uninitiated. But if you know what to expect, there is nothing like it to make you feel you are truly in Morocco.

The tayeba at a hammam will wash you with a kessel scrubbing glove.

HOW TO USE THE HAMMAM

Hammams may be simple places (left), or they may be more elaborate and upscale (right).

ORIGINS

Islamic public baths were originally cold, and only men were permitted to use them. When the prophet Mohammed came to believe that hot water could promote fertility, the heated hammam (meaning "spreader of warmth") was inaugurated, and its use was extended to women. It soon became central to Muslim life, with several in each city, town, and village annexed to the mosque, to make hygiene available to everyone in accordance with the laws of Islam. The hammam's popularity also increased because the heat was thought to cure many types of diseases. The price of entry was—and still is—kept low so that even the poorest can afford it. Unlike the Roman baths, which were large, open, and designed for socializing, Moroccan hammams are mostly small, enclosed, and dimly lighted to inspire piety and reflection. In time the hammams drew people to socialize, especially women, whose weekly visits became so important to them—the only time they were allowed to leave the confines of their house—that it eventually was viewed as a right.

CHOOSE A LOCATION

If you're looking for an authentic experience, head to a public hammam. If you're shy, have a higher budget, or seek a more luxurious experience, head to a private one. But realize that all hammams are sex-segregated. When looking for a public hammam, ask at your hotel about public hammam that are welcoming to foreigners. Avoid hammams with seedy reputations. Entry to a public hammam is usually 10 DH; private hotel hammams cost 200–500 DH. Upscale spa treatments can add 800–1000 DH.

WHAT TO BRING

In a public hammam, take basic toiletries: soap, shampoo, comb and/or hairbrush, razor, a towel (women should bring an extra towel to wear as a turban when you leave, as hair dryers are not permitted), and a spare pair of underwear. You may also want to bring a pair of flip-flops, as the hammam's tiled floors are slippery and hot. Buy a small plastic water jug, scrubbing glove called a kessel (or kees, or kis), the dark olive soap called *savon noir,* and mineral-laden clay for conditioning hair and skin called *rhassoul* from a local grocer or pharmacy.

Don't bring any valuables; you'll leave your belongings in an open cubby (the attendants watch diligently over these, so bring 5–10 DH for a tip). If you hire a *tayeba,* an assistant, who will basically do everything from start to finish for you, tip 20–50 DH. Private hammams usually provide individual bags containing everything you need.

HAMMAM ETIQUETTE

The hammam is generally relaxed, with the echo of voices and splashing water resounding from each room. As a tourist, you may be stared at, but a big smile will ease anxiety. A warm *salaam* when you arrive will help break the ice. Once you have stripped down to your underwear and stored your bagged belongings in a cubby, take two buckets from the entry room and enter the hammam. Most hammams consist of three interconnected rooms, usually dimly lit from tiny windows in a small, domed roof. The floors are often white marble tiles—both hot and slippery—so tread carefully. The first room is warm, the next hot, and the last is the hottest.

Choose a spot in the hot room first. Then go to the taps and fill your buckets, one with hot water, the other with cold for mixing. Go back and rinse your sitting area, and sit on a mat (which is usually provided). You can either stay here to let your pores open or go to the hottest room for 15 minutes or so.

Apply the olive soap over your body. Sit for a while before rinsing it off, then begin scrubbing your skin with the kessel mitt. Particularly in women's hammams, one of the other bathers may offer to scrub your back; it's polite to allow her to scrub yours and offer to scrub hers in return. Now rinse off with jugs of water mixed from the hot and cold buckets. You may refill your buckets at any time. Apply the rhassoul over your hair, and comb or brush until it's silky smooth, then repeat.

Finally, lather your body with regular soap, followed by a final all-over rinse, including rinsing your sitting area clean before leaving. Wrapped in your towel, you can relax back in the changing room before dressing and going out-side. If you hired a tayeba, pay him or her now, and tip the attendant who looks after the belongings. (Moroccan women never leave a hammam with exposed wet hair, and you may want to wrap yours with a towel or scarf as well; this isn't such a big deal for men.)

Private hammams follow the same ritual. Towels are usually supplied or rented. Specialized products are available for purchase. In hotels and upscale spas, you won't need to take anything with you, as attendants, towels, and all products are included in the fee. Tayebas in private hammams should be tipped 40–60 DH.

HAMMAN VOCABULARY

Kessel: Scrubbing glove made from coarse natural or synthetic fabric; used for exfoliation.

Savon noir: organic molasses-like paste derived from black olives; used as cleanser.

Rhassoul: natural clay from Middle Atlas rich in mineral salts; used to condition the hair and skin.

Tayeba or ghalassa: attendant who will fill water buckets, wash, and scrub you.

SAFETY TIPS

■ Not all public hammams are welcoming to foreigners.

■ Avoid going to public hammams on crowded Thursday evenings, and on Friday and Saturday afternoons.

■ Drink plenty of water before entering a hammam.

■ If you feel hot at any point, exit quickly and head for a cooler room.

GOLF

Marrakesh's popularity as a golfing destination is booming and there are now nine golf courses in and around town, with more under construction.

Al Maaden Golf Resort. This 18-hole, Kyle Phillips–designed course opened in 2010 with square bunkers, geometric water features, and fairways between the resort villas. Along the way admire the huge, modern, outdoor sculpture park, then wind down at the clubhouse. ⊠ *Sidi Ben Youssef Ali, old rte. de Ouarzazate, Palmery* ☎ *0524/40–40–00* ⊕ *www.almaaden.com ⅂. 18 holes. 7266 yards. Par 72. Green Fee: 650 DH ⌁ Facilities: Driving range, putting green, pitching area, golf carts, pull carts, caddies, rental clubs, pro shop, golf academy/lessons, restaurant, bar.*

Golf Amelkis Club. The 27-hole Golf Amelkis Club, designed by Cabell B. Robison, offers plenty of challenges. Unwind afterward with a drink at the bar in the kasbah-style clubhouse. ⊠ *Km 12, rte. de Ouarzazate, Palmery* ☎ *0524/40–44–14* ⊕ *www.golfamelkis.com ⅂. 27 holes (3 9-hole courses). 11,600 yards. Par 72. Green fee: 600 DH ⌁ Facilities: driving range, putting green, pitching area, golf carts, pull carts, caddies, rental clubs, pro shop, golf academy/lessons, restaurant, bar.*

Palm Golf Club. The Robert Trent Jones Sr.–designed course at the Palmeraie Golf Palace Hotel, 7 km (4½ miles) north of town in the Palmery, has 27 holes (an 18-hole course and a 9-hole course) and remains one of the most popular courses in Marrakesh. It's playable all year round and is suitable for players of all standards. ⊠ *Palmeraie Golf Palace Hotel, Circuit de la Palmeraie, Palmery* ☎ *0524/30–63–66* ⊕ *www. palmgolfclubmarrakech.com ⅂. 18 holes. 4102 yards. Par 72. 9 holes. 2000 yards. Par 36. Green fee: 600 DH ⌁ Facilities: Driving range, putting green, pitching area, golf carts, pull carts, caddies, rental clubs, pro shop, golf academy/lessons, restaurant, bar.*

Royal Golf Club. The long-established Royal Golf Club, founded in 1933, is a tree-filled haven, with a 27-hole course 7 km (4 miles) south of Marrakesh on the old Ouarzazate road. The casual Club House restaurant is open to nongolfers and has a delightful shaded terrace for a light and inexpensive lunch. ⊠ *Km 7, rte. de Ouarzazate, Palmery* ☎ *0524/40–98–28* ⊕ *www.royalgolfmarrakech.com ⅂. 27 holes. 6492 yards. Par 72. Green fee: 600 DH ⌁ Facilities: Driving range, putting green, pitching area, golf carts, pull carts, caddies, rental clubs, golf academy/lessons, restaurant, bar.*

HORSEBACK RIDING

Les Cavaliers d'Al Hamra. This French-run riding club caters mostly to the expat community, but it's open to tourists for lessons at the riding center arena and also for trekking out into the local countryside. A 90-minute ride costs 200 DH per person. ⊠ *Km 15, rte. de Fès, Palmery* ☎ *0600/39–17–83* ⊕ *www.cavalieralhamra.com.*

Les Cavaliers de l'Atlas. Half-day and full-day trekking excursions on horseback are offered from this ranch in the Palmery from 400 DH for two people, for two hours. Both novices and experienced riders are catered to. Horseback riding out into the countryside at Lake Lalla Takerkoust can also be arranged, with transportation included. The riding center is located near the Namaskar Palace Hotel. ⊠ *Bab Atlas, off rte. de Fès, near Namaskar Palace Hotel, Palmery* ☎ *0672/84–55–79* ⊕ *www.lescavaliersdelatlas.com.*

QUAD BIKING

Quad bikes and sand buggies are available for hire on the outskirts of Marrakesh, with most of the outfitters taking advantage of the sandy tracks of the Palmery for a half day or so of fun, but some can organize treks that range farther afield, to the Agafay desert or Lalla Takerkoust.

Dunes & Desert Exploration. For those who like the more adrenaline-pumping entertainment of quad bikes, this outfitter is a one-stop shop who can also arrange camel rides in the Palmery, hot-air-balloon rides, mountain biking, or even white-water rafting excursions in the Ourika Valley. ☎ *0524/35–41–47* ⊕ *www.dunesdesert.com.*

FAMILY **Kech Motor Bike.** Outside the city, this outfitter organizes quad-biking excursions from one hour to four days in the Agafay desert region or around Lalla Takerkoust, 30 minutes from Marrakesh. Prices start from 400 DH per hour and include transport to the site from your hotel. Children from five years old can participate in a learning session on miniquads. Cash only. ⊠ *Km 28, rte. de Barrage* ☎ *0673/74–99–39* ⊕ *www.quads-marrakech.com.*

SWIMMING

If your riad or hotel lacks a pool, you may find that a nearby hotel will let you use their facilities for a small fee.

Beldi Country Club. For a tranquil and elegant afternoon by the pool and away from the throngs in town, consider the Beldi Country Club, 6 km (3¾ miles) outside the city. A day pass, including lunch on the shaded terrace, use of sunbeds, and use of the pool, is 370 DH; use of the pool alone is 200 DH. ⊠ *Km 6, rte. de Barrage* ☎ *0524/38–39–50* ⊕ *www.beldicountryclub.com* ☉ *Closed Jan.–Mar.*

Jnane Tamsna. This boutique hotel in the Palmery allows nonguests access to its lush gardens and two large outdoor pools. The cost is 380 DH per person and includes lunch. Tennis is also available, and reservations are required. ⊠ *Douar Abiad, Circuit de la Palmeraie, Palmery* ☎ *0524/32–84–84* ⊕ *www.jnane.com.*

Nikki Beach. The Palmery is home to the grown-up Nikki Beach, which comprises a huge pool and restaurant area. Showing off the body beautiful, sipping cocktails, and looking supercool is more important here than swimming. There's even a DJ spinning some tunes in the evening. The resort has proven a bit too gaudy for some visitors: drinks are massively overpriced, a lounger costs from 500 DH for the day, and weekends a minimum spend of 1,000 DH is required. It's for adults only (over 18 years). ⊠ *Circuit de la Palmeraie, Palmery* ☎ *0524/36–87–27* ⊕ *www.nikkibeach.com* ☉ *Closed Jan.–Mar.*

FAMILY **Oasiria.** The jewel in Marrakesh's aqua-park crown is Oasiria, where children enjoy a kids' lagoon, pirate ship, wave pool, inner-tube ride, and three twirly waterslides, while parents chill out at any of the five cafés and snack restaurants. There are two heated swimming pools for adults only (one indoors for winter use) and a free shuttle bus from near Koutoubia Mosque or from Harti Gardens in Guéliz during summer months. ⊠ *Rte. de Barrage, 4 km (2½ miles) from town* ☎ *0524/38–04–38* ⊕ *www.oasiria.com* ▨ *190 DH* ☉ *Closed Oct.–Apr.*

TANGIER AND THE MEDITERRANEAN

WELCOME TO TANGIER AND THE MEDITERRANEAN

TOP REASONS TO GO

★ **Tangier:** As the capital of the Tangier-Tetouan region in Morocco's industrial heartland, Tangier has been at the center of Moroccan culture since the 5th century BC. Today, it continues to draw visitors with its breathtaking views and friendly locals.

★ **The Rif Mountains:** Running parallel to the Mediterranean coast for 200 km (125 miles), the Rif Mountains span from Cap Spartel and the Strait of Gibraltar to northern Morocco's most scenic areas.

★ **Tetouan:** Overlooking the verdant Martil Valley, Tetouan is famous for its Hispano-Moorish architecture and medina.

★ **Chefchaouen:** This charming blue-and-white mountain stronghold is one of Morocco's fairy-tale towns offering some of the most beautiful views in the country.

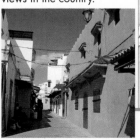

1 Tangier. The sights, sounds, and aromas of Morocco are never better highlighted than in this tumultuous collision of Rifi Berber, Arabic, and European cultures. Tangier conveniently and uniquely offers within its small borders lively souks, laid-back cafés and bars, access to both the Atlantic and the Mediterranean, and plenty of flora and fauna for nature lovers to explore.

2 The Ceuta Peninsula. Taking its name from the Spanish enclave of Ceuta, the Peninsula is home to glorious beaches and modern resort towns along the coast of the Strait of Gibraltar and the Atlantic Ocean. The Cap Spartel lighthouse marks the meeting place of the Mediterranean and Atlantic.

3 Chefchaouen and the Rif. At the very tip of North Africa, Chefchaouen only opened to Christians in the 20th century and has since become a favorite of locals and tourists alike. The pure mountain air, the cool, blue-and-white medina, and the slow pace of life encapsulate another era.

GETTING ORIENTED

3

Tangier's long and varied history, as well as its location directly across from mainland Europe, has produced a unique and diverse culture filled with traces of the past. Founded by the Carthaginians in the 5th century BC and colonized by the Romans, Arabs, Portuguese, and French over the following centuries, the city has combined the architecture, cultures, and culinary traditions from each civilization that has sought to capture it. The fertile lands throughout the Rif Valley and the deep-sea fishing areas along the Ceuta Peninsula have produced successful commercial industry, contributing to the wealth of the local economy. Tangier's underrated but famed exports include olives and world-famous perfumes.

MOROCCAN WRITERS

Morocco has a rich literary tradition. Marrakesh's Koutoubia Mosque, the city's largest, derives its name from the Arabic word for librarian. Dating to the 12th century, it served not only as an important place of worship but also as a library and the world's first marketplace for manuscripts.

(above) Koutoubia Mosque, Marrakesh (opposite page, bottom) Tahar Ben Jelloun (opposite page, top) Siham Benchekroun

Moroccan scribes have been writing about the world since the 14th century, when the *Rihla* (*The Journey*) recounted the story of the Moroccan Islamic scholar Ibn Battuta, who traveled an astounding 75,000 miles over 30 years. By the 20th century, when dramatic political changes inspired a new generation of Moroccan writers, much of the writing turned inward to address domestic issues. Contemporary Moroccan authors touch upon a remarkably diverse range of topics, including such controversial subjects impacting Moroccan society as gender roles, discrimination, poverty, and class division, by writers who create their works in Arabic, French, Berber, and English.

EXPATS IN MOROCCO

Since the 1950s, Tangier and the surrounding towns and villages have acted as a refuge for the world's most influential literary figures. Tennessee Williams, Allen Ginsberg, and Jack Kerouac called Tangier home, while George Orwell once visited under an alias as he reported on the political leanings of the various newspapers on sale at the time.

Five of the brightest lights in Moroccan letters can be discovered in translation (though sometimes only in import editions).

DRISS CHRAÏBI

Novelist, radio producer, and commentator Driss Chraïbi writes novels that address themes of colonialism, the clash between cultures, and the treatment of women within Muslim society. Many of his works are semiautobiographical. His works include *Le Passé Simple* (*The Simple Past*), *Les Boucs* (*The Butts*), *La Civilisation, Ma Mère* (*Mother Comes of Age*), and his autobiography *Vu, Lu, Entendu* (*Seen, Read, Heard*).

ABDELKEBIR KHATIBI

A playwright, novelist, literary critic, and scholar, Abdelkebir Khatibi often incorporated political and social issues into his novels during his most productive periods, the 1960s and '70s. His novels include *La Mémoire Tatouée* (*Tattooed Memory*), *Amour Bilingue* (*Bilingual Love*) and *La Blessure du Nom Propre* (*The Wound Under Its Own Name*).

TAHAR BEN JELLOUN

Born in 1944 to a Fez shopkeeper, Tahar Ben Jelloun is considered one of North Africa's most successful authors. Both a poet and novelist, he has received international acclaim for his works, which provide an insight into Moroccan

culture on a variety of controversial themes such as gender identity, sexuality, and male domination within the society. Novels include *The Sand Child*, *Harrouda*, *Racism Expliqué à Ma Fille* (*Racism Explained to My Daughter*), and *La Nuit Sacrée* (*The Sacred Night*).

SIHAM BENCHEKROUN

A doctor, journalist, and writer, Siham Benchekroun is known as much in the West for her pioneering work in medical journalism as for her novels and poetry, which often focus on the lives of Moroccan women. They include the novels *Oser Vivre* (*Dare to Live*) and *Chama*, as well as *À toi* (*For You*), a compilation of poems. Though available in French, none of her books have been translated into English.

RITA EL KHAYAT

Anthropologist, psychologist, and feminist scholar, Rita El Khayat has written more than 30 books focusing predominately on psychiatry and anthropology. She was a moving force in the late 1990s in Morocco's movement to modernize the country's family law code. In 2008, she was nominated for the Nobel peace prize. *Open Correspondence*, published in 2010, is a compilation of enlightening correspondence between El Khayat and Abdelkebir Khatibi.

TAHAR BEN

Updated
by Joe
Worthington

Nestled between the Mediterranean Sea and the backbone of the Rif Mountains, Tangier and the surrounding Tangier-Tetouan region hold all the *Arabian Nights* allure that many people associate with the country—as well as an energy unparalleled in the rest of Morocco.

The ancient cities of Tangier and Tetouan offer a glimpse of evolving urban Morocco with their Arab-inspired sophistication, European dress and languages, palm-lined boulevards, and extensive infrastructure for travelers. Here the vast majority of the population is under 25, and the streets are full of children until late in the evening, especially in the summer months. Tangier is in sharp contrast to the villages and small towns along the Rif Mountains routes, where regional dress and a traditional, agricultural way of life persist. As you travel farther east, the language shifts from Arabic to Rifi Berber (Tarifit), spotted with Spanish and French.

PLANNING

WHEN TO GO
The region has a temperate, coastal climate throughout the year, with the traditional high season lasting from late July to the end of August. In Tangier and along the Mediterranean Coast, winter brings rain and surprisingly cold temperatures, whereas the summer months of June through September see hot and sunny days. The Rif Mountains are perfect for skiing in the winter, when thick snow covers the entire range. Spring and summer bring an influx of tourists to the region, during which time the airports and seaports get busier, rooms are hard to find, and the medina, cafés, and beaches overflow with visitors.

PLANNING YOUR TIME
First-time visitors to the region would best use their time by basing themselves in Tangier. The city's bustling medina and abundance of accommodations ensure a good starting point for exploring all that the surrounding area has to offer. Traveling to Tetouan and Chefchaouen is possible by taking CTM buses; however taking a taxi directly from

Tangier is much easier (fares should be decided before departing). It's possible to see the major points of the region in a week, but it's best to spend at least four days in Tangier and two days in any other town or city visited to truly get a sense of this unique corner of Morocco. Be sure to plan ahead of time to secure desired accommodations and any necessary travel arrangements, as the region is sparsely connected in comparison to other major city hubs.

GETTING HERE AND AROUND

AIR TRAVEL

Tangier–Ibn Battouta Airport is becoming more popular for both full-service and low-cost airlines, offering domestic and international connections. Tetouan's smaller regional Sania Ramel Airport connects to a small number of domestic and European cities.

BOAT AND FERRY TRAVEL

Ferry travel is a popular way to get to the Tangier region, especially from Europe. The Tanger-Med cargo port is now being used more as a passenger terminal, with connections to and from Algeciras, Gibraltar, Genoa, and Barcelona. Tanger Ville is a passenger port with connections from major cruise lines.

BUS TRAVEL

CTM buses offer intercity transportation between Tangier and regional towns and villages.

CAR TRAVEL

Renting a car in Tangier to explore the region is possible and manageable (though automatics are still very scarce and roads tend to get very busy during the summer months), as is hiring local drivers (and their cars) for varying lengths of time through local travel agencies. You can also haggle with taxi drivers who may allow you to hire their services for the day to travel to areas directly surrounding Tangier. The latter may work best for those looking to explore the region immediately surrounding Tangier.

TAXI TRAVEL

Grands taxis (taxis that travel fixed routes indicated by their parking stations and leave only when full, meaning with six people) are good ways to get from point to point. They travel between cities as well as along fixed routes within Tangier. To avoid a squeeze or unpredictable delay, offer to pay for more than one spot. There are also *petits taxis* (these are either yellow or blue with a horizontal yellow stripe) that can be flagged down on the roadside and will transport passengers between Tangier and Tetouan; meters should be used for fair pricing.

TRAIN TRAVEL

Frequent intercity train connections can be found between the Tanger Ville train station and Marrakesh, Rabat, Fez, and Casablanca; prices are very cheap, often even for first-class tickets. Trains also depart from Tangier to the popular seaside resort of Asilah and the Algerian border at Oujda.

GUIDES AND TOURS

In the port area there are still plenty of fake guides wanting to show you around. It is possible to negotiate tours with these locals for a small fee, but be aware that you might not be getting your money's worth. Most licensed guides sport a badge and work for tour companies; you can also find them in any tourist office or book one online in advance.

RESTAURANTS

As much of a mosaic as the region itself, northern Moroccan cuisine combines influences from several other cultures with added spices and native ingredients—and notably features Spanish tapas (sans ham, though there is a cured turkey variety that is mischievously called *jambon de dinde,* or "ham of turkey"). Tapas are one way to roll here, as you can eat a filling meal for free with the purchase of a few beers at many of the bars. Tagines are made with particular flair in the north, where olives and spices are local. The abundance of fresh seafood makes it a natural choice in coastal areas. Fresh grilled sardines, shrimp, and calamari are standard fare here, as are larger more-gourmet Mediterranean catches such as *pageot* (red sea bream), swordfish, sole, St. Pierre (John Dory), and *dorado* (sea bream). A local delicacy that can be purchased on almost every street corner within the medina is the *brouchette,* a kebab filled with swordfish, vegetables, and spices. There is no shortage of restaurants and cafés in Tangier and the major regional towns, but they tend to get quite busy in the summer months, and the most popular restaurants require reservations.

HOTELS

Accommodations in the north range from opulent to downright spare, with everything in between. Other than at the height of the summer tourism season, you'll have a range of options in most areas. Hotels in Tangier can be on a par with those of Europe, especially those at the heart of the Medina, but the farther you venture off the beaten path, the farther you might feel from Tangier's five-star welcome. Particularly in some of the smaller cities east of Chefchaouen and Tetouan, hotels lack the amenities to call themselves "top-tier." Look a bit closer, though—what they lack in luxury these hotels often make up in charm, character, and, most of all, location.

Many hotels and B&Bs in the region don't take debit or credit cards, so it's always advisable to pay online in advance or be prepared to pay with cash. During high season, prices tend to rise quite drastically, but booking ahead can secure some superb rooms. *Hotel reviews have been shortened. For full information, visit Fodors.com.*

WHAT IT COSTS IN DIRHAMS			
$	**$$**	**$$$**	**$$$$**
Restaurants	under 100 DH	100 DH–150 DH	151 DH–200 DH	over 200 DH
Hotels	under 500 DH	500 DH–1,000 DH	1,001 DH–1,500 DH	over 1,500 DH

Restaurant prices are the average cost of a main course at dinner, or if dinner is not served, at lunch. Hotel prices are the lowest cost of a standard double room in high season.

3

TANGIER

15 km (9 miles) across Strait of Gibraltar from Algeciras, Spain; 350 km (220 miles) north of Casablanca; 278 km (172 miles) north of Rabat.

A refreshing alternative to more popular Moroccan tourist hubs like Marrakesh and Agadir, the city of Tangier makes for a great weekend trip from Europe during the spring and summer months. Giddy from the rush provided by crossing the Strait of Gibraltar from the European continent to Africa, first-time visitors may find the Tangier port such a rude awakening that they fail to see the beauty of the place. Mobs of faux guides and bona fide hustlers greet the arriving ferries, hungry for greenhorns to fleece in any way they can. Once you hit your stride and start going places with confidence, Tangier has a charm that this raucous undercurrent only enhances: crumbling kasbah walls, intimate corners in the serpentine medina, piles of bougainvillea, French balconies, Spanish cafés, and other remnants of times gone by.

Grab a seat at a sidewalk café and you'll begin to see how dramatically the urban brouhaha is set against the backdrop of the turquoise Mediterranean. Tangier is a melting pot—a place where it's not uncommon to see sophisticated Moroccans sharing sidewalks with rural Rifi Berbers wrapped in traditional striped *mehndis* (brightly striped blankets women wear tied around their waists) and eccentric expatriates, as well as the new generation of fashion-conscious teenagers. This is also Hercules's city, and recently, rudimentary graffiti tags in the empty lots have sported this name; musclemen advertise fitness clubs and burgeoning gymnasts and acrobats, many of whom then join the world's foremost circuses and shows, can be spotted practicing on the beaches and in the parks.

GETTING HERE AND AROUND
AIR TRAVEL
Tangie–Ibn Battouta Airport is just 15 km (9 miles) from Tangier's city center and is accessible by taxis located outside of the airport terminal. Several airlines fly to Tangier through European gateways, including Air Arabia Maroc (from London Gatwick and Amsterdam), Iberia (from Madrid), Royal Air Maroc (from several European cities); Ryanair (from Brussels, Paris, and others), and Vueling (from Barcelona). Many of the airlines have local offices.

Contacts Air Arabia Maroc ☎ 0802/00–08–03 toll-free in Morocco (call center based in Casablanca) ⊕ www.airarabia.com. **Corendon Dutch Airlines** ⊕ www.

corendon.com. **Germanwings** ☎ 871/894–3395 in UK ⊕ www.germanwings. com. **Iberia** ☎ 0539/39–31–56 ⊕ www.iberia.com. **Jetairfly** ☎ 70/22–00–00 in Belgium ⊕ www.jetairfly.com. **Royal Air Maroc** ☎ 0539/37–46–31 ⊕ www. royalairmaroc.com. **Ryanair** ⊕ www.ryanair.com. **Vueling** ☎ 931/518–158 in Spain ⊕ www.vueling.com.

BOAT AND FERRY TRAVEL

Ferry travel is a popular option for tourists and locals alike, with frequent connections from Algeciras and Tarifa. A number of ferry companies operate routes across the Strait of Gibraltar.

The Spanish ferry company FRS operates a regular 60-minute service between Tarifa and Tanger Ville (the city's port; 395 DH per passenger, 1,450 DH per car); a 90-minute service between Algeciras and Tanger-Med (250 DH per passenger, 1,295 DH per car); and a once-weekly 90-minute service between Gibraltar and Tanger-Med (520 DH per passenger, 1,845 DH per car). Trasmediterranea and Balearia also operate services from Algeciras, while Grandi Navi Veloci and Grimaldi Lines offer ferries from Barcelona. Cruise ships regularly dock in Tanger Ville.

While Tanger Ville is the main ferry port at the heart of Tangier, Tanger-Med (which is about two hours away along the cost) is equally viable thanks to its complimentary coach service to Petit Socco (a main square) in Tangier.

Many ferry companies also offer hydrofoil trips, which are the most comfortable modes of transport across the Strait. Be aware that on very windy days, the sea can get choppy and it's not uncommon for ferries to turn around; if this happens, be sure to ask for a refund.

Contacts Balearia ☎ 0539/93–44–63 in Tangier ⊕ www.balearia.com. **FRS** ☎ 0539/94–26–12 Tangier ⊕ www.frs.es. **Grandi Navi Veloci** ☎ 038/80–00–20 in Tangier ⊕ www.gnv.it. **Grimaldi Lines** ☎ 00531/11–11–11 in Tangier ⊕ www.grimaldi-lines.com. **Port Tanger-Med** ☎ 0801/00–50–60 toll-free in Morocco, 00539/33–71–55 outside Morocco ⊕ www.tmsa.ma. **Port Tanger-Ville** ☎ 0539/33–23–32 ⊕ www.sapt.ma. **Southern Ferries Ltd** ☎ 0844/81–7785 in the U.K. ⊕ www.southernferries.co.uk. **Trasmediterranea** ☎ 902/45–46–45 in Spain ⊕ www.trasmediterranea.es.

BUS TRAVEL

Tangier-Tetouan's regional bus operator is CTM. Several buses run daily between Tangier, Tetouan, Chefchaouen, Al Hoceima, Nador, and many other cities within the region. The company even has an overnight 10-hour bus to Marrakesh, as well as a 5½-hour bus to Casablanca.

Contacts CTM Tangier ☎ 0539/32–03–83 local, 0522/54–10–10 countrywide ⊕ www.ctm.ma.

CAR TRAVEL

If you want to rent a car to explore this region of Morocco on your own time, there are major car-rental companies operating in Tangier. Cards can be rented out of the city center, at the airport, and at ferry ports.

Contacts Aircar ☎ 0539/33–51–21 ⊕ www.aircar.ma. **Avis** ✉ 54, bd. Pasteur ☎ 0539/93–46–46 ⊕ www.avis.com. **Budget** ✉ Tangier-Med Port ☎ 0531/06–09–52 ⊕ www.budget.com. **Europcar** ✉ 87, bd. Mohammed V

☎ *0539/94–19–38* ⊕ *www.europcar.com.* **Hertz** ✉ *36, bd. Mohammed V* ☎ *0539/32–21–65* ⊕ *www.hertz.co.uk.*

TAXI TRAVEL

In the new part of the city, abundant petits taxis are the safest and most efficient way to get around. Petits taxis have a meter, so make sure to insist that the driver turns it on. You can wave one down by indicating the general direction you wish to travel. If the driver is going your way, he'll stop. For longer distances, or if you are among a group of four or more, you'll need the larger grand taxi, which can be called from most major hotels. A 10-minute petit taxi ride should cost about 9 DH to 11 DH; in a grand taxi (by yourself), the same journey would be about 30 DH. At night the fare increases by half. From the port and airport, the price should be 20 DH to 30 DH and 100 DH to 160 DH, respectively, depending if it's day or night. Make sure to agree on a price before departing.

TRAIN TRAVEL

Tangier is served by ONCF, the Moroccan rail service, with connections to Casablanca (6 hours), Marrakesh (10½ hours), and Fez (8½ hours). Tangier Ville train station is 3 km (2 miles) outside of the city, a short taxi ride from the Medina. First-class accommodations or sleeper cars are recommended for longer journeys, especially overnight ones. Regional trains also link to the seaside town of Asilah.

Train Contacts Office National des Chemins de Fer (*ONCF*). ☎ *0890/20–30–40* ⊕ *www.oncf.ma.*

SAFETY

Tangier has become a much safer place since it became the favorite, prodigal son of the current king, who recognized its potential to be a great tourist destination and subsequently increased police presence. Using common sense when exploring by day and staying out of dark alleys at night will help keep you out of harm's way. When in doubt about walking through dimly lighted areas, take a taxi. The medina in Tangier can be dangerous at night. Tangerines are known as late sleepers, so don't be surprised that the streets are usually empty and stores shut until 10 am. Tourists should keep a photocopy of their passports with them at all times in case the police ask to see it.

VISITOR INFORMATION

Tangier's tourist information center is open daily and can usually supply information about local events as well as brochures and some rudimentary maps, but if you need or want a good city map, you'll have to buy one.

Contacts National Tourism Office ✉ *Av. Pasteur* ☎ *0539/94–18–37* ⊕ *www. visitetanger.com.*

EXPLORING

MEDINA

TOP ATTRACTIONS

Fodor'sChoice **Tangier American Legation.** As the first American public property outside
★ of the United States, the Tangier American Legation pays testament
to the long-standing relationship between Morocco and the United
States. Since the building was donated to the U.S. government by Sultan Moulay Suliman in 1821, the museum has amassed a large collection of paintings, books, maps, and portraits. In the adjoining Forbes
Museum, not-to-be-missed miniature depictions of famous battles
take place daily. Other displays showcase the original correspondence
between George Washington and the sultan, honoring the 1777 recognition of the United States by the Moroccan head of state. There's
also an amusing letter home from a panicked ambassador who was
given an unusual goodwill gift of friendship by the Moroccan people: a
now-extinct Barbary lion. ⊠ 8, Zankat d'Amérique ☎ 0539/93–53–17
⊕ www.legation.org ⊗ Mon.–Thurs. 10–1 and 3–5, Fri. 10–noon and
3–5, weekends by appointment.

Cinema Rif. This bustling cinema and cultural center, the Cinémathèque
de Tanger, is housed in a renovated, whitewashed 1938 theater and
offers retrospective screenings and cutting-edge films across two screens.
Old Spanish film flyers dazzle from under the glass at the café, where
there is a full menu of curious, ciné-inspired cocktails. Wi-Fi is also
available. The colorful, comfy chairs spill out onto the legendary Grand
Socco. ⊠ Grand Socco, pl. du 9 Avril ☎ 0539/93–46–83 ⊕ www.
cinemathequedetanger.com ⊡ 20 DH.

Fodor'sChoice **Kasbah.** Sprawling across the ancient medina's highest point, Tangier's
★ Kasbah can be blinding at midday as the infamous Mediterranean sun
bounces off the pristine white walls, but the narrow streets give ample
shade and breeze later in the afternoon, and it is a pleasant place to
spend some time. Modified since the Roman era, its impressive wall is
a relic of the Portuguese in the 16th century. During early Arab rule it
was the traditional residence of the sultan and his harem. The Kasbah
has always been shared by Moroccans and foreign residents alike—and
particularly in the International Zone era. It is also the site of some of
the best hotels in the city. The Kasbah Square is the site of snake tamers
for tourists (imported from Marrakesh), and also the iconic Bab el Bhar,
a literal hole in the wall that offers a glorious view of the Atlantic and
Spain (only 20 miles away), alternately advancing and receding with
the currents of the Strait. There is also Bab el-As'aa (Door of the Rod),
a beautiful worn zellij gate that used to be the site of punishments, and
Bab Haha, which must speak for itself. You can reach the Kasbah by
passing through Bab el Fahs ("Checkpoint Gate" in Arabic) into the
medina from the Grand Socco and climbing Rue d'Italie and entering
through the Kasbah gate, Bab el Kasbah, at the top or by winding up
the medina's rue des Chrétiens to the Kasbah area.

Petit Socco. Tennessee Williams based his play Camino Real on this
square—and it is indeed dramatic, with a cast of characters passing
through at any time of the day who are bound to give you a taste of

Tangier

KEY

- ① Exploring sights
- ① Hotels & Restaurants

TANGIER HISTORY

Tangier's strategic position at the juncture of the Mediterranean Sea and Atlantic Ocean has long been hotly contested. Following ancient Carthaginian, Roman, and then Arab conquerors, Portugal seized Tangier in the 15th century, only to hand it over to Britain in the 17th century as part of Catherine of Braganza's dowry on her marriage to King Charles II (a dowry that also included Bombay). England's control of Tangier was short-lived; in 1685 it fell into the hands of the Arab sultan Moulay Ismail. The French came to Tangier in 1912, but not without disputes from England and continuous scurries for control, so that by 1923 Tangier was governed by international authority. The city's international status, complete with special tax laws and loose governance, attracted an international crowd. In the first half of the 20th century,

Tangier was a sumptuous, rather anarchic sensory feast that drew artists, writers, diplomats, heiresses, and free spirits from all over the world. Rumor has it that Allied secret agents from across the world used Tangier as a meeting base during World War II.

After Moroccan independence from French rule in 1956, Tangier was incorporated into the kingdom of Morocco. The international population—and investors—dwindled, and the city's magnificence retreated to the realm of myth. Modern-day Tangier is much more subdued than the sybaritic haven of the glory days, yet it still has a distinct chiaroscuro appeal. Like Morocco's distinctive *zellij* tiles, the city is an amalgam—in this case of various periods and nationalities—that appears to change shape depending on the angle from which it's viewed.

Moroccan daily life. It has a theatrical range of seating, which is split among the three main cafés—parterre (Tingis), orchestra (Centrale), or balcony (Fuentes). The Fuentes used to be the German post office in the International Zone period—supposedly the most reliable one before the Germans fled during WWII. It's a great place to take a break before plunging back into the souks that surround it, or let gravity take you down past the Grand Mosque to the viewing platform looking out onto the port.

WORTH NOTING

Grand Mosque. The towering white-and-green-tile minaret of the largest mosque in the city makes it one of the most recognizable attractions in Tangier's medina. Built in 1685 (on the ruins of a destroyed European-built church) under the orders of the Sultan Moulay Ismail, it was a tribute to and celebration of Morocco's return to Arab control. While only Muslims are allowed to enter the mosque, its vibrant exterior make it a great spot for photos as you wander through the medina. ✉ *Rue Siaghine.*

Kasbah Museum. Constructed by the 17th-century sultan Moulay Ismail, this was the Kasbah's palace. The sultan's former apartments now house an interesting Moroccan-art museum, with mosaic floors, carpets, traditional Fez furniture, jewelry, ceramics, leather, daggers, illuminated manuscripts, textiles, and historic, finely crafted examples of carved

A fishing trawler returns to Tangier's harbor after a long day at sea.

and painted cedar ceilings. The marble columns in the courtyard were taken from the ancient Roman city of Volubilis. Don't miss the mosaic *Voyage of Venus* or the life-size Carthaginian tomb. Exit the palace via the former treasury of Moulay Ismail, the Bit el Mal; look for the giant knobby wooden boxes that once held gold and precious gems. ⊠ *Pl. de la Kasbah, rue Ibn Abbou* ☎ *0539/93-20-97* 🖃 *10 DH* ☀ *Wed.– Mon. 9–4.*

VILLE NOUVELLE

TOP ATTRACTIONS

Fodor'sChoice ★

Grand Socco. Tangier's chief market area in times past, the Grand Socco (a combination of French and Spanish meaning "great souk")—and otherwise "place du 9 Avril," which corresponds to the date of a famous speech made by King Mohammed V on the occasion of independence—now serves as a local transportation hub. Bab el Fahs, the main door to the medina, stands at the bottom. As late as the 1940s, when the new city was just beginning, the door was locked at night to seal off outsiders, thus its name, literally "Inspection Gate." You'll find plenty of cafés around Grand Socco, many of which offer amazing views of the sea. ⊠ *Rue de la Liberté.*

Mendoubia Gardens. Directly opposite Cinema Rif stands the former residence of the Mendoub—the sultan's representative on the governing commission during the international years—now a flourishing park. Flanked by a row of French colonial–era buildings, it's popular with young couples and local families on weekends. On a peak of the central hill, surrounded by historic cannons, an engraved stone monument

Tangier's Grand Socco is a popular destination both day and night.

displays the speech King Mohammed V gave to the French asking for Moroccan independence in 1947. ⊠ *Av. Sidi Bou Araqia*.

Place de France. Famous for its café scene in the first half of the 20th century, place de France is one of Tangier's main squares and is named for the French consulate located in one corner of the square. The square fills up after about 6 pm for a nightly promenade. During World War II, legend has it that the square was a popular haunt for European secret agents and shady deals.

Fodor's Choice ★

St. Andrew's Church. While Morocco is now a Muslim country, this towering Anglican church still stands as a vestige of Tangier's international days. Consecrated in 1905, on land granted by Queen Victoria, you'll get a sense of the flourishing interfaith relations that Tangier was once famous for in the church's interior; the Lord's Prayer is engraved in Arabic behind the altar and quotes from the Koran appear across the Moorish-style walls. A cemetery surrounds the church and holds graves of British and Commonwealth soldiers who died fighting in North Africa during World War II. The caretaker is almost always on site, and for a small tip (20 DH), he will astound you with his knowledge about the church and Tangier in general. ⊠ *Rue d'Angleterre* ☉ *Daily 9–5*.

WORTH NOTING
Mohamed Drissi Gallery of Contemporary Art. Located in the stately former British Consulate building built in 1890 and surrounded by a lovely garden, this gallery, run by Morocco's ministry of culture, shows mostly traveling exhibitions. ⊠ *52, rue d'Angleterre* ☎ *0539/94–99–72* ☉ *Wed.–Mon. 9–1 and 2–6*.

Place des Canons. Located in the place de France, the so-called "Wall of Lazies" is where you'll find three cannons standing on a viewing platfom, pointed in the direction of Spain; some say this is meant to stop Spanish invaders, or perhaps the French, the British, or the Portuguese. On a clear day it's possible to see the faint outline of Spain on the horizon; freshly roasted nuts from the many vendors make for a tasty snack as you take in the view.

WHERE TO EAT

Tangier's cuisine is a unique mishmash unlike anywhere else in North Africa, where Moroccan, French, Spanish, and even British flavors combine to create a wonderfully diverse culinary scene. Thanks to the proximity of the Mediterranean, very fresh seafood is prominent on menus, while traditional dishes like tagine, couscous, and *baissara*, a bean soup, are available nearly everywhere. The city's top hotels house restaurants that serve unique and sometimes opulent dishes, while you can buy brouchettes or mouthwatering *harira* soup at street vendors for very cheap.

MEDINA

$$$
MOROCCAN

✕ **El Korsan.** One of Tangier's most reliable restaurants, El Korsan is located in the peerless El Minzah hotel with a kitchen that serves traditional Moroccan cuisine in the most sumptuous manner possible. Specialties include succulent *mechoui* (roasted lamb or mutton), slow-cooked tagines, and couscous. The food is excellent, the staff is attentive, and the décor is classically Moroccan, with soaring arches and handicrafts. Andalusian music is performed nightly. $ *Average main: 160DH* ⊠ *El Minzah, 85, rue de la Liberté* ☎ *0539/93–58–85* ⊕ *www. leroyal.com/morocco* ⌚ *Reservations essential* ☉ *No lunch.*

$$$$
FRENCH
Fodor's Choice
★

✕ **El Morocco Club.** In 1931 an American architect renovated a Tangerine mansion and turned it into this restaurant and piano bar, which has become the go-to gathering place for expats in Tangier. Currently run by a duo hailing from Belgium, a limited but still impressive menu features foie gras, beef filets, and *tartelettes au citron meringuée* (lemon meringue tarts). The café terrace, located under a century-old ficus tree, offers slightly more affordable salads and sandwiches and is an excellent choice for dining when the weather's nice. $ *Average main: 390DH* ⊠ *Pl. du Tabor* ☎ *0539/94–81–39* ⊕ *www.elmoroccoclub.ma* ⌚ *Reservations essential* ☉ *Closed Mon.*

$
MOROCCAN

✕ **Hammadi.** Decorated in an over-the-top Moroccan style, with banquettes covered with sumptuous pillows and rich brocades, Hammadi (named after the affable owner) is not to be missed. With a live band playing traditional Andalusian music and several nightly shows, including belly-dancing, it is anything but dull. The place is definitely touristy, but it also has a charm. Try the house pastilla, chicken tagine, or *kefta* (beef patties) along with a steaming cup of freshly brewed mint tea. $ *Average main: 60DH* ⊠ *2, rue de la Kasbah* ☎ *0539/93–45–14.*

$$$$
SEAFOOD
Fodor's Choice
★

✕ **Hotel Nord-Pinus.** Boasting an unforgettably romantic ambience, this world-class restaurant serves traditional Moroccan dishes with a creative twist. Along with dishes like chicken and raisin tagine (cooked on a traditional open fire), there's a splendid array of vegetarian dishes such as the eggplant caviar. Most of the seafood is local and freshly caught, and the vegetables are transported to the restaurant by local women from the nearby Rif Mountains. Almost as delicious as the food is the windowed balcony overlooking the sea and out to Gibraltar. Call ahead to find out the exact menu as it changes daily. $ *Average main: 225DH* ✉ *11, rue Riad Sultan* ☎ *0539/22–81–40* ⊕ *www.nord-pinus-tanger. com* ⌲ *Reservations essential.*

$$
FRENCH

✗ **Maison Kayser.** Renowned French pastry chef Eric Kayser brings a highly trained staff to this café-restaurant that offers an array of French goodies like baguettes, cakes, doughnuts, and *choux* buns. As you walk in, the modernist and simplistic features immediately hit you, making for a cool and relaxing change from the busy streets of Tangier. Grab a pastry and marvel at its intricate design as you relax and people-watch. French coffee and Moroccan mint tea are also available. Note that it's open daily, but only until noon. $ *Average main: 100DH* ✉ *Rue des Amoureux, near the Spanish Consulate* ☎ *0539/33–16–83* ⊕ *www. maison-kayser.com/en* ☾ *No dinner.*

VILLE NOUVELLE

$
MOROCCAN

✗ **Agadir.** This cozy restaurant offers an expansive menu of traditional Moroccan cuisine, with a number of delicious tagines (try the lamb and prune, or chicken with vegetables). The harrira soup makes a good starter. There's also plenty of Continental fare; both wine and beer are available. Retro warm colors make this simple room seem romantic and relaxed. It's a great place to go after a long day of sightseeing, but not if you're starving: expect a bit of wait, as the one waiter is also the chef. $ *Average main: 70DH* ✉ *Rue Prince Heritier* ☎ *0668/82–76–96* ▭ *No credit cards.*

$
MOROCCAN

✗ **Darna.** Located in an old British prison, the women's section of this multidimensional nonprofit vocational training center, whose name means "Our House," prepares scrumptious home-style lunches. The restaurant is a favorite of Tangier's expat community, not least for its sun-drenched patio and remarkably vivacious fig tree growing out from cheerful tiles. Traditional couscous is served on Friday and should not be missed. Check out the textile shop or the bath products and jewelry after a delicious lemon tart or chocolate mousse dessert. Darna also offers a four-handed massage in the beauty salon. $ *Average main: 50DH* ✉ *Rue Jules Cot, off pl. du 9 Avril* ☎ *0539/94–70–65* ⊕ *www. alliancesdarna.ma.*

$$$$
FRENCH
Fodor's Choice
★

✗ **La Fabrique.** Owners Nicolas and Christine Samet have cleverly combined French cuisine with New York design to create this industrial-style two-story restaurant. The ground floor has leather couches and bar stools, perfect for a pre-meal aperitif, while upstairs the traditional French chef serves courses such mince of lamb confit Provençale, Burgundy snails, and tonka-bean-and-chestnut cake. There's a different special every day. After 8 pm, the place gets a bit quieter and a lot more romantic. $ *Average main: 850DH* ✉ *Résidence Salima I, 7, rue d'Angleterre* ☎ *0539/37–40–57* ⊕ *www.lebalcondetanger.com/ la-fabrique* ☾ *Closed Sun.*

$$
MOROCCAN

✗ **Restaurant Lounge Oriental Palace.** Lively belly dancers move between the tables at this chic lounge in an opulent banquet hall with carved ceilings and authentic tile work. Superb dishes such as lamb with prunes are sure to satiate a gourmet palate, while a typical Mediterranean St. Pierre gets a fresh spin with Moroccan spices. In the summe, chefs are flown in from Thailand to delight diners with traditional Thai cuisine. You'll need to take a small blue taxi to get here. [$] *Average main: 120DH* ✉ *International Continental Hotel, 3, rue de Cordoue Park Brooks* ☎ *0539/93–79–45* 🌐 *www.intercontinental-tangier.com* ✍ *Reservations essential.*

$$$ MOROCCAN 🍴 **Saveurs de Poisson.** The owner, Mohammed Belhadj, is a colorful Tangerine local obsessed with Popeye, the restaurant's mascot, and he likes to explain the beneficial health effects of each recipe on the menu. The menu and the price are fixed, so there's no choice; just sit down and be prepared for four courses served in large tagines to be shared by the table. The main course is always the catch of the day, which is served grilled and as kebabs—it's usually St. Pierre, dorado, or sole. The meal is followed by a dessert of roasted pine nuts with strawberries (in season) covered in local honey. You'll be served special fruit juice based on prunes and infused with flowers, cloves, and other secret ingredients, and a souvenir earthenware mug is usually part of the price. [$] *Average main: 165DH* ✉ *2, Escalier Waller, down from El Minzah hotel* ☎ *0539/33–63–26* ✍ *Reservations essential* 💳 *No credit cards* ⏱ *Closed Fri.*

WHERE TO STAY

Whether the style is sparse modernism or over-the-top opulence, Tangier is all about leisure and luxury, sometimes with a vintage or old-world feel. Add Morocco's famous hospitality and Tangier's plethora of gorgeous views (it's almost impossible to find a place to stay that doesn't offer breathtaking views of the sea or over the medina) and you have an unforgettable experience.

MEDINA

$$ B&B/INN 🏨 **Albarnous Maison d'Hôtes.** The rooms are named after notable Tangerine residents, such as Ibn Battuta and Paul Bowles, at this Moroccan-Italian-inspired hotel, one of the most famous in the city. **Pros:** friendly atmosphere; cozy. **Cons:** can be difficult to locate; very busy area. [$] *Rooms from: 900DH* ✉ *18B, Ahmed Cheikh Ben Ajiba* ☎ *0539/37–19–19* 🌐 *www.albarnoustanger.com* 🛏 *4 rooms, 1 suite* 🍽 *Breakfast.*

$$ HOTEL Fodor's Choice ★ 🏨 **Dar Nour and Le Salon Bleu.** In the center of the old medina and boasting a 360-degree view encompassing the city, the Atlantic, the Strait of Gibraltar, the Bay of Tangier, and Spain, this "House of Light" is partly built right on the Kasbah's western ramparts. **Pros:** personal attention; cozy atmosphere. **Cons:** as with everywhere in the Kasbah, you must climb up before you can come down again; a little confusing to find. [$] *Rooms from: 720DH* ✉ *20, rue Gourna* ☎ *0662/11–27–24, 0654/32–76–18* 🌐 *www.darnour.com* 🛏 *3 rooms, 7 suites* 🍽 *Breakfast.*

$$ HOTEL 🏨 **Hotel Continental.** Morocco's very first hotel was built in 1865 in the Victorian style—appropriately, since Queen Victoria's son Alfred was the first official guest. **Pros:** great views; excellent location; good value. **Cons:** not all rooms are air-conditioned; some renovated rooms are

This elaborately tiled room is in the Hotel Continental.

impersonal. [$] *Rooms from: 510DH* ✉ *36, Dar Baroud* ☎ *0539/93–10–24* 🌐 *www.continental-tanger.com* 🛏 *56 rooms* 🍴 *Breakfast.*

$$$$ HOTEL **Hotel Nord-Pinus.** At the highest point in Tangier's medina, Hotel Nord-Pinus offers outstanding views of the mountains and Straits of Gibraltar afar and the bustling crowds below. **Pros:** antique but chic décor; close to the medina; spectacular views. **Cons:** difficult to get to in a taxi or car; expensive. [$] *Rooms from: 1690DH* ✉ *11, rue du Riad Sultan, Kasbah* ☎ *0593/22–81–40* 🌐 *www.nord-pinus-tanger.com* 🛏 *5 rooms* 🍴 *Breakfast.*

$$ HOTEL **La Maison de Tanger.** Every room in this traditional hotel is completely unique, each individually decorated and with balconies looking out to the hotel gardens and the sea in the distance. **Pros:** intimate and relaxed atmosphere; great staff. **Cons:** hard to find in the medina. [$] *Rooms from: 845DH* ✉ *9, rue Al Mabara, Kasbah* ☎ *0539/93–66–37* 🌐 *www.lamaisondetanger.com* 🛏 *5 rooms, 3 suites* 🍴 *Breakfast.*

$$ B&B/INN **La Tangerina.** Across from the outer wall of the Kasbah, this four-story hotel is minimally decorated in a Sahara-safari style with large palms among other plants, black-and-white-checker floors, and beautiful carpets. **Pros:** beautiful setting; stunning views from balcony. **Cons:** many rooms face into the center of the house only, though it is usually quite serene. [$] *Rooms from: 715DH* ✉ *19, rue du Riad Sultan* ☎ *0539/94–77–31* 🌐 *www.latangerina.com* 🛏 *10 rooms* 🍴 *Breakfast.*

$$ B&B/INN **Riad Dar Sultan.** Several styles of carpet create a chaotic harmony that makes this exotic abode exactly what you would expect to find in the Kasbah. **Pros:** in the heart of the medina; romantic atmosphere. **Cons:** a bit hard to find. [$] *Rooms from: 900DH* ✉ *49, rue Touila* ☎ *0539/33–60–61* 🌐 *www.darsultan.com* 🛏 *6 rooms* 🍴 *Breakfast.*

VILLE NOUVELLE

$$$$
HOTEL
El Minzah. Built in 1930, Tangier's top hotel offers a helpful staff in Ottoman costume, beautiful gardens, an elegant patio, the constant sound of falling water from the capacious courtyard, and fine views over the Strait of Gibraltar. **Pros:** great service; excellent facilities. **Cons:** not in the medina; pricey. $ *Rooms from: 1605DH* ⊠ *85, rue de la Liberté* ☎ *0539/93–58–85, 0539/33–34–44* ⊕ *www.leroyal.com/morocco* ⤳ *125 rooms, 15 suites* ❂| *Breakfast.*

$
B&B/INN
El Muniria. Made famous as the favorite hotel of the Beat Generation writers, El Muniria still offers clean and comfortable rooms, a lovely garden, and Madame Rabia, the charming proprietress. **Pros:** nice views; away from the crowd. **Cons:** on poorly lit alley; area can get sketchy at night. $ *Rooms from: 160DH* ⊠ *1, rue Magellan* ☎ *0539/93–53–37* ⤳ *8 rooms* ⊟ *No credit cards* ❂| *Breakfast.*

$$
B&B/INN
Rembrandt. While the rooms have little in the way of real Tangerine style, this hotel does have a somewhat nostalgic feel to it, thanks in part to the eclectic blend of furnishings and artwork found throughout. **Pros:** near nightlife; easily accessible by foot or vehicle. **Cons:** inauthentic décor; tends to be filled with tour groups. $ *Rooms from: 680DH* ⊠ *Bd. Mohammed V* ☎ *0539/93–78–70* ⊕ *www.hotel-rembrandt.com* ⤳ *63 rooms, 6 suites* ❂| *Breakfast.*

$$$
HOTEL
FAMILY
Tanjah Flandria. On Ville Nouvelle's main thoroughfare, this modern, jet-set chic hotel has a rooftop pool and a pleasant, atmospheric lounge-bar with bay views. **Pros:** recently renovated; central location for beach and medina; friendly staff. **Cons:** international décor unspecific to Tangier. $ *Rooms from: 1200DH* ⊠ *6, bd. Mohammed V, off bd. Pasteur* ☎ *0539/93–32–79* ⤳ *146 rooms, 4 suites* ❂| *Breakfast.*

NIGHTLIFE

Tangier's nightlife begins with the early-evening promenade and café hour, from about 6 to 9, when the streets teem with locals and expats alike. While in the winter the nightlife scene can be lacking, in spring and summer many beachfront cafés are full well into the night. Late dining is another mainstay of Tangerine nightlife, with many restaurants open past 10 pm—rare in Morocco and, along with tapas, another example of Spanish influence in the region.

Tangier has plenty of vibrant cafés, where writers and other creative types go to talk and mingle. Due to its Islamic roots, the nightlife scene tends to be dominated by men, with women typically patronizing the *salons de thé* instead. Major hotels have piano bars where much of the city's business is undertaken as cigar smoke drifts through the air.

There is also an abundance of discos throughout the main areas of Tangier, which are open well into the early hours of the morning; be aware that the common assumption is that women who attend these discos are "working."

MEDINA
CAFÉS
Café Centrale. Ringside seating at the greatest show on Earth can be had at Café Centrale, which sits on the Petit Socco. It's a good place to catch your breath with a *panaché orange* (orange-flavor fruit shake) and a *croque-monsieur* (grilled cheese sandwich) or a full meal of succulent lamb chops as you watch the strange cast of characters wander past. ⊠ *Petit Socco, Medina* ☎ 0539/07–92–83.

Gran Café de Paris. With its tufted brown leather seats, impeccable service, mirrors galore, and a wall covered with fading photographs of Volubilis and woodcarvings of astrological creatures, Gran Café de Paris will make you feel like you're back in the 1950s with Burroughs (he wrote here), or in *The Bourne Ultimatum* (it was filmed here as well as on the rooftops of Tangier). This is a perfect place to watch the *paseo* (evening stroll) on the boulevard or the Wall of the Lazies. Have an orange juice or a Nescafé with milk (*café au lait*). ⊠ *Pl. de France, Medina.*

Les Fils du Detroit. Andalusian musicians hold jam sessions every night around 5 or 6 in the closet-size Les Fils du Detroit. Sometimes your presence is enough to get the band going. You'll pay just the price of a mint tea, but it's nice to leave a tip for the musicians. ⊠ *Pl. du Méchouar, off pl. de la Kasbah, Medina.*

VILLE NOUVELLE
BARS
Atlas Bar. Although it has a speakeasy exterior and sometimes a burly security guard at the front door, Atlas Bar is cute and mild-mannered on the inside. At the center is an island bar surrounded by high bar stools. The best part, however, is the generous selections of tapas served with every drink. ⊠ *30, rue Prince Heritier, Ville Nouvelle.*

OFF THE BEATEN PATH

Cabaña. Though it's just beyond the city center, Cabaña feels like you've stepped onto Gilligan's Island. You'll be greeted by monkeys and tropical fragrances at this cliffside bar and restaurant. Enter a campground, pass monkeys and banana tree groves, and head to the platform with two restaurants, a pool (open 10 am–6 pm), and a patio for dancing. Tell the taxi driver to take you to "Camping Miramonte" in Marshan. ⊠ *Camping Miramonte, next to the Royal Palace, Marshan* ☎ 0539/26–03–86 ⊕ *www.campingmiramonte.com.*

Les Passagers de Tanger. This restaurant-bar is remarkable for its wonderful view over the Grand Socco and for its theme nights with dancing. The outdoor patio is pleasant day or night while the inside is plain, with sepia-tone snapshots of modern Tanjawis lining the walls. You can come here if you're craving otherwise-illicit Serrano ham, but expect to pay a price to satisfy your hunger. For a snack, try the red and black olive tapenade that resembles caviar. ⊠ *4, pl. du 9 Avril, on the Grand Socco, 3rd fl., Ville Nouvelle.*

Number One Bar. This renovated apartment with pink walls and an impressive collection of memorabilia from the last 20-odd years gives you the feeling that you are behind the scenes of the myth. Karim, the bar's owner, has great taste in blues and jazz and lived in America for ten years. The low-lit outpost occupies the building on the corner across from the Rembrandt hotel, where boulevard Pasteur ends. Though the tapas are a bit pricey, an adjoining restaurant is also a decent option for dinner. ✉ *1, bd. Mohammed V, Ville Nouvelle* ☎ *0539/94–16–74.*

Tanger Inn. A best late-night libation at the Tanger Inn is the opportunity for literary nostalgia. Knowing that your bar stool may have supported the likes of William Burroughs, Allen Ginsberg, Jack Kerouac, Paul Bowles, Jean Genet, Tennessee Williams, or Federico García Lorca always adds a dash of erudition to your cocktail. Approaching from boulevard Mohammed V with a friend is advisable, as the area can be sketchy by night. On weekends the place is unmanageably packed with young locals and is anything but smoke-free. ✉ *El Muniria, 1, rue Magellan, Ville Nouvelle.*

CAFÉ

Café Hafa. West of the Kasbah overlooking the Strait of Gibraltar and set up on seven levels plunging toward the sea, this laid-back cliffside café has become the favorite sunset-watching haunt of the Tangier glitterati. Waiters impressively deliver 16 steaming and sticky cups of tea at a time despite swarms of bees that thankfully don't sting very often. People will test if you've been to Tangier by whether or not you have been here. Eggs and traditional pea soup (*baissara*) are also available. ✉ *Av. Mohammed Tazi, Ville Nouvelle.*

DANCE CLUBS

Chellah Beach Club. Especially lively and highly recommended on summer nights, Chellah Beach Club is tucked among the clubs along the strip on Tangier Bay. Dine or have drinks accompanied by a Copacabana-style jazz band that has the dance floor swinging from 9 until the crowd disperses. There is also a popular open-mic night Monday from 9 to 11 that attracts all kinds of local talent. ✉ *Av. Mohamed VI, Ville Nouvelle* ☎ *0539/32–50–68.*

Morocco Palace. An energetic dance hall with a live band, the singers' vocals here can be jarring—the flat tones come out of *sheikhates* (female Arabic vocalists from Morocco) traditions. The star *lotar* player, who accompanies belly-dancing shows, is a truly amazing musician and plays three sets a night, at 11 pm, 1 am, and 3 am. ✉ *11, av. du Prince de Moulay Abdellah, Ville Nouvelle* ☎ *0539/93–86–14.*

Regine Club. A favorite of weekending Spaniards, local professionals, and hip twentysomethings, the dance floor here gets steamier and steamier as the night goes on. The music is typical, somewhat bland Mediterranean House with some flashes back to the 1980s, whose pop stars line the walls after your descent down a funhouselike mirrored entrance and stairway. ✉ *8, rue el Mansour Dahbi, Ville Nouvelle* ☎ *0539/34–02–38.*

SHOPPING

Shopping in Tangier can be just as mystifying and thrilling as it is in Marrakesh. Be ready to haggle for better prices; learning a few numbers in Arabic helps to earn the respect of vendors and makes it more likely you'll get a good deal. Ville Nouvelle boutiques offer standard

Moroccan items, such as carpets, brass, leather, ceramics, and clothing at higher—but fixed—prices. The more unusual and creative high-quality items, however, are mostly in the specialty shops throughout the medina. Don't be afraid to stop at small, unnamed stores, as these often stock real off-the-beaten-path treasures.

MEDINA

ANTIQUES

Boutique Majid. One of the finest antiques shops in Morocco, Boutique Majid has a wide collection of antique textiles, silks, rich embroideries, rugs, and Berber jewelry (often silver with coral and amber), as well as wooden boxes, household items, copper, and brass collected from all over Africa on his yearly scouting trips. Prices are high, but the quality is indisputable. As master showman and proprietor Abdelmajid says, "It's an investment!" International shipping is available. ⊠ *66, rue des Chrétiens, Medina* ☎ *0539/93–88–92* ⊕ *www.boutiquemajid.com.*

CRAFTS

Boutique Marouaini. The simple Boutique Marouaini sells ceramics, wood, rugs, clothing, and metalware, as well as paintings by local artists at very reasonable prices. ⊠ *65, rue des Chrétiens, Medina* ☎ *0539/33–60–67.*

Coin de l'Art Berbère. The extensive collection of rugs at Coin de l'Art Berbère includes samples from the Middle and High Atlas regions, made by Saharan and southern Berber tribes. Check out the collection of doors, locks, windows, and boxes from southern Morocco and the Sahara, and get ready to haggle over prices. ⊠ *53, rue des Chrétiens, Medina* ☎ *0539/93–80–94.*

PERFUMES

Fodor's Choice
★

Parfumerie Madini. Founded in 1919 in the heart of Tangier's medina, this world-famous perfume house produces some of the world's longest-lasting and most highly regarded Oudh fragrances. The parfumerie is owned by Sidi Madini and has been passed down through his family for 500 years. Some of the most recognizably branded perfumes and eau de toilettes are made here, including Coco Chanel, Dior, and Allure, alongside locally based essential-oil perfumes. You can purchase a 50 ml bottle for around 50 DH. ⊠ *14, rue Sebou* ☎ *0539/93–43–88* ⊕ *www. madini.ma.*

VILLE NOUVELLE

ANTIQUES

Galerie Tindouf. Across from the Hotel Minzah is this pricey antiques shop specializing in clothing, home furnishings, and period pieces from old Tangier, with an especially large inventory of older rugs. The owners also run the Bazaar Tindouf, right down the street, which sells modern Moroccan crafts in ceramics, wood, iron, brass, and silver, plus embroidery and rugs. The staff here won't give you the hard sell. ⊠ *72, rue de la Liberté, Ville Nouvelle* ☎ *0539/93–86–00* ⊕ *www.gallerytindouf.com.*

CRAFTS

Dar D'Art. This "house of art" showcases local artists all year round in a plethora of media and styles, but mostly non-orientalist paintings. Ask to be shown the stock, as well, for the gallery artists. The owner,

Choukri, is charming and knowledgeable about the small but strong art scene in Tangier and Morocco. ⊠ *6, rue Khalid Matran, Ville Nouvelle* ☎ *0539/37–57–07* ⊕ *www.dardart.com* ⊘ *Daily 10–1 and 3–7, or by appointment.*

Ensemble Artisanal. The fixed-price, government-regulated Ensemble Artisanal offers handicrafts from all over Morocco. The store is a little pricey, but it's a good place to develop an eye for quality items and their market prices before you hit the medina shops. You can also custom emboss or cover bound books in leather. ⊠ *Rue de Belgique at rue Ensallah, 3 blocks west of pl. de la France, Ville Nouvelle* ☎ *0539/93–78–41.*

Fondoq Shejrah. This weaving cooperative is housed on the second floor of an old stable and inn whose name translates to "tree hotel" and overlooks what used to be the large courtyard where visitors parked horses. Weavers and their looms are tightly packed into nooks that are also shops, with walls lined in naturally dyed blankets, throws, curtains, linens, thick wool djellabas and synthetic silk scarves all hot off the looms. As the cooperative is unmarked from the outside, it is best if a local shows you the portal that leads into the complex, which is below restaurant Saveurs de Poisson, the Waller steps, and the chicken coop alley. ⊠ *Rue el Oualili, below and to the right of Waller steps and rue de la Liberté, Ville Nouvelle.*

SPORTS AND THE OUTDOORS

Taking a nature walk through the surrounding hills, cliffs, and beaches is a perfect way to see the diverse fauna of the region, especially in the summer months when flowers are in bloom. Jet-skiing along the coast and golfing on the ever-increasing number of courses are also becoming more popular.

BEACHES

The one constant across Tangier and northern Morocco is outstanding beaches. From crowded city beaches to miles of empty space, from fine sand to high cliffs, you'll find whatever combination of leisure, civilization, and scenery you have in mind on these shores.

GOLF

Golf, the favorite sport of the late King Hassan II, has quickly spread throughout Morocco.

Royal Golf de Tánger. The 18-hole Royal Golf de Tanger, founded in 1914, is one of two premier courses in the north and is located 3 km (2 miles) outside of the city center. The course measures 6605 yards and is par 70. The greens fee is 400 DH for 18 holes and 50 DH for practice. ⊠ *Rte. de Boubana* ☎ *0539/93–89–25* ⊕ *www.royalgolftanger.com.*

THE CEUTA PENINSULA

The Ceuta Peninsula offers such splendid views and gentle breezes that it is difficult not to recommend it if you have the time and curiosity to spend a day there. The N16 coast road east from Tangier hugs the edge of the Strait of Gibraltar all the way to the Djebel Musa promontory and Cap Spartel.

CAP SPARTEL

16 km (10 miles) west of Tangier.

Minutes from Tangier is the jutting Cap Spartel, the African continent's extreme northwest corner. Known to Romans as Ampelusium ("cape of the vines"), this fertile area sits high above the rocky coast. A shady, tree-lined road leads up to the summit, where a large lighthouse has wonderful sweeping views out over the Mediterranean at the very point where it meets the Atlantic.

GETTING HERE AND AROUND
Cap Spartel is most easily reached by grand taxi from Tangier.

EXPLORING

Fodor's Choice ★ **Cap Spartel Lighthouse.** Built by Sultan Mohammed III in 1864, this lighthouse has been maintained by Britain, France, Spain, and Italy until Morocco's independence from France in 1956. From atop a cliff at the northernmost point of the African continent, the area around the lighthouse offers amazing views of the Straits of Gibraltar. On a clear day, it is possible to look out on the horizon and see the meeting point of the dark blue Atlantic and the turquoise Mediterranean.

FAMILY **Caves of Hercules.** Five kilometers (3 miles) south of the cape are the so-called Caves of Hercules, a popular tourist attraction tied to the region's relationship with the mythical hero, who was said to rest here after his famous labors. Inhabited since prehistoric times, the caves were used more recently to cut millstones, hence the hundreds of round indentations on their walls and ceiling otherwise attributed to Hercules' clawing fingers. The caves are known for their windowlike opening in the shape of the African continent, through which the surf comes crashing into the lagoon and lower cave. Legend has it that the cave leads to a tunnel that crosses through the Strait of Gibraltar, leading you to the other side of the Mediterranean. Here you can buy souvenirs and have a camel ride in the parking lot. 🎟 5 DH 🕐 *Daily 9–1 and 3–6.*

NEED A BREAK? Above and to the right of the entrance to the Caves of Hercules, follow the tiled wall down to a path leading to a small, unnamed platform café. Run by a fellow named Abdelkader, this tiny café is the prime spot from which to view the caves from the outside. Its small wicker seats are ideal places to take in the stunning Atlantic views and to look down at local fishermen trying their luck on the rocks below while bold divers jump from the cliff. The café also offers a hidden secret. The small gray door near the kitchen opens into a two-story dining room inside Abdelkader's own personal cave; he will serve up one of his wonderful tagines while the surf's sound echoes off the cool cave walls.

Cotta. Approximately 7 km (4½ miles) south of Cap Spartel, look down toward the beach and you'll see the ruins of the 3rd century BC Roman town of Cotta. It was known for its production of *garum,* an

Cap Spartel's lighthouse looks out over the Mediterranean and the Atlantic.

anchovy paste that was exported throughout the Roman Empire. All that remains of the town now are the foundations of buildings, baths, and villas. You can walk to the site from the road or, more easily, from Robinson Beach.

Rmilet Park. Halfway to Cap Spartel, Rmilet is a park popular with local families on weekends. It has shady pine, mimosa, and eucalyptus groves, as well as acrobats, ponies, drum circles, and humble kebab huts at the end of the path in a parking lot with incredible views. Here you can also see the abandoned house of Ion Perdicarus and imagine his kidnapping by the Rifi bandit El Raissouni, with whom he later became friends. It's a great stop-off or day-trip for a few hours with the family. The café across from the main entrance offers yet another stunning and unusual view of Tangier.

WHERE TO STAY

$$$$ HOTEL **Hotel Andalucia Golf.** This luxury hotel is a haven for golf fans, with its location adjacent to the Royal Golf de Tangier course. **Pros:** good for business services; friendly staff. **Cons:** need to drive into the city; room décor does not reflect Moroccan culture. [$] *Rooms from: 2000DH* ✉ *Rte. de Cap Spartel* ☎ *0539/93–64–66* 🌐 *www.hotelandalucia.ma* 🛏 *131 rooms, 13 suites* 🍴 *Breakfast.*

$$$$ HOTEL **Hotel Mirage.** Located above the Caves of Hercules, this modern resort has traditional touches, a local art gallery, and an appropriately stunning 180-degree view of horizon. **Pros:** great service; excellent facilities; peaceful setting. **Cons:** 20-minute drive or taxi-ride from the city. [$] *Rooms from: 2400DH* ✉ *Grotte de Hercules, rte. de Cap*

Spartel ☎ *0539/33–33–31* 🌐 *www.lemirage-tanger.com* 🛏 *25 bungalows* 🍴 *Breakfast.*

SPORTS AND THE OUTDOORS

BEACHES

Cap Spartel's beaches vary widely from wide inlets to long stretches of sand. Ashakar is a public beach with three parts: the first is level with the road while the following two, more highly recommended, are accessed by descending steep steps down cliffs and sometimes flowering dunes, and eventually becomes Robinson Beach.

FAMILY **Robinson Beach.** Just west of Tangier, the area's most famous beach on the far Atlantic coast offers several uninterrupted miles of fine, silky sand and good waves ideal for families and surfers alike. Like its counterpart at Tarifa across the Straits of Gibraltar, there is generally a lot of wind around Robinson, making it also ideal for windsurfing. This is the last beach on the Atlantic before its waters merge with those of the Mediterranean at Cap Spartel, so the winds and current can be tricky. Staying close to shore is recommended for safety. **Amenities:** food and drink; water sports. **Best for:** snorkeling; walking; windsurfing. ✉ *Plage Municipale, off av. Mohamed VI, Tangier.*

ASILAH

40 km (25 miles) southwest of Tangier.

Known as one of the country's most artistic communities, the sleepy fishing village of Asilah hosts a two-week festival every year in August in which artists from all over the world are invited to paint murals on the city's walls. Asilah was conquered by the Portuguese in 1471, and its Old Town retains a Portuguese feel. There are several relaxing beaches here, and restaurants that offer some of the area's best fresh seafood dishes.

GETTING HERE AND AROUND

Asilah can be reached from Tangier by either a grand taxi or a CTM bus, which leaves from Tangier's central bus station near Petit Socco.

WHERE TO EAT

$ SPANISH 🍴 **Casa Garcia.** People flock to this unassuming seafood restaurant for no-nonsense fresh fish and langoustines. You can be sure you're being served the catch of the day. Unlike its neighbors, this place serves alcohol. Weekend afternoons can be a difficult time to find a table as whole families join tables banquet-style. [$] *Average main: 75DH* ✉ *51, rue Moulay Hassan Ben el Mehdi* ☎ *0539/41–74–65* 💳 *No credit cards.*

$$ MOROCCAN 🍴 **Oceano Casa Pépé.** Reliable and friendly, this small restaurant is located outside Bab el Kasaba, the Old Town's main gate. The anchovy appetizer is not to be missed, and neither is the paella. The selection of tapas makes this place popular with groups. [$] *Average main: 100DH* ✉ *Rte. de Rabat* ☎ *0539/41–73–95* 💳 *No credit cards.*

$ PIZZA FAMILY 🍴 **Yali's Restaurant.** This unassuming pizzeria among a strip of similar restaurants along the old medina wall stands out for the unbeatable freshness of its fare, which is best at lunchtime. Specialties include a pleasantly spiced and salted catch-of-the-day served with the traditional fresh pureed tomato dip. Crispy pizzas are especially good for the kids and the staff is very friendly. [$] *Average main: 60DH* ✉ *Av. Hassan II, in the Town Center* ▭ *No credit cards.*

WHERE TO STAY

$$ HOTEL 🏨 **Al Alba.** Offering impeccably neat and tidy traditional-style rooms, this hotel gestures at cloud and sky with its blue stained-glass skylights and patios. **Pros:** staff is helpful; offers full board upon request. **Cons:** not in the medina proper. [$] *Rooms from: 900DH* ✉ *35 Nakhil* ☎ *0539/41–69–23* 🌐 *www.asilahalalba.com* 🛏 *7 rooms, 3 suites* 🍴 *Multiple meal plans.*

$$ B&B/INN 🏨 **Dar Manara.** Renting a room here really means that you have the whole house and its various atmospheres to explore and enjoy, complete with a festive Moroccan tent on the rooftop. **Pros:** in the heart of the medina. **Cons:** small; need to book ahead. [$] *Rooms from: 650DH* ✉ *23 M'Jimaa St.* ☎ *0539/41–69–64* 🌐 *www.asilah-darmanara.com* 🛏 *5 rooms* ▭ *No credit cards* 🍴 *Breakfast.*

LARACHE

80 km (50 miles) southwest of Tangier.

Known primarily for its proximity to the ruins of the ancient town of Lixus, Larache is worth a stop for a stroll along the Balcon Atlantico, a seaside promenade that runs along the rocky shore. There are numerous cafés on the promenade where you can enjoy a fruit drink. Another enjoyable walk is to French writer Jean Genet's grave in the Catholic Cemetery just south of the medina. It's near the Muslim graveyard, which boasts decorative tile graves and dramatic views.

Larache's sleepy plaza feels like Spain all over again. Many of the people in this town grew up speaking Spanish as their first language and even attending Spanish Catholic schools—a few nuns still live here. Visible from afar, the 16th-century Geubibat Fort sits atop the highest cliff in Larache. The mouth of the snaking Loukos River is the fabled site of the Garden of Hesperides where Hercules picked his golden apples.

GETTING HERE AND AROUND

Larache can be reached from Tangier by either a grand taxi or a CTM bus, which leaves from Tangier's central bus station.

EXPLORING

Fodor's Choice ★ **Lixus BC.** You may have heard of Volubilis, Morocco's most famous Roman ruins in Meknès, but on the Loukkos River, Lixus BC is a lesser-known but no-less-impressive site just 45 minutes away from Tangier. The main attractions are an amphitheater, a column-lined road, a mosaic of the sea-god—half man, half crab—and the religious center of the town, high on the hill, which retains the foundations for the places of worship of each civilization to have settled there. The hill held great importance to a series of seafaring civilizations, starting with the Phoenicians in the 7th century until the time of the Arabs. The guides at the entrance are official and informative. They are paid by the government to do their job, but appreciate a tip. 🎟 *Free (tips appreciated)* ⏲ *Daily 9–6.*

WHERE TO STAY

$ HOTEL **La Maison Haute.** Located in the Kasbah, and offering great rooftop views of the city and ocean, this little gem of a hotel is hidden behind an unassuming exterior. **Pros:** friendly staff; great location. **Cons:** steep steps; not all rooms have bathrooms. [$] *Rooms from: 415DH* ✉ *6, Derb Ben Thami* ☎ *065/34–48–88* 🌐 *lamaisonhaute.free.fr* 🛏 *7 rooms* 🍴 *Breakfast.*

CEUTA

94 km (58 miles) northeast of Tangier.

A sleepy enclave that makes for an ideal getaway from the hustle and bustle of Tangier's hectic medina and the often crowded beaches, Ceuta was once ones of the finest cities in northern Morocco, prospering under Spanish rule. Originally thriving under its Arab conquerors, the city was extolled in 14th-century documents for its busy harbors, fine educational institutions, ornate mosques, and sprawling villas. Smelling prosperity, the Portuguese seized Ceuta in 1415; the city passed to Spain when Portugal itself became part of Spain in 1580, and it remains under Spanish rule today. The town's Arabic name, Sebta, comes from the Latin *septum* from *sepir* ("to enclose").

Ceuta's strategic position on the Strait of Gibraltar explains its ongoing use as a Spanish military town (many of the large buildings around the city are military properties). There has been little argument from Morocco to claim the small peninsula; this can be explained by a desire not to lose Spanish support for Moroccan rule over the Western Sahara, and also to maintain steady relations with Spain in general. Walls built by the Portuguese surround the city and are, together with the ramparts, impressive testimony to the town's historic importance on European–Near Eastern trade routes.

Now serving mainly as a port of entry or departure between Spain and Morocco, Ceuta's heyday has long since passed, though the mere existence of this Hispano-African hybrid that has successively belonged to Phoenicians, Carthaginians, Romans, Vandals, Byzantines, Arabs, Portuguese, and Spaniards is staggering, and it remains an important transportation base between Africa and Europe.

GETTING HERE AND AROUND

Ceuta can be reached from Tangier by either a grand taxi or a CTM bus, which leaves from Tangier's central bus station.

Trasmediterranea operates four ferries a day from Algeciras, Spain to Ceuta, a trip that takes approximately 70 minutes (340 DH for passenger; 1,405 DH for car).

Upon arrival in Ceuta you will be greeted with a lengthy passport check and stamping process (sometimes taking up to 45 minutes) while passing through several checkpoints. Note that euros are the standard currency here, with dirhams only accepted in some establishments. Cash machines are available downtown and usually give the best exchange rate. Ceuta also uses Spanish as the official language, and when calling

Ceuta from Morocco or from overseas, you must use the Spanish country code (34).

ESSENTIALS

Visitor Information Ceuta Tourist Information ⊠ *Baluarte de los Mallorquines, Ceuta, Spain* ☎ *0856/20–05–60 for Edrissis, 0956/50–62–75 for Estación Marítima* ⊕ *www.ceuta.es.*

EXPLORING

Castillo del Desnarigado. Located just under Ceuta's lighthouse, and named for a flat-nosed Berber pirate who made the cove his home in the 1417 after escaping from an Algerian mining prison, the fort was built here in the 19th century and now houses a military museum showcasing the evolution of weapons from the 16th to 19th century. You can look out across Ceuta's port and, on clear days, drink in a stunning view of Gibraltar from the ramparts. ⊠ *Carretera Del Hacho* ☎ *956/51–40–66 in Spain* 🖃 *Free* ⊙ *Weekdays 9:30–1, Sat. 11–1:30.*

Foso de San Felipe. St. Philip's Moat was built in 1530 by Portuguese crusaders to strengthen the town's fortifications. Crossing the moat gives you grand views of the ramparts, including their inner walls and structures. ⊠ *Calle de la Independencia.*

Plaza de África. A lovely Andalusian-style space, the plaza is the heart of the old city. Check out the noteworthy war memorial, honoring those who took part in the Spanish invasion of Morocco in 1859. Flanking the main plaza is a pair of impressive churches, both built on the sites of former mosques. To the north is the church of Nuestra Señora de África (Our Lady of Africa), an ornate baroque structure much frequented by *ceutíes* (residents of Ceuta) looking for peace and quiet. On the southern end of Plaza de África, look for the city's cathedral. Constructed in an 18th-century baroque style—much like Nuestra Señora de África—it is larger and lushly ornate.

WHERE TO EAT

Much like Ceuta itself, the city's cuisine is a hybrid of Spanish and Moroccan influences. With the Mediterranean at its doorstep, Ceuta's culinary expertise lies in seafood. From shrimp sautéed in a spicy pepper sauce to creamy baked whitefish dishes and enormous grilled sardines to Spanish-style cold anchovy, garlic, and olive-oil tapas, Ceutan seafood is an experience not to be missed. Moroccan influences are present in the form of couscous, as well as sweet-salty combinations such as prunes with roast lamb. A favorite pastime here is eating jamón serrano and drinking wine (both very difficult to do just a few minutes away in Islamic Morocco).

$$$$
SEAFOOD
✕ **El Club Nautico C.A.S.** Modest on the inside, but offering a lovely view and a waterfront location, this port restaurant's a catch for its daily offerings of fresh seafood. Enter through the aging revolving door and be pleasantly surprised. Be careful: Ceuta's port has two yacht clubs, and while this restaurant is very good, the other is quite bad. 🖃 *Average main: 226DH* ⊠ *Muelle Deportivo* ☎ *956/51–37–53.*

$
SPANISH
✕ **La Esquinita Iberica.** For an inexpensive and pleasurable snack, head to this no-nonsense tapas bar near La Plaza Nuestra Señora de Africa,

where the treats come with your drink. Try the *insalata russo* (a Spanish take on the Russian salade Olivier), a Spanish tortilla (mix between an omelet and potato pancake), or some pure jamón serrano with bread. [$] *Average main: 57DH* ✉ *4, Calle Jaudenes* ☎ *0956/51–61–04 in Spain.*

$$$ SPANISH
🍴 **Parador la Muralla Ceuta Restaurant.** Generally considered Ceuta's best restaurant, this charming dining room with exposed beams and tropical plants serves classic Andalusian dishes such as seafood paella, stuffed shrimp, shellfish in sauce, and creative daily specials. Dramatic lighting is provided by Andalusian lanterns hanging from the high ceiling in a romantic constellation. [$] *Average main: 170DH* ✉ *Gran Hotel Parador–La Muralla, 15, Pl. de África* ☎ *956/51–49–40 in Spain* ✍ *Reservations essential.*

WHERE TO STAY

$$$ HOTEL
🏨 **Gran Hotel Parador–La Muralla.** An aging monument—but still one of your best options in Ceuta—La Muralla is conveniently located on the main square, with views of the well-maintained garden, changeable sea, or the plaza itself. **Pros:** central location; good restaurant; relaxing. **Cons:** rooms can be stuffy; service is slow. [$] *Rooms from: 1380DH* ✉ *15 Pl. Nuestra Señora de África* ☎ *956/51–49–40 in Spain* 🌐 *www.parador.es* 🛏 *77 rooms, 29 suites* 🍽 *No meals.*

$$$ B&B/INN
🏨 **TRYP Ceuta.** On a busy street in Ceuta's commercial center, the TRYP offers comfort and amenities within walking distance of the main sights. **Pros:** good location close to the port and heliport; modern building and amenities. **Cons:** stuffy rooms; details sometimes shabby; service not always attentive. [$] *Rooms from: 1065DH* ✉ *3, Av. Alcalde Sánchez Prados* ☎ *956/51–12–00 in Spain, 888/956–3542 toll-free in the U.S.* 🌐 *www.solmelia.com* 🛏 *121 rooms* 🍽 *No meals.*

SPORTS AND THE OUTDOORS

BEACHES

The northern Mediterranean beaches, centered on Cap Malabata, between Tangier and Ceuta, are some of the region's finest. Their water is a typical Mediterranean turquoise, and secluded spots are easy to come by if you take the time to look.

The road south from Ceuta to Martil passes more than 32 km (20 miles) of modern beach resorts that offer a wide array of sports and activities. These good, if somewhat touristy, family beaches are heavily populated in summer. You could say that this is north Africa's answer to Spain's Costa del Sol.

El Chorrillo Beach. Ceuta's most frequented beach both day and night, El Chorrillo offers perfect sun rays in the morning and a calm Mediterranean atmosphere after dark. The sand is very fine and white, the water is relatively calm all year round, and the undertow is unthreatening. **Amenities:** parking; toilets; water sports. **Best for:** sunrise; sunset; swimming; windsurfing. ✉ *Just off Av. Martinez Catena.*

KAYAKING

Kayak Aventura. You can take a waterborne tour around Ceuta's fortifications, enter the moats and canals of El Foso (literally "moat" or "trench") by day, or you can tour the glowing and ancient walls by

3

night. The company also offers excursions to the natural cliffs, pools, and beaches around the peninsula, all in single or double kayaks. Opt to snorkel if you like, or more hearty souls can venture all the way to La Isla Perejil. Regularly scheduled guided nightly excursions leave at 7 pm and cost a mere €10. Otherwise, call ahead and reserve any time of day for an excursion suitable for adults or children. ✉ *Playa de la Ribera* ☎ *0676/27–80–86 in Morocco* ⊕ *www.ceutakayak.com.*

SAILING
El Puerto Deportivo. This company advises on sailboat charters or windsurfing equipment rental. ✉ *Puerto de Ceuta* ☎ *956/51–37–53 in Spain.*

SCUBA DIVING
Ceuta-Sub. This company gives classes and runs dives in select locations around the peninsula. ✉ *Club Santo Ángel, Ctra. de San Amaro* ☎ *0669/28–80–00 in Morocco.*

EN ROUTE
Winding south out of Ceuta, back into Morocco, the N13 road follows the coast toward Martil. The road gives you easy access to a string of well-developed beach resorts that combine modern amenities with gorgeous Mediterranean sands and north Moroccan charm.

RESTINGA-SMIR

18 km (11 miles) south of Ceuta, 42 km (26 miles) east of Tangier.

Until recently, Restinga-Smir was a small fishing village, but development has come quickly: it's now one of the region's priciest summering spots, Morocco's version of the Côte d'Azur in France. Rimmed by a long, uninterrupted coastline, the beaches here have yellow sand and are protected from wind. An amusement park, Smir, has roller coasters for kids; outfitters in the port area offer other diversions such as windsurfing, horseback riding, miniature golf, tennis, and camping, all of which your hotel can arrange. Marina Smir is lined with shops, cafés, and small restaurants geared toward tourists and affluent locals. Most upscale restaurants are in the hotels, but the seafood places on the marina are all good bets, grilling up the catch of the day in a pleasant outdoor atmosphere.

GETTING HERE AND AROUND
Restinga-Smir can be reached from Tangier by either a grand taxi or a CTM bus via Tetouan.

KABILA

20 km (12 miles) south of Ceuta, 114 km (71 miles) east of Tangier.

Kabila is quite literally a tourist village: a sprawling complex complete with hotel, villas, a helpful staff, a shopping center, and a marina with restaurants. The beaches—the majority of which are reserved for resort guests—are spotless (if a bit grainier than those farther north and south). Well-kept grounds and plenty of flowers keep the area green. Think California, with Moroccan food and décor. To arrange sailing and other outdoor activities, call Hotel Kabila.

GETTING HERE AND AROUND

Kabila can be reached from Tangier by either grand taxi or a CTM bus via Tetouan.

WHERE TO STAY

$$$$
RESORT

Hotel Kabila. No expense was spared in creating this full-blown tourist resort, which has rooms furnished with a distinctively Rifi Berber flair, featuring regional handicrafts, and with its own patio (or, on upper floors, a balcony). **Pros:** exotic experience; plenty of activities. **Cons:** outdated main building; service spotty. $ *Rooms from: 1602DH* ✉ *Rte. de Tetoun Ceuta* ☎ *0539/66–60–13* ⊕ *www.kabilahotel.com* ⟲ *92 rooms, 4 suites* ⊚ *Breakfast.*

TETOUAN

40 km (24 miles) south of Ceuta, 57 km (35 miles) southeast of Tangier on the N2.

Andalusian flavor mingles with the strong Rifi Berber and traditional Arab identities of the majority of the populace to make Tetouan a uniquely Moroccan fusion of sights and sounds. Tetouan's medina, a UNESCO World Heritage Site, remains largely untouched by tourism and retains its quotidian life and authenticity. The name Tetouan itself comes from the Tarifi (Rifi) Berber word for "the springs," to which the city owes its numerous fountains and gardens.

Nestled in a valley between the Mediterranean Sea and the Rif Mountains' backbone, the city of Tetouan was founded in the 3rd century BC by Berbers, who called it Tamuda. Romans destroyed the city in the 1st century AD and built their own in its place, the ruins of which you can still see on the town's edge. The Merenids built a city in the 13th century, which flourished for a century and was then destroyed by Spanish forces, which ruled intermittently from the 14th to the 17th century. The medina and kasbah that you see today were built in the 15th and 16th centuries and improved upon thereafter: Moulay Ismail took Tetouan back in the 17th century, and the city traded with the Spanish throughout the 18th. Tetouan's proximity to Spain, and especially to the enclave of Ceuta, kept its Moroccan population in close contact with the Spanish throughout the 20th century. As the capital of the Spanish protectorate from 1913 to 1956, Tetouan harbored Spanish religious orders that set up schools here and established trading links between Tetouan, Ceuta, and mainland Spain. Their presence infused the city with Spanish architecture and culture. Peek into the vintage cinemas you see along the way, such as the Spanish-built Teatro Espagnol just off of place Feddane, for a hint at the opulence of a bygone era.

GETTING HERE AND AROUND

Tetouan has a small airport, the Sania Ramel Airport, that's just 5 km (3 miles) outside town, with flight connections to Casablanca and Al Hoceima with Royal Air Maroc; to Liege with Jetairfly; and to Amsterdam with Corendon Dutch Airlines.

CTM is the region's main bus company and runs several buses daily to Tangier, Chefchaouen, Al Hoceima, and Nador.

Tetouan was the capital of Spanish Morocco in the early 20th century.

ESSENTIALS

Bus Contacts CTM Tetouan ⊠ *Av. Hassan II* ☎ *0539/96–16–88* ⊕ *www.ctm. co.ma.*

Visitor Information Tetouan Tourism Office ⊠ *30, av. Mohammed V* ☎ *0539/96–19–15.*

EXPLORING
TOP ATTRACTIONS

Medina. Tetouan's medina is one of Morocco's most active and interesting, and includes a rectilinear Jewish quarter, or Mellah, as well as exceptional 19th-century Spanish architecture from the period of the protectorate. Note the constantly flowing fountains, such as the one in the corner of Souk el Fouki; they are supplied by underground springs that have never failed and have never been explained. Crafts, second-hand clothing, food, and housewares markets are scattered through the medina in charming little squares such as Souk el Houts el Kadim (the old fish market) and L'Wusaa. Kharrazin is where animal hides are hung to dry in the sun, and through a door to the north you'll find *debbagh,* or the traditional leather treatment baths. Tetouan's medina is fairly straightforward, so don't hesitate to deviate from the main path and explore; it's hard to get lost. There are also plenty of options for refreshment. ⊠ *Rue Terrafin at Bab er-Rouah.*

Place Feddane (*Mechouar Saaid*). If you follow the pedestrian avenue Mohammed V past Spanish houses with wrought-iron balconies and tilework, you will eventually flow into place Feddane, the open square near the Royal Palace, unusually located in the very center city and a central gathering place in the evening. On the east side look up to see Dar Tair (the "House of the Bird"), an old Spanish apartment building crowned with a majestic bronze statue of a man fighting an eagle. The square is also the entrance point to Bab er-Rouah, the historical covered market on the north side, the Mellah and M'sala on the east and south, and rue Zawiya, where you'll find a few nice eating options. ⊠ *East end, av. Mohammed V.*

Place Moulay Mehdi. A leisurely stroll through Tetouan begins most naturally in the place Moulay Mehdi, a large plaza ringed with cafés, a post office, and the Spanish Eglise Nuestra Señora de Las Victorias aglow with strings of lights in the evening. It is often the site of outdoor concerts and evening snack vendors and strollers. ⊠ *Bd. al- Moukaouama, near bd. Mohammed V.*

WORTH NOTING

Archaeological Museum. West of place Feddane, this three-room museum holds a large collection of Roman mosaics and statuettes, coins, bronzes, and pottery found at various sites in northern Morocco such as Lixus and Cotta, as well as pictures of the archaeological site of Tamuda (recalling Stonehenge), where Anteus is fabled to have been buried after his battle with Hercules. The garden paths are rimmed with Jewish tombstones marked with pre-Columbian motifs brought back from South America and elaborate calligraphic Muslim tombstones. ⊠ *Av. Ben Hassan* ☎ *0539/96–48–43* 🎫 *10 DH* ⊗ *Mon.–Sat. 10–6.*

Dar San'aa (*School of Arts and Crafts*). Located across from Bab al Okla, this living museum founded by the monarchy has been considered the premier school in Morocco for the creation and preservation of traditional Andalusian, Berber, and Arab-influenced crafts and interior design since 1919. The school has resided in its current, architecturally significant Moorish-Andalusian home since 1928. The architectural splendor includes a colonnade inscribed with Kufic inscriptions, stained-glass details, and a green-tile exterior in the style of Fez. There's no shop inside, but on the other hand you can hone your skills for the souks without being hassled. ☎ *0539/97–27– 21* ⊗ *Weekdays 8–4:30.*

Ethnographic Museum of Tetouan. Transformed into a museum in 1948, the Ethnographic Museum is housed in the former fortress of the sultan Moulay Abderrahman, built around 1830 and surrounded by an Andalusian garden. The museum has a wonderful collection of traditional Moroccan costumes, jewelry, embroidery, weapons, musical instruments and other handcrafted objects. The most elaborate displays are of the accoutrements of Tetouani wedding ceremonies, which are among the most elaborate of Moroccan wedding attires and mixed with Jewish traditions. ⊠ *Av. Skala Bab El Oukla* ☎ *0539/97–05–05* 🎫 *10 DH* ⊗ *Mon.–Sat. 9–4.*

WHERE TO EAT

In recent years the town has seen an expanding number of good restaurants; though a fair percentage of them are foreign-owned, they still retain local charm. Otherwise, street delicacies are best here. Local specialties, found especially in the Mellah, for example at the corner of Rue al-Quds, are not to be missed. You may wish to sample *z'az'a* (a shake), flan *beldi* (meaning it is made with fresh country milk and eggs), and a pastry soaked in honey called *aslia*.

$ ╳ **La TouRouge.** Located in the wall of the old medina next to Ryad al
CAFÉ Ocha and overlooking Moulay Rachid Garden (otherwise known as "lovers' garden" with its large rock face), this small, hip café offers an umbrella-shaded patio, good espresso, and sandwiches; it often hosts informal concerts. This is a nice place for a break from the winding, narrow streets of M'sala in the outer Medina. $ *Average main: 75DH* ✉ *Av. Hassan I, next to Ryad al Ocha 9, Medina* ☎ *0539/71–31–32* ▭ *No credit cards.*

$ ╳ **Restaurant El Reducto.** Located next to the Mellah, this restaurant in
MOROCCAN a Spanish-run hotel is one of few options for a great homemade meal short of—but in truth, not much different from—being invited into a Tetouani home. Fine Moroccan and Spanish dishes in the restaurant include a most refined chicken pastilla, fish *briwat* (spicy fish turnovers), delicious nut-based pastries, and Spanish *croquetas* (croquettes), but picky eaters can also get delicious hamburgers. Alcohol is available. $ *Average main: 100DH* ✉ *Mechwar, 38, Essaid Zanqat Zawya Kadiriya* ☎ *0539/96–81–20* ⊕ *www.riadtetouan.com.*

$ ╳ **Restaurant Palace Bouhlal.** This palatial house was built in the 19th
MOROCCAN century and has colorful, finely painted floral doors and zellij columns. The traditional menu includes a sampling of Moroccan dishes including harira, couscous, kebabs, mint tea, and dessert. Be aware that the place is often used for tour groups and weddings. $ *Average main: 80DH* ✉ *48, Jamaa Kebir* ☎ *0670/85–95–63* ⌫ *Reservations essential* ▭ *No credit cards.*

$ ╳ **Restaurant Restinga.** Look closely at the south facade of this pedes-
MOROCCAN trian street lined with stores, and you'll see a small arch that leads into a simple courtyard with a large white ficus tree as its centerpiece. This is Restaurant Restinga. Try one of the traditional tagines with lamb or chicken or the platter of *friture de poisson,* which usually includes sole, *merlan* (whiting), calamari, *rouget* (red mullet), and shrimp. Dining is available inside or in the breezy courtyard. Service is friendly, and beer and wine are available. The restauarant also serves complimentary tapas with each order of alcohol. $ *Average main: 50DH* ✉ *21, bd. Mohammed V* ☎ *0539/96–35–76* ▭ *No credit cards.*

WHERE TO STAY

$$ ⊡ **Blanco Riad.** Run by Spanish owners since 2009, this beautiful, crisp,
HOTEL upscale riad once served as the Spanish consulate. **Pros:** peaceful atmo-
Fodor'sChoice sphere; historic setting. **Cons:** must reserve ahead for the restaurant;
★ pricey. $ *Rooms from: 1000DH* ✉ *25, rue Zawiya* ☎ *0539/70–42–02* ⊕ *www.blancoriad.com* ⬿ *8 rooms* ⊠❘ *Breakfast.*

$$ ⊡ **Hotel and Restaurant El Reducto.** Friendly, quadrilingual hosts Ruth and
HOTEL Brahim bring enthusiasm and warmth to this hotel and restaurant, making it one of the best options in Tetouan. **Pros:** nice staff; great views. **Cons:** the busy restaurant in the courtyard can make rooms noisy until late at night. $ *Rooms from: 750DH* ✉ *Mechwar, 38, Essaid Zanqat Zawya Kadiriya* ☎ *0539/96–81–20* ⬿ *7 rooms* ⊠❘ *Breakfast.*

$ ⊡ **Hotel Oumaima.** Moments from place Moulay Mehdi, this simple
B&B/INN hotel's private bathrooms with showers are the only luxury, but what

the hotel lacks in amenities it makes up for in convenience. **Pros:** great price; central location. **Cons:** can be noisy at night; rooms need renovations. $ *Rooms from: 309DH ⊠ 10, rue du 10 Mai ☎ 0539/96–34–73 ⤳ 36 rooms ▭ No credit cards ⚭ No meals.*

$

HOTEL

⚉ **Hotel Panorama.** Unreproachably clean, this new budget hotel boasts views of the mountains (either Jbel Ghorghiz and Jbel Derssa) across the valley from Tetouan from several of the rooms. **Pros:** clean; nice staff. **Cons:** on the outskirts of the new city; very basic hotel. $ *Rooms from: 400DH ⊠ Av. Moulay el-Abbas ☎ 0539/96–49–70 ⊕ www. panoramavista.com ⤳ 63 rooms ▭ No credit cards ⚭ No meals.*

SHOPPING

The most interesting shopping is found in the medina where *mendils,* the bright, multicolor cloth used by farmers from the Rif for all-purpose protection from the elements, are made and sold in a little square northeast of Bab er-Rouah. Wood and leather are other artisanal products to look for in the medina.

Ensemble Artisanal. This is a government-sponsored crafts center where rug weavers, leather workers, woodworkers, and jewelry designers manufacture and sell their wares. Prices are not negotiable here, but the value is excellent, especially if you factor in saved haggling time. ⊠ *Av. Hassan I ☎ 0539/99–20–85.*

CHEFCHAOUEN AND THE RIF

The trip south from Tetouan to Chefchaouen takes you through fertile valleys where locals sell produce along the road, sheep graze in golden sunshine, and the pace of life slows remarkably from that of the regions just to the north. The route from Chefchaouen to Al Hoceima winds through the spectacular scenery of the Rif, northern Morocco's highest mountains.

CHEFCHAOUEN

64 km (38 miles) south of Tetouan, 98 km (61 miles) southeast of Tangier.

Nestled high in the gray Rif Mountains, Chefchaouen, known as the "Blue City," is built on a hillside, and is a world apart from its larger, Spanish-style neighbors. The pace of life here seems somehow in tune with the abundant natural springs, wildflowers, and low-lying clouds hovering above the surrounding mountains. From Rifi Berbers dressed in earth-tone wool *djellabas* (long, hooded robes) and sweaters (ideal for cold, wet Rif winters) to the signature blue-washed houses lining its narrow streets, Chefchaouen has managed to maintain its unique identity.

Founded in 1471 by Moulay Ali ben Rachid as a mountain base camp for launching attacks against the Portuguese at Ceuta, Chefchaouen, historically off-limits to Christians until recently, had been visited by only three Europeans when Spanish troops arrived in 1920. Vicomte Charles de Foucauld—French military officer, explorer, and missionary—managed to make it inside the walls disguised as a rabbi in 1883. In 1889 British journalist Walter Harris, intrigued by the thought of a city closed to Westerners a mere 97 km (60 miles) from Tangier, used a similar strategy to gain access to Chefchaouen while researching his book *Land of an African Sultan*. The third visitor, American William Summers, was less lucky and was caught and poisoned in 1892.

Chefchaouen's isolationism had increased with the arrival of Muslims expelled from Spain at the end of the 15th century and again at the start of the 17th. Jews expelled from Spain with the Muslims chose various shades of blue for the facades of their houses, while the Muslim houses remained green or mauve. When the Spanish arrived in 1920 they were stunned to find Chefchaouen's Sephardic Jews speaking and writing a medieval Spanish dialect that had been extinct in Spain for four centuries. The medina has been walled since its earliest days, and is still off-limits to cars.

Somehow, even the burgeoning souvenir shops don't make much of a dent in the town's mystique. Chaouen, as it's sometimes called, is an ideal place to wander through a tiny medina, walk up into the looming mountains above the valley, and sip mint tea in an open square. No other place in Morocco has Chefchaouen's otherworldly, bohemian appeal—a place that ranks as a consistent favorite among travelers to the region.

GETTING HERE AND AROUND

CTM is the region's bus company with several buses daily between Tangier, Tetouan, Al Hoceima, and Nador. Grand taxis can be taken from Tangier or Tetouan directly to Chefchaouen for around 60 DH each way.

ESSENTIALS

Bus Contacts CTM ☎ *0539/98–76–69* ⊕ *www.ctm.co.ma.*

Visitor Information Chefchaouen Tourist Information ✉ *Pl. de Mohammed V.*

EXPLORING

OFF THE BEATEN PATH

Akshour Waterfall and God's Bridge. Two waterfalls and a natural bridge both located a short walk from the village of Akshour, a 40-minute drive from Chefchaouen toward Oued Laou on the coast, are the highlights of any trip into the heart of the Rif mountains. The path to the first waterfall is an easy 45-minute walk. From there, you have the option of continuing on a five- to six-hour round-trip hike to a second, much larger waterfall. On the other side of the river, you can either head up on a very steep path to the so-called "God's Bridge" itself, a natural bridge, or follow the canyon to a view from below. Be prepared to wade a little if the water is high. Small bungalow cafés offering vegetable tagines and mint tea sprinkle the path, as do wildflowers and small wildlife. Be aware that some locals will try to sell you things, some of them illegal. ✉ *Akshour.*

Talassemtane National Park. Established in 1989, Talassemtane National Park is just outside Chefchaouen's city walls. The 145,000-acre expanse boasts a Mediterranean ecosystem that hosts a unique variety of

Moroccan pine as well as more than 239 plant species, many of which are endangered, such as the black pine and the Atlas cedar. There are short day hikes, and more ambitious hikes along a large loop trail. ✉ *3, rue Machichi* ☎ *039/98–72–67.*

WHERE TO EAT

$ MOROCCAN 🍴 **Café Kasbah.** Located just across from the 500-plus-year-old *fondeq* (horse stable hotel), this unassuming restaurant is itself a renovated old fondeq. Away from the chaos of the main plaza, it has intimate booths offering a much-welcome egress from the hot sun. Starry-night colored tiles on fantastic iron chairs add to the magic of the colorful surroundings. It's open continually from 7 am to midnight. [$] *Average main: 50DH* ✉ *Pl. Uta el Hammam* ☎ *0539/88–33–97* 💳 *No credit cards.*

$ MOROCCAN 🍴 **Casa Aladdin.** This three-story riad has two terraces and is decorated with more experimental mixed-media approaches to the standard blue street scenes than you can shake a stick at. The main dishes can be hit or miss (tagines are the best bet), but the bird's-eye views over the main square are unique, and the fresh dairy products on the reasonably priced prix-fixe menu are local and scrumptious: the goat cheese salad appetizer and the fresh yogurt and cinnamon dessert are both highly recommended. And it's open late. [$] *Average main: 75DH* ✉ *17, rue Targui* ☎ *0539/98–90–71* 💳 *No credit cards.*

WHERE TO STAY

$ B&B/INN 🏨 **Caiat Lounge Refuge.** An excellent base camp from which to explore the Rif, this eco-friendly oasis in the mountains is actually a plateau of cute houses across from a dramatic valley. **Pros:** small and friendly; scenic. **Cons:** very basic amenities. [$] *Rooms from: 450DH* ✉ *Jemaa El Oued, Km 12 on road between Chefchaouen and Oued Laou, Asmetan* ☎ *0666/28–87–15* 🌐 *www.caiat.com* 🛏 *5 houses, 7 rooms* 🍽 *Multiple meal plans.*

$$ HOTEL 🏨 **Casa Hassan-Dar Baibou.** Renowned throughout Morocco, this 350-year-old family home houses an excellent restaurant with a handful of guest rooms. **Pros:** friendly atmosphere; a real bargain. **Cons:** need to reserve far ahead in high season. [$] *Rooms from: 850DH* ✉ *22, rue Targui* ☎ *0539/98–61–53* 🌐 *www.casahassan.com* 🛏 *24 rooms* 🍽 *Some meals.*

$ HOTEL 🏨 **Hotel Dar Mounir.** This sleek and chic B&B was designed by a local painter Al-Haoulani, whose paintings also decorate the walls. **Pros:** great staff and interior design. **Cons:** neighborhood can be noisy at night. [$] *Rooms from: 300DH* ✉ *Pl. Uta Hammam, Kadi Alami Hay Souika* ☎ *0539/98–82–53* 🌐 *www.hotel-darmounir.com* 🛏 *11 rooms* 🍽 *Breakfast.*

$ HOTEL 🏨 **Hotel Parador.** Ideally situated on the medina's edge, the simple and plain Hotel Parador was originally built in the 1920s as the Spanish governor's house. **Pros:** comfortable rooms; friendly atmosphere, parking available. **Cons:** little of the charm of the old city. [$] *Rooms from: 500DH* ✉ *Pl. el Mahkzen* ☎ *0539/98–63–24* 🌐 *www.hotel-parador.com* 🛏 *34 rooms, 4 suites* 🍽 *Breakfast.*

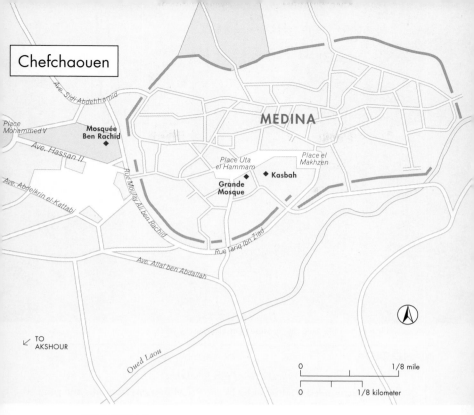

Chefchaouen

MEDINA

Place
Mohammed V

Mosquée
Ben Rachid

Place Uta
el Hammam

Place el
Makhzen

Grande
Mosque

Kasbah

Ave. Sidi Abdelhamid

Ave. Hassan II

Ave. Abdelkrin el Kattabi

Rue Moulay Ali ben Rachid

Rue Tariq Ibn Ziad

Ave. Allal ben Abdallah

Oued Laou

TO
AKSHOUR

0   1/8 mile

0   1/8 kilometer

SHOPPING

Chefchaouen is one of the north's best places to shop for quality traditional crafts. Wool items and leather goods are the main local export:
look in small medina stores for thick blankets, rugs, bags, and shoes.

Abdellah Alami. This shop sells nothing but bronze products, made by
a family of bronze workers who produce some of this region's finest
handmade plates, bowls, and trays. Prices are reasonable, and the selection is vast. ⊠ *257, Onsar Rasselma* ☎ *0539/98–73–03.*

Artisanal Chefchaouen. The small cooperative workshop Artisanal Chefchaouen produces beautiful, inexpensive hand-painted wooden boxes,
shelves, birdcages, chests, and mirrors of extremely high quality. ⊠ *Pl.
el Makhzen, in parking lot of Hotel Parador.*

Casa Marbella/Coin de l'Artisanat. Accredited by the Moroccan Ministry
of Industry and Artisanal Commerce, Casa Marbella/Coin de l'Artisanat
creates some of the country's finest zellij work, as well as metalwork,
pottery, silver filigree, and bronze. Traditional henna application is also
available for women. Prices are reasonable, and orders can be shipped
via airmail around the world. Retain all receipts and the store's contact
information if you choose to ship directly. ⊠ *40, rue Grandade Hay
Andalouss* ☎ *0539/98–71–20.*

Chefchaouen is known as the "blue city" because of its blue-washed walls.

AL HOCEIMA

215 km (133 miles) east of Chefchaouen.

Surrounded on three sides by the Rif Mountains' foothills and rimmed on the fourth by turquoise Mediterranean waters, Al Hoceima is a dominating town atop rolling hills. The town perches directly over a stunning turquoise bay and, while it isn't nearly as developed as Tangier and Tetouan, its natural sights and exquisite coastline make it the perfect place to relax for a day or two.

Established by the Spanish in 1925 as Villa Sanjuro, Al Hoceima was built as a stronghold against Rifi Berber rebellions. Al Hoceima is now proudly Berber, and Berber flags and signs are becoming more and more prominent. The king recognized *Tamazight*—a general term that encompasses six different Berber dialects, four of which are in use by Morocco's Berber population—as Morocco's second official language, alongside Arabic. Tarifit (Rifi Berber) is spoken by about 4 million people in the Rif Valley, sometimes exclusively of any other language, though there are many Spanish words.

The finest Spanish edifice in the town is the beautifully tiled **Collège Espagnol** (Spanish College) at the end of boulevard Mohammed V. The Old Town is centered on the pretty, Art Deco **place du Rif.** There are few sights here, but you can wander the town's markets, kick back at a café, and just enjoy the relative quietude. In the Ville Nouvelle, the clifftop **place Mohammed VI,** just above the main beach, is the focal point of the evening *paseo* (promenade) and has a fun sidewalk punctuated by fountains. Festivals and citywide events are held here in the summer months, when many expatriate Al Hoceimans residing in Europe return home on vacation.

GETTING HERE AND AROUND

Al Hociema's Cherif Al Idrissi Airport, located just 17 km (11 miles) southeast of the town, connects to Amsterdam, Brussels, Casablanca, and Tetouan with Royal Air Maroc; Amsterdam with Corendon Dutch Airlines; Brussels with Jetairfly; and Amsterdam and Rotterdam with Transavia.

CTM buses operate several daily services to Tangier, Tetouan, Chefchaouen, and Nador. If you're driving yourself, the N2 cuts easts toward Nador and Melilla, and there is also a scenic coastal road from Tetouan to Al Hoceima.

ESSENTIALS

Bus Contacts CTM ⊠ 46, pl. Rif ☎ 039/98–22–73 ⊕ www.ctm.co.ma.

Visitor Information Al Hoceima Tourism Office ⊠ Rue Al Hamra, Calabonita ☎ 0539/98–11–85.

DRIVING IN THE RIF

If you decide to continue on from Chefchaouen, remember that driving at night can be dangerous in the Rif Valley, where a false roadblock of stones can lead to robberies or forcible purchase of *kif* (hashish). Especially around Ketama, never accept invitations to private village ceremonies or even a mint tea, as this is usually a setup of some kind: someone slips a package of kif into your car and then the police are suddenly interested in searching your vehicle. Remember that kif, though prevalent, is illegal, and punishments for drug crimes in Morocco are extremely harsh.

EXPLORING

The real reasons to come to Al Hoceima are the many beaches. The main city beach, **Plage Quemado,** sits in a natural bay formed by mountains on each side. The water is crystal clear, perfect for snorkeling and scuba diving, and you can rent equipment from a hut on the beach. (Be sure to check the equipment carefully before use.) Near Quemado Beach is Al Hoceima's port, where several restaurants cook up wonderfully fresh seafood. The coastline outside of town is equally as scenic; the beach at **Asfiha,** located 1 km (½ mile) west of the city, stretches around the bay with miles of uninterrupted, fine, ash-color sand. It is a popular family resort and is usually very crowded in summer, with many beachside bungalow-cafés in which to hide from the sun and have tea or lunch. The beach is very much worth a trip, for from here you can see the tiny Spanish rock fortress **Peñon de Alhuceimas,** meaning "Lavendar Rock." **Souani Beach** is a nice small bay backed by a pine forest, a perfect place for a picnic.

WHERE TO EAT AND STAY

$ ✕ **Club Nautique.** Fresh, simply grilled fish and other seafood reign
SEAFOOD supreme here, along with several resort-style bars placed strategically around the two terraces and captain's cabin–style interior; there is a large selection of Moroccan wines on offer, with Gerrouane being a good bet. The house salads are well prepared and can be made to suit the size of your party. The views of the bay and local fishing boats from

the outdoor tables are stunning. [$] *Average main: 70DH* ✉ *Port d'Al Hoceima* ☎ *0539/98–14–61* 💳 *No credit cards.*

$$$$ HOTEL 🏨 **Chafarina's Beach.** This tourist complex 4 km (2 miles) north of Al Hoceima and overlooking Bouskour (the King's favorite public beach in the area) offers kitschy Romanesque decadence in the communal areas with beautiful sweeping views over the Mediterranean, aquatic and sports activities, and a splendid dining hall. **Pros:** lively in summer; plenty of activities. **Cons:** can be deserted in the off-season. [$] *Rooms from: 1650DH* ✉ *Tala Youssef, Plage Bouskour* ☎ *0539/84–16–01* 🛏 *30 suites* 🍴 *Breakfast.*

$$ HOTEL 🏨 **Hotel Amir Plage.** In a cove of its own between the Kalah Bonita bus station and the Place du Rif, this hotel sits directly on its beach. **Pros:** on the water; very private; reasonable prices. **Cons:** down a steep driveway; small beach can be crowded in peak season. [$] *Rooms from: 800DH* ✉ *Plage du Matadero* ☎ *0539/98–32–90* 🌐 *www.hotelamirplage.com* 🛏 *22 rooms, 10 suites* 🍴 *Breakfast.*

$$$ HOTEL 🏨 **Suites Hotel Mohammed V.** Al Hoceima's grand old hotel has sleek, chic, remodeled rooms (albeit in a sanatorium style) and bungalows for guests to choose from. **Pros:** away from the hubbub; near the beach. **Cons:** rooms a bit utilitarian. [$] *Rooms from: 1100DH* ✉ *Pl. de la Marche Verte* ☎ *0539/98–22–33* 🌐 *www.hotelsuitesmohammedv.com* 🛏 *30 suites* 🍴 *Breakfast.*

SPORTS AND THE OUTDOORS

BEACHES

The area around Al Hoceima has some of North Africa's finest Mediterranean beaches. Quemado Beach, a busy urban strip in Al Hoceima proper, is a cove tucked between large hills, with fine sand and crystalline water; during a simple swim you can see coral and schools of fish below. There are plenty of beaches to explore just outside—for instance, Tala Youssef, just west of Al Hoceima, where King Mohammed VI spends his summer holidays.

To the east, the beaches beyond Nador such as Kariet Arkmane, Ras Kebdana, and Saïdia are quieter and less well equipped for family activities, but excellent for relaxing and communing with nature.

RABAT AND
CASABLANCA

WELCOME TO RABAT AND CASABLANCA

TOP REASONS TO GO

★ **Rabat's Kasbah des Oudayas:** Rabat's medieval Kasbah des Oudayas, the Oudayas Gardens, and the Oudayas Museum overlook the mouth of the Oued Bou Regreg river and the city of Salé beyond.

★ **Casablanca's Tour Hassan II:** The largest mosque in Africa and the seventh largest in the world, this modern extravaganza makes elaborate use of traditional Moroccan craftsmanship.

★ **Colonial France's southern Riviera:** The alpine colony at Casablanca's Quartier des Habous and La Corniche managed to bring parts of France to North Africa.

★ **Casablanca's southern beaches:** For a refreshing ramble along a largely unspoiled coastline with not much more going on than surfable waves crashing in from the Atlantic, the beaches between Casablanca and El Oualidia are some of the world's best.

1 Rabat. Visitors are enticed by the beautiful tranquillity of Rabat, with its Moorish gardens bordered by charming cafés. They marvel at the Hassan Tower, which has overlooked the city for eight centuries, and the Mohammed V Mausoleum. The Musée Archéologique houses the country's most extensive collection of archaeological artifacts. Golf fanatics may play at the Royal Golf Dar Es-Salam, while beach lovers will enjoy the shore south of Rabat.

2 Around Rabat. Bird lovers should consider a day at Lake Sidi Bourhaba, near Mehdiya Plage, known for its nearly 200 species of birds. For those captivated by Morocco's medinas, the nearby city of Salé feels entirely different from Rabat, and shoppers will enjoy Salé's pottery shops. The beaches of Skhirat, Oued Cherrat, and Bouznika are breathtaking.

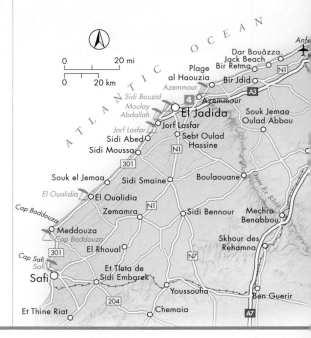

3 Casablanca. With its spacious avenues of contemporary and Hispano-Moorish structures, Art Deco architecture, public fountains, and spacious shoreline, Casablanca appeals to Western visitors. Modern structures amid a mosque shooting its laser beams to Mecca underscore Casablanca's eclectic spirit. An appealing blend of East and West, it successfully balances history and innovation.

4 Around Casablanca. Dar Bouazza, an eclectic fishing village and resort town, has great beaches and several oceanfront restaurants. Azemmour has a whitewashed medina and artsy atmosphere. El Jadida was built by the Portuguese and feels quite different from other Moroccan cities, as well as offering more dining and lodging options.

GETTING ORIENTED

You can easily drive to Rabat from the northern cities of Tangier or Tetouan on the newer highway, although the older, slower coastal road is still open. From there, you can go on to Casablanca, Azemmour, and El Jadida, where the highway ends. The coastal road will lead you further south from this point—a good idea if you wish to explore the southern beaches, Essaouira, Marrakesh, or the Atlas Mountains. Either way you'll absorb plenty of coastal scenery. If you're flying into Casablanca but have limited time to spend in the region, you may want to go straight to Rabat, as it's only an hour and a half from the airport by car or train and is richer in traditional sights.

THE ROMANS IN MOROCCO

Rome's influence in the Maghreb was geographically limited, but for 300 years it was of strategic importance and a source of vast wealth for the empire. The breathtaking archaeological remains, especially at Volubilis, point to Rome's commitment to the region.

(above) A Roman mosaic at the ruins at Volubilis (opposite page, bottom) Several columns that remain standing from the basilica (opposite page, top) The triumphal arch, which was restored in 1932

By the 3rd century BC, Carthage (modern-day Tunis) had caught the attention of Rome, who eyed it with a desire that epitomized the empire's insatiable appetite for expansion. A trio of Punic Wars, spanning 100 years, caused Rome to fear for its future. However, Carthaginian potency waned with the death of Hannibal, and in 146 BC, after a three-year siege, Carthage was finally crushed. Rome annexed North Africa and now controlled the Mediterranean. The region was divided among various client kings, headed by the Numidian prince Jugurtha. When he attempted to unify the kingdoms in revolt, Rome had no choice but to act. In 106 BC, after a six-year war, Jugurtha was dead and Rome's grip on North Africa left unchallenged—at least for another 60 years, that is.

VOLUBILIS

Volubilis was home to Juba II and his son Ptolemy. Under this cultured duo, the city blossomed and continued to thrive well after Rome's departure in the 3rd century AD. After a millennium of constant occupation, the city was plundered for its stone in the 17th century by Moulay Ismail, but what remains is simply stunning—one reason the ruins were named a UNESCO World Heritage Site.

JULIUS CAESAR

Following Julius Caesar's march on Rome in 49 BC, Republican resistance had been growing, and nowhere more rapidly than in North Africa. Caesar arrived there in 47 BC with 30,000 men. One year later, at Thapsus (in present-day Tunisia), his outnumbered legions soundly defeated the armies of King Juba of Numidia (in present-day Algeria) and Republican forces led by Scipio. Over the following months, resistance was crushed throughout North Africa, and Rome's grip on the Maghreb became tighter than ever.

KING JUBA II

Despite his father's allegiances, Juba II was installed as the client king of Numidia and later Mauretania. Juba had been educated in Rome and was a sophisticated and respected monarch. While living in Volubilis with his wife Cleopatra Selene (daughter of Antony and Cleopatra), he wrote many geographical and historical works. It was under his rule that the city flourished and became a showcase for palatial architecture as well as a center for commerce.

Juba II was of Berber descent and co-ruled with his son Ptolemy, nurturing their comfortable relationship with Rome, even asking for (and receiving) military assistance in crushing a violent Berber rebellion in AD 24.

CALIGULA AND CLAUDIUS

In AD 40, all of that was to change with the arrival of the notoriously unstable Caligula who, in a fit of jealousy, had Ptolemy murdered and then declared an end to Berber autonomy. Unsurprisingly, the province rose up in a bloody revolt that was eventually put down by Emperor Claudius.

Claudius divided the province into Mauretania Caesariensis (West Algeria) and Mauretania Tingitana (Morocco) whose capital was Tingis, present-day Tangier. Rome developed existing towns rather than starting new settlements, and Volubilis in particular benefited. It exported vast quantities of olive oil and wheat to Rome, eventually supplying fully two-thirds of that city's food.

POST-ROMAN OCCUPATION

In 285 Rome called a halt to its ambitions in Africa and left the region after 300 years of almost undisputed occupancy. A small garrison remained, and Morocco remained part of the Roman empire until the 5th century AD. Roman influence in the Maghreb was confined to the northwest of the country and stopped just north of Rabat. Although relatively brief and limited, the Roman presence has left Morocco architectural remains to rival any in North Africa.

Updated by
Olivia Gun-
ning Bennani

As two of Morocco's most modern and elegant cities, Rabat and Casablanca straddle the North Atlantic coast, welcoming visitors with their varied histories and blossoming cultures.

As the political capital of Morocco, Rabat is a surprisingly sedate city that brims with historical interest and splendid architecture from both Arab and Art Deco periods. The royal city boasts many monuments from successive Arab dynasties as well as a simple unmarked cave on the coast that is thought to be one of the first sites ever inhabited by humans. Rabat and her twin city, Salé, watch one another over the river Bou Regreg, where they both offer traditional medinas full of market bustle as well as some of the most important historical sights in the country.

No more than 100 km (62 miles) southwest of Rabat is Casablanca, once a Berber town and now a thoroughly modern city, developed by the French since 1912 until Moroccan independence. Morocco's main industrial and commercial axis stretches from Casablanca to Kenitra, making the city the undisputed commercial capital with rich strata of history piled everywhere.

Despite the historical riches, Rabat, Casablanca, and its surrounding towns are somewhat removed from the pressures of the larger tourist centers like Marrakesh, Fez, and Agadir. Quite apart from the gentle climate, you'll generally find yourself—unlike in, say, Fez—free to wander around relatively unhassled.

The Atlantic breakers roll in all along the rest of Morocco's North Atlantic coast, contrasting markedly with the placid waters of Morocco's Mediterranean coast. From here, the ocean stretches due west to the United States. Much of this coast is lined with sandy beaches, and dotted with simple white *koubbas,* the buildings that house a Muslim saint's tomb.

What you can really sample when visiting this region is the urban side of North Africa, which overflows with modern structures in industrial, commercial, and leisure terms. Yet the old has not been ousted, so expect conspicuous contrasts: traditional dress alongside contemporary

European designers and ancient Moorish edifices not far from trendy restaurants bubbling over with international tourists and young locals.

PLANNING

WHEN TO GO

During the summer months of July, August, and the first part of September, temperatures are hot, beach towns are crowded, and hotels tend to be more packed and expensive. April through June and October, the weather is delightful—easily warm enough to enjoy the beaches (although it may be too cold to swim)—and most coastal resorts are pleasantly empty. If you don't want to swim or sunbathe, you can sightsee from November to March (and even then the weather can be quite warm). The relatively cold period lasts from around early December through the end of February; temperatures on the coast can plunge to 4°C–6°C (39°F–43°F).

PLANNING YOUR TIME

Most flights to this region land in Casablanca, so it's probably most logical to start there. After spending a few days exploring this economic heart of Morocco, you'll probably be in search of some peace, so head north towards Rabat, stopping at Mohammedia for an afternoon. While in Rabat, spend a few days admiring the magnificent architecture, elegant restaurants, and lively medina. For even more peace, skip farther north to Moulay Bousselham, a bird-lover's haven. To explore the southern parts of the area, stop by Azemmour and El Jadida on your way to Oualidia. To complete this tour fully, you'd need a good two weeks, but many people prefer to focus on just the two cities—with brief day trips to some surrounding beach towns.

GETTING HERE AND AROUND

AIR TRAVEL

The only major airport in this region of Morocco is Casablanca's Mohammed V International Airport, which is located about 25 km (16 miles) south of the city. It's the most common international gateway for Americans traveling to Morocco. Many airlines fly direct from Middle Eastern and European cities, as well as those in the United States and Canada. Casablanca, Rabat, and other destinations in the region can be easily reached via the numerous train, shuttle, or taxi services located outside the arrivals terminal.

BUS TRAVEL

You can reach some outlying destinations by bus if you don't wish to drive, but the trips can be less than comfortable and long. Always make sure you use a reputable bus company.

CAR TRAVEL

If your stay in this region is limited to Casablanca and Rabat, you won't need a car at all. If, however, your aim is to relax in small coastal towns like Moulay Bousselham and El Oualidia, a car is far more useful than the slow and complicated public transportation to those places.

TRAIN TRAVEL

There is excellent nonstop train service almost hourly between Casablanca and Rabat (even more frequently at the beginning and end of the day). This is the best way to move between the cities. You can travel onward to Tangier, Fez, Meknès, Marrakesh, and a few other destinations by train. This can be a comfortable and reasonably priced way to travel in Morocco.

SAFETY

Official guides in Morocco are identified by large, brass badges. Be wary of the numerous unofficial guides, generally young men, who will offer to find you a hotel, take you on a tour of the city, or, in some cases, find hashish, or *kif,* for you. Some will falsely claim to be students who merely wish to practice their English. To avoid these hustlers, you should appear confident and aware of where you are going. If you feel bullied or harassed, do not hesitate to summon police. As in any large city, pickpockets exist, and you should be alert and aware of your surroundings while walking around the city. Be careful to keep essential documents out of reach; an inside pocket is the most sensible, since bag-grabbing (often by motorcyclists) is quite common.

RESTAURANTS

Morocco's northern Atlantic coast is its center of seafood par excellence. Along the entire coast the menus are remarkably similar: *salades* (salads), *crevettes* (prawns), *friture de poisson* (fried fish and octopus), *calamar* (squid), and various kinds of fish. *Fruits de mer* are always shellfish and prawns, not fish. In addition to seafood, Casablanca and Rabat offer many types of international cuisine—Italian and other Mediterranean restaurants, as well as Asian and even American eateries—and, of course, traditional Moroccan fare and French cuisine. Although it's tempting to think you can find good Moroccan restaurants anywhere, the best ones on this stretch of the coast are really limited to Casablanca and Rabat. (Moroccans eat Moroccan cuisine in the home, so when they dine out, they tend to want something more unusual.)

HOTELS

It's always a good idea to book ahead in this part of the country, as Rabat and Casablanca fill up with business travelers, and the beach resorts are packed in summer months. Casablanca has branches of the familiar international business hotels, and most business hotels in both Casablanca and Rabat will discount their published rates by applying corporate rates at the drop of a company's name. In the smaller coastal resorts you'll typically find midrange sea-view hotels with pools, but increasingly these towns also offer smaller, more personalized, bed-and-breakfast-type lodgings. *Hotel reviews have been shortened. For full information, visit Fodors.com.*

WHAT IT COSTS IN DIRHAMS				
	$	$$	$$$	$$$$
Restaurants	under 80 DH	80 DH–120 DH	121 DH–160 DH	over 160 DH
Hotels	under 900 DH	900 DH–1,500 DH	1,501 DH–2,000 DH	over 2,000 DH

Restaurant prices are the average cost of a main course at dinner, or if dinner is not served, at lunch. Hotel prices are the lowest cost of a standard double room in high season.

FESTIVALS
Le Festival de Casablanca, a citywide arts event, attracts international visitors every July. L'Boulevard, which takes place in early or late summer, is an annual competition among local and foreign artists and is popular with the younger crowd. Rabat's Mawazine festival, usually in May, has achieved international recognition, bringing high-quality performers to Morocco. Note that exact festival dates vary according to Ramadan; many festivals are not held during their usual period due to the holiday, so scheduling can be unpredictable.

RABAT

40 km (25 miles) southwest of Kenitra, 91 km (57 miles) northeast of Casablanca.

Rabat is an excellent place to get acquainted with Morocco, as it has a medina and an array of historical sites and museums, yet exerts significantly less of the pressure that most foreign travelers experience in a place like Fez. You'll generally find yourself free to wander and browse without being hassled to buy local wares or engage a guide. As a diplomatic center, Rabat has a large community of foreign residents. Attractive and well kept, with several gardens, it's arguably Morocco's most pleasant and easygoing city as far as tourists are concerned.

Rabat was founded in the 12th century as a fortified town—now the Kasbah des Oudayas—on a rocky outcrop overlooking the River Bou Regreg by Abd al-Mu'min of the Almohad dynasty. Abd al-Mu'min's grandson, Yaqoub al-Mansour, extended the city to encompass the present-day medina, surrounded it with ramparts (some of which still stand), and erected a mosque, from which the unfinished Hassan Tower protrudes as Rabat's principal landmark. Chellah, a neighboring Roman town now within Rabat, was developed as a necropolis in the 13th century.

In the early 17th century Rabat itself was revived with the arrival of the Muslims, who populated the present-day medina upon their expulsion from Spain. Over the course of the 17th century the Kasbah des Oudayas grew notorious for its pirates, and an independent republic of the Bou Regreg was established, based in the kasbah; the piracy continued when the republic was integrated into the Alaouite kingdom and lasted until the 19th century. Rabat was named the administrative capital of the country at the beginning of the French protectorate in

1912, and it remained the capital of the Alaouite kingdom when independence was restored in 1956.

The city has grown considerably over the last 20 years, and today it has many important districts outside the kasbah, the medina, and the original French Ville Nouvelle. These include L'Océan, the seaside area that was once Spanish and Portuguese (during the French protectorate); Hassan, the environs of the Hassan tower; Agdal, a fashionable residential and business district; Ryad, an upscale residential district; and Souissi, an affluent enclave of wealthy folks and diplomats. Take a ride in a taxi, a tram, or your own car around the various neighborhoods to get a real understanding of the city as a whole.

GETTING HERE AND AROUND

AIR TRAVEL

For international visitors, Rabat is best reached via Casablanca's Mohammed V International Airport. Rabat-Salé Airport, which has only domestic flights, is 10 km (6 miles) northeast of the capital. The train service from Casablanca's airport into Rabat is reliable and frequent.

BUS TRAVEL

The bus station in Rabat is on the outskirts of the city in a neighborhood known as Kamara; from there you can take a taxi or a city bus into town.

Bus Information CTM ⊠ *2, av. Hassan II* ☎ *0535/28–14–86* ⊕ *www.ctm.co.ma.*

CAR TRAVEL

You may prefer not to hire a car if you are only visiting Rabat and Casablanca, but if you want to explore further, one may be helpful. Major international agencies do have rental outlets in Rabat or at the domestic airport.

Rental Cars Avis ⊠ *7, rue Abou Faris el Marini* ☎ *0537/72–18–18* ⊕ *www.avis.com.* **Budget** ⊠ *Rabat-Salé Airport* ☎ *0530/20–05–20* ⊕ *www.budget.com.* **Hertz** ⊠ *Rabat-Salé Airport* ☎ *0537/82–97–00* ⊕ *www.hertz.com.*

TAXI TRAVEL

Rabat's *petits taxis,* which are blue, can get you easily from Point A to Point B, and you'll find them just about everywhere in town. A typical metered fare will cost you about 15 to 20 DH (after 9 pm there is a 50% surcharge to the metered fare).

TRAIN TRAVEL

Rabat has two train stations: Rabat-Agdal, on the outskirts of town toward Casablanca, and Rabat-Ville, closer to most hotels and attractions. Rabat is three hours by train from Meknès, four hours from Fez, and four hours from Marrakesh. All these trains also call at Casablanca. In addition, there are overnight trains from Rabat to Oujda, and three direct trains daily to Tangier, which also have bus connections from an intermediate stop (just before Asilah) to Tetouan. Casablanca's tramway costs 6 DH per ride and is an excellent way to get around the city.

Train Contacts Office National des Chemins de Fer ⊠ *8 bis, rue Abderrahmane el Ghafiki* ☎ *0890/20–30–40* ⊕ *www.oncf.org.ma.*

GUIDES AND TOURS

Guided tours of several cities in this region are best reserved in your home country. Generally speaking, you can't buy a place on a local guided tour upon arrival the way you can in many other countries.

Atlas Voyages. Operating out of Rabat, this professional agency offers almost any kind of tour or break you could desire, from a Rif mountain escape to an urban exploration of one of the Kingdom's regal cities. They cater to all budgets and group sizes, and are flexible in terms of trip type, from off-road trekking to luxury palatial getaways. ☎ 0802/00–20–20 ⊕ www.atlasvoyages.com.

SAFETY

Rabat is considered one of the safest, least harried cities in Morocco. Travelers can generally expect minimal harassment from vendors and fake tour guides. Nonetheless, streets can be somewhat desolate after sundown, so visitors may prefer to use taxis then.

EXPLORING

TOP ATTRACTIONS

Archaeological Museum. Opened in 1931, the Musée Archéologique holds prehistoric, Roman, and Islamic-period artifacts discovered throughout the country. The emphasis is on Roman pieces, including many inscribed tablets; the Chellah and Volubilis sites are particularly well represented, and there's an ample collection of Roman bronze items. Also on display is a plaster cast of the early human remains found at Harhoura Beach, on the coast south of the city. ✉ 23, rue Al Brihi, Ministères ☎ 0537/70–19–19 ⊕ www.minculture.gov.ma 🖃 10 DH ⊗ Wed.–Mon. 9–4:30.

Fodor's Choice ★

Chellah Ruins and Gardens. Chellah was an independent city before Rabat ever existed. It dates from the 7th or 8th century BC, when it was probably Phoenician. You'll see the remains of the subsequent Roman city, Sala Colonia, on your left as you walk down the path. Though these remnants are limited to broken stone foundations and column bases, descriptive markers point to the likely location of the forum, baths, and market. Sultan Abu Saïd and his son Abu al Hassan, of the Merenid dynasty, were responsible for the ramparts, the entrance gate, and the majestic portals. The Merenids used Chellah as a spiritual retreat, and at quiet times the *baraka* (blessing) of the place is still tangible.

The entrance to the Merenid sanctuary is at the bottom of the path, just past some tombs. To the right is a pool with eels in it, which is said to produce miracles—women are known to toss eggs to the eels for fertility. The ruins of the mosque are just inside the sanctuary; you can still see the beautiful arches and the *mihrab* (prayer niche). Storks nest on the impressive minaret. On the far side of the mosque is a beautiful wall decorated with Kufi script, a type of Arabic calligraphy characterized by right angles. To the left of the mosque is the *zaouia* (sanctuary), where you can see the ruins of individual cells surrounding a basin and some ancient mosaic work. Beyond the mosque and zaouia are some beautiful, well-maintained walled gardens. Spring water runs through the gardens at one point, and they give the Chellah a serenity that's quite extraordinary considering that it's less than a mile from the center of a nation's capital. From the walled gardens you can look out over the River Bou Regreg: you'll see cultivated fields below, and cliffs across the river. On the right is a hill with a small white koubba. ■ **TIP→ Tour groups are elsewhere at lunchtime, so try to come then to experience the Chellah at its most serene.** ✉ *Chellah* 🎟 *10 DH* ⏲ *Daily 9:30–5:30 (or until sunset if earlier).*

Hassan Tower. At the end of the 12th century, Yaqoub al Mansour—fourth monarch of the Almohad dynasty and grandson of Abd al Mu'min, who founded Rabat—planned a great mosque. Intended to be the largest mosque in the Muslim world, the project was abandoned with the death of al Mansour in 1199. A further blow to the site occurred with the strong tremors of the 1755 Lisbon earthquake, and this tower is the only significant remnant of al Mansour's dream. A few columns remain in the mosque's great rectangular courtyard, but the great tower was never even completed (which is why it looks too short for its base). Note the quality of the craftsmanship in the carved-stone and mosaic decorations at the top of the tower. From the base there is a fine view over the river. Locals come here at dawn to have their wedding photos taken. ✉ *Hassan* 🎟 *Free.*

Fodor's Choice ★ **Kasbah des Oudayas.** The history of the Kasbah is the early history of Rabat. Built on high ground over the mouth of the Bou Regreg river and the Atlantic, the Kasbah was originally built here for defensive purposes. Still inhabited, it originally comprised the whole of the city, including the castle of Yaqoub al Mansour.

Walk up the steps to the huge, imposing ornamental gate, built, like Bab Rouah, by the Almohads. The gate's interior is now used for art exhibits. Enter the Kasbah and turn right into Rue Jama (Mosque Street). The **mosque,** which dates from Almohad times (it was built in the mid-12th century), is on the left; it was supposedly reconstructed in the late 18th century by an English Muslim—Ahmed el Inglizi. Continue to the end of the road past a house called Dar Baraka, and you'll emerge onto a large platform overlooking the Bou Regreg estuary. Here you have a magnificent view across the river to the old quarter of Salé, and you can walk down to the water's edge. Go back along Rue Jama until you come to Rue Bazo on the left; this winds down the Kasbah past picturesque houses. Turn left, walk to the bottom of the street, and proceed down to the banks of the Bou Regreg river to see the beautiful **Jardin des Oudayas** (Oudayas Garden), a walled retreat that you can explore at your leisure. The garden was laid out in the early 20th century (and is now wheelchair accessible), but its enclosure dates from the beginning of the present Alaouite dynasty in the 17th century.

At the top of the garden, accessible by a bridge across a pool, is the **Musée des Oudayas** (Oudayas Museum), which holds various objects of traditional Moroccan art. The museum is set in a house built by Moulay Ismail in the traditional style, with rooms arranged around a courtyard. Thanks to fortuitous design, the rooms get sun in winter but not in summer. The two most valuable items are the 12th- or

Rabat

Oued Bou Regreg

MELLAH

Av. Al Marsa

Bab El Mellah

R. des Consuls

Av. Moulay Ismail

MEDINA

Av. Chellah

Parc du Triangle de Vue

CENTRE VILLE

R. Souika

R. Sidi Fatah

Rue Boukroun

Av. Mohammed V (El Gzah)

Pl. Achouhada

Bab Bouiba

Bab Al Had

Av. Jazirat Al Arab

Av. Al Mouqawama

Bd. Hassan II

R. Mansour Addahbi

R. Patrice Lumumba

R. Mekka

R. Al Marinhyine

R. Al Mourabattine

R. Abdelmomen

Av. Al Mouahidine

Av. Al Alaouine

R. Attar ben Abdellah

Av. Abou Inan

R. Soukarno

Bd. Mohammed V

Gare Rabat Ville

Djemâa Sunna

Av. Ibn Toumert

R. Loubnane

Av. Moukhtar Gazouili

Av. Abdelkrim Al Khattabi

Rue Sénégal

Bd. Al Maghrib al Arabi

Pl. Italia

Bd. Hassan II

Av. Mali

Pl. Russia

Av. Jean Jaurès

Av. Pasteur

R. Descartes

Bab Rouah

R. Abdiwahed

R. Abou Chouaib

Adoukkali

R. Al Marrakchi

Stade Olympique

Av. Al Mouqawama

Av. Madagascar

Av. Tonkin

R. Qadi Ayad

Av. Al Ghazali

Bd. Annasr (Av. de la Victoire)

R. Ibn Khaldoune

R. Oqba

R. Ibn Hazm

Av. Sidi Mohamed ben Abdellah

Av. Mohamed Zerktouni

Bab Tamesna

Pl. Ibn Al Widane

Jardin d'Essais

R. Al Battani

R. Ibn Hajar

R. Al Achaari

Bab Marrakech

R. Innaouen

TO AGDAL

13th-century Almohad Koran and the medieval astrolabe; other exhibits include Andalusian musical instruments, clothing, jewelry, and pottery from Fez. Leave the garden by the wrought-iron gate at the top and turn left as you come out to exit the Kasbah by the lower gate. ■TIP→ **You may be approached by a potential guide at the entrance, but you won't really need one.** ⊠ *Oudayas Museum, 1, bd. Al Marsa, Medina* 🕾 *0537/73–15–37* 🖼 *Kasbah free, museum 10 DH* ☉ *Kasbah freely accessible, museum Wed.–Mon. 9:30–4.*

NEED A BREAK?

Oudayas Café. The Oudayas Café is an excellent place to pause for a drink or snack; the shady terrace is decorated with mosaic tilework and looks across the river to Salé. There is always tea for sale and someone is usually passing around Moroccan pastries. ⊠ *Oudayas Museum, 1, bd. Al Marsa, Medina* 🕾 *0537/73–15–37.*

Mohammed V Mausoleum. Resting place of King Mohammed V, who died in 1961, the mausoleum is adjacent to the Hassan Tower and, thanks to a commanding position above the river, is similarly visible to anyone approaching Rabat from Salé. The tomb itself is subterranean; the terrace that overlooks it is approached by steps on each side. Looking down, you're likely to see someone ritually reading the Koran. Beyond the central sarcophagus of King Mohammed V are those of his sons Prince Moulay Abdallah and King Hassan II, who was interred here in July 1999 as world leaders stood by for his state funeral. Designed by a Vietnamese architect and built between 1962 and 1966, the tomb is cubical, with a pyramidal green-tile roof, a richly decorated ceiling, and onyx interior walls. A mosque, built at the same time, adjoins the tomb. ⊠ *Hassan.*

WORTH NOTING

Bab Rouah (*Gate of the Winds*). Currenly an art gallery, this city gate was built by Yaqoub al Mansour in 1197. To see it, go outside the city walls and look to the right of the modern arches. Originally a fortification, the gate has an elaborately decorated arch topped by two carved shells. The entrance leads into a room with no gate behind it; you have to turn left into another room and then right into a third room to see the door that once led into Rabat. ⊠ *1, av. de la Victoire, Centre Ville* 🖼 *Free* ☉ *Daily 8:30–noon and 2:30–7:30.*

Lalla Soukaina Mosque. Built in the 1980s by King Hassan II in honor of his granddaughter, this mosque is proof that the tradition of Moorish architecture that produced the Court of Lions in Granada's Alhambra is alive and well. Notice the exquisite sandstone work on the walkways surrounding the mosque, and look up at the colorfully painted geometrical designs on the ceilings. The mosque is surrounded by immaculately kept gardens. Non-Muslims may not enter, but there's plenty to admire from outside. ⊠ *Edge of Souissi, beyond Ibn Sina Hospital, Souissi.*

Rabat Zoological Gardens. Here most of the animals have relatively wide enclosures and plenty are at ease in the local climate. The zoo is divided into themes: mountains, desert, savannah, and the tropics; plus there's an aviary, water area, and an educational farm. You can see Atlas lions (which only exist in captivity), elephants, giraffes, hippos, fennec foxes, and hordes of magnificent oryx and gazelles. ✉ *Annexe 23 ème, Cité Yaacoub el Mansour* ☎ *0537/29–38–94* 🌐 *www.rabatzoo.ma* 🎟 *50 DH* 🕒 *Daily 10–5:30.*

Royal Palace (*Mechouar*). Built in the early 20th century, Morocco's Royal Palace is a large, cream-color building set back behind lawns. Its large ornamental gate is accented by ceremonial guards dressed in white and red. The complex houses the offices of the cabinet, the prime minister, and other administrative officials. Don't stray from the road down the middle of the complex; the palace is occupied by the royal family and closed to the public. ✉ *Mechouar.*

Sunna Mosque. Rabat's most important mosque was built in the 1960s, but because it was designed in a traditional Maghrebi style, it was sheltered from the architectural anarchy of the time and remains beautiful and dignified today. In their day the French wanted to extend Avenue Mohammed V through this site, but the Moroccans resisted, and thanks to the martyrs of that confrontation, the mosque stands here on the site of an earlier one. Non-Muslims may not enter. ✉ *At the top of Ave. Mohamed V, Centre Ville.*

WHERE TO EAT

$ MOROCCAN 🍴 **Dar Naji.** This authentically Moroccan restaurant is a trusted eatery among locals and offers visitors a truly medina-esque vibe. Prices are always low here, but the attention to the quality of the salads, tagines, and couscous dishes is unrelenting. [$] *Average main: 60DH* ✉ *Bab Al Had, rue Jazirat Al Arab, Medina* ☎ *0661/33–19–43* 💳 *No credit cards.*

$$$$ MOROCCAN 🍴 **Dinarjat.** This palatial restaurant offers guests traditional Moroccan meals, although the beautiful ambience of its setting in a medina house is its crowning glory. Live Andalusian music creates a charming background. Start your à la carte meal with a spread of Moroccan salads, and then savor classic dishes like tagines or couscous. You can get here from boulevard Laalou, not far from the Kasbah des Oudayas; in the evening a man stands at the nearest entrance to the medina with a lantern, ready to guide you to the restaurant. [$] *Average main: 250DH* ✉ *6, rue Belgnaoui, Medina* ☎ *0537/70–42–39* 🌐 *www.dinarjat.com.*

$$ ITALIAN 🍴 **La Mamma.** Rabat's original Italian restaurant is still the city's firm favorite. Pastas, pizzas, and grilled meats are excellent here, as are the pitchers of sangria. From the central brick oven to the garlands of garlic hanging from the rafters, the atmosphere is homey Italian kitchen. Though the place is always bustling, service is fast. [$] *Average main: 100DH* ✉ *6, Zankat Tanta, Centre Ville* ☎ *0537/70–73–29.*

$$$$ FRENCH 🍴 **Le Goéland.** Located near the flower market on Place Petri, Le Goéland is an elegant restaurant specializing in fresh fish with a warm yet dignified atmosphere. The French cuisine and the service are excellent, although the prices are a little higher than many other places in Rabat. The catch of the day is showcased on ice near the entrance and the meats are well prepared. Try the huge and elegantly presented turbot encrusted in salt, and for dessert a delicious café *liégeois* (iced coffee with ice cream and whipped cream). [$] *Average main: 280DH* ✉ *9, rue Moulay Ali Cherif, Hassan* ☎ *0537/76–88–85* 🕒 *Closed Sun.*

$$$$ BRASSERIE Fodor's Choice ★ 🍴 **Le Grand Comptoir.** Seemingly straight out of the 1930s, Le Grand Comptoir is a quintessential Parisian brasserie offering classic French food alongside a good wine list. The restaurant prides itself on using fresh and local ingredients, although it also stays faithful to the French culinary traditions it emulates. It's also the go-to place for a cocktail and for live music; DJs and bands play on Thursday, Friday, and Saturday nights. [$] *Average main: 300DH* ✉ *279, av. Mohamed V, Centre Ville* ☎ *0537/20–15–14.*

$$$ MOROCCAN 🍴 **Le Petit Beur.** If you're looking for genuine local food, you'll appreciate Le Petit Beur, aka Dar Tagine, which has it all: couscous, brochettes, tagines, and *harira* (bean-based soup with vegetables and meat). The pretty tiled walls and painted ceilings give you the impression of dining in richer surroundings than the moderate prices and casual mood suggest. In true Moroccan spirit, it can get a bit noisy. [$] *Average main: 150DH* ✉ *8, rue Dumas, Centre Ville* ☎ *0537/73–13–22.*

$$$$ JAPANESE 🍴 **Matsuri.** This Japanese restaurant chain has restaurants in several Moroccan cities and serves good quality food. The selection of fish, though limited, is always very fresh, and the staff are helpful. You can get quick service if you are in a hurry. Alcohol is available. [$] *Average main: 220DH* ✉ *155, av. Mohamed VI, rte. de Zaers, Souissi* ☎ *0537/75–75–72.*

$$$ FRENCH 🍴 **Paul.** Café, bakery, and distinguished French restaurant all rolled into one, Paul is one of Agdal's most popular spots. In the evening there is a variety of fish, game, meat dishes, and some good salads. The *salade fraicheur* (fresh salad) is fantastic, while fish lovers will enjoy the *espadon* (swordfish) and *rouget grillé* (grilled red snapper). The filet de boeuf is also very popular. Desserts abound, with the *tarte fine aux pommes* (apple tart) and crème brûlée highlighting the menu. During the day, you can lunch on delicious quiches, sandwiches, and crêpes. The kitchen stays open late, and the menu changes seasonally. The bakery is a standout in its own right, and makes what may be the best fresh-baked bread in town. [$] *Average main: 150DH* ✉ *82, av. Nations Unies, Agdal* ☎ *0537/67–20–00* 🌐 *www.paul.fr.*

$$$$ MEDITERRANEAN 🍴 **Picolo's.** This friendly restaurant serves Mediterranean cuisine in a charming setting with warm service. It offers a broad selection of fish, meat, and pasta dishes. The *brochettes de poisson* (fish kebabs) are worth a try, as is the 100% homemade goat cheese ravioli, which is utterly delicious. The restaurant has a beautiful airy garden and intimate tables amid the greenery. [$] *Average main: 250DH* ✉ *149, rte. des Zaers, Souissi* ☎ *0537/63–69–69.*

$$$$ FRENCH 🍴 **Restaurant Cosmopolitan.** Set in an exquisite Art Deco villa, this exceptionally refined French place specializes in fine cuisine. It has a swish yet sunny garden patio; inside the dining rooms stretch out with French poise. If you want to do it properly, you'll go for the *escargots en fazzoletti* (snails) followed by the filet de boeuf, although there are some great fish choices too. You don't want to miss trying a rum baba with Chantilly cream for dessert. The wine list is excellent and service is immaculate. [$] *Average main: 180DH* ✉ *Av. Ibn Toumart, Centre Ville* ☎ *0537/20–00–28.*

$$$
SEAFOOD
✕**Restaurant de la Plage–La Table des Gourmets.** Located near the kasbah and overlooking the river, you couldn't ask for a more glorious spot. The menu's almost as good as the view; the John Dory with mushroom cream sauce and Spanish-style dorado are particularly sought-after. The dessert menu features a truly depraved fondant au chocolat as well as a practically perfect lemon tart. $ *Average main: 160DH* ⊠ *Plage des Oudayas, Medina* ☎ *0537/20–29–28.*

$
MOROCCAN
✕**Tajine wa Tanjia.** This is the place to discover a national delicacy, the *tanjia* (a type of casserole cooked in a large earthen jar), along with other Moroccan dishes. It's authentic and friendly, with very reasonable prices. $ *Average main: 70DH* ⊠ *9, rue Baghdad, Hassan* ☎ *0537/72–97–97* ▭ *No credit cards.*

$$
FRENCH
Fodor'sChoice
★
✕**T'y Potes.** An enchanting restaurant set among verdant and shady gardens, T'y Potes offers a menu that strives to encapsulate Brittany, France, so think luscious salads and buckwheat crêpes oozing with any ingredients you can imagine, as long as they're (mostly) French. You can also try tartines—another Brittany specialty—open-faced sandwiches with fancy spreads. Try the heavenly goat cheese salad to start and then get into the spirit with the *tartiflette galette,* a French dish of potatoes, onions, and cheese cooked into a round crust. Finish with what's possibly the earth's most delicious crêpe—apple in salty caramel with vanilla ice cream. The experience is made even better by the fantastic service and the pleasant and knowledgeable staff. Alcohol is served. $ *Average main: 80DH* ⊠ *11, rue Ghafsa, Hassan* ☎ *0537/70–79–65* ⊕ *www.typotes.com* ☽ *No lunch Mon.; no dinner Sun.–Wed.*

WHERE TO STAY

$
HOTEL
Ibis Moussafir. The Ibis Moussafir is adjacent to the Rabat-Agdal train station—that is, the first station you come to from Casablanca. **Pros:** wonderfully comfortable; good breakfast; near business district. **Cons:** views are not impressive. $ *Rooms from: 646DH* ⊠ *32, rue Abderrahmane el Ghafiki, Agdal* ☎ *0530/20–03–93* ⊕ *www.ibis.com/gb/hotel-2036-ibis-rabat/index.shtml* ⤳ *95 rooms, 4 suites* ⦿ *Breakfast.*

$$
HOTEL
La Tour Hassan. If you want a luxury hotel that reflects classic Moroccan architecture, the Tour Hassan is ideal. **Pros:** located in city center; authentic décor. **Cons:** rooms in north wing are near a nightclub and can be loud. $ *Rooms from: 1220DH* ⊠ *26, rue Chellah, Hassan* ☎ *0537/23–90–00* ⊕ *www.latourhassan.com* ⤳ *122 rooms, 18 suites* ⦿ *Breakfast.*

$$
HOTEL
Le Diwan Rabat. Built on a busy intersection, this luxury hotel, part of the MGallery-Accor chain, is remarkably quiet inside. **Pros:** beautiful facility; free guarded parking lot. **Cons:** rates are high for the area. $ *Rooms from: 1100DH* ⊠ *Pl. de l'Unité Africaine, Hassan* ☎ *0537/26–27–27* ⊕ *www.accorhotels.com/gb/hotel-2820-le-diwan-rabat-mgallery-collection/index.shtml* ⤳ *88 rooms, 6 suites* ⦿ *No meals.*

$$
HOTEL
Riad Azhara. This exceptionally original riad has only four rooms and suites spread over an enormous and incredibly stylish space. **Pros:** great décor; intimate. **Cons:** parts of the terrace don't have barriers, so children should be supervised at all times. $ *Rooms from: 970DH* ⊠ *11,*

Rabat's Kasbah des Oudayas is visible behind fishing boats overturned on the banks of the Oued Bou Regreg.

rue Skaia Belmekki, Medina ☎ *0537/20–20–28* ⊕ *www.riadazahra.com* ☞ *3 suites, 1 room* ¶Ol *Breakfast.*

$$
HOTEL
Fodor's Choice
★

🏨 **Riad Kalaa.** This 17th-century traditional medina house is built around a courtyard, with a fantastic terrace and views of Rabat's rooftops, making it one of the most beautiful riads in town. **Pros:** very idyllic; comfort in supreme style. **Cons:** difficult to find, although the riad will send someone to meet you on request. $ *Rooms from: 1180DH* ⊠ *3–5, rue Zebdi, Medina* ☎ *0537/20–20–28* ⊕ *www.riadkalaa.com* ☞ *5 rooms, 10 suites* ¶Ol *Breakfast.*

$
B&B/INN

🏨 **Riad Marhaba.** This comfy and well-furnished riad has a welcoming atmosphere with a room and suites that retain their authentic features. **Pros:** friendly and comfortable. **Cons:** a little tricky to find, although locals will help you out. $ *Rooms from: 600DH* ⊠ *Rue Açam, Medina* ☎ *0654/12–60–42* ☞ *4 suites, 1 room* ▭ *No credit cards* ¶Ol *Breakfast.*

$$$$
HOTEL

🏨 **Sofitel Rabat Jardin des Roses.** This luxury hotel subtly combines modernity with traditional Moroccan handicrafts. **Pros:** a true luxury five-star hotel; beautiful grounds. **Cons:** expensive. $ *Rooms from: 2080DH* ⊠ *Quartier Aviation, Souissi* ☎ *0537/67–56–56* ⊕ *www. sofitel.com* ☞ *202 rooms, 27 suites* ¶Ol *Multiple meal plans.*

$$$$
HOTEL
Fodor's Choice
★

🏨 **Villa Mandarine.** This quite spectacular villa in the residential neighborhood between Agdal and the Royal Palace offers all you need to be truly at ease: smart hosts, savvy fellow guests, and outstanding French and Moroccan cuisine with a contemporary slant. **Pros:** romantic setting; relaxing hammam. **Cons:** no public transportation. $ *Rooms from: 2100DH* ⊠ *19, rue Ouled Bou, Souissi* ☎ *0537/75–20–77* ⊕ *www.villamandarine.com* ☞ *31 rooms, 5 suites* ¶Ol *Breakfast.*

NIGHTLIFE

BARS AND CLUBS

5th Avenue. Rabat's Manhattan disco scene takes place here, complete with wanna-be models waiting to be discovered and DJs spinning all kinds of tunes. ✉ *4, rue Bin Alaouidan, Agdal* ☎ *0537/77–52–54.*

Amnesia. Rabat's original nightclub has been going strong for over 25 years and still pulls in crowds, with weekends getting especially wild. The massive building can hold over a thousand clubbers, while the mostly house and R&B music blasts. Be aware that the drinks aren't cheap here and the entry price is always changing—sometimes bouncers do let you in for free, though. ✉ *18, rue Monastire, Medina* ☎ *0612/99–11–90.*

Cabane Bambou. This club is a fantastic place to enjoy some quality music and African rhythms. It's open late and gets pretty busy since there's no cover charge. ■ TIP→ **Women might feel more comfortable if accompanied by a man.** ✉ *6, rue de Tindouf, Hassan* ☎ *0537/26–28–61.*

Fodor'sChoice
★
Le Bistrot du Pietri. Inside the Pietri Urban Hotel is Rabat's most popular jazz restaurant, which invites superb musicians to play every Tuesday, Friday, and Saturday night. Expect anything from bebop and Latin to jazz fusion. The food is excellent too, with the menu embodying a good deal of Mediterranean taste with a little inventiveness from the chef. ✉ *4, rue Tobrouk* ☎ *0537/70–78–20* ⊕ *www.lepietri.com.*

Le Dhow. For a fun drinking experience climb aboard the Dhow, which is actually a boat on the Bou Regreg River. There are three different decks where you can eat, drink, and people-watch. There is, naturally, a distinct nautical theme. At night, the nearby Oudayas Kasbah illuminates the twinkling lights of the walled medina across the street. ✉ *Quai de Bou Regreg, av. Al Marsa, Medina* ☎ *0537/70–23–02* ⊕ *www.ledhow.com.*

Upstairs Bar. This is one of the hottest places to be at night for both upscale Rabatis and the expat crowd. ✉ *8, av. Michliffen, Agdal* ☎ *0537/67–41–11.*

SHOPPING

In addition to finding traditional Moroccan furniture, clothing, artwork, and other locally made crafts, Rabat, like other major Moroccan cities, is becoming more and more European in terms of shopping options and access to clothing and other imported products. The Agdal neighborhood has a high concentration of furniture and antiques stores, while the lower part of **avenue Mohammed V** is a good place to buy traditional Moroccan clothing.

ANTIQUES

Arabesques. This shop carries beautiful carved-wood furnishings, leather-covered chests, iron-frame mirrors, painted screens, and countless other decorative items. There are new pieces as well as some older treasures to be found. Prices may be a bit higher than in the souks, but you'll get less hassle from the shopkeepers. ✉ *61, rue Fal Ould Oumeir, Agdal* ☎ *537/68–02–55.*

CRAFTS

Coté Maisons. Brimming with the most beautiful of decorative items, Coté Maisons is an excellent source for classy souvenirs. From delicate Moroccan teapots to fabulously stylish hand-of-Fatima pouches (with the signature Moroccan tassel), it's impossible to leave with your hands empty. Local artisans' collections are regularly highlighted. ✉ *23, rue Dayet Ifrah, Agdal* ☎ *0537/77–70–66* ☉ *Closed Sun.*

Ensemble Artisanal. Near the River Bou Regreg is a series of small workshops where you can see artisans create Morocco's various handicrafts: everything from traditional mosaic tilework, embroidery, leatherwork, traditional shoes, and painted wood to brass, pottery, and carpets. You can buy the items at fixed prices, which are a little higher than well-negotiated prices in nearby Rue des Consuls but which save you the trouble of bargaining. ✉ *6, Tarik el Marsa, Espace les Oudayas, Medina* ☎ *0537/73–05–07* 💲 *Free.*

Rue des Consuls. The medina's Rue des Consuls is the place to shop for handicrafts and souvenirs in Rabat: it's pedestrian-only, has a pleasant atmosphere, and imposes no real pressure to buy, aside from the typical encouragements. Here you can find carpets, Berber jewelry, leather goods, wooden items, brass work, traditional clothing, and slippers, among other treasures. You can peruse Zemour carpets (striped in white and burgundy) from Khémisset, near Meknès; deep-pile Rabati carpets, in predominantly blue-and-white designs; and orange, black, and white Glaoui rugs. Some of the larger shops take credit cards. ■TIP➔ **Try to visit rue des Consuls on a Monday or Thursday morning when the entire street turns into a carpet market.** ✉ *Medina.*

HAMMAMS

La Tour Hassan Hammam. Built in 1914 next to the famous unfinished tower of the Moorish Hassan Mosque, this elegant yet affordable hotel spa offers a hammam, massage, sauna, Jacuzzi, and beauty treatments. ✉ *26, rue Chellah, Hassan* ☎ *0537/70–42–01* 💲 *250 DH* ☉ *By appointment.*

SHOPPING CENTERS AND MALLS

Mega Mall. If you want a rather non-Moroccan experience, or are just in the mood for some hassle-free shopping, Rabat's MegaMall will do the trick. Following the design of a typical American mall, it has over 80 moderate to high-end local and European stores, a food court, bowling alley, and ice-skating rink. ✉ *Km 4.2, av. Mohammed VI, Souissi* ☎ *0537/75–75–75* ⊕ *www.megamall.ma.*

SPORTS AND THE OUTDOORS

GOLF

Fodor'sChoice
★
Royal Golf Dar es Salam. The most famous golf course in Morocco is on the road toward Romani, at the far edge of Souissi on the right. Designed by Robert Trent Jones, it's considered one of the 50 best courses in the world. There are two 18-hole courses and one 9-hole

course in 162 verdant acres. ✉ *Km 9, av. Mohammed VI–Rte.des Zaers, Souissi* ☎ *0537/75–58–64* ⊕ *www.royalgolfdaressalam.com.*

AROUND RABAT

SKHIRAT BEACH

20 km (12 miles) southwest of Rabat.

Southwest of Rabat, towards Casablanca, is the lovely Skhirat Beach. Since it's close to the capital, Skhirat is perfect for either an afternoon at the beach or a weekend away. Home of the luxurious L'Amphitrite Palace Hotel, it's also the site of the 1971 attempt to assassinate the former King Hassan II during his birthday gala at the Royal Palace of Skhirat.

GETTING HERE AND AROUND

While it's easiest to go by car to Skhirat, you can also take the train from Rabat Ville station to Bouznika station. From there, take a taxi to the Plage Bouznika (5 DH). Grands taxis also go from Rabat to Skhirat (9 DH).

EXPLORING

Dar Es-Soltane Cave (*Les Grôttes de Harhoura*). On the other side of the coastal road, roughly level with Contrabandiers but under some white, Spanish-style apartments, is a cave with iron railings in front of it. There's no sign to identify the cave, and you can't go inside, but this site, known as El Harhoura or the Dar Es-Soltane caves, is one of the earliest known sites of human habitation. Casts of the pre-historic human skeletons found here are on display in Rabat's archaeological museum. ✉ *Av. Moustapha Assayeh, Temara, Rabat.*

Contrabandiers Beach. Temara Plage is connected to the next beach, Contrabandiers, which is longer and has finer sand, by a walkway across the rocks. It's a pretty bay that draws in throngs of sunbathers, swimmers, and surfers in summer. As is always the case on this coastline, currents can be extremely dangerous, so make sure you're a strong swimmer if you attempt to swim. Locals will rent you a beach umbrella, and there are usually several vendors who walk up and down the coast selling ice cream and other snacks. **Amenities:** food and drink. **Best for:** surfing; swimming; walking. ✉ *Skhirat.*

Skhirat Plage. To say that Skhirat Plage is loved by Moroccans during the summer months is quite the understatement. It's graced by a long stretch of fine, golden sand, perfect for strolls year-round. Like many of the Northern Atlantic beaches, this is a surfing spot, as the plethora of boards reveals. Swimmers love it too, but beware of dangerous currents; lifeguards are not always present. The beach lies just beyond the Royal Palace of Skhirat. **Amenities:** food and drink. **Best for:** surfing; swimming; walking. ✉ *Skhirat.*

FAMILY **Temara Plage.** A small yet pretty bay beach, Temara Plage is rather empty during colder months, but very much the opposite in summer. The sand here is golden and fine, and there's a bank of rocks for those into rockpooling. The beach can be reached by car from the R322 from

Rabat, or from the highway. Otherwise, take the train from Rabat and get off at Temara station; the beach is a short walk away. **Amenities:** lifeguards (during summer); food and drink. **Best for:** sunsets; swimming; walking. ⊠ *Rabat.*

WHERE TO STAY

$$$$ 🛏 **L'Amphitrite Palace.** This luxury hotel is a palace on a splendid beach
HOTEL   where you can watch surfers, chat with fishermen, and soak in the crashing Atlantic. **Pros:** modern building; fresh décor; beautiful beach. **Cons:** very expensive. Ⓢ *Rooms from: 2300DH* ⊠ *Skhirat Plage, Skhirat* ☎ *0537/62–10–00* ⊕ *www.lamphitrite.com* ⤳ *178 rooms, 14 suites* �’◎❘ *Breakfast.*

OUED-CHERRAT

36 km (22 miles) from Rabat.

Oued Cherrat is a small beach area with superb ocean views and excellent surf conditions. Once a wild and relatively unfrequented stretch of sand, it's now a lot more popular and development is truly underway, although it's still less crowded than other North Atlantic beaches during the summer months.

GETTING HERE AND AROUND

Coming by car, take the highway from Rabat towards Casablanca, taking the Bouznika exit and then the coastal road towards Oued Cherrat. You can also take a train from Rabat Ville station; they leave each hour, on the hour, to Bouznika station. From there, taxis to the Plage Oued Cherrat are around 7 DH. Grands taxis also go from Rabat to Bouznika (15 DH).

EXPLORING

Bouznika Bay. This bay is one of the prettiest in the region and much loved by both Rabat and Casablanca locals. For this reason, it gets very crowded in the summer, when everyone hits the golden sands and surfers stream into the waves. It's a lovely place out of season too—perfect for picnicking and rockpooling (exploring the tide pools). **Amenities:** food and drink; lifeguards; parking (5 DH–10 DH). **Best for:** surfing; swimming; walking. ⊠ *Plage de Bouznika, Rabat.*

WHERE TO EAT

$$$$ ✕ **Eden Wed Food and Beach Club.** This excellent place to eat, drink, and
SEAFOOD   disconnect serves fresh food that's mostly fish based, with juicy salads and proper desserts thrown in. The location is fabulous—right on the beach, with areas for eating and relaxing separated by rustic bamboo canes. There's a beach volleyball area and petanque ground, too. The atmosphere is gentle; families, surfers, sporty types, and sun lovers will all be at home here. It also serves alcohol. Note that while it's officially only open from April to November, groups can (and often do) reserve off-season. Ⓢ *Average main: 180DH* ⊠ *Résidence Eden Island, rte. Cotière de Rabat, Oued-Cherrat* ☎ *0661/29–69–38* ⊘ *Closed Dec.–Mar.*

SPORTS AND THE OUTDOORS

FAMILY **Blue Surf School.** Right on the Oued Cherrat Beach, this club offers water-sports activities and lessons, from surfing and paddleboarding to beach volleyball and canoeing, as well as yoga and percussion classes. You can also rent equipment to do any of the above if you already know what you're doing. ⊠ *Résidence Eden Island, Oued-Cherrat* ☎ *0651/22–60–36.*

SALÉ

37 km (23 miles) southwest of Kenitra, 13 km (8 miles) northeast of Rabat across river.

Morocco's second-most-populated city, Salé, was probably founded around the 11th century. In medieval times it was the most important trading harbor on the Atlantic coast, and at the beginning of the 17th century it joined Rabat in welcoming Muslims expelled from Spain. Rabat and Salé were rival towns for more than 100 years following this, but Rabat eventually gained the upper hand. Today Salé is rather shabby, but still an important cradle of Moroccan history. The medina is worth the journey both for its monuments and its genuine authenticity. Expect to see more people in traditional dress or practicing traditional crafts than you would in most other Moroccan large-city medinas.

GETTING HERE AND AROUND

The Rabat–Salé tramway provides the ideal option for traveling between the two cities, costing just 6 DH per ride. Buses and taxis are also options.

TIMING AND PRECAUTIONS

Most travelers visit Salé just for the day. Salé is a relatively safe city, with very little harassment. If you feel threatened, do not hesitate to summon police.

EXPLORING

Salé's most interesting sights are located in and around the medina. A good place to start a tour of Salé is at the entrance to the medina, near the Great Mosque, which you can access from the road along the southwest city wall. Don't worry if you lose track of where you are in the medina; many a shop will distract you, but you're never far from an entrance gate.

Abou el Hassan Merenid Medersa. Turn left around the corner of the Great Mosque, and you'll see on your right the Abou el Hassan Medersa, built by the Merenid sultan of that name in the 14th century and a fine example of the traditional Koranic school. Like the Bou Inania in Fez or the Ali ben Youssef in Marrakesh, this medersa has beautiful intricate plasterwork around its central courtyard, and a fine *mihrab* (prayer niche) with a ceiling carved in an interlocking geometrical pattern representing the cosmos. Upstairs, on the second and third floors, you can visit the little cells where the students used to sleep, and from the roof you can see the entire city. ⊠ *Rue Ash al Shaiara* 🖼 *10 DH* ☉ *Daily 10–1 and 3–6.*

Battlements and Fortresses of Salé. A heavily fortified town for many centuries, Salé still has many traces of this eventful history preserved within its old medina walls. Many landmarks in the area have been named as national heritage sites or monuments. **Borj Bab Sebta** is an 11th-century, square-shape fortress situated at the Sebta gate into the old medina. **Borj Adoumoue,** also called the Old Sqala, is an 18th-century bastion, where cannons gaze over the waters to this day. **Borj Roukni,** also called Borj Kbira, or the large fortress, is a semicircular, 19th-century edifice built to counter attacks by the French. **Borj al-Mellah** is at the entrance to the old Jewish quarter. There's also a fantastic kasbah (although in need of preservation) known as the **Gnawa Kasbah,** built by Moulay Ismail in the 1700s. ✉ *Medina.*

Fodor's Choice ★ **Complexe des Potiers.** Salé is well known throughout the country, and beyond, for its local pottery design and tradition. This pottery complex (just off the road toward Fez, to the right after the river from Rabat) is a whole series of pottery stores, each with its own style. Other crafts have been added, notably bamboo and straw work and mosaic-tile furnishings. The shops inside the large central building carry a variety of handicrafts at rather high prices. There is often the chance to chat with a potter and maybe even try your own hand at the craft. ✉ *Oulja, rte. Ain Houalla.*

Djemâa Kabir (*Great Mosque*). A few steps from the Sidi Abdellah ben Hassoun tomb is the great mosque known as Djemâa Kabir, a beautiful 12th-century mosque built by the Almohad dynasty. It's also the third-largest mosque in Morocco after the Hassan II in Casablanca and the Kairaouine in Fez. Non-Muslims cannot enter.

Sidi Abdellah ben Hassoun Tomb. One of the streets in Salé's medina is Zanqat Sidi Abdellah ben Hassoun—named after the town's patron saint. His magnificent tomb is situated here. He died in Salé in 1604. ✉ *Zanqat Sidi Abdellah ben Hassoun.*

Zaouia Tijania. Just before the tomb of Sidi Abdellah ben Hassoun is the *zaouia* (an Islamic school) of the Tijani order, a mystical Sufi Islamic sect founded by Shaykh Ahmad al-Tijani (1739–1815).

WHERE TO EAT AND STAY

$$$$ MEDITERRANEAN 🍴 **Al Marsa.** When Salé's marina was built, it brought with it a couple of swanky restaurants including Al Marsa—meaning "port" in Arabic—which serves Spanish food in a glass-encased building brimming with white-cloth tables overlooking the river Bou Regreg. The owners are also fishmongers, so you can be sure that any seafood sold is entirely fresh. The *suprême de Saint-Pierre* (John Dory) in lemon butter is quite sublime while the vermicelli paella is no less than festive. On the sweet-side, don't miss the *tocino de cielo,* a thick heavenly custard dripping in caramel. If Spanish cuisine isn't your thing, Al Marsa has a sister restaurant right next door, also called Al Marsa, serving Italian dishes. [$] *Average main: 220DH* ✉ *Port de Plaisance, Marina de Bou Regreg* ☎ *0537/84–58–18* 🌐 *www.almarsarestaurants.ma.*

$ **The Repose.** This outstanding riad is a veritable sanctuary set over
HOTEL three floors and run by a lovely Anglo-Moroccan couple. **Pros:** excep-
FAMILY tional food; restful environment; conscientious staff. **Cons:** can be
Fodor's Choice hard to find. $ *Rooms from: 600DH* ✉ *17, Zankat Talaâ, Ras Chejra,*
★ *Medina* ☎ *0537/88–29–58* ⊕ *www.therepose.com* ⬅ *1 room, 3 suites*
⦿ *Multiple meal plans.*

SHOPPING
Souk Laghzal. A couple of times a week, usually Tuesday and Thursday,
a local auction is held in the wool market square. This is a quirky event
where a crowd sits in a circle around the auctioneer, who sells off some
unpredictable items that might include an old kaftan, a plastic chandelier, or a beautiful pottery piece—you never can guess. Just before this
area is a type of clothing rummage sale where heaps of garments are
sold at very low prices. As the square's name would suggest, this is also
a wool area; you can buy dyed wool on one side of the square and wool
products (carpets and the like) on the other. ✉ *Medina.*

SIDI-BOUKNADEL

18 km (11 miles) northeast of Rabat.

Sidi-Bouknadel (also known as Bouknadel) isn't accessible from the
autoroute, but its attractions lie to the north, halfway between Kenitra
and Rabat, and are accessible via the coastal road from either of the
two.

GETTING HERE AND AROUND
Taxis run regularly from Salé to Sidi-Bouknadel in summer. If travel-
ing from Rabat by bus, board Bus No. 13 at avenue Moulay Hassan in
Rabat. You can take the same bus back to Rabat from Sidi-Bouknadel.
Taxis can be chartered to and from Rabat, Salé, and Kenitra through-
out the year.

TIMING AND PRECAUTIONS
Most travelers visit Sidi-Bouknadel for the day en route to Rabat or on
their way north. Sidi-Bouknadel is generally safe, with minimal has-
sling of visitors. The beach, however, is rather secluded after sundown,
so caution is advised for those desiring an evening walk on the shore.

EXPLORING
Belghazi Museum. In 1991 an entrepreneurial craftsman named Abdelila
Belghazi was contracted to carve cedar decorations for the huge sliding
domes on the Prophet's Mosque in Medina, Saudi Arabia. Thanks to
this windfall, he established a workshop in this building in Bouknadel
and founded the Belghazi Museum to exhibit his collection of traditional Moroccan art. Patronized (that is, publicly supported) by Princess
Lalla Meriam, it is the first private museum in the country and houses
a far larger collection than any state museum. On display are pottery,
wood carvings, embroidery, manuscripts, musical instruments, agricultural tools, and weapons. One interesting room is full of Moroccan
Jewish art, such as wedding clothes and temple furnishings. ✉ *Km 17,
rte. de Kenitra* ☎ *0537/82–21–78* ⊕ *www.museumbelghazi.com* 🎟 *50
DH* ⊗ *Daily 9–6.*

FAMILY   **Jardins Exotiques** (*Exotic Gardens*). South of Sidi Bouknadel are the extraordinary Jardins Exotiques, created in the mid-20th century by a Frenchman named François, who used to play classical music to his plants. The gardens were originally planned to represent different regions, such as Polynesia, China, and Japan. They're a haven for birds and frogs, and the profusion of walkways and bridges makes them a wonderful playground for children. Since François's death, the gardens have been maintained by the government and a touching poem by François about his life forms an epitaph at the entrance. ☎ *0537/82–27–56* ⊕ *www.jardinsexotiques.com* ✉ *5 DH* ⊙ *Daily 9–6:30.*

Plage des Nations. This magnificent beach is so long that even during the busiest times you'll find some space along the stretch. The water is swimmable, but there may be strong currents, so caution should be observed. The sands are cleaned daily in summer, although some litter is possible in colder months. It's a hot spot for surfers and paragliders; sunbathers can rent a parasol from a local for reasonable prices. The beach is accessed by driving along the Route de Kinetra from Salé or by taking Bus No. 9 from Bab Khemiss in Salé. **Amenities:** food and drink; lifeguards. **Best for:** surfing; swimming; walking.

MEHDIYA PLAGE

40 km (25 miles) northeast of Rabat.

If you are traveling by car along the coast north of Rabat (toward Moulay Bousselham) and are in the mood for a beach stroll, Mehdiya Plage, which is about 11 km (7 miles) west of Kenitra, will do the trick. Its long, sandy beach is known for good surfing as well as swimming, although the strong undertow along Morocco's Atlantic coast is widely feared and respected. There's a great daily fish market where prawns are among the fresh (and inexpensive) treats on offer, and a handful of beachside cafés.

GETTING HERE AND AROUND

You can take a shuttle train (every 30 minutes) from Rabat to Kenitra, but to reach Mehdiya Plage you must still drive or take a taxi from there. Mehdiya Plage is really best seen as a brief stopover when you are driving north from Rabat.

EXPLORING

Lake Sidi Bourhaba. Slightly inland from Mehdiya is the lovely freshwater Lake Sidi Bourhaba, internationally famous for the number and variety of birds that pass through on their way to the south side of the Sahara desert. Ornithologists flock here nearly as eagerly as the itinerant birds themselves, looking especially for the rare marbled teal along with another 200 species. ✉ *Kenitra.*

MOULAY BOUSSELHAM

46 km (29 miles) southwest of Larache, 82 km (51 miles) northeast of Kenitra, 150 km (93 miles) northeast of Rabat.

The laid-back fishing village of Moulay Bousselham is very popular with Moroccans in summer, but is all but empty in cooler weather. It's made up of little more than a single street with a smattering of cafés and souvenir shops. Moulay Bousselham's lagoon and beach are breathtaking. Its sandbar is somewhat dangerous for swimmers due to a rapid drop-off that causes a continual crash of breaking waves. However, this is one of northern Morocco's prime bird-watching locations, with boat trips organized to see thousands of birds—herons, pink flamingos, sheldrakes, and gannets. The best time for watching birds is just after dawn. The whole area is considered a wetland and thought to be protected by the Ramsar Convention (an international treaty working for the conservation of wetlands) and the village's two patron saints.

GETTING HERE AND AROUND

Moulay Bousselham has a train station with daily service from Larache and Rabat. There are frequent buses and taxis to Moulay Bousselham from Souk el-Arba du Rharb, which is accessible from Rabat and Larache by grand taxi.

TIMING AND PRECAUTIONS

Most travelers stay in Moulay Bousselham for a couple of nights. Moulay Bousselham is generally considered safe, with most annoyances stemming from vendors hawking their wares. The village becomes desolate after sundown, so it's wise to take the usual precautions.

ESSENTIALS

Visitor Information Mansouri el Boukhary Tourism Association ☎ *0663/09–37–94.*

EXPLORING

Merdja Zerga (*Blue Lagoon*). Moulay Bousselham is at the head of Merdja Zerga (the Blue Lagoon), which gives its name to the 17,000-acre national park that contains it. This is a major stopover for countless birds migrating from Norway, Sweden, and the United Kingdom to Africa: the birds fly south at the end of summer and stop at Merdja Zerga in September, October, and November before continuing on to West Africa and even as far as South Africa. They stop off again on their way back to Europe in spring, so spring and fall are the best times for bird-watching. The pink flamingoes on their way to and from Mauritania are particularly spectacular.

Moulay Bousselham's Tomb. A the foot of the village, near the sea, you'll find the tomb of Moulay Bousselham. Like Sidi Abdel Jalil's tomb, it is a white building capped with a dome; Sidi Abdel Jalil's tomb, however, is somewhat smaller.

WHERE TO STAY

$
B&B/INN
Hôtel Le Lagon. With panoramic views over the inland lagoon and the Atlantic as well, this comfortable hotel has breezy rooms and a spacious terrace for breakfast or evening meals. **Pros:** good views; affordable. **Cons:** poor access to public transportation. $ *Rooms from: 300DH* ⌧ *Le Lagon, Front de Mer* ☎ *0537/43–26–50* 🛏 *30 rooms* ▬ *No credit cards* ⦿*Breakfast.*

$
B&B/INN
La Maison des Oiseaux. This sweet yet fading B&B has a beautiful garden. **Pros:** friendly atmosphere; very genuine. **Cons:** difficult to find;

can't be booked online. $ *Rooms from: 350DH* ☎ *0537/43–25–43* ⇗ *8 rooms (6 with bath)* ⊟ *No credit cards* ⦿❘ *Breakfast.*

CASABLANCA

91 km (57 miles) southwest of Rabat.

Casablanca is Morocco's most modern city, and various groups of people call it home: hardworking Berbers who came north from the Souss Valley to make their fortune; older folks raised on French customs during the protectorate; devoted Muslims; wealthy business executives in the prestigious neighborhoods of California and Anfa; new and poor arrivals from the countryside, living in conspicuous shantytowns; and thousands of others from all over the kingdom who have found jobs here. There is also a fair-size expat population, including many French people. The city has its own stock exchange, and working hours tend to transcend the relaxed pace kept by the rest of Morocco.

True to its name—*casa blanca* in Spanish (white house), which, in turn, is Dar el-Beida in Arabic—Casablanca is a conglomeration of white buildings. The present city, known colloquially as "Casa" or "El Beida," was only founded in 1912. It lacks the abundance of ancient monuments that resonate in Morocco's other major cities; however, there are still some landmarks, including the famous Hassan II Mosque.

GETTING HERE AND AROUND

AIR TRAVEL

From overseas, Casablanca's Mohammed V Airport is the best gateway to Morocco itself: you'll find a well-maintained arrivals hall, relatively efficient and courteous staffers, and a not-so-complicated continuation of your journey by train or car. Trains connect the airport to the national network from 7:35 am to 10:30 pm, and taxis are available to the city of Casablanca at relatively expensive but fixed rates (250 DH–300 DH).

BUS TRAVEL

Buses are fine for short trips, such as from Casablanca to El Jadida or Safi, but trips longer than a couple of hours can be interminable, hot, and dusty. Inquire at the station for schedule and fare information. In Casablanca the Compagnie de Transports au Maroc (CTM) bus station is by far the most convenient, since the other stations are on the outskirts of town.

Contacts CTM Casablanca ✉ *23, rue Léon l'Africain, Centre Ville* ☎ *0522/54–10–10* ⊕ *www.ctm.co.ma.*

CAR TRAVEL

You may not want a car if you are staying in Casablanca, as driving here is almost a hazardous sport, but it is possible to rent one if you are planning to explore the country. Others may prefer moving onto their next destination, such as Fez or Marrakesh, before renting a car.

Rental Cars Avis ✉ *19, av. des Forces Armées Royales, Centre Ville* ☎ *0522/31–24–24* ⊕ *www.avis.com.*

CLOSE UP

The Legend of the Blue Lagoon

The legend of the Blue Lagoon and Moulay Bousselham dates from the 10th century, when the saint Saïd ben Saïd immigrated to the Maghreb from Egypt, following a revelation instructing him to pray where the sun sets over the ocean. He had a disciple called Sidi Abdel Jalil who, legend tells, saw Saïd ben Saïd fishing one day with a hook and asked him why a man with such great powers needed a hook. To show that he needed no such aids himself, Sidi Abdel Jalil put his hands into the water and pulled out fish as numerous as the hairs on his hand. Provoked by this act, Saïd ben Saïd took off his *selham* (cloak), swept it along the ground, called out, "Sea, follow me," and proceeded to walk inland. He did not stop until he had walked 10 km (6 miles). The sea followed him, and so the lagoon was formed. After this, Saïd ben Saïd was called Moulay Bousselham—"Lord, Owner of the Cloak." Both Moulay Bousselham and Sidi Abdel Jalil are buried in the town.

4

TRAIN TRAVEL

Casablanca has three train stations: Casablanca Port, Casablanca, and Casablanca l'Oasis (the former two both downtown, the latter in the Oasis neighborhood). By train you can travel quickly and pleasantly to Marrakesh, Fez, Rabat, Tangier, and smaller towns like El Jadida and Azemmour. Direct trains from the airport go to both Casa Voyageurs and l'Oasis. Trains to Rabat depart hourly. (The train is by far the best way to move between Casablanca and Rabat.) Casablanca is less than three hours by train from Marrakesh (nine trains daily), 3½ hours from Meknès (eight trains daily), and 4½ hours from Fez (nine trains daily). In addition, there are overnight trains from Casablanca to Oujda (three daily, 10 hours) and direct trains daily to Tangier (three daily, six hours).

Contacts Office National des Chemins de Fer, Casa-Oasis ⊠ *Rte. de l'Oasis* 🕾 *0890/20–30–40.* **Office National des Chemins de Fer, Casa-Port** (*O.N.C.F.*). ⊠ *Bd. Houphouet Boigny, Medina* 🕾 *0890/20–30–40* ⊕ *www.oncf.org.ma.* **Office National des Chemins de Fer, Casa-Voyageurs** (*O.N.C.F.*). ⊠ *Bd. Mohammed V, Centre Ville* 🕾 *0890/20–30–40* ⊕ *www.oncf.org.ma.*

TRAM TRAVEL

The tramway has given the city something to be very proud of: it's safe, clean, affordable, and runs on time, which is no mean feat in Casablanca. With the tram, you can easily navigate from some of Casablanca's major locations, such as the Ain Diab beach area, the old pedestrianized town center around boulevard Mohammed V, and the old medina. It also makes a link between some of the city's more affluent areas and the less salubrious suburbs. For now, the tram comprises 48 stations that run along one major line which forks at one end, meaning there are three possible terminuses. The website includes a route finder and downloadable plan.

Tickets cost 6 DH. The tram runs from 5:30 am to 10:30 pm on weekdays and until 11:30 pm on weekends. ⊕ *www.casatramway.ma.*

GUIDES AND TOURS

Visit Morocco. Based in Casablanca, this well-run travel agency has years of experience and a helpful staff who are able to arrange almost any kind of trip you can imagine. It also has a good hand on the cultural events of the country, including the world-famous traditional music parties and the glitzy film festivals. ⊠ *3, rue Ahmed Ben Bouchta, Val d'Anfa* ☎ *0522/36–16–32* ⊕ *www.visitmorocco.ma.*

TIMING AND PRECAUTIONS

Many visitors spend at least a couple of nights in Casablanca, often using it as a base to visit other places in the area. As in any large city, travelers should be cautious at night when walking in the city center and around the old medina. It is best to use a taxi late at night when returning from a restaurant or the nightclubs.

EXPLORING

TOP ATTRACTIONS

Fodor'sChoice **Abderrahman Slaoui Museum.** One of the city's few museums, the Abder-
★ rahman Slaoui is hidden away in a splendid Art Deco villa. Permanent exhibits feature a collection of the nation's treasures, including delicate crystal perfume bottles, vintage prints, and 300-year-old jewelry from Fez. The museum also has a small café with lovely bay windows. ⊠ *12, rue du Parc, Centre Ville* ☎ *0522/20–62–17* ⊕ *www.musee-as.ma* ⊠ *30 DH* ☉ *Tues.–Sat. 10–6.*

Habous. At the edge of the new medina, the Quartier des Habous is a curiously attractive mixture of French colonial architecture with Moroccan details built by the French at the beginning of the 20th century. Capped by arches, its shops surround a pretty square with trees and flowers. As you enter the Habous, you'll pass a building resembling a castle; this is the Pasha's Mahkama, or court, completed in 1952. The Mahkama formerly housed the reception halls of the Pasha of Casablanca, as well as a Muslim courthouse; it's currently used for district government administration. On the opposite side of the square is the Mohammed V Mosque—although not ancient, this and the 1938 Moulay Youssef Mosque, in the adjacent square, are among the finest examples of traditional Maghrebi (western North African) architecture in Casablanca. Look up at the minarets and you might recognize a style used in Marrakesh's Koutoubia Mosque and Seville's Giralda. Note also the fine wood carving over the door of the Mohammed V. The Habous is well known as a center for Arabic books; most of the other shops here are devoted to rich displays of traditional handicrafts aimed at locals and tourists. ■ TIP→ This is the best place in Casablanca to buy Moroccan handicrafts. You can also buy traditional Moroccan clothes such as kaftans and *djellabas* (long, hooded outer garments). Immediately north of the Habous is Casablanca's Royal Palace. You can't go inside, but the outer walls are pleasing; their sandstone blocks fit neatly together and blend well with the little streets at the edge of the Habous. If you want to experience the heart of the Habous, take a traditional bath within the arches of **Hammam Chiki**, the city's most famous bathhouse. ⊠ *Habous.*

Casablanca

ATLANTIC OCEAN

OLD MEDINA

Bd. ben Abdellah
Bd. Sidi Mohammed
Bd. Sour Jdid
Bd. de Tiznit
Bd. de la Corniche
R. de Tarayo
R. de Goulmina
Bd. Mohamed Zerktouni
Bd. Moulay Youssef
Bd.
R. de Grenade
Bordeaux
Bd. Ziraqui
Bd. du Marechal Fayolle
Bd. Tahar el Alaoui
Bd. des Almohades
R. Houphouet Boigny
Pl. de Marrakesh
Pl. des Nations Unies
Av. de Royal
Bd. Mohammed
Av. du Phare
Bd. Jouffroi
Bd. Abdellatif
Bd. Ziraqui
Bd. d'Anfa
Bd. Moulay Youssef
Pl. de la Fraternité
Av. de l'Armée Royale
Av. Moulay Hassan 1er
Bd. de Hassan
Av. de Paris
RACINE
rond point des Sports
rond point Racine
Place Mohammed V
Bd. Rachidi
ANFA
Bd. d'Anfa
Rue de Normandie
Bd. Massira
Khadra
Bd. Mohammed Zerktouni
Av. Moussa ben Noussair
rond point de l'Unité Africaine
Arab League Park
Av. de Mers Sultan
MAARIF
Rue Platon
Bd. Bir Anzarane
Bd. Brahim Roudani
Bd. d'Avril
Av. Hassan II
Rond Point Hassan II
Bd. Mohamed Zerktouni
rond point d'Europe
R. des Hôpitaux
R. de Ceuta
Bd. Hamza Ibn Abdelmouttalib
Bd. Yacoub el Mansour
Rte. d'El Jadida
Bd. Abdelmoumen
R. Tarik Ibnou Ziad
Av. du 2 Mars

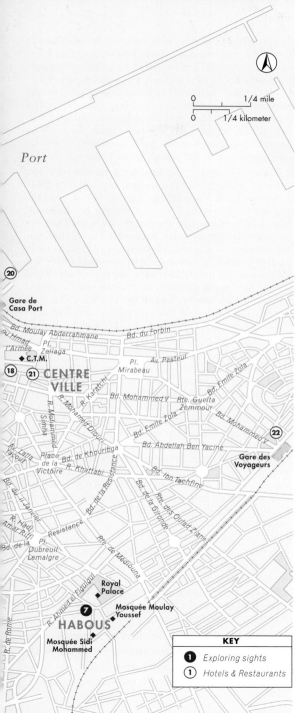

Port

0 — 1/4 mile
0 — 1/4 kilometer

Gare de
Casa Port

Bd. Moulay Abderrahmane
au Hmad   Bd. du Forbin
l'Armée Pl.
Zellaga
◆ C.T.M.

Pl.   Av. Pasteur
Mirabeau
**CENTRE
VILLE**

R. Karatchi
Bd. Mohammed V Rte. Guelta
R. Mohamed Diouri Zemmour
Bd. Mohammed V
R. Mohamed
Smiha Bd. Emile Zola
Bd. Emile Zola
Bd. Mohammed V

Av. Lalla
Yacout Bd. Abdellah Ben Yacine
Place Bd. de Khouribga
de la R. Khattabi
Victoire

Bd. du 11 Janvier
R. Hadj
Amar Riffi
Resistance
R. Pl.
Dubreuil
Lemalgre
Bd. de la

Gare des
Voyageurs

Rte. des Oulad Ziane
Bd. de la Résistance
Rte. de Mediouna

R. de Rome

R. Ahmed el Figuigui
7
HABOUS
Mosquée Sidi
Mohammed

**Royal
Palace**
Mosquée Moulay
Youssef

KEY

1 *Exploring sights*
(1) *Hotels & Restaurants*

Hassan II Mosque. Casablanca's skyline is dominated by this massive edifice. No matter where you are, you're bound to see it thanks to its attention-grabbing green-tile roof. The building's foundations lie partly on land and partly in the sea, and at one point you can see the water through a glass floor. The main hall holds an astonishing 25,000 people and has a retractable roof so that it can be turned into a courtyard. The minaret is more than 650 feet high, and the mezzanine floor (which holds the women's section, about 6 feet above the main floor) seems dwarfed by the nearly 200-foot-high ceiling. Still, the ceiling's enormous painted decorations appear small and delicate from below.

Funded through public subscription, designed by a French architect, and built by a team of 35,000, the mosque went up between 1987 and 1993 and is now the third-largest mosque in the world, after the Haramain Mosque in Mecca and the Prophet's Mosque in Medina. It was set in Casablanca primarily so that the largest city in the kingdom would have a monument worthy of its size. Except for Tin Maland, this is the only mosque in Morocco that non-Muslims are allowed to enter. ■TIP→ **If you fly out of Casablanca, try to get a window seat on the left for a good view of the mosque in relation to the city as a whole.** Right next to the mosque is the "*médiathèque*," which contains a fantastic public library and occasionally hosts talks and workshops. ⊠ *Bd. de la Corniche, Medina* ☎ *0522/48–28–86* ⊕ *www.fmh2.ma/mediatheque* 🖅 *120 DH* ☉ *Guided tours Sat.–Thurs. at 9, 10, 11, and 2 (all visits by guided tour)*.

Place Mohammed V. This is Casablanca's version of London's Trafalgar Square: it has an illuminated fountain, lots of pigeons, and a series of impressive buildings facing it. Coming from the port, you'll pass the main post office on your right, and on your left as you enter the square is its most impressive building, the courthouse, built in the 1920s. On the other side of avenue Hassan II from the post office is the ornate Bank Al Maghrib; the structure opposite, with the clock tower, is the Wilaya, the governor's office. The more modest buildings on the right side of the square house the notorious customs directorate (where importers' appeals against punitive taxes stand little chance). To avoid confusion, note that place Mohammed V was formerly called place des Nations Unies and vice versa, and the old names still appear on some maps. Now that the tram serves this area, it's easy to here from nearly anywhere else in the city. ⊠ *Centre Ville*.

WORTH NOTING

Corniche. Get a feel for Casa's Atlantic setting by stopping at a Corniche café and basking in the sun and breeze. On weekends, this area is bursting with people settling in the seafront line of cafés and restaurants, basking in the beach resorts, and walking up and down the wide pavement. In the evenings, nightclubs and bars open their doors to all different types of partygoers. ⊠ *Ain Diab*.

■ NEED A
BREAK?

La Sqala Cafe Maure. Situated within an 18th-century Portuguese fortress, La Sqala enchants with its plethora of beautiful gardens, patio, greenery, and fountains. It may serve the best Moroccan breakfast in town, and if you want a quick snack while sightseeing, the pastries and mint tea are a great

bet. La Sqala also serves lunch and dinner, offering a perfect mix of traditional but tasteful Moroccan design and atmosphere coupled with splendid Moroccan salads and tagines. ✉ ***Bd. des Almohades, Medina*** ☎ ***0522/26-09-60*** 🌐 ***www.restopro.ma/lasqala.***

Venezia Ice. After strolling along the Corniche, take a break and relax on the trendy Venezia's terrace and enjoy one of their 60 flavors of ice creams and sorbets. ✉ ***Above Tahiti Beach Club, La Corniche, Ain Diab*** ☎ ***0522/79-83-64.***

Old Medina. The simple whitewashed houses of the medina, particularly those closest to the harbor, form an extraordinary contrast to Morocco's economic and commercial nerve center just a few hundred yards away. European consuls lived here in the 19th century, the early trading days, and there are still a youth hostel and a few very cheap hotels within. Today it boils over with busy Moroccan shoppers, vendors, beggars, and locals. The medina has its own personality and charm due in part to the fact that Moroccans living in more affluent areas may never even enter it. Near place des Nations Unies a large conglomeration of shops sells watches, leather bags and jackets, shoes, crafted wood, and clothes. ✉ *Medina.*

Sidi Abderrahman. If you follow the Corniche to its southwestern edge, you will see the tomb of Sidi Abderrahman, a Sufi saint, just off the coast on a small island. Moroccans come to this shrine if they are sick or if they feel they need to rid themselves of evil spirits. Before the bridge was built in 2013, it was accessible only at low tide, at which point you would simply walk to the small conglomeration of white houses, built practically one on top of the other. Non-Muslims are allowed to visit the tiny island and have their futures told by a resident fortune-teller, although access to the shrine itself is prohibited. The other side of the island is one of the most exciting places in Casablanca to sit and watch the wild Atlantic swell. Be sensitive to the people who live here, as they will not appreciate being taken for museum objects and may object to having their pictures taken. **TIP→ On the sands, just in front of the tomb, you can enjoy some snails, or pancakes if you prefer, and Moroccan mint tea along with the locals.** ✉ *Ain Diab.*

WHERE TO EAT

$$$$ FRENCH
🍴 **A Ma Bretagne.** This restaurant is along the Corniche, past Sidi Abderrahman, and serves French provincial cuisine. The setting is modern and elegant, with hardwood floors, sleek columns, and wall-to-wall oceanview windows. The menu excels in its fish and shellfish dishes—the prawns make an excellent starter, and the grilled fish is particularly good. For sweets lovers, the warm chocolate tart is spectacular. [$] *Average main: 200DH* ✉ *Bd. de la Corniche, Sidi Abderrahman, Ain Diab* ☎ *0522/36-21-12.*

$$$ MOROCCAN FAMILY
🍴 **Al-Mounia.** Casablanca's first and most cherished Moroccan restaurant has a lovely patio with a centuries-old tree. The excellent cooking is all Moroccan, so expect couscous, tagines, and the like, but with a

refined touch. The salads are delectable, and the tagines bubble with the most sensational of perfumes. You can dine in rooms decked with quintessential Moroccan décor or take to the outdoor terrace in balmy weather. [$] *Average main: 130DH* ✉ *95, rue Prince Moulay Abdallah, Centre Ville* ☎ *0522/22–26–69* ⏲ *Closed Sun.*

$$$$ FRENCH Fodor's Choice ★ 🍴 **Brasserie la Bavaroise.** At Brasserie la Bavaroise, you'll experience a seriously culinary atmosphere and a menu awash with delectable French dishes. One of the most popular menu items is the filet steak with three sauces, while the *vacherin glacé* (a white cheese) with red fruit makes for an amazing dessert. While this place is definitely sophisticated, it's certainly not stuffy. [$] *Average main: 190DH* ✉ *133, rue Allal Ben Abdellah, Centre Ville* ☎ *0522/31–17–60* 🌐 *restopro.ma/bavaroise.*

$$ SPANISH 🍴 **Casa José.** This elegant and quintessentially Spanish tapas restaurant is a favorite among Casablancans and always abuzz with diners and drinkers. That makes it a great place to meet locals, and, in addition, women can come here on their own and feel entirely comfortable. If you're lucky enough to meet the owner, George, he'll recount his fabulously interesting life in Morocco and elsewhere. Products are local and fish is supplied daily. Typical options include calamari and patatas bravas; for those missing pork, there's even real chorizo. There are also local and international wines and beers. [$] *Average main: 90DH* ✉ *Bd. Felix Houfouet Boigny, Centre Ville* ☎ *0655/05–78–51.*

$ CAFÉ 🍴 **Freshandco.** Whether you're looking for a light bite or something more substantial, Freshandco has a good selection of dishes for all tastes. Sandwiches are prepared on site using fresh ingredients, many of which are organic. You can eat at one of the cute wooden tables inside or opt for takeaway. They'll deliver to your hotel, too. [$] *Average main: 65DH* ✉ *2, rue Theophile Gautier, Gautier* ☎ *0522/26–00–81* ⏲ *Closed weekends.*

$$$$ JAPANESE 🍴 **Kaiten.** With ever-expanding Asian food options in Casablanca, this is still one of the city's best Japanese restaurants. The menu includes a large selection of sushi, sashimi, maki, and other specialties served in an elegant and fashionable atmosphere. It's pricey but worth it. There are also choices for those who don't like sushi. [$] *Average main: 200DH* ✉ *18, rue Oumaima Sayeh, Racine* ☎ *0522/39–87–66.*

$$$ TAPAS 🍴 **La Bodega.** Every night is fiesta night at La Bodega. Opposite the central market, the restaurant offers a warm and colorful atmosphere with a lively Spanish and Latin flavor. There's live music each night by theme—Tuesday is salsa night, with a professional salsa dancer to give tips if you feel like improving your moves. Stop by for tapas and a drink or stay for a full meal. The menu is typically Latin; try the *jamón serrano* (thinly sliced, dry-cured Spanish ham) or fried calamari to start. Then, savor the chicken fajitas or paella before finishing up with the heavenly *croustillant au chocolat* (a type of chocolate crust dessert). If you can still move afterwards, step onto the dance floor and bust some moves. [$] *Average main: 145DH* ✉ *129, rue Allal ben Abdellah, Centre Ville* ☎ *0522/54–18–42* 🌐 *www.bodega.ma* ⏲ *No lunch Sun.*

$$$ MODERN FRENCH Fodor's Choice ★ 🍴 **La Cantine de Charlotte.** A splendid and cute restaurant in the elegant Gautier quarter of town, La Cantine de Charlotte showcases chef Richard Meyniel's unrivaled culinary skills. The menu changes frequently, but is always a fabulous mix of refined yet innovative. While there's an

inescapable penchant for luxurious components like lobster, asparagus, oysters, etc., there's also a good amount of local and fresh ingredients too. It's small and intimate, decorated with easy French chic, and service is unobtrusive and efficient, but friendly. [$] *Average main: 160DH* ✉ *3, rue Abou Adil El Allaf, Gautier* ☎ *0522/27–23–00* 🕒 *Closed Sun.*

$$$$ BISTRO 🍴 **Le Bistro Chic.** This place prides itself on its wine list, treating customers to a fantastic range of French and other wines. There's a proper bistro ambience in the restaurant area, while the mezzanine bar offers small plates and appetiers, including a very respectable cheese board. The beef carpaccio is highly praised, as is the roast salmon. There are reasonable prix-fixe menus for both lunch and dinner. [$] *Average main: 180DH* ✉ *8, rue Taha Houcine, Gautier* ☎ *0522/29–78–78* 🌐 *www.bistrot-chic.com* 🕒 *Closed Sun.*

4

$$$$ FRENCH 🍴 **Le Cabestan.** Offering spectacular views of the Atlantic Ocean in a great location near the Corniche lighthouse, this restaurant offers fine Mediterranean cuisine. It also doubles as a lively bar and club, drawing in a cocktail and champagne loving crowd until very late. Look down from a window seat onto blue rock pools as you savor delicious fish dishes. To wind down, you might have *tarte fine caramélisée aux pommes d'oulmès* (caramelized apple tart). [$] *Average main: 200DH* ✉ *90, bd. de la Corniche, Phare d'el Hank, Ain Diab* ☎ *0522/39–11–90* 🌐 *www.le-cabestan.com* 🕒 *Closed Sun.*

$$$$ THAI 🍴 **Mai Thai.** Casablanca's most adored Thai restaurant is frequented by a rather affluent clientele. Set in a renovated villa, it's booked up nearly every night. Menu favorites include the pad thai and shrimp rolls. There's also a fabulous bar and a gorgeous garden, although sadly there are no tables outside. Occasionally, musicians are brought in for some live music. [$] *Average main: 180DH* ✉ *408, bd. Driss Slaoui* ☎ *0522/95–02–34* 🕒 *Closed Mon.*

$$$$ SPANISH 🍴 **Paco Petit Rocher.** For fine dining with a fantastic view, you should head to the super-elegant Paco Petit Rocher. It sits in an unrivaled position, gazing over the sublime Atlantic waves and the Hassan II Mosque. Expect delicious Spanish-infused cuisine and good wine. [$] *Average main: 240DH* ✉ *Complexe au Petit Rocher, bd. de la Corniche, Ain Diab* ☎ *0522/36–26–26.*

$$ FRENCH FUSION 🍴 **Paul.** An outlet of a French café, bakery, and restaurant group, Paul is housed in the beautiful Art Deco Villa Zevaco. Whether for breakfast, lunch, or afternoon tea, Paul's terrace is always full of customers thanks to the fabulous garden and unparalleled pastries, breads, and cakes. Try the Royal, a decadent, chocolate mousse–like cake, or the mille-feuille, which melts in the mouth. The rustic breads are beloved throughout the city. At lunchtime, try the fresh salads or croque-monsieurs. [$] *Average main: 90DH* ✉ *Angle bd. d'Anfa at bd. Moulay Rachid, Anfa* ☎ *0522/36–60–00* 🌐 *www.boulangeries-paul.com.*

$$ SEAFOOD 🍴 **Restaurant du Port de Peche.** Tucked away inside the port, this is perhaps Casablanca's most treasured fish restaurant and thus draws a crowd at lunchtime. What to choose depends on what's been caught that day, so be sure to ask the servers for advice. To find the place, enter the port by the gate and turn left toward the fishing port. If you're arriving on foot, don't let the strong port odors deter you—the restaurant's

Casablanca has lively nightlife and dining scenes.

interior is clean and fresh. $ *Average main: 120DH* ⊠ *Port de Pêche, Medina* ☏ *0522/31–85–61.*

$$
SEAFOOD
✕ **Taverne du Dauphin.** One of the city's oldest fish places, the Dauphin is an alternative to the more expensive places offering fish and seafood, making it typically very busy. It's well placed in the town center, near the port and on the edge of the medina. Some tables spill out onto the pavement. $ *Average main: 100DH* ⊠ *115, bd. Félix Houphouet Boigny, Medina* ☏ *0522/22–12–00* ⊕ *www.taverne-du-dauphin.ma* ☉ *Closed Sun.*

$$
ITALIAN
✕ **Toscana.** With its quality food and reasonable prices, Toscana is the city's original Italian eatery. You can't go wrong with the divine pasta *melanzane* (eggplant) or any of the pizzas. There's also a nice selection of meat and fish dishes for larger appetites. Don't expect a lot of elbow room in the stylish interior, but enjoy the lively buzz. Service is wonderfully fast in spite of the always-full house. $ *Average main: 90DH* ⊠ *7, rue Yaalal Ifrani, Racine* ☏ *0522/36–95–92.*

$
CAFÉ
✕ **Tulik.** Casablanca's original salad bar offers a breath of fresh air for travelers looking for a healthier lunch option. You can put your own salad together from fresh vegetables, protein options, and homemade dressings. Tulik also offers homemade quiches, soups, and tarts. It's conveniently located near one of the main shopping districts. $ *Average main: 70DH* ⊠ *Rue Assilme, Racine* ☏ *0526/92–21–31* ▭ *No credit cards* ☉ *Closed Sun. No dinner.*

WHERE TO STAY

$$
HOTEL
Barceló Casablanca. Ideally located on Casablanca's Boulevard Anfa, this hotel is a perfect for business travelers. **Pros:** great location; full business hotel. **Cons:** no gym or pool. $ Rooms from: 1400DH ⊠ 139, bd. Anfa, Racine ☎ 0522/20–80–00 ⊕ www.barcelo.com ⟋ 83 rooms, 2 suites ⦿ Breakfast.

$$$$
HOTEL
Hotel & Spa Le Doge. Le Doge is a charming refuge amidst the cacophony of Casablanca and the first Relais & Chateaux property in Morocco. **Pros:** staff attentiveness; great restaurant for dinner. **Cons:** difficult to find. $ Rooms from: 3200DH ⊠ 9, rue du Docteur Veyre ☎ 0522/46–78–00 ⊕ www.hotelledoge.com ⟋ 3 rooms, 13 suites ⦿ Breakfast.

$
HOTEL
Hotel Bellerive. Although it's fading a bit, this budget hotel and its ocean views still retain a certain charm. **Pros:** easy on the wallet; good for families with young children. **Cons:** bland décor; rooms facing street are noisy. $ Rooms from: 575DH ⊠ Bd. de la Corniche, Ain Diab ☎ 0522/79–75–04 ⟋ 37 rooms ⦿ Breakfast.

$
HOTEL
Hotel Ibis Casa Voyageur. This Ibis is right next to the Casablanca Voyageurs train station, which makes it very convenient for those catching the train to or from the airport. **Pros:** friendly staff; near public transportation. **Cons:** uncreative atmosphere. $ Rooms from: 550DH ⊠ Av. Ba Hmad, pl. de la Gare–Casa Voyageurs, Centre Ville ☎ 0522/40–19–84 ⊕ www.ibishotel.com ⟋ 106 rooms ⦿ Breakfast.

$$$$
HOTEL
Hyatt Regency Casablanca. Casablanca's most conspicuous hotel occupies a large site next to place des Nations Unies. **Pros:** plenty of shopping nearby; great views. **Cons:** too kitschy for many travelers. $ Rooms from: 2500DH ⊠ Pl. des Nations Unies, Centre Ville ☎ 0522/43–12–34 ⊕ www.casablanca.regency.hyatt.com ⟋ 222 rooms, 33 suites ⦿ No meals.

$$$
HOTEL
Fodor's Choice
★
Kenzi Tower. The 28th floor of Casablanca's Twin Center, the modern and elegant Kenzi Tower offers a stunning view of the city, the Atlantic ocean, the Hassan II Mosque, and the port. **Pros:** fantastic views; excellent location. **Cons:** too large and impersonal at times. $ Rooms from: 1750DH ⊠ Bd. Zerktouni, Maarif ☎ 0522/97–80–00 ⊕ www.kenzi-hotels.com ⟋ 190 rooms, 47 suites ⦿ No meals.

$$
HOTEL
Royal Mansour Meridien. The Royal Mansour has long been one of the better hotels in Casablanca, especially for those looking for traditional luxury. **Pros:** plenty of amenities; doting staff; impressive gym. **Cons:** a little tired in places; in need of a makeover. $ Rooms from: 1430DH ⊠ 27, av. des FAR, Centre Ville ☎ 0522/31–30–11 ⊕ www.lemeridien-casablanca.com ⟋ 182 rooms, 23 suites ⦿ No meals.

NIGHTLIFE

Most Casablanca nightlife for the young and wired develops out along the boulevard de la Corniche, a 30 DH to 35 DH taxi fare from the center of town. Exceptions are the major hotel discos such as the Black House in the Hyatt Regency.

BARS AND PUBS

La Suite. This place is packed any night of the week with a local crowd devoted to music, dancing, drinking, and socializing. There are often themes like wine-and-cheese night or ladies' night, and DJs regularly spin to a lavish party crowd. There are frequent happy-hour deals and an excellent food menu as well. ⊠ *54, rue Jean Jaurès, Gautier* ☎ *0522/20–13–14.*

Le Chester's. If you can find room, squeeze in and soak up one of Casablanca's most popular drinking establishments. The long bar was clearly designed to welcome a large number of punters, and it does just that every night. Expect the DJ to whirl out some party sounds, and if there's a big soccer game, you can be sure Chester's showing it. You can order bar snacks or take a table in the restaurant area if you need more substantial refreshments. ⊠ *3, rue Abou Faraj Al Asbahani, Racine* ☎ *0522/94–12–82.*

Rick's Café. Located within the walls of a restored medina riad, Rick's Café evokes, of course, the romantic Casablanca from the classic Humphrey Bogart film—which wasn't actually shot here. The pianist, Issam, plays jazz nightly and also organizes jam sessions. Service is efficient and the menu blends American, French, and local cuisines. You can dine while sitting atop a high stool at the bar or settle in at one of the intimate tables. The cocktails are perfectly crafted and there's a comprehensive wine list. ⊠ *248, bd. Sour Jdid, pl. du Jardin Public, Medina* ☎ *0522/27–42–07* ⊕ *www.rickscafe.ma.*

Rose Bar. Inside the Cabestan restaurant is the Rose Bar, a lively place that draws the glitterati of the city who drink, dance, and gossip the night away beneath the DJ's watchful eye. The spectacular coastal views and briny air add to the unforgettable experience. ⊠ *Cabestan, 90, bd. de la Corniche, Ain Diab* ☎ *0642/79–22–62* ⊕ *www.le-cabestan.com.*

DANCE CLUBS

B-Rock. This is a haunt for musicians as well as local music enthusiasts. Expect live music every night and be sure to check out the open-jam night on Sunday. ⊠ *55, bd. de la Corniche, Ain Diab* ☎ *0614/38–76–34.*

Brooklyn Bar. In you're looking for a place to drink and dance, head to Brooklyn Bar, which seamlessly blends the nightlife scenes of New York City and Casablanca. ⊠ *56, bd. de la Corniche, Ain Diab* ☎ *0661/25–96–98.*

SHOPPING

Every year, Casablanca becomes more and more a cosmopolitan city, with a significant selection of European stores and priding itself on the availability of fashionable Western clothing. The greatest concentration of clothing boutiques by far is found in the Maarif area, on both sides of boulevard Massira Al Khadra, near boulevard Zerktouni. Here you'll find the Twin Center shopping mall, European stores like Zara, Mango, and Massimo Dutti, and all manner of specialty stores from Belgian chocolatiers to fashionable shoe stores to Portuguese porcelain warehouses.

ANTIQUES

Maarif. Aside from the two large shopping malls, the main shopping center of Casablanca is Maarif, just south of Boulevard Zerktouni. The maarif market is famous among Casablancans, stocking fruits, vegetables, fish, spices, and olives, as well as flowers and argan-oil products. On the other side of boulevard Massira el Khadra, you'll find a good deal of European stores such as Zara, Pimkie, Mango, and Massimo Dutti. Maarif also hosts many specialty stores from Belgian chocolatiers to Portuguese porcelain warehouses. Built on a grid, you'll find that the lower part, nearer boulevard Bir Anzarane, is more traditional, with lots of hole-in-the-wall places selling local products.

CRAFTS

The best place to shop for souvenirs and handicrafts in Casablanca is the **Quartier des Habous.** It offers the best variety and prices, but you should still try to get an idea of the market prices before starting to bargain. In close proximity to Casa's luxury hotels, the shops lining the **boulevard Houphouet Boigny** offer few bargains, and their business is mostly geared to tourists. They do present a broad sampling of all things Moroccan however, and are convenient for last minute, one-stop shopping. For hassle-free shopping, Coté Maisons has high quality artisanal products, often with a modern flair.

Coté Maisons. The beautifully designed products at this sumptuous boutique are irresistible, making Coté Maisons the ultimate place for high-end souvenirs. All items are produced according to artisanal tradition but with a definite dash of contemporary chic. ⊠ *10, rue Molièere, Racine* ☎ *0522/39–11–47.*

Thema Maison. Moroccan themes in household paraphernalia are the rule at Thema Maison, a good choice for drapes, pillows, or minor decorative trinkets. ⊠ *27, rue Houssine Ben Ali, Centre Ville.*

HAMMAMS

The following hammams are open to all (even nonguests, if in a hotel). *(For more on the hammam experience, see the illustrated feature in Chapter 2.)*

PUBLIC HAMMAMS

Hammam Le Pacha. Popular with Moroccans, this is one of the most frequented private baths in Casablanca; use of the hammam with combo exfoliation/soaping costs 100 DH; massage cost an additional 130 DH; towels are 30 DH. ⊠ *484, bd. Gandhi* ☎ *0522/77–42–41* 🖃 *50 DH* 🖃 *No credit cards.*

Hammam Ziani. This is an authentic hammam offering a range of typical services, such as exfoliation and soaping. It also has packages that include massages and algae wraps. ⊠ *5, rue Abou Rakrak* ☎ *0522/31–96–95* ⊕ *www.hammamziani.ma* 🖃 *60 DH* 🖃 *No credit cards.*

SHOPPING CENTERS/MALLS

Anfa Place. This shopping mall overlooks the sea opposite the Abdul-Aziz Saud Mosque, right before the Megarama cinema. There is a fair selection of shops—mostly clothing and accessories—although there are also stores selling music, books, and cosmetics, as well as a supermarket. Right outside, you'll find a host of restaurants and cafés mostly overlooking the beach, which can also be accessed. ⊠ *Bd. de la Corniche, Ain Diab* ☎ *0522/95–46–46* ⊕ *www.anfashopping.com.*

FAMILY **Morocco Mall.** Located at the end of the corniche, just after the Sidi Abderrahman Islet, is Africa's second-largest mall. It features all kinds of stores and a sizeable food court. There's also an IMAX theater, a large supermarket, and an adventure playground for kids that includes an ice rink. ⊠ *Corner of bd. de la Corniche and bd. de L'Ocean, Ain Diab* ☎ *0801/00–12–30* ⊕ *www.moroccomall.net.*

SPORTS AND THE OUTDOORS

BEACH CLUBS

FAMILY **The Tahiti Beach Club.** The most polished of a series of semiprivate clubs along the Corniche in Ain Diab that are also open to the public is the Tahiti Beach Club. Entry here is 250 DH per person during the week and 400 DH on the weekend. Along with sun and sand, the Tahiti offers many recreational activities appealing to adults and children alike. It has 10 pools, four top-notch restaurants with views of the ocean, a spa, a well-equipped gym, playgrounds, and a surf school. ⊠ *Bd. de la Corniche, Ain Diab* ☎ *0522/79–80–25* ⊕ *www.tahitibeachclub.ma.*

AROUND CASABLANCA

MOHAMMEDIA

25 km (16 miles) north of Casablanca

A short drive from Casablanca, Mohammedia and the surrounding area has a long stretch of pretty bays, which draw in droves during the summer. It was originally a port town and currently has a delightful harbor and yacht club and a good choice of fish restaurants, as well as a food market. Charming wooden beach houses line the coast. North of town, the beaches are good for swimmers, surfers, and sunbathers alike although currents here can be dangerous.

On Saturday, there is a souk at Al Alia, a southeastern district of Mohammedia. It's a grand event for locals, and you can see donkeys, horses, and traps as well as walkers flocking towards it for miles. You'll find everything and everyone from confit camel meat to dentist chairs.

GETTING HERE AND AROUND

Trains from the Casablanca Port station leave every half hour to Mohammedia (18 minutes, 15 DH). A grand taxi from Casablanca costs approximately 10 DH, while a bus will cost you 6 DH.

In Mohammedia, you can take a relatively inexpensive petit taxi, with a minimum fare of 7 DH.

EXPLORING

FAMILY **Plage Les Sablettes.** This long sandy bay attracts droves of surfers, sunbathers, and families in summer when temperatures can get very high. **Amenities:** none. **Best for:** sunbathing; swimming; walking. ✉ *Bd. Hassan II, Mohammedia.*

WHERE TO EAT AND STAY

$$ ✕ **Restaurant du Parc.** As its name suggests, the Restaurant du Parc sits
SEAFOOD on the park, in a 1950s building with a terrace for diners. As is almost always the case in Mohammedia, the menu bears a distinct fish and seafood theme, so your choices will depend on what's been caught that day. Some options might be grilled John Dory, paella, or king prawns. It also offers a good selection of meat dishes and some Moroccan fare. If you're feeling like something lighter, the *salade pecheur* (seafood salad) or the vegetarian salad are good options. Desserts include crêpe suzette and profiteroles. $ *Average main: 100DH* ✉ *Bd. Zerktouni, on the corner opposite the park, Mohammedia* ☎ *0523/32–22–11* ⊕ *www. restaurantduparc.ma.*

$$$$ ✕ **Restaurant du Port.** The most famous place to eat in town is the gastronomic fish restaurant, Restaurant du Port. The splendid menu isn't
SEAFOOD cheap, but it's worth every last dirham. Try the sea bass carpaccio with
Fodor'sChoice coriander and argan oil and then move on to the roasted monkfish
★ medallions with cèpes. If you've got room afterwards, don't miss the heavenly raspberry tiramisù. $ *Average main: 165DH* ✉ *1, rue du Port, Mohammedia* ☎ *0523/32–24–66* ⊕ *www.restoport.ma.*

$$$ ⛱ **Hotel Aventi.** This is a rather lavish place, embracing dozens of swish
HOTEL rooms and suites, several restaurants and bars, pools, a spa, and a nightclub. **Pros:** a well-run establishment; the only really luxe place in town. **Cons:** rather large thus less appealing to those who prefer an intimate ambience. $ *Rooms from: 1793DH* ✉ *Av. Moulay Youssef, Mohammedia* ☎ *0523/30–68–00* ⊕ *www.avantimohammedia.com* ⇆ *138 rooms, 18 suites, 1 villa* ⎟◯⎟ *Breakfast.*

NIGHTLIFE

Le Roof. A superb place to have a drink, this classy bar sits above the boat-shape Restaurant du Port and draws in a fun-loving crowd on a regular basis. Le Roof also features DJs, making this the chic place to party as the sun sets over the ocean across the way. ✉ *1, rue du Port, Mohammedia* ☎ *0523/32–24–66* ⊕ *www.roof.ma* ◯ *Closed Sun.*

SPORTS AND THE OUTDOORS

FAMILY **Bautilus.** Since Mohammedia is essentially a port town, the thing to do
Fodor'sChoice here is try your hand at sailing, the ideal way to explore the coast. Begin-
★ ners and more experienced sailors alike will be able to pick among a choice of small boats, from catamarans to motorboats. Bautilus is run by Mark and Mehdi, two experienced and passionate sailors who can also fix up fishing trips as well as water activities such as wakeboarding. Sailing lessons start at 300 DH and motorboat trips costs 2,000 DH for a half day or 3,000 DH for a full day. Canoe trips are priced at 300 DH per person for groups of eight or more. ✉ *Base Nautique de Mohammedia* ☎ *0665/19–69–87, 0645/46–02–28* ⊕ *www.bautilus.com.*

4

DAR BOUAZZA

20 km (12½ miles) southwest of Casablanca.

A beach town on the outskirts of Casablanca, Dar Bouazza used to be quite small but is expanding quickly, as the swell of villas and apartments can attest to. A haunt for the Casablanca expat community, the town has a curious mix of traditional locals—fisherman, surfers, rural families—and Americans and Europeans. These expat residents, along with well-off Moroccans looking to relax and get away from the stresses of Casablanca, have spurred an increase in entertainment and leisure activity in this small town. Surfing, Jet-skiing, beachside dining with live music (and wine), a water park, and a spa are all options. If you are just looking for a relaxing day at the beach, Dar Bouazza is a good choice. Stop at any of the free public beaches for some fun in the sun.

GETTING HERE AND AROUND

Renting a car is the best option for visiting the area. Head out of Casablanca south on the route d'Azemmour, and take the first right exit down to Plage Oud Merzeq.

Grand taxis from the southern end of Casablanca, in Hay Hassani, can also take you to Dar Bouazza, but specify that you are going to the beach, because some of the taxis don't take the beach road and continue on directly south. The trip costs 10 DH per person.

EXPLORING

FAMILY **Jack Beach.** The most visited beach in Dar Bouazza is a great place for swimming, surfing, and strolling in the summer. On the far side, there's a tidal pool area and, when the tides are low, the long stretches of soft sand are quite divine for strolling and exploring the coast. **Amenities**: food and drink. **Best for**: surfing; swimming; walking. ✉ *Rte. P3012.*

La Ferme Pedagogique. A sublime spot for both adults and children, this farm is a superb place to disconnect from the chaos and clamor of the city. Here you can discover organic plants and herbs, as well as visit and look after animals, all offered with an environmentally friendly mindset. If you want to picnic, they'll even make you up a fantastic basket. ✉ *Rte. d'Azemmour, 18 km (11 miles) from Casablanca* ☎ *0540/02–67–17, 0662/41–42–28* 🌐 *www.lafermepedagogique.ma* 🎟 *20 DH* 🕒 *Tues.–Sun. 9–6.*

WHERE TO EAT AND STAY

$$ FRENCH 🍴 **Emo'Sens Beach.** All day long, locals come in and out of this fantastic deli-restaurant-café, thanks to its gourmet menu and cute décor. Take a seat at a garden bench or an indoor stool and sample the menu created by the epicurean owner and chef. From fish dishes and hearty risottos to sumptuous salads and huge burgers, you'll no doubt leave a happy customer. For dessert, there are French-style tarts delicately garnished with colorful fruit, among other sweet delicacies. [$] *Average main: 80DH* ✉ *Rte. P3012* ☎ *0522/91–55–39* 🌐 *www.emo-sens.com.*

$$ DELI Fodor's Choice ★ 🍴 **Natty Natty.** If you are in the mood for a picnic on the beach, or perhaps a gourmet ice cream, Natty Natty is the best bet. Owned by a young Frenchman, this specialty deli has a fantastic selection of cheeses, fresh pasta, Spanish hams, specialty preserves, and heaps more. Don't

miss the French Brittany crêpes made with sarrasin. Service is fantastic and the atmosphere relaxed. Bring a bottle of wine from Casablanca since there is no place to buy alcohol in Dar Bouazza. $ *Average main: 100DH* ⊠ *Dar Kouch* ☎ *0660/72–03–70* ⊟ *No credit cards.*

$$
SEAFOOD
FAMILY
✕ **Sunny Beach.** The food served at Sunny Beach is focused on fresh fish cooked to order, with some salads and desserts thrown in as well. Kids will be eager to play in the sand, and there are some lounge chairs available for sunbathers and tired parents. It's a great place to put your feet up, sip a local wine, and enjoy the waves. The paella and calamari are firm favorites. $ *Average main: 95DH* ⊠ *Tamaris 1* ☎ *0663/71–73–53* ⊕ *www.sunnybeachonline.com.*

$$
HOTEL
🛏 **Hotel des Arts.** This hotel was designed by a resident architect—it's fun, laid back, and unique; the suites are designed to resemble the architectural style of cities throughout the world: New York, Barcelona, Paris, etc. **Pros:** ideal location; interesting design. **Cons:** expensive for the area; service is slack. $ *Rooms from: 1300DH* ⊠ *1120, Jack Beach* ☎ *0522/96–54–50* ⤵ *22 rooms, 28 suites* ⦿ *Breakfast.*

SPORTS AND THE OUTDOORS

SURFING

Glisse School. If you feel like trying your hand at surfing, Glisse School on Jack Beach has excellent instructors—some of whom speak English. The rates are very reasonable and it's open year-round. A 1½-hour lesson including equipment costs 200 DH. ⊠ *Jack Beach* ☎ *0669/79–69–60.*

WATER PARKS

FAMILY **Tamaris Aquaparc.** When children are looking for some thrills, Morocco's largest water park will do the trick. Open from May to September, it's full of slides, fountains, and any other water-ride fun you can think of, as well as places to dine. It gets very busy in hot weather when sweltering Casablancans look for somewhere to cool off. ⊠ *Km 15, rte. d'Azemmour* ☎ *0522/96–53–69* ⊕ *www.tamaris-aquaparc.com* 🎟 *160 DH* ⊙ *May–Sept., daily 10–6:30.*

AZEMMOUR

75 km (46 miles) southwest of Casablanca.

Azemmour, situated on both the banks of the Oum Errabi River and the Atlantic Ocean, is a fantastic weekend or day trip from Casablanca. The small town boasts a quintessential Portuguese medina, warm locals, and an artistic influence that gives the charming town a unique flavor. The Portuguese built Azemmour in 1513, and it proudly claims Estavanico, or "Stephan the Black," as a former resident. Estavanico, born in 1500 into slavery, was the first North Africa–born person to arrive in what now is the United States. Traveling with Álvar Núñez Cabeza de Vaca, he was one of just four survivors of the Spanish Narvéaz expedition.

GETTING HERE AND AROUND

Train service from Casablanca to Azemmour leaves from the l'Oasis station, with trains running about every two hours. With a car, the drive from Casablanca to Azemmour takes about an hour. Buses also run regularly between the two cities. If you are staying in one of the small riads, take a petit taxi from the train or bus station (about 7 DH) to one of the doors of the Azemmour medina. Once at an entrance to the medina, it's best to call the riad where you are staying to have an escort take you from the medina entrance to the premise. The small medina streets and alleys are a gentle maze, and not easy to navigate alone—but once you've spent some time walking the streets, you'll get your bearings. What's more, most locals are friendly and will try to help if you become lost.

Bus Contacts CTM ⊕ *www.ctm.ma.*

Train Contacts Office National des Chemins de Fer ☎ *0890/20–30–40* ⊕ *www.oncf.ma.*

EXPLORING

To fully enjoy the attractions within the medina, it's best to arrange for a guide from your riad. The medina is divided into three parts: the Mellah, the kasbah, and the old medina. While the medina retains much of its traditional charm, the artistic influence of local and foreign artists can also be seen. Azemmour's unique lighting has attracted many artists, who have chosen to set up shop in here. As you wander through the streets, murals by artists are a delightful surprise throughout the medina; it's worth stopping into one of the studios to see the artists at work. The medina's art gallery as well as the local rug weaver are also worth visits.

It's also worth exploring the new town, which is located on the opposite side of the road to the traditional medina. Here you can visit the tomb of Sidi Bouchaib, a saint recognized for his abilities to heal dementia. Only Muslims can go in, but everyone can go into the initial porch and watch pilgrims enter, or just admire the architecture outside. From there, wander down through the busy thoroughfare, boulevard Ahmed Choufani, which is unfrequented by tourists but full of busy locals. It's flanked by a multitude of hole-in-the-wall shops selling traditional wares, many of which are related to healing and spells. Expect to find anything from leeches and fox tails to animal bones, all used in traditional medicine.

Ahmed el-Amine. Perhaps the most recognized of Azemmour's resident artists, Ahmed el-Amine has been painting in and around the medina for more than a decade. ⊠ *6, Derb el-Hantati* ☎ *0523/35–89–02.*

Galerie Akwas. The medina's original art gallery exhibits the work of visual artists from across the nation. It was founded by Abderrahmane Rahoul, director of the Ecole Supérieure des Beaux Arts in Casablanca, a well-known and highly respected visual artist himself. ⊠ *Bab El Makhzen.*

FAMILY **Plage Al Haouzia.** Before the Mazagan Resort was built, you could walk the beach right up to El Jadida from Azemmour. While this is no longer possible, the beach is still fantastic and one of the cleanest beaches on the coast. There's also a shipwreck that's fun to explore. **Amenities:** food and drink; lifeguards. **Best for:** sunsets; surfing; swimming; walking.

WHERE TO STAY

Azemmour's tourism infrastructure is in its infancy, so restaurant and accommodation options are sparse. That being said, Azemmour has some fantastic riads that offer great accommodations and dining. Staying at one of the smaller, more intimate riads and taking advantage of Mazagan's facilities for dining or daytime use is an economical option.

$ | **Dar Nadia.** Set in the old Jewish quarter, otherwise known as the
B&B/INN | Mellah, this set of three houses joined together is a fantastic ramble of pleasant and comfortable rooms. **Pros:** clean and authentic; very homey. **Cons:** can be hard to find. $ *Rooms from: 450DH* ✉ *3, rue Souika El Malah, Azemmour Medina* ☎ *0523/35–84–72* ⬧ *5 rooms* ═ *No credit cards* ⦿ *Breakfast.*

$ | **Dar Wabi.** A traditional medina riad, Dar Wabi offers a tranquil and
B&B/INN | concealed treat. **Pros:** friendly, at-home atmosphere. **Cons:** difficult to find. $ *Rooms from: 800DH* ✉ *Azemmour Medina, Derb Daïra* ☎ *0661/15–10–26* ⊕ *www.darwabi.over-blog.com* ⬧ *5 rooms* ═ *No credit cards* ⦿ *Breakfast.*

$ | **L'Oum Errabia.** This divine guesthouse is positioned at the river's edge
HOTEL | and effortlessly juggles a mixture of charm and chic. **Pros:** fabulous
Fodor's Choice | design and atmosphere; great location. **Cons:** can be noisy if very busy.
★ | $ *Rooms from: 800DH* ✉ *17, Impasse Chtouka* ☎ *0523/34–70–71* ⊕ *www.azemmour-hotel.com* ⬧ *9 rooms* ⦿ *Breakfast.*

$ | **Riad 7.** Comprising a series of pretty and compact rooms, Riad 7
B&B/INN | is decorated with a contemporary slant while still preserving the traditional Moroccan features of the ancient building. **Pros:** centrally located in the old medina; traditional building. **Cons:** some rooms are dark. $ *Rooms from: 500DH* ✉ *2, Derb Chtouka* ☎ *0661/38–34–47, 0523/34–73–63* ⊕ *www.riad7.com* ⬧ *4 rooms, 1 suite* ⦿ *Breakfast.*

SHOPPING

Mohamed Janati. Besides being one of Azemmour's friendliest faces, the multilingual Mohamed Janati is a skilled weaver. Working at his traditional loom, he's happy to invite you in for tea, a chat, and an introduction to his weaving process. His rugs, covers, and scarves are absolutely beautiful and sold at reasonable prices. Mohamed also doubles as a chef and you can order pastilla or tagines from him. ✉ *229, Derb Eddira, Azemmour Medina* ☎ *0644/15–99–93.*

SPORTS AND THE OUTDOORS

In addition to water sports like Jet-skiing, surfing, and kayaking, boat trips and fishing excursions along the river can be arranged by the riads. Beaches just south of the city are also beautiful for a stroll or swim.

EL JADIDA

99 km (62 miles) southwest of Casablanca.

El Jadida has a fabulous 16th-century Portuguese medina, a UNESCO World Heritage Site, a large, sandy bay, and a promenade lined with palm trees and cafés. The name El Jadida means "the New" and has alternated more than once with the town's original Portuguese name, Mazagan.

GETTING HERE AND AROUND

Train service to El Jadida is limited, and the train station is inconveniently located 4 km (2½ miles) south of town. Buses are fine for trips from Casablanca to El Jadida. Frequent buses also come from the south from Safi and Oualidia. In El Jadida, one bus station, Gare Routière, serves all the bus companies and the grand taxis.

El Jadida has inexpensive metered petit taxis. For local runs, however, it is always advisable to establish an agreed-upon fare before getting in. The going rate for local trips is around 10 DH. The taxi station is next to the bus station. The larger, more-roadworthy grand taxis are available for intercity journeys, such as El Jadida to Oualidia (50 DH) or for longer trips to Marrakesh (70 DH) or Essaouira (65 DH).

Bus Information CTM ⊠ *Av. Mohammed V* ☏ *0522/54–10–10* ⊕ *www.ctm. co.ma.*

Train Information Office National des Chemins de Fer ⊠ *4 km(2 miles) south of El Jadida* ☏ *0890/20–30–40* ⊕ *www.oncf.org.ma.*

TIMING AND PRECAUTIONS

Most travelers stay in El Jadida for one night or two. El Jadida is generally considered safe. However, the Cité Portugaise area is poorly lighted at night and the new town has a few seedy bars and nightclubs. Visitors should exercise caution if visiting after sundown.

ESSENTIALS

Visitor and Tour Information El Jadida Délégation de Tourisme ⊠ *Av. Jaich el-Malaki* ☏ *0523/34–47–88.*

EXPLORING

Cité Portugaise. To get to El Jadida's main attractions, the Portguese ramparts, otherwise known as the Cité Portugaise, drive south along the coastal road until you see a sign, although its hard to miss the sight of the beautiful ancient stone walls. The Portuguese city was originally a rectangular island with a bastion on each corner, connected to the mainland by a single causeway. Take the entrance on the right where you'll see that the original Portuguese street names have been retained.

Fortress. At the end of the Rua da Carreira, you can walk up ramps to the walls of the fortress. Looking down from the fortress, you'll see a gate that leads directly onto the sea and, to the right, El Jadida's fishing harbor.

Jewish cemetery. El Jadida was once home to a very large Jewish population, which you can still see traces of in the city's Mellah, the Jewish quarter of the old medina. If you walk around the walls to the other side of the fortress, you can look down on the Jewish cemetery.

Mosque. Beyond the cistern is a fine old mosque; its original construction makes it one of the focal points of the city. The white minaret has five sides, all with rounded edges.

Our Lady of the Assumption. Walk down Rua da Carreira (rue Mohammed Al Achemi), and you'll see on the left the old Portuguese church, Our Lady of the Assumption, built in 1628 with a roof from the French period.

El Jadida's Portuguese cistern was where water was stored when the town was the fortress of Mazagan.

Portuguese Cistern. Beyond the mosque on Rua da Carreira, you'll see on the left an old Portuguese cistern, where water was stored when El Jadida was the fortress of Mazagan (some say the cistern originally stored arms). A small amount of water remains to reflect the cistern's Gothic arches, a lovely effect. El Jadida's cistern was not rediscovered until 1916, when a Moroccan Jew stumbled on it in the process of enlarging his shop—whereupon water started gushing in. ⊠ *Rua da Carreira* 🎫 *10 DH* 🕙 *Daily 9–1 and 3–6:30.*

Sidi Bouzid Beach. This beautiful stretch of sand extends away from El Jadida; you can access it by taking the coastal road about 5 km (3 miles) out of town. It's an ideal place for a stroll or watching the sunset. Swimming is great here too, although currents can be strong. **Amenities:** food and drink; lifeguards. **Best for:** surfing; swimming; walking.

NEED A BREAK? **Requin Blue.** Right near Sidi Bouzid, the Requin Bleu serves a wide variety of fresh seafood and fish dishes. ⊠ *Centre Balnéaire, Sidi Bouzid* 🎫 *0523/34-80-67* ⊕ *www.requinbleu.com.*

WHERE TO EAT

$ — MOROCCAN ✕ **Café do Mar.** This cute café is spread over a number of floors, and offers fabulous crêpes made with buckwheat according to Brittany, France tradition. Get yourself a good-quality coffee or a thirst-quenching juice while spoiling yourself with some divine Moroccan pastries. $ *Average main: 60DH* ⊠ *Cité Portuguaise* 🎫 *0523/37–34–00* ⊕ *www.liglesia. com/cafedomar.html.*

$$$ — MOROCCAN ✕ **La Capitainerie.** Within the ramparts there is not much in terms of sit-down dining, save for La Capitainerie. The menu revolves around

seafood with a Moroccan edge. You can order à la carte or choose a fixed-price menu; both change daily. Located in a restored sea captain's house, the dining room is a real highlight: the décor focuses on highlighting local tradition with a number of period objects. It overlooks the esplanade and has a decent wine list. $ *Average main: 130DH* ⊠ *Cité Portuguaise* ☎ *0523/37–34–00.*

$$
SEAFOOD
✗ **Restaurant du Port.** This is the city's old-school fish restaurant, located between the port and the ramparts and serving fresh fish and seafood straight out of the water. While the menu depends on the day's catch, you can't go wrong with the calamari and sole. You can also sit at the bar and dine tapas-style, while enjoying the reasonably priced alcohol selection. The décor is quintessentially yesteryear nautical Morocco, with low ceilings and wood paneling. $ *Average main: 80DH* ⊠ *Port d'El Jadida* ☎ *0523/34–25–79* ▭ *No credit cards* ☉ *No dinner Sun.*

$
SEAFOOD
✗ **Tchikito.** For good fresh fish, local ambiance, and low prices, Tchikitos is the way to go. This is a no-frills, no-thrills, easy-on-the-wallet restaurant just outside the medina walls. Be prepared to meet lots of locals as this seems to be everyone's favorite fish place. $ *Average main: 40DH* ⊠ *4, rue Smiha* ☎ *0523/37–18–19* ▭ *No credit cards.*

WHERE TO STAY

$
B&B/INN
🏠 **Dar Al Manar.** This delightful guesthouse just out of town is an ideal place to unwind. **Pros:** beautiful natural setting; intimate atmosphere. **Cons:** a little out of town. $ *Rooms from: 800DH* ⊠ *B.P. 229* ☎ *0523/35–16–45* ⊕ *www.dar-al-manar.com* ⇆ *5 rooms* ¶◎¶ *Breakfast.*

$$
HOTEL
🏠 **Liglesia.** One of Morocco's most wonderfully chic hotels is built within the walls of an old Spanish church, in the heart of the ancient Portuguese city walls. **Pros:** very unique location; gorgeous building. **Cons:** if you stay in the converted church, breakfast is in a different building. $ *Rooms from: 1500DH* ⊠ *Eglise Espagnole, Cité Portuguaise* ☎ *0523/37–34–00* ⊕ *www.liglesia.com* ⇆ *13 rooms, 2 suites* ¶◎¶ *Breakfast.*

$$$$
HOTEL
FAMILY
🏠 **Mazagan Beach Resort.** Mazagan is a spectacular luxury resort between Azemmour and El Jadida. **Pros:** luxury accommodations; beautiful setting; lots of leisure activities. **Cons:** not accessible by public transportation. $ *Rooms from: 2600DH* ⊠ *Mazagan Beach Resort* ☎ *0523/38–80–60* ⊕ *www.mazaganbeachresort.com* ⇆ *468 rooms, 32 suites* ¶◎¶ *Breakfast.*

$$
RESORT
🏠 **Pullman Mazagan Royal Golf & Spa.** The large, well-appointed rooms of this luxury hotel are brightened by cheery turquoise and yellow linens and blue-striped armchairs. **Pros:** quiet area; good for golf; on the beach. **Cons:** no public transportation. $ *Rooms from: 1250DH* ⊠ *Km 7, rte. de Casablanca* ☎ *0523/37–91–00* ⊕ *www.pullmanhotels. com* ⇆ *117 rooms, 10 suites* ¶◎¶ *Breakfast.*

SPORTS AND THE OUTDOORS

GOLF

Mazagan Golf Club. The Mazagan Golf Course is a links course, meaning the course literally links the land with the sea. Designed by South African golfer Gary Player, this par-72, 18-hole golf course follows the natural contours of the dunes and has spectacular panoramic sea views.

Green fees are 750 DH. ✉ *Mazagan Beach Resort* ☎ *0523/38–80–80* ⊕ *www.mazaganbeachresort.com.*

Royal Golf El Jadida. This 18-hole course next to the Atlantic is still worth a visit, even though it pales in comparison to the newer, neighboring Mazagan Beach Resort course. Green fees are 370 DH. ✉ *Km 7, rte. de Casablanca* ☎ *0523/35–41–50* ⊕ *www.royalgolfeljadida.com.*

EN ROUTE To leave El Jadida in the direction of El Oualidia, follow signs to Jorf Lasfar. Jorf Lasfar itself is the site of a chemical plant responsible for serious pollution in this region. After this, the coastal road becomes more scenic, passing fertile fields and lagoons. It's also quite an agricultural region and many salt mines are found here.

EL OUALIDIA

4

175 km (109 miles) southwest of Casablanca, 89 km (55 miles) southwest of El Jadida. From El Jadida, follow sign to Jorf Laser.

As you enter El Oualidia you'll see salt pans at the end of a lagoon. This town is famous for its oysters, and if you visit the oyster parks, you can eat oysters after learning how they're cultivated. (Oyster Park 7 is most renowned.) Turn right in the center of town to reach the beach. El Oualidia's bay is arguably one of the most picturesque places on Morocco's entire Atlantic coast. The fine sand is gently lapped by the placid sapphire lagoon, and in the distance white breakers of the sea collide beyond the cliffs. The beach is surrounded by a promontory to the south, a gap where the sea enters the lagoon, an island, and another promontory to the north. Around the corner is a beach that seems wholly untouched: sandy bays and dunes bearing tufts of grass alternate with little rocky hills. The summer months see a large influx of travelers and beach campers here, and thus far less tranquillity.

There aren't many "sights" in El Oualidia, but if you have a car, it's worth taking a drive south along the coastal road from El Oualidia to Essaouira, which has magnificent views, especially in spring, when the wildflowers are out. There is a souk in town on Saturday.

GETTING HERE AND AROUND
Grands taxis and local buses offer services to Essaouira and El Jadida. Both depart from a stop near the post office on the main road. There is also regular bus service north and south. If you are traveling by car from Marrakesh, follow the road to Safi and take the scenic coast road to Oualidia. If you are driving from El Jadida, follow the coast road down to Oualidia and allow extra time for possible congestion.

Bus Information CTM ✉ *El Jadida–Safi Rd.* ☎ *0523/34–26–64* ⊕ *www.ctm.ma.*

TIMING AND PRECAUTIONS
El Oualidia is a great choice for a stopover on the way to or from the north or south or as a destination of its own for a relaxing beach weekend.

WHERE TO EAT AND STAY

$$ SEAFOOD 🍴 **Ostrea II.** Just after the entrance to this small town, you'll see a sign for Ostrea II pointing right towards the lagoon. Head down the twisty road and you'll find this famed eatery overlooking the water and the oyster park. There's an outside terrace where you can watch boats row by as well as an indoor dining room if it gets chilly. The menu mostly consists of various types of seafood, but the reason most people come is for the oysters (the crab is pretty popular too). There's a respectable wine list and a nice choice of classic desserts like French apple tart. [$] *Average main: 100DH* ☎ *01672/50–05–55.*

$$$$ HOTEL Fodor's Choice ★ 🏨 **La Sultana Oulidia.** Breathtakingly beautiful and discrete, this luxurious boutique hotel on a secluded corner of Oulidia's lagoon is worth the price if you are in the mood to be truly pampered. **Pros:** great location; excellent facilities; flawless service. **Cons:** expensive. [$] *Rooms from: 3400DH* ✉ *3, Parc a huitres* ☎ *0523/36–65–95* 🛏 *11 suites* 🍽 *Breakfast.*

$$$ HOTEL 🏨 **L'Hippocampe.** This family-run hotel overlooks the lagoon, offering direct access to the beach. **Pros:** easy beach access; friendly staff. **Cons:** few amenities. [$] *Rooms from: 1600DH* ✉ *Oualidia Plage* ☎ *0523/36–61–08* 🌐 *www.hippocampeoualidia.com* 🛏 *23 rooms, 2 suites* 🍽 *Multiple meal plans.*

$ HOTEL 🏨 **Hotel Restaurant à l'Araignée Gourmande.** This hotel overlooks the beach and lagoon and is a good place to eat. **Pros:** tasty food. **Cons:** could do with a lick of paint. [$] *Rooms from: 300DH* ✉ *Oualidia Plage* ☎ *0523/36–61–44* 🌐 *www.araignee-gourmande.com* 🛏 *45 rooms* 🍽 *Breakfast.*

SPORTS AND THE OUTDOORS

SURFING

Gentle waves make El Oualidia's lagoon a great place to learn how to surf. Experienced surfers will find waves to their liking on the straightforward Atlantic beaches south of town; one of the better ones is called Mateisha Plage (in the Moroccan dialect) or Tomato Beach.

Surfland. This surfing school in El Oualidia runs surfing holidays, including English-speaking instructors and camping accommodations for both adults and children. It's 200 DH per lesson with equipment provided. Surfers staying elsewhere can join up without a reservation if there's enough space. ✉ *B.P. 40, Oualidia, El Jadida* ☎ *0523/36–61–10.*

FEZ AND THE
MIDDLE ATLAS

With Meknès, Volubilis, and Moulay Idriss

Visit Fodors.com for advice, updates, and bookings

WELCOME TO FEZ AND THE MIDDLE ATLAS

TOP REASONS TO GO

★ **Go back in time:** Fez el-Bali is the world's largest active medieval city and promises a sensorial vacation from modern life.

★ **Indulge your senses in the Meknès food souk:** On the Place el-Hedime sample famous olives, aromatic spices, and dried fruit, available in a dizzying array of colors and flavors.

★ **Explore an archaeological gem in Volubilis:** A short trip from Meknès, these well-preserved Roman ruins are considered the most impressive in the country.

★ **Ski the Moroccan Aspen:** Attracting both royalty and the Moroccan elite, the highest peak of the Michlifen ski resort rises to 6,500 feet.

★ **Take an overland adventure:** Two of the most stunning sights in the Middle Atlas are the cascading waterfalls of Ouzoud and the Friouato caves near Taza.

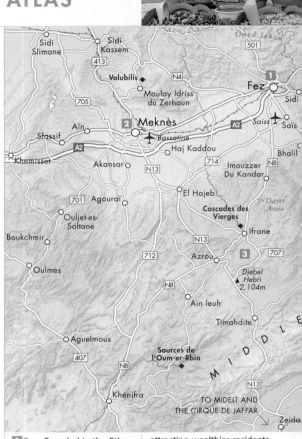

1 Fez. Founded in the 8th century on the banks of the Fez River by Moulay Idriss, Fez remains Morocco's grandest and oldest imperial city. Within the medieval stone walls of the medina there are two distinct historic areas: Fez el-Bali (Old Fez) and Fez el-Djedid (New Fez). Farther south, the Ville Nouvelle (New Town) is a modern district built in 1912,

attracting wealthier residents and strong commercial activity. The city's labyrinthine heart is the medina, enclosing historic minarets, souks, mosques, museums, fountains, and squares that get the well-deserved attention of most visitors throughout the year.

2 Meknès. Founded in the 11th century by the Almoravids, Meknès became an

GETTING ORIENTED

Situated between the mountainous Middle Atlas and valleys of the Rif, Fez and Meknès are rewarding visits with historic monuments, sumptuous palaces, imposing ramparts, and vibrant markets. Fez is by far the more significant destination. Meknès is a calmer city to experience authentic local life, with fewer tourists and hustlers. Side trips to the Roman ruins in Volubilis and sacred village of Moulay Idriss are highly recommended if time permits. The Middle Atlas, the northernmost part of the three Atlas Mountain chains, is a brief surprise on the way to or from the Sahara. Explore provinces like Ifrane, considered "Morocco's Switzerland," Berber cities of Azrou and Sefrou, beautiful forests, picturesque mountain ranges, and the canyons of the Cirque du Djebel Tazzeka near Taza.

5

imperial city under the rule of Sultan Moulay Ismail. The city has three distinct areas—the ancient medina with its central Place el-Hedime; the Imperial City, which contains the most impressive monuments; and the Ville Nouvelle (New Town).

3 The Mediterranean Middle Atlas. The northern Middle Atlas begins south and east of Fez and stretches southwest. The Azrou Cedar Forest and the Djebel Tazzeka Massif above Taza are the main attractions in this heavily forested northern zone, along with the ski region near Ifrane and the rugged Cirque de Jaffar at the more barren southern edge.

Updated by
Sarah Gilbert

Designated as UNESCO World Heritage Sites, Fez and Meknès are, respectively, the Arab and Berber capitals of Morocco, ancient centers of learning, culture, and craftsmanship.

Recognized as Morocco's intellectual and spiritual center, Fez has one of the world's oldest universities as well as the largest intact medieval quarters. It is the country's second-largest city (after Casablanca) with a population of approximately 1 million. Meknès, with nearly 850,000 inhabitants, offers a chance to experience all the sights, sounds, and smells of Fez on a slightly smaller, more manageable scale. Both Fez and Meknès still remain two of Morocco's most authentic and fascinating cities, outstanding for their history and culture, and Fez rivals Marrakesh as a top tourist destination and host of international events and festivals.

In between Fez and Marrakesh, the Middle Atlas is a North African arcadia, where rivers, woodlands, and valley grasslands show off Morocco's inland beauty. Snowy cedar forests, ski slopes, and trout streams are not images normally associated with the country, yet the Middle Atlas unfolds like an ersatz alpine fantasy less than an hour from medieval Fez. To remind you that this is still North Africa, Barbary apes scurry around the roadsides, and the traditional *djellaba* (hooded gown) and hijab appear in ski areas.

Most travelers to Morocco can get a glance of the Middle Atlas as they whiz between Fez and Marrakesh, or between Meknès and points south. The central highland's Berber villages, secret valleys, scenic woods, dramatically barren landscapes, and hilly plains blanketed with olive groves lie in stark contrast to the exotic imperial cities. For this reason alone, the region is rewarding to discover for its integrity and authenticity.

PLANNING

WHEN TO GO

Busloads of tourists and intense heat tend to suppress the romance of just about anything. Try to visit Fez and Meknès between September and April, before the high season or extreme heat makes it uncomfortable to sightsee. Spring is really the best time to visit any part of Morocco.

The Middle Atlas is relatively cool year-round, and often snowbound mid-winter with temperatures dropping below 0°C (32°F). For skiing or driving through the snow-filled Michlifen mountain region or Azrou Cedar Forest (occasionally snowed in from January to March, but normally well plowed), come between December and April. April through June is the best time to hike. The high tourist season in the mountains runs mid-March through summer. The most popular festival is the annual Fes Festival of World Sacred Music, currently held in June.

PLANNING YOUR TIME

If you're short of time, Fez should be your priority. The ancient monuments of the medina and the leather tanneries can be explored in one or two days, although you should devote longer to losing yourself in the medieval city's labyrinthine alleyways. A third day could be spent visiting the smaller and more manageable imperial city of Meknès and the impressive Roman ruins of Volubilis. With more time and transport—a rental car or tour—Fez makes the ideal base for day trips to alpine-style Ifrane and the Middle Atlas towns of Sefrou and Azrou. If you really want to experience Berber culture, spend the night in the troglodyte village of Bhalil; or visit the Holy City of Moulay Idriss, just a stone's throw from Volubilis. If you have over a week to spare and really want to get off the beaten path, Midelt in the southern reaches of the Middle Atlas is the base for driving the spectacular Cirque de Jaffar and climbing Djebel Ayachi.

GETTING HERE AND AROUND

Most tourists visiting the Middle Atlas set down in Fez, the region's largest city. Traveling within Fez is best done on foot, but taking a petit taxi to points of interest such as the Ville Nouvelle is an inexpensive option. To visit Meknès or Volubilis, take a train, bus, grand taxi (negotiate a price before the journey), or tour. To visit the Middle Atlas, you'll need a car or a tour.

AIR TRAVEL

Flights to Fès-Saïss Airport operate regularly from international and domestic destinations. But you can't fly directly into Fez from the United States. You must connect in Europe or Casablanca. Upon arrival, petits taxis wait outside the airport terminal and train station and carry two to four people. Grands taxis carry six people. Avoid unofficial drivers who hang around the terminals and charge false rates. Taxis should have their meters running. Most drivers request cash payment.

BUS TRAVEL

The CTM is Morocco's best bus company and has service from most major cities to Fez and Meknès. You can reach some destinations in the Middle Atlas by bus, but ultimately, you're going to have to drive or take a taxi or tour.

CAR TRAVEL

The easiest way to tour the well-paved regions in and around Fez and the Middle Atlas is by car. The best map to use is the Michelin Map of Morocco 959; if you can't find this map at home, ask your car-rental company to provide one. A map is a necessity if you plan to venture far from the beaten path. Road signs at major intersections in larger cities are well marked to point you in the right direction. Little white pillars alongside routes indicate distance in kilometers to towns. Traveling farther afield into the Middle Atlas, many secondary roads are unpaved and require a four-wheel-drive vehicle. Through mountain passes, roads can be dangerously narrow, steep, and winding.

TRAIN TRAVEL

Fez and Meknès are served by the ONCF train station that goes east to Oujda, south to Marrakesh, and west to Tangier, Rabat, and Casablanca. Fez and Meknès are also connected by regular local trains, a 45-minute trip.

RESTAURANTS

Every Moroccan city has its own way of preparing the national dishes. *Harira,* the spicy bean-based soup filled with vegetables and meat, may be designated as Fassi (from Fez) or Meknessi (from Meknès) and varies slightly in texture and ingredients. Note that few of the basic medina restaurants in Fez and Meknès are licensed to serve alcohol. Proprietors generally allow oenophiles to bring their own wine, as long as they enjoy it discreetly. Larger hotels and luxury *riads* (renovated guesthouses and villas) have well-stocked bars that serve wine, beer, and cocktails, as do more upscale restaurants.

Most of the Middle Atlas hotels we recommend have fair to excellent restaurants, but venture to stop at small-town crossroads or souks for a homemade bowl of harira for 5 DH or less. Note: some locals may frown upon alcohol of any kind. Be discreet if you carry your own wine or beer.

HOTELS

Hotels in Fez range from the luxurious and the contemporary to more personal, atmospheric riads that offer everything from an Arabian Nights fantasy to authentic traditional living, and more upscale but still boutique versions, such as Palais Amani. Hotels in or near the Fez el-Bali are best, as the medina is probably what you came to see. In Meknès, there is a more limited choice, with a few gems competing at the top end. In the Middle Atlas, the resort of Michlifen Ifrane Suites and Spa draws local elite for its Anglo-European styling. The Middle Atlas offers a selection of good hotels. Some of the inns and auberges off the beaten path should be thought of as shelter rather than full-service hotels, as lodging tends to be unmemorable. *Hotel reviews have been shortened. For full information, visit Fodors.com.*

WHAT IT COSTS IN DIRHAMS				
	$	$$	$$$	$$$$
Restaurants	under 200 DH	200 DH–300 DH	301 DH–400 DH	over 400 DH
Hotels	under 1,200 DH	1,200 DH–1,600 DH	1,601 DH–2,000 DH	over 2,000 DH

Restaurant prices are the average cost of a main course at dinner, or if dinner is not served, at lunch. Hotel prices are the lowest cost of a standard double room in high season.

SAFETY

In general, Fez and Meknès are safe cities. In Fez—less in Meknès—pickpocketing and unwanted hassle from hustlers and faux guides will be the biggest concern. Harassment from those offering to be tour guides or drivers is best avoided by smiling and firmly saying "no thank you," preferably in French or Arabic. Try not to become visibly agitated, as it could exacerbate the situation.

You can safely explore Fez medina during the day, but ask at your hotel if there are any areas you should avoid after dark. If you get off track, turn around and head back to a more populated area. If you are followed, enter a store, hotel, restaurant, or café and ask for help. At night, poorly lit medina alleyways can be intimidating but are not necessarily unsafe. Often hotels and restaurants will dispatch someone to escort you to your destination.

From December through January, heavy snowfall may cover Middle Atlas roads; however, the snow-removal systems in places such as the Azrou Cedar Forest are relatively good, with cleared driving routes. More remote roads (marked in white on the Michelin map of Morocco) will be difficult to access or completely closed in snowy conditions. Driving off-road or to natural sites such as the Cascades d'Ouzoud in winter, when snowfall can be significant, is not advised.

FEZ

Fez is one of the world's most spectacular city-museums and an exotic medieval labyrinth—mysterious, mesmerizing, and sometimes overwhelming. Passing through one of the *babs* (gates) into Fez el-Bali is like entering a time warp, with only the numerous satellite dishes installed on nearly every roof as a reminder you're in the 21st century, not the 8th. As you maneuver through crowded passages illuminated by shafts of sunlight streaming through thatched roofs of the *kissaria* (covered markets), the cries of *"Balek!"* ("Watch out!") from donkey drivers pushing overloaded mules—overlapped with the cacophony of locals bartering, coppersmiths hammering, and the *muezzin,* the city-wide call to prayer—blend with the strong odors of aromatic spices, curing leather, and smoking grills for an incredible sensorial experience you will never forget.

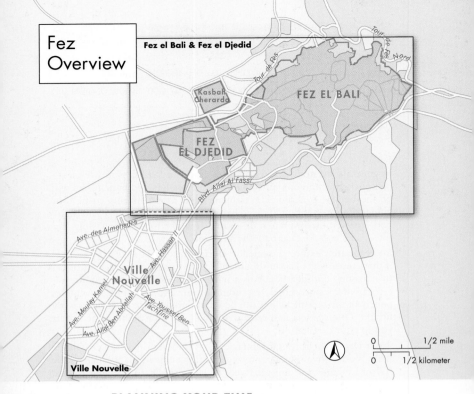

Fez
Overview

Fez el Bali & Fez el Djedid

Tour de Fes
Tour de Fes Nord
Kasbah Cherarda
FEZ EL BALI
FEZ EL DJEDID
Blvd. Allal Al Fassi

Ave. des Almohades
Ave. Hassan II
Ville Nouvelle
Ave. Moulay Kamel
Ave. Allal Ben Abdallah
Ave. Youssef Ben Tachfine

Ville Nouvelle

0   1/2 mile
0   1/2 kilometer

PLANNING YOUR TIME
FESTIVALS

Fes Festival of World Sacred Music. Sponsored by the Foundation of Fez, a nonprofit association working to maintain the city's cultural heritage, the Fes Festival of World Sacred Music focuses on a different theme each year and has become an international favorite, attracting some of the world's finest musicians and intellectual scholars for the Fes Forum roundtable debates. Concerts are held in diverse venues across the city, from the imposing Bab Al Makina to the beautiful gardens of the Dar Batha Musuem. There are also free concerts, including Sufi Nights, held daily in a palatial dar. ☎ 0535/74–05–35, 0535/74–06–91 ⊕ www. fesfestival.com.

GETTING HERE AND AROUND

Fez is an enigmatic, exotic city best explored on foot. Walking beneath one of the imposing arched babs and into the medina's maze of cobbled streets stimulates all the senses. Summer months can be unbearably hot with little air circulation, especially along canopied and crowded alleyways. The best time to tour is the morning; crowds and temperatures won't be too intense. Nights are cool throughout the year with a refreshing desert breeze. Remember that Friday is a traditional day of prayer, and many establishments in the medina are closed.

AIR TRAVEL

The main gateway to the region is Fès-Saïss Airport. Driving to down-town Fez takes about 30 minutes. A taxi will cost around 200 DH; a local bus from the Ville Nouvelle around 5 DH.

BUS TRAVEL

Hourly CTM buses cover the Fez–Meknès route. The trip takes about one hour and costs 25 DH. The bus to Marrakesh takes about nine hours and costs 175 DH. The bus to Casablanca takes around five hours and costs 100 DH. The bus to Tangier takes around six hours and costs 115 DH.

Bus Contacts CTM ⊠ *Pl. Atlas, Ville Nouvelle* 🕾 *0535/62–20–41* ⊕ *www.ctm.ma.*

CAR TRAVEL

You will not want a car in Fez. Indeed, a car would probably impede your ability to negotiate the city. But if you plan to explore the Middle Atlas region, or if you are beginning a larger trip to Morocco in Fez, then a car may be appropriate and even necessary.

Rental Cars Avis ⊠ *50, bd. Chefchaouni, Ville Nouvelle* 🕾 *0525/62–69–69* *.***Budget** ⊠ *Fès-Saïss Airport* 🕾 *0532/03–09–21.* **Hertz** ⊠ *Av. Lalla Meryem, Ville Nouvelle* 🕾 *0535/62–28–12* ⊕ *www.hertz.com.*

TAXI TRAVEL

Grands taxis are large, usually shared taxis (up to six passengers) that make long-distance runs between cities. This can be faster, more com-fortable, and better value than bus travel. The local petits taxis are metered, take up to four passengers, and may not leave the city limits. If the driver refuses to turn on the meter or agree to a reasonable price, don't hesitate to get out. There is a 50% surcharge after 8 pm.

TRAIN TRAVEL

Trains run between Fez and Meknès each day. They cost from 20 DH and take 45 minutes. There are seven daily trains to Casablanca (five hours, from 110 DH) via Rabat (four hours, from 80 DH). There are five daily trains to Marrakesh (eight hours, from 195 DH). The train to Tangier takes five hours and costs from 105 DH. The Fez train station is on the north side of the Ville Nouvelle, a 10-minute walk from the center of town, and a 10 DH taxi ride from the medina.

Train Information Fez Train Station ⊠ *Av. des Almohades, Ville Nouvelle* 🕾 *0535/93–03–33.*

GUIDES AND TOURS

There's much to be said in favor of employing a good guide in Fez: you'll be left alone by faux guides and hustlers, and if your guide is good you'll learn much and be able to see more of your surroundings than when having to read and navigate as you move around. On the other hand, getting lost in Fez el-Bali is one of those great travel experiences. Maps of the medina really do work, and there are now numerous signs on medina walls pointing you to important sites, restaurants, and hotels.

The tourist office and your hotel are the best sources for official guides vetted by the ONMT. An official guide costs around 300 DH for a half day and around 500 DH for a full day, more if you include touring regions or special destinations by car.

Cafe Clock Cooking Workshop. At Cafe Clock's one-day cooking workshop you'll uncover the secrets of Moroccan cooking from souk to plate. Fassi cuisine originated in the fondouks where numerous cultures—Andalusian, Indian, and Persian among them—crossed paths, and you'll start by choosing a menu of salad, main course, and dessert. Then shop for ingredients in the souk with one of the cafe's Moroccan chefs before rustling up everything from tagines to couscous in the kitchen—or on the roof terrace for larger groups—and sitting down to enjoy the fruits of your labor. ⊠ *7, Derb el Magana, Fez el-Bali* ☎ *0535/63–78–55* ⊕ *www.cafeclock.com* ⊠ *600 DH.*

Fodor'sChoice
★
Culture Vultures Fez. Fez is undoubtedly Morocco's capital of art and crafts, and Culture Vultures leads an interactive small-group tour of the workshops of traditional craftsmen: weavers, coppersmiths, tanners, tile makers, and more. As well as gaining an insight into the daily lives of the artisans, you can try your hand at their various crafts. The tour ends at an artisanal training center funded by the Mohammed V Foundation, where around 500 students between the ages of 16 and 30 are being taught more than 40 different traditional crafts. Tours run from Saturday to Thursday with a maximum of six people. ☎ *0645/22–32–03* ⊕ *www.culturevulturesfez.org* ⊠ *From 847 DH.*

Fodor'sChoice
★
Plan-it Fez. This outfitter offers engaging cultural tours, from unveiling the medina's secrets on the Architecture and Islamic Gardens Tour to culinary adventures on the excellent Souk Tasting Trails tour. Or join a family as they shop for produce in their local souk, pick up bread at their neighborhood *farran* (bakery), then learn how to preserve lemons, make mint tea, and conjure up typical salads and a tagine of your choice in the kitchen of their traditional dar. You'll end by sitting down with the family to share the meal in true Moroccan style. This outfitter also run day trips beyond Fez—take a Roman picnic to Volubilis, barter at the carpet auction in Khenifra, or hike through the Rif Mountains—and excursions to the Sahara. ☎ *0535/63–87–08* ⊕ *www.plan-it-fez. com* ☉ *From 900 DH.*

VISITOR INFORMATION
Contacts Fez Tourist Office ⊠ *Pl. Mohammed V, Ville Nouvelle* ☎ *0535/62–47–69.* **ONMT** ⊠ *Pl. Mohammed V, Ville Nouvelle* ☎ *0535/62–47–69.*

EXPLORING

FEZ EL-BALI

Fez el-Bali is a living medieval city, crafts workshop, and market that has changed little in the past millennium. With no cars allowed and some 1,000 very narrow *derbs* (dead-end alleys), it beckons the walker on an endless and absorbing odyssey. Exploring this honeycomb of ancient alleyways with often chaotic crowds, steep inclines, and pitted cobblestone steps is a challenging adventure. Fez isn't really yours, however, until you've tackled it on your own, become hopelessly lost a few times, and survived to tell the tale.

TOP ATTRACTIONS

Andalusian Mosque. This mosque was built in AD 859 by Mariam, sister of Fatima al-Fihri, who had erected the Kairaouine Mosque on the river's other side two years earlier with inherited family wealth. The gate was built by the Almohads in the 12th century. The grand carved doors on the north entrance, domed Zenet minaret, and detailed cedarwood carvings in the eaves, which bear a striking resemblance to those in the Musée Nejjarine, are the main things to see here, as the mosque itself is set back on a small elevation, making it hard to examine from outside. ⊠ *Rue Nekhaline* ⚅ *Entrance restricted to Muslims.*

Attarine Medersa. Named for local spice merchants known as *attar,* the Attarine Medersa (Koranic School of the Spice Sellers) was founded by Merenid Sultan Abou Saïd Othman in the 14th century as a students' dormitory attached to the Kairaouine Mosque next door. Its graceful proportions, elegant, geometric carved-cedar ornamentation, and excellent state of preservation make it one of the best representations of Moorish architecture in Fez. ⊠ *Boutouil Kairaouine* ☽ *Daily 9–1 and 3–6:30.*

Fodor's Choice ★ **Bab Boujeloud.** Built in 1913 by General Hubert Lyautey, Moroccan commander under the French protectorate, this Moorish-style gate is 1,000 years younger than the rest of the medina. It's considered the principal and most beautiful point of entry into Fez el-Bali. The side facing towards Fez el-Djedid is covered with blue ceramic tiles painted with flowers and calligraphy; the inside is green, the official color of Islam— or of peace, depending on interpretation. ⊠ *Pl. Pacha el-Baghdadi.*

Batha Musuem (*Museum of Moroccan Arts*). Housed in Dar Batha, a late-19th-century Andalusian palace built by Moulay el Hassan, the museum of Moroccan Arts has one of Morocco's finest handicrafts collections. The display of pottery, for which Fez is particularly famous, includes rural earthenware crockery and elaborate plates painted with geometric patterns. Other displays feature embroidery stitched with real gold, astrolabes from the 11th to the 18th century, illuminated Korans, and Berber carpets and kilims. ⊠ *Dar Batha, Pl. de l'Istiqlal, entrance on Mahaj el Methab* ☎ *0535/63–41–16* 💴 *10 DH* ☽ *Wed.– Mon. 8:30–noon and 2:30–6.*

Bou Inania Medersa. From outside Bab Boujeloud you will see this medersa's green-tile tower, generally considered the most beautiful of the Kairaouine University's 14th-century residential colleges. It was built by order of Abou Inan, the first ruler of the Merenid dynasty, which would become the most decisive ruling clan in Fez's development. The main components of the medersa's stunningly intricate decorative artwork are: the green-tile roofing; the cedar eaves and upper patio walls carved in floral and geometrical motifs; the carved-stucco midlevel walls; the ceramic-tile lower walls covered with calligraphy (Kufi script, essentially cursive Arabic) and geometric designs; and, finally, the marble floor. Showing its age, the carved cedar is still dazzling, with each square inch a masterpiece of handcrafted sculpture involving long hours of the kind of concentration required to memorize the Koran. The black belt of ceramic tile around the courtyard bears Arabic script reading, "This

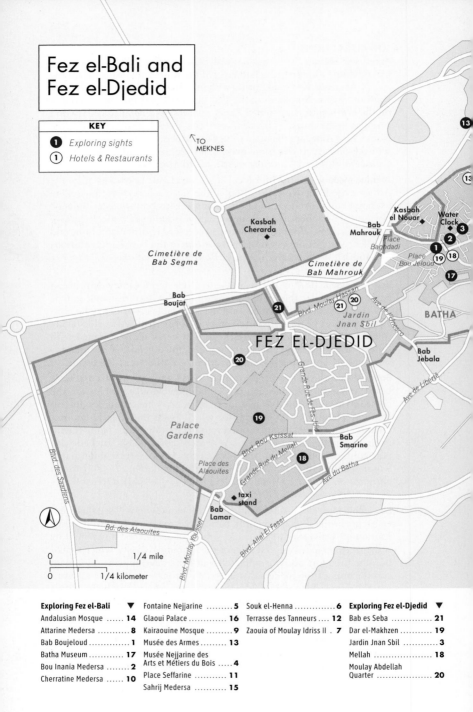

Fez el-Bali and Fez el-Djedid

KEY

- **1** *Exploring sights*
- **(1)** *Hotels & Restaurants*

TO MEKNES

Cimetière de Bab Segma

Kasbah Cherarda

Cimetière de Bab Mahrouk

Kasbah el Nouar

Water Clock

Bab Mahrouk

Place Bagdadi

Place Bou Jeloud

Bab Boujat

Blvd. Moulay Hassan

Jardin Jnan Sbil

BATHA

FEZ EL-DJEDID

Bab Jebala

Ave de l'Unesco

Ave. de Liberté

Palace Gardens

Grande Rue de Fes-Jdid

Blvd. Bou Ksissat

Bab Smarine

Grande Rue du Mellah

Ave. du Batha

Place des Alaouites

taxi stand

Bab Lamar

Blvd. des Saadiens

Blvd. Moulay Youssef

Bd. des Alaouites

Blvd. Allal El Fassi

0   1/4 mile
0   1/4 kilometer

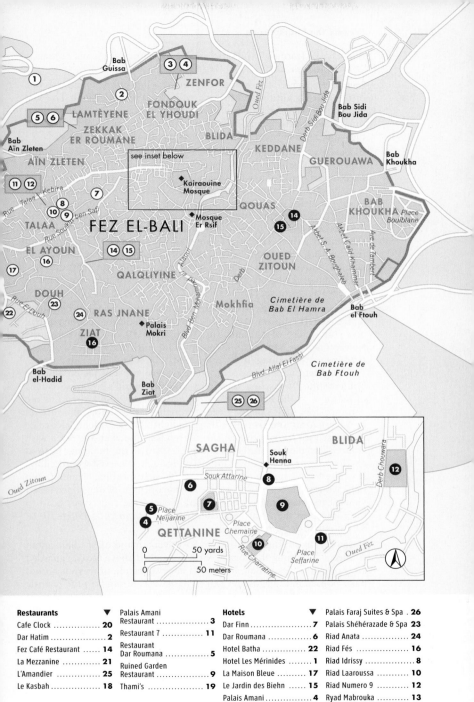

Restaurants ▼

Hotels ▼

is a place of learning" and other such exhortatory academic messages. ✉ *Talâa Kebira* 🖼 *10 DH* ☉ *Daily 9–7.*

Fontaine Nejjarine. This ceramic-tile, cedar-ceiling public fountain is one of the more beautiful and historic of its kind in Fez el-Bali. The first fountain down from Bab Boujeloud, Fontaine Nejjarine seems a miniature version of the Nejjarine fondouk, with its geometrically decorated tiles and intricately carved cedar eaves overhead. ✉ *Pl. Nejjarine.*

Glaoui Palace. Among the medina's many hidden palaces, the extraordinary Dar al Glaoui is one of its most atmospheric. The Pasha of Marrakesh's second home—he ruled over most of southern Morocco in his day—has fallen into disrepair since Morocco's independence from France in 1956, when his power waned. But amid the crumbling ruins, evidence of its former grandeur is visible in the exquisite cedarwood doors, intricate stucco, tiled salons, and the carved wooden balconies that line its patios. The large estate was comprised of 17 buildings and two gardens, with ornate salons, an enormous kitchen, Koranic school, garages, stables, a harem, and a hammam. Abdou—an artist and one of the remaining family members—or his sister will show you some of its treasures. ✉ *1, rue Hamia Douh, Ziat* ☎ *0667/36–68–28.*

Fodor's Choice
★ **Kairaouine Mosque.** This is considered one of the most important mosques in the Western Muslim world. One look through the main doorway will give you an idea of its immensity. With about 10,760 square feet, the Kairaouine was Morocco's largest mosque until Casablanca's Hassan II Mosque came along in the early 1990s. Built in AD 857 by Fatima, the daughter of a wealthy Kairaouine refugee, the mosque became the home of the West's first university and the world's foremost center of learning at the beginning of the second millennium. Stand at the entrance door's left side for a peek through the dozen horseshoe arches into the *mihrab* (marked by a hanging light). An east-facing alcove or niche used for leading prayer, the mihrab is rounded and covered with an arch designed to project sound back through the building. Lean in and look up to the brightly painted and intricately carved wood ceiling. If you're lucky enough to visit during the early morning cleaning, two huge wooden doors by the entrance swing open, providing a privileged view of the vast interior. For a good view of the courtyard, head to the rooftop of the Attarine Medersa. ✉ *Bou Touil* ☎ *0535/64–10–16* ☞ *Entry restricted to Muslims.*

Musée des Armes. Built in 1582 under the command of Saadian sultan Ahmed el-Mansoor, this former fortress perched above the city guarded and controlled Fez el-Bali. In 1963, a huge collection of weapons originally housed in the Museum Dar el-Batha was brought to the historic site, creating the interesting display in what is now the Museum of Arms. Sabres, swords, shields, and armor from the 19th century showcase the history of how arms played a social role in tribal hierarchy. Of importance is the arsenal of sultans Moulay Ismail and Moulay Mohammed Beh Abdellah—the elaborate Berber guns encrusted in enamel, ivory, silver, and precious gems date back to the 17th century. ■TIP➔ **Walk up to the crenellated rooftop in late afternoon for a**

The dye vats of the Terrasse des Tanneurs may be pleasing to the eye, but they are not pleasing to the nose.

beautiful panoramic view of the city. ⊠ *Borj Nord* ☎ *0535/64–52–41* 🎟 *10 DH* ⊙ *Wed.–Mon. 8:30–noon and 2:30–6.*

Musée Nejjarine des Arts et Métiers du Bois. The 14th-century Nejjarine fondouk, or Inn of the Carpenters, is now home to a fascinating museum. The three-story patio displays Morocco's various native woods, 18th- and 19th-century woodworking tools, and a series of antique wooden doors and pieces of furniture. For 10 DH enjoy mint tea on the rooftop terrace with panoramic views over the medina. Don't miss the former jail cell on the ground floor, or the large set of weighing scales, a reminder of the building's original functions—commerce on the ground floor and lodging on the levels above. ■ TIP➜ Check out the palatial, cedar-ceiling public bathrooms, certainly the finest of their kind in Fez. ⊠ *Pl. Nejjarine* ☎ *0535/74–05–80* 🎟 *20 DH* ⊙ *Daily 10–5.*

Place Seffarine. This wide, triangular souk of the *dinandiers,* or coppersmiths, is a welcome open space, a comfortable break from tight crags and corners. Donkeys and their masters wait for transport work here, and a couple of trees are reminders this was once a fertile valley alongside the Fez River. Copper and brass bowls, plates, and buckets are wrought and hammered over fires around the market's edge, where the smells of soldering irons and donkey droppings permeate the air. Look towards the Kairaouine Mosque at the top of the square to see the Kairaouine University library, which once housed the world's best collection of Islamic literature but is only open to Muslim scholars. ⊠ *Pl. Seffarine.*

Souk el-Henna. This little henna market is one of the medina's most picturesque squares, with a massive, gnarled fig tree in the center and rows of spices, hennas, kohls, and aphrodisiacs for sale in the tiny stalls around the edges. The ceramic shops on the way into the henna souk sell a wide variety of typically blue Fassi pottery. At the square's end is a plaque dedicated to the Maristan Sidi Frej, a medical center and psychiatric and teaching hospital built by the Merenid ruler Youssef Ibn Yakoub in 1286. Used as a model for the world's first mental hospital—founded in Valencia, Spain, in 1410—the Maristan operated until 1944. ⊠ *Derb Fakharine.*

Fodor's Choice **Terrasse des Tanneurs.** The medieval tanneries are at once beautiful, for
★ their ancient dyeing vats of reds, yellows, and blues, and unforgettable, for the malodorous smell of decaying animal flesh on sheep, goat, cow, and camel skins. The terrace overlooking the dyeing vats is high enough to escape the place's full fetid power and get a spectacular view over the multicolor vats. Absorb both the process and the finished product on Chouara Lablida, just past Rue Mechatine (named for the combs made from animals' horns): numerous stores are filled with loads of leather goods, including coats, bags, and *babouches* (traditional slippers). One of the shopkeepers will hand you a few sprigs of fresh mint to smother the smell and explain what's going on in the tanneries below—how the skins are placed successively in saline solution, quicklime, pigeon droppings, and then any of several natural dyes: poppies for red, turmeric for yellow, saffron for orange, indigo for blue, and mint for green. Barefoot workers in shorts pick up skins from the bottoms of the dyeing vats with their feet, then work them manually. Though this may look like the world's least desirable job, the work is relatively well paid and still in demand for a strong export market. ⊠ *Chouara Lablida.*

Zaouia of Moulay Idriss II. Originally built by the Idriss dynasty in the 9th century in honor of the city's founder—just 33 at the time of his death—this *zaouia* (sanctuary) was restored by the Merenid dynasty in the 13th century and has became one of the medina's holiest shrines. Particularly known for his *baraka* (divine protection), Moulay Idriss II had an especially strong cult among women seeking fertility and pilgrims hoping for good luck. The wooden beam at the entrance, about 6 feet from the ground, was originally placed there to keep Jews, Christians, and donkeys out of the *horm,* the sacred area surrounding the shrine itself. Inside the horm, Moroccans have historically enjoyed official sanctuary—they cannot be arrested if sought by the law. You may be able to catch a glimpse of the saint's tomb at the far right corner through the doorway; look for the fervently faithful burning candles and incense and the tomb's silk-brocade covering. Note the rough wooden doors themselves, worn smooth with hundreds of years of kissing and caressing the wood for baraka. ⊠ *Bou Touil, on north side of mosque* ⊙ *Daily 24 hrs* ☞ *Entrance restricted to Muslims.*

WORTH NOTING

Cherratine Medersa. Recent restoration against humidity and other natural agressions has kept this important historical site intact. Constructed in 1670 by Moulay Rachid, this is one of Fez's two Alaouite medersas. More austere than the 14th-century medersas of the Merenids, the Cherratine is more functional, designed to hold over 200 students. It's interesting primarily as a contrast to the intricate craftsmanship and decorative intent of the Merenid structures. The entry doors beautifully engraved in bronze lead to the *douiras,* narrow residential blocks consisting of a honeycomb of small rooms. ⊠ *Derb Zaouia* 🖂 *20 DH* ☉ *Daily 9–1 and 3–6:30.*

Fondouk Tsetouanien. Named for the traders from Tétouan who traded and lodged here, this fondouk is the medina's most original with its jumble of balconies, ground-floor scales, and rug and leather dealers. The fondouks were great centers of ribaldry and intrigue in the Middle Ages—some sense of this seems to have survived the passage of time. ⊠ *Bou Touil, near the Kairaouine Mosque.*

FEZ EL-DJEDID
TOP ATTRACTIONS

Fez el-Djedid (New Fez) lies southwest of Bab Boujeloud between Fez el-Bali and the Ville Nouvelle. Built after 1273 by the Merenid dynasty as a government seat and stronghold, it remained the administrative center of Morocco until 1912, when Rabat took over the role and diminished this area's visibility and activity. The three distinct segments of Fez el-Djedid consist of the Royal Palace in the west, the Mellah or Jewish Quarter in the south, and Muslim District in the east.

Bab es Seba. Named for the seven brothers of Moulay Abdellah, who reigned during the 18th century, the Gate of Seven connects two open spaces originally designed for military parades and royal ceremonies, the Petit Méchouar and Vieux Méchouar, now known as Moulay Hassan II Square. It was from this gate that Prince Ferdinand, brother of Duarte, king of Portugal, was hanged head-down for four days in 1437 after being captured during a failed Portuguese invasion of Tangier. ⊠ *Av. Moulay Hassan.*

Dar el-Makhzen. Fez's Royal Palace and gardens are strictly closed to the public, but even from the outside they're an impressive sight. From Place des Alaouites, take a close look at the door's giant brass knockers, made by artisans from Fez el-Bali, as well as the imposing brass doors themselves. Inside are various palaces, 200 acres of gardens, and parade grounds, as well as a medersa founded in 1320. One of the palaces inside, Dar el-Qimma, has intricately engraved and painted ceilings. The street running along the palace's southeast side is Rue Bou Khessissat, one side of which is lined with typically ornate residential facades from the Mellah's edge. ⚠ Note: Security in this area is high and should be respected. Guards watch visitors carefully and will warn that photographs of the palace are forbidden; cameras are sometimes confiscated.

Jardin Jnan Sbil. Gardens play an important role in Moroccan culture, and this gorgeous green space just outside the medina walls is one of the oldest in Fez. Once part of the Royal Palace, it was donated to the city in the 19th century by Sultan Moulay Hassan. Because of its importance, the garden recently underwent four years of restoration to return it to its former splendor, and it reopened to the public in 2011. Now a stroll around its shady pathways, with time to admire its many towering palms, rose bushes, lakes, and fountains, is the perfect escape from the medina's hubbub. ⊠ *Av. Moulay Hassan.*

Mellah. With its characteristically ornate balconies and forged-iron windows, the Mellah was created in the 15th century when the Jews, forced out of the medina in one of Morocco's recurrent pogroms, were removed from their previous ghetto near Bab Guissa and set up as royal financial consultants and buffers between the Merenid rulers and the people. Fez's Jewish community suffered repressive measures until the beginning of the French protectorate in 1912. Faced with an uncertain future after Morocco gained independence in 1956, nearly all of Fez's Jews migrated to Israel, the United States, or Casablanca. ■ TIP➔ **Head to the terrace of Danan Synagogue on Rue Der el-Ferah Teati for a panoramic view of the district.** ✛ *Accessible via Place des Alaouites or Bab el-Mellah.*

WORTH NOTING

Moulay Abdellah Quarter. Built by the Merenids as a government seat and a stronghold against their subjects, this area lost its purpose when Rabat became the Moroccan capital under the French protectorate in 1912. Subsequently a red-light district filled with brothels and dance halls, the quarter was closed to foreigners for years. Historic highlights include the vertically green-striped **Moulay Abdellah Mosque** and the **Great Mosque Abu Haq,** built by the Merenid sultan in 1276.

VILLE NOUVELLE

The 20th-century Ville Nouvelle is a modern neighborhood built by the French, with tree-lined avenues, contemporary hotels, fashionable boutiques, and upscale residences. Considerable commercial development is taking place to attract younger, affluent Fassis. There are no outstanding historical sites, but visit this area for newer cafés, restaurants, and lodging.

WHERE TO EAT

In the country's culinary capital, foodie pleasures are everywhere: from simple food stalls and cafés to gourmet Moroccan fare in ancient palaces, traditional Moroccan recipes given a contemporary twist by innovative chefs, and French- and Mediterranean-influenced dishes. For something quick and filling, you can always grab a 10 DH bowl of cumin-laced pea or bean soup at one of the many stands and stalls near the medina's main food markets just inside Bab Boujeloud, or take a sightseeing break with a honey-laden pastry and some fresh mint tea. For a heartier meal, there's grilled meat, slow-cooked tagines, and vegetable-topped couscous. Taste Fassi specialties on a fascinating street-food tour, and don't leave without sampling pigeon pastilla, a heavenly combination of sweet and sour flavors. It's often made with chicken nowadays, but the Ruined Garden, in the medina, will cook the authentic dish to order with a day's notice.

FEZ EL-BALI

$ ✕ **Cafe Clock.** Set in the heart of the medina, this cross-cultural café
ECLECTIC   spread over two traditional dars is a Fez institution. It's the perfect
Fodor's Choice   place to take a sightseeing break with a tea or mocktail, or a bite from
★   the eclectic menu, like the justly famous camel burger. It's vegetarian-friendly, too. But the Clock is much more than a café: if you want to

learn to cook Moroccan cuisine, pick up some Moroccan Arabic, try your hand at calligraphy, learn to play the oud, or have a henna tattoo, just check out its cultural program. ■ **TIP→ It's cash only, but dollars and euros, as well as dirham, are accepted.** [$] *Average main: 95DH* ✉ *7, Derb el Magana* ☎ *0535/63–78–55* 🌐 *www.cafeclock.com* 💳 *No credit cards.*

$ MOROCCAN 🍴 **Dar Hatim.** They say the best Moroccan food is served at home, and Dar Hatim is the next-best thing. In a tucked-away corner of the Mellah, the old Jewish quarter of the medina, a local family has turned its living room and courtyard into a superb restaurant. Fouad will guide you to the restaurant, while his wife and mother are in the kitchen preparing the traditional Moroccan dishes. In the convivial, exquisitely tiled dining room, you can choose from four different three-course set menus. There's always a selection of Moroccan salads, freshly baked bread, and succulent olives, along with tagines, couscous, and pastillas; vegetarians can be catered to as well. ■ **TIP→ They don't serve alcohol but will open any wine or beer you want to bring.** [$] *Average main: 170DH* ✉ *19, Derb Ezaouia Fandak Lihoudi* ☎ *0535/52–53–23, 0666/52–53–23* ✍ *Reservations essential.*

$ MEDITERRANEAN FAMILY 🍴 **Fez Café Restaurant.** This popular bistro-style café-cum-restaurant is set in the delightful medina oasis of Jardin des Biehn. The daily changing chalkboard and à la carte menu reflects the Moroccan chef's love of Gallic gastronomy. He happily mixes Moroccan and French culinary influences, using fresh ingredients from the market and the owners' organic garden. Feast on fillet steak or fish; vegetarians are well catered-to, with delicious quiches, soups, and salads. Eat alfresco in the garden, on the rooftop under the sun and stars, or in the brightly colored interior room with lots of creative decorative touches, including nods to the Biehns' Provençal roots. ■ **TIP→ Cooking classes with the chef are available upon request.** [$] *Average main: 150DH* ✉ *13, Akbat Sbaa, Douh* ☎ *0535/63–50–31* 🌐 *www.jardindesbiehn.com/en/restaurant* ✍ *Reservations essential* ⏲ *Closed Thurs.*

$$ MOROCCAN 🍴 **L'Amandier.** This fine-dining Moroccan restaurant sits on the top floor of Palais Faraj, with stunning views over the twinkling lights of the medina. The décor is sleek and sophisticated, the service is attentive, and the chef has re-created age-old Fassi recipes that have been passed down through the generations. Start with a selection of cooked vegetable salads—smoky eggplant, carrots glazed with honey, delicately spiced roasted peppers. Then try one of the slow-cooked tagines, such as the chicken with pumpkin jam or the lamb shoulder, which falls off the bone. [$] *Average main: 220DH* ✉ *Palais Faraj, Bab Zhiat, Quartier Ziat* ☎ *0535/63–53–56* 🌐 *www.palaisfaraj.com/EN/restaurants* ✍ *Reservations essential* ⏲ *No lunch.*

$ MEDITERRANEAN FAMILY 🍴 **Le 44.** Tired of tagines? Family- and vegetarian-friendly cafe-restaurant Le 44 serves up pasta dishes, fresh salads, and soups, as well as delicious French desserts like tarte tatin. This light, bright, contemporary riad is set down a winding derb off the Talaa K'bira (there are signs) and you can take a well-earned break from pounding the pavement with a tea, coffee, or soda, as well as exotic local fruit juices, such as almond, avocado, and date on the roof terrace. There's Wi-Fi too. [$] *Average* *main: 50DH* ✉ *44, Derb Bensalem-Talaa Kbira* ☎ *0634/70–75–13* ⏲ *Closed Mon.*

$ MOROCCAN
🍴 **Le Kasbah.** Spread over several floors, the rooftop tables of this good-value restaurant just below Bab Boujeloud offer an entertaining view of the street life below. The menu is standard tourist fare—mixed grill, tagines, couscous—so you're probably better off sticking to an afternoon mint tea with pastries. The location is the thing: the three pavement tables make for great people-watching. [$] *Average main: 70DH* ✉ *Rue Serrajine* ☎ *0535/74–15–33.*

$$$ MOROCCAN
🍴 **Palais Amani Restaurant.** Dining under the stars in this Andalusian-style oasis is a delight, surrounding by citrus trees and next to a twinkling fountain. The chefs take traditional recipes and give them a contemporary presentation, creating a daily changing three-course dinner using seasonal produce from the market. Perhaps a fava bean soup or a beef-and-artichoke tagine will be on the menu. They also have an à la carte menu, for lunch as well as dinner, with Mediterranean favorites, such as duck breast and fries. On the roof terrace you'll find a tapas menu and a good mojito, or you can dine inside the Art Deco–influenced dining room. [$] *Average main: 395DH* ✉ *Palais Amani, 12, Derb el Miter, Oued Zhoune, Fez el Bali, Fez* ☎ *0535/63–32–09* 🌐 *www.palaisamani.com.*

$$$ ECLECTIC Fodor's Choice ★
🍴 **Restaurant 7.** The city's most chic riad-turned-restaurant has become a base for pop-ups from globally renowned chefs. Jerome Waag from Alice Waters's Chez Panisse in California was the first, with more top chefs to follow for residencies of between one and four months. Their brief: to use whatever's inspired them at the market that day to create a cross-culinary, four-course, prix-fixe menu. Dishes such as chilled fava-bean-and-almond soup and farm chicken braised with fresh figs and anise seed appear on the nightly changing chalkboard menu, while the restaurant's pared-down interior eschews Morocco's traditional color palette in favor of black-and-white tiles, bright white walls, and striking contemporary art prints. [$] *Average main: 320DH* ✉ *7, Zkak Rouan* ☎ *0535/63–89–24* 🌐 *www.restaurantnumero7.com* ✍ *Reservations essential* 💳 *No credit cards* ⏲ *Closed Mon. and Tues. No lunch.*

$$ MEDITERRANEAN Fodor's Choice ★
🍴 **Restaurant Dar Roumana.** One of the city's best eateries is set in the strikingly beautiful courtyard of hotel Dar Roumana. French chef Vincent Bonin has created a Mediterranean menu with a Moroccan twist that makes the most of seasonal produce fresh from the markets and top local producers. Creative salads, such as figs with crispy pancetta, local goat cheese, and date dressing, are followed by a meat or fish dish—perhaps a perfectly cooked veal T-bone or pan-fried John Dory—and a sumptuous dessert, like *vacherin* (cow's milk cheese) and black cherries or Sephardic bitter orange and almond cake. There's an excellent wine list too. [$] *Average main: 275DH* ✉ *Dar Roumana, 30, Derb El Amer, Zkak Roumane* ☎ *0535/74–16–37* 🌐 *www.darroumana.com* ✍ *Reservations essential* ⏲ *Closed Sun. No lunch.*

$ MOROCCAN FAMILY Fodor's Choice ★
🍴 **Ruined Garden Restaurant.** This British-run alfresco restaurant, set in the romantic remains of a ruined riad, comes complete with crumbling mosaic floors, fountains, and lush foliage. The à la carte menu and daily specials are prepared using fresh produce from the souk: think salads such as *zaalouk* (smoky eggplant, tomato, and paprika puree) and street food–style dishes like sardines marinated in *chermoula* (a marinade,

5

including herbs, oil, lemon juice, and garlic) with a polenta batter and mini *maakouda* (spiced battered potato cakes in a rich tomato sauce). Tea and cakes are also served all day, as well as a variety of juices and smoothies, like date milk and orange-blossom water. ■**TIP**➜ **You can also preorder delicious Fassi specialty pigeon pastilla and seven-hour cooked Mechoui lamb a day in advance.** $ *Average main: 100DH* ✉ *Sidi Ahmed Chaoui, Siaj* ☎ *0649/19–14–10* ⊕ *www.ruinedgarden. com* ⊗ *Closed Wed.*

$ ✕ **Thami's.** One of the worst-kept secrets of locals and expats, Thami's is

MOROCCAN the perfect place to enjoy a delicious, well-priced meal with the added bonus of first-rate people-watching. Close to the Bab Boujeloud at the top of one of the medina's busiest thoroughfares, Thami's has expanded over the years from a single table and four chairs under the shade of a mulberry tree to a full-fledged restaurant. What hasn't changed is the friendly service and the simple, cheap, and fresh dishes on offer, from the popular kefta-and-egg tagine to hearty bowls of harira. $ *Average main: 30DH* ✉ *44, rue Sarrajine, near Bab Boujeloud at the top of the Tala'a Sghira* ☎ *0660/43–35–05* ▭ *No credit cards.*

FEZ EL-DJEDID

$ ✕ **La Mezzanine.** Just a five-minute walk from the medina, this lounge-

MOROCCAN bar and restaurant is a haven of Fassi cool. It's undergone a modern Moroccan redesign and now the air-conditioned interior is cool white tadelakt with splashes of vivid red. The roof terrace with its lounging cushions and oversize lanterns is the perfect place for a sunset drink overlooking the lush Jnan Sbil gardens. Or enjoy a casual meal of salads (the Caesar is particularly good) and fusion tapas, such as Roquefort-filled *briouates* (spicy dumplings). Naturally, this chic oasis managed by an equally hip and friendly staff is outfitted with Wi-Fi and a sound system. $ *Average main: 80DH* ✉ *17, Kasbat Chams* ☎ *0611/07–83–36* ▭ *No credit cards* ⊗ *Closed Mon.*

VILLE NOUVELLE

$$ ✕ **MB Fès.** The minimalist design of this restaurant-lounge—one of the

MEDITERRANEAN city's most stylish eateries—channels industrial chic with rough-hewn stone walls, slate floors, and floor-to-ceiling windows, complemented by sleek, contemporary furniture. The menu combines French-influenced fare, with dishes such as *magret de canard* (duck breast) and sole meunière, and international favorites such as Caesar salad and hamburger, backed up with an impressive wine list. After dinner, head to the upstairs bar to lounge on a leather sofa with a creative cocktail. $ *Average main: 200DH* ✉ *12, rue Ahmed Chaouki* ☎ *0535/62–27–27* ⊕ *www.mbrestaurantlounge.com* ✎ *Reservations essential.*

WHERE TO STAY

Staying in Fez's medina offers such a unique experience that you're best off choosing a hotel either in or very near medieval Fez el-Bali. Choose an atmospheric riad, boutique hotel, or resort-style hotel. There are also some good new hotels in the Ville Nouvelle. There are no hotels in Fez el-Djedid.

Restaurant ▼

MB Fès 1

Hotels ▼

Hotel Sahrai 1

Barceló Fès Medina 2

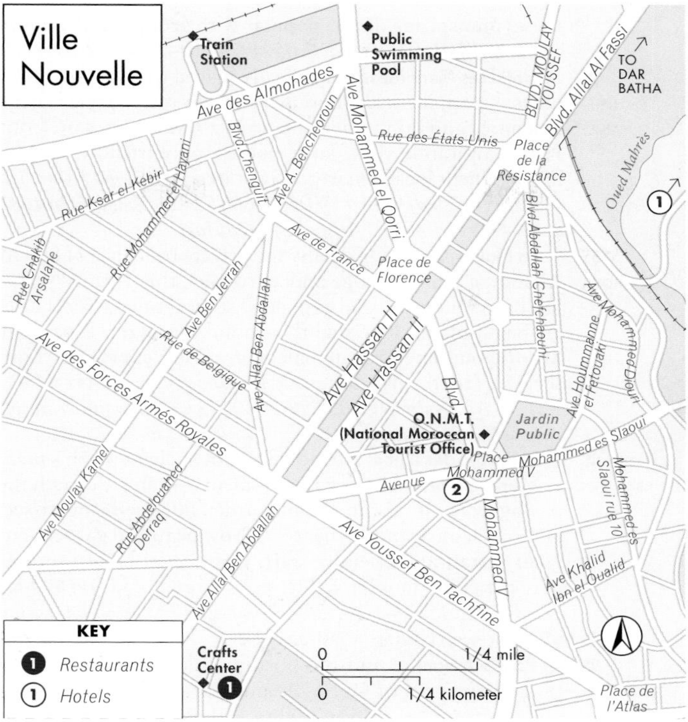
Ville Nouvelle
Train Station
Public Swimming Pool
BLVD. MOULAY YOUSSEF
Blvd. Allal Al Fassi
TO DAR BATHA
Ave des Almohades
Ave Mohammed el Qorri
Blvd. Chenguit
Ave A. Bencheroun
Rue des États Unis
Place de la Résistance
Oued Mahrès
Rue Ksar el Kebir
Rue Mohammed el Hayani
Ave de France
Place de Florence
Blvd. Abdallah Chefchaouni
Rue Chakib Arsalane
Ave Ben Jerrah
Ave Allal Ben Abdallah
Rue de Belgique
Ave Hassan II
Ave Hassan II
Ave Mohammed Diouri
Ave Hoummanne el Fetouaki
Blvd.
Ave des Forces Armés Royales
O.N.M.T. (National Moroccan Tourist Office)
Jardin Public
Place Mohammed V
Avenue Mohammed es Slaoui
Mohammed es Slaoui rue 10
Mohammed V
Ave Moulay Kamel
Rue Abdelouahed Derraq
Ave Allal Ben Abdallah
Ave Youssef Ben Tachfine
Ave Khalid Ibn el Oualid
KEY
Restaurants
Hotels
Crafts Center
0 1/4 mile
0 1/4 kilometer
Place de l'Atlas

FEZ EL-BALI

$ B&B/INN FAMILY 🏨 **Dar Finn.** The former home of the Pasha of Tazi has been restored to its former splendor by a British couple, who have created five rooms and two enormous suites—the Pacha Suite was once his office—large enough for families. **Pros:** plenty of outside space; central location. **Cons:** may be too intimate for some; Wi-Fi patchy in the upstairs rooms. [$] *Rooms from: 935DH* ✉ *27, Zkak Rouah, Chrablyine* ☎ *0655/01–89–75, 0535/74–00–04* 🌐 *www.darfinn.com* 🛏 *5 rooms, 2 suites* 💳 *No credit cards* 🍴 *Breakfast.*

$ B&B/INN Fodor's Choice ★ 🏨 **Dar Roumana.** The House of the Pomegranate is a sumptuously restored residence, with five stunning suites that showcase the work of Fez's famous artisans in their carved cedarwood doors and lofty ceilings, mosaic tile floors, and intricate plasterwork. **Pros:** beautiful décor; great service; excellent restaurant. **Cons:** hard to find (but they have a porter); steep stairs to upper-floor rooms. [$] *Rooms from: 952DH* ✉ *30, Derb el Amer, Zkak Roumane* ☎ *0535/74–16–37* 🌐 *www.darroumana.com* 🛏 *5 suites* 🍴 *Breakfast.*

$ HOTEL 🏨 **Hôtel Batha.** Just outside the medina entrance near Bab Boujeloud, the popular Batha has an excellent location, good-value rooms—spacious, clean, and comfortable, if a little dated—and the all-important air-conditioning. **Pros:** central location; family-friendly pool. **Cons:** street

5

noise; uninspiring décor; popular with groups. [$] *Rooms from: 680DH* ✉ *Pl. de l'Istiqlal, Batha* ☎ *0535/74–10–77* 🛏 *62 rooms* 🍴 *Breakfast.*

$$ HOTEL FAMILY 🏨 **Hôtel Les Mérinides.** Strategically placed to overlook the city, Les Mérinides is popular with those who seek a resort-style hotel with modern amenities and don't mind the drive a few minutes up from the medina. **Pros:** panoramic view; large pool; family-friendly. **Cons:** dated décor; inconvenient location; expensive rates. [$] *Rooms from: 1380DH* ✉ *36, Chrablyne Borj Nord* ☎ *0535/64–52–26* 🌐 *www.hotel-lesmerinides.com* 🛏 *96 rooms, 7 suites* 🍴 *Breakfast.*

$$$$ HOTEL 🏨 **La Maison Bleue.** Originally the private residence of Sidi Mohammed el Abaddi, a famous judge and astrologer, this 19th-century family home has been renovated and expanded several times over the years, and now it's beginning to fray slightly around the edges. **Pros:** central location; historic building; private balconies. **Cons:** expensive rooms; unreliable service; faded furnishings. [$] *Rooms from: 2134DH* ✉ *33, Derb El Mitter, Ain Asliten* ☎ *0535/63–60–52* 🌐 *www.maisonbleue.com* 🛏 *18 rooms* 🍴 *Breakfast.*

$$ B&B/INN 🏨 **Le Jardin des Biehn.** Attracting a global clientele, this *maison d'hôtes* is a serene experience from the moment you step through the ocher-color passageway into the luxuriant garden filled with sweet-scented jasmine and roses, olive and citrus trees. **Pros:** beautiful garden; creative rooms; great restaurant; friendly staff. **Cons:** may be too intimate for some; may get chilly in winter. [$] *Rooms from: 1455DH* ✉ *13, Akbat Sbaa, Douh* ☎ *0535/74–10–36, 0664/64–76–79* 🌐 *www.jardindesbiehn.com* 🛏 *4 rooms, 5 suites* 🍴 *Breakfast.*

$$ HOTEL Fodor's Choice ★ 🏨 **Palais Amani.** Amid the bustling alleyways near the tanneries and the parking area of Oued Zhoune, the eco-friendly Palais Amani is an unexpected oasis of tranquillity and elegance that has garnered much attention. **Pros:** personalized service; spacious rooms; elegant design; elevator. **Cons:** no pool; down a dark derb. [$] *Rooms from: 1385DH* ✉ *12, Derb el Miter, Oued Zhoune* ☎ *0535/63–32–09* 🌐 *www.palaisamani.com* 🛏 *15 rooms* 🍴 *Breakfast.*

$$$$ HOTEL 🏨 **Palais Faraj Suites & Spa.** Housed in a lavish 19th-century former palace set just outside the medina walls, the 25 suites blend contemporary furnishings with acres of marble, intricately carved cedarwood, ornate zellij tiling, and sparkling chandeliers—the work of a four-year renovation led by experts in Moorish architecture. **Pros:** spacious; first-rate facilities; large swimming pool; road access. **Cons:** not in the thick of the medina; not as intimate as a riad. [$] *Rooms from: 2576DH* ✉ *Bab Ziat, Quartier Ziat* ☎ *0535/63–53–56* 🌐 *www.palaisfaraj.com* 🛏 *25 suites* 🍴 *Breakfast.*

$$$ HOTEL 🏨 **Palais Sheherazade & Spa.** Set in the former home of a 19th-century minister, the Palais Sheherazade is a perfect expression of traditional style, with spectacular woodwork and tranquil views onto the vast courtyard. **Pros:** spacious rooms; central location; luxurious spa. **Cons:** expensive restaurant. [$] *Rooms from: 1909DH* ✉ *23, Arsat Bennis Douh* ☎ *0535/74–16–42* 🌐 *www.sheheraz.com* 🛏 *24 suites* 🍴 *Breakfast.*

$ B&B/INN 🏨 **Riad Anata.** The Belgian owner has given this traditional house a lighter, more contemporary feel, while staying true to its Moroccan

At sunset, Fez begins to come alive with lights.

roots, decorating the five rooms—named after colors—in pale tones, with smooth tadelakt walls and splashes of vibrant color from throws, rugs, and local artwork. **Pros:** personal service; close to taxis and parking. **Cons:** lacks ornate Moroccan décor; could be too small for some. $ *Rooms from: 1120DH* ⊠ *Derb el-Hamia* ☎ *0535/74–15–37* ⊕ *www.riad-anata.com* ⤳ *5 rooms* ⟨⟩ *Breakfast.*

$$$$ 🏨 **Riad Fès.** For an architecturally refined interpretation of riad living,
HOTEL   head to this luxurious hotel: a perfect blend of character, modern convenience, creature comforts, and outstanding service. **Pros:** quiet location; luxurious appointments; hammam. **Cons:** very expensive. $ *Rooms from: 2500DH* ⊠ *5, Derb Ibn Slimane Zerbtana* ☎ *0535/74–12–06* ⊕ *www.riadfes.com* ⤳ *30 rooms, 14 suites* ⟨⟩ *Breakfast.*

$ 🏨 **Riad Idrissy.** After a meticulous restoration, this delightful British-run
B&B/INN   riad's triple-height courtyard and five rooms are resplendent with dazzling zellij tiles and ornate stuccowork. **Pros:** charming and attentive
Fodor's Choice   staff; access to the Ruined Garden restaurant in the mornings; roof
★   terrace. **Cons:** may feel too small and personal for some; steep stairs to upper-floor rooms. $ *Rooms from: 727DH* ⊠ *Derb Idrissy* ⊕ *www.riadidrissy.com* ⤳ *5 rooms* ⟨⟩ *Breakfast.*

$$ 🏨 **Riad Laaroussa.** Built around a lush courtyard garden—a tranquil
B&B/INN   oasis from the medina's mayhem right on the doorstep—this 17th-
Fodor's Choice   century palace had fallen into disrepair before being rescued and rebuilt
★   by its French-American owners, utilizing the skills of the city's finest craftsmen. **Pros:** attentive service; central location; garden. **Cons:** may be too relaxed for some; steep stairs to upper-floor rooms. $ *Rooms from: 1232DH* ⊠ *3, Derb Bechara* ☎ *0674/18–76–39* ⊕ *www.riad-laaroussa.com* ⤳ *4 rooms, 4 suites* ⟨⟩ *Breakfast.*

$ ☖ **Riad Numero 9.** It's just like staying at a friend's house, a friend with
B&B/INN impeccable taste that is, and what it lacks in size—there are just three
bedrooms set around the courtyard, each on a different level—it more
than makes up for in style. **Pros:** perfect for small groups; central location. **Cons:** the smallest room is not en suite; windows open onto the
courtyard. **$** *Rooms from: 1121DH* ✉ *9, Derb Lamsside, Zkak el Ma*
✍ *stephen@riad9.com* ⊕ *www.riad9.com* ↘ *3 rooms* ▭ *No credit
cards* †◎| *Breakfast.*

$ ☖ **Ryad Mabrouka.** This carefully restored Andalusian townhouse in
B&B/INN the heart of the medina is consistently a pleasure: every detail is polished, from magnificent doors and crafted furnishings to a pretty interior garden with well-maintained pool. **Pros:** central location; elegant
rooms; good service; terrace. **Cons:** not for families with young children. **$** *Rooms from: 1175DH* ✉ *25, derb el Miter* ☎ *0535/63–63–45*
⊕ *www.ryadmabrouka.com* ↘ *2 rooms, 6 suites* †◎| *Breakfast.*

VILLE NOUVELLE

$ ☖ **Barceló Fès Medina.** Despite its name, this contemporary hotel—the
HOTEL Spanish chain's second in Morocco—sits in a prime spot at the edge
of the Ville Nouvelle, with stellar views over the medina. **Pros:** located
between old and new Fez; swimming pool; contemporary design. **Cons:**
not in the medina; lacks the intimacy of a riad. **$** *Rooms from: 952DH*
✉ *53, av. Hassan II* ☎ *0535/94–88–00* ⊕ *www.barcelo.com* ↘ *125
rooms, 9 suites* †◎| *Multiple meal plans.*

$$$$ ☖ **Hotel Sahrai.** Perched on a hill looking down on the medina, this
HOTEL boldly designed and ultrastylish boutique hotel has brought a new
level of contemporary luxury to Fez. **Pros:** stylish, contemporary décor;
choice of restaurants and bars. **Cons:** not for those looking for traditional Moroccan style; expensive rates. **$** *Rooms from: 2002DH* ✉ *Bab
Lghoul, Dhar el Mehraz* ☎ *0535/94–03–32* ⊕ *www.hotelsahrai.com*
↘ *36 rooms, 14 suites* †◎| *Breakfast.*

NIGHTLIFE

The Ville Nouvelle has a more active nightlife in Fez, though many of
the best hotel bars are in or near the edge of the medina.

FEZ EL-BALI

BARS

Bar at the Hôtel les Mérinides. This open-air bar and lounge overlooking the medina is a popular watering hole with live music at night,
a wide selection of alcoholic and nonalcoholic beverages, and one
of the best panoramic views in the city. ✉ *36, Chrablyne Borj Nord*
☎ *0535/64–52–26.*

Fodor's Choice **Le Golden Bar.** This Art Deco–influenced bar attracts sophisticated locals
★ and visitors as much for the medina views as the creative cocktails.
Perched atop the hotel Palais Faraj, with sweeping vistas on three sides,
you can sample a well-crafted cocktail, a glass of fine local wine, or
beer from a comfortable couch. This intimate spot also hosts live music
and DJs on weekend nights. There's also a large alfresco terrace overlooking the jumble of medina rooftops. ■ **TIP→** Get there for sunset to

watch the old city turn to gold. ⊠ *Palais Faraj, Bab Ziat, Quartier Ziat* ☏ *0661/07–46–99* ⊕ *www.palaisfaraj.com.*

VILLE NOUVELLE

BARS

The Rooftop. Perched on top of the Hotel Sahrai, the equally chic Rooftop bar draws a sophisticated crowd. The indoor-outdoor bar, with its expanse of wood, local stone, and glass, finished off with designer seating and ambient lighting, hosts top DJs on weekends. But the real star of the show is the view over the old ciy. There are plenty of luxurious alfresco daybeds to lounge on, so grab a creative cocktail and a front-row seat and watch the sun set as the medina fills with twinkling lights. ⊠ *Hotel Sahrai, Bab Lghoul, Dar el Mehraz* ☏ *0535/94–03–32* ⊕ *www.hotelsahrai.com.*

SHOPPING

FEZ EL-BALI

Fez el-Bali is a gigantic souk. Embroidery, pottery, leather goods, rugs and carpets, copper plates, brass pots, silver jewelry, textiles, babouches, and spices are all of exceptional handmade quality and sold at comparatively low prices, considering the craftsmanship that has remained authentic for nearly a thousand years.

CRAFTS

Au Petit Bazar de Bon Accuiel. Fassi dealer Mohamed Benabdejlil's store isn't cheap, but it's got an interesting selection of antiques, textiles, and Berber jewelry—and be sure to look upstairs. ⊠ *35, Talaa Seghira.*

Les Mysteres de Fes. This small store is packed with fascinating pieces of jewelry, antiques, handmade objects, and furniture. ⊠ *53, Derb bin Lemssari, Sidi Moussa* ☏ *0535/63–61–48.*

Maison de Broderie et de Brocart de Fes. Discover the intricate work of local embroiderers, including beautiful tablecloths and napkins. ⊠ *2, Derb Blida* ☏ *0535/63–65–46.*

Place Seffarine. The picturesque Place Seffarine is the place for all things metal: bowls, boxes, candleholders, and ornate lamps. And you can watch the artisans as they rhythmically hammer the copper and brass into shape outside their workshops. ⊠ *Pl. Seffarine.*

Terrasse de Tannerie. Shop for butter-soft bags, slippers, and jackets at this labyrinthine shop overlooking the tanneries. Be sure to bargain. ⊠ *10, Hay Labilda Chouara* ☏ *0535/63–66–25.*

FOOD

Herboristerie Seddik. In this quaint shop, the shelves are stacked with herbs, spices, and all kinds of traditional beauty products such as argan oil, as well as flower extracts and medicinal plants. ⊠ *15, Hay Lablida, near the Chouara Tannery.*

HAMMAMS AND SPAS

Palais Amani Spa. Indulge in a luxurious hammam experience at this cross between a traditional hammam and a European-style spa. Palais Amani's mosaic-tiled hammam offers a private, romantic, candlelit

Continued on page 250

THE AUTHENTICITY OF ARTISANSHIP
Traditional Moroccan Crafts

Shopping in Morocco is an experience you will never forget. In cities like Marrakesh and Fez, the souks are both magical and chaotic, their narrow alleyways overflowing with handcrafted products created using centuries-old techniques.

by Victoria Tang

Open bazaars and medieval markets display the bright colors, bold patterns, and natural materials found throughout Morocco's arts and crafts tradition. Items are proudly made in artisan workshops dating back to ancient times.

Handmade Moroccan arts and crafts demonstrate the influence of Berber, Arab, Andalusian, and European traditions. Using natural resources like copper, wool, silver, wood, clay, and indigenous plants, artisans and their apprentices incorporate symbolic motifs, patterns, and color into wood carvings, textiles, ceramics, jewelry, slippers, clothing, and other decorative arts. Traditional processes from the Middle Ages are still used in many cases and can be observed from start to finish. Be prepared to negotiate a good price for anything you would like to buy: bartering here is expected and considered an art form in itself.

(top left) Ceramic tagines (top right) leather slippers (bottom right) perfume bottles

THE BEST OF MOROCCAN GOODS

Visiting Morocco's souks also gives you the opportunity to view the techniques still used to mass-produce a wide assortment of authentic goods by hand. While prices in Morocco may not be as cheap as they once were, hand-crafted goods can be found at any price point. Even the highest-quality pieces are half of what you'd pay back home.

LEATHER

Moroccan leather, known as *maroquinerie*, has been sought after worldwide. Fez and Marrakesh have extensive working tanneries, producing large quantities of items for export. Sold inexpensively in local markets are bags, belts, luggage, jackets, vests, and beautifully embroidered goat skin ottomans. Leather and suede *babouches* are the ultimate house slippers; myriad colors and styles are available, and they make an inexpensive gift.

SPICES

Markets overflow with sacks of common spices used extensively in local cuisine and natural healing treatments. To create tajines and couscous back home, look for cayenne, cumin, turmeric, cinnamon, ginger, paprika, and saffron. Ask shopkeepers to blend *ras el hanout*, an essential mixture of ground aromatic spices including cardamon, nutmeg, and anise used for stews and grilling.

SILVER

The most popular silver jewelry in Morocco is crafted by Berbers and Arabs in the southern High Atlas and in the Anti-Atlas Mountains. Taroudant and Tiznit are the most well-known jewelry-producing areas. Desert nomads—Touaregs and Saharaouia—craft silver items for tribal celebrations. Smaller items include fibulas (ornamental clasps to fasten clothing), Touareg "crosses," delicate filigree bracelets, and hands of Fatima (or *khamsa*, meaning five, for the five fingers) that are said to offer protection from the evil eye. There's also a good variety of Moroccan Judaica that includes silver *yads* (Torah pointers), Torah crowns, and menorahs. Silver teapots, serving trays, and decorative pieces capture the essence of Moroccan metalwork with geometric designs and ornate detail.

ARGAN OIL

Much valued by the Berbers, argan oil has been used for centuries as an all-purpose salve, a healthy dip for homemade bread, protection for skin and nails, a treatment for scars and acne, a hair conditioner, a skin moisturizer, and even a general cure for aches and pains. With its strong nutty and toasty flavor, argan oil is popularly sold in the food souks of Essaouira, Marrakesh, and Meknès in its purest form for culinary use. The oil is often mixed with other essential oils for beauty and naturopathic treatments.

The Origins of Argan: The oil from the Argania spinosa, a thorny tree that has been growing wild in Morocco for some 25 million years, is a prized commodity. Today, the tree only grows in the triangular belt along Morocco's Atlantic coast from Essaouira down to Tafraoute in the Anti-Atlas Mountains and eastward as far as Taroudant. It takes about 35 kg (77 pounds) of sun-dried nuts to produce one liter of oil.

TEXTILES

For centuries, weaving in Morocco has been an important artisanal tradition to create beauty and spiritual protection. Looms operate in medina workshops, while groups of tribal nomads can be seen weaving by hand on worn carpets in smaller villages. The best buys are multicolored silk-and-gold thread scarves, shawls, and runners, as well as hand-embroidered fabrics used for tablecloths, decorating, and traditional caftans and djellabas.

WOOD

From the forests of the Rif and Middle Atlas, cedar wood is used to create beautiful *mashrabiyya* latticework often found on decorative household chests, doors, and tables. Essaouira is the source of all thuya-wood crafts. Here, only the gnarled burls that grow out of the rare coniferous tree's trunk are used to carve a vast variety of objects, from tiny boxes and picture frames to trays, games, and even furniture often decorated with marquetry in ebony and walnut.

(top) Pressing argan oil in a traditional press
(bottom) argan oil and its source

MOROCCAN POTTERY

 Morocco has earned a reputation as one of the world's best producers of artisanal ceramics. Decorative styles, shapes, and colors vary from city to city, with three major areas producing the best. From platters and cooking vessels to small pots decorated with silver filigree, this authentic craft makes for an inexpensive, high-quality, and practical souvenir.

FEZ

Morocco's most stunning ceramics are the distinctive blue-and-white *Fassi* pieces. Many of the pieces you'll find actually have the word *Fas* (the Arabic pronunciation of Fez) written in Arabic calligraphy and incorporated into geometric designs. Fassi ceramics also come in a beautiful polychrome of teal, yellow, royal blue, and burgundy. Another design unique to Fez is the simple *mataysha* (tomato flower) design. You'll recognize it by the repetition of a small, four-petal flower design. Fez is also at the forefront of experimental glazes—keep your eyes out for solid-color urns of iridescent chartreuse or airy lemon yellow that would look at home next to a modernist piece by Philippe Starck or Charles Eames.

(top) Blue-and-white Fassi ceramics (left) Moroccan teapot

SAFI

Safi's flourishing pottery industry dates to the 12th century. Produced near the phosphate mines known as Jorf el Asfar (*asfar*, like *safran*, means yellow), because of the local yellow clay, the pottery of Safi has a distinctive mustard color. The potters' elaborate designs and colors rival those of Fez but are in black with curving lines of leaves and flowers, with less emphasis on geometric patterns. The pottery is predominantly overglazed with a greenish blue, though brown, green, and dark reds are also used.

SALÉ

In Salé, potters work on the clay banks of the River Bou Regreg estuary to produce glazed and unglazed wares in classic and contemporary styles, from huge garden urns to delicate dinner sets.

(top) Safi ceramic teapots

ASSESSING POTTERY

Look for kiln markings left after the ceramics have been fired. Pottery fired en masse is put in the kiln on its side, so the edges of bowls are often painted after they have been fired. The paint tends to flake off after a while, giving the bowls a more rustic, or antiqued, look.

Another technique for firing en masse is to stack the bowls one on top the other. This allows for the glazing of the entire piece but results in three small marks on both the inside and outside of bowls from the stands on which they were placed. Small touch-ups tend to disrupt the fluidity of the designs, but such blemishes can be used as a bargaining angle to bring down the price.

You can spot an individually fired piece by its lack of any interior faults. Only three small marks can be seen on the underside of the serving dish or bowl, and the designed face should be immaculate. These pieces, often large, intricately glazed serving pieces, are the most expensive that you'll find.

THE ART OF NEGOTIATION

Everywhere in Morocco you will haggle and be hustled by experienced vendors who pounce on you as soon as you blink in their direction. Your best defense is the proper mindset. For your first souk visit, browse rather than buy. Wander the stalls and see what's for sale. Don't enter stores or make eye contact with vendors, or you will certainly be pulled in. You can also visit one of the state-sponsored artisan markets found in most large Moroccan cities, where prices are rather high but fixed.

Once you've found what you want to buy, ask the price (in dirhams). Stick to the price you want to pay. The vendor will claim you are his first customer and never look satisfied. If he won't decrease the price far enough, walk away. Chances are the vendor will run after you, either accepting your best offer or making a reduction.

MOROCCAN RUGS

 Moroccan rugs vary tremendously in quality and design. There are basically two types: urban (*citadin*) and rural (Berber); each type has endless varieties of shapes, sizes, and patterns. In general, smaller bazaars in the souks carry rural rugs, while larger bazaars and city stores carry a selection of both.

URBAN RUGS

Urban rugs have been woven in Morocco since the 18th century. They have higher knot counts (they're more "finely" woven) than the rural rugs, which technically makes them of higher quality. Urban rugs typically have seven colors and varied patterns including bands of different colors with geometric and floral designs. They are woven by women in cooperatives, Rabat and Salé being the main centers, but also in Meknès, Fez, and Marrakesh.

RURAL CARPETS

Rural carpets, some of which are known as *kilims* (tapestry weave or flat weave) are identified first by region and then by tribe. They are mostly woven by hand in the Middle Atlas (**Azrou** and **Oulmes**) and on the plains around Marrakesh (**Chichaoua**) by women. They're dark red and made of high-quality wool and have bands of intricate geometric designs. A single rug can take weeks or months to complete. No two rugs are ever alike.

BUYING TIPS

■ **Check the color.** If artificially aged, the back will be lighter than the front. Natural dyes are very bright but usually uneven. Artificial dyes can bleed when swiped with a damp cloth.

■ **Check the weave's knot count.** Urban carpets should have a high knot count—about 100 per square inch.

■ **The age of rugs.** Rugs don't have labels with identification, provenance, or origin date. Rural rugs are rarely more than 50 years old.

■ **Carpet Prices.** Good-quality rugs are expensive. Expect to pay 200 DH to 750 DH per square foot. Flat-weave rugs are generally cheaper than pile rugs. Cotton is much less expensive than wool. It's worth taking the time to check comparable prices at one of the fixed-price state-run cooperatives.

OTHER RUG-PRODUCING REGIONS

Middle Atlas rugs are widely available in the town of **Khemisset**, between Meknès and Rabat, where the highly detailed red-striped *zemmour* rugs sell at near wholesale prices. In the mountains north of Fez the women of the **Beni Ouarain** tribe weave rugs with patterns of fine stripes in black and white; they also weave the thick beige pile rugs with cross-hatching that have now become popular with U.S. and European interior designers.

The flat-weave rugs of the High Atlas Mountains (**Aït Ouaourguite**, near Ouarzazate) have a natural background with beige and brown stripes. The wool-pile rugs from this region have alternating soft plush pile with intricate woven motifs—diamonds, zigzags, and tattoo-like motifs in warm tones like mustard-yellow and tomato-red—and are most plentiful in **Taznakht** and the **Tifnout Valley.**

The white, sequined blanket-like rugs displayed on rural roadsides are made in the Middle and High Atlas, and are used both practically and ceremonially, their sequins prized for their reflection of light. Natural dyes are still used for most Berber rugs: orange from henna, blue from indigo, yellow from saffron, and red from the indigenous madder plant.

HAOUZ

The four principal carpet-producing tribes are the **Rehamna, Oulad bou Sbaa, Ahmar** and **Chiadma.** There are two carpet types: reddish-orange monochrome style and the *zarbia*, noted for its enigmatic motifs.

(top left) A modern rug showroom (top right) a rug souk (bottom right) flat-weave kilims treatment that, unlike a local hammam, couples can enjoy together. Follow up with a relaxing massage using organic products in one of the treatment rooms. Not all the therapists speak English, so if it's your first time at a hammam, ask the English-speaking front desk to explain the treatment in advance. ⊠ *Palais Amani, 12, Derb el Miter, Oued Zhoune.*

Spa Laaroussa. After a hard day's sightseeing, there's no better place to relax and unwind than Riad Laaroussa's beautifully restored 17th-century bathhouse. This private space is covered with dark Carrara marble and, as you steam, you'll be treated to an aromatic body scrub and face mask of *rhassoul* clay, mined in the Atlas mountains. Afterwards, indulge in one of the city's best massages with essential oils infused with fragrant orange blossom and jasmine. They treat up to two people (women and/or men) at the same time, and it gets busy, so book in advance. ⊠ *3, Derb Bechara* ⊕ *www.riadlaaroussa.com.*

METAL
La Maison Bouanania. For ornate bronze lanterns, copper plates, heavy silver jewelry inlaid with semiprecious stones, visit La Maison Bouanania. ⊠ *6, Derb ben Azahoum, Talâa Kebira* ☎ *0535/63–65–66.*

L'Art du Bronze. Hundreds of bronze, copper, and silver objects, antique and new, are sold at affordable prices. ⊠ *35, Talaa Sghira* ☎ *0535/74–02–77.*

Le Trésor Mirinides. All sorts of jewelry and artisanal Moroccan articles are sold at this friendly shop. ⊠ *22, Ain Alou* ☎ *0535/63–44–81.*

POTTERY
Maison Sahara. Stop by this shop to browse the famous Fassi blue-and-white pottery, from delicate dishes to large tagines. ⊠ *9, pl. Nejjarine* ☎ *035/63–45–22.*

RUGS
La Petite Maison Berbere. In the not-so-petite emporium of Fassi carpet expert Bouzidi Idrissi Mohamed, carpets and rugs of every size, shape, and color are piled floor to ceiling, including brightly colored, tightly woven kilim; shaggy wool Beni Ourain; and other signature styles from the Middle and High Atlas tribes. The staff are charming, but be prepared to bargain hard to get the price down. ⊠ *79, Talâa Kbira, near the Honey Souk* ☎ *0535/63–77–41.*

TEXTILES
Chez Alibaba. For a huge selection of Berber fabrics, artisanal kaftans, and djellabas, this friendly boutique carries some of the best. ⊠ *7, Derb el Mitter* ☎ *0535/63–69–32.*

VILLE NOUVELLE
CRAFTS
Ensemble Artisanal. It's a haul across town on the southeastern edge of the city, but those who make the trek to Ensemble Artisanal will have the rare treat of seeing a cooperative of artisans working on everything from leather to copper to pottery and wood. The Ensemble is also useful if you want to comparison shop: you can get a sense of how the fixed prices here line up with the prices you find in the medina. ■TIP→ The

ironsmith's lanterns here are of a quality you won't easily find in the medina. ⊠ *Av. Allah ben Abdullah* ☎ *0535/62–27–04, 0535/62–56–62.*

Les Poteries de Fès. The famous blue-and-white Fassi pottery is made here. You can see how craftsmen mold, glaze, and paint plates, dishes, bowls, and all things ceramic, as well as piece together mosaics with classic zellij tiling. From Bab el-Ftouh it's a 20-minute walk west or a petit taxi ride to the new potters' quarters. ⊠ *32, Aïn Nokbi* ✛ *Take Rte. N6 Sidi Hrazem* ☎ *0535/76–16–29.*

MEKNÈS

60 km (37 miles) west of Fez, 138 km (85 miles) east of Rabat.

Meknès occupies a plateau overlooking the Bouefekrane River, which divides the medina from the Ville Nouvelle. Meknès's three sets of imposing walls, architectural Royal Granaries, symmetrical Bab Mansour, and spectacular palaces are highlights in this well-preserved imperial city. Less inundated with tourists and more provincial than Fez, Meknès offers a low-key initiation into the Moroccan processes of shopping and bargaining. The pace is slower than Fez and less chaotic. Whether it was post–Moulay Ismail exhaustion or the 1755 earthquake that quieted Meknès down, the result is a pleasant middle ground between the Fez brouhaha and the business-as-usual European ambience of Rabat.

GETTING HERE AND AROUND

AIR TRAVEL

Fès-Saïss Airport serves both Fez and Meknès. The taxi or bus ride from there into Meknès takes about 50 minutes and costs around 330 DH.

BUS TRAVEL

Regular CTM buses cover the Fez–Meknès route hourly. There are buses to Casablanca (around four hours, 90 DH), Tangier (around six hours, 90 DH), and Marrakesh (around eight hours, 165 DH).

Bus Contacts CTM Meknes. ⊠ *Av. des FAR, Ville Nouvelle* ☎ *0535/52–25–83 for call center* ⊕ *www.ctm.ma.*

CAR TRAVEL

You don't need (and probably don't want) a car if you are just visiting Fez and Meknès; however, if you want to explore the immediate region of the Middle Atlas, a car (or car and driver) will be crucial since these places can be difficult to reach by bus or grand taxi.

Rental Cars Meknes Car ⊠ *Av. Hassan II, Ville Nouvelle* ☎ *0535/51–20–74.*

TAXI TRAVEL

Grands taxis carry up to six passengers and make long-distance runs between Fez and Meknès. This can be faster, more comfortable, and a better value than bus travel.

Metered petits taxis take up to four passengers, but may not leave the city limits. If the driver refuses to turn on the meter or agree to a reasonable price, do not hesitate to get out. There is usually a 50% surcharge after 8 pm.

TRAIN TRAVEL

The most convenient train station in Meknès is the Rue el-Amir Abdelkader stop close to the administrative center of the city. If you're coming from Tangier, this will be the first stop; from Fez it will be the second. All trains stop at both stations.

PLANNING YOUR TIME

Meknès is a beautifully intact medieval city, easily explored in a short excursion from Fez. From the central Place el-Hedime you can discover the medina's network of small open and covered streets flanked by shops, artisan studios, and food stalls. To see the Imperial City quarter, take a petit taxi or a more atmospheric *calèche* (horse-drawn carriage).

FESTIVALS

Meknès International Animated Film Festival. Meknès's annual international animated film festival (FICAM) takes place each spring at the French Institute. ⊕ *www.ficam.ma.*

VISITOR INFORMATION

Contacts Meknès Tourist Office ⊠ *Pl. Administrative, Ville Nouvelle* ☎ *0535/51–60–22.*

EXPLORING

THE IMPERIAL CITY

Haras Régional de Meknès. Purebred Arabian and Berber horses and fine hybrids are treated like royalty at this 165-acre equestrian breeding and training farm used for Morocco's military until 1947. Under the direction of the Ministry of Agriculture, it's become the largest national stud ranch with around 270 horses identified by plaques on their stable walls: red for Arabians, green for Berber stallions and mares, and red and green for hybrids. Manicured pastures, multiple dressage and jumping quarters, and a 30-acre hippodrome showcase these spectacular "horses of the Maghreb," and Haras organizes regional competitions in Fez, Khénifra, Meknès, Khémisset, and the world-renowned Horse Festival in Tissa. ⊠ *El Hajeb* ☎ *0535/53–97–53.*

Fodor's Choice ★ **Heri el Souani** (*Royal Granaries*). Also known as Dar el-Ma (Water Palace) for the Agdal Basin reservoir beneath, the granaries were one of Moulay Ismail's greatest achievements and are the first place any Meknessi will take you to give you an idea of the second Alaouite sultan's grandiose vision. The Royal Granaries were designed to store grain as feed for the 10,000 horses in the royal stables—not just for a few days or weeks but over a 20-year siege if necessary. Ismail and his engineers counted on three things to keep the granaries cool enough that the grain would never rot: thick walls (12 feet), suspended gardens (a cedar forest was planted on the roof), and an underground reservoir with water ducts under the floors. The high-vaulted chamber on the far right as you enter has a 30-foot well in its center and a towpath around it—donkeys circulated constantly, activating the waterwheel in the well, which forced water through the ducts and maintained a stable temperature in the granaries. Out behind the granaries are the remains of the royal stables, roofless after the 1755 Lisbon earthquake. Some

1,200 purebreds, just one tenth of Moulay Ismail's cavalry, were kept here. Stand just to the left of the door out to the stables—you can see the stunning symmetry of the stable's pillars from three different perspectives. The granaries have such elegance and grace that they were once called the Cathedral of Grain by a group of Franciscan priests, who were so moved that they requested permission to sing religious chants here. Acoustically perfect, the granaries and surrounding park are now often used for summer concerts and receptions. They're 2 km (1¼ miles) south of Moulay Ismail's mausoleum, so take a taxi in hot weather. ⌨ *10 DH* ☻ *Daily 9–noon and 3–6:30.*

BAB MANSOUR AND THE MEDINA

A walk around Bab Mansour and Place el-Hedime takes in nearly all of Meknès's major sites, including Moulay Ismail's mausoleum and the Prison of the Christian Slaves.

TOP ATTRACTIONS

Bab Mansour. Widely considered North Africa's most beautiful gate, this huge horseshoe-shape triumphal arch was completed in 1732 by a Christian convert to Islam named Mansour Laalej (whose name means "victorious renegade") and looms over the medina square. The marble Ionic columns supporting the two bastions on either side of the main entry were taken from the Roman ruins at Volubilis, while the taller Corinthian columns came from Marrakesh's El Badi Palace, part of Moulay Ismail's campaign to erase any vestige of the Saadian dynasty that preceded the Alaouites. Ismail's last important construction project, the gate was conceived as an elaborate homage to himself and strong Muslim orthodoxy of the dynasty rather than a defensive stronghold—hence, its intense decoration of green and white tiles and engraved Koranic panels, all faded significantly with age. French novelist Pierre Loti (1850–1923) penned the definitive description of Bab Mansour: "rose-hued, star-shaped, endless sets of broken lines, unimaginable geometric combinations that confuse the eye like a labyrinthine puzzle, always in the most original and masterly taste, have been gathered here in thousands of bits of varnished earth, in relief or recessed, so that from a distance it creates the illusion of a buffed and textured fabric, glimmering, glinting, a priceless tapestry placed over these ancient stones to relieve the monotony of these towering walls." ✉ *Rue Dar Smen, in front of the pl. el-Hedime.*

Bou Inania Medersa. Begun by the Merenid sultan Abou el-Hassan and finished by his son Abou Inan between 1350 and 1358, the Meknès version of Fez's residential college of the same name is arguably more beautiful and better preserved than its better-known twin. Starting with the cupola and the enormous bronze doors on the street, virtually every inch of this building is covered with decorative carving or calligraphy. The central fountain is for ablutions before prayer. Head upstairs to visit the small rooms that overlook the courtyard. These housed the 60 communal *tolba,* or student reciters. ■TIP➔ **The rooftop terrace has one of best panoramic views of Meknès's medina.** ✉ *Rue des Souks es Sebbat* ⌨ *10 DH* ☻ *Weekdays 9–noon and 3–6.*

Meknès

MEDINA

OLD
MELLAH

NEW
MELLAH

DAR
EL KEBIRA

DAR
EL MAKHZEN

IMPERIAL
CITY

Royal Golf Gardens

Place El
Berdaine

Zaouia of Sidi
Mohammed
ben Aïssa

Rue Sebat

Palais des
Idrissides

Place
el-Hedim

Place Lalla
Aouda

Bab
er-Rih

Bab
el Qari

Blvd. Circulaire

Rue El Hanaya
Nasseria

Rue Zaida
Soufra

Rue Karmouni

Rue Karaftoun

Rue Zidine Abderrazak

Rue Djemma
Zitouna

Blvd. El Haboul

Rue Andalous

R. el Meriniyne

Rue Farhat Hachad

Av. el Mouga

Rue Omane el Moutahida

Av. Moulay Ismail

Blvd. Circulaire

Av. Sidi Abd el Mahjoub

Rue des Moulins

Rue Rouamzine

Rue Dar Smen

Av. du Mellah

Rue Sekakine

Av. Zine el Abidine

Oued Boufekrane

Blvd. Abderrahman
Ibn Zidane

Blvd. Mers

Assaragh

Rue
Rue Diba

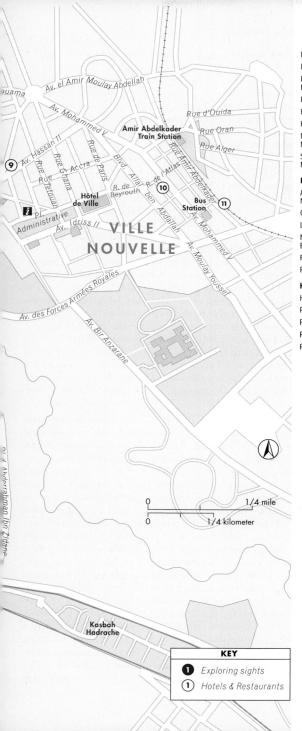

KEY

❶ *Exploring sights*

① *Hotels & Restaurants*

Dar Jamai. This 19th-century palace just inside the medina was built by the same family of *viziers* (high government officials) responsible for the Palais Jamaï hotel in Fez. The building itself is exquisite, especially the second-floor carved-cedar ceilings, interior Andalusian garden, and *menzah* (pavillion), which now houses the ethnographic **Museum of Moroccan Art** with an important collection of carpets, jewelry, ceramics, needlework, and woodwork. ■ TIP→ Facing away from Bab Mansour, the ceramics stalls on Place el-Hedime's left side sell oversize tagine pots for as little as 15 DH to 20 DH. ⊠ *Rue Sekkakine, off pl. el-Hedime* 🖃 *10 DH* ☺ *Wed.–Mon. 9–1 and 3–6:30.*

Moulay Ismail Mausoleum. One of four sacred sites in Morocco open to non-Muslims (the others are Casablanca's Hassan II, Rabat's Mohammed V Mausoleum, and Rissani's Zaouia of Moulay Ali Sherif), this mausoleum was opened to non-Muslims by King Mohammed V (grandfather of Mohammed VI) in honor of Ismail's ecumenical instincts. An admirer of France's King Louis XIV—who, in turn, considered the sultan an important ally—Moulay Ismail developed close ties with Europe and signed commercial treaties even as he battled to eject the Portuguese from their coastal strongholds at Asilah, Essaouira, and Larache. The mausoleum's site once held Meknès's Palais de Justice (Courthouse), and Moulay Ismail deliberately chose it as his resting place with hopes he would be judged in his own court by his own people. The deep ochre-hue walls inside lead to the sultan's private sanctuary, on the left, heavily decorated with colorful geometric zellij tiling. At the end of the larger inner courtyard, you must remove your shoes to enter the sacred chamber with Moulay Ismail's tomb, surrounded by hand-carved cedar-and-stucco walls, intricate mosaics, and a central fountain. ⊠ *Rue Sarag, near Bab er-Rih* 🖃 *Free* ☺ *Sat.–Thurs. 9–noon and 3–6.*

Sidi Mohammed ben Aïssa Mausoleum. Built in 1776 by Sultan Sidi Mohammed ben Abdellah, the *zaouia* of Sidi Mohammed ben Aïssa is the focal point of the legendary Aïssaoua cult, known for such voluntary rituals as swallowing scorpions, broken glass, and poison; eating live sheep; and cutting themselves with knives in prayer-induced trances. Ben Aïssa was one of Morocco's most famous saints. He was said to have made a pact with the animal world and possessed magical powers, such as the ability to transform the leaves of trees into gold and silver coins. Thought to have been a 17th-century contemporary of Moulay Ismail (1646–1727), Ben Aïssa was known as the protector of Moulay Ismail's 50,000-man workforce and persuaded hungry laborers that they were able to eat anything at all, even poisonous plants, glass, or scorpions. Ben Aïssa went on to become the general protector of all his followers. The cult of Aïssa is still around, and has in fact proliferated throughout North Africa to Algeria and beyond. Every year, during Ben Aïssa's *moussem* (pilgrimage) on the eve of the birth of the prophet Mohammed, members of the Aïssaoua fraternity from all over North Africa gather at the shrine. Processions form and parade through Meknès, snakes are charmed, and the saint's followers perform ecstatic dances, often imitating the behavior of certain animals. Although some of the Aïssaoua's more brutal practices have been outlawed, this moussem

A horse-drawn calèche is a more relaxing and traditional way to tour Meknès.

remains one of Morocco's most fascinating events. ✉ *Bd. Circulaire s/n* ⊙ *Daily 9–noon and 3–6* ☞ *Entry restricted to Muslims.*

WORTH NOTING

Habs Qara (*Prison of Christian Slaves*). After you pass through Place Lalla Aouda and Bab Filala, the pyramid-shape dome on the right side of the next square is the Koubba al Khayatine (Tailors' Pavilion), named for the seamsters who sewed military uniforms here. Originally known as the Koubbat as-Sufara (Ambassadors' Pavilion), this was where Moulay Ismail received ambassadors from abroad. The stairs to the right of the pavilion entrance lead down to storage chambers originally built as a prison by the Portuguese architect Cara, himself a prisoner who earned his freedom by constructing these immense subterranean slave quarters. Go below to see where the 60,000 slaves (of which 40,000 were reportedly Christian prisoners of war) were shackled to the wall, forced to sleep standing up, and ordered to work on the sultan's laborious building projects. Ambassadors visiting Meknès to negotiate the ransoms and release of their captive countrymen were received in the pavilion above, never suspecting that the prisoners were directly below them. ✉ *Pl. Lalla Aouda* 🖾 *10 DH* ⊙ *Daily 9–1 and 3–6.*

WHERE TO EAT

There are only a few culinary gems in Meknès, but chances are you'll want to sample local delicacies, snack on exotic dried fruits, and savor the ritual sweet pastries and mint tea, purported to be the best in the country. Good cafés and restaurants are scattered in the medina (many near the Place el-Hedime). Avenues Mohammed V and Hassan II in

The souks of Meknès are smaller and easier to navigate than those of Fez.

the Ville Nouvelle provide a wide choice of Moroccan and French or Mediterranean dishes.

$ MOROCCAN 🍴 **Collier de la Colombe.** A five-minute walk to the left inside Bab Mansour, this graceful medina space with intricate carvings, giant picture windows, and terraces overlooking the Boufekrane River and Ville Nouvelle is a good place to enjoy authentic Moroccan specialties. The menu is classic Moroccan, with highly recommended pastilla (a house specialty), tender grilled lamb, spicy beef brochettes, and mouthwatering fish tagines. Local Moroccans regularly line up and wait for choice seating on the panoramic rooftop terrace. Prices are a steal for the experience and quality of cooking. Alcohol is served. [$] *Average main: 90DH* ✉ *67, rue Driba, via Bab Mansour and P. Lalla Aouda, Ville Nouvelle* ☎ *0535/55–50–41* 🌐 *www.lecollier.amawebs.com.*

$ FRENCH 🍴 **Le Relais de Paris.** Need a break from tagine? This chain of French restaurants provides some of the best traditional cuisine in town. Le Relais de Paris offers a prix-fixe and à la carte menu in a relaxing atmosphere overlooking Mt. Zerhoun and a lovely garden. Gastronomic delights on offer include classic steak frites, braised lamb, eggplant-and-goat-cheese lasagna, and addictive chocolate profiteroles. [$] *Average main: 120DH* ✉ *46, rue Oqba Ibn Nafia, Ville Nouvelle* ☎ *0535/51–54–88.*

$ MOROCCAN 🍴 **Metropole Restaurant and Brasserie.** On the corner near the central food market, this family-friendly, heavily tiled eatery serves a daily menu of traditional Moroccan fare, all at reasonable prices. The menu includes savory lamb tagine and couscous, but the restaurant specializes in freshly grilled chicken brochettes. [$] *Average main: 100DH* ✉ *12, av. Hassan II, Ville Nouvelle* ☎ *0535/52–25–76* 💳 *No credit cards.*

$ ✕**Restaurant Marhaba.** Fuel up at this canteen-style eatery for outstand-
MOROCCAN   ing Moroccan cheap eats. Start with freshly made Berber bread and
thick harira. Share a plate of grilled brochettes and *makouda* (potato
fritters). Portions are generous, and a full meal will cost less than a cup
of coffee back home. [$] *Average main: 25DH* ✉ *23, av. Mohammed V*
☎ *0535/52–16–32* ▭ *No credit cards.*

$ ✕**Restaurant Omnia.** Seek out this lovely family-run restaurant in the
MOROCCAN   heart of the medina serving incredibly delicious cuisine with warm
smiles in an authentic traditional atmosphere. The selection of Moroccan salads, spicy harira, and couscous or tagine are part of a set menu
that finishes off with mint tea and honey-laden pastries. As an added
bonus the prices are attractively low. [$] *Average main: 45DH* ✉ *8, Derb*
Ain el Fouki, Quartier Rouamzine ☎ *0535/53–39–38* ▭ *No credit*
cards.

WHERE TO STAY

Meknès has not yet attracted the same level of commercial development
and active restoration of riads as Fez, although there are an increasing
number of places to stay in the medina. For more updated accommodations, there are several decent hotels in the Ville Nouvelle that are
reasonably priced and a short walk or taxi ride from the train station.

$ ⛶ **Hôtel Akouas.** With a friendly staff, Hôtel Akouas has adequate Art
HOTEL   Deco–inspired rooms with satellite TVs, air-conditioning, and heat.
Pros: central location; small pool; free Wi-Fi. **Cons:** can get noise
from nightclub; plain décor. [$] *Rooms from: 440DH* ✉ *27, rue Amir*
Abdelkader ☎ *0535/51–59–67* ⊕ *www.hotelakouas.com* ⇘ *50 rooms*
♟❘ *Breakfast.*

$ ⛶ **Palais Didi.** Next to Bab Mansour and steps from the Moulay Ismail
HOTEL   Mausoleum, this stately 18th-century palace has ground-floor suites
composed of a bedroom, drawing room, and handsome tiled bathroom,
all arranged around a classical patio and fountain. **Pros:** medina location; panoramic terrace; small pool. **Cons:** some rooms old-fashioned;
relatively expensive. [$] *Rooms from: 700DH* ✉ *30, Derb Hammam*
Moulay Ismail ☎ *0535/55–85–90* ⊕ *www.palaisdidi.com* ⇘ *8 rooms,*
4 suites ▭ *No credit cards* ♟❘ *Breakfast.*

$ ⛶ **Riad d'Or.** Traditional styling in this basic bed-and-breakfast pro-
B&B/INN   vides the Moroccan home experience, and visitors on a budget will find
decent amenities for the price, including a quality restaurant, clean pool,
and panoramic terrace to sunbathe or relax, with great views over the
Imperial City. **Pros:** central location near Place el-Hedime; large, well-
appointed rooms; small pool. **Cons:** can be noisy; unreliable heat and
air-conditioning. [$] *Rooms from: 560DH* ✉ *17, rue Ain el Anboub, at*
rue Lalla Alcha Adoula, Hammam Jdid-Bab Issy ☎ *0535/53–38–71*
⊕ *www.riaddor.com* ⇘ *20 rooms* ▭ *No credit cards* ♟❘ *Breakfast.*

$ ⛶ **Riad Felloussia.** Set in the heart of Meknès, between place el-Hedime
B&B/INN   and the medina, the five suites—some of which are split-level—of this
Fodor's Choice   lovely riad are full of character, decorated with traditional furniture,
★   Berber rugs, and African art. **Pros:** friendly service; central location.
Cons: may be too small for some; no air-conditioning. [$] *Rooms from:*

560DH ✉ *23, Derb Hammam Jdid, Bab Aissi* ☎ *0535/53–08–40* 🌐 *www.riadfelloussia.com* 🛏 *5 suites* 💳 *No credit cards* 🍴 *Breakfast.*

$ B&B/INN 🏠 **Ryad Bahia.** This 14th-century family house has been lovingly restored by a couple with years of experience working as Meknès guides and is an impressive anthology of ceramic, rug weaving, and woodworking crafts tucked away on the medina just a few steps from the Dar Jamai museum on the place el-Hedime. **Pros:** medina location; outstanding service; family-friendly atmosphere. **Cons:** long walk from parking lot; no alcohol allowed on premises. [$] *Rooms from: 670DH* ✉ *Derb Sekkaya, between pl. el-Hedime and Bouanania Medersa, just behind Dar Jamai museum, Tiberbarine* ☎ *0535/55–45–41* 🌐 *www.ryad-bahia.com* 🛏 *13 rooms* 🍴 *Breakfast.*

NIGHTLIFE

A somewhat seedy bar and disco scene thrives in the hotels around the train station in the Ville Nouvelle. The bar at **Le Relais de Paris** is a good choice for a quiet drink, or for a livelier scene try the nightclub at **Hotel Rif**, where sometimes you'll hear traditional Gnaoua, sometimes Western folk music.

Summer concerts in the **Heri el-Souani** are favorites of Meknès music lovers. Check with the tourist office for dates and dress warmly—the 12-foot walls built to cool oats and barley chill people as well.

SHOPPING

The diminutive Meknès souk, as with Meknès generally, seems somehow easier to embrace than Fez. Getting lost here is difficult; it just isn't that big. Meknès's merchants and craftsmen can be as exceptional as those in Fez, and what's more, they're easier to negotiate with. Just be prepared, if you try to tell a rug salesman that you're pressed for time, to hear, "Ah, but a person without time is a dead person."

THE SOUKS

Beginning from the Place el-Hedime, just past the pottery stands brimming with colorful tagine vessels, a narrow corridor leads into the **Souk Atriya,** the food souk, with a wonderful display of everything from spices to dried fruit to multicolor olives. The **Souk Nejjarine,** the woodworkers' souk, leads into the rug and carpet souk. Farther on in this direction is the **Souk Bezzarine,** a general flea market along the medina walls. Farther up to the right are basket makers, iron smiths, leather workers, and saddle makers, and, near Bab el-Djedid, makers of odd items like tents and musical instruments. The Souk es-Sebat begins a more formal section, where each small section is devoted to a specific craft, beginning with the *babouche* (leather slipper) market. If you are in the market for a carpet, then follow signs to the **Palais des Idrissides,** a wonderful 14th-century palace and carpet emporium.

CRAFTS

Centre Artisanale. The government-run Centre Artisanale is, as always in Moroccan cities, a good place to check for fixed-price, quality hand-crafted products and prices before beginning to haggle in the souks. ✉ *Av. Zine el-Abidine* ☎ *0535/53–08–08.*

Palais de l'Artisan. A specialist in damascening (watered steel or silver inlay work), Palais de l'Artisan sells jewelry, souvenirs, and decorated pottery. ✉ *11, Koubt Souk Kissaria Lahrir* ☎ *0535/53–35–02.*

FOOD

Souk Atriya. The food souks and *kissaria* (covered market) run along one side of the medina square. A tour through this gastronomic oasis stuffed with all manner of products heaped in elaborately arranged cones and pyramids—prunes, olives, spices, nuts, dates, and sugary pastries in every conceivable shape and color—is a veritable feast for the senses. The variety of olives on display and the painstaking care with which each pyramid of produce has been set out daily is nearly as geometrically enthralling as the decorative designs on the Bab Mansour. Look for the bustling fish stalls for seafood of all kinds straight from the Atlantic, an hour's drive away. ■TIP➡ The kissaria is a good place to stock up on Moroccan spices and aromatic herbs. ✉ *Pl. el-Hedime.*

RUGS

Palais des Idrissides. Much more than a carpet emporium, this magnificent 14th-century palace built by the cult of the Idrissid dynasty is a treasury of art, artisanship, and architecture not to be missed. The multilingual proprietors deliver a memorable discourse on the house's history and craftsmanship before moving on to an eloquent and entertaining history and ethnographical portrait of Berber kilim and carpet creation. The unusual carved and inlaid ceilings of olive wood, rather than the customary cedar, are extraordinarily rich and ornate. The sloped floor, built for drainage, is made of Carrara marble, in exchange for which Morocco used to trade sugar. The large grandfather clocks were gifts of Louis XIV, allegedly bestowed on the sultan to ease Ismail's chagrin at the refusal of Louis's daughter, Princesse de Conti, to marry him. This carpet and kilim cooperative displays work from the 45 Berber tribes that have traditionally lived near Meknès, each with its own symbols and techniques. ⇨ *For tips on buying rugs, see the Shopping feature earlier in this chapter.* ✉ *11, rue Kermouni* ☎ *0535/55–78–92.*

SIDE TRIPS FROM FEZ AND MEKNÈS

Volubilis and Moulay Idriss are highly recommended side trips from Fez and Meknès. Volubilis was the Roman Empire's farthest-flung capital, and Moulay Idriss has Morocco's most sacred shrine, the tomb of founding father Moulay Idriss I. Both sites are key to an understanding of Moroccan history. It's possible to see both places in one day, and, if you don't have your own transport, most tours from Meknès or Fez will cover both, although you may not spend as much time in Moulay Idriss as it deserves. If you have to choose between trips to Volubilis and Moulay Idriss, go with the former. The Roman ruins at Volubilis are some of the best archaeological treasures in the country.

Another option is to head over to Oulmès (81 km [50 miles] from Meknès) for an excursion farther into the countryside.

MOULAY IDRISS

23 km (14 miles) north of Meknès, 3 km (2 miles) southeast of Volubilis, 83 km (50 miles) west of Fez.

Moulay Idriss is Morocco's most sacred town, the final resting place of the nation's religious and secular founder, Moulay Idriss I. It is said that five pilgrimages to Moulay Idriss are the spiritual equivalent of one to Mecca, earning it the nickname the poor man's Mecca. Non-Muslims are not allowed inside the tomb at all, and until 2005 were not allowed to spend the night in town. A splash of white against Djebel (Mt.) Zerhoun, the picturesque town tumbles down two hillsides. The pace of life is leisurely, visits are normally hassle-free, and people watching in the main square offers a view of Moroccan life that hasn't changed for centuries.

Moulay Idriss attracts thousands of pilgrims from all over Morocco to its moussem in late August or early September. Non-Muslims are welcome to attend the secular events, which are a fascinating glimpse into Islamic life and celebrations.

GETTING HERE AND AROUND
Buses (15 DH) leave Meknès for Moulay Idriss every 15 minutes from 6 am until 10 pm. Or take a grand taxi from the Institut Français de Meknès (Rue Ferhat Hachad, between the medina and the Ville Nouvelle) for 10 DH.

TIMING AND PRECAUTIONS
Moulay Idriss is a holy town and requires utmost respect for sacred rituals and customs, so act and dress respectfully. Each Saturday there's a lively local market. During Ramadan, most shops and restaurants are closed during the day, but you can buy picnic food from the market or eat on the terrace at the hotel Dar Zerhoune. It's thoughtful not to eat and drink on the street during this time.

EXPLORING
Moulay Idriss Medersa. An outstanding historic site from the Merenids, the Moulay Idriss Medersa was built in the 14th century by sultan Abou el Hassan. Hidden in the town's steep and twisting streets, the medersa's striking cylindrical minaret constructed in 1939 is the only one of its kind in Morocco, standing as testimony to Turkish and Arab influences. Originally built with materials from Volubilis, the minaret is decorated with green ceramic tiles bearing inscriptions of the 114 *suras* (chapters) of the Koran. ☞ *Entry restricted to Muslims.*

Sidi Abdellah el Hajjam Terrace. From the Sidi Abdellah el Hajjam Terrace, in the Khiber quarter, you will have the best vantage point to see the holy village of Moulay Idriss and its sacred sanctuaries. A casual and friendly café on the top level is the perfect place to enjoy Moroccan

The moussem in Moulay Idriss draws pilgrims from far and wide in late August or early September.

morsels while sipping a cool beverage and taking in the view. The adjoining quarter across the gorge is called Tasga.

Zaouia of Moulay Idriss I. This important shrine and mausoleum of the Idrissid dynasty's patriarch is off-limits to non-Muslims, marked by a wooden bar to restrict access. For a good view, climb to a vantage point overlooking the religious sanctuary—the hike up one of many hills through the town's surrounding alleys is invigorating and a symbolic bow to Morocco's secular and spiritual history.

WHERE TO EAT AND STAY

The main street through Moulay Idriss (up to the parking area just in front of the mausoleum) has a line of small restaurants serving everything from brochettes of spicy meat to harira. In front, you'll see stands where tagines cook over hot coals for hours until the meat is tender; the kefta tagine is the one to try.

$$$$ MOROCCAN 🍴 **Scorpion House.** Set high on a hillside, looking down on the jewel-like town of Moulay Idriss, the Scorpion House is the personal retreat of the owner of Café Clock in Fez. He's put his own unique stamp on this beautiful property: inside, whitewashed interiors are filled with eclectic, retro furniture, global vintage finds, and Moroccan art; outside, multilayered, plant-filled terraces and gardens look over the jumble of whitewashed houses and mosques. It's a bespoke experience so doesn't come cheap—many of the staff are brought in from Fez just to serve you. But indulging in a long, leisurely lunch or sunset dinner of freshly prepared Moroccan dishes with a contemporary twist, with the sacred city as a backdrop, is certainly something to savor. **■ TIP→ They can cater to a maximum of 30 people.** [$] *Average main: 3355DH* ✉ *54,*

Drouj El Hafa ☎ *0655/21–01–72* 🌐 *www.scorpionhouse.com* ✍ *Reservations essential* 💳 *No credit cards.*

$ B&B/INN Fodor's Choice ★ 🏨 **Dar Zerhoune.** With a prime perch atop a hill, overlooking the tranquil Holy City of Moulay Idriss, this welcoming, Western-owned guesthouse is the perfect place to unwind after the hurly-burly of Fez. **Pros:** friendly staff; roof terrace; free Wi-Fi. **Cons:** no air-conditioning; no TV (but books and board games are available); cash only. [$] *Rooms from: 530DH* ✉ *42, Derb Zaouk, Tazga* ☎ *0535/54–43–71* 🌐 *www.darzerhoune.com* 🛏 *6 rooms* 💳 *No credit cards* 🍴 *Breakfast.*

VOLUBILIS

28 km (17 miles) northwest of Meknès, 88 km (53 miles) northwest of Fez, 3 km (2 miles) west of Moulay Idriss.

Volubilis was the capital of the Roman province of Mauritania (Land of the Moors), Rome's southwesternmost incursion into North Africa. Favored by the confluence of the rivers Khoumane and Fertasse and surrounded by some of Morocco's most fertile plains, this site has probably been inhabited since the Neolithic era.

Volubilis's municipal street plan and distribution of public buildings are remarkably comprehensible examples of Roman urban planning. The floor plans of the individual houses, and especially their incredibly well-preserved mosaic floors depicting mythological scenes, provide a rare connection to the sensibilities of the Roman colonists who lived here 2,000 years ago.

If you prefer to see Volubilis on your own without a guide (less informative but more contemplative), proceed through the entrance, and make a clockwise sweep, starting at the newly built, contemporary visitor center. After crossing the little bridge over the Fertasse River, climb up to the plateau's left edge, and you'll soon come across a Berber skeleton lying beside a sculpture with his head pointed east, a deliberate placement suggesting early Islamization of the Berber populace here.

GETTING HERE AND AROUND

Volubilis is a 30-minute drive north from Meknès, and an hour's drive from Fez. Sometimes marked on road signs as "Oualili," Volubilis is beyond Moulay Idriss on Route N13, which leaves R413 to head northeast 15 km (9 miles) northwest of Meknès. Grands taxis to Volubilis are available from Meknès and Fez, for around 200 DH and 400 DH respectively. From Moulay Idriss there are shuttles to Volubilis (5 DH). From Fez, the only regularly scheduled bus connection to Volubilis is via Meknès.

TIMING AND PRECAUTIONS

Volubilis is an expansive site that requires intense walking and sun exposure. Tour earlier in the day or late in the afternoon, wear a hat, and carry a water bottle.

VISITOR INFORMATION

Contacts **Volubilis Visitor Center** ✉ *Main Gate.*

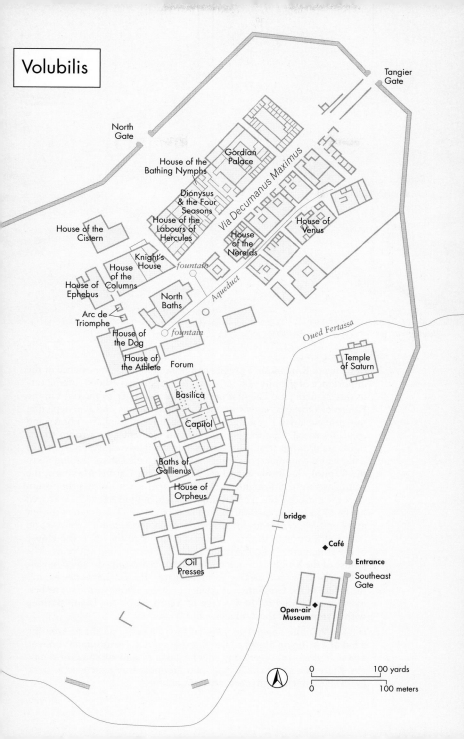

Volubilis

Tangier Gate

North Gate

Gordian Palace

House of the Bathing Nymphs

Via Decumanus Maximus

Dionysus & the Four Seasons

House of the Labours of Hercules

House of Venus

House of the Cistern

Knight's House

fountain

House of the Columns

House of the Nereids

House of Ephebus

North Baths

Aqueduct

Arc de Triomphe

House of the Dog

fountain

Oued Fertassa

House of the Athlete

Forum

Temple of Saturn

Basilica

Capitol

Baths of Gallienus

House of Orpheus

bridge

◆ Café

Entrance

Southeast Gate

Oil Presses

Open-air Museum ◆

0   100 yards

0   100 meters

Volubilis was the Roman capital of Mauritania.

EXPLORING

Remains of **Roman olive presses** can be seen to the left, evidence of the importance of the olive-oil industry that supported 20,000 inhabitants of this 28-acre city. The first important mosaics are to the right in the **House of Orpheus**, consisting of a dolphin mosaic and one depicting the Orpheus myth in the Tablinum, a back room used as a library and receiving room. Past the public **Baths of Gallienus**, in a room to the right, are a dozen sets of footprints raised slightly above floor level in what was a communal bathroom. The wide-paved street leading up to the **Capitol**, the **Basilica**, and the **Forum** is the **Cardus Maximus**, the main east–west thoroughfare of any Roman town. Across the forum were the market stalls. The **Triumphal Arch**, built in AD 217, destroyed by the 1755 Lisbon earthquake and restored in 1932, is down to the left at the end of **Decumanus Maximus**, the main north–south street. As you look south through the arch, the first building to the left is the **House of the Dog**, named because of an unearthed bronze dog sculpture. The **House of the Knight** has an incomplete but beautifully designed mosaic of Dionysus. Beyond the northernmost gate—the **Tangier Gate**—stands the **Palace of the Gordians**, the residence of the administrators. The best mosaics are found in the **Cortege of Venus**. Look for **Diana Bathing with Nymphs** and the **Abduction of Hylas**.

▓TIP→ Volubilis can get very hot, as the ruins offer no shade. Wearing a hat and bringing plenty of water are essential. The ground is uneven and sometimes rocky, so bring your best pair of walking shoes or sneakers. There is a small shady café built around a tree near the car park, for drinks, snacks, and more substantial bites.

Arch of Caracalla. Rising out of fertile plains and olive groves, the impressive triumphal arch of Volubilis is the center point of the ancient Roman site. Decorated only on the east side, it is supported by marble columns, built by Marcus Aurelius Sebastenus to celebrate the power of Emperor Caracalla.

Dionysus and the Four Seasons. Along the Decumanus Maximus, the small spaces near the street's edge held shop stalls, while mansions—10 on the left and 8 on the right—lined either side. The house of Dionysus and the Four Seasons is about halfway down the Decumanus Maximus; its scene depicting Dionysus discovering Ariadne asleep is one of the site's most spectacular mosaics.

House of Orpheus. One of the most important houses in the Roman ruins is the House of Orpheus, the largest house in the residential quarter. Three remarkable mosaics depict Orpheus charming animals with his lyre, nine dolphins symbolizing good luck, and Amphitrite in her sea horse–drawn chariot. Head north from here to explore the public Baths of Gallienus and free-standing Corinthian pillars of the Capitol.

Fodor's Choice
★
House of Venus. Volubilis's best set of mosaics, not to be missed, is in the House of Venus. Intact excavations portray a chariot race, a bathing Diana surprised by the hunter Actaeon, and the abduction of Hylas by nymphs—all still easily identifiable. The path back down to the entrance passes the site of the Temple of Saturn, across the riverbed on the left.

House of the Bathing Nymphs. Named for its superb floor mosaics portraying a bevy of frolicking nymphs in a surprisingly contemporary, all but animated, artistic fashion, the House of the Bathing Nymphs is on the main street's right side. The penultimate house has a marble bas-relief medallion of Bacchus. As you move back south along the next street below and parallel to the Decumanus Maximus, there is a smaller, shorter row of six houses that are worth exploring.

House of the Ephebus. The ancient town's greatest mansions and mosaics line the Decumanus Maximus from the town brothel north to the Tangier Gate, which leads out of the enclosure on the uphill end. One of the most famous is the House of the Ephebus, just west of the Triumphal Arch, named for the nude ivy-crowned bronze sculpture discovered here (now on display in Rabat). The *cenacula,* or banquet hall, has colorful mosaics with Bacchic themes. Opposite the House of the Ephebus is the House of the Dog, where a bronze canine statue was discovered in 1916 in one of the rooms off the *triclinium,* a large dining room.

WHERE TO STAY

$
HOTEL
Hôtel Volubilis Inn. Surrounded by olive groves high on a hillside, this comfortable hotel has exceptional views from its pool and terrace over the valley to the southwest. **Pros:** bar; outstanding views. **Cons:** popular with tour groups; relatively expensive. $ *Rooms from: 640DH ⊠ Rte. de Volubilis (N13), Douar Fartassa Oualili, Moulay Idriss Zerhoun* ☎ *0535/54–44–05, 0661/63–84–22* ⤳ *50 rooms* ○ *Breakfast.*

5

THE MEDITERRANEAN MIDDLE ATLAS

Spreading south and east of Fez, the northern Middle Atlas is drained by the River Moulouya en route to the Mediterranean Sea near the Algerian border. The Azrou Cedar Forest and the Djebel Tazzeka Massif above Taza are the main attractions in this heavily forested northern zone, along with Midelt and the Cirque de Jaffar at the more barren southern edge.

GETTING HERE AND AROUND

The Fès-Saïss Airport serves the Middle Atlas as well as Fez and Meknès. Azrou, Ifrane, Sefrou, Imouzzer du Kandar, Beni-Mellal, Azilal, Midelt, Kasba Tadla, and Khénifra are all served by CTM buses, if somewhat sporadically and at unsocial hours. The bus from Casablanca to Ifrane to Azrou takes six hours from beginning to end; the one from Meknès to Azrou to Midelt takes four to five hours total.

If you have any intention of wandering into the overlands, you must use a four-wheel-drive vehicle. Ensure your car is equipped with a spare tire and emergency fuel. Depending on where you're coming from, it's best to rent a car in Fez or Meknès. *(For more information, see the Fez and Meknès sections earlier in the chapter.)*

Bus Contacts La Gare Routière de Midelt ✉ *N13, Midelt.*

The contacts here organize tours beyond their immediate towns, so feel free to check out any of these when planning your trip.

HIKING AND TREKKING

Major treks arise from the Djebel Ayachi Massif, south of Midelt, as well as above Beni-Mellal, Azilal, and Demnate. The Tessaout gorges above Lac des Aït-Aadel, west of Demnate, have some of Morocco's best and most spectacular long-distance trekking.

HORSEBACK RIDING

For the equestrian, several stables offer mountain or rural outings on horseback. Try the Centre Equestre et de Randonnée.

Le Centre Equestre et de Randonnées Aïn Amyer. On the outskirts of Fez, Le Centre Equestre et de Randonnées Aïn Amyer has 20 horses in its stables and many of them are the famous Moroccan Barb species, a desert breed with stamina. Depending on the time you have, it's possible to go on a ride of several hours into the countryside. You can also take private classes at the center. ✉ *Aïn Amyer, Rte. d'Immouzzer, Fez* ⊕ *www.marocrandocheval.ma.*

FISHING

Morocco, surprisingly, offers trout fishing in the foothills of the High Atlas and in the Azrou Cedar Forest. European brown trout and rainbows, nearly all stocked fish or descendants of repopulated fisheries, thrive in select highland environments. March through May are the prime angling months. Permits and further orientation are available through the Administration des Eaux et Forêts offices in Rabat.

Administration des Eaux et Forêts ✉ *605, Rabat-Chellah, Rabat* ☎ *0537/76–00–38, 0537/76–00–41* ⊕ *www.eauxetforets.gov.ma.*

RAFTING

One of best ways to see Morocco is through the natural beauty of its flowing rivers and dramatic canyons. Morocco Rafting specializes in river-rafting tours. Adventure holidays are available with a range of activities that combine rafting, kayaking, canyoning, and tubing.

Morocco Rafting. This company—open since the late 1990s—specializes in white-water rafting tours on the Ahansei, Oum Er Rbia, Ourika, and Nifiss rivers. ✉ *Rue Beni Marine, Marrakesh* ☎ *0614/97–23–16* 🌐 *www.rafting.ma.*

TAZA

120 km (72 miles) east of Fez.

An important capital during the Almohad, Merenid, and early Alaouite dynasties (11th to 16th centuries), Taza was used as a passage into Morocco by the first Moroccan Arabs—the Idrissids—and nearly all successive invaders en route to Fez. Fortified and refortified over the centuries, the city, located in the mountain pass known as the Taza Gap separating the Rif from the Middle Atlas Mountains, is marked by a medina that houses a 14th-century medersa and four mosques.

5

ESSENTIALS

Bus Contacts Taza CTM Terminal ✉ *Pl. de l'Indépendance* 🌐 *www.ctm.ma.*

EXPLORING

First constructed in the 12th century, the haunting city walls have been in various states of renovation. Accessing the main entry point, the Bab er-Rih (Gate of the Wind) leads up to a beautiful panoramic view of the Djebel Tazzeka hills. Through the center of town, walk the main street that connects the medina's four principal mosques—the Grande Mosquée, the Sidi Azouz mosque, the Mosquée du Marché, and the Andalous Mosque.

Grande Mosquée. With its perforated cupola, the Great Mosque is a historically significant UNESCO World Heritage Site. Dating from the 12th century, the mosque, founded by Sultan Abd el-Moumen, is possibly the oldest Almohad structure in existence and believed to predate the mosque at Tin Mal. Of architectural importance are the mosque's inscribed three-ton chandelier and intricately designed windows and doorways. ✣ *Walk towards Bab er-Rih past the medina.*

Souks. Set around the Mosquée du Marché, or Market Mosque, Taza's untouristy souks and the covered stalls of the kissaria are worth exploring. Look out for the shaggy cream-wool rugs with black geometric markings made by the Beni Ourain tribe.

WHERE TO EAT AND STAY

$ MEDITERRANEAN 🍴 **Les Deux Rives.** This small Mediterranean restaurant offers light entrées including salads, soups, and pizzas. [$] *Average main: 40DH* ✉ *20, av. Oujda* ☎ *0535/67–12–27* 💳 *No credit cards.*

$ HOTEL 🏨 **Grand Hôtel du Dauphiné.** Though the period charm has diminished, this budget hotel offers clean rooms, shuttered balconies at the front, and agreeable service. **Pros:** very central; close to public transportation.

Cons: no heat in winter; most rooms don't have en suite bathrooms; old-fashioned décor; cash only. [$] *Rooms from: 290DH* ✉ *Pl. de l'Indépendance, Ville Nouvelle* ☎ *0535/67–35-67* 🛏 *26 rooms* 💳 *No credit cards* 🍴 *Breakfast.*

AROUND TAZA

The 123-km (76-mile) loop around the Cirque du Djebel Tazzeka southwest of Taza is one of the most varied and spectacular day trips in the Middle Atlas. Packing a range of diversions from picnicking by the waterfalls of Ras el-Oued to spelunking in the Gouffre du Friouato (Friouato Caves), reaching the summit of the 6,494-foot Djebel Tazzeka, or navigating the gorges of the Oued Zireg, this tour is geared for the serious adventurer. Without stops, the entire multisurface drive takes approximately five hours. The S311 road south from Taza is narrow and serpentine. The Cascades of Ras-El, 10 km (6 miles) south of Taza, is the first stop. The Parc National de Tazzeka has tranquil picnic spots. The right fork on the S311 brings you to the Friouato Caves within the park, while the left path leads out to the lake bed of Dayat Chiker, most impressive in springtime when subterranean waters keep it filled.

Beyond the caves, the road climbs through a pine forest to the village of Bab Bou Idir, abandoned except in summer when the campground and chalets fill with vacationers. After another 8 km (5 miles), the right-hand fork leads 9 km (5½ miles) to the crest of Djebel Tazzeka, 6,494 feet, a tough climb by car or on foot. Your reward is the unique view over the Rif and south to the Middle Atlas.

From Djebel Tazzeka there are another 38 km (23 miles) north along the spectacular Zireg river gorges to Sidi Abdallah des Rhiata, where you can get on the N6 back to Taza or Fez. ⚠ **The 7-km (4½-mile) track to the crest of Djebel Tazzeka is a dangerous drive in bad weather.**

Friouato Caves. One of the most breathtaking natural sights in the Middle Atlas, the Friouato Cave complex, 26 km (16 miles) from Taza, includes North Africa's deepest caverns—they extend steeply down 520 stairs to a depth of 590 feet. Explored by the eminent French speleologist Norbert Casteret in 1930, the caves consist of various large chambers filled with enormous stalagmites in strange and fantastic shapes and colors. Chambers such as the Salle de Lixus, the Salle de Draperies, and the Salle Casteret lead through what has been referred to as an underground palace. This experience is not advised for claustrophobes or the faint-of-heart (or -knee). The caves are muddy and wet, the climb down and back is strenuous, and opportunities for minor injuries are many since you must squeeze through narrow crevices and slick passageways. As with many caves, the Friouato Caves are home to a large colony of bats. Proper hiking footwear and waterproof warm clothes are recommended, as are powerful flashlights; you can rent protective clothing and helmet lights for 50 DH. 🎟 *Admission 5 DH, guide 200 DH* 🕓 *Daily 8–6.*

SEFROU

33 km (20 miles) southeast of Fez, 136 km (84 miles) southwest of Taza.

A miniature Fez at an altitude of 2,900 feet, the small town of Sefrou lies in the fertile valley of the River Agdal. Once known as the Jardin du Maroc, it actually predates Fez and was the first stop on the caravan routes between the Sahara and the Mediterranean coast. It was originally populated by Berber converts to Judaism, who came north from the Tafilalt date palmery and from Algeria in the 13th century. The town remained a nucleus of Jewish life until 1956, when, upon the country's declaration of independence from France, virtually all of the Jewish community fled Morocco.

EXPLORING

Sefrou is a picturesque ancient walled city whose medina is well preserved and worth a visit. With cooler temperatures than nearby Fez, it makes a pleasant summer day trip. Wander around the Mellah quarter, one of the oldest in Morocco, and explore the tranquil medina and the covered souks, where the stalls are set behind bright-green shutters. The town is most noted for its annual Fête des Cerises, or Cherry Festival, that celebrates the yearly harvest in mid-June with food, music, dance, and cultural activities including crowing the Cherry Queen.

5

Kef el-Moumen. During the town's famous Cherry Festival in June, a procession ventures across the Aggai River to the Kef el-Moumen cave containing the prophet Daniel's tomb, a pilgrimage venerated by Jews and Muslims alike. According to legend, seven followers of Daniel slept here for centuries before miraculously resuscitating.

Lalla Rekia. West of Sefrou is the ancient fountain of Lalla Rekia, believed to contain miraculous holy water to cure mental illness. Some visitors still bring jugs to the spring to carry away alleged healing benefits from the fount's source. The area is best accessed by rental car or taxi, as public transportation in the area is limited.

Sidi Lahcen Ben Ahmed. The zaouia of Sidi Lahcen Ben Ahmed is the final resting place of this 17th-century saint.

OFF THE BEATEN PATH

Gallery H'biza and Culture Vultures. Culture Vultures, an avant-garde arts and culture organization, runs a small, contemporary-art gallery and gift shop housed in the old fondouk in the heart of Sefrou's medina. H'biza translates as "small loaf of bread," and in a Moroccan proverb represents an opportunity not to be turned down. They work with local artists, so pop into their office to see what artists-in-residence and presentations they have coming up. ⇨ *Culture Vultures runs an excellent tour in Fez visiting the craftspeople of the medina; see Guided Tours.* ✉ *Pl. Huddadine* ☎ *0645/22–32–03* 🌐 *www.culturevulturesfez.org.*

WHERE TO STAY

$ B&B/INN 🏨 **Dar Attamani.** Down a narrow alleyway in the heart of the medina, this atmospheric 19th-century Jewish merchant's house has been turned into a basic but charming B&B. **Pros:** central location; terrace. **Cons:** difficult to find; not all rooms are en suite. [$] *Rooms from: 400DH* ✉ *14, Bastna* ☎ *0645/29–89–30* 🌐 *www.darattamani.com* 🛏 *5 rooms* 💳 *No credit cards* 🍴 *Breakfast.*

$ B&B/INN Fodor's Choice ★

Dar Kamal Chaoui. In the tranquil troglodyte village of Bhalil, Kamal and Bea Chaoui have turned their family home into a delightful B&B with four rooms thoughtfully decorated with local touches—perhaps a donkey pannier or an intricately painted wooden door as a headboard—all with handwoven blankets across the beds. **Pros:** charming owners; interesting village; good walking. **Cons:** quiet area; off the beaten track. [$] *Rooms from: 670DH* ✉ *60, Kaf Rhouni, Bhalil* ☎ *0678/83–83–10* 🌐 *www.kamalchaoui.com* 🛏 *4 rooms* 🍴 *Breakfast.*

OFF THE BEATEN PATH

Bhalil. The small Berber village of Bhalil is an off-the-beaten-track gem, around 5 km (3 miles) from Sefrou. Built across a hillside, the picturesque pastel-colored houses that line the narrow, winding streets may appear conventional from the outside, but step inside and you'll discover that many of them are built into the rock face. This design keeps out the scorching summer heat, as well as the icy winter chill, and Bhalil's modern-day troglodytes normally use the cave as a living and dining space. This tranquil village is set at the foot of Djebel Kandar, and it makes a good base for walking, from leisurely rambles to more strenuous all-day hikes. **■ TIP→ You'll often find the women of Bhalil sitting outside their houses sewing intricate djellaba buttons.**

IFRANE

25 km (15 miles) southwest of Imouzzer du Kandar, 63 km (39 miles) southwest of Fez.

Built in 1929 during the French protectorate to create a *poche de France* (pocket of France) for expatriate French diplomats, administrators, and business personnel, Ifrane's alpine chalets, contemporary villas, and modern boulevards have become the place to see and be seen for local elite, whose wealth is visibly flaunted with Western designer clothing in European-style cafés and a luxury resort and spa overlooking the Azrou Cedar Forest. Nicknamed "Morocco's Switzerland," Ifrane sits at an altitude of 5,460 feet and is visibly well maintained with manicured gardens, tree-lined streets, and Swiss-style architecture. As a royal mandate, the Al Akhawayn University, an English-language public university with an American curriculum, opened in the mid-1990s and has become one of the country's finest.

ESSENTIALS

Taxis **Ifrane Taxi Stand.** The taxi stand is located about a half mile from the village square behind the central market. ✉ *Ifrane–Meknès Rd.*

Visitor Information **Délégation du Tourisme d'Ifrane** ✉ *Av. Mohammed V* ☎ *0535/56–68–21* 🕒 *Weekdays 8:30–12:30 and 2:30–6:30.*

EXPLORING

Known primarily as an upscale ski-resort town, Ifrane is also famous for its cold-water trout fishing and hiking trails around the **Cascades des Vierges** (Waterfall of the Virgins). Zaoula de Ifrane, a small village just north of the city, is home to local artisans. Near the well-photographed stone Atlas lion statue in the center of town, the royal palace of the ruling Alaouite dynasty is still in use by the ruling kingdom and off-limits to the general public, with extraordinarily high security in the area.

The scenery around Ifrane is almost alpine; it's not uncommon to see sheep grazing on the hillsides.

WHERE TO EAT AND STAY

$
INTERNATIONAL
FAMILY

✕ **La Paix.** On the ground floor of the Appart Hotel, this airy, modern eatery is a family-friendly restaurant–pizzeria–tea salon, popular with both locals and visitors. The menu offers a range of international dishes, as well as authentic Moroccan tagines and steak frites, plus tasty soups, salads, pizzas, and delicious desserts, smoothies, and milk shakes. $ *Average main: 60DH* ✉ *Appart Hotel, Av. de la Marche Verte* ☎ *0535/56–66–75* ▭ *No credit cards.*

$$$$
RESORT
Fodor's Choice
★

▦ **Michlifen Ifrane Suites and Spa.** Less than an hour south of the world's largest medieval city at Fez, this five-star resort hotel perched atop a hill is a stunningly luxurious retreat near the Michlifen ski slopes that continues to attract wealthy locals. **Pros:** beautiful views; sumptuous rooms and spa; sports center. **Cons:** limited public transportation; very expensive rates (but check for offers). $ *Rooms from: 4000DH* ✉ *Av. Hassan II, Ville d'Ifrane* ☎ *0535/86–40–00, 0535/86–41–00* ⊕ *www. michlifenifrane.com* ⤵ *71 rooms* ◎| *Breakfast.*

SPORTS AND THE OUTDOORS

SKIING

Michlifen and Djebel Hebri are the two ski resorts nearest Ifrane and within day-trip range of Fez. If your expectations are modest, a day on the slopes is a pleasant option—there are four trails that are relatively simple. Skis and sleds can be rented at the resorts.

AZROU

17 km (10 miles) southwest of Ifrane, 67 km (40 miles) southeast of Meknès, 78 km (47 miles) southwest of Fez.

Occupying an important junction of routes between the desert and Meknès and between Fez and Marrakesh, Azrou—from the Berber word for "rock"—is a significant ancient Berber capital named for the city's quarry of black volcanic rocks. It was one of Sultan Moulay Ismail's strongholds after he built an imposing fortress here (now in ruins) in 1684. For centuries Azrou remained unknown, a secret mountain town that invading forces never fully located, thanks in part to a cave system designed for concealment and protection. Enjoy the mellow pace and lifestyle of traditional Berber mountain life. The interesting Tuesday souk gets crowded, but the small medina is normally comparatively tranquil. Just before Azrou, the enormous freshwater lake of Dayet Azrou is a popular spot for picnics. You can take a boat out on the water, although swimming is not allowed.

EXPLORING

The heaving Tuesday souk is held in an open area 1½ km (1 mile) to the northeast of the town. It attracts locals from many neighboring towns for its vast selection of local produce, plastic goods, clothes, and more. Place Mohammed V is the tranquil main square, where you'll find several cafés and shops.

Azrou Cedar Forest. The Azrou Cedar Forest is a source of great pride throughout the country. Moroccan cedars, some more than 400 years old, grow to heights of close to 200 feet and cover some 320,000 acres on the slopes of the Middle Atlas, the High Atlas, and the Rif at altitudes between 3,940 and 9,200 feet. Cedar is much coveted by woodworkers, particularly makers of stringed musical instruments. Living among the enormous cedars to the south of Azrou are troops of bold Barbary macaques and birdlife ranging from the redheaded Moroccan woodpecker to owls and eagles. Flora include the large-leaf peony, the scarlet dianthus, and the blue germander, all of which attract butterflies, including the cardinal and the colorful sulfur Cleopatra. You can pick up information, guides, and maps of the forest showing trails and hikes at the Ifrane Tourist Office *(⇨ see Ifrane, above)*.

Ensemble Artisanale d'Azrou. Azrou's artisan center, just off the P24 to Khénifra (and a mere five-minute walk from Place Mohammed V), is a collection of small crafts shops selling carpets, kilims, stone, and cedar carvings. ⊘ *Closed Fri.*

Lycée Tariq Ibn Ziyad. Seeing a Berber center, the French established the Collège Berbère here in an attempt to train an elite Berber opposition to the urban Arab ruling class; both Arabic and Islam were prohibited. After independence, the movement faded. The Berber college became an Arabic school and was renamed the Lycée Tariq Ibn Ziyad. With nearly 400 locals matriculated, it now teaches a progressive curriculum and hosts international exchange students. ⊠ *Bd. Prince Heritier Sidi Mohammed* ☎ *0535/56–24–16.*

WHERE TO EAT AND STAY

$ CAFÉ 🍴 **Patisserie Azrou.** This corner café, located near the mosque in the city center, is typically smoky and dark and male-dominated on the ground floor but more pleasant and spacious upstairs or outdoors. The coffee is flavorful and the service friendly. [$] *Average main: 20DH* ✉ *Pl. Hassan II* 💳 *No credit cards.*

$ HOTEL 🏨 **Hôtel Panorama.** Up on a hill near Azrou's center, this rustic hotel has good views over the forest and town as well as a decent restaurant and reliable heating—more than welcome during Azrou's long, snowy winters. **Pros:** Wi-Fi; quiet location. **Cons:** a bit dated; some staff don't speak English. [$] *Rooms from: 420DH* ✉ *Rue el-Hansali, Hay Ajelabe* ☎ *0535/56–20–10* 🛏 *36 rooms* 🍽 *Breakfast.*

$$ HOTEL 🏨 **Palais des Cerisiers.** Situated close to the village center en route to the Azrou Cedar Forest, this pretty, Alpine-style hotel is set in a stone mansion on verdant grounds and well equipped with classic wood furnishings, air-conditioned and centrally heated rooms, serene mountain views, and a large pool. **Pros:** tranquil atmosphere; pool. **Cons:** service may be slow. [$] *Rooms from: 1250DH* ✉ *Rte. Cèdre Gouraud, Hay Ajelabe* ☎ *0535/56–38–30* 🌐 *www.lepalaisdescerisiers.com* 🛏 *14 rooms, 4 suites, 2 apartments* 🍽 *Breakfast.*

SOURCES DE L'OUM-ER-RBIA

57 km (35 miles) southwest of Azrou.

An unexpected natural wonder in the middle of the country, the 40 freshwater and seven saltwater springs that arise from the River Oum-er-Rbia are best approached from Azrou and Aïn Leuh through the cedar forest. Flowing across nearly the entire Moroccan heartland from the Middle Atlas to the Atlantic Ocean (at Azemmour, south of Casablanca), the great Oum-er-Rbia, Morocco's longest river, has been diverted, dammed, and largely destroyed over the years in favor of irrigation and hydroelectric projects. The sources are now impressive for the great volume of crystal clear water bursting from the adjoining mountain's side, part of the Djebel Hebri Massif and the Michlifen ski area's snow runoff. The Aguelmane Azigza (Lake Azigza), another 20 km (12 miles) south of the sources on Route 3211, is equally impressive, with stunning red cliffs surrounding undulating blue-green waters.

Kayaking trips are only available during April, and possibly March or early May, depending on weather conditions. Several tour companies offer memorable itineraries by experienced instructors who provide kayak clinics on the scenic Ahansal.

MIDELT

206 km (124 miles) southeast of Khénifra, 232 km (144 miles) south of Fez, 126 km (76 miles) north of Er-Rachidia.

Midelt itself is flat, nondescript, and not worth a special trip, but for the more adventurous, the nearby Cirque de Jaffar and Djebel Ayachi definitely are, and Midelt is the logical base for these excursions. The town itself has an interesting carpet souk with rugs in original geometric designs and kilims made by Middle Atlas Berber tribes.

EXPLORING

Atelier de Tissage–Kasbah Myriem. The Atelier de Tissage–Kasbah Myriem is a workshop run by the Notre Dame d'Atlas convent and monastery since 1925. Off the road to the Cirque de Jaffar, en route to Tattiouine and surrounded by trees, it is a good place to buy local Berber carpets, blankets, and hand-embroidered textiles of all kinds as well as to chat with the benevolent French Franciscan nuns, all of whom are experts on Moroccan weaving. On site is a small church with an icon of the Seven Sleepers of Ephesus, a legend referenced in both Christianity and Islam. ☎ *0664/44–73–75* 🕒 *Daily 8–noon and 2–5:30.*

Cirque de Jaffar. You'll need four-wheel drive to tackle the notoriously rough but spectacular 80-km (48-mile) loop through the Cirque de Jaffar, a verdant cedar forest running around the Ayachi peak's lower slopes. The 12,257-foot **Djebel Ayachi,** the dominant terrain feature in the Atlas Mountains south of Midelt, was long thought to be Morocco's highest peak before Djebel Toubkal, south of Marrakesh, was found to be 13,668 feet. The view of this snowcapped (from December to March) behemoth from the eponymous hotel's roof is inspiring. If you have time for serious exploration, the 130-km (78-mile) loop around through Boumia and Tounfite will take you across the immense Plateau de l'Arid, through the gorges of the upper Moulouya river valley, and into the Cirque de Jaffar on your way back into Midelt. Seasoned adventurers with four-wheel drive might be tempted to bivouac in the Cirque de Jaffar and climb Djebel Ayachi. After that, the route over to Tounfite on the right fork of Route 3424 is another exotic journey. Even more rugged still is the left fork, Route 3425, over the 10,749-foot Djebel Masker to Imilchil.

Gorges d'Aouli. Off the beaten track, a digression from Midelt takes you to the silver and lead mines at the Gorges d'Aouli, a 24-km (14-mile) round trip negotiable by a standard car. Formed by the Oued Moulouya—Morocco's longest river, flowing all the way to the Mediterranean—the gorges are sheer rock walls cut through the steppe.

WHERE TO EAT AND STAY

$ MOROCCAN 🍴 **Restaurant de Fes.** This small restaurant offers delicious Moroccan dishes, including tasty vegetarian tagines and seven different salads in the three-course set menu. It tends to attract groups. [$] *Average main: 80DH* ✉ *2, av. Mohammed V.*

$ HOTEL 🏨 **Kasbah Asmaa.** Mountains and gardens encircle this kasbah-style hotel—an unexpected oasis in this part of the Middle Atlas—a few miles from Midelt center. **Pros:** large pool; convenient stopover; friendly staff. **Cons:** some rooms may be shabby; attracts large tour groups; cash only. [$] *Rooms from: 500DH* ✉ *Rte. d'Er Rachidia* ☎ *0535/58–04–05* 🛏 *40 rooms, 7 suites* 💳 *No credit cards* 🍽 *Breakfast.*

6

THE HIGH ATLAS

WELCOME TO
THE HIGH ATLAS

TOP REASONS TO GO

★ **Hike North Africa's tallest peak:** Djebel Toubkal, which soars to 13,671 feet, is only a two-day climb. Trekkers can find everything they need at the base of the mountain.

★ **Legendary hospitality:** Many travelers say their favorite experiences involve staying with a traditional Berber family and engaging in simple pleasures such as rambling, horseback riding, and bird-watching.

★ **Adrenaline junkies getting their fix:** From quad biking to skiing to skydiving and hot-air ballooning, outdoor activities in magical surroundings abound. Even just driving through the jaw-dropping mountains can be an adventure, with panoramas you have to see to believe.

★ **Berber tradition and culture:** Life in the Atlas has barely altered over hundreds of years. While the arrival of electricity and new roads has brought changes, you'll still find Berber culinary, agricultural, linguistic, and artisanal heritage alive and well.

1 The Central High Atlas. Forested with olive groves and live oaks on their lower slopes, the rugged mountains to the south of El-Ksiba and Beni-Mellal offer memorable trek and jeep excursions and form a striking contrast to Azilal's lush Cascades d'Ouzoud and Demnate's natural bridge at Imi-n-Ifri.

2 The Aït Bougmez Valley. This Berber heartland (also known as the valley of happiness) lies beneath the protective shadow of Mt. M'Goun—Morocco's second-highest peak. It's an exquisite place to walk, cycle, discover local culture, and absorb that Atlas air.

3 Imlil. A village between Marrakesh and Mt. Toubkal, Imlil is the center of adventure tourism in Morocco. Trekkers en route to the mountain stop here for rest, relaxation, and to breathe in the fresh mountain air so rarely found elsewhere.

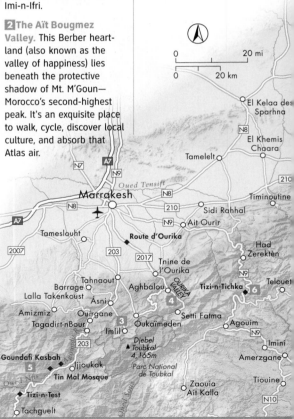

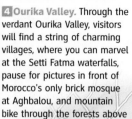

4 **Ourika Valley.** Through the verdant Ourika Valley, visitors will find a string of charming villages, where you can marvel at the Setti Fatma waterfalls, pause for pictures in front of Morocco's only brick mosque at Aghbalou, and mountain bike through the forests above Tahannout.

5 **To Tizi-n-Test.** The pass southwest of Marrakesh leads to the trekking center of Ouirgane and on to Taroudant.

GETTING ORIENTED

The two routes over the Tizi-n-Test (Test Pass) and Tizi-n-Tichka (Tichka Pass) are spectacular. For serious trekking, the area around Imlil is justifiably famous. There are also less strenuous walks along many of the dirt roads in the region, for instance along the Agoundis River. Alternatively, visitors can make the hotels around Ouirgane their base, exploring the area on mule back or simply lounging by the pool. The Tin Mal Mosque and the Goundafi Kasbah can easily be reached from Ouirgane on a day trip. The Aït Bougmez Valley leads deep into the mountains to reveal a cornucopia of rich verdure, staggering ranges, and Berber traditions, practically unchanged for centuries.

6 **To Tizi-n-Tichka.** Completed in 1936, the Tizi-n-Tichka can be a daunting prospect. Though the road is safer and wider than the one over the Tizi-n-Test, it can be a dangerous drive, particularly in winter weather conditions. Still, the views from the pass are like nothing else.

TREKKING IN THE ATLAS

There are few better antidotes to the marvel-ous mayhem that is Marrakesh than the clear air and amazing vistas offered by the High Atlas Mountains. From gentle strolls through unspoiled Berber villages to full-blown, week-long mountain treks, outfitters can cater to all levels of experience and budget.

(above) Two trekkers walking along a river in the Central High Atlas (opposite page, bottom) walking in the Tizi-n-Tichka pass (opposite page, top) a terrace restaurant with a view of the snow-covered Atlas peaks

Most travelers to the High Atlas associate it with one thing: Djebel Toubkal, North Africa's highest peak, scraping the clouds at 13,671 feet. It is indeed a mag-nificent sight, and for most of the year is a relatively easy climb. From late April to early October a strong pair of legs (and boots) will suffice. As the focal point of the range, Djebel Toubkal is very popular in high season, but over its 600-plus-mile length, the High Atlas has over 400 peaks that exceed 10,000 feet, so there are plenty of alternatives. In typical Moroccan style, flexibility is the name of the game. Pretty much any type or length of trek can be organized, from a half-day excursion to a lengthy expedition involving mules and guides. Your level of fit-ness will determine which you choose.

SAFETY ADVICE

Never walk alone. Always tell someone where you are going, and when you hope to return. Take suitable quantities of food; warm, lightweight cloth-ing; a hat and sunscreen; and a first-aid kit and water-purifying tablets (not bottled water). Most important, wear comfort-able boots. Litter and general pollution are a growing problem, so please leave no traces of your visit.

It is generally agreed that the launch point for any foray into the High Atlas is the small, albeit largest, Berber village in the region, Imlil. Here, accommodations are both plentiful and cheap, though they can be a little faded. Moreover, Berber hospitality is included, on which one cannot put a price.

In the shadow of Djebel Toubkal, Imlil is unprepossessing but has a purposeful bustle, offering all that is necessary for a trek. Everything is for hire: boots (though bring your own if possible), jackets, sleeping bags, crampons, and even a mule, which can carry the loads of four people, including children, over most terrain.

What sets the High Atlas apart from the rest of Morocco is not only its stunning geography and the Berber tradition that lives on here, but also its relative proximity to lively urban centers such as Marrakesh and Essaouira, a fact that should be exploited.

GUIDES

Detailed maps are scarce, but with a guide you shouldn't need one, and Imlil seems bursting with people willing to lead an expedition. They vary widely in competence and legitimacy. Official guides can be found at the Bureau des Guides et des Accompagnateurs à Imlil, in the main square, but don't completely rule out those attached to local hotels. In terms of cost, expect to pay 350 DH

to 400 DH each for one day. Mules come in at a very reasonable 100 DH. Bargaining is permitted, but make sure you know what you're paying for: food and overnight stays are sometimes not included.

TREKKING ROUTES

The choice of route will depend upon your level of experience, the season, the time available, and the budget. The obvious option is to attack Djebel Toubkal—you can be up and down in two days. Head south from Imlil past Sidi Chamarouch and make the easy ascent. Overnight on the mountain in the Neltner hut (a common shelter before the peak) and proceed to the summit in the morning.

Those with more time and stamina may opt for a circular route, east from Imlil. Over five days, you might visit Tacchedirt, Tizi Likemt (at an impressive 11,663 feet), spend the second night at Azib Lkemt, and the third in Amsouzerte. To the west, Lac d'Ifni (a serene mineral-rich lake) awaits, then back to the Neltner hut before descending to Imlil. Those wishing to contrast the trekking experience with a luxurious stay in beautiful surroundings may visit Ouirgane, the reservoir at Lalla Takerkoust, or the Route de l'Ourika, where many top hotels and welcoming guesthouses await.

6

Updated by
Olivia Gun-
ning Bennani

The High Atlas region is made for outdoor adventures—the perfect antidote to the concentration and animation of Marrakesh. You can hang glide, ski, hot-air balloon, quad bike, and ride mules, but perhaps best of all, you can walk. And if trekking in the snowy mountain ranges for days on end with only Berber women and their mules for friends isn't your thing, you can always wimp out and drive.

But the truth is, there's nothing wimpy about it. The roads career around bends for miles on end, carving their way through the rock. You and your fellow passengers will "ooh" and "aah" at every vista and every new combination of snow and sun. Stretching from the ocean to the desert, the mountain scenery is utterly compelling.

The High Atlas Mountains rise as a natural fortress between the fertile Haouz Plain around Marrakesh and the deserts of the south. Trapping moisture that blows in from the Atlantic, the mountains pass this bounty along to the land and to the thin rivers that vanish into the southern desert. To reach the mountains, even today's travelers must go through one of the routes guarded by age-old passes: Tizi-n-Test in the west or Tizi-n-Tichka in the east. They benefit from some glorious spots to stay, and the chance to take a quiet look at some intriguing relics of Moroccan history.

PLANNING

WHEN TO GO

For some the High Atlas is at its best in April, when the trees are flowering and the mountains are still cloaked in white. High-country hiking is safest and easiest in late summer. Winter can be cold but very peaceful, and on sunny days the lower passes just south and north of Imlil and the area around the Agoundis can make for pleasant day hikes. The high passes should be attempted in winter only by serious alpinists with serious gear, and even in summer the higher peaks should be approached with caution.

FESTIVALS

The most famous of festivals in this region is the Imilchil Marriage Festival, held each year in September. Legend has it that a "Romeo and Juliet" story happened here ages ago; since then, an annual festival is held for young people to choose their own partner. Though lately the festival has been attracting more and more tourists, it's still a sight to behold. The Setti Fatma Moussem, held in August, still contains the religious elements of a *moussem* (pilgrimage festival). Foreigners are welcome and will be pulled into the games and entertainment.

PLANNING YOUR TIME

There is so much to see in this region, and since the roads are narrow and serpentine, slopes are steep, and terrain is bumpy, allow plenty of time for getting around. A full two weeks is recommended to truly experience the Atlas, but a shorter 7-to-10-day trip could also be done. Start off in either Ourika or Tahannout to get acquainted with the region, while any mountain hike will truly begin in Imlil. The village of Tacchedirt is worth the five-hour trek, as is the more demanding two-day ascent to the great Toubkal. Afterwards, explore the route to the pretty village of Ouirgane, and, to complete a circle back in the Marrakesh direction, stop at the barrage of Lalla Takerkoust, a pretty settlement with some pleasant eateries and accommodations.

Alternatively, you can take the Rte. 210 out of Marrakesh, heading towards Ouzoud Falls, before continuing on to the reservoir Bin el-Ouidane. From here, head back down through Azilal and further south to the magnificent valley of Aït Bougmez, which can serve as a base for trekking.

GETTING HERE AND AROUND

While there's no air travel directly into the High Atlas, getting to the region isn't as difficult as it seems.

AIR TRAVEL

The closest airport is Marrakesh Menara, both to the Central High Atlas regions east of the city and to the areas south of Marrakesh, including the Ourika Valley. Many of the better hotels can arrange direct airport transfers from Marrakesh on your behalf, though the trip may come at an additional charge.

BUS TRAVEL

You can also hop on a bus from an airport or another major city, but this kind of travel can be time-consuming. If going to Azilal or other areas north and east of Marrakesh, try to avoid the marathon bus that goes from Marrakesh to Fez (via Beni-Mellal); buses run from Beni-Mellal up to Azilal, a common departure point for hiking excursions, departing approximately every three hours between 7 am and 4 pm. Buses also reach destinations in the High Atlas south of Marrakesh.

CAR TRAVEL

Unless you are taking a guided excursion, a car is the best way to explore off the beaten path at your own pace. If you have any intention of wandering into the hinterland independently, be sure you're driving a four-wheel-drive vehicle, and consider carrying more than one spare as well as emergency fuel. It's best to rent a car in Marrakesh and travel on from there. *See* ⇨ *Chapter 2, Marrakesh, for more information on rental cars.*

TAXI TRAVEL

You can also take a *grand taxi,* a large, usually white, beige, or even light-turquoise Mercedes, which can take up to six passengers, to many of these destinations. Agree on and settle the fare prior to setting off.

SAFETY

The High Atlas is no longer the wily region it used to be, but travelers should take precautions. Rural sentiments are quite different from urban ones, so women should dress more conservatively than in larger cities. The biggest safety concern is, of course, for trekkers; beginners should consult a local expert or join a group.

RESTAURANTS

There are a few excellent restaurants in some of the major hotels, but beyond these, fare is limited mostly to what's available in small hotel restaurants and cafés—mostly tagines. Avoid alcohol except in hotels. In general, drinking won't raise any eyebrows as long as you're among other tourists, but the practice of carrying wine and spirits into the backcountry is not appreciated by villagers. Alcohol is *haram* (forbidden by the Koran), but on a more earthly level it's simply not very socially acceptable.

HOTELS

Some more sophisticated hotels in the High Atlas are located in or around Ouirgane, Lalla Takerkoust, and Ourika, which are quickly becoming sought-after refuges from the sometimes excessive stimulation of Morocco's cities. There are a couple of stunning kasbahs around Imlil. Most other lodging in the region consists of inexpensive *gîtes* (backpackers' refuges). Heterosexual couples staying in private homes while trekking will be assumed to be married. It's best not to disabuse your hosts of their assumptions. If one member of the heterosexual couple is Moroccan, a marriage certificate is likely to be required. *Hotel reviews have been shortened. For full information, visit Fodors.com.*

WHAT IT COSTS IN DIRHAMS			
$	**$$**	**$$$**	**$$$$**
Restaurants	under 90 DH	90 DH–120 DH	121 DH–150 DH	over 150 DH
Hotels	under 400 DH	400 DH–650 DH	651 DH–1,000 DH	over 1,000 DH

Restaurant prices are the average cost of a main course at dinner or, if dinner is not served, at lunch. Hotel prices are the lowest cost of a standard double room in high season.

WHAT TO WEAR

As weather in this region can be unpredictable, it's best to bring layers. Having a wool sweater or fleece pullover is a necessity, as it can get quite frigid at night. Solid footwear, such as boots or sneakers, is important. Sandals are socially acceptable and a sturdy, sensible pair can be useful for strolls, although not for demanding hikes. Both women and men should dress conservatively. Women will be better received by locals if they wear longish sleeves, avoiding short skirts and short shorts. Both genders should be aware that pants are more practical when mule riding, unless you are accomplished at riding sidesaddle.

TOURS

A good local tour guide will be able to plan with you, and accompany you, on a thorough visit of the region. As well as organizing accommodations and transport (which can be a headache), they'll be able to point you in the right direction of safe and appropriate treks and worthwhile points of interests while supplying all the cultural information you may require. There is also the language advantage; remember that in the mountains, Arabic or a Berber dialect is mostly spoken and a language-savvy guide is an invaluable asset. Be sure to research tour guides and companies in advance as there are some less reputable organizations around.

Action Sport Loisirs. This is a bike-tour company that offers mountainbiking and cycling activities from Marrakesh into the High Atlas. It can fix up any kind of bike tour, from gentle track riding to rougher trips for the more fearless. Meals can also be incorporated into the tours. Trips range from half days to several days of intensive biking. A day's biking costs around 750 DH. ✉ *1, bd. Yacoub El Mansour, Guéliz, Marrakesh* ☎ *0661/24–01–45* ⊕ *www.marrakechbikeaction.com.*

Ame d'Aventure. This organization is comprised of a team of awardwinning guides who possess valuable local, geographical, and cultural knowledge as well as language skills. Each guide is fully trained, and the company offers a range of activities from mountain trekking and cross-country biking to desert camel rides. It caters to individuals and groups of all sizes and budgets. ✉ *81, rue Tensift, Guéliz, Marrakesh* ☎ *0661/43–00–15* ⊕ *www.ameaventure.com.*

THE CENTRAL HIGH ATLAS

Deep in the Berber heartland, the Central High Atlas is relatively unscathed by modernity. While most areas enjoy electricity and roads, there are still hamlets quite cut-off from such contemporary comforts. Expect the most jaw-dropping of scenery—at times gently dipping, occasionally plunging theatrically, and always housing exquisitely pretty and simple villages constructed from the soil on which they stand. The region's crowning glory is Mt. M'Goun, which stretches up over 13,000 feet, making it the second-highest peak in North Africa.

IMILCHIL

113 km (70 miles) southwest of Midelt, 150 km (93 miles) northeast of Marrakesh.

The joy of a visit to Imilchil is in the journey; however, if you find yourself in the area during August or September, you'll have an extra reason to visit. The September (sometimes late-August) moussem, which brings the Aït Haddidou tribe together to marry off eligible (but not always fully consenting) young people, is an event that over time has become more of a tourist attraction than a marriage mart. The surrounding **Plateau des Lacs** (Plateau of the Lakes) includes the lakes of Iseli and Tislit

CLOSE UP

The Berbers

Berbers, or Imazighen, as they often prefer, are the ancestral people of North Africa west of the Nile (the area known as the Maghreb). They live in every part of Morocco and move in every social class, from the poorest rural farms to the wealthiest neighborhoods in Rabat. The word "Berber" is thought by many to derive from "barbarian," used by the Romans to describe foreigners, especially those from the untamed hinterlands of their empire. Berbers themselves are manifold, dividing into three broad groups: Masmouda, Sahanja, and Zénètes. Although there were numerous Berber-speaking Jewish communities until the mid-20th century (when many moved to Israel at its foundation in 1948), the population is now almost entirely Muslim.

LANGUAGE
There are three main divisions of the Berber language: Taririft in the Rif area; Tamazight in the Mid-Atlas; and Tashelhit in the Anti-Atlas and Souss. However, the divisions don't necessarily match the broad groups mentioned here. High Atlas Berbers

call themselves Ishelhin, and also speak Tashelhit. The language seems to have arrived with migrants from somewhere in the Middle East at least 3,000 years ago, perhaps in several waves.

THE BERBER WAY
Attention to local sensitivities is much appreciated and often rewarded with the celebrated Amazigh hospitality. Smiling goes further than anything in creating good will. Dressing modestly is always appreciated. Smoking is an urban phenomenon, so everyone (particularly women) should smoke discreetly. Many High Atlas villagers are outraged that their children behave as beggars by demanding money, pens, or sweets from foreigners; the polite way to refuse is to say, "*Allah esahel,*" which means "God make it easy on you." If you would like to contribute something to these regions, do so through an official channel, such as Pack for Purpose, ⊕ *www.packforapurpose.org*. Always ask permission before you photograph Moroccans.

(His and Hers, or Fiancé and Fiancée). Lac Tislit is 5 km (3 miles) from Imilchil, while Iseli is another 10 km (6 miles) east. You can visit both of these lakes in one trip, but be careful if the weather is wet, as the tracks leading to the lakes can get muddy, making it easy for cars to get stuck.

GETTING HERE AND AROUND
Some people will approach Imilchil from Midelt (*see ⇨ Chapter 5, Fez and the Middle Atlas*). To reach Imilchil from the west, leave Beni Mellal on Avenue 20 Août Ex (N50), and shortly after take Route Principale 24. Continue on the P3221. After 5 km (3 miles), take the N8 for 44 km (27 miles), then take a right onto the R317 and continue for 119 km (74 miles), arriving at Imilchil after a total of about 170 km (105 miles) and three hours' driving.

BENI-MELLAL

198 km (123 miles) northeast of Marrakesh, 30 km (18 miles) south of Kasba Tadla, 211 km (127 miles) southwest of Azrou.

Ringed with fortifications built by Moulay Ismail in 1688, this rapidly growing country town nestles in the shadow of 7,373-foot Djebel Tassemit, surrounded by verdant orchards that are well irrigated by the Bin-el-Ouidane reservoir, 59 km (35 miles) to the southwest. Beni-Mellal is largely modern and of little tourist interest, but its Tuesday souk, known especially for its Berber blankets with colorful geometric designs, is an event to catch. ■ **TIP→ The 10-km (6-mile) walk up to the Aïn Asserdoun spring and the Kasbah de Ras el-Aïn is well worth the haul for the gardens and waterfalls along the way and the views over the olive groves and the Tadla Plain.**

GETTING HERE AND AROUND

Beni-Mellal can be reached by bus, grand taxi, or car from Marrakesh.

ESSENTIALS

Bus Contacts Beni-Mellal CTM Station ✉ *Bd. El Hansalli* ☎ *0523/48–39–81.*

Visitor Infomation Délégation du Tourisme de Beni-Mellal ✉ *Immeuble Chichaoua, av. Hassan II* ☎ *0523/48–87–27.*

WHERE TO EAT AND STAY

$ MOROCCAN 🍴 **SAT Agadir.** This small and traditional restaurant offers light salads as well as meat dishes. The upper dining-room area offers a view of the square. [$] *Average main: 23DH* ✉ *155, bd. El Hansali* ☎ *0523/48–14–48.*

$$$ HOTEL 🏨 **Hôtel Ouzoud.** Although regarded as Beni-Mellal's best hotel, its simple décor is perhaps not what one would expect from a four-star establishment. **Pros:** more amenities than anywhere else; pretty gardens. **Cons:** lacks charm; can be noisy at night. [$] *Rooms from: 850DH* ✉ *Rte. de Marrakech* ☎ *0523/48–37–52, 0523/48-98-22* 🛏 *56 rooms* 🍽 *No meals.*

AZILAL

171 km (103 miles) northeast of Marrakesh, 86 km (52 miles) southwest of Beni-Mellal on the S508, off the P24.

Azilal is a small garrison town, rather uninteresting to tourists but useful as a jumping-off point for routes into the southern highlands, especially toward the M'Goun Massif in the High Atlas, north of Ouarzazate. The gravel trails south of here become a maze of loops and tracks, great for exploring, but the main route forks 28 km (17 miles) after Aït Mohammed. To the right (southwest), the 1809 road descends into the Aït Bougmez valley, passing *ksour* (villages or tribal enclaves) at El Had and Agouti and looping eventually back to Aït Mohammed after a tough, tremendous 120-km (72-mile) trek that's much more effectively absorbed on foot than from a car.

GETTING THERE AND AROUND

Unless you are driving, the only practical way to get to Azilal is by bus or grand taxi from Beni-Mellal or Marrakesh.

6

CLOSE UP

The Imilchil Moussem

Every year scores of people get married at the three-day moussem, the engagement festival that takes place at Imilchil every August or September, at the northern end of the Todra Gorges. The reason? Long ago Iseli and Tislit, a young man and woman from opposing tribes, fell in love. Sound familiar? It's Shakespeare with a twist. The warring tribes were so angered by their love that they separated the pair, whereupon they wept and wept until their tears formed the two lakes that rest there today. They threw themselves in and drowned. The villagers were so shocked that they vowed to honor their love henceforward, and started the ceremony in their honor.

ESSENTIALS

Visitor Infomation Délégation du Tourisme d'Azilal ✉ *Av. Mohammed V* ☎ *0523/45–87–22.*

EXPLORING

The left (northeast) fork takes the 1807 road through the Tizi-n-Ilissi Pass to the Zaouia Ahanesal shrine and eventually reaches the 260-foot rock formations known and marked on the Michelin 742 National as **La Cathédrale des Rochers** (Cathedral of Rocks) for its resemblance to the spiky spires of a Gothic cathedral. The road eventually becomes 1803 and passes through a live-oak forest to reach the Bin-el-Ouidane reservoir after 113 km (68 miles) of slow, though wildly scenic, driving.

CASCADES D'OUZOUD

153 km (95 miles) northeast of Marrakesh, 22 km (14 miles) northwest of Azilal.

No trip to the Atlas would be complete without a stop at these impressive falls, which are approachable from the S508 via the 1811. You will most likely hear the roaring water before you get your first glimpse, especially in late spring when the melting snow swells the rivers. The cascades, which are a popular destination for holidaying Moroccan families, as well as foreigners, are rarely seen without a rainbow halo. On the way back down, wild Barbary apes play in the trees—avoid feeding them as they can get aggressive. Locals say the apes fall into three categories: those liking olives, those liking tourists, and those disliking both and preferring to hide in holiday season. If you are lucky, you might spot the youngsters swinging through the phone lines.

There are a number of pop-up snack places, which are not always the most reliable in terms of hygiene; and while the colorful boats that sashay towards the gushing torrent may look attractive, they may not be the most secure. Remember that swimming in the basin carved out of the rock at the base of the falls is strictly forbidden.

The Imilchil wedding moussem draws more than just happy couples; livestock vendors are also there in full force.

Downstream, past the Ouzoud falls on the 1811 road, is the Berber hillside village of **Tanaghmelt**. Nicknamed "the Mexican village," the small community is connected by a web of narrow alleyways and semi-underground passages. You may also wish to continue up the 1811 (toward the P24) to see the **river gorges** of the Oued-el-Abid.

GETTING THERE AND AROUND
Around 170 km (105 miles) of reasonably good road separate Marrakesh from the Cascades d'Ouzoud, a journey that takes some two to three hours of driving; however, this is a worthwhile and popular day trip. Leaving Marrakesh, take the Fez road (N8). Continue for around 60 km (37 miles). Turn right toward Azilal (the S508). Approximately 20 km (12 miles) before Azilal, turn left, following signs to Ouzoud.

WHERE TO STAY

$$$
HOTEL
FAMILY

La Kasbah d'Ouzoud. It's hard to guess that this Kasbah is new in town as the owners have built it in accordance with tradition, using baked earth bricks (and some cement) for the thick walls, resulting in a flawless and peaceful retreat that's cool in summer and cozy in winter. **Pros:** beautiful building; obliging staff; lush gardens. **Cons:** a bit out of town, so you'll have to drive or walk a bit to get to the falls. $ *Rooms from: 720DH ⊠ C/R Ait Taguelle* ☎ *0523/42–92–10* ⊕ *www.kasbahouzoud. com* ⤳ *6 bungalows, 5 rooms, 2 suites* ⃝| *Breakfast.*

$$$
HOTEL
Fodor's Choice
★

Riad Cascades d'Ouzoud. After the hair-raising, hairpin bends leading to the Cascades, you may find it hard to leave this stylish yet unspoiled riad. **Pros:** a perfect blend of elegance and comfort; welcoming and authentic; amazing location; the owners are very friendly and knowledgeable about the Atlas. **Cons:** some rooms on the small side; the

CLOSE UP

Moroccan Wines

During their occupation of the Maghreb, the Romans exercised their viticulture skills and exploited the climate and the soil, but upon their departure, and with the strengthening of Islam, the grapes literally withered on the vine. Under the French protectorate the vineyards were revived, but fell into state hands once they left in 1956, marking a second decline in production. The French once again took the helm in the 1990s, replacing all the vines and planting them in sand, which maintains the heat and kills phylloxera (the organism that

once decimated French vineyards in the 19th century). The harvest is at the end of August and bottling takes place in France. The reds are quite low in tannin, the whites reasonably sharp and benefit from chilling. Wines of note are Médallion and Volubilis (reds and whites), both at the high end of the price range, but don't exclude bargains like the tasty Guerrouane Gris (a slightly orange-colored rosé) or the Président Sémillon Blanc. Look out for Gérard Depardieu Lumiere, a syrah blend produced from the vineyards of the larger-than-life French actor.

walkway in front can get busy with tourists. $ *Rooms from: 710DH* ✉ *Cascades d'Ouzoud* ☎ *0523/42–91–73* ⊕ *www.ouzoud.com* 🛏 *8 rooms, 1 suite* ⦾ *Multiple meal plans.*

DEMNATE

72 km (43 miles) southwest of Azilal, 158 km (95 miles) southwest of Beni-Mellal, 99 km (59 miles) east of Marrakesh.

Demnate is a modest market center to which villagers from the neighboring hills and plains bring multifarious produce, especially for the Sunday souk held outside the walls. Once famed for its ceramics artisans, Demnate still has some traditional kilns. The rectangular ramparts are made of an unusual ocher-color *pisé* (clay) and pierced by two monumental portals; within is a kasbah built by T'hami el-Glaoui. As you approach the town, look out for the government-built dam, towering above the road.

GETTING HERE AND AROUND
The best way to get to Demnate is by car. If you don't want to rent one, you could always go for the more expensive option of hiring a driver, leaving you free to enjoy the scenes passing by your car window.

EXPLORING
Imi-n-Ifri. Up a 6-km (4-mile) piste above Demnate is the natural stone bridge Imi-n-Ifri, where the diminutive River Mahseur has carved out a tunnel inhabited by hundreds of crows. A path twists down through the boulders and under the "bridge," where stalactites and sculpted hollows dramatize the natural rock formations. Women come to bathe in the stream because it is said to bring them good luck, but the crows are considered harbingers of doom. The legend associated with these birds—a St. George and the Dragon–type saga in which a lovely maiden is saved from an evil genie who, when destroyed by the brave hero, dematerializes into crows—is told in several variations by imaginative guides.

THE AÏT BOUGMEZ VALLEY

Also known as the valley of happiness, this Atlas valley was basically cut off from the rest of the world until 2001; before then, only a narrow, overgrown track led into the heavenly series of hamlets perched above a river and the richest of flora. Here, slopes dotted with beehives lead down into a grove of walnut and apple trees. The valleys are filled with vegetables and fruit grown using traditional farm techniques; there's not a tractor in sight, only donkeys, simple ploughs, and one seriously hard-working community.

Today, there is a road that leads to Aït Bougmez and, with the arrival of electricity in 2006, the area has begun to attract visitors. Hikers enjoy the challenge of M'Goun, Morocco's second-highest peak, while others prefer exploring the steep pathways on mountain bikes. For the less ambitious, just hiking through the rich fields at the base of the valley and enjoying the pure, refreshing air is an experience.

Almost all houses here continue to be made from the traditional pisé bricks and baked earth, and you'll notice that most have living roofs, since sheaves of grasses are incorporated into the structure. One of the prettiest sights is the poppies peeping from them in spring. Life here is very simple, so don't expect any luxury spa hotels. There are also no restaurants in Aït Bougmez, but you can have a meal in practically any guesthouse with a little advance notice.

Remember that you are deep in the mountains, and safety is vital. It is easy to get lost. And be aware that much of this terrain is totally deserted for miles and miles on end. In winter, it gets incredibly cold and it's not uncommon to have minor snowstorms. Do not go unaccompanied unless you are very well equipped and experienced.

GETTING HERE AND AROUND

From Marrakesh, expect to spend five hours getting to the Aït Bougmez valley. Leaving Marrakesh on the Route de Fez, take the right turn after 60 km (37 miles) towards Azilal. From Azilal, follow signs to the Aït Bougmez valley. It's a long, but bewitchingly beautiful road that calls for careful, unhurried driving through mountain roads that are almost exclusively U-shaped. It's also possible to reach Aït Bougmez by grand taxi from Marrakesh with a change at Azilal. This is a much less comfortable and rather more frightening way, but it's possible. Be aware that the last taxi leaves Azilal around 2 pm in order to make it to Aït Bougmez before nightfall.

EXPLORING

FAMILY **Prehistoric dinosaur footprints.** Kids and adults alike love treading in these giant tracks of both carnivorous and herbivorous dinosaurs that are estimated to be about 185 million years old. There are several dinosaur-footprint sites in the region, but the easiest to find are those in the village of Ibaklliwane. As the road leads into the Aït Bougmez hamlets, it splits in two—this is actually a double valley. Follow the right-hand branch, leading into Tabant, the main village complete with a couple of cement structures, a school, and an administrative building. Follow

this track for about 1½ km (1 mile) past the schoolhouses into the village of Ibaklliwne, where you'll find the dinosaur footprints on the hillside. ✉ *Ibaklliwane.*

Sidi Moussa Marabout. A 2½-hour walk from the base of the valley will take you to the steep slope of Sidi Moussa Hill. Here stands a circular earthen building, a shrine to the saint Sidi Moussa (*Moussa* means "Moses" in Arabic) which dates to at least 200 years ago. Sidi Moussa, revered for his skills in curing infertility, was buried here, and his tomb once attracted many visitors, although few still make the pilgrimage. Women thought to have fertility issues would leave a garment at the door and then spend the night inside. For a time the building was used as a collective granary before being restored by the Titmit Village Association. A guard will serve you a glass of tea and give you a tour (pay him about 10 DH—all proceeds go to the Association).

WHERE TO STAY

$$$ HOTEL Fodor's Choice ★ 🏨 **Dar Itrane.** Tucked into the village of Imghlaus, Dar Itrane is an inconspicuous gemstone of a lodge, with little that isn't utterly charming. **Pros:** delightful and helpful staff; appealing rooms; very good facilities. **Cons:** not all rooms have great views. [$] *Rooms from: 880DH* ✉ *Imghlaus Village* ☎ *0610/08–69–30* 🌐 *www.origins-lodge.com/FR/Dar_Itrane* 🛏 *17 rooms* 🍴 *Some meals.*

$ B&B/INN 🏨 **Gite Aït Ayoub.** This charming family village house is clean and beautifully placed amid the overgrown green of the valley. **Pros:** genuine Berber home; comfy beds; owner is extremely knowledgeable. **Cons:** showers cost extra (10 DH) and are outside (although there is a toilet inside). [$] *Rooms from: 160DH* ✉ *Ibakaliwane Village* ☎ *0671/19–22–87* 🌐 *www.aitayoub-voyages.com* 🛏 *4 rooms* 💳 *No credit cards* 🍴 *Multiple meal plans.*

$$$ HOTEL FAMILY 🏨 **Touda Ecolodge.** This fantastic lodge occupies a prize position in the valley's deepest village, standing atop a hill with an unbeatable vantage point. **Pros:** magnificent views; well-equipped accommodations; photography course and cooking lessons offered. **Cons:** the road to get here may be difficult for some vehicles. [$] *Rooms from: 990DH* ✉ *Village Zawyat Oulmzi* ☎ *0033/683617991 in France, 0662/14–42–85 in Morocco* 🌐 *www.touda.fr* 🛏 *8 rooms* 🍴 *Some meals.*

SHOPPING

Women's Cooperative of Imghlaus. In the village of Imghlaus, up a dusty slope is a small, unassuming hut where you'd never know that inside was a veritable furor of singing voices and busy fingers. Squashed inside the diminutive hut, about 15 women create exquisite carpets in an organized production line. This cooperative is part of a fair-trade program that ensures the creators get the profits, with no middlemen involved. You can witness the fabrication process from beginning to end: the wool being cleaned, brushed, spun, and then fed through the loom. They'll also show you the natural tints they use: walnut for brown, petals for yellow, and a scarlet root for red. It can take two to three months to complete a rug. Design is important here; in Aït Bougmez, expect to find a certain

6

motif repeated, and the older women may have this same motif tattooed on their chins or foreheads, an ancient tradition, which revealed identity and was seen as beautiful. Prices vary, but expect a minimum of approximately 1,000 DH for a medium-size rug. You can buy directly here, or order online and have it mailed. ⊠ *Imghlaus* ⊕ *www.theanou.com.*

SPORTS AND THE OUTDOORS

TREKKING

An entire book would be necessary to make a comprehensive list of all the trekking possibilities available here. While the biggie is obviously M'Goun, a certain fitness level is required to complete it, so don't ignore other possibilities. Within one day, you can trek to the crest of Adazene, the mountain pass of Tizi'n Aït Imi, or hike to Aït Ours. It's important to remember that these mountains can be extremely dangerous. Unless very experienced, make sure you have a trusted guide. Most guesthouses can provide official guides for treks in the region, and will be able to advise you on the most appropriate trek.

IMLIL

64 km (40 miles) southeast of Marrakesh.

The village of Imlil is the preeminent jumping-off point for the high country, a vibrant mountain retreat whose existence has been given over to preparing walkers for various climbs around the peaks. It's a growing hub filled with guides, rooms of varying price and quality, and equipment-rental shops. Imlil is a long strip of a village, built up around the main road. The main square is a parking area, often crammed with the camper vans and cars of trek-minded travelers. Simple terraced cafés teem with *accompagnateurs* (guides), locals offering lodging in their homes, and mule owners renting the services of these essential means of mountain transport. ⚠ **Storms may occasionally make the road into town impassable or treks to neighboring settlements impossible. Consider this if you're heading up in rough weather.**

GETTING HERE AND AROUND

Rental cars are available from numerous international and local agencies in Marrakesh. You can get as far as Asni by bus (20 DH to 30 DH from Marrakesh, heading to Taroudant), and then for 15 DH get a seat in a grand taxi to Imlil. If you're moving between high-end hotels, ask how much it would cost to hire a private car and driver; from Marrakesh, this will typically be about 950 DH for up to four passengers.

TIMING AND PRECAUTIONS

Depending on how adept you are at trekking, you could enjoy hiking for a day or spend an entire week trekking the region. The best time to visit is early or late summer or early fall, but winter is best avoided except for the most avid of outdoors enthusiasts.

Visitor and Tour Information Bureau des Guides ⊠ *Village Center* ☎ *0524/48–56–26* ⏱ *Daily 8:30–6:30.*

EXPLORING

Djebel Toubkal. You can unlock the adventurer inside by scaling this peak, the highest in North Africa. In truth, there are several ways to make the ascent, from hikes lasting several days to gentler—and briefer—options: from Neltner Hut, the summit is achievable in around four hours. Take into consideration the time of year; winter is a season only for experienced climbers, while spring is breathtaking (in every sense), with snowy mountains framed by the fields of fruit blossoms and wildflowers below. Ascents start from the small, buzzing village of Imlil, where guides and necessary equipment may be secured. The road to Imlil is a left turn off the S501 (the Tizi-n-Test road that leads south from Marrakesh), just after Asni. The 17-km (11-mile) stretch is a spectacular expanse of scrub and cacti, which reaches out to the very foot of Ouanoukrim Massif. ■TIP→ **For the best views try and time your arrival on the peak for late morning.**

WHERE TO EAT

Food can be pretty basic in Imlil (primarily consisting of cafés that provide skewers and tagines), so if you're looking for something more gourmet, you may wish to seek out Kasbah du Toubkal, a 10-minute hike through the town. (There is a reception center on the main street.) The kasbah provides excellent Moroccan dishes to nonguests, in magnificent surroundings. Otherwise, most guesthouses will offer a full, home-cooked meal to nonguests.

$$ ✕**Café Aksoual.** A rustic establishment that is popular with locals and
MOROCCAN hikers out to experience the "real" Morocco, Café Aksoual offers traditional dishes: tagines, skewers, bread, and salads, all washed down with eyelid-flickeringly sweet mint tea. Look out for locals texting: it is a intriguing fact that although neighboring villages have only the most basic running water, electricity, and troubled cell reception, Imlil boasts its very own cell tower. $ *Average main: 110DH* ✛ *The restaurant is before the main square in Imlil, on the right as you approach from Asni* ▭ *No credit cards.*

WHERE TO STAY

Some of Imlil's hotels are right on the main square as you enter the village, but there are plenty more tucked away. Given the rise in popularity for treks in the region, there is now a good choice of hotels catering to a variety of tastes and budgets. They can range from mattresses on the floor of someone's home to opulent suites in luxurious accommodations. A great way to meet locals and see everyday Moroccan life is to stay in a private home for about 100 DH a night per person. If you go this route, pay special attention to etiquette suggestions and make sure you find out before nightfall what and where the bathroom facilities are. Bring your own toilet paper if you'd rather not go all that local.

$ ▦ **Auberge Zaratoustra.** This renovated and very pretty auberge is run by
B&B/INN a friendly couple who offer convivial service and excellent home-cooked cuisine (the couple met in the culinary milieu) with a refined touch. **Pros:**

run with care and attention; great food; warm welcome. **Cons:** can be tricky to find. ⓢ *Rooms from: 320DH* ☎ *0661/74–09–68* 🛏 *5 rooms, 5 studios* ⦿ *Multiple meal plans.*

$$ 🏨 **Hotel and Café Soleil.** This simple, authentic hotel and café is on the
HOTEL main square of Imlil. **Pros:** great local color; hotel can organize treks and tours and will hold luggage for trekkers. **Cons:** basic accommodations. ⓢ *Rooms from: 600DH* ⊠ *Village Square* ☎ *0524/48–56–22* ⊕ *www. hotelsoleilimlil.com* 🛏 *12 rooms* 🚫 *No credit cards* ⦿ *Some meals.*

$$$$ 🏨 **Kasbah du Toubkal.** Thank your stars that the short trek to this stun-
HOTEL ning, yet simple Kasbah keeps some guests away, so you can gaze over
Fodor'sChoice the snowcapped Atlas peaks in peace. **Pros:** freedom to inhale in the
★ crisp air in near solitude; excellent on-site hammam; hotel can organize tours, including a packed lunch. **Cons:** luxury comes at a price, even though 5% of room prices goes back to the local community; must travel on a mule to get here. ⓢ *Rooms from: 1790DH* ⚓ *Follow main road through Imlil and go right at fork, follow the signs up the hill, and keep going until you reach the top* ☎ *0524/48–56–11* ⊕ *www. kasbahdutoubkal.com* 🛏 *12 rooms, 3 Berber salons (no en-suite facilities), 2 suites, 1 house, 1 dorm* ⦿ *Breakfast* ⌓ *2-night minimum.*

$$$$ 🏨 **Kasbah Tamadot.** Should Hollywood set-makers get to work on a super-
HOTEL deluxe Moroccan mountain retreat, they might come up with something like this. **Pros:** heaven on earth; 20% of your breaktaking bill goes to the local Berber community. **Cons:** far removed from real Morocco; children only allowed certain times of the year; expensive. ⓢ *Rooms from: 5600DH* ⊠ *Rte. d'Imlil, Asni* ⚓ *The kasbah is just after Asni on road to Imlil, on the left* ☎ *877/577–8777 in U.S. (toll-free), 0524/36–82–00* ⊕ *www.virgin.com/kasbah* 🛏 *24 rooms including 6 tented Berber-style suites* ⦿ *Breakfast.*

$ 🏨 **Refuge de Club Alpin Français.** This is one of a series of refuges main-
B&B/INN tained by an association of French mountaineering buffs and is a good place to pick up a guide or information; you can also stay here in one of the basic rooms. **Pros:** a relaxing, no-nonsense place to be; mules, as well as guides, can be arranged through the hotel. **Cons:** very basic rooms. ⓢ *Rooms from: 145DH* ⊠ *Across main square from Café Soleil* ☎ *0524/48–51–22* ⊕ *www.cafmaroc2011.ffcam.fr* 🛏 *23 rooms* 🚫 *No credit cards* ⦿ *Multiple meal plans.*

OURIKA VALLEY

The Ourika Valley is the gateway to the High Atlas peaks, leading out of fuming Marrakesh into the fresh coolness of the mountains. It's a popular place to go for those in need of respite from the clamor and chaos of the city, but who don't want to travel far. Only 20 minutes outside of Marrakesh, you can see green gorges, sparkling yellow wheat fields at the foot of snowcapped mountains, and the ferocious flush of the Ourika River, where women wash clothes in the spray of waterfalls at the roadside. At the very end of the valley is Setti Fatma, a great base for trekkers. From here, explore stacked Berber villages with flat roofs as red as the earth they're built from. The only vertical line that breaks the slither of horizontal roofs is that of the village mosque, whose

The Kasbah de Toubkal, a luxury hotel, sits high above the village of Imlil.

minaret towers above all. You can stay at a guesthouse (often advertised as having a farm or garden) and spend a day or two lounging amid the exotic flowers, dipping in and out of a pool, strolling through fields, and feasting on homemade Moroccan food.

You can take a grand taxi from Marrakesh (10 DH to Ourika, 20 DH to Setti Fatma); there are five daily buses (6 DH to Ourika).

ROUTE DE L'OURIKA

As you leave Marrakesh on the P2107, you travel through a rich plain with the Atlas peaks above. This is known as the Route de l'Ourika, and is a good place to spend a night cooling off from the furnace that is Marrakesh. Since the plains are so generously watered by the Atlas slopes above, you'll find a lot of luscious vegetation, much different than the scorched terrain nearby. Anticipate reams of olive, citrus, and fig trees, and boughs bending with flowers. There are a number of guesthouses, kasbahs, and minifarms along the way offering comfy accommodations, home-cooked food, and fresh air.

GETTING HERE AND AROUND

If you have a car, then follow the Avenue Mohamed VI out of Marrakesh and onto the P2017 (aka Route de l'Ourika). Buses (6 DH) and grand taxis (10 DH) can also be taken from Marrakesh or you can contact a reliable company to get a good car and driver.

WHERE TO STAY

$$ ☷ **La Ferme Berber.** This is a quirky and charming place to stay, eat, relax, **HOTEL** and rejuvenate. **Pros:** comfortable and peaceful; great food. **Cons:** the pool is quite small. $ *Rooms from: 520DH* ✉ *Km 9, rte. de l'Ourika*

☎ *0661/92–09–41* 🌐 *www.lafermeberbere.com* 🛏 *6 rooms, 4 suites, 2 tents* 🍴 *Breakfast.*

$$ HOTEL FAMILY 🏨 **Le Bled.** This homely guesthouse is only a 20-minute drive from the center of Marrakesh, yet couldn't be more of a contrast. **Pros:** suites have private gardens; lots to keep kids amused; wonderful homemade food. **Cons:** can get busy on weekends; rooms are less comfortable than suites. [$] *Rooms from: 650DH* ✉ *Douar Coucou, Taseltanet* 🌐 *www.lebledmarrakech.com* 🛏 *4 rooms, 3 suites* 🍴 *Breakfast.*

$$$ HOTEL 🏨 **Quaryati.** This plush ecolodge is hidden in the lush plains beneath the Atlas through which the Route de l'Ourika runs. **Pros:** luxurious but still ethical; large swimming pool. **Cons:** lawn area could do with some extra shade. [$] *Rooms from: 950DH* ✉ *Douar Tounsi, Sidi Abdallah Ghiat* ☎ *0619/00–00–06* 🌐 *www.quaryati.com* 🛏 *26 rooms, 8 suites, 3 pavilions* 🍴 *Breakfast.*

TNINE DE L'OURIKA

35 km (22 miles) south of Marrakesh.

Tnine de l'Ourika is a small village easily explored on foot, with its Monday souk ranking among the best in the region. Aside from that, the only thing to see is the local *zaouia* (sanctuary) and the ruins of an ancient kasbah. However, there are two must-see sights nearby.

To get to either Nectarome or La Safranière (two magnificent gardens), take the left turn at Ourika for the road that heads for Tnine de l'Ourika and Dar Caid Ourika. The turn is signposted to both Nectarome and La Safranière, but easy to miss. La Safranière is down one of the first left turns down a small track (signposted); Nectarome is also a left, a little farther up (also signposted); then through a gate on the left after a few minutes' drive. Any local can give directions. If you are looking to take a break in Ourika, have a cool drink on the terrace of the stunning Kasbah Bab Ourika, which perches above the village.

GETTING HERE AND AROUND

Tnine de l'Ourika is best reached by car or grand taxi, though a few buses stop here on their way to Oukaïmeden.

EXPLORING

La Safranière de l'Ourika. Just before the turn to Nectarome, La Safranière de l'Ourika has guided tours around its gardens of the valuable saffron plant. For the ultimate saffron experience, go around the end of October into mid-November, when the plants are in flower and you can even participate in the picking and drying process. There are plenty of other plants and trees to admire, as well as a few farm animals. ✉ *Ferme Boutouil, Takateret* ☎ *0661/15–34–15* 🌐 *www.safran-ourika.com* ⏲ *Daily 8–6; harvest season daily 7–6.*

Nectarome. The absolute pièce de résistance of any visit to the Ourika Valley is a trip to Nectarome, the region's first aromatic garden. It produces essential oils for massages, spas, and hammams in the classiest of hotels and riads back in Marrakesh. Started by two Moroccan brothers (one a biochemist, the other a pharmacist), it grows 50 species of aromatic and medicinal plants, all in 2½ acres of beautifully maintained

Oukaïmeden is the most popular ski resort in Morocco.

and colorful gardens. They pick the plants on site, then extract, process, and bottle the oil in the top-secret perfume workshop. You can take a guided tour (80 DH) through the grounds and learn about the healing properties of each plant (lavender for rest; rosemary for blood circulation; thyme for digestion; geraniums for menopause, etc.), or wander on your own (20 DH). You can also have an essential-oils open-air pedicure in specially constructed basins dug into the ground (80 DH for 20 minutes) or bake your own Berber bread in one of three types of clay oven to accompany your breakfast (50DH). Whatever you do, don't miss the seven-plant tea infusion, taken in a garden gazebo or Berber tent, or the boutique, where you can buy the goods. ■ TIP→ Don't munch on the leaves of the oleander rose; they're pretty on the outside but poisonous on the inside. Two leaves are enough to kill a man. ⊠ B.P. 142 ☎ 0524/48–21–49 ⊕ www.jardin-bioaromatique-ourika. com ⊗ Winter daily 9–5; summer daily 9–6:30.

SETTI FATMA

Once you arrive at Setti Fatma, some 65 km (40 miles) from Marrakesh, you'll notice the increase in crowds and, of course, an increase in eating, lodging, and shopping options. Setti Fatma is not the most restful village in the valley, but it's convivial, bubbling with activity. One of the main reasons people make their way to Setti Fatma is to visit the seven waterfalls—a two-hour climb from the village center. It's also a great setting-off point for walks into the mountains, where you can explore villages inaccessible by road.

GETTING HERE AND AROUND

A few kilometers along the 2017 from Tnine de l'Ourika, the road forks. Bear left towards Setti Fatma and the full beauty of the Ourika valley awaits you. Walnut trees line the river which rushes to serve a number of pretty villages leading to Setti Fatma. The tiny village of Aghbalou is especially pretty, and a lovely place to spend a night.

WHERE TO EAT AND STAY

$ MOROCCAN 🍴 **Restaurant-Hotel Azilal.** For only 50 DH, you can get a great meal here consisting of three courses made entirely by the family's mother. Go for a classic Moroccan salad (tomatoes and peppers) and a tagine of your choice and eat on the quaint platform overlooking the river. It's simple and very Moroccan. There's supposed to be Wi-Fi, but you may need to check if it's working. [$] *Average main: 50DH* ✉ *Setti Fatma* ✥ *Near the entrance of the village on the right, with an eating area on the opposite side* ☎ *0668/88–37–70* 💳 *No credit cards.*

$ MOROCCAN 🍴 **Timichi.** You need to cross a rickety bridge to get to this restaurant, which buzzes with the hum of local chatter, the sound of the trickling river, and the occasional Berber musician. The menu is predictable, with Moroccan salads, tagines, and a variety of sodas, but it's very tasty and the location is a great vantage point for people-watching. It also has some basic triple rooms with shared showers up the very steep staircase. [$] *Average main: 60DH* ✉ *Setti Fatma, Ourika at the end of the village, on the left, over the last makeshift footbridge* ☎ *0668/94–48–67* 💳 *No credit cards.*

$$ HOTEL FAMILY 🏨 **Auberge Le Maquis.** One of the valley's first lodges, this friendly option guarantees excellent service, good food, and a snug bed for prices that won't break the bank. **Pros:** fantastic welcome; free Wi-Fi throughout; central heating (a rare find in these parts). **Cons:** occasional noise from the road. [$] *Rooms from: 580DH* ✉ *Km 45, Aghbalou* ☎ *0524/48–45–31* 🌐 *www.le-maquis.com* 🛏 *10 rooms, 1 suite* 🍽 *Breakfast.*

$ B&B/INN 🏨 **Hotel Asgaour.** This simple yet comfortable hotel is probably the best of the lodging options in the center of the village. **Pros:** central location; clean; owners make a real effort. **Cons:** rooms with windows overlooking the road may be noisy. [$] *Rooms from: 200DH* ✉ *Setti Fatma, Ourika, just inside the village on the right-hand side of the road* ☎ *0524/48–52–94* 🛏 *26 rooms* 💳 *No credit cards* 🍽 *No meals.*

SPORTS AND THE OUTDOORS

TREKKING

Bureau des Guides. For treks around the area, consult Hassan Aït Brahim at the Bureau des Guides just inside the village of Setti Fatma. Prices vary, depending on group size and distance. ✉ *On the right after Hotel Azgour, Setti Fatma* ☎ *0673/52–09–07.*

SHOPPING

Small stands line the road from before Ourika to Setti Fatma, selling crafts, pottery, and the carpets for which the Berbers are so famous. Many of these small stands supply the great boutiques and bazaars of Marrakesh, so if you're in the mood for bargain hunting, you're likely to find a better deal here. Two shops stand out, a couple of kilometers apart and both a few kilometers before the right turn to Oukaïmeden (heading south), as the road starts to climb.

La Source de Tapis. A Berber women's cooperative with more than 7,000 carpets on sale, five hundred women from villages all over the region bring their carpets down to this enormous three-level shop, and are paid when their own carpet sells. There's a plethora of choices, but it's a particularly good source for embroidered rugs. Expect to be offered an 8-foot by 5-foot rug for 2,500 DH to 3,000 DH. The shop also ships. ✉ *Amassin, 39 km (23 miles) from Marrakesh on the P2017* ☎ *0524/48–24–58.*

Pottery at Le Kasbah de Tifirte. This is a marvelous emporium of tagine pots, plates, and vases. You can watch experts sitting at a clay wheel knock off a tiny tagine pot and lid within minutes, judging everything expertly by eye and experience. Pieces are then fired in a kiln, decorated, and fired again. It's an excellent place to learn the difference between *tadelakt*, a hand-polished finish that takes an entire day, and painted stucco imposters. A half day in the workshop costs 70 DH although prices for groups can be negotiated. ✉ *Amassin, 39 km (24 miles) from Marrakesh on the P2017* ☎ *0667/34–49–06.*

OUKAÏMEDEN

20 km (13 miles) from Imlil.

While you probably didn't go to Morocco for the snow, if Vail's novelty value has worn off and you have a day or two to kill, then a bit of powder isn't out of the question. The ski station at Oukaïmeden is becoming an increasingly popular retreat and a good place for novices to get in some practice without the stress of jam-packed slopes. A range of walks is available outside the ski season.

Unless you're Moroccan, or a ridiculously enthusiastic ski bum, it's highly unlikely you'll arrive with any of the right gear. Numerous shops are ready to help out. As in the souk, nothing has a fixed price, so you may need to bargain. As a general rule, expect to pay around 150 DH per day for some warm clothing, boots, skis, and poles. The next step is getting to the ski lift, which is in fact a frustratingly long distance away (particularly in ski boots). To ride on the big lift to the very top of the mountain (known as the *télésiège* in French) a lift pass costs 100 DH per day; access to the six smaller chairlifts (*téléskis*) costs 50 DH per day.

Although Oukaïmeden is small, don't think its 20-odd *pistes* (runs) are basic. Apart from three green (easy) runs and four blue (medium), everything else is either red (advanced) or black (difficult). Only red and black runs go down the télésiège, so go ready for a challenge. The long red run starts to the right of the lift drop-off point—everything else to the left is black, and with names like Combe du Mort (Vale of Death) they aren't for the fainthearted. It's currently undergoing massive investment. The ski season lasts from December until late March.

GETTING HERE AND AROUND

Transport can be a problem here, as a grand taxi from Marrakesh will drop you off, but might prove unreliable for collection. There is no scheduled bus service. In the busy ski season, you should find shared taxis or even minibuses shuttling between the resort and Marrakesh.

Otherwise, consider taking a tour of Oukaïmeden with an operator such as the U.K.-based Do Something Different, or call a car and driver from a reliable company, such as the excellent El Jarssi Transport.

ESSENTIALS

Guides and Tours **Do Something Different** ☏ *(44) 0208/0903790 in the U.K.* ⊕ *www.dosomethingdifferent.com.* **El Jarssi Transport** ☏ *0661/32–07–58.*

TIMING AND PRECAUTIONS

For skiers, Oukaïmeden is often a day trip from Marrakesh. There are a few hotels for those wishing to spend the night. Oukaïmeden, being a resort, is extremely safe. Just be sure to bring warm clothes.

WHERE TO EAT AND STAY

$$$$
FRENCH
FAMILY

✕ **Chez Juju.** There are few options in terms of lodging and dining in Oukaïmeden, but if you feel like a hearty meal, then head for the hotel Chez Juju. Whether you choose to just eat here or to stay the night as well, you'll instantly appreciate Juju's yesteryear feel, modeled after alpine-style accommodations. The restaurant has been operating for more than 60 years and serves up distinctly French dishes such as cassoulet and tartiflette, alongside some Moroccan choices like tagines. There's a bar too. If you choose to lodge here, the rooms are comfortable enough, albeit a tad basic. Ⓢ *Average main: 160DH* ✉ *Village Center, Oukaïmeden* ☏ *0524/31–90–05* ⊕ *www.hotelchezjuju.com.*

$
B&B/INN

🏠 **Club Alpin Français.** Offering a safe place to sleep for trekkers, skiers, and summer ramblers alike, this very simple and basic dormitory-style accommodation is clean and well run. **Pros:** a relaxing, clean and no-nonsense place to be; hotel can organize treks. **Cons:** very basic accomodation. Ⓢ *Rooms from: 110DH* ✉ *Oukaïmeden, on the right as you first enter town* ☏ *0524/31–90–36* ⊕ *www.ffcam.fr* ⤴ *158 beds (82 dormitory-style and a total of 76 beds in rooms for 4 or 8 people)* ▭ *No credit cards* ⏺ *Multiple meal plans.*

TO TIZI-N-TEST

To the west of Djebel Toubkal the southern road from Marrakesh through Asni and Ouirgane carves its way through the High Atlas Mountains and offers spectacular views all the way to the Tizi-n-Test pass and beyond. Ouirgane is a great base for trekking and playing in the hills, and has some fantastic lodging options. South of Ouirgane is best done as a road trip, with stops for occasional sights and breathtaking views.

LALLA TAKERKOUST LAKE

Thanks to the abundance of water, the Lalla Takerkoust dam is a good cooling-off point in the region. Fed by the river Oued Nfis, the lake has a shoreline stretching 7 km (4 miles) and offers fabulous views of High Atlas peaks. It was originally made by the French to ensure the surrounding Houz Plains were watered. There are various activities available such as trekking and horseback riding, as well as water sports (although the ethics of such activities on a reservoir are somewhat questionable), and an increasing number of hotels and guesthouses.

GETTING HERE AND AROUND

If you have your own car, take the R203 out of Marrakesh, in the direction of Tahannout and Asni. After around 5 km (3 miles), take the R209, better known as the Route du Barrage, off to the right. Continue until you reach the village of Lalla Takerkoust.

Otherwise, the village can be reached from Marrakesh by bus or grand taxi. The problem with both of these options is that you'll be dropped in the village of Lalla Takerkoust and will need to continue to the lake either on foot or with a local taxi, who will charge at least 100 DH. The easiest option is to ask your hotel for help. Most will organize a taxi transfer for you, charging around 170 DH for the entire journey from Marrakesh.

EXPLORING

FAMILY **Lalla Takerkoust Lake.** This reservoir is around 80 years old and a very established feature of the region, built by the French during the protectorate period. The water level fluctuates depending on rainfall and snowmelt, as it is fed from the mountains above. There are a few Jet Skis available to rent and take on the lake, which is not illegal but still questionable, given that this is a working reservoir. Swimming is forbidden since there is no lifeguard, but it's not uncommon to see people taking a dip, especially in the hotter months when temperatures rise. The most popular activity here is simply walking around the lake, which affords lovely views of the region as well as the local birdlife.

6

WHERE TO STAY

$$$ HOTEL FAMILY **Jnane Tihihit.** Not far from the lake, this paradisiacal farm and guesthouse hides out behind the dusty, unassuming village of Makhfamane. **Pros:** exemplary gardens; total immersion in nature; delicious food. **Cons:** the road to get here is very bumpy; natural pool might not be to everyone's tastes. *Rooms from: 852DH ✉ Douar Makhfamane ☎ 0670/96–59–70 🌐 www.riad-t.com/jnane-tihihit 15 rooms Breakfast.*

$$$ HOTEL **Kasbah Igoudar.** About a 20-minute drive from the lake, the authentically built Kasbah Igoudar sits amid 50 acres of olive trees, creating a secluded and romantic spot that invites relaxation. **Pros:** quiet and remote; great for real detachment; free transfer from airport to the hotel. **Cons:** standard rooms are rather small; might be too secluded for some. *Rooms from: 969DH ✉ Rte. d'Amizmiz, 7 km (4 miles) before Amizmiz coming from Marrakesh ☎ 0663/77–89–44 🌐 www.kasbah-igoudar.com 12 rooms, 3 suites Breakfast.*

$$ HOTEL **Le Petit Hotel du Flouka.** Set over a series of terraces leading down to the lake, this elegantly refurbished hotel is both relaxing and friendly. **Pros:** congenial ambience; tasteful décor; great views. **Cons:** can get crowded on Sunday. *Rooms from: 550DH ✉ Rte. 203, Lalla Takerkoust 🌐 www.leflouka.com 11 rooms, 4 suites Breakfast.*

SPORTS AND THE OUTDOORS

HORSEBACK RIDING

Les Cavaliers de L'Atlas. This is a reputable equestrian company that organizes all kinds of horseback excursions in the region. You can take a horse or pony out for anything from two hours to the whole day. It's a great way to discover the area and experience the lake or the nearby Agafay Desert from a different vantage point. Prices range from

400 DH for two hours, 780 DH for a half day, and 980 DH for a full day, including meal and transfer if needed. ✉ *Lalla Takerkoust Lake* ☎ *0672/84–55–79* 🌐 *www.lescavaliersdelatlas.com.*

TAHANNOUT

35 km (22 miles) from Marrakesh.

The town of Tahannout is the capital of the Al Haouz province not too far outside Marrakesh. While most of the buildings on the main stretch of road here are rather uninteresting, there's a weekly Tuesday souk and a Jewish cemetery to be explored. But what's really interesting about Tahannout is the gorgeous surroundings; this is an area to explore, with something for all energy levels, and is relatively untouched by tourists so far.

GETTING HERE AND AROUND

If driving from Marrakesh, take the R203 road in the direction of Tahannout and Taroudant for about 30 km (20 miles). Follow signs through Tahannout to Asni in order to reach the most interesting accommodations and sights.

EXPLORING

Just outside of Tahannout towards Asni you can access the forest of **Toubkal National Park**. This is an area of extraordinary natural beauty that's worth exploring either on foot or by mountain bike. Alternatively, hike through the captivating Sidi Fares Valley or visit the clusters of Berber villages alongside the Ighighayne River. For the more ambitious, the summit of Mt. Khelout (5,068 feet) is a fair challenge, as is the Foudrar Ridge (5,541 feet). A new road leading from Tahannout to Oukaïmeden, has improved access to the Atlas peaks. You can rent walking and biking equipment from Kasbah Angour and other guesthouses in the area.

WHERE TO STAY

$$$$ HOTEL FAMILY 🏨 **Kasbah Angour.** This grand Kasbah stands proudly atop a hill offering jaw-dropping views of the surrounding mountain slopes, including Mt. Angour to the south. **Pros:** all rooms and suites are excellent; splendid views from every room; staff members speak English. **Cons:** difficult to access without a car or organized transport. [$] *Rooms from: 1750DH* ✉ *Just off the 2028, Douar Toufsirine* ☎ *0524/43–81–03* 🌐 *www.kasbahangour.com* 🛏 *22 rooms, 3 suites* 🍴 *Breakfast.*

SPORTS AND THE OUTDOORS

FAMILY **Terres d'Amanar.** A great place for both energetic children and adventurous adults, this large activity park is built on the side of the breathtaking hillside and offers plenty of activities like zip lining, archery, horseback riding, pottery, and more. You can reserve activities in advance, or just show up and have the kids enjoy the playground. Transport and transfers from the airport can be provided on request. Hotel and restaurant facilities are also available here, including rooms (1,368 DH), tents, and luxurious ecolodges. ✉ *Douar Akli, Tahanoute, El Haouz* ☎ *0524/43–81–03* 🌐 *www.terresdamanar.com.*

OUIRGANE

60 km (37 miles) south of Marrakesh.

Ouirgane is one of Morocco's more luxurious bases for mountain adventures. It doesn't have the highest peaks, but it has a glorious choice of charming hotels and day trips that take in captivating scenery toward the mountainous Tizi-n-Test to the south. You can climb Djebel Toubkal in three days or stay up in the High Atlas for a little longer, safe in the knowledge that you have a snug hotel waiting for you back in Ouirgane. Even if you keep close to town, you can explore the surrounding hills on two "wheels" (foot or bicycle) or four (mule, horse, or quad bike) with ease. In town there's a lively morning souk on Thursday. For many, Ouirgane is just a pleasant stop before tackling Tizi-n-Test. But the charming village has a few auberges that make it a good starting point for treks.

GETTING HERE AND AROUND

If you have your own car, Ouirgane is a fairly short drive from Marrakesh. Failing that, a grand taxi costs 25 DH per person from Marrakesh; taxis from Tnine de l'Ourika are available for about 20 DH. The cheapest way is by bus (15 DH), which leaves Marrakesh's Gare Routière five times daily. However, it's easier to make the journey in hired vehicles, often with a hired driver.

EXPLORING

Mouflon Rouge. Although counting sheep isn't everyone's idea of fun, seeking out Morocco's wild Berber sheep (*mouflon* in French, *aoudad* in Tashelhit) at the Mouflon Rouge will by no means put you to sleep. The wooly creatures are famed throughout the region, and can be seen at a lovely viewing area just before Ouirgane. It's worth it to see what all the fuss is about. ✛ *On approach to Ouirgane from the north, look for a right turn signposted to "La Bergerie" near the village of Marigha. Keep going south on main road for about ½ km (¼ mile), then take a left turn for the viewing area, which parallels Ouirgane River.*

Salt Mines. It is worth negotiating the pot-holed road to the salt mines just off the Amizmiz road (stop at the turning for the Amizmiz road and walk the last part). For centuries, the Berbers have produced salt here but today's relatively low value of the once highly prized natural commodity has greatly endangered the livelihoods of the salt-mining families. To support them, be sure to flag down a merchant as you see him riding from village to village on his donkey and if you tour the mines, tip the miners. ■ TIP➔ **Don't go on a Saturday as that is when they make their way to the souk at Asni.** ✛ *From Ouirgane, take the Amizmiz Rd.*

Shrine of Haïm ben Diourne. Site of one of the few Jewish festivals still held in Morocco, this complex contains the tombs of Rabbi Mordekai ben Hamon, Rabbi Abraham ben Hamon, and others. The shrine, known locally both as the "tigimi n Yehudeen" and "marabout Juif" ("House of the Jews" in Arabic and French, respectively), is a large white structure. The moussem generally happens in May. Tip the gatekeeper after a tour—anything between 5 DH and 15 DH is fine. ✛ *About 4 km (2½ miles) outside Ouirgane, the shrine is accessible on foot or by mule in less than an hour, or you can drive right up to gate on a dirt piste. Turn* *left after about 1 km (½ mile) at Ouirgane's souk; follow the road as it winds through village until you reach a pink cubic water tank. Turn right and go to the end of road, about 3 km (2 miles).*

WHERE TO EAT AND STAY

$$$
MOROCCAN
FAMILY

✕ **Chez Momo.** Nestled in the foothills of the mountains near Ouirgane, at Chez Momo you can sip a cocktail by the small pool or have a barbecued dinner seated on one of the chairs fashioned from tree trunks. It is well worth sampling the Berber cuisine, such as corn or barley couscous or vegetarian tagine, accompanied by homemade tanourt bread with oranges and cinnamon to follow. After such a feast you may find yourself inquiring about one of the seven cozy rooms and six suites (priced around 750 DH), to which a breakfast of morning coffee and *beghrir* (pancakes) is brought to your door. $ *Average main: 140DH* ✉ *Rte. d'Asni, Km 61 from Marrakesh* ✢ *The dirt road to Chez Momo is roughly 1 km (½ mile) south of the bridge over the Ouirgane River. Turn right at the sign and continue about 164 ft. downhill. Turn right again and park among the olive trees* ☎ *0524/48–57–04, 0661/58–22–95* ⊕ *www.aubergemomo.com.*

$$$$
FRENCH

✕ **La Bergerie.** This delightful restaurant and guesthouse combines shaker style with *Little House on the Prairie.* French owner Françoise has devised a menu with both excellent French and Moroccan dishes and offers a full bar (something of a rarity in these parts). Specialties include wild boar, frog's legs, and the wonderful *souris d'agneau* (a rich dish of slow-cooked lamb shank). The attached inn has 10 standard rooms (1,080 DH for half board, but check for discounts), four bungalows for two people sharing, and three family suites which accommodate up to four. Be sure to say hello to Mimi, the establishment's sleek ginger cat. $ *Average main: 180DH* ✉ *Marigha, Rte. de Taroudant, Km 59, Asni* ☎ *0524/48–57–17, 0661/15–99–06* ⊕ *www.labergerie-maroc.com.*

$$$$
HOTEL

⊡ **Domaine de la Roseraie.** The Grande Dame of this part of the Atlas, La Roseraie is plush but slightly fading. **Pros:** rooms hidden in private natural parkland; kids under 6 stay free; nice views. **Cons:** quite costly for faded splendor. $ *Rooms from: 1350DH* ✉ *Rte. de Taroudant, Km 60* ☎ *0524/48–56–94, 0524/43–91–28* ⊕ *www.laroseraiehotel.com* ⤴ *21 rooms, 21 suites* ❏ *Some meals.*

SPORTS AND THE OUTDOORS

"Sights" aside, by far the best thing to look at here is the surrounding countryside with its poppies, yellow wheat, snowcapped mountains, rushing rivers, and glorious, looming hills. You can get out there in so many different ways, and your hotel (or a better-equipped one nearby) is the best way to rent equipment for outdoor activities.

BIKING

You can rent bikes from La Roseraie, or, for the cheapest option, La Bergerie (from 20 DH an hour). Quad-biking adventurers can rent the beasts from Au Sanglier Qui Fume for 300 DH an hour (550 DH for half a day).

HORSEBACK RIDING

For horseback riding, La Roseraie is *the* place for the entire region. You can rent horses for local rides or for full-blown tours in the mountains, complete with food and lodging in Atlas villages. Prices start at 200 DH for an hour. As there might be an additional levy elsewhere, it's best to come straight here.

WALKING

Every hotel will be able to fix you up with a walking guide to wander the local hills and rivers, dropping in on the salt mines, the remains of the Jewish settlement, and a Berber house, as you like. It's also only three days on foot (with the help of a mule or two) to the summit of Djebel Toubkal. The route bypasses Imlil altogether, a significant benefit for anyone keen to avoid the trekker base camp.

TIZI-N-TEST

The road to Tizi-n-Test is one of Morocco's most glorious mountain drives. The route south from Ouirgane to Tizi-n-Test takes you through the upper Nfis Valley, which was the spiritual heart of the Almohad Empire in the 12th century and later the administrative center of the Goundafi *caids* (local or tribal leaders) in the first half of the 20th century. It's best enjoyed as a day trip by car from Ouirgane, especially as lodging options are seriously basic and few. There are plenty of cafés on the way, however, and a great stop off at Tin Mal Mosque.

The route to Tizi-n-Test clings to the mountainside, sometimes triple-backing on itself to climb the heights in a series of precipitous hairpin bends. It's often only a narrow single lane, with sheer drops, blind corners, and tumbling scree. Expect every bend to reveal a wide and furiously fast Land Rover coming right at you, or worse, a group of children playing soccer. Honk as you round sharp corners, and give way to traffic climbing uphill. There is no need to pick up hitchhikers, as they are most probably just moving from one nearby village to another. However, if asked for water, you can stop and hand over any spare water bottles through the window.

GETTING HERE AND AROUND

To drive the stunning mountain road that winds south toward Tizi-n-Test, you'll need transport. You can pick up a bus (a scary option) or a grand taxi (only slightly better) from Ouirgane. Better still to opt for individual transport. It is most advisable to hire a car and driver through one of the better hotels in Marrakesh (or a good hotel around Ouirgane). Otherwise, the member of your party brave enough to volunteer to drive will need all his or her concentration for the treacherous bends and will miss the splendid scenery.

EXPLORING

Goundafi Kasbahs. Most of the massive Goundafi Kasbahs, strongholds of the Aït Lahcen family that governed the region until independence in 1956, have long since crumbled away. But just past the small village of Talat-n-Yacoub, look up. A great hulking red Kasbah sits at the top of the hill, amid a scene that is today eerily peaceful, with hawks nesting among the scraps of ornately carved plaster and woodwork still clinging to the

The Tin Mal Mosque is one of only two mosques in Morocco that non-Muslims may enter.

massive walls. Built as a counterpart to the original Goundafi redoubt in Tagoundaft, the Kasbah is a compelling testament to the concentration of power in an era said to be governed "tribally." Locals say the hands of slack workers were sealed into the Kasbah's walls during construction. There's usually not a tourist in sight. Better yet, its future is secure, since it has been bought for conversion into a restaurant, what will surely become one of the best-placed spots to eat in the area. It's a rocky, although fairly easy, walk up to it. From the Kasbah you can see the Tin Mal Mosque to the south, across the juncture of the Nfis and Tasaft rivers. Just southeast are the mines of Tasaft. The Ouanoukrim Massif (the group of big mountains at the center of the High Atlas Mountains) dominates the view to the north. ⊠ *Above Talat-n-Yacoub, about 40 km (25 miles) south of Ouirgane, Talat-n-Yacoub.*

Tin Mal Mosque. One of only two mosques in the country that non-Muslims may enter (the other is Casablanca's enormous Hassan II mosque), Tin Mal sits proudly in the hills and is well worth a visit. Built by Ibn Tumart, the first Almohad, its austere walls in the obscure valley of the Nfis formed the cradle of a formidable superstate and was the birthplace and spiritual capital of the 12th-century Almohad empire. Today the original walls stand firm, enclosing a serene area with row after row of pale brick arches, on a huge scale built to impress. ■ TIP➜ **Admission to the mosque is free, but tip the guardian anything between 5 DH and 20 DH and he'll show you around and explain a little of the history.** ⊠ *Talat-n-Yacoub* ✛ *The signposted turnoff for mosque is about 4 km (2½ miles) south of Talat-n-Yacoub. Turn right, cross bridge, and follow path up other side of valley.*

Tizi-n-Test. The pass climbs up to a staggering 6,889 feet and provides extraordinary views to the north towards the mountain peaks and south towards the Souss valleys. It's a hair-raising road trip calling for low gears and snail-like speeds, but the views are worth every second. ⊠ *76 km (47 miles) southwest of Ouirgane.*

WHERE TO EAT AND STAY

$
CAFÉ

✕ **La Haute Vue.** This small café right at the summit of Tizi-n-Test is the perfect place to take in the astounding view with some Berber biscuits and mint tea on beautiful wrought-iron chairs made by the owner's son. It's also a good spot to stop on the road and wander up the hills. Although the restaurant has a hotel attached, it's best avoided. $ *Average main: 60DH* ⊠ *Tizi-n-Test summit: 6,889 ft.* ☎ *0661/40–01–91* ▭ *No credit cards.*

$
B&B/INN

⊞ **La Belle Vue.** A kilometer down the road from Tizi-n-Test, this concrete block of a hotel has a totally different *belle vue* (beautiful view) from the café at the top. **Pros:** breathtaking views from the café; spotless rooms; reasonable prices. **Cons:** shared bathrooms; disappointing views from the rooms. $ *Rooms from: 160DH* ⊠ *Tafingoulte, 1 km (½ mile) south of Tizi-n-Test summit* ☎ *0667/59–57–58* ⇗ *12 rooms* ▭ *No credit cards* ⦿*Some meals.*

TO TIZI-N-TICHKA

The scenery around the Tichka Pass is peaceful and more low-key than the rest of the High Atlas. It's soothing and stunning in equal measure, a good bet for stimulating walks and a relaxing hotel stay. If you're just passing through en route to the southern oases, the vista from the Tichka road itself is amazing—especially in spring—and the Glaoui Kasbah at Telouet is worth a look.

TIZI-N-TICHKA

110 km (68 miles) southeast of Marrakesh.

Winding its way southeast toward the desert, the Tichka Pass is another exercise in road-trip drama. Although the road is generally well maintained and wide enough for traffic to pass—and lacks the vertiginous twists of the Tizi-n-Test—it still deserves respect. Especially in winter, take warm clothes with you, as the temperature at the pass itself can seem another latitude entirely from the balmy sun of Marrakesh. ■TIP→ **Sometimes gas can be difficult to find, particularly unleaded, so fill up before you hit the mountains. There's a station at the town of Aït Ourir, on the main road to Ouarzazate.**

The road out of Marrakesh leads you abruptly into the countryside, to quiet olive groves and desultory villages consisting of little more than a *hanut* (convenience store) and a roadside mechanic. You'll pass the R'mat River, the Oued Zat, and the Hotel Hardi. From here the road begins to rise, winding through fields that are either green with barley and wheat or brown with their stalks. At Km 55 you'll encounter the Hotel Dar Oudar in Touama. In springtime magnificent red poppies dot the surrounding fields.

On the way up into the hills, look for men and boys, often standing in the middle of the road, waving shiny bits of rock. These are magnificent pieces of quartz taken from the mountains that they sell for as little as 5 DH. On your left at Km 124 from Marrakesh you'll see the **Palais-n-Tichka,** a sort of Wal-Mart for these shiny minerals, as well as other souvenirs. It's also a good restroom stop.

The road begins to climb noticeably, winding through forests and some of the region's lusher hillsides. A broad valley opens up to your left, revealing red earth and luminously green gardens. At Km 67 stands Mohammad Noukrati's Auberge Toufliht. From Toufliht there is little between you and the Tichka Pass but dusty villages, shepherds, and rock. You might find a decent orange juice, trinket, or weather-beaten carpet in villages like Taddert, but you'll probably feel pulled toward the pass. The scenery is rather barren, and as the naked rock of the mountains begins to emerge from beneath the flora, the walls of the canyon grow steeper and more enclosing.

Around Km 105 you'll see several waterfalls across the canyon. The trail down is precipitous but easy enough to follow; just park at the forlorn-looking refuge and the Café Tichka at Km 108. The trail winds to the left of the big hill, then cuts to the right and drops down to the falls after a short walk of half an hour or so. The Tichka Pass is farther along, at 7,413 feet above sea level. Depending on the season and the weather, the trip over the pass can take you from African heat to European gloom and back.

NEED A BREAK?

La Maison Berbère. This rest stop has made more of an effort than most of the others on this route, with a high-ceiling and traditionally decorated salon permeated by the unmistakable smell of real coffee. Take a late breakfast or a tagine on the terrace at the back, overlooking a small garden and poppy-dotted fields. ✉ ***Rte. de Ouarzazate, 5 km (3 miles) before Taddert*** ☎ ***0524/37–14–67*** 🕒 ***Daily 6–5.***

WHERE TO EAT AND STAY

$ MOROCCAN

🍴 **Dar Oudar.** More a restaurant with rooms than an out-and-out hotel, this is a good stop-off point before the climb to the Tichka Pass. The kitchen is justifiably proud of its reputation and makes delicious french fries, as well as tagines and grills. The *kefta* (spiced minced beef) brochettes are outstanding. If you want to stay the night, rooms are 200 DH, with breakfast at 25 DH. [$] *Average main: 60DH* ✉ *Km 56, Rte. de Ouarzazate* ☎ *0524/48–47–72* 🌐 *www.daroudar.moonfruit.fr* 💳 *No credit cards.*

$ B&B/INN

🏨 **Auberge Toufliht.** At this basic hotel, beer, wine, and cocktails are available (as the "Speciale" sign indicates) and the place has a pleasantly rowdy feel, particularly on weekends. **Pros:** sweet little touches; charming rooms. **Cons:** can get noisy; sometimes closed without warning. [$] *Rooms from: 220DH* ✉ *P31, Toufliht, 67 km from Marrakesh (135 km from Ouarzazate)* ☎ *0524/48–48–61* 🛏 *9 rooms, with baths* 💳 *No credit cards* 🍽 *No meals.*

$$
HOTEL
Fodor'sChoice
★

I Rocha. Hidden on a promontory above Tizirine, a somewhat inhospitable Berber town, this is one of the best lodges in the region. **Pros:** lovely terrace; sparkling rooms; hotel can arrange cooking courses, trekking, or star-gazing by telescope. **Cons:** wine prices are very inflated. $ *Rooms from: 550DH ⊠ Tizirine ⊕ Take a signposted left at Tizirine (also called Douar Tisselday), halfway down the main road that runs from Tizi-n-Tichka to Ouarzazate. Follow a steep dirt track for 500 ft.* ☎ 0667/73–70–02 ⊕ *www.irocha.com* ⤵ *7 rooms* ⊟ *No credit cards* ⦿ *Some meals.*

$
HOTEL

Le Coq Hotel Hardi. The riverside Hardi makes a reasonable base for exploring Marrakesh from the relative peace of the countryside. **Pros:** cozy poolside seating; well-manicured gardens. **Cons:** rooms are bare; restaurant is overpriced. $ *Rooms from: 350DH ⊠ Rte. d'Ouarzazate, Pont du Zat, Ait Ouir, 38 km from Marrakesh* ☎ 0524/48–00–56 ⊕ *www.lecoq-hardi.com* ⤵ *23 rooms, 1 suite* ⦿ *Breakfast.*

TELOUET

116 km (72 miles) southeast of Marrakesh, 20 km (12 miles) east of P31.

The main reason for visiting this otherwise unremarkable village is to see the incredible kasbah of the Glaouis (which is sometimes referred to simply as "Kasbah Telouet"). Built in the 19th century, the kasbah is now in near ruin, but the interior still hints of the luxury that once was.

It was from Telouet that the powerful Glaoua family controlled the caravan route over the mountains into Marrakesh. Although the Goundafi and Mtougi caids also held important High Atlas passes, by 1901 the Glaoua were on the rise. Having secured artillery from a desperate Sultan Moulay el-Hassan, the Glaoua seized much of the area below the Tichka Pass, and were positioned to bargain when the French arrived on the political scene. The French couldn't have been pleased with the prospect of subduing the vast, wild regions of southern Morocco tribe by tribe. Thus the French-Glaoua alliance benefited both parties, with Mandani el-Glaoui ruling as Grand Vizier and his brother Tuhami serving as pasha of Marrakesh.

GETTING HERE AND AROUND

Getting to Telouet isn't always easy. The best way, aside from with a tour group, is to take a grand taxi from Marrakesh or drive yourself.

TIMING AND PRECAUTIONS

The kasbah itself takes no more than three hours to explore. Take care, as parts of it are beginning to crumble.

EXPLORING

Kasbah Telouet. About five minutes south of Tizi-n-Tichka is the turnoff for the Glaoui Kasbah at Telouet. The road is paved but narrow, and winds from juniper-studded slopes down through a landscape of low eroding hills and the Assif-n-Tissent (Salt River). In spring, barley fields soften the effect, but for much of the year the scene is rather bleak.

Parking for the Kasbah is down a short dirt road across from the nearby auberge Chez Ahmed. Entry is free, but you should tip the parking attendant and the guardian of the gate. Inside, walking through dusty courtyards that rise to towering mud walls, you'll pass through a series of

6

gates and big doors, many threatening to fall from their hinges. Different parts are open at different times, perhaps according to the whims of the guard. Most of the Kasbah looks ravished, as though most of the useful or interesting bits had been carried off when the Glaoui reign came to its abrupt end in 1956. This sense of decay is interrupted when you get upstairs: here, from painted wood shutters and delicately carved plaster arabesques to exquisitely set tile and broad marble floors, you get a taste of the sumptuousness the Glaoui once enjoyed. Because it was built in the 20th century, ancient motifs are combined with kitschy contemporary elements, such as traditionally carved plaster shades for the electric lights. The roof has expansive views. There have been talks of restoring the entirety of the Kasbah to its former glory, but there have been no signs of restoration so far.

NEED A BREAK?

Chez Ahmed. A small but clean café and guesthouse is located next door to the Kasbah Telouet parking lot. Owner Ahmed is highly knowledgeable of Glaoui history, and he can organize tours of the surrounding area. He is also happy to sit and chat as well as feed you well for around 70 DH. ■ TIP→ If you do not wish to take a tour, politely make this known toward the beginning of the conversation. ☎ *0524/89–07–17*.

WHERE TO STAY

$$$$ HOTEL Fodor's Choice ★ 🏨 **Domaine Malika.** This small boutique hotel would not be out of place in one of the world's hippest capitals: how wonderful, then, that it is here in the High Atlas. **Pros:** light-hearted, tasteful, and unique décor; hotel will organize tours, airport transfers, and cooking lessons. **Cons:** the place is very small, so book ahead. [$] *Rooms from: 1750DH* ✉ *Ouirgane* ✣ *From Marrakesh, take the Taroudant road in the direction "Tahnanaoute." Before Ouirgane, in Douar of Maghira, turn right toward Amizmiz. The hotel is 500 meters ahead on left* ☎ *0661/49–35–41* 🌐 *www.domaine-malika.com* 🛏 *7 rooms* ⏲ *Closed early Dec.* 🍴 *Breakfast.*

$$$$ HOTEL Fodor's Choice ★ 🏨 **Kasbah Bab Ourika.** This luxurious retreat is a delightful example of how to build a near-perfect romantic getaway that's ecofriendly to boot. **Pros:** an ambience that's hard to top; staff can arrange activities and treks in the area. **Cons:** the road to the kasbah is bumpy. [$] *Rooms from: 1980DH* ✉ *Ourika Valley Atlas Mountains, Tnine de l'Ourika* ☎ *0668/74–95–47, 0661/63–42–34* 🌐 *www.kasbahbabourika.com* 🛏 *20 rooms, 7 suites, 2 bungalows, 1 apartment* 🍴 *Breakfast.*

$$$$ HOTEL 🏨 **Widiane Suites and Spa.** This hotel offers a level of luxury unusual in Morocco's mountains. **Pros:** the place to go to treat yourself; the hotel can arrange a wide variety of activities in the area. **Cons:** opulence on this scale jars somewhat with the rural simplicity of surroundings; expensive. [$] *Rooms from: 2250DH* ✉ *Chemin du Lac de Ben el-Ouidane, Ben el-Ouidane* ☎ *0523/44–27–76* 🌐 *www.widiane.net* 🛏 *31 rooms* 🍴 *Some meals.*

THE GREAT
OASIS VALLEYS

WELCOME TO
THE GREAT OASIS VALLEYS

TOP REASONS TO GO

★ **Desert dreams:** Live out those Lawrence of Arabia fantasies by sleeping on dunes under the stars.

★ **Dadès Gorge:** Follow mountain trails through some of Morocco's most beautiful scenery.

★ **Kasbah trail:** Marvel at and stay in ancient strongholds that dot the landscape.

★ **Morocco's Hollywood:** Spot celebs in Ouarzazate, home to visiting film crews.

★ **Flower power:** Visit the Valley of Roses in spring to see endless specimens in the wild.

1 Ouarzazate. Ouarzazate (pronounced wah-zaz-zatt) is a natural crossroads for exploring southern Morocco. The town has a wide range of accommodations as well as a few sights that can fill up a day. Most important, Ouarzazate has excellent road connections, putting the entire region within reach.

2 The Dadès and Todra Gorges. These sister canyons, located within about two hours' drive from each other northeast of Ouarzazate, have been carved into the rocks over millennia by the snowmelt waters of the High Atlas. Trekking, mountain biking, and rock climbing are favorite activities for tourists.

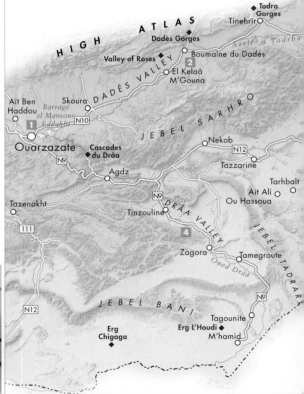

3 **To Merzouga and the Dunes.** If you opt to visit the south of Morocco, then it's almost criminal not to at least spend a night in the Sahara. The village of Merzouga is readily accessible by road, and the dunes of Erg Chebbi can be reached on foot or by camel.

4 **The Drâa Valley.** This fertile valley—extending along the shores of Morocco's longest river from Agdz, through Zagora as far as M'Hamid—offers one of the most colorful and diverse landscapes in the kingdom. For those heading into the dunes at Erg Chigaga, Zagora is your last contact with modern services such as banks, pharmacies, and gas stations.

GETTING ORIENTED

The Great Oasis Valleys cover a huge area, in a sort of lopsided horseshoe from Ouarzazate (the largest town in the northwest corner), east past the magnificent Dadès and Todra gorges on the northern road, south to the dunes at Merzouga, and looping back west on the southern road through the Drâa Valley to Zagora, M'Hamid, and the great expanse of desert that reaches all the way across Erg Chigaga to Foum Zguid. To miss any of these roads would be to miss some of Morocco's most characteristic immensity—wide-open spaces and tundralike desolation.

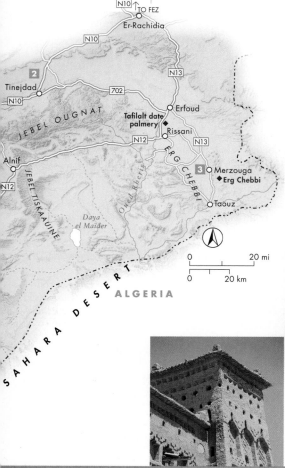

7

By Rachel Blech

Morocco without the Sahara is like Switzerland without the Alps, and a desert sojourn is fundamental to an understanding of the country. After you've seen the Atlas Mountains, followed by palmeries and kasbahs, a trip down to the desert may seem a long way to go to reach nothing, and some Moroccans and travelers will warn you against it. Don't listen to them.

The void you encounter in the Sahara will remind you why prophets and sages sought the desert to purge and purify themselves. Unless you have oodles of time, though, you'll have to choose between the dunes of Erg Chebbi at Merzouga and Erg Chigaga beyond M'Hamid, which are separated by 450 km (279 miles) of hard driving.

Of course, a vacation in the valleys isn't just about sublime Saharan sand. The asphalt might end and the desert begin at Merzouga and M'Hamid, but in between are the oases flanked by the Todra and Dadès gorges—sister grand canyons separating the High Atlas from the Djebel Sarhro Massif. Both of these dramatic gorges appeal to hikers, and the Todra is a hot spot for climbers as well.

Permeating it all is a palpable sense of history. Once, the caravan routes from the Sudan, Timbuktu, and Niger to Marrakesh and Fez passed through Morocco's Great Oasis Valleys, and these played a crucial role in the region's past. From the Drâa Valley came the Saadian royal dynasty that ruled from the mid-12th to mid-17th century, and from the Ziz Valley and the Tafilalt oasis rose the Alaouite dynasty, which relieved the Saadians in 1669 and which still rules (in the person of King Mohammed VI) in 21st-century Morocco.

PLANNING

WHEN TO GO

You'll pay lower off-season rates and encounter fewer convoys of tourists if you travel the oasis routes in early December or mid-January through early March. High season begins in mid-March but doesn't fully kick in until April or Easter (whichever comes first). The Christmas and New Year period is also popular; if you want to visit a desert camp then, it's wise to book at least two months ahead. Summer is extremely hot in the desert and some hotels close during July and August, especially if this coincides with the holy month of Ramadan. If you plan to visit the Sahara in summer, traveling east via the Dadès and Todra gorges to Merzouga is slightly easier since the shaded depths of the canyons offer some respite from the sun. ■TIP➜ **Keep yourself stocked up on bottles of water: it's very hot.**

PLANNING YOUR TIME

Doing the entire Great Oasis Valleys circuit is a serious undertaking, and you might miss the best parts for all the whirlwind traveling. So it's important to set priorities and carefully plan your itinerary. You could easily spend 14 days exploring. Allow at least five to seven if you want to include hiking time and a trip into the Sahara; then decide which dunes you want to discover—Erg Chebbi or Erg Chigaga.

From Ouarzazate, allot a minimum of two days to reach Erg Chebbi, traveling east through the Todra Gorge and Dadès Valley to Merzouga (this allows for an overnight stop in the Todra Gorge en route). On the return leg you can circle along the southern flanks of the Djebel Sarhro, passing via traditional villages like Nekob, into the Drâa Valley before arriving in Ouarzazate again.

Reaching Erg Chigaga from Ouarzazate requires a 4x4 vehicle and at least two days of driving (this again allows for an overnight stop). Head south through the Drâa Valley, admiring Agdz and Zagora en route to M'Hamid; then continue off-road for about 50 km (31 miles) to the dunes. Returning to Ouarzazate, drive the route in reverse or loop back via Foum Zguid.

GETTING HERE AND AROUND

The most convenient arrival and departure points for touring this vast region are the towns of Ouarzazate (if you're traveling from Marrakesh and the Atlantic coast) or Er-Rachidia (if you're traveling from Fez, Meknès, or the Mediterranean coast). Given a choice, opt for Ouarzazate, as it is an interesting town in its own right. Ouarzazate is a key transport hub for forays into the Dadès and Todra gorges, the Drâa Valley, and the desert regions beyond Zagora. Er-Rachidia, aside from being a stop for those en route to Erfoud, Rissani, and Merzouga, is itself of little interest to travelers.

AIR TRAVEL

Royal Air Maroc (⊕ *www.royalairmaroc.com*) serves Ouarzazate's Taourirt International Airport, offering direct flights daily from Casablanca and multiple ones per week from Paris. The airline also connects Casablanca with Er-Rachidia thrice weekly and Zagora twice weekly.

Petits taxis (local taxis) provide ground transport from these airports; however, if you need to catch an early return flight, it's best to arrange transportation back to the airport through your hotel the night before.

BUS TRAVEL

There are no train connections south of Marrakesh. Compagnie du Transports au Maroc (locally known as CTM) and Supratours buses run to Ouarzazate, through the Drâa Valley, and down to Zagora and M'Hamid, but busing around southern Morocco is not recommended unless you don't mind assuming a full-time study of transport logistics.

CAR TRAVEL

The only practical way to tour the Great Oasis Valleys is by car. Being surrounded by gorgeous, largely unexplored hinterlands—like the Todra or Dadès gorges—without being able to explore safely and comfortably defeats the purpose of coming down here. Driving the oasis roads requires full attention and certain safety precautions: slow down when cresting hills, expect everything from camels to herds of sheep to appear in the road, expect oncoming traffic to come down the middle of the road, and be prepared to come to a full stop if forced to the right and faced with a pothole or other obstacle. If you haven't rented a car someplace else, you can rent one on arrival in Ouarzazate.

Rental Cars **Europcar** ⊠ *Av. Mohammed V, pl. 3 Mars, Ouarzazate* ☎ *0524/88–20–35* ⊕ *www.europcar.ma.* **Hertz** ⊠ *35, av. Mohammed V, Ouarzazate* ☎ *0524/88–20–84* ⊕ *www.hertz.com.* **Tafoukt Cars** ⊠ *88, rue er-Rachidia, Ouarzazate* ☎ *0524/88–26–90.*

WHAT TO DO

Hikes, treks, and even camel safaris can be the highlight of any trip through the southern oases, dunes, or gorges. The main roads through the region are all paved, making most places accessible in a rental car or taxi; a 4x4 will be required for venturing across country between the two gorges or into the desert on any road marked as a *piste* (an unpaved backcountry road). In both the Dadès and Todra gorges it is well worth giving yourself time to hike; employ the services of a local guide who knows the area intimately and can provide more spectacular perspectives on the canyons and local life. The Todra Gorge is also prime territory for rock climbers, but it is advisable to bring your own gear. North of Msemrir, a trekker with a fly rod in his backpack might even find a trout or two. Serious trekking adventures through the M'Goun Massif (above the Dadès Valley) or around Djebel Sarhro, south of Tinerhir, are by far the best way to see this largely untouched Moroccan backcountry. For exploring the desert either at Merzouga or M'Hamid it is best to travel by camel, or if budget allows by 4x4. Wonderful multiday camel treks can take you through the lower reaches of the Drâa Valley oasis and into the dunes.

SAFETY

You shouldn't have problems traveling this part of Morocco, but always exercise caution if going into remote areas. Don't stop for hitchhikers or for people whose cars have broken down, as there are still some dishonest individuals wanting to take advantage of tourists.

Be prepared to be followed by local kids who may want to engage you in conversation. Rather than money, give them items such as pens or pencils. If they are selling homemade handicrafts, then of course give them a few dirhams for their efforts.

■ TIP➔ Where possible, make sure you engage a qualified guide through one of the official Bureaus de Guides—this is especially important when trekking in the desert or mountains.

RESTAURANTS

In the rural areas outside of Ouarzazate there are virtually no restaurants, just tatty streetside cafés. Lunch stops, complete with bathroom facilities, are best found in the hotels and auberges listed; for evening meals it is best to book your accommodation with half board. Far from the set-menu cuisine of Morocco's urban palaces, the fare you'll be served along the southern oasis routes tends to be hearty and simple. *Harira* (a tomato and lentil soup) is more than welcome as night sets in and temperatures plunge. *Mechoui* (roast lamb) is a standard feast—if you can order it far enough in advance. Some of the best lamb and vegetable tagines in Morocco are simmered over tiny camp stoves in random corners and campsites down here. You may want to keep a bottle of wine in the car or in a day pack, as many restaurants (even in hotels) don't serve alcohol, but have no problem with customers bringing their own. Always ask first, though, as some places object.

HOTELS

Hotels on the southern oasis routes generally range from mediocre to primitive, with several charming spots and a few luxury establishments thrown in. Come with the idea that running water and a warm place to sleep are all you really need, and accept anything above that as icing on the cake. Bedding down outdoors on hotel terraces is common (and cheap) in summer, as are accommodations in *khaimas* (Berber nomad tents). The night sky is so stunning here that spending at least one night *à la belle étoile* (beneath the stars) seems almost mandatory. Any of the desert hotels and guesthouses in Merzouga or M'Hamid will be able to arrange an unforgettable night under canvas, along with the necessary camel or 4x4 vehicle to get there. Basic bivouac camps, costing around 250 DH per person per night, typically have mattresses on the floor of large Berber tents and a shared bathroom block. Luxury tented camps—featuring private safari-style tents with Berber rugs, plush furnishings, and en-suite chemical toilets—fulfill the Arabian Nights "glamping" fantasy; rates start at around 1,500 DH per person. Whatever you choose, bear in mind that many lodgings in remote areas still don't accept credit cards; double check the terms of payment and be sure to have sufficient cash on hand if required. *Hotel reviews have been shortened. For full information, visit Fodors.com.*

Rose petals are offered along the roadside at a rose moussem.

	WHAT IT COSTS IN DIRHAMS			
	$	$$	$$$	$$$$
Restaurants	under 70 DH	71 DH–100 DH	101 DH–150 DH	over 150 DH
Hotels	under 450 DH	451 DH–700 DH	701 DH–1,000 DH	over 1,000 DH

Restaurant prices are the average cost of a main course at dinner, or if dinner is not served, at lunch. Hotel prices are the lowest cost of a standard double room in high season.

FESTIVALS

Each year villages here host a number of *moussems* (festivals) that are linked to the religious or agricultural calendar. These usually feature feasting, dancing, traditional music, and possibly a wonderful display of horsemanship called a fantasia. The downside is that they often don't have specific dates, so encountering one is largely a matter of luck. That said, there are a few festivals you can largely rely on: the **Rose Festival** of Kelaâ M'Gouna (Dadès Valley) in early May; the **International Nomads Festival** in M'Hamid el Ghizlane (Drâa Valley) in mid-March; and the **Erfoud Date Festival** (Ziz Valley) in October. Check with the local tourist office or a nearby hotel for the exact dates about a month ahead of your visit.

OUARZAZATE

204 km (127 miles) southeast of Marrakesh, 300 km (186 miles) southwest of Erfoud.

An isolated military outpost during the years of the French protectorate, Ouarzazate—which means "no noise" in the Berber Tamazigh language—long lived up to its name. Today, however, the town is Morocco's Hollywood, and moviemakers can regularly be found setting up shop in this sprawling desert crossroads with wide, palm-fringed boulevards. Brad Pitt, Penélope Cruz, Angelina Jolie, Samuel L. Jackson, Cate Blanchett, and many more have graced Ouarzazate's suites and streets; and a film school here provides training in the cinema arts for Moroccan and international students. Yet despite the Tinseltown vibe and huge, publicly accessible film sets, Ouarzazate retains a laid-back atmosphere, making it a great place to sit at a sidewalk café, sip a café noir, and spot visiting celebs—or at least have a chat with the locals, who'll happily recount their experience working as an on-set extra (at its peak in the late 1990s, the movie industry provided casual work for almost half of the local population). Not surprisingly, though, the main attraction is still the cinematic surrounding terrain that made Ouarzazate a mainstay for filmmakers in the first place: namely, the red-glowing kasbah at Aït Ben Haddou; the snowcapped High Atlas and the Sahara, with tremendous canyons, gorges, and lunarlike steppes in between.

GETTING HERE AND AROUND

The center of Ouarzazate is easily explored on foot. Avenue Mohammed V, the main street, runs from east to west with shops, cafés, banks, pharmacies, and tour agencies all along its length. Most hotels are near the Kasbah Taourirt; however, a cluster of boutique guesthouses dot the outlying palm groves, across the bridge in the direction of Zagora. If you're staying at the latter—or visiting the film studios—you'll need to rent a car or rely on cabs.

AIR TRAVEL

There are daily flights to Ouarzazate's Taourirt International Airport from Casablanca and twice-weekly ones from Paris. The airport is 3 km (2 miles) from the town center and can be reached by petits taxis.

BUS TRAVEL

Ouarzazate is well served by buses from Marrakesh (4 hours), Agadir (8½ hours), Casablanca (8½ hours), Taliouine (3½ hours), Taroudant (5 hours), Tinerhir (5 hours), Er-Rachidia (6 hours), Erfoud (7 hours), Zagora (4½ hours), and M'Hamid (7 hours). CTM buses run from the eastern end of Avenue Mohammed V. Supratours buses run from the western end of Avenue Mohammed V. Other public buses run from the *gare routière* (bus station) about 2 km (1 mile) from the town center, just off the N9 route to Marrakesh. Shared *grands taxis* (long-distance taxis) will also bring you here from Marrakesh, Er-Rachidia, Agadir, and Zagora; these can be hired for private day excursions, too.

Bus Contacts CTM Ouarzazate ⊠ *Av. Mohammed V, next to main Post Office at the east end* ☎ *0524/88–24–27* ⊕ *www.ctm.ma.* **Supratours** ⊠ *Av. Mohammed V* ☎ *0524/88–56–32* ⊕ *www.oncf.ma.*

CLOSE UP

Camel or Jeep?

Visitors who are cash-rich and time-poor are likely to plump for travel by 4x4, especially to the desert south of M'Hamid that stretches west to Foum Zguid. Getting to Erg Chigaga, for example, takes two hours by four-wheel drive and at least two days by camel. There are also great off-road routes around Zagora, M'Hamid, and Foum Zguid for those who love four-wheel-drive adventures. Some even prefer to go by quad bikes, which are also readily available.

But spare a thought for the poor desert, which thrives on being alone and slowly buckles under the weight of car fumes, carelessly discarded rubbish, and intrusive revving and whooping in an otherwise noiseless environment. Camels may take longer, but they're quieter, more authentic, and fit with the nomadic way of life.

GUIDES AND TOURS

Many travel agents and tour companies in Ouarzazate offer day excursions as well as longer outings that might include nights in the Dadès and Todra gorges or Saharan camping and camel trekking. You'll find them along Avenue Mohammed V, in the Place el-Mouahidine, and frequently attached to hotels—just be sure to shop around and ask exactly what is being included in price (e.g., 4x4, driver, guide, meals, hotels, camel trip, etc.). Visitors who'd rather do a DIY driving tour will find car rental agencies along Avenue Mohammed V, too. ■ TIP→ If you book a desert tour in Ouarzazate, you'll avoid being hassled by touts when you reach Merzouga or M'Hamid.

Cherg Expeditions. Private day trips through the valleys and gorges or into the mountains to discover amethysts are led by Cherg Expeditions. You can sign on for multiday desert tours, too. Nearby destinations include the Fint Oasis and the kasbahs at Aït Ben Haddou. ✉ *2, pl. el Mouahidine* ☎ *0524/88–79–08, 0661/24–31–47* ⊕ *www.cherg.com.*

Ksour Voyages. This full-service travel agency organizes tours and 4x4 excursions to the Sahara and Great Oasis Valleys from Ouarzazate. Nationwide itineraries are also available. ✉ *11, pl. du 3 Mars* ☎ *0524/88–28–40* ⊕ *www.ksour-voyages.com.*

Zbar Travel. Well-priced tours and excursions throughout southern Morocco are offered by Zbar Travel, a respected English-speaking agency with a second office in M'Hamid. ✉ *12, pl. Al Mouahadine* ☎ *0668/51–72–80* ⊕ *www.zbartravel.com.*

TIMING AND PRECAUTIONS

For those traveling to the desert, this is an important town for stocking up on cash and purchasing essentials like maps, batteries, and other supplies. If you're heading south to M'Hamid, it's also the last town where you will find a supermarket selling wine, beer, and liquor.

VISITOR INFORMATION

Contacts Ouarzazate Delegation de Tourisme ✉ *297, av. Mohammed V* ☎ *0524/88–24–85* ⊗ *Closed weekends.*

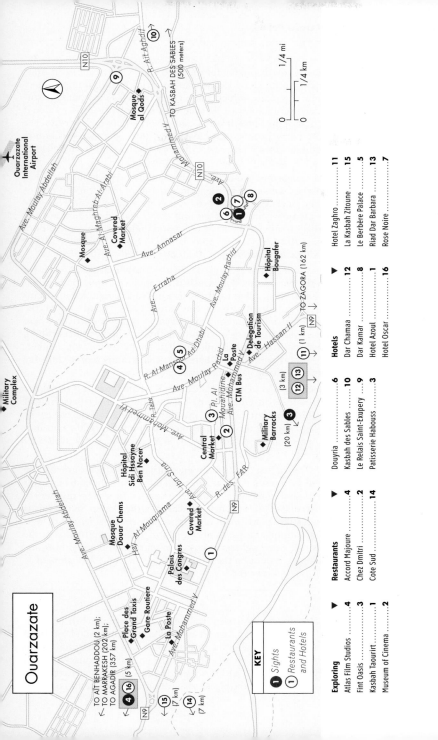

Ouarzazate

→ TO AÏT BENHADDOU (2 km);
→ TO MARRAKESH (202 km);
→ TO AGADIR (357 km)

Ouarzazate International Airport ✈

Military Complex ◆

Mosque al Qods ◆

Covered Market

Mosque ◆

TO KASBAH DES SABLES (500 meters) →

R. Aït Aghdif →

Ave. Mohammed V

Ave. Al-Maghreb Al-Arabi

Ave. Moulay Abdellah

Ave. Annasar

Ave. Erraha

Ave. Moulay-Rachid

Hôpital Bougafer ◆

Hôpital Sidi Hssayne Ben Nacer ◆

Mosque Douar Chems ◆

Palais des Congres ◆

Place des Grand Taxis

Gare Routière

La Poste

Ave. Mohammed V

Covered Market

R. des FAR

R. Al Mansour Ad-Dhabi

R. Al Mouqouama

Ave. Ibn Sina

Ave. Mohammed VI

R. Ibn Taza

Central Market

Pl. Al Mouahidine

Ave. Mohammed V

La Poste

CTM Bus

Delegation Ave. de Tourisme

Ave. Hassan II

Military Barracks ◆

TO ZAGORA (162 km) →

(1 km) →

(3 km)

(20 km) →

N9

N10

N10

N9

N9

1/4 mi

1/4 km

0

0

KEY

◆ Sights 1

▼ Restaurants and Hotels 1

Exploring ◆

Atlas Film Studios **4**

Fint Oasis **3**

Kasbah Taourirt **1**

Museum of Cinema **2**

Restaurants ▼

Accord Majoure **4**

Chez Dmitri **2**

Cote Sud **14**

Douyria **6**

Kasbah des Sables **10**

Le Relais Saint-Exupery **9**

Patisserie Habouss **3**

Hotels ▼

Dar Chamaa **12**

Dar Kamar **8**

Hotel Azoul **1**

Hotel Oscar **16**

Hotel Zaghro **11**

La Kasbah Zitoune **15**

Le Berbère Palace **5**

Riad Dar Barbara **13**

Rose Noire **7**

EXPLORING

Atlas Studios. If you're looking for things to do in Ouarzazate, visit Atlas Studios, next to the Hotel Oscar. Flanked with beautiful impropriety by two giant Egyptian statues, these are Morocco's most famous studios. Guided tours start every 45 minutes, and the price is discounted if you're a guest of the hotel. It isn't Disney World, but you do get a sense of just how many productions have rolled through town—including Hollywood blockbusters like *The Mummy* and *Gladiator,* and classics films like *Cleopatra* and *Lawrence of Arabia.*

For another angle on the Ouarzazate film industry, check out the rather grand-looking kasbah off to the right just out of town on the way to Skoura. One enterprising local producer, frustrated by the increasingly expensive charges being levied on film crews wanting to film around real kasbahs, decided to build his own and undercut the competition. ✉ *Tamassint, Km 5, rte. de Marrakesh, next to Hotel Oscar* ☎ *0524/88–22–23* ⊕ *www.studiosatlas.com* 🖃 *50 DH* ☉ *Daily 8:30–7:15.*

Fint Oasis. About 20 km (12 miles) outside of town, heading south via Tarmigte, the picturesque Fint Oasis is a popular destination for day-trippers. The track leading to it is rough but can be handled in a standard vehicle if you drive with extreme care. Head off-road towards the dark, rocky escarpment and the track eventually meets the river, where palm trees spring into view. You can walk through Berber villages along the riverbed and stop for a simple lunch at one of the few local auberges. ■TIP➡ **Many agencies in Ouarzazate can arrange half- or full-day guided visits to the oasis.** ✉ *Tarmigté.*

Kasbah Taourirt. Once a Glaoui palace, the Kasbah Taourirt is the oldest and finest building in Ouarzazate. This rambling edifice was built of *pisé* (a sun-dried mixture of mud and clay) in the late 19th century by the so-called Lords of the Atlas. You can hire a guide at the entrance to take you around for about 100 DH. ✉ *Av. Mohammed V* 🖃 *20 DH* ☉ *Daily 8–4:30.*

FAMILY **Museum of Cinema.** Just opposite the entrance to Kasbah Taourirt, at the top of the steps, is a small private museum full of paraphernalia left over from movies shot in the area. Although many of the sets on display are from French films that were never released in the United States, this is still an interesting spot to visit. It's refreshingly cool inside, and there is a room with antique movie cameras, props, and clapperboards at the back. Kids will enjoy ogling the costumes, sitting on the royal throne, or even hanging around in the Roman dungeon. ✉ *Av. Mohammed V, opposite Kasbah Taourirt* ☎ *0524/89–03–46* 🖃 *30 DH.*

WHERE TO EAT

$$ ✗**Accord Majeure.** Popular with tourists and expats, Accord Majeure
FRENCH   is a friendly French-style bistro that serves consistently good food and Moroccan wines. The menu focuses mostly on classic dishes like boeuf bourguignon, but there are also interesting culinary detours—such as Thai curry, Italian pasta, and fresh seafood (a rarity in this part of the country). Take a seat on the pleasant outdoor terrace or in the convivial

The busy Atlas Studios is one of the top attractions in Ouarzazate.

dining room. $ *Average main: 100DH* ✉ *Quartier Mansour Eddahbi, opposite Le Berbère Palace hotel* ☎ *0524/88-24-73* ✷ *Closed Sun. and Ramadan.*

$$
✕ Chez Dimitri. If Ouarzazate is the crossroads of the southern oasis routes, Chez Dimitri is at the heart of it. Founded in 1928 as the town's first store, gas station, post office, telephone booth, dance hall, and restaurant, this eatery may look unimpressive on an initial sweep down Ouarzazate's banal main drag, but the food—whether Greek, Moroccan, or even Thai—is invariably excellent. The owners are friendly and helpful, and the signed photographs of legendary movie stars on the walls are sometimes enhanced by real stars at the next table. $ *Average main: 100DH* ✉ *22, av. Mohammed V* ☎ *0524/88-73-46* ⊕ *www.dimitri-restaurant-ouarzazate.com.*

INTERNATIONAL

$$
✕ Coté Sud. An enterprising Spaniard established this restaurant–cum–cultural center outside Ouarzazate, near Tifoultoute kasbah. The architecture is stark, blending 21st-century modernism with southern Moroccan tradition, and the menu is comprised of Spanish and French dishes, which can be enjoyed in the cool, elegant dining room or on the outdoor terrace. The site—which also includes a bar, art gallery, and cinema—is a little on the quiet side but hopefully will flourish with time. $ *Average main: 90DH* ✉ *Tifoultoute, 10 km (6 miles) west of Ouarzazate* ✛ *From Ouarzazate, take the road to Tifoultoute kasbah (turning left at Al Baraka petrol station)* ☎ *0540/01-93-87* ⊕ *www.cotesud-maroc.com* ⊟ *No credit cards.*

SPANISH

$$
✕ Douyria. This *douyria*, or small house, is run by French-Moroccan couple Alexandra and Driss. Building up from the base of an old pisé home alongside the Kasbah Touarirt, Douyria marries tradition with

MOROCCAN

contemporary flair. There are two Moroccan salon-style dining areas, with bold color schemes of lilac and lime, and the creative menu offers an interesting selection of starters and mains. If you are willing to go with something exotic, try goat cooked in argan oil and sesame, or camel tagine with figs and almonds. The small terrace has wonderful views towards the lake at Ouarzazate. Actor Sir Ben Kingsley is a fan, as the guestbook will testify. Alcohol is served. $ *Average main: 80DH* ⊠ *Taourirt, next to Kasbah Touarirt* ☎ *0524/88–52–88* ⊕ *www.restaurant-ouarzazate.net.*

$$$
INTERNATIONAL
Fodor's Choice
★
✕ **La Kasbah des Sables.** Fine cuisine and an evocative setting combine to make dining at La Kasbah des Sables a special event. French owner Brigitte engaged local artisans to create something magical at the edge of Ouarzazate. Upon entering, you're greeted by a wall of lanterns reflected in a central pool, and meals are served in are six intimate areas, each with different decorative scheme (imagine a Berber salon or a patio with tables on terraces surrounded by water). The food is imaginative, too, mixing French-Moroccan influences in dishes such as confit of rabbit, with spices, honey, and peach sauce. $ *Average main: 120DH* ⊠ *Hay Aït Qdif* ☎ *0524/88–54–28* ⊕ *www.lakasbahdessables.com* ⊘ *Closed July.*

$$$
MOROCCAN
✕ **Le Relais Saint-Exupéry.** In a town not renowned for its dining scene, this restaurant stands out. Although the checkered floor tiles and red tablecloths give it the air of a French bistro, the cuisine is high Moroccan with French panache. Owner Jean-Pierre is an active subscriber to the slow food ethic, and his house specialties include *pastilla* (salty-sweet pigeon in puff pastry) and camel meat with pureed potato, served in a Malian ginger sauce. There are several four-course set menus available, but you can request à la carte choices as well. $ *Average main: 140DH* ⊠ *13, Moulay Abdellah, Quartier el Qods* ☎ *0524/88–77–79* ⊕ *www.relais-ouarzazate.com* ⊘ *Closed for Ramadan.*

$
CAFÉ
✕ **Patisserie Habouss.** If you've got time to relax in Ouarzazate, there's no place better for people-watching than the terrace of Patisserie Habouss. Locals and visitors can be found indulging in its famous homemade gâteaux or honey-soaked Moroccan pastries accompanied by cinnamon coffee or freshly squeezed fruit juice. As the sun sinks, witness the sleepy place el-Mouahidine transform into a busy evening marketplace. ■ TIP➔ **A small restaurant on the upper terrace of the café serves regional food at very reasonable prices.** $ *Average main: 40DH* ⊠ *Pl. Al Mouahidine* ☎ *0524/88–26–99.*

WHERE TO STAY

$$
B&B/INN
⌂ **Dar Chamaa.** Poised on the outskirts of town, Dar Chamaa is a boutique riad that offers a contemporary take on traditional design. **Pros:** good service; stylish accommodations with lots of mod-cons. **Cons:** away from the town center. $ *Rooms from: 700DH* ⊠ *Tajda, 8 km (5 miles) south of Ouarzazate center* ✛ *From Ouarzazate center, follow the road to Zagora across the bridge and then turn left into the palm groves (just after Hotel les Jardins de Ouarzazate)* ☎ *0524/85–49–54* ⊕ *www.darchamaa.com* ⤶ *18 rooms, 2 suites* ⦿I *Breakfast.*

$$$$
B&B/INN

Dar Kamar. For anyone seduced by tales of Glaoui wealth and influence, this 17th-century pasha's courthouse has magisterial appeal. **Pros:** beautiful interiors; doting service. **Cons:** cheaper rooms (3rd category) get little daylight. $ *Rooms from: 1200DH* ⊠ *45, Kasbah Taourirt* ☎ *0524/88–87–33* ✎ *www.darkamar.com* ↪ *12 rooms, 2 suites* ❙⊙❙ *Breakfast.*

$
HOTEL

Hotel Azoul. Built in the style of an old kasbah, this small family-owned hotel on the main strip is a cut above the other budget lodgings in the area. **Pros:** central location; interesting design. **Cons:** bedrooms are cramped (choose a suite if possible); breakfast is an additional 30 DH per person. $ *Rooms from: 440DH* ⊠ *Av. Mohammed V, 330 ft. on left after pl. du 3 Mars* ☎ *0524/88–30–15* ⊕ *www.hotelazoul.com* ↪ *8 rooms, 4 suites* ❙⊙❙ *No meals.*

$$
B&B/INN
FAMILY

Hotel Oscar. This modest hotel, located next door to Atlas Studios, often serves as a base for the production crew when films are being shot on location. **Pros:** ideal for families with children; good restaurant with set lunch and dinner menus (135 DH). **Cons:** far from town center. $ *Rooms from: 600DH* ⊠ *Tamassint, Km 5, rte. de Marrakesh* ☎ *0524/88–22–23* ⊕ *www.hotel-oscar-ouarzazate.com* ↪ *56 rooms, 8 suites* ❙⊙❙ *Breakfast.*

$
B&B/INN

Hotel Zaghro. This budget hotel just outside town will appeal to travelers looking for a no-frills stop-over. **Pros:** friendly staff; easy on the wallet. **Cons:** only 30 rooms have air-conditioning; some rooms share bathrooms; filled with tour groups $ *Rooms from: 300DH* ⊠ *Tabount, Km 1.5, rte. de Zagora, south of town, over bridge on the road to Zagora* ☎ *0524/85–41–35* ⊕ *www.hotel-zaghro.com* ↪ *55 rooms* ❙⊙❙ *Breakfast.*

$$
B&B/INN

La Kasbah Zitoune. This kasbah-style hotel sits in a remote location on the site of an ancient olive grove (hence the name, Arabic for "olive"). **Pros:** peaceful and spacious surroundings; fantastic views across the Ouarzazate palmery to the Kasbah Tiffoultoute. **Cons:** no pool; lack of communal living areas; food quality is patchy. $ *Rooms from: 560DH* ⊠ *Zone Touristique de Tiffoultoute, 10 km (6 miles) west of Ouarzazate* ☎ *0524/88–70–14* ⊕ *www.kasbahzitoune.com* ↪ *10 rooms, 3 suites* ❙⊙❙ *Breakfast.*

$$$$
HOTEL

Le Berbère Palace. Movie stars and magnates tend to stay at Ouarzazate's only 5-star hotel when working on location. **Pros:** plenty of creature comforts; top-notch service. **Cons:** breakfast is an extra 150 DH per person; air-conditioners are too close to the bed for comfort. $ *Rooms from: 2500DH* ⊠ *Av. Al Mansour Eddahbi* ☎ *0524/88–31–05* ⊕ *www.hotel-berberepalace.com* ↪ *160 rooms, 89 suites* ❙⊙❙ *No meals.*

$$
B&B/INN

Riad Dar Barbara. Run by an English-Moroccan couple, this guesthouse in a residential neighborhood on the outskirts of Ouarzazate has huge rooms with traditional décor, air-conditioning and heating, and en-suite bathrooms. **Pros:** friendly English-speaking staff; spacious rooms; Wi-Fi in the reception area. **Cons:** bathrooms need updating; no pool. $ *Rooms from: 500DH* ⊠ *Tajda, 8 km (5 miles) south of Ouarzazate* ☎ *0524/85–49–30* ⊕ *www.riaddarbarbara.com* ↪ *8 rooms* ▭ *No credit cards* ❙⊙❙ *Breakfast.*

7

$$$ B&B/INN **Rose Noire.** Using traditional Berber construction and decorative techniques, Jmiaa and Bernard Rose lovingly restored a 300-year-old riad in the kasbah; its charming rooms, arranged around a courtyard that's open to the sky, include nice touches like handwoven carpets and genuine artifacts. **Pros:** beautiful building; welcoming hosts; tasty meals. **Cons:** hard to find; not for those with mobility issues. [$] *Rooms from: 850DH* ✉ *Quartier de la Mosquée, Kasbah Taourirt* ☎ *0524/88–20–16* 🌐 *www.maisondhote-rosenoire.com* 🛏 *5 rooms, 2 suites* 🍴 *Breakfast.*

SHOPPING

Labyrinthe du Sud. You'll discover a treasure trove of antiques, carpets, Touareg and Berber jewelry, and trinkets at Labyrinthe du Sud. Credit cards are accepted. ✉ *Rte. de la Kasbah des Cigognes, Tajda* ☎ *0524/85–42–43* 🌐 *www.labyrinthe-sud.jimdo.com.*

SPORTS AND THE OUTDOORS

FOUR-WHEELING

Quads Aventures. You can rent quad bikes from Quads Aventures at the entrance to Atlas Studios, on the main Marrakesh road. They're good for day trips to the natural and historic wonders that have become backdrops to blockbuster films, including the kasbah at Aït Ben Haddou and a plateau used in *Gladiator.* The outfitter also rents canoes, great for the sparkling lake just southeast of town. Two hours of quad-biking costs 750 DH per person with reductions for groups. ✉ *Km 5, rte. de Marrakech, next to entrance to Atlas Studios* ☎ *0524/88–40–24* 🌐 *www.quadsaventures.com.*

HAMMAMS AND SPAS

The following hammams and spas are open to all (even nonguests, if in a hotel).

Caravan des Épices. This herbs and spice merchant sells every kind of medicinal root, leaf, mineral, spice, and ointment that you could imagine. On-site hammam services are also available by advance reservation. ✉ *Rue El Mansour Eddahbi* ☎ *0524/89–05–06* 🌐 *www.caravane-epices.com* 🎟 *Hammam with exfoliation 250 DH, massage with essential oils 200 DH.*

Hammam. There is a newly built public hammam in the center of town, next to Patisserie Habouss on Place Al Mouahidine. You can buy black soap and exfoliation gloves at the door. ✉ *Pl. Al Mouahadine* 🎟 *Hammam 10 DH, with exfoliation 50 DH* 💳 *No credit cards.*

Le Berbère Palace. A common destination for movie stars filming in the nearby studios, this Kasbah-style hotel has a deluxe hammam "Oasis," sauna, and Jacuzzi that are open to non-guests. Advance booking required. ✉ *Av. El Mansour Addahbi* ☎ *0524/88–31–05* 🌐 *www.hotel-berberepalace.com* 🎟 *Hammam 150 DH, 250 DH with exfoliation (30 mins)* 🕒 *Daily 10–8.*

AÏT BEN HADDOU

30 km (19 miles) northwest of Ouarzazate.

The *ksar* (fortified village) at Aït Ben Haddou is something of a celebrity itself. This group of earth-built kasbahs and homes hidden behind defensive high walls has come to fame (and fortune) as a backdrop for many films, including David Lean's *Lawrence of Arabia,* Ridley Scott's *Gladiator,* and Oliver Stone's *Alexander.* Of course, it hasn't always been a film set. It got going in the 11th century as a stop-off on the old caravan routes, with salt heading one way and ivory and gold heading back the other. Strewn across the hillside and surrounded by flowering almond trees in early spring, the red-pisé towers of the village fortress resemble a sprawling, dark-red sand castle. Crenellated and topped with an ancient granary store, it's one of the most sumptuous sights in the Atlas. The ksar is a UNESCO World Heritage Site.

When not teeming with camera crews, it can get inundated with visitors desperate to capture the postcard-perfect snap. But you can usually manage a moment or two alone with the ksar to take in its beauty, no matter how many people are there.

GETTING HERE AND AROUND

The village is easily reached by road. There are very few buses to Aït Ben Haddou, so if you don't have a car the best and cheapest option is to charter a grand taxi in Ouarzazate. On arrival, you'll find two main entrances to the kasbah. The first, by the hotel-restaurant La Kasbah, has ample safe parking and you can cross the riverbed via stepping-stones. Farther down the road is the second entry point opposite the Riad Maktoub. Here you can leave your car at the side of the road and then take a short stroll to a footbridge across the river to the kasbah.

TIMING AND PRECAUTIONS

The narrow road to Aït Ben Haddou is filled with vehicles traveling faster than they should. Proceed with caution and keep well over to the right, giving way to anything bigger than you. To reach the kasbah itself involves crossing a river, the Oued Mellah; however, a footbridge and new pathways up through the kasbah have been built by locals and have made exploration much easier and safer than ever before.

WHERE TO EAT

There are a few café-restaurants on the roadside close to the parking areas of Aït Ben Haddou. However, you should avoid those with all the tour buses parked outside as quality is invariably poor. Lodgings like Riad Maktoub or Ksar Ighnda, listed below, offer reliable alternatives—both are open to the general public for lunch or dinner.

WHERE TO STAY

$ B&B/INN 🏨 **Auberge Ayouze.** This restored pisé home maintains an aura of authenticity thanks to typical architectural features, like carved Berber motifs and ceilings woven from reeds and date palms. **Pros:** great value; authentic setting. **Cons:** no pool; not much English spoken; only two rooms have heating and air-conditioning. [$] *Rooms from: 310DH* ✉ *Douar Asfalou, 2 km (1 mile) north of Aït Ben Haddou* ☎ *0524/88–37–57* 🌐 *www.auberge-ayouze.com* 🛏 *6 rooms* 🍴 *Breakfast.*

$$$
B&B/INN
⊞ **Kasbah Ellouze.** Next to the old kasbah of Tamdaght, the rustic Kasbah Ellouze (Kasbah of Almonds) is brimming with character. **Pros:** kasbah setting; helpful staff; great food. **Cons:** rooms are dark and cold in winter; hot water not always reliable. [$] *Rooms from: 950DH ⊠ Tamdaght, 5 km (3 miles) north of Aït Ben Haddou on P1506 ☎ 0524/89–04–59 ⊕ www.kasbahellouze.com ⤳ 10 rooms, 3 suites ⊟ No credit cards ⊘ Closed Jan. and July ¶○¶ Some meals.*

$$$
HOTEL
⊞ **Ksar Ighnda.** The most upmarket accommodations in the village, Ksar Ighnda stands on the grounds of an old mud-built ksar—though only the original olive trees remain in the garden near the pool. **Pros:** spacious gardens and common areas. **Cons:** standard rooms are small; restaurant serves average quality meals and meager breakfasts. [$] *Rooms from: 990DH ⊠ Douar Asfalou, 2 km (1 mile) east of Aït Ben Haddou ☎ 0524/88–76–44 ⊕ www.ksar.ighnda.net ⤳ 44 rooms, 6 suites ¶○¶ Breakfast.*

$
HOTEL
⊞ **La Kasbah.** Better suited to large tour groups than independent travelers, the key attraction of this hotel is an uninterrupted view of the kasbah. **Pros:** good food and facilities; stunning views; spacious bungalows have private terraces. **Cons:** lacks a personal touch. [$] *Rooms from: 400DH ⊠ Complexe Touristique ☎ 0524/89–03–08 ⊕ www.hotel-lakasbah.com ⤳ 90 rooms, 10 suites ¶○¶ Breakfast.*

$$
B&B/INN
⊞ **Riad Caravane.** Recently opened by French couple Andréa and Vincent, Riad Caravane has stylish rooms, a roof terrace looking out to the kasbah, and a small dipping pool. **Pros:** chic design; village atmosphere. **Cons:** some rooms are small; hard to find. [$] *Rooms from: 660DH ☎ 0524/89–09–16 ⊕ www.riad-caravane.com ⤳ 5 rooms, 3 suites ⊟ No credit cards ⊘ Closed for Ramadan ¶○¶ Breakfast.*

$$
B&B/INN
⊞ **Riad Maktoub.** A short walk from the entrance to the kasbah, this family-run guesthouse offers Berber-style accommodations with comfortable beds, air-conditioning, and tiled bathrooms. **Pros:** family business; great views from the terrace; close to the village. **Cons:** service is lacking; rooms cold in winter. [$] *Rooms from: 500DH ☎ 0524/88–86–94 ⊕ www.riadmaktoub.com ⤳ 15 rooms, 8 suites ¶○¶ Breakfast.*

SKOURA

50 km (31 miles) southwest of El Kelaâ M'Gouna, 42 km (26 miles) northeast of Ouarzazate.

Surprisingly lush and abrupt as it springs from the tawny landscape, Skoura deserves a lingering look for its kasbahs and its rich concentration of date palm, olive, fig, and almond trees. Pathways tunnel through the vegetation from one kasbah to another within this fertile island—a true oasis, perhaps the most intensely verdant in Morocco. ■ TIP➔ Skoura is such a pleasant and magical place to hole up that if you're on a grand tour of the Great Oasis Valleys, it's well worth considering staying here rather than in often-lackluster Ouarzazate.

With so many grand deep-orange-hue kasbahs in Skoura, a tour of the Palmery is compulsory. The main kasbah route through Skoura is approached from a point just over 2 km (1 mile) past the town center toward Ouarzazate. The 18th-century **Kasbah Aït Ben Moro** is the first fortress on the right (now restored and converted to a hotel); you can leave your car at the hotel, which will happily arrange for a local guide to take you through the Palmery, past the Sidi Aïssa *marabout* (shrine to a learned holy man). Alternatively, continue along the main road for a few hundred meters till you find the Museum of Skoura. By the Amerhidil River is the tremendous **Kasbah Amerhidil,** the largest kasbah in Skoura and one of the largest in Morocco. The partially renovated edifice is open to the public.

Down the (usually bone-dry) river is another kasbah, **Dar Aït Sidi el-Mati,** while back near the Ouarzazate road is the **Kasbah el-Kabbaba,** the last of the four fortresses on this loop. North of Skoura, on Route 6829 through Aït-Souss, are two other kasbahs: **Dar Lahsoune,** a former Glaoui residence, and, a few minutes farther north, the **Kasbah Aït Ben Abou,** the second largest in Skoura after the Amerhidil.

EXPLORING

Museum of Skoura. Constructed and entirely funded by schoolteacher Abdelmoula el Moudahab, this small but fascinating private museum houses a collection of traditional Berber costumes, artifacts, manuscripts, and antiques belonging to several generations of local families. Abdelmoula, who speaks good English, can explain tribal differences and describe the various types of kasbahs and holy shrines found in the Skoura region. ✉ *Douar Ihzgane* ☎ *0524/85–23–68* 🌐 *www.musee-theatre-skoura.com* 🎟 *20 DH.*

7

WHERE TO STAY

$$ B&B/INN 🏨 **Chez Talout.** Run by one of Morocco's friendliest hoteliers, this farmhouse is worth the trek for Talout's warm welcome, wonderful food, and roof-terrace views across the Palmery to Skoura's kasbahs. **Pros:** excellent cuisine; lovely pool **Cons:** well off the beaten track. [$] *Rooms from: 660DH* ✉ *Ouled Aarbia* ✥ *7 km (4½ miles) before Skoura if coming from Ouarzazate, turn left off main road just after Idelssane* ☎ *0662/49–82–83* 🌐 *www.talout.com* 🛏 *12 rooms, 2 suites* 💳 *No credit cards* 🍴 *Breakfast.*

$$$$ HOTEL ALL-INCLUSIVE 🏨 **Dar Ahlam.** If money is no object, then consider a stay in this restored 19th-century kasbah, one of Morocco's most exclusive and sumptuous hideaways. **Pros:** heavenly accommodations; pampering beyond your wildest dreams. **Cons:** rates are well beyond the reach of most mortals. [$] *Rooms from: 12,650DH* ✉ *Kasbah Madihi, Skoura Palmery* ☎ *0524/85–22–39* 🌐 *www.darahlam.com* 🛏 *13 suites, 1 villa* 🕒 *Closed Aug.* 🍴 *All-inclusive.*

$$$ B&B/INN 🏨 **Kasbah Aït Ben Moro.** This stunning hotel is a converted 18th-century desert castle that overlooks the Palmery, the Kasbah Amerhidil, and the High Atlas Mountains. **Pros:** charming host; swimming pool and pretty terraces; true kasbah experience. **Cons:** rooms and stairways are poorly lit; meals can be mediocre. [$] *Rooms from: 770DH* ✉ *Douar Taskoukamte, 2½ km (1½ miles) west of Skoura* ☎ *0524/85–21–16* 🌐 *www.kasbahaitbenmoro.com* 🛏 *13 rooms, 4 suites* 🍴 *Breakfast.*

The Kasbah Amerhidil is the largest in Skoura.

$$$
B&B/INN
FAMILY
Fodor's Choice
★

🍴 **Les Jardins de Skoura.** Styling itself as a *"maison de repos,"* this restored farmhouse casts such a spell over guests that many of them find it difficult to leave, staying on for days in its warm, lazy embrace. **Pros:** idyllic surroundings, excellent facilities. **Cons:** may be too isolated for some. ⓢ *Rooms from: 880DH ⊠ Skoura Palmery ✛ 2 km (1 mile) before Skoura (from direction of Ouarzazate), and after passing Kasbah Aït Ben Moro follow yellow arrow signs for left turn, additional 4 km (2½ miles) of track to get to house ☎ 0524/85–23–24 ⊕ www.lesjardinsdeskoura.com ⇨ 5 rooms, 3 suites ▭ No credit cards ⊗ Closed July ⏍ Breakfast.*

SPORTS AND THE OUTDOORS

FOUR-WHEELING

X.trem Explorer. On the way into Skoura, coming from the direction of Ouarzazate, look out for signs on your left to X.trem Explorer. Based at the Dar Ikram guesthouse, it runs dune-buggy excursions around the sands, palms, and kasbahs. ⊠ *Dar Ikram, 5 km (3 miles) southwest of Skoura ☎ 0666/43–53–77 ⊕ www.darikram.net.*

HORSEBACK RIDING

Skoura Equestrian Centre. This well-run spot just outside of town offers professional English-speaking riding instruction, as well as horseback excursions around the kasbahs of Skoura oasis; expect to pay 300 DH for two hours or 500 DH for a full day with picnic lunch. The center is managed by Sport-Travel Maroc in Marrakesh. Book in advance. ⊠ *2 km (1 mile) north of Skoura on the road to Toundout ☎ 0661/43–21–63.*

EL KELAÂ M'GOUNA

24 km (15 miles) southwest of Boumalne du Dadès, 92 km (57 miles) northeast of Ouarzazate.

The region known as the Valley of the Roses essentially forms a triangle, stretching north to Bou Thaghrar and west to Boumalne du Dadès from Kelaâ M'Gouna. It is in fact a confluence of several valleys that meet at the village of Bou Thaghrar. The local Berber population cultivates the Rosa Damascena on the slopes of the High Atlas, and the richness of the soil boosts the pigment of the blooms. Throughout the drive from Kelaâ M'Gouna to Boumalne du Dadès (N10) you'll see thousands of small pink Persian blossoms dividing the fields and fringing the highway. To reach the terraced rose gardens higher up in the Valley of the Roses, take the signposted route north from Kelaâ M'Gouna as far as Bou Thaghrar. From there you have to proceed on foot. Guides are essential and can be found in Bou Thaghrar for about 250 DH per day.

GETTING HERE AND AROUND

Kelaâ M'Gouna, on the main route from Ouarzazate to Boumalne du Dadès, is served by buses and grands taxis from both directions. The route N10 is a principal road and easily navigable. There are minibuses in Kelaâ M'Gouna for tourists visiting the Valley of the Roses.

TIMING AND PRECAUTIONS

Exploring the Valley of the Roses can take anything from a day to a week, depending on how much hiking you want to do. The best time to visit is during Kelaâ M'Gouna's three-day Rose Festival, held annually at harvest time in early May. On Wednesday there is a lively local souk.

WHERE TO STAY

$$
B&B/INN
🏠 **Kasbah Itran.** Teetering on the edge of a precipice with stupendous views over the Valley of Roses, Kasbah Itran offers quirky, colorful accommodation inside its high stone walls; tasteful rooms all have open fireplaces (recently modernized to reduce fumes) and are suffused with incense and cinnamon from the kitchen. **Pros:** stunning valley views; atmospheric rooms. **Cons:** not all rooms have air-conditioning and three have shared bathrooms; English-speaking staff not always available; patchy service. $ *Rooms from: 550DH* ✉ *Douar Mirna, 4 km (2½ miles) north of Kelaâ M'Gouna on road to Bou Thrarar* ☎ *0524/83–71–03* ⊕ *www.kasbahitran.com* 🛏 *11 rooms* ▬ *No credit cards* ⊘ *Some meals.*

$$$
HOTEL
FAMILY
🏠 **La Perle du Dadès.** Between Kelaâ M'Gouna and Boumalne du Dadès, this restored riverside kasbah is an ideal base for exploring both the Valley of Roses and the Dadès Gorge. **Pros:** lots of leisure activities; imaginative design. **Cons:** a little hard to find; not much English spoken; beds are low and uncomfortable. $ *Rooms from: 825DH* ✉ *16 km (10 miles) northeast of El Kelaâ M'Gouna on N10; 7 km (4½ miles) south of Boumalne du Dadès* ✛ *Turn right onto a small track at the village of Souk el-Khemis and cross the dried Dadès riverbed* ☎ *0524/85–05–48* ⊕ *www.perledudades.com* 🛏 *8 rooms, 7 suites* ▬ *No credit cards* ⊘ *Breakfast.*

SPORTS AND OUTDOORS

Bureau de Guides Kelaâ M'Gouna. Aziz Boullouz heads up the Bureau des Guides in Kelaâ M'Gouna. He can organize walking tours of the underexplored Valley of Roses, M'Goun Massif, the Jbel Saghro, and remote trekking regions. ✉ *Zaouite Aguard* ☎ *0662/13–21–92.*

THE DADÈS AND TODRA GORGES

The drive through Morocco's smaller versions of the Grand Canyon is stunning, and the area merits several days' exploration. The Dadès Gorge is frequented more by independent travelers than tours, while the Todra is much more about mass-organized tourism. So many buses stop at the most beautiful point that you almost forget it's supposed to be beautiful. If you avoid lunchtime (when all the tour buses disgorge), and venture on, there are some great walks and lovely spots where you can feel much more alone.

THE DADÈS GORGE

Boumalne du Dadès is 53 km (33 miles) southwest of Tinerhir, 116 km (72 miles) northeast of Ouarzazate.

Snaking its way up from Boumalne du Dadès, the narrow roadway that is gradually swallowed up by the gorge is captivating. Along the route you'll see sprawling, emerald-green valleys and classic kasbahs set against a backdrop of surreal wind-sculpted, geological formations. The immensity of the gorge itself is a humbling reminder of our own vulnerability to the forces of nature and time. The switchback road helter-skelters to the end of the tarmac at Msemrir, but (in good weather) you can loop across to Todra Gorge in a 4x4 vehicle or continue northwards on a rocky piste to Imilchil. The scenery of the Dadès Gorge is astounding, and if you can break away on foot to explore further, you will encounter Berber nomad families living in caves and rocky crags carved into the mountainside.

GETTING HERE AND AROUND

The easiest access point for the Dadès Gorge is the town of Boumalne du Dadès, which is linked to Ouarzazate in the west and Er-Rachidia in the east by the N10. CTM buses frequent this route, providing transportation to and from Boumalne du Dadès. The road through the gorge itself is paved as far as Msemrir. Traveling beyond Msemrir requires a four-wheel-drive vehicle, and even then only if conditions are right. The piste routes can be treacherous, especially during the rainy season between December and February. If you do not have your own transport, grands taxis from Boumalne du Dadès will take you on the scenic drive.

Bus Contacts CTM. Although there is no longer a CTM bus office in Boumalne du Dadès, tickets can be purchased from shops along the main street displaying the yellow sign reading, "Espace Service." ✉ *Av. Mohammed V, Boumalne du Dadès* ⊕ *www.ctm.ma.*

TIMING AND PRECAUTIONS

The Dadès Gorge is beautiful all year. In summer the steep canyon walls and rushing rivers are refreshing after the heat of the desert. In winter, however, the region gets considerable rainfall that makes the pistes impassable. Always ensure you have a full tank of gas, a spare tire, and plenty of water if embarking on cross-country routes.

VISITOR INFORMATION

Contacts **Bureau des Guides a Boumalne du Dadès.** ⊠ *Av. Mohammed V, just after the bridge on left (if coming from Dadès Gorge), next to WafaBank, Boumalne du Dadès* ☎ *0667/59–32–92.*

EXPLORING

The town of **Boumalne du Dadès** marks the southern entrance to the Dadès Gorge, which is even more beautiful—longer, wider, and more varied—than its sister, the Todra Gorge. The 63 km (39 miles) of the Dadès Gorge, from Boumalne through Aït Ali and on to Msemrir, are paved and approachable in any kind of vehicle. Beyond that are some great rocky mountain roads for four-wheel-drive vehicles with good clearance. Boumalne itself is only of moderate interest, though the central market square is a good vantage point for a perusal of local life. The shops Artisanale de Boumalne and Maison Aït Atta merit a browse for their local products at local prices, particularly rosewood carvings and rosewater.

The lower Dadès Gorge and the Dadès River, which flows through it, are lined with thick vegetation. While the Todra has its lush date palmery, the Dadès has figs, almonds, Atlas pistachio, and carob trees. A series of kasbahs and *ksour* (plural of *ksar,* or fortified house) give way to Berber villages such as Aït Youl, Aït Arbi, Aït Ali, Aït Oudinar, and Aït Toukhsine—*aït* meaning "of the family" in the Tamazight Berber language.

Two km (1 mile) up the road from Boumalne is the **Glaoui Kasbah,** once part of the empire of the infamous pasha of Marrakesh, T'hami el-Glaoui. The ksour at **Aït Arbi** are tucked neatly into the surrounding volcanic rock 3 km (2 miles) farther on from Glaoui Kasbah.

Ten km (6 miles) from Aït Arbi is the village of Aït Sidi Boubker in the **Tamlalt Valley,** mostly known for the bizarre red rock formations called "Les Doigts de Singes" (or "Monkey's Fingers") after their curiously organic shapes carved by water and wind. A little further beyond them are more sculpted rocks known as the "Valley of Human Bodies," where local legend says that lost travelers died of hunger and were transformed into rocks. After Aït Oudinar, where most of the lodging options are clustered, the road crosses a bridge and gets substantially more exciting and empty, and the valley narrows dramatically, opening up around the corner into some of the most stunning views in the Dadès. Six km (4 miles) north of the bridge, the **Hôtel la Kasbah de la Vallée** has basic accommodations, a restaurant, and a licensed bar. A few kilometers from here, a staggering series of hairpin bends descend into the belly of the camera-ready canyon.

Aït Hammou, the next village, is 5 km (3 miles) past the Kasbah de la Vallée. It makes a good base camp for walking and climbing north to vantage points over the Dadès River or, to the east, to a well-known cave with stalactites (ask the Hôtel la Kasbah de la Vallée for directions). At the top of the gorges is **Msemrir,** a village of red-clay pisé ksour that has a café with guest rooms. To go farther from Msemrir, you'll need four-wheel drive to follow the road (R704) that leads north over the High Atlas through Tilmi, the Tizi-n-Ouano, and Agoudal to Imilchil and eventually up to Route P24 (N8), the Marrakesh–Fez road. The road east from Msemrir climbs the difficult Route 3444, always bearing right, to another gorgetop town, Tamtattouchte. It makes for a great off-road drive.

WHERE TO EAT

Like other rural locales, the Dadès Gorge has few dining options, but lunch is served at most of the small auberges and touristic hotels: as long as you turn up between midday and 3 pm, when the tagines are bubbling, you should be able to find a table. Chez Pierre and Dar Jnan Tiouira *(see below)* are particularly noted for their excellent food.

WHERE TO STAY

$
B&B/INN
Auberge des Peupliers. An ideal base for anyone craving simple Berber hospitality, Auberge des Peupliers has cozy accommodations with distinctive clay sinks, electric heating, and en-suite showers. Newer rooms include traditional features (like carved motifs) and face out across the gorge. **Pros:** friendly, helpful service. **Cons:** older rooms look shabby. $ *Rooms from: 300DH* ⊠ *Ait Ouffi, rte. de Dadès Gorge, 27 km (17 miles) north of Boumalne du Dadès* ☎ *0524/83–17–48* ⊕ *www. aubergedespeupliers.net* ⤳ *12 rooms* ═ *No credit cards* ⑩ *Some meals.*

$$
B&B/INN
Fodor'sChoice
★
Chez Pierre. Clinging to the rocky face of the Dadès Gorge, this guesthouse is by far the nicest place to both eat and stay in the area. **Pros:** beautiful situation; great service and décor. **Cons:** property and rooms accessed via steep stairways. $ *Rooms from: 550DH* ⊠ *Rte. de Dadès Gorge, 27 km (17 miles) north of Boumalne du Dadès* ☎ *0524/83–02–67* ⊕ *www.chezpierre.org* ⤳ *8 rooms, 1 suite* ⑩ *Breakfast.*

$$$$
B&B/INN
Dar Jnan Tiouira. This newly built kasbah has been a labor of love. **Pros:** fabulous location; great food; luxurious rooms. **Cons:** hazardously steep ramps and stairs throughout; staff not always on hand. $ *Rooms from: 1250DH* ⊠ *Aït Ouffi, rte. de Dadès Gorge, 22 km (13½ miles) north fromBoumalne du Dadès* ☎ *0667/35–18–60* ⊕ *www. darjnantiouira.com* ⤳ *5 rooms, 2 suites* ═ *No credit cards* ⑩ *Some meals.*

$$
B&B/INN
Hôtel la Kasbah de la Vallée. Halfway between Boumalne and Msemrir, this hotel overlooks one of the most dramatic parts of the canyon. **Pros:** owners have in-depth knowledge of area; plenty of activities. **Cons:** lots of tour groups. $ *Rooms from: 560DH* ⊠ *Aït Oufi, 27 km (16 miles) north of Boumalne du Dadès* ☎ *0524/83–17–17* ⊕ *www.kasbah-vallee-dades.com* ⤳ *40 rooms, 2 suites* ═ *No credit cards* ⑩ *Some meals.*

$$$
HOTEL
FAMILY
Hotel Xaluca Dadès. Part of the Spanish Xaluca chain, this vast hotel offers high-quality accommodation in a region which generally lacks luxury. **Pros:** spacious, airy lounges; plenty of family amenities. **Cons:** located at edge of Boumalne, far from the gorge; ugly architecture; popular with tour groups. $ *Rooms from: 990DH* ⊠ *Rte. de Er-Rachidia,*

Boumalne du Dadès ☎ *0524/83–00–60* 🌐 *www.xaluca.com* 🛏 *104 rooms, 2 suites* 🍴 *Breakfast.*

$ B&B/INN 🏨 **Kasbah de Victor.** Perched on a promontory, the tiny Kasbah de Victor has stunning views of the Dadès Gorge and is popular with families who enjoy the garden and outdoor pool (though it is ice-cold most of the year). **Pros:** heating in winter; terrace salon has wonderful views. **Cons:** remote location; pool not well maintained; owner not always on site to ensure quality. [$] *Rooms from: 400DH* ✉ *31 km (19 miles) north of Boumalne du Dadès* ☎ *0622/29–02–68* 🛏 *4 rooms* 💳 *No credit cards* 🍴 *Some meals.*

SPORTS AND THE OUTDOORS

Mohamed Amgom. An experienced local Berber guide, Mohamed Amgom offers treks in the Dadès Valley for 400 DH per day. He can also organize four-wheel-drive vehicles for excursions throughout the Dadès and Todra gorges and works with his brother at the Hotel la Kasbah de la Vallée. ☎ *0666/59–41–42.*

THE TODRA GORGE

194 km (121 miles) northwest of Rissani, 184 km (114 miles) northeast of Ouarzazate.

The towering limestone stacks of the Todra Gorge are breathtakingly beautiful, as is the winding route upwards from Tinerhir which leads you there through delightful groves of date palm, pomegranate, fig, and olive trees. The namesake river that carved the gorge also feeds vegetation, forming the Todra Oasis—Morocco's highest—cradled in the southern slopes of the High Atlas. This whole mountainous area is the heartland of the Aït Atta tribe of Berbers, who have inhabited the region for centuries. Today it's also a top spot for trekking and rock climbing. Local hotels can organize guided hikes lasting several hours or several days. Mountaineers, ascending from the oasis to the steep cliffs of the gorge above, will also find plenty to keep them occupied, including several technical climbs for the experienced and some newer sections marked out for novices. Although hotels here may be able to offer you a guide and climbing equipment, the quality and condition of the latter cannot be vouched for, so bring your own or sign on for an organized tour run by a reputable outfitter.

GETTING HERE AND AROUND

The town of Tinerhir (also spelled "Tinghir"), on the main N10 route from Ouarzazate and Er-Rachidia, is the most convenient access point for visiting the Todra Gorge. Long-distance buses travel here from Agadir, Casablanca, Marrakesh, Fez, Meknès, and Rabat. Buses also arrive from Ouarzazate (five hours), Er-Rachidia (three hours), and Erfoud (four hours); most stop on Avenue Mohammed V, on the northern side of the main square.

To reach the gorge, take route R703 (3445) north toward Tamtattouchte, and follow the riverbed upwards for about 15 km (9 miles). If you don't have your own vehicle, you can catch a grand taxi to take you up through the Todra palmery as far as the Todra Gorge; the 30-minute

Continued on page 346

SEEING THE

Life's truly picture-perfect moments come few and far between: a sea of sand dunes, shimmering gray, yellow, orange, and red throughout the day, is one of them. The Sahara is the most beautiful, enigmatic, and awe-inspiring natural wonder that you can experience in Morocco—but if at all possible, don't rush through the experience.

SAHARA

by Rachel Blech

The Touareg freedom fighter Mano Dayek once wrote, "The desert will not tell you about itself—it is a way of life". The nomadic tribes of "Blue Men" who have lived for generations in the Moroccan Sahara understand this better than most. The desert is partly a state of mind that requires you to bow to nature in the search for humility, so prepare yourself for enlightenment here amongst the billowing *ergs* (dunes), stark stony *hamada* (plains), and scattered oases.

Should you have time for it, an expedition into the deeper desert provides a glimpse into a forgotten world. You may enter the desert by camel or jeep, but you will be able to sleep in a traditional bedouin tent or something even more comfortable and luxurious. You may even have the opportunity to snowboard down the dunes.

DID YOU KNOW?

Merzouga is best known for the magnificent, undulating dunes at Erg Chebbi, but nearby there is also a seasonal salt lake, Dayet Sjiri, the largest natural body of water in Morocco.

POINTS OF ENTRY

The two main desert destinations in Morocco are very different—Merzouga lies 9 hours' drive due east of Ouarzazate via the Dadès and Ziz valleys; M'Hamid is 5 hours' drive south of Ouarzazate via the Drâa Valley.

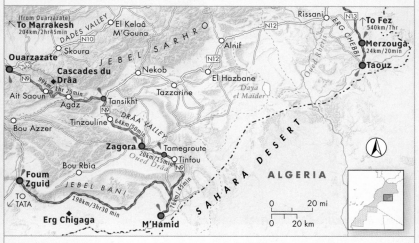

MERZOUGA

From Fez, Merzouga is the most convenient overnight desert stop. The onward route then takes you through the Todra and Dadès gorges before reaching Ouarzazate. The dunes near Merzouga, called Erg Chebbi, have sand piled high like a fancy hairdo, and you can dip your toe in as you like. The desert is easily accessible by road right to the edge of the golden sands. Here you can spend a night very happily in an oasis bivouac camp, sleeping under the stars, and another back in Merzouga at an auberge or luxury hotel with majestic dune views. ■TIP→ To escape from other travelers seeking solitude, head for the northernmost or southernmost tip of the dunes—away from the village of Merzouga.

M'HAMID

M'Hamid is the best entry point for the more adventurous and is the easiest place to reach if you are coming from Marrakesh. The paved road ends in the village, and beyond there's nothing but desert scrub, stony hamada, and soft dunes. Erg Chigaga is the star attraction, some 50 kms distant from the village. The sands go on for miles, and excursions by 4x4, camel, or a combination of both can be for as long or short as you like. Typically, a one-night trip by camel from M'Hamid gets you to nearby Erg L'Houdi (The Dunes of the Jews); four days round-trip gets you to Erg Ezahaar (The Screaming Dunes), and five days gets you to the highest dunes in the region, Erg Chigaga.

OTHER HIGHLIGHTS

ERG CHIGAGA

Erg Chigaga can be reached by desert *piste* (unsealed dirt road) in a 4x4 in around three hours, so an overnight getaway is possible. Alternatively, a two-day camel trek from M'Hamid will get you to Erg Chigaga, and you can book a 4x4 vehicle to bring you back the next day. Bivouacs in Erg Chigaga range from simple, nomad-style shared camps to super-deluxe private encampments.

OUARZAZATE

There are no dunes in Ouarzazate, but it's a great place to pick up a rental vehicle, bus, or taxi to take you to either Merzouga or M'Hamid. You can book a private tour with one of the many agencies in town. Tight on time? Fly to Ouarzazate airport from Casablanca.

ZAGORA

The desert vibe really kicks in at Zagora, which is itself an interesting town to visit. Unfortunately, the small sand dunes nearby give only a tiny taste of the desert; M'Hamid is where the Sahara truly begins. Take the extra two-hour drive to the end of the road if you possibly can. In Zagora you can arrange any kind of extended desert tour that will combine the desert at M'Hamid, the dunes of Erg Chigaga, the dried Lake Iriki, and a return via Foum Zguid. Or you can take a quick camel trek down through the Drâa Valley.

(top) A kasbah in Ouarzazate (top right) Merzouga dunes (center) a camel caravan (bottom right) riding motorcycles on the dunes

TINFOU

Less than an hour south of Zagora, there is little to see in Tinfou other than an isolated sand dune with a few bivouac camps and camel rides. Nearby is the Kasbah Hotel Sahara Sky, which has a state-of-the-art observatory for astronomy enthusiasts.

TAOUZ

This tiny village at the very end of the paved road after Merzouga is where the desert closes in. Here you can visit the gnaoua musicians at nearby Khamlia, and from Taouz you can take off-road excursions on complicated desert pistes heading southwest to eventually reach the village of Tagounite (just north of M'Hamid) on the N9/P31. This is at least a 9-hour drive and not recommended without a professional local driver/guide.

FOUM ZGUID

If you are traveling from Ouarzazate or Marrakesh, the dunes of Erg Chigaga can be reached more quickly by entering the desert at Foum Zguid rather than traveling the length of the Drâa Valley to M'Hamid, though most guided trips still leave from M'Hamid. The trip from Ouarzazate to Foum Zguid takes four hours by road and off-road piste to Erg Chigaga, skirting Jbel Bani on the old Paris–Dakar rally trail for another three hours.

TATA

Although it does not serve as a portal to the desert dune regions, Tata is a good base for excursions to the Akka oasis and the prehistoric rock-carvings at Oum el-Alek, Tircht, and Aït Herbil. You can pick up a local guide in Tata to show you the best archeological sites.

WILL I FRY? (AND OTHER QUESTIONS)

A typical desert bivouac camp in the Sahara

WILL I FRY?

Temperatures can reach 55°C (131°F) in June, July, and August. If you must go in summer, take sunset camel rides into the dunes, spend the night, and head back at dawn. The best (and busiest) time is between March and early May. October to February is nice, too, although it can be very cold at night from December through February.

WHAT SHOULD I WEAR?

Cover up with light layers. Loose-fitting clothes (e.g. knee-length shorts or baggy cotton pants and trekking sandals) are best for summer. In winter, lightweight walking boots or sneakers, long pants, T-shirts, long-sleeve tops, and a thick fleece should suffice, but bring something warmer for the night.

WHAT ABOUT MY HEAD?

It's essential to have a head covering to protect you from both sun and sand at any time of year. Donning the *sheish* (turban), beloved of Saharoui and Berbers, is really fun. Knot the end of a lightweight dyed fabric (most often blue), and put it on your head. Wrap the rest

around your head and take the end across your nose and tuck it in.

WHAT IF I PREFER SKIING?

Believe it or not, you're in the right place. If camels, four-wheel drives, and long walks don't interest you, think of the sands as a miraculous cross between snow and sea. Most of the desert tour companies in Merzouga or M'Hamid have skis, sand-boards, and body-boards for hire. Make sure you ask an expert if the sand is suitable. Be warned though... there are no lifts to get you back up the dunes!

DO I EVEN NEED A GUIDE?

The desert is unforgiving, and the inexperienced can easily become the expired. You should never attempt to visit the desert without an experienced guide. If you arrive in Merzouga or M'Hamid without having pre-booked a guided tour, make sure your guide is legitimate. While guiding visitors around the desert has kept hard-up locals in cash for years, you should be on the look-out for people on buses whose "uncle" has a place you can stay in for cheap. These people are almost always touts working on commission. Likewise, some may try to convince you that there is a "better" alternative to the auberge you pre-booked. The best way to avoid hassles is to make all arrangements in advance and arrange pick-up if you don't have your own transportion, or a roadside meeting if you do.

WHICH DUNES SHOULD I VISIT?
The impressive Erg Chebbi, near Merzouga, are more amenable to a quick in/out overnight, but they are a full 10-hour drive from Fez or two full days hard driving from Marrakesh. Erg Chebbi is very impressive, and solitary spots can be found on the fringes, with a good range of basic to deluxe accommodations. Southwest of M'Hamid, however, you have eye-popping dunes that stretch for miles, including the Erg Chigaga. Ideally, allow at least two days (by camel) to get there from M'Hamid, but a round-trip from Marrakesh is possible in three days with a 4x4.

WHAT ESSENTIAL ITEMS SHOULD I BRING?
Bring enough cash to see you through several days; sunscreen; sun glasses or a visor; eco-friendly toiletries; toilet paper; bottled water (at least three liters per day per person); zip-up plastic bags for keeping sensitive items free of sand; a flashlight with spare batteries; a basic first-aid kit; and a road map or GPS if you are driving to your starting point on your own. A sense of humor comes in handy too.

Gazing out on the desert

WHERE SHOULD I STAY?
In the desert, of course! Most tour operators, hotels, and auberges have their own permanent tented camps (*bivouacs*) hidden among the oases and dunes. Tents are usually good for between 2 and 4 people, but you can generally have a tent to yourself if traveling alone. If you want to keep the stars within eyeshot all night, you can also just sleep on a blanket over the sands. Most fixed camps have a restaurant tent (some serving alcohol), separate toilets, and washing facilities of some kind. In Merzouga and M'Hamid, at the edge of the desert, there are also traditional auberges and plusher hotels of varying grades of luxury (some even have swimming pools).

WILL I BE SAFE?
Yes, if you use your common sense. Do not stray far from your group or your guide: it is very easy to get disorientated in the dunes as they all look alike; you can quickly lose sight of your camp or your vehicle.

WHAT IS THERE TO DO IN THE DESERT?

You might think there's not much to do in the desert, but when there are no shops, no electricity, and no running water, just getting by becomes wonderfully time-consuming. You can cook bread in the sand; count stars until the sky caves in; climb to the crest of the dunes at sunset; and listen to hypnotic Berber drumming deep into the night.

Camel trips are de rigueur and in Erg Chebbi, near Merzouga, they rarely last more than three hours, with dinner generally waiting for you at your chosen bivouac camp. Beyond M'Hamid, farther south, there's a much greater range of desert terrain to explore. Away from the fixed camps, the experience of camping *sauvage*, with just a nomad guide and camel for

company, gives a much better understanding of the real desert way of life.

For thrill-seekers there are quad bikes and buggies for desert safaris, or you can try your skills at boarding down the high dunes. Alternatively, just take it easy and watch the changing moods, colors, and textures of the dunes all day long.

GREAT DRIVES: TODRA GORGE

If you have a four-wheel-drive vehicle with good clearance, you can take the adventurous route from the top of the Todra Gorge: pop over into the Dadès Gorge by the difficult but passable Route 3444 from Aït Hani (first village after Tamtattouchte) to **Msemrir.** If you try this by jeep, take the second left after Tamtattouchte up a steep incline. Go right at the first fork, left at the second fork, and right at the third fork. Travel 6 km (4 miles) to the next fork, where you take the road on the left. From there it's a slow 45 km (28 miles) to Msemrir. Hikers in top condition can

do this as well, forming an ideal five- or six-day walk up the Todra and over to, down, and out the Dadès Gorge, including one night camping between Tamtattouchte and Msemrir.

Other four-wheel-drive options include continuing north to Agoudal and Imilchil (⟹ *see Chapter 5, Fez and the Middle Atlas*), or heading east through Aït Hani, Tiidrine, and Assoul to Rich, a tortuous but stunningly beautiful route on which you ford several (shallow) rivers and see no one except Berber villagers and the occasional nomad.

drive should cost about 20 DH per person. There are also minibuses that transport locals to the villages above the Todra Gorge; you can ask to be dropped off on the way through.

Bus Contacts CTM Tinerhir ✉ *Av. Hassan II, next to the main square* ☎ *0524/83–43–79* ⊕ *www.ctm.ma.*

TIMING

The steep sides of the gorge can often mean that the route through the gorge itself is in shade, but the effect of angled sunlight shifting across the rock face during the day creates a sublime canvas of red and orange. Mid- to late afternoon is deemed the best time to visit.

EXPLORING

The 15-km (9-mile) drive up from Tinerhir to the beginning of the Todra Gorge will take you through lush but slender palmeries, sometimes no wider than 100 feet from cliff to cliff. An inn and a café await near the spring, but you're better off not stopping, as the site itself isn't remarkable, and the concentration of hustlers and over-helpful children is dense.

The 66-foot-wide entrance to the Todra Gorge, with its roaring clear stream and its 1,000-foot-high rock walls stretching 325 feet back on either side, is the most stunning feature of the whole canyon, though the upper reaches aren't far behind. The farther off the beaten path you get, the more rewarding the scenery; a walk or drive up through the gorge on paved roads to Tamtattouchte is particularly recommended. There are some marked trails leading from Le Festival hotel.

From the thin palmery along the bottom, the walls of the Todra Gorge remain close and high for some 18 km (11 miles), dappled only with occasional families of nomads tending sheep, goats, or camels up on the rocks. Colorfully attired young Berber shepherdesses may appear from nowhere; sometimes you can hear them singing Berber melodies from high in the crags, their sounds echoed and amplified by the rock walls of the canyon. Eagles nest in the Todra, along with *choughs* (red-beaked rooks), rock doves, and blue rock thrushes.

La Source des Poissons Sacrés (Springs of the Sacred Fish), about halfway to the beginning of the gorge, is so named for the miracle performed by a sage, said to have struck a rock once to produce a gushing spring, and twice to produce fish. Today the sacred source is frequented by young Berber women who are experiencing difficulties in conceiving children. (It is rumored that bathing in the water has about an 80% success rate.) You can also stop here to camp and have a refreshing drink.

Museum of the Oasis. This small but ambitious community-oriented spot is well worth a stop if you're driving east from Tinerhir toward Merzouga. Housed in the 19th-century ksar of El Khorbat, it contains old maps, photos, antiques, and exhibits that document the traditional lifestyle of the southern oasis, with proceeds going to development and educational projects in the village. After perusing the displays, you can browse for locally made items at the craft workshop, and then enjoy a meal or spend a night in the atmospheric El Khorbat guesthouse ($$)—both are part of the same tourism initiative. ✉ *Tinejdad, 48 km (31 miles) east of Tinerhir* ☎ *0535/88–03–55* 🌐 *www.elkhorbat.com* 🎫 *20 DH.*

WHERE TO STAY

$$ B&B/INN 🏨 **Auberge Baddou.** This small hotel is a worthy choice for budget accommodations at the far northern end of the Todra Gorge. **Pros:** spotless rooms; friendly service. **Cons:** rather isolated in unattractive village; cheaper rooms have shared bathrooms; central heating is an extra 150 DH per night in winter. [$] *Rooms from: 500DH* ✉ *Aït Hani, Tamtatouchtte, 29 km (18 miles) north of Tinerhir* ☎ *0672/52–13–89* 🌐 *www.aubergebaddou.com* 🛏 *16 rooms, 2 suites* 💳 *No credit cards* 🍴 *Some meals.*

$$ B&B/INN 🏨 **Dar Ayour.** This pretty guesthouse sits at the edge of the river amid fig trees, olives, and date palms with the walls of the Todra Gorge towering above. **Pros:** peaceful setting; small outdoor swimming pool. **Cons:** some rooms very small; bathrooms are basic. [$] *Rooms from: 660DH* ✉ *Km 17, rte. des Gorges de Todra, Douar Tizgui* ☎ *0524/89–52–71, 0672/52–12–51* 🌐 *www.darayour.com* 🛏 *16 rooms, 2 suites* 🍴 *Some meals.*

$$ B&B/INN FAMILY 🏨 **Le Festival.** Made from the same mountain rock that surrounds it, this quirky eco-hotel is owned and operated by the charming Addi Sror, who speaks excellent English. **Pros:** dramatic isolation; great meals; environmentally sensitive. **Cons:** castle and cave rooms 200 DH–300 DH extra per night; few in-house amenities; three rooms in main house share a bathroom. [$] *Rooms from: 500DH* ✉ *Rte. de Todra Gorge, 5 km (3 miles) north of the Todra Gorge, 12 km (7 miles) south of Tamtattouchte* ☎ *0661/26–72–51* 🌐 *www.aubergelefestival-todragorge.com* 🛏 *15 rooms* 💳 *No credit cards* 🍴 *Some meals.*

SPORTS AND THE OUTDOORS

Climb Morocco. This Marrakesh-based rock-climbing outfit was established by two young Americans with AMGA qualifications and a passion for climbing. They can fix you up with transportation to Todra, equipment, accommodations, and guided instruction for beginners and experienced climbers alike. ☎ *0650/79–95–88* ⊕ *www.climbmorocco.com.*

TO MERZOUGA AND THE DUNES

This particular southeastern corner holds some of Morocco's greatest sights, principally the Sahara's picture-perfect undulating dunes near Merzouga, and the Tafilalt date palmery. Now that the road to Merzouga is completely paved, you can drive straight there without stopping; this allows you to avoid Er-Rachidia (a colonial town with little to offer) and even Erfoud, though you may want to pause in the latter to take advantage of the town's supermarkets, banks, and pharmacies. ■TIP➡ **When traveling anywhere in the desert, ensure you have enough cash, batteries, bottled water, and toiletries to see you through for several days until you get to a major town.**

EN ROUTE

Approaching Erfoud from the direction of Tinejdad, you can't help but notice the hundreds of holes that start appearing along both sides of the road about 27 km (17 miles) before you reach town. Although they resemble giant molehills, the holes are actually wells called *khettara.* Part of an ancient Persian-designed irrigation system, which was first brought to Morocco by the Arabs in the 12th century, these wells access water from the natural water table, channeling it through underground canals to different palm groves. On the left-hand side of the road, as sand dunes begin to pile up, look for the ones dug to irrigate the Tafilalt Oasis back in the 14th century. Local guide **Said Ouatou,** who can be found in a Bedouin tent beside the road (also on the left), will explain the science and history. ■TIP➡ **Be careful if you have young children: the edges of the wells can crumble.**

ERFOUD

81 km (50 miles) south of Er-Rachidia, 300 km (186 miles) northeast of Ouarzazate.

Any expedition to Erg Chebbi will entail passing through—or possibly spending a night in—Erfoud. Formerly a French administrative outpost and Foreign Legion stronghold, this frontier town on the Algerian border has a definite Wild West (in this case, Wild South) feel to it. Erfoud's finest architectural feature is the main gate into the medina, designed in the typical Almohad style with flanking crenellated bastions and an intricately carved stucco portal. Practical-minded travelers will also be interested in the grid of low, dusty red buildings that house banks, shops, and such. Hotels here tend to be large and impersonal, but film buffs will appreciate the fact that they've catered to the cast and crew of blockbusters such as *The Mummy* and *Prince of Persia,* which were shot in the surrounding desert.

The military fortress at Borj-Est, just across the Ziz to the east, provides the best possible view over the date palmery, the desert, and Erfoud from its altitude of 3,067 feet above sea level. Near the Borj-Est are quarries famous for their black marble, one of Erfoud's principal products; this luxurious solid is surprisingly rich in petrified marine fossils.

GETTING HERE AND AROUND

Erfoud sits at the southern end of the Ziz Oasis. From the north, the only way here is the N13 via Er-Rachidia. From Ouarzazate, take the N10 and turn onto the R702 just after the village of Tinejdad. This direct route avoids Er-Rachidia.

Buses to Erfoud depart from Er-Rachidia (1½ hours), Fez (11 hours), Rissani (1½ hours), and Tinerhir (4 hours). From Er-Rachidia you can take buses to Ouarzazate, Marrakesh, Midelt, and Meknès.

Bus Contacts CTM Erfoud ✉ *Complex Commerciale, Av. Mohammed V* ☎ *0535/57–68–86* 🌐 *www.ctm.ma.*

TIMING AND PRECAUTIONS

The biggest annual event is the Erfoud Date Festival, which coincides with the date harvest in October (the exact days vary from year to year). As with all the Moroccan Sahara regions, the best way to avoid excessive heat is to come between February and May or September and November.

EXPLORING

FAMILY **Tahiri Museum of Morocco.** Midway between Erfoud and Rissani, this private museum is hard to miss—just look for the giant replica dinosaurs standing outside. Take a peek inside at the interesting, well-presented collection curated by Moroccan paleontologist Brahim Tahari; it includes fossils, bones, minerals, flints, crystals, and assorted oddities. ■ **TIP→ There's a shop attached if you want to purchase your own bit of prehistory.** ✉ *Km 17, Rte. de Rissani* 🎟 *Free (donations welcome).*

7

WHERE TO EAT

When hunger hits, your best option is to head to one of the hotels listed below. That said, there are a few simple eateries along the main street in the town center.

$$ MOROCCAN 🍴 **Pizzeria-Restaurant des Dunes.** If you're craving pizza, try this tourist-friendly spot just opposite the gas station as you enter Erfoud from the direction of Er-Rachidia. It serves standard pies plus a local variation on the theme called *madfouna tafilalt* (aka "Berber pizza"), which is a baked flat bread stuffed with meat. Tagines and pastillas are also available. Dine in or take a seat on the terrace. [$] *Average main: 80DH* ✉ *Av. Moulay Isamil* ☎ *0535/57–67–93* 🌐 *www.restaurantdesdunes.com* 💳 *No credit cards.*

WHERE TO STAY

$$ HOTEL 🏨 **Hotel Kasbah Tizimi.** This faux 1960s kasbah is popular with package-tour operators, but it's a decent midrange place for independent travelers to stop on the way to or from the desert as well. **Pros:** reasonable prices; nice pool and patio area. **Cons:** filled with tour groups; substandard bathrooms. [$] *Rooms from: 660DH* ✉ *Rte. de Jorf* ☎ *0535/57–61–79* 🌐 *www.kasbahtizimi.com* 🛏 *72 rooms, 6 suites* 🍽 *Breakfast.*

$$$ HOTEL 🏨 **Kasbah Xaluca.** In a desert town that lacks any character-filled boutique accommodations, the rambling Kasbah Xaluca is the best choice available and offers a sense of authenticity combined with luxury facilities. **Pros:** pretty pool area; attentive service; all mod-cons. **Cons:** distance from dunes; full of tour groups. [$] *Rooms from: 990DH*

✉ *Maadid, 5 km (3 miles) north of Erfoud, on road to Er-Rachidia* ☎ *0535/57–84–50* ⊕ *www.xaluca.com* ⇆ *110 rooms, 24 suites, 8 bungalows* ⵏ⊙⵿ *Breakfast.*

SHOPPING

No trip to Erfoud is complete without a visit to one of the many marble and fossil workshops. This section of desert was once a rich seabed filled with many types of marine creatures that no longer exist. Trilobites, urchins, ammonites, and other fossils are abundant in the local stone, and huge slabs are quarried, dissected, polished, and shaped here to create all manner of objects from tabletops to pendants. Most of the workshops give demonstrations as well as exhibit the finished articles.

Fossiles d'Erfoud. This fossil showroom, workshop, and factory has English-speaking owners who are happy to show individuals and groups around the facilities. The showroom has just about every object you might imagine could be made from fossils, and there are plenty of un-"improved" fossils to go around as well. Credit cards are accepted and international shipping can be arranged. ✉ *107, av. Moulay Ismail* ☎ *0535/57–60–20* ⊕ *www.fossilesderfoud.com.*

RISSANI

17 km (11 miles) south of Erfoud, 40 km (25 miles) northwest of Merzouga.

Rissani stands on the site of the ancient city of Sijilmassa, Morocco's first independent southern kingdom, which flourished from the 8th to the 14th century. Founded in 757 by dissident Berbers, who had committed the heresy of translating the Koran to the Berber language (Islamic orthodoxy forbids translation from the Arabic of the direct revelations of God), Sijilmassa prospered from the natural wealth of the Tafilalt oasis and the Tafilalt's key role on the Salt Road to West Africa. But the city was almost completely destroyed by civil strife in 1393; archaeological excavations are now attempting to determine its former size and configuration. All that remains of Sijilmassa today is the excellent 13th-century gate Bab Errih, notable for the green ceramic-tile frieze over its three horseshoe arches.

GETTING HERE AND AROUND

There are two main routes into Rissani, the N12 from Tazzarine (west) or the N13 from Erfoud (north). Buses arrive from Erfoud (1½ hours), Er-Rachidia (3 hours), Meknès (8 hours), Tinejdad (3½ hours), Tinerhir (4 hours), and Zagora (10 hours). Grands taxis run to Erfoud and Merzouga. CTM buses operate from the main square, while other companies use the bus station just outside the arched entrance to the town.

Bus Contacts CTM Rissani ✉ *Rue Hassan II, opposite the Protection Civil building and near the entrance to the market* ☎ *0535/57–50–53* ⊕ *www.ctm.ma.*

TIMING

Rissani hosts a souk on Sunday, Tuesday, and Thursday.

EXPLORING

Modern Rissani is known as the cradle of the Alaouite dynasty, of which King Mohammed VI is the still-reigning sultan. The well-marked Circuit Touristique guides you through the main remnants of the Alaouite presence here. The **Zaouia of Moulay Ali Sherif,** the mausoleum of the dynasty's founder, is 2 km (1 mile) southeast of the center of Rissani. Next to the zaouia is the **Ksar Akbar,** to which rebellious Alaouite family members and the wives of deceased sultans were exiled. Moulay Ismail had two of his sons sent here to put some distance between his heirs and his power base at Meknès. The **Ksar Oualad Abdelhalim,** the largest and most impressive of these Alaouite structures, is 1 km (½ mile) beyond Ksar Akbar; it was built in 1900 for Sultan Moulay el-Hassan's older brother, who had been named governor of Tafilalt. After Ksar Oualad Abdelhalim, loop around past the remaining ksour and climb the high ground at **Tinrheras,** an excellent lookout point over the Tafilalt.

The drive back north from Merzouga through Rissani brings you to the **Tafilalt date palmery.** The presence of a million-plus date palms here seems doubly miraculous after you have seen the desert. The palmery is a phenomenon created by the parallel Ziz and Rheris rivers, which flow within 3 to 5 km (2 to 3 miles) of each other for 26 km (16 miles).

Here's how to navigate Rissani without resorting to outside assistance. On the approach to Rissani from Erfoud is the first of two gates. Just after the first gate, follow the road as it curves left; don't take a right-hand fork for the "Circuit Touristique." You'll quickly reach town, at which point you'll go under a second arch. Ahead are the walls of the kasbah. Turn right so that they are on your left, and follow them until the road ends in a T-junction. Turn left, keep left at the next fork, and you should be on the road that winds through the palmery and leads, eventually, to the dunes.

WHERE TO STAY

$$$
B&B/INN

Kasbah Ennasra. Constructed using traditional materials and designs, the Kasbah Ennasra has a laid-back charm. **Pros:** friendly, English-speaking staff. **Cons:** far from the dunes; pool unheated in winter; rooms are poorly lit. *Rooms from: 825DH ⊠ Ksar Labtarni, rte. de Rissani, 2 km (1 mile) north of Rissani 0535/77–44–03 ⊕ www. ennasra.com ⟳ 13 rooms, 4 suites ⊚ Breakfast.*

MERZOUGA

53 km (33 miles) southeast of Erfoud, 134 km (83 miles) southeast of Er-Rachidia.

Merzouga has an ever-expanding strip of hotels and guesthouses, with options ranging from simple to sublime. The village's main draw, though, is the easy access it offers to Erg Chebbi, where the sand soars as high as 815 feet. A sunrise trip to the dunes has become a classic Moroccan adventure. A series of café-restaurant-hotels overlooks Erg Chebbi, and most run camel excursions to the top as well as to oases where you can spend the night in permanent bivouacs. Some tour operators now offer exclusive and luxurious camps tucked in dunes away from the crowds—picture tents kitted out with woven carpets, antiques, lanterns, four-poster beds, and en suite washing facilities. You can also expect chilled champagne and fine dining by candlelight, but be prepared—paradise doesn't come cheap! ■TIP→ Between Erg Chebbi and the town, have a look at the underground aqueduct, Merzouga's main water supply. It's flowing (oozing) proof that sand dunes form as a result of moisture, which causes the sand to stick and agglomerate.

GETTING HERE AND AROUND
The N13 from Erfoud can now be driven in an ordinary car. Minibuses and grands taxis bring tourists from Rissani and Erfoud.

GUIDES AND TOURS
Once in Merzouga you get around either by foot, camel, or 4x4. If you haven't come on an organized tour, the hotel or guesthouse you choose will be able to make arrangements for you, using their own local guides and bivouac camps.

Adventures with Ali. Ali Mouni, owner of the Nomad Palace hotel, is a reliable and professional local operator; he can organize anything from short camel treks to longer desert safaris and overnight stays at one of the area's nicest standard bivouacs. Private desert events can also be arranged. ⊠ *Nomad Palace, 6 km (4 miles) south of Merzouga on road to Taoz* ☎ *0661/56–36–11* ⊕ *www.adventureswithali.com.*

Omar Berhi Camel Trekking. Omar grew up in the desert south of Merzouga and now lives near the dunes in the village of Hassi Labied. He leads one- to three-night camel treks into the Erg Chebbi dunes, charging around 400 DH per person per night. ⊠ *Hassi Labied* ☎ *0662/34–48–16* ⊕ *www.cameltrekking.com.*

Your Morocco Tour. This U.S.-Moroccan agency can organize tours from Marrakesh or Fez that include a night spent at its luxury bivouac in the dunes of Merzouga. The price (about 1,800 DH per person with dinner, breakfast, drinks, and the camel trek) is built into the cost of a longer tour package. ☎ *0662/34–48–16* ⊕ *www.your-morocco-tour.com.*

TIMING AND PRECAUTIONS
In summer, prepare for the extreme daytime heat by bringing sunglasses, sunblock, and plenty of bottled water. In winter, the nights can be viciously cold, so pack extra layers if camping out. ■TIP→ The fine sand of the Sahara will find its way into everything. Carry zip-top plastic bags for keeping items sand-free, especially electronic equipment and cosmetics.

EXPLORING
Dayet Srji. Near the dunes, this seasonal salt lake is a surprising sight—it's filled in early spring with pink flamingos.

Fodor'sChoice
★
Erg Chebbi. In most cases your hotel is your best bet for an organized tour of Erg Chebbi. Every auberge near the dunes is there because it's a prime jumping-off point for a sunrise or sunset journey, either on foot or by camel. Most auberges have their own permanent bivouac in the dunes, often not far from others but generally fairly well concealed—which lets you pretend no one else is around even if they are. Most bivouac areas are organized into series of small tents for couples and larger groups, so you don't have to share with everyone. If you want to

The magnificent dunes at Erg Chebbi are just outside of Merzouga.

be utterly private, make sure your auberge doesn't share a tented site with any other, or ask to camp in the dunes on your own.

For anything more than camel riding and staying in a desert oasis, such as quad biking, you'll need to go to the right hotel (Tombuctou rents quads) or a local rental agent. Most auberges can get their hands on four-wheel drive, even if they don't always have them onsite.

WHERE TO STAY

Thanks to the recent arrival of reliable electricity and Internet access, the number of lodging options has greatly increased. There are nearly 100 guesthouses and hotels to choose from in the area, but the best are north of Merzouga in the desert village Hassi Labied; these also benefit from being closest to the towering sands. All will be able to arrange a night's stay in a bivouac camp, and you can usually return to the hotel for a shower the morning after.

$$ B&B/INN 🏨 **Kasbah Erg Chebbi.** Appropriately named after the sand dunes everyone is here to see, this typical Saharan option is one of the closest auberges to Erg Chebbi. **Pros:** helpful, English-speaking staff; close to dunes. **Cons:** no air-conditioning or heating. [$] *Rooms from: 600DH* ✉ *2½ km (1½ miles) north of Hassi Labied* ☎ *0670/77–83–15* 🌐 *www.kasbahergchebbi.com* 🛏 *22 rooms, 4 suites* 💳 *No credit cards* 🍴 *Some meals.*

$$ B&B/INN 🏨 **Kasbah Mohayut.** A mud-built auberge in the Saharan tradition, Kasbah Mohayut has comfortable, air-conditioned rooms that are decorated in the local style (think tiled floors, date-palm ceiling, wrought-iron beds, and colorful rugs); there are also spacious family suites with huge king-size beds, a salon, and a private terrace looking out to the dunes. **Pros:** right beside the dunes; pretty pool. **Cons:** this part of dunes is

often busy with other tourists. ⓢ *Rooms from: 600DH* ✉ *1½ km (1 mile) south of Hassi Labied* ☎ *0666/03–91–85* ⊕ *www.hotelmohayut. com* 🛏 *20 rooms, 6 suites* ⑪ *Some meals.*

$$$$
HOTEL
FAMILY

🏨 **Kasbah Tombuctou.** Another of the Xaluca luxury hotels, this rather ostentatious faux kasbah rises from the sand like a mirage; crenulated turrets and inner corridors lead to attractive, air-conditioned rooms with huge en suite bathrooms finished in colored tadelakt. **Pros:** magnificent view of the dunes; luxurious lodgings; Wi-Fi throughout. **Cons:** lights in rooms are very dim. ⓢ *Rooms from: 1118DH* ✉ *1½ km (1 mile) south of Hassi Labied, Hassi Labied* ☎ *0535/57–70–91* ⊕ *www. xaluca.com* 🛏 *72 rooms, 5 suites* ⑪ *Some meals.*

$$
B&B/INN

🏨 **Ksar Sania Eco-Lodge.** At the edge of the Sahara, this unique French-owned eco-lodge lets guests bed down in handsome, hexagonal bungalows that are built from straw-covered mud; the rooms are very spacious and stylish, with tasteful furnishings, rich colors, and traditional ceilings. **Pros:** highly original concept; environmentally friendly. **Cons:** service can be slack. ⓢ *Rooms from: 600DH* ✉ *2 km (1 mile) south of Merzouga* ☎ *0535/57–74–14* ⊕ *www.auberge-ksarsania-merzouga. com* 🛏 *14 rooms, 1 suite, 5 huts* ▭ *No credit cards* ⊘ *Closed during Ramadan when it falls in summer* ⑪ *Some meals.*

$$
B&B/INN

🏨 **Nomad Palace.** Ali Mouni's clean, comfortable auberge has an excellent location at southern end of Erg Chebbi, far from other lodgings. **Pros:** full range of desert and mountain activities available; great facilities; removed from the crowds. **Cons:** food is unimaginative; Wi-Fi is intermittent. ⓢ *Rooms from: 700DH* ✉ *6 km (4 miles) south of Merzouga on road to Taoz* ☎ *0535/88–20–89* ⊕ *www.hotelnomadpalace. com* 🛏 *31 rooms, 4 suites* ▭ *No credit cards* ⑪ *Some meals.*

$$$
B&B/INN

🏨 **Riad Madu.** Opened in 2013 by the Annam brothers from Merzouga, Riad Madu is a cut above the other Saharan inns dotting the edge of the Erg Chebbi dunes. **Pros:** shiny and new; enthusiastic staff; half-board meal plan available. **Cons:** other desert hotels nearby; some problems with air-conditioning. ⓢ *Rooms from: 870DH* ✉ *Hassi Labied, 5 km (3 miles) north of Merzouga* ☎ *0535/57–87–40* ⊕ *www.riadmadu.com* 🛏 *8 rooms, 4 suites* ▭ *No credit cards* ⑪ *Breakfast.*

$$
B&B/INN

🏨 **Sahara Garden Kasbah & Bivouac.** Situated far from the madding crowd at the northern tip of Erg Chebbi, Sahara Garden has 10 perfectly comfortable guest rooms in the main building—but the adjacent eco-oriented bivouac is a bigger draw. **Pros:** stunning location; deluxe camping. **Cons:** difficult to find. ⓢ *Rooms from: 500DH* ✉ *Hassi Labied, 17 km (10½ miles) north of Merzouga* ✣ *Follow the signs to Hotel Yasmina* ☎ *0670/18–13–94* ⊕ *www.sahara-garden.com* 🛏 *10 rooms, 6 deluxe tents, 30 standard tents* ⑪ *Some meals.*

SPORTS AND THE OUTDOORS

Les Petales de Merzouga. Bikes and four-wheel-drive vehicles can be rented through Les Petales de Merzouga. Camel treks can also be arranged. ☎ *0618/76–79–90* ⊕ *www.quadmaroc.net.*

DJEBEL SARHRO AND NEKOB

95 km (59 miles) east of Agdz, 165 km (103 miles) southwest of Rissani.

If you pick the southern oasis route, don't miss the chance to stay in Nekob, Morocco's most kasbah-filled village. Locals have come up with all sorts of reasons for why there are 45 of them. The amusing and believable theory is that members of a rich extended family settled here in the 18th and 19th centuries and quickly set to work trying to out-build and out-impress each other. There's little in the way of showing off in the village today. The children are wild and the place a little untouched for the moment.

Visitors can pick up handcrafted carpets and head scarves made by local women at the weekly Sunday souk, or simply sit back, stare over the palmery, and savor the experience. If you're looking for a more active alternative, the trekking potential north of town stretches as far as Boumalne du Dadès, 150 km (93 miles) away and on the northern oasis route. It's a five-day hike to Tagdift or Iknioun.

GETTING HERE AND AROUND

Nekob lies on the southern oasis route between Agdz and Rissani, skirting the southern slopes of the Djebel Sarhro. Minibuses and grands taxis travel here from Rissani, Zagora, and Ouarzazate.

Exploring the mountain ranges and peaks of Djebel Sarhro requires a four-wheel-drive vehicle.

Contacts Bureau des Guides. An official Bureau des Guides, run by Mohamed YaaQoub, can organize hiking trips in the Djebel Sarhro for an afternoon or several days. ✉ *Town center* ☎ *0667/48–75–09* ⊕ *www.moroccotrek.net.*

EXPLORING

Djebel Sarhro Massif. The wonderfully panoramic oasis Route 6956/R108 (which becomes 3454/N12 after Tazzarine) still appears as a desert piste on some Moroccan road maps, but it has been paved. Indeed, it's one of the safest, fastest, least crowded roads in Morocco, and it offers unparalleled views up into the Djebel Sarhro Massif and all the way over to the Tafilalt date palmery. Count on four hours for the 233-km (140-mile) trip from Route P31/N9 (the Ouarzazate–Zagora road) to Rissani, in the date palmery.

NEED A BREAK?

Auberge Kasbah Meteorites. Morocco is a magnet for fossil fans, and much of the activity centers around the town of Alnif, on Route 3454/N12 between Rissani and Tazzarine. About 13 km (8 miles) west of Alnif is Auberge Kasbah Meteorites where you can enjoy a simple lunch, a dip in the immaculate pool, and a two- to three-hour excursion with a guide who'll show you the best place to hunt for fossils and ancient stone carvings. There are also 30 bright, clean bedrooms should you decide to stay over so you can explore the region in greater detail. ✉ *Ksar Tiguima, 13 km (8 miles) west of Alnif* ☎ *0535/78–38–09* ⊕ *www.kasbahmeteorites.com.*

7

WHERE TO STAY

$$ B&B/INN **Auberge Ennakhile Saghro.** This charming auberge has an entrancing view of the palmery below and offers either budget rooms with either shared or private en-suite bathrooms in the "kasbah" wing; the latter have ingenious fittings where the shower base is made from a couscous pan and the water flows from a honey jar. **Pros:** sublime views; plenty of activities; swimming pool. **Cons:** only nine rooms have private bathrooms. [$] *Rooms from: 580DH* ✉ *N'kob, at Erfoud end of town* ☎ *0524/83–97–19, 0672/64–15–11* 🌐 *www.kasbah-nkob.com* 🛏 *15 rooms* 💳 *No credit cards* 🍴 *Some meals.*

$$$ B&B/INN **Baha Baha.** At the edge of the village, the wooden gates of Kasbah Baha Baha open into a huge garden with a shimmering pool and the truest rendition of a traditional kasbah that you're likely to find. **Pros:** restored kasbah full of traditional style; grounds have emerald lawns and kitchen gardens. **Cons:** older rooms have no bathroom or air-conditioning; stairways are narrow and steep. [$] *Rooms from: 750DH* ✉ *Village de N'Kob* ✥ *Follow signs to right from main road if heading west* ☎ *0524/83–97–63* 🌐 *www.kasbahabahaha.com* 🛏 *11 rooms, 4 suites* 💳 *No credit cards.*

$$$ B&B/INN FAMILY **Kasbah Hotel Aït Omar.** The premier address in the village of Nekob, this old family kasbah has been lovingly restored to high specifications by a German couple who fell in love with it, the village, and the local Berber people. **Pros:** very comfortable; great service; environmentally friendly ethic. **Cons:** awkward, steep stairways. [$] *Rooms from: 990DH* ✉ *Village N'Kob* ☎ *0524/83–99–81* 🌐 *www.hotel-aitomar.de* 🛏 *4 rooms, 10 suites/apartments* 💳 *No credit cards* ⏲ *Closed July and Aug.* 🍴 *Breakfast.*

$$$ B&B/INN **Kasbah Imdoukal.** This gorgeous Moroccan-owned kasbah sits in the heart of the village. **Pros:** in the center of Nekob; plenty of atmosphere. **Cons:** prices are a bit high. [$] *Rooms from: 770DH* ✉ *Village N'Kob* ☎ *0524/83–97–98* 🌐 *www.kasbahimdoukal.com* 🛏 *18 rooms, 2 suites* 💳 *No credit cards* 🍴 *Breakfast.*

THE DRÂA VALLEY

Morocco's longest river, the Drâa once flowed all the way to the Atlantic Ocean just north of Tan-Tan, some 960 km (597 miles) from its source above Ouarzazate. With the sole exception of a fluke flood in 1989—the only time in recent memory that the Drâa completed its course—the river disappears in the Sahara southwest of M'Hamid, some 240 km (150 miles) from its headwaters. The Drâa Valley and its palmery continue nearly unbroken from Agdz through Zagora to M'Hamid, forming one of Morocco's most memorable tours.

As wild as you may have found certain parts of Morocco thus far, the trip down to the Sahara will seem more so, something like steady progress into a biblical epic. The plains south of Ouarzazate give way to 120 km (75 miles) of date palmeries and oases along the Drâa River, and between Agdz and Zagora more than two-dozen kasbahs and ksour line both sides. The occasional market town offers a chance to mingle with the diverse peoples you'll see walking along the road in black shawls.

Though most of the inhabitants are in fact Berbers, the Drâa Valley is also home to Arabs, small communities of Jews or the Mellahs they once inhabited, and numerous Haratin (descendants of Sudanese slaves brought into Morocco along the caravan routes that facilitated salt, gold, and slave trading until late in the 19th century).

After Zagora and Tamegroute, the road narrows as the Tinfou Dunes rise to the east and, farther south, a maze of jeep tracks leads out to Erg L'Houdi (Dune of the Jew). Finally, in M'Hamid el Ghizlane (Plain of the Gazelles), with sand drifting across the road and the Drâa long since gone underground, there is a definite sense of closure—the end of the road.

AGDZ

69 km (43 miles) southeast of Ouarzazate.

Agdz, at the junction of the Drâa and Tamsift rivers, marks the beginning of the Drâa palmery. A sleepy market town and administrative center, Agdz (pronounced *ah*-ga-dez) has little to offer at first glance other than the 5,022-foot peak Djebel Kissane and the Kasbah Dar el-Glaoui. But in the palm groves at the edge of town you'll discover some gorgeous boutique hotels; these make an ideal base for a day or two of hiking and exploring. From Agdz south to M'Hamid, the P31/N9 road follows the river closely except for a 30-km (19-mile) section between the Tinfou Dunes and Tagounite.

GETTING HERE AND AROUND

Agdz is served by buses and grands taxis traveling between Ouarzazate and Zagora. The trip takes approximately two hours from either town.

TIMING AND PRECAUTIONS

A great time to visit is in October when the date harvest is in full swing. The market is stacked with boxes of the most delicious and succulent varieties. ■TIP→ **Schistosomiasis, a parasite, has been reported in the Drâa River, so don't be tempted to swim or even wade across.**

EXPLORING

Kasbah Timidarte. Eight km (5 miles) south of Tamnougalt on the P31/N9 road, Kasbah Timidarte was built in the 17th century by the local population. Recently restored, it now operates as rustic little guest house with rooms from 300 DH. ■TIP→ **For an informed guide to the history of the region and the kasbahs, contact Hussein Achabak, who leads this eco-tourism initiative.** ☎ *0668/68–00–47 for Hussein Achabak* ⊕ *www. kasbahtimidarte.com.*

Ksar Igdâoun. The truncated pyramidal towers and bastions of the Ksar Igdâoun are visible 15 km (9 miles) past the turnoff onto Route 6956/R108 to Tazzarine. There used to be three gates to the ksar: one for Jews, one for other people who lived nearby, and one for the local governor. ☞ *10 DH.*

Tamnougalt. Lining virtually the entire Drâa Valley from Agdz to Zagora are some two dozen ksour and kasbahs on both sides of the river. Perhaps the most amazing ksour in this region are at Tamnougalt, 6 km (4 miles) south of Agdz—the second group of red-pisé fortifications on the left. The resident Berber tribe, the Mezguita, governed its own independent republic from here until the late 18th century; the crenellated battlements and bastions were a necessary defense against desert nomads. For a deeper understanding of the tribe's traditional way of life, peruse the displays of farming and household implements in Tamnougalt's Kasbah des Caids du Mezguita museum. Occupying a restored 16th-century edifice, it is run Hassan Aït el Caid (a descendant of the original caids, who controlled the trade caravans passing through the region). Hassan can also take you on a walking tour through the village and the oasis, and explain the local Berber tribes and their origins en route. Donkey treks and picnic can be arranged as well. 🌐 *www.kasbah-des-caids.com* 🎫 *Museum 20 DH.*

OFF THE BEATEN PATH

Cascades du Drâa. Look for the turnoff to the Cascades du Drâa (also known as the Cascades de Tizgui) on the left, 30 km (19 miles) south of Ouarzazate and 10 km (6 miles) before Agdz. ■TIP→ **The 10-km (6-mile) track down to the waterfalls is steep but paved and best traversed in a 4x4.** Over thousands of years, the water has carved out natural pools that are ideal for a refreshing dip. Prolonged drought in the region has reduced the falls' dramatic impact; however, with palm trees, figs, and oleander flowers springing from the rocks, they are still worth a detour in autumn or spring.

WHERE TO EAT

If you're passing though at lunchtime, the town has a slim selection of cafés; alternately you can continue on to Chez Yacob *(see below)*, located south towards Zagora in the village of Tamnougalt.

$ MOROCCAN FAMILY

🍴 **Agdz Café Restaurant.** Located at the edge of town as you arrive from the direction of Ouarzazate, this terrace café with easy parking outside is a good place to stop for lunch or a beverage break. It serves tagines, brochettes, salads, and other snacks; the clean bathrooms are an added bonus. [$] *Average main: 60DH* ☎ *0524/84–38–00* 💳 *No credit cards.*

WHERE TO STAY

$$$ B&B/INN

🏨 **Bab el Oued.** Six freestanding rooms await guests at this handsome ecolodge. **Pros:** beautiful location; environmentally sensitive. **Cons:** food quality inconsistent; rooms are dark and poorly lighted. [$] *Rooms from: 825DH* ✉ *Tamnougalte* ☎ *0540/06–66–04* 🌐 *www.babelouedmaroc.com* 🛏 *2 rooms, 4 suites* 💳 *No credit cards* 🍽 *Breakfast.*

$$ B&B/INN

🏨 **Chez Yacob.** Wander through the heavy wooden door into this renovated kasbah at midday, and its tiny central courtyard will be packed to the rafters with lunching tour groups—a big thumb's-up for the kitchen, with the added bonus that you can bring your own wine and beer. **Pros:** full of charm; great views over palmery. **Cons:** very little parking space; rooms are dark. [$] *Rooms from: 600DH* ✉ *6 km (4 miles) from Agdz on route to Zagora* ☎ *0524/84–33–94* 🌐 *www.lavalleedudraa.com* 🛏 *8 rooms, 1 suite* 💳 *No credit cards* 🍽 *Some meals.*

$$$ B&B/INN

🏨 **Dar Qamar.** Nestled among the crumbling old kasbahs and palm groves of the Drâa Valley, this French-run boutique guesthouse has rooms that range from small doubles to spacious suites with four-poster beds; the cheaper choices are rather cramped, but all have air-conditioning, en-suite bathrooms with tadelakt polished-plaster finishes, and good hot showers. **Pros:** charming location; great hosts; Wi-Fi. **Cons:** not much English spoken. $ *Rooms from: 770DH* ⊠ *Douar Asslim* ☎ *0524/84–37–84* ⊕ *www.darqamar.com* ↩ *5 room, 2 suites* ⑩ *Breakfast.*

$$$
B&B/INN
FAMILY
Fodor's Choice
★

🏨 **Kasbah Azul.** The aptly named "House of Peace" is tucked away in the palm groves outside Agdz. **Pros:** beautiful setting; great for kids **Cons:** expensive; books up quickly. $ *Rooms from: 940DH* ⊠ *Douar Asslim, 2.5 km (1 mile) north of Agdz* ☎ *0524/84–39–31* ⊕ *www. kasbahazul.com* ↩ *4 rooms, 3 suites* ⊗ *Closed during Ramadan (call ahead)* ⑩ *Breakfast.*

TINZOULINE

59 km (37 miles) southeast of Agdz, 130 km (81 miles) southeast of Ouarzazate.

Tinzouline holds an important weekly souk. If you're here on a Monday, take this opportunity to shop and make contact with the many peoples of this southern Moroccan region where Berber, Arab, Jewish, and Haratin communities have coexisted for centuries. The Tinzouline ksour are clustered around a majestic kasbah in the middle of an oasis that includes several villages. Tinzouline is also one of the most important prehistoric sites in pre-Saharan North Africa: from the ksour a 7-km (4½-mile) gravel path leads west of town to cave engravings depicting mounted hunters. These drawings are attributed to Iron Age Libyo-Berbers, lending further substance to the theory that Morocco's first inhabitants, the Berbers, may have originally come from Central Asia via central and eastern Africa.

ZAGORA

95 km (59 miles) southeast of Agdz, 170 km (106 miles) southeast of Ouarzazate.

Zagora is—and does feel like—the boundary between the Sahara and what some writers and travelers have referred to as "reality." After Zagora, time and distance are measured in camel days: a famous painted sign at the end of town (near the impressive new Zagora Province offices) features a camel and reads, "Tombouctu 52 Days"—that is, "52 days by camel." M'Hamid, 97 km (60 miles) farther south, marks the actual end of the paved road and the beginning of the open desert, but Zagora is where the sensation of being in the desert kicks in.

On your way out of town, heading across the bridge signposted toward M'Hamid, you'll find the town of Amezrou and in it, the fascinating **Kasbah des Juifs** (Kasbah of the Jews).

GETTING HERE AND AROUND

Zagora is easily reached by the main road from M'Hamid and Ouarzazate. Buses and grands taxis navigate this route. The town's CTM bus station is on the main street, which has been upgraded, widened, and embellished with fountains to trumpet its status as provincial capital. Zagora itself is easy to explore on foot or by inexpensive petit taxi.

Numerous local tour agencies offer camel trips, oasis treks, and desert camping.

Bus Contacts CTM Zagora ⊠ 37, bd. Mohammed V ☎ 0524/84–73–27 ⊕ www. ctm.ma.

GUIDES AND TOURS

Caravane du Sud. This family-run agency specializes in the desert regions and villages around Zagora. Local guides with an eco-tourism ethos lead 4x4 and camel tours. ☎ 0524/84–75–69, 0661/87–68–74 ⊕ www. caravanesud.com.

Tombouctour. Long-established Tombouctour organizes tours throughout Morocco; the local office in Zagora will set up overnight excursions or desert safaris for travelers turning up at its door. ⊠ 79, av. Mohammed V ☎ 0524/84–82–07 ⊕ www.tombouctour.com.

EXPLORING

Amezrou. Three km (2 miles) south of Zagora, Amezrou is famous for its Jewish silversmiths, who made decorative jewelry in this small village until the creation of the Israeli State in 1948, when all but 30,000 of Morocco's 300,000 Jews left for Israel. Berber craftsmen continue the tradition in the Mellah here. It's an interesting stop if you don't mind the clamor of children eager to be hired as your guide.

Djebel Zagora. The town's promontory, capped by an 11th-century Almoravid fortress, is an excellent sunset vantage point—it overlooks the Drâa palmery with the distant Djebel Sarhro Massif to the north and the Tinfou Dunes to the south. Djebel Zagora is reached via the first left turn south of the Kasbah Asmaa hotel; there's also a twisting footpath up the 3,195-foot mountain from the hotel itself.

Ksar Tissergate Museum. Deep within the evocative alleys of the Ksar Tissergate—a 17th-century fortified village—this fascinating museum displays local costumes, agricultural implements, domestic utensils, jewelry, and other artifacts. Unlike most museums in southern Morocco, exhibits here have explanations in English. ⊠ Next to Kasbah Ziwana, 8 km (5 miles) from Zagora on the road to Ouarzazate ☎ 20 DH.

WHERE TO EAT

$ ✕ **Le Dromadaire Gourmand.** Having hung up his *sheshe* (turban) after
MOROCCAN   years of guiding tourists through the desert, Mustapha el-Mekki has established what has rapidly become one of the most popular eateries in Zagora. Little by little the restaurant was built and today serves regional specialties such as *tagine de mariage* (a slow-cooked casserole of beef with apricots, prunes, and almonds) and a Drâa Valley vegetable soup. There's a sidewalk terrace café and spacious, cool interior with Berber motifs carved into the walls. You can bring your own wine or beer. $ Average main: 70DH ⊠ Av. Mohammed V, near TOTAL gas station ☎ 0661/34–83–94 ⊕ www.dromadaire-gourmand.com ▭ No credit cards.

Zagora is the last major town before the Sahara really begins at M'Hamid.

WHERE TO STAY

$$$$
B&B/INN
Fodor's Choice
★

🏠 **Azalai Desert Lodge.** Hidden within the Drâa Valley oasis, the Azalai Desert Lodge is a luxurious Moroccan-owned retreat with secluded gardens, creative cuisine, and an interior that has been featured in several prestigious design magazines. **Pros:** luxury at the edge of the desert; beautiful décor. **Cons:** no Wi-Fi; remote location. $ *Rooms from: 1450DH* ⊠ *Tissergate, 7 km (4 miles) north of Zagora* ⊕ *www. azalaidesertlodge.com* 🛏 *6 rooms, 2 suites* ⊟ *No credit cards* ⊗ *Closed July and Aug.* ⋈ *Some meals.*

$
B&B/INN

🏠 **Dar Raha.** You'll get an authentic village experience (at minimal cost) by staying in this restored family home in the heart of Amezrou, just outside Zagora. **Pros:** feels like living with the locals; thoughtful touches include djellabas and slippers for guests; Wi-Fi throughout. **Cons:** shared bathrooms. $ *Rooms from: 400DH* ⊠ *Rue el-Ghzaoui, Amezrou, 2 km (1 mile) southeast of Zagora on road to M'Hamid* 📞 *0524/84–69–93* ⊕ *www.darraha.com* 🛏 *9 rooms* ⊗ *Closed July and Aug.* ⋈ *Breakfast.*

$$
B&B/INN
FAMILY

🏠 **Kasbah Sirocco.** A popular pit-stop on the way to the desert, Kasbah Sirocco has clean, functional rooms; all have air-conditioning, and most have views of the relaxed pool terrace. **Pros:** great pool; full range of services. **Cons:** can be noisy. $ *Rooms from: 660DH* ⊠ *Amezrou, 2 km (1 mile) southeast of Zagora on road to M'Hamid* 📞 *0524/84–61–25* 🛏 *20 rooms* ⋈ *Breakfast.*

$$
B&B/INN

🏠 **Kasbah Ziwana.** If you're fed up with faux kasbahs, then here's the real deal. **Pros:** comfortable rooms in an genuine kasbah; modern bathrooms. **Cons:** lack of natural light; few amenities. $ *Rooms from: 660DH* ⊠ *Ksar Tissergate, 8 km (5 miles) from Zagora on the road* *to Ouarzazate* ☎ *0524/84–70-61* ⊕ *www.kasbah-ziwana-zagora.com* ⇥ *13 rooms* ▭ *No credit cards* †⊙† *Some meals.*

$$
HOTEL
▦ **Palais Asmaa.** An impressive red carpet leads into this long-established "palace" hotel, which caters largely to tour groups. **Pros:** good range of facilities; reasonably priced; attractive pool. **Cons:** full of tour groups; rooms could stand a makeover; no elevator. $ *Rooms from: 600DH* ✉ *Rte. de M'Hamid* ☎ *0524/84–75–91* ⊕ *www.asmaa-zagora.com* ⇥ *75 rooms, 5 suites* †⊙† *Breakfast.*

$$$
B&B/INN
▦ **Riad Dar Sofian.** Originally built as a family home, this rambling three-story riad is full of over-the-top Moroccan décor, with stucco plasterwork, colorful mosaic tiling, ornate ceilings, and antique furnishings competing for attention. **Pros:** lots of creature comforts; Wi-Fi; lovely pool. **Cons:** mismatched decor; no elevator. $ *Rooms from: 880DH* ✉ *Amazraou* ☎ *0524/84–73–19* ⊕ *www.riaddarsofian.com* ⇥ *10 rooms* †⊙† *Breakfast.*

$$$$
B&B/INN
▦ **Riad Lamane.** Gorgeous gardens and chic design in an oasis setting ensure this place stays popular year after year. **Pros:** the shaded gardens and pool are a paradise. **Cons:** service can be sluggish and food mediocre; busy with tour groups at lunch; poor Wi-Fi connection. $ *Rooms from: 1200DH* ✉ *Amezrou, at end of town towards M'Hamid* ☎ *0524/84–83–88* ⊕ *www.riadlamane.com* ⇥ *7 rooms, 1 suite, 7 bungalows, 5 tents* †⊙† *Some meals.*

TAMEGROUTE

18 km (11 miles) southeast of Zagora.

Tamegroute (literally "the last town before the border," an accurate toponym when the Algerian border was closer than it is now) is the home of the **Zaouia of Sidi Mohammed Ben Naceur,** a sanctuary devoted to this extraordinary *marabout* (sage). Closed to non-Muslims, the sanctuary itself can be admired from the outside—the door bears an intricately decorated archway of carved cedar and stucco. The surrounding courtyard is perennially filled with dozens of psychiatric patients hoping for miraculous cures or just for charity from the Naciri brotherhood. Outside to the left, the old subterranean slave quarters of the "underground kasbah" are still inhabited by descendants of Sudanese slaves.

GETTING HERE AND AROUND
M'Hamid-bound buses from Zagora stop at Tamegroute, but they arrive in the evening. For a day trip, it is best to hire a grand taxi or drive yourself.

TIMING
A visit to Tamegroute will take no more than two hours.

EXPLORING
Ceramics Cooperative. Don't miss Tamegroute's ceramics cooperative at the south end of the library, medersa, and slave quarters. The characteristic rough, green-glazed pottery sold here is all handmade. Other brightly colored and patterned objects are invariably from other regions and may have been mass-produced. ■TIP➔ **Check the underside of items to see the markings that identify their true origins.**

KSOUR AND KASBAHS

Ksour (plural for *ksar*) are fortified villages with many homes lining narrow alleys, whereas kasbahs are fortified castles belonging to a single family and often contain their own granary, or agadir. Moroccan ksour and kasbahs are all built of *pisé*, a sun-dried mixture of mud and clay. The Erfoud–Ouarzazate road through the Dadès Valley is billed as the "Route of the Thousand Kasbahs," with village after village of fortified pisé structures, many decorated with carved and painted geometrical patterns (the more intricate the motif, the wealthier the owner). The Drâa Valley is also rimmed with kasbahs and ksour for the length of the Agdz–Zagora road. Highlights of the Dadès route are the Kasbah Amerhidil, at the Skoura oasis, and the Aït Ben Haddou kasbahs, near Ouarzazate; showstoppers in the Drâa Valley include the 16th-century ksour at Tamnougalt, just south of Agdz, and the 17th-century Ksar Tissergate, just north of Zagora—both now feature interesting museums. Increasingly, these historic structures are being restored and converted into guesthouses. Fitting one out with modern amenities while maintaining its architectural integrity is no easy task for owners, but staying in one that achieves the perfect balance is an unforgettable experience for guests.

Fodor'sChoice ★ **Medersa.** Just north of the Zaouia of Sidi Mohammed Ben Naceur is a 17th-century medersa that still lodges 400 students preparing for university studies. The accompanying Koranic library once held the largest such collection in Morocco, with 40,000 volumes on everything from mathematics, philosophy, medicine, and astronomy to linguistics and Berber poetry. The remaining tomes are plenty impressive: a genealogy of the prophet Mohammed, manuscripts adorned with goldleaf, a medical book with afflictions written in red and remedies in black, and hand-illuminated manuscripts penned in mint (green), saffron (yellow), and henna (red) on gazelle hide. Ask for a look at the 13th-century algebra primer with Western Arabic numerals, which, though subsequently abandoned in the Arab world, provided the basis for Western numbers. There is no official admission charge, but a small donation is expected (20 DH).

M'HAMID

68 km (42 miles) south of Tinfou, 97 km (60 miles) south of Zagora, 260 km (161 miles) southeast of Ouarzazate, 395 km (245 miles) southwest of Rissani.

Properly known as M'Hamid el-Ghizlane, or Plain of the Gazelles, M'Hamid neatly marks the end of Morocco's Great Oasis Valleys and the end of the asphalt road. It was once an outpost for the camel corps of the French Foreign Legion, and a large military barracks reminds visitors that the Algerian border is not far away. Looking at modern M'Hamid—a one-street village with overeager tour companies hustling for business—you may wonder what's worth defending, but consider the obvious upside. The Sahara awaits at the end of the main street, making this a vital departure point for desert forays, most notably to Morocco's highest dunes at Erg Chigaga, 50 km (31 miles) west.

In the palm groves just before M'Hamid, the outlying villages of Ouled Driss and Bounou have interesting kasbahs that can be visited. A short hop across the dried river bed of the Drâa, next to M'Hamid's mosque, takes you toward the site of the original village, some 2 km (1 mile) away, where a 17th-century Jewish-built kasbah is still inhabited by the local Haratin population.

The sand drifting like snow across the road (despite the placement of palm-frond sand breaks and fences), the immensity of the horizon, plus the patient gait of camels combine to produce a palpable change in the sense of time and space at this final Drâa oasis. The ocean of dunes 7 km (4½ miles) beyond M'Hamid will satisfy any craving for some real Saharan scenery.

GETTING HERE AND AROUND
M'Hamid is the last village before the pavement ends. Buses arrive here twice daily from Marrakesh via Zagora and Ouarzazate. Grands taxis and minibuses also make the journey to and from Zagora.

GUIDES AND TOURS
Arriving in M'Hamid without having already reserved accommodations or excursions can be intimidating due to fiercely competing touts. That said, there are several local agencies to choose from if you want to trek or take a 4x4 expedition deeper into the dunes and surrounding desert.

Bivouac Sous Les Étoiles. The excursion menu of this French-Moroccan agency includes a day trip by donkey cart through nearby oases and villages, with a break for lunch in a traditional family home (400 DH per person). Overnight camel treks and 4x4 tours are available, too. ⊠ *Village center* ☎ *0524/84–61–75* ⊕ *www.bivouacsouslesetoiles.org.*

Caravan of Dreams. Run by Ali Laghfiri, who grew up in the village of M'Hamid, this German-Moroccan outfit offers camel treks and 4x4 excursions to a picturesque camp in the Erg Lehoudi dunes. Cooking and drumming lessons at the camp can also be arranged. ⊠ *Village center* ☎ *0670/02–00–33* ⊕ *www.caravane-de-reve.com.*

Nomadic Life. Khalifa Mharzi is a qualified, English-speaking desert guide who specializes in cross-country bike rides. He can also set up camel treks and bivouacs. ⊠ *Village Center* ☎ *0662/84–26–76* ⊕ *www.nomadiclife.info.*

Sahara Services. This full-service travel agency offers camel treks to the nearby dunes of Erg Lehoudi and 4x4 trips to a luxury bivouac in Erg Chigaga from its office in M'Hamid. ⊠ *Village Center* ☎ *0661/77–67–66* ⊕ *www.saharaservices.info.*

Zbar Travel. The local office of Zbar Travel serves as a launchpad for sand-boarding adventures, camel treks, and 4x4 outings. The agency also has a very comfortable bivouac camp in the dunes of Erg Chigaga. ⊠ *Main St., on right as you enter village* ☎ *0668/51–72–80* ⊕ *www.zbartravel.com.*

TIMING AND PRECAUTIONS

M'Hamid has a Monday souk that's famous for the occasional appearance of nomadic, trans-Saharan traders of the Reguibat tribe. Much chronicled by writer Paul Bowles, these ebony-skinned fellows habitually wear the indigo sheish, a linen cloth wrapped around the head and face for protection from the elements. The dye from the fabric runs, tingeing the men's faces blue and leading to their nickname, the "Blue Men." Don't expect too much in the way of merchandise, though; the souk has lost much of its appeal in recent years. Noteworthy annual events include the International Nomads Festival, staged in mid-March to promote understanding of the nomadic traditions of the Moroccan Sahara; and a world music festival called Taragalte, which takes place in the nearby dunes in November. ■TIP→ **Many hotels and desert camps close during July and August due to the unbearable heat.**

EXPLORING

Fodor's Choice ★

Erg Chigaga. The splendid Erg Chigaga dunes are the principal reason why visitors make the trek south to M'Hamid. Wild, remote, and largely unspoiled, they're only accessible by heading west out of the village on 50 km (31 miles) of dusty and stony pistes. The journey takes three hours in a 4x4 vehicle or three days on a camel, though hurried jet-setters bound for Erg Chigaga's luxury bivouac camps sometimes come by helicopter direct from Marrakesh. Morocco's highest dunes, rising almost 1,000 feet, are approached by crossing smaller dunes, *hammada* (rocky Martian-like terrain), and flat expanses which are sometimes flooded in winter. A few nomadic families still live in the region, herding their camels and goats through the pasture which can be surprisingly lush. ⊠ *50 km (31 miles) west of M'Hamid.*

Ksebt el-Allouj. The ruins of the ksar Ksebt el-Allouj, dating from the Saadian dynasty, lie across the Drâa riverbed on the other side from the village from M'Hamid, about 2 kms (1 mile) from the town center. The ksar is uninhabited and is interesting to poke around in.

OFF THE
BEATEN
PATH

Erg L'Houdi (*Dune of the Jew*). Between the sand dunes at Tinfou and the village of M'Hamid lies more dramatic scenery. The first pass through the Djebel Bani is the Anagam, after which the road leaves this dry steppe and enters a lush palmery. Note that as you approach the Algerian border, just 50 km (31 miles away), you might be asked for your passport by police controls at Tagounite—a routine check of no consequence. After Tagounite, a second pass (noticeable by the ridge that looks like a tagine!) is called Tizi-Beni-Selmane. From here the road descends to the turnoff for Erg L'Houdi (The Dune of the Jews), a favorite spot for bivouacs. Dozens of sets of four-wheel-drive tracks mark the way to the dune, some 5 km (3 miles) from the P31/N9. ■TIP→ **The route is not suitable for standard cars. From M'Hamid, the trip to the dunes takes around two hours on the back of a camel.**

WHERE TO STAY

$$$

HOTEL
FAMILY

▥ **Chez le Pacha.** One of a string of kasbah-style hotels in palm groves as you approach M'Hamid, Chez le Pacha is a well-run establishment that offers a lot at a reasonable price. **Pros:** stylish accommodations; helpful staff. **Cons:** the half-board plan is compulsory. Ⓢ *Rooms from: 1000DH*

✉ Bounou, 5 km (3 miles) north of M'Hamid ☎ 0524/84–86–96 🌐 www.chezlepacha.com 🛏 12 rooms, 4 suites, 10 huts 🍴 Some meals.

$$$ B&B/INN 🏨 **Dar Azawad.** Having changed hands, this boutique guesthouse doesn't deliver the exceptional service of yesteryear; however, it can still be relied on to provide comfortable, stylish lodgings in an oasis setting. **Pros:** lovely suites loaded with mod-cons; pool heated year-round. **Cons:** service can be sluggish; pushy to sell desert trips. [$] *Rooms from: 770DH ✉ Douar Ouled Driss ☎ 0524/84–87–30 🌐 www.darazawad.com 🛏 9 rooms, 4 suites, 8 tent rooms 🕓 Closed July 🍴 Breakfast.*

$$$$ B&B/INN Fodor's Choice ★ 🏨 **Jnan Lilou.** French-run Jnan Lilou feels like a little piece of paradise at the edge of the oasis. **Pros:** pretty location; handsome bungalows; friendly service. **Cons:** very little English spoken. [$] *Rooms from: 1430DH ✉ Ouled Driss ☎ 0671/51–74–77 🌐 www.jnanlilou.com 🛏 3 rooms, 4 suites 💳 No credit cards 🕓 Closed July 🍴 Some meals.*

$$$$ HOTEL 🏨 **Kasbah Azalay.** The only luxurious lodging actually in the village of M'Hamid is this Spanish-owned kasbah hotel at the edge of the palmery. **Pros:** plenty of creature comforts; magnificent pool and spa. **Cons:** lack of communal terraces or salons for socializing; often empty; overpriced. [$] *Rooms from: 1100DH ✉ M'Hamid el-Ghizlane ☎ 0524/84–80–96 🌐 www.azalay.com 🛏 38 rooms, 5 suites 🍴 Breakfast.*

$$ B&B/INN 🏨 **Le Drom' Blanc.** Hidden in the palm groves of Bounou, this guesthouse has simple en-suite rooms set around a central patio, plus nomad-style tents and self-contained pisé bungalows in the garden. **Pros:** secluded location in palm groves; one wheelchair-accessible room. **Cons:** rooms are very dark; not much English spoken. [$] *Rooms from: 580DH ✉ Bounou, 5 km (3 miles) north of M'Hamid ☎ 0524/84–68–52 🌐 www.ledromblanc.com 🛏 4 rooms, 6 tents, 3 bungalows 🍴 Breakfast.*

AGADIR AND
THE SOUTHERN
ATLANTIC COAST

With Essaouira and the Anti-Atlas

WELCOME TO AGADIR AND THE SOUTHERN ATLANTIC COAST

TOP REASONS TO GO

★ **Catch a wave:** The magnificent Atlantic coastline draws hundreds of surfers and other watersports fanatics every year to ride its huge breaks and test their wits against the winds.

★ **Satisfying seafood:** Whether you are haggling down by Essaouira port for your own fish or enjoying the day's catch at an upscale restaurant in Agadir's marina, both cities are a seafood-lover's paradise.

★ **Family fun:** Donkey and camel rides, swimming pools, and ice-cream stalls make Agadir heaven for children, while stylish resort hotels serve up every luxury Mom and Dad could possibly want.

★ **Walking in the Anti-Atlas:** Enjoy the spectacular scenery around Tafraoute and the pretty villages of the Ammeln Valley, without another tourist in sight.

★ **Taroudant:** Explore the authentically Moroccan walled city with its strong crafts tradition, fascinating souks, and some lovely boutique hotels.

1 Agadir. Agadir is essentially a large, regional trading city fronted by Morocco's premier beach resort. Long popular with European sun worshipers and tourists, visitors spend most of their time on the sweeping sandy beach at the south end of which are a number of all-inclusive and five-star resort hotels. You can find some less crowded local beaches to the north and south; the Souss Massa National Park is also nearby.

2 Essaouira. Essaouira is quieter and more emblematically Moroccan than Agadir, though it's becoming more popular, with bus tours coming for the day from Marrakesh or Agadir. The beach stretches for miles in a curving bay, but an almost constant breeze means most visitors are attracted by the car-free medina and the busy port with its fresh-fish restaurants.

3 The Souss Valley and Anti-Atlas. The region around the Anti-Atlas Mountains, comprising Taroudant, Tafraoute, and Tiznit, is relatively undiscovered by tourists, attracting nature lovers, walkers, and climbers instead. It's easily reached from family-friendly Agadir, providing a completely different kind of travel experience.

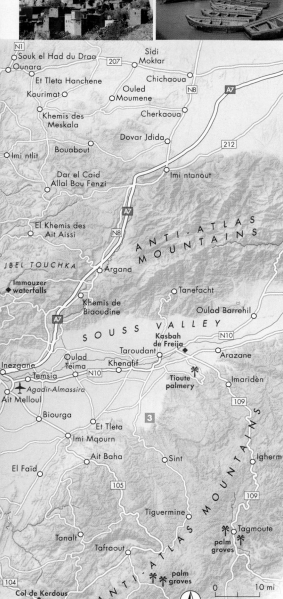

GETTING ORIENTED

Morocco's southern coastal towns might be just a few hours from bustling Marrakesh, but their laid-back vibe makes you feel you're a world away. Moroccans and Europeans flock to this region in summer for the sea breeze, the sandy beaches, the luxurious resorts, or the numerous festivals that ensure that there's always music in the air. This is also *argan* country: otherwise known as "Morocco gold," this tree's oil is changing the economic prospects of local women and the beauty regimes of women across the world.

8

THUYA: BURIED TREASURE OF THE ATLAS

Coveted since Roman times, Morocco's rare and beautiful thuya wood is particular to the western foothills of the Atlas Mountains. In modern times, this material remains synonymous with wealth, being the first burled wood used for luxury dashboards in the Rolls-Royce.

(above) Thuya wood boxes may be carved and polished or inlaid. (opposite page, bottom) A carved thuya wood cup (opposite page, top) The seed cones of the thuya tree, a relative of the cedar

At first glance, the thuya tree, a rather unassuming Atlas conifer, is underwhelming. The tree's foliage is rather scrubby while its trunk has unknotted, bland wood. However, the roots hold a treasure trove of beauty—this is from where thuya wood's natural burled grain and complex markings come. For the Berbers of the Middle Atlas, the thuya industry is a vital aspect of the local economy. Fathers hand down the skills necessary to select, harvest, and work the wood. Theirs is the delicate job of measuring and cutting the root pieces into a variety of shapes and sizes. So precious is it—and so brittle—that any slip of the hand spells catastrophe.

SPOTTING REAL THUYA WOOD

Genuine thuya is a reddish brown color and has myriad darker, knotty whorls, closely resembling burr walnut and bird's-eye maple. Beware of traders offering larger pieces such as dining tables and storage chests, which may not be genuine. Carved pieces (other than antiques) tend to be small. The most popular items found in souks and stores are boxes, bowls, place mats, and penholders.

THE SCENT

Thuya's scent, nature's guard against parasitic attack, once made it a prized ingredient of ancient lore. The Greeks named the tree *thuya* (pronounced *twee-ya*), which means "sacrifice." They used its distilled essence to produce incense for religious ceremonies. As with cedar, its close relative, thuya's distinctive aroma remains decades after the wood is cut. Today, the scent is more likely to feature in aromatherapy rather than ritual.

SUSTAINABLE HARVESTING

With the substantial part of the tree securing so many livelihoods, its sustainability is of great importance. Not long ago, a demand from collectors overseas, and a national desire for impressive furnishings had endangered the supply of thuya. Since the 1990s, the Moroccan government has been working on a program to protect the future of the precious Atlas forests and establish a replanting program. Today, the thuya industry is closely controlled. Artisans are encouraged to turn their attentions to small, delicate pieces and inlays, thus leaving the majority of trees in the forests to grow to maturity. Massive pieces, such as the doorways and carved furnishings favored by the ancient Romans, are rare. If you are lucky enough to sleep in a house with a thuya ceiling, it is almost certainly renovated or reclaimed rather than new.

THE CRAFT OF CARVING

The majority of Berber woodworkers now operate in cooperatives, ensuring that the bulk of profits pass directly to the artisans themselves. They, in turn, hand their skills on to their teenage apprentices, while educating them in the environmental issues so key to their future. Tradition dictates that men perform the artistically skilled part of the production process, including both carving and decoration. Women and children polish and feed the intricate grain. These cooperatives are also turning their attention to maximizing sustainable by-products of the thuya. A pine-scented oil, for example, is extracted from the resin and is valued in both aromatherapy and homeopathy. The sap also yields a lacquer and varnish, used widely by local craftsmen.

BUYING THUYA

Although you can find thuya wood products everywhere in Morocco, those wishing to buy articles fashioned from this beautiful wood are most likely to find reasonably priced items on Morocco's Atlantic coast, such as in Essaouira and Agadir. Check prices prior to purchase at one of the many outlets available online; try to buy from a cooperative to ensure your money goes to the craftsmen rather than wholesalers and middlemen.

8

Updated by
Lynn Sheppard

While they're both on the coast and they both have beaches that people rave about, Essaouira and Agadir couldn't be more different. A hippie hangout whose secret travelers refused to reveal for years, Essaouira is only now coming into the limelight as a mainstream destination, but it nevertheless retains its slightly "other" feel. Windy beaches attract water-sports enthusiasts rather than sunseekers, and riad-hotels cater to independent travelers.

Agadir, on the other hand, was made for mass tourism. It's a modern resort city with every kind of singing, dancing, and casino-betting distraction on hand along with long stretches of hot, sandy beaches, and calm seas perfect for sunbathing families. Both, however, have lively ports worth seeing in action and superb fresh fish and seafood. Between the two are less frequented spots good for diving, surfing, windsurfing, kite-surfing, kayaking, and bodyboarding, or, for the less active, sunbathing and just hiding out from the world a little.

For those wanting to get closer to nature, head inland southeast of Agadir, and you'll find fruit orchards, argan trees, saffron crocus fields, pretty painted villages, and kasbahs. The plains of the Souss Valley and the jagged Anti-Atlas Mountains provide stunning vistas with plenty of scope for adventure. The picturesque walled town of Taroudant has historic sights and markets that attract day-trippers from Agadir, but it is also a great base for exploring and trekking into the Anti-Atlas or western High Atlas mountains. A very worthwhile circuit from Taroudant will include the towns of Tafraoute and Tiznit. Tafraoute is famed for its scenic backdrop of towering granite boulders, almond blossoms, blue-painted rocks, and nearby rock carvings, while the 19th-century walled town of Tiznit is famed for its silversmiths and jewelry souk.

Whether your interests involve holing up in luxury or diving into the surf, this coastal area has a great deal to offer. For nature lovers and culture vultures there are ancient medinas, kasbahs, pretty villages, and wilderness all within easy reach.

PLANNING

WHEN TO GO

Unlike inland destinations that get too hot in summer, high season for the coast is July and August, with peaks at Christmas, New Year's Day, and June. The best months for visiting may be September and October, when it's off-season but still warm. Summer tends to be busy with vacationing Moroccan families; spring in Agadir is the main season for vacationers and families from abroad. Surfers and water-sports fans come year-round, although early spring is by far the best time for surf.

In the Souss Valley, spring is the most spectacular time to visit, when almond trees and wildflowers are in bloom, the harvest is near, and the weather is sunny but not too hot. Fall temperatures are moderate, but landscapes are a bit drabber after the summer harvest. As long as rains don't wash out the roads, winter is pleasant as well—it is particularly popular for climbers in the mountains. Coastal areas are mild, although inland temperatures can be cold and heated rooms hard to find. If you must come in summer, stick to the coast: even an hour inland, in Taroudant, the July and August heat is unbearable in all but the nighttime hours.

PLANNING YOUR TIME

Most visitors to the region fly into Agadir or reach Essaouira from Marrakesh. Both cities easily warrant more than just a day trip, so it's worth booking at least a couple of nights in a local riad. You can decide to stick to just one city, but many people decide to hit up both while in the area. From Agadir, the Anti-Atlas region is easily accessible in day excursions or with an overnight stay in Tafraoute or Taroudant. These trips can be arranged with a rental car or through one of the many local travel agencies. The area further south of Agadir, where the desert meets the ocean, is beautiful, and has a fascinating and turbulent history of occupation and independence, but requires a longer trip as distances are great and public transport very limited. If you are fortunate to be traveling to any of the region's towns during a festival, book accommodations well in advance.

GETTING HERE AND AROUND

AIR TRAVEL

The key international air hub in the region is Agadir, although visitors based in Essaouira may fly in to Marrakesh or Essaouira itself. Agadir's Al Massira Airport is 35 km (21 miles) east of town. *Grands taxis* (large shared taxis for up to six passengers) to downtown Agadir are a fixed price of 200 DH, but many drivers expect you to haggle. There is also a shuttle bus (4 DH) every 30 minutes from the airport to nearby Inezghane (13 km [8 miles] southeast of Agadir) where several bus services and grand taxis provide connections to other southern destinations as well as to the main bus station in Agadir. Otherwise, your hotel will usually be happy to arrange your airport transfer.

BUS TRAVEL

There is frequent bus service offered by both CTM and Supratours connecting to Essaouira, Marrakesh, and Casablanca, as well as grand taxis that travel between cities.

CAR TRAVEL

A freeway now connects Marrakesh and Agadir and has cut travel times considerably; the journey takes approximately three hours. Explorations of the area around Taroudant and Tafraoute can be done as side trips from Agadir. If you don't want to drive yourself, one of the most enjoyable ways to cover this broad area is to organize a tour through one of several agencies based in Agadir. You can rent a car in either Agadir or Essaouira if you want to explore the region at your own pace.

SAFETY

Essaouira and Agadir are quite safe, with almost no violent crime. Lone female travelers will feel more comfortable in these towns than in some other parts of Morocco. Travelers should keep an eye on their personal belongings, however, as pickpockets are common, especially during festival time when the streets are jam-packed.

RESTAURANTS

All along the coast you can get great grilled and battered fresh fish and seafood that's inexpensive and tasty at any time of day. For a better fish experience, go to a restaurant and try fish tagine or skewered and marinated fish brochettes. International cuisine is also readily available in both Agadir and Essaouira.

HOTELS

You'll find a full range of options, from small budget hotels to Agadir's five-star behemoths. In Essaouira, many old traditional family homes, or *riads,* have been restored and converted to beautiful guesthouses. In summer it's best to reserve rooms in advance, and for the more upscale boutiques, you may have to book several months in advance whatever the time of year. There's also an increasing number of rental apartments in Essaouira and "apartment hotels" in Agadir; both offer self-catering options.

The Souss has some choice small hotels ranging from simple *auberges* (inns) and restored riads to former palaces and one luxury hotel that's among the best in Morocco. *Hotel reviews have been shortened. For full information, visit Fodors.com*

WHAT IT COSTS IN DIRHAMS			
$	$$	$$$	$$$$
Restaurants under 70 DH	71 DH–90 DH	91 DH–110 DH	over 110 DH
Hotels under 450 DH	451 DH–700 DH	701 DH–1,000 DH	over 1,000 DH

Restaurant prices are the average cost of a main course at dinner or, if dinner is not served, at lunch. Hotel prices are the lowest cost of a standard double room in high season.

FESTIVALS

Agadir and Essaouira are music hotspots, so it is no surprise that both cities host popular music festivals. Held in July, Agadir's Festival Timitar celebrates native Berber music, while Essaouira's world-famous Festival of Gnaoua, held each June, hosts international musicians as well as native ones. Various towns around the Anti-Atlas have developed festivals to celebrate aspects of local culture, including in Taroudant (focusing on traditional music every June); Tafraoute (celebrating the almond blossom in February); and Tiznit (honoring the Amazigh New Year in January).

AGADIR

270 km (168 miles) southwest of Marrakesh, 460 km (285 miles) south of Casablanca.

Agadir is, above all else, a holiday resort, so don't hope for a medina, a souk, or a kasbah (although it does have all three, after a fashion). Think sun, sea, and sand. These are what it does best, as hundreds of thousands of visitors each year can testify.

There's no reason to begrudge the city its tourist aspirations. Razed by an earthquake in 1960 that killed 15,000 people in 13 seconds, Agadir had to be entirely rebuilt. Today it's a thoroughly modern city where travelers don't think twice about showing considerable skin, and Moroccans benefit from the growing number of jobs.

There's a reason why this popular European package vacation destination is overrun with enormous, characterless beachfront hotels. The beach, all 10 km (6 miles) of it, is dreamy. A 450-yard-wide strip, it bends in an elegant crescent along the bay, and is covered with fine-grain sand. The beach is sheltered and safe for swimming, making it perfect for families. Farther north, where small villages stand behind some of the best waves in the world, is a surfers' paradise.

Even if you have no interest in surfing, diving, jet-skiing, golf, tennis, or horseback riding down the beach, you can treat Agadir as a modern bubble in which to kick back. It's equipped with familiar pleasurable pursuits—eating, drinking, and relaxing next to the ocean—and modern amenities such as car-rental agencies and ATMs. It isn't quite Europe, but neither is it quite Morocco.

GETTING HERE AND AROUND

Most travelers fly directly into Agadir's Al Massira airport. Although there are no direct flights from North America, connections from Casablanca and European airports are easy. Inexpensive buses are easy ways to get here from Essaouira, Marrakesh, and beyond. If all else fails, grands taxis can take you just about anywhere for the right price.

Once in Agadir, you'll find that downtown is easily navigable on foot, although you may prefer to taxi in from your hotel. The city's orange petits taxis are easy to flag down. Agadir also has many car-rental agencies, including Hertz and Avis.

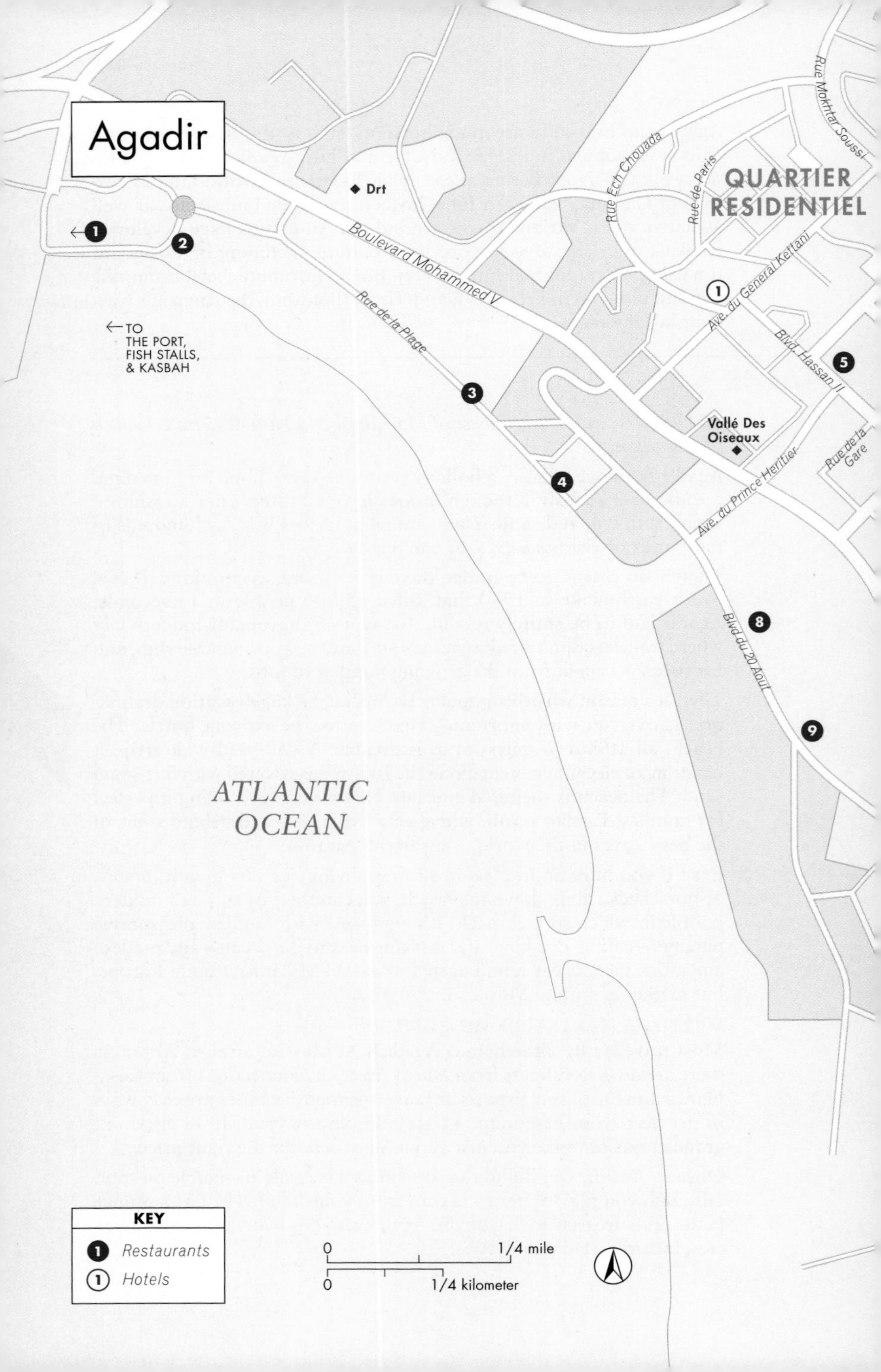
Agadir
Drt
Boulevard Mohammed V
Rue de la Plage
Rue Ech Chouada
Rue de Paris
Rue Mokhtar Soussi
QUARTIER RESIDENTIEL
Ave. du General Kettani
Blvd. Hassan II
Vallé Des Oiseaux
Rue de la Gare
Ave. du Prince Heritier
Blvd du 20 Aout
TO THE PORT, FISH STALLS, & KASBAH
ATLANTIC OCEAN
KEY
Restaurants
Hotels
0
1/4 mile
0
1/4 kilometer

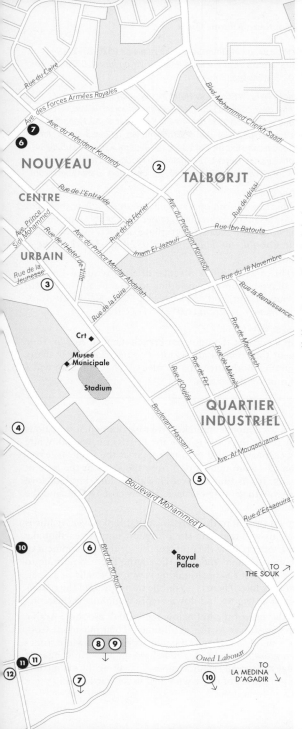

Restaurants ▼

Hotels ▼

Bus Contacts CTM ✉ *94, av. Mokhtar Soussi, Inezgane* ☎ *0528/83–22–94* ⊕ *www.ctm.ma.* **Supratours** ✉ *In the Gare Routière Voyageurs* ☎ *0528/22–40–10, 0528/84–12–07* ⊕ *www.supratours.ma.*

Rental Car Contacts Avis ✉ *Bungalow Hotel Marhaba, av. Mohammed V* ☎ *0528/82–14–14for downtown, 0528/83–92–44 for airport* ⊕ *www.avis.com.* **Dan Car** ✉ *Av. Mohammed V* ☎ *0528/84–46–00.* **Europcar** ✉ *Av. Mohammed V, near Hotel Tulip* ☎ *0528/84–02–03 for downtown, 0528/83–90–66 for airport* ⊕ *www.europcar.com.* **Exotik Cars** ✉ *5, av. Général Kettani* ☎ *0528/84–11–42* ⊕ *www.exotikcars.net.* **Hertz** ✉ *Bungalow Marhaba, av. Mohammed V* ☎ *0528/84–09–39 for downtown, 0528/83–90–71 for airport* ⊕ *www.hertz.com.*

GUIDES AND TOURS

Complete Tours. This English-run operation based in Agadir with offices in Marrakesh and Casablanca can put together your whole trip, including hotels, excursions, and meals—everything, in fact, but the flight. ✉ *26, Immeuble Oumlil, Av. Hassan II* ☎ *0528/82–34–01* ⊕ *www. complete-tours.com.*

Massira Travel. This agency offers a range of trips with an English-speaking guide all over Morocco, including to Essaouira, Marrakesh, Imouzzer, Tafraoute, Tiznit, and farther afield. ✉ *25, bd. du 20 Août, next to L'Orange Bleue restaurant* ☎ *0528/84–77–13.*

VISITOR INFORMATION

You can pick up a copy of the bilingual French–English *Agadir Tour Guide* magazine or the French-only *Agadir Premiere Le Mag* in many shops and restaurants. Both offer a better idea of what's on than will a trip to the local tourism delegation.

EXPLORING

For those looking for a more comprehensive tour of town, a ridiculous yet amusing way to see the town is with the Petit Train, a small white tram with three carriages pulled by a motorcar at the front. It leaves every 35 minutes (9:15 am until 6 pm) from the kiosk at the base of Vallée des Oiseaux. It's as touristy as a Hawaiian shirt, but kids love it and it's a great way to get off your feet. Tickets cost 18 DH, and the ride lasts 40 minutes.

FAMILY **Kasbah.** High up on the hill to the northwest that looks over Agadir is the old kasbah. This was the main site of Agadir until an earthquake razed the city in 1960, creating the opportunity for the development of modern Agadir, which stands today to the south. There is nothing to see of the former city, but the breathtaking views, especially at sunset, make the trip worthwhile. There is no public transport and the road is steep, so arrange your trip up and down before beginning the ascent.

Emblazoned on the side of the hill below the kasbah are three Arabic words that keep guard over Agadir at all times. Their meaning? God, country, and the king. By day they're a patchwork of huge white stones against the green grass. By night they're lighted up powerfully against the dark. The huge hill is really a burial mound, covering the old medina and the impromptu graves of those who died in the earthquake.

FAMILY **La Medina d'Agadir.** In Ben Sergao, a few miles south of Agadir on
Fodor'sChoice the Inezgane road, is a remarkable 13-acre project orchestrated by
★ Moroccan-born Italian decorator-architect Coco Polizzi. He dreamed
of replacing the medina Agadir lost to the 1960 earthquake with a
new medina on his own land. This combination of living ethnological
museum and high-quality bazaar was finally completed in 2007 by
hundreds of Moroccan craftsmen following centuries-old techniques.
Each stone is laid by hand, and the buildings are made of earth, rock
from the Souss, slate from the High Atlas, and local woods such as
thuya and eucalyptus. Decorations follow both Berber and Saharan
motifs. Mosaic craftsmen, painters, jewelers, a henna artist, metalwork-
ers, and carpenters welcome spectators as they practice their crafts (and
welcome customers for the results) in workshop nooks throughout the
medina. The medina also houses restaurants, shops, and even an amphi-
theater. ⊠ *La Medina d'Agadir, Bensergao* ☎ *0528/28–02–53* ⊕ *www.
medinapolizzi.com* 🎫 *40 DH* ⊗ *Daily 9–6.*

Fodor'sChoice **Musée Municipale du Patrimoine Amazighe.** Agadir's municipal museum
★ celebrates the Berber Amazigh heritage of the region and features collections of photography, jewelry, artifacts, and local handicrafts as well as
temporary exhibits. It's worth a visit to learn about the symbolism seen
in Berber carpet and jewelry, and about the *igouder* (plural of *agadir,*
a communal granary) of the local villages. If you're lucky, there may
be an English-speaking intern on hand to guide you around. ⊠ *Passage at Souss, Av. Hassan II* ☎ *0528/82–16–32* 🎫 *20 DH* ⊗ *Mon.–Sat.
9:30–5:30.*

FAMILY **Souk Al Had.** In the northeastern corner of the city is a daily bazaar selling souvenirs, household goods, and the produce of the fertile Souss
plains. You'll need to bargain hard. ⊗ *Tues.–Sun.*

Souss Massa National Park. Just south of Agadir, beyond the Souss River
reaching to the mouth of the River Massa, is the Souss Massa National
Park. Stretching down to Aglou Plage, it was created in 1991 and is
currently under the management of Morocco's High Commission for
Water and Forests. The park is a breeding ground for a number of
indigenous and migratory bird species, including the bald ibis. There
are also captive-breeding programs for four threatened North African
antelope and gazelle species, as well as for ostriches, which were previously extinct in Morocco since 1945.

Tours are available within the park, which also contains a number of
guesthouses and other accommodation options. Many of these support
sustainable tourism and offer bird- and animal-watching excursions.
⊠ *Parc National de Souss Massa, Inezgane* ☎ *0528/33–38–80.*

FAMILY **Vallée des Oiseaux** (*Valley of the Birds*). It's not so much a valley as a
pleasure garden connecting Avenue Hassan II to the beach. It not only
has birds, but also monkeys, fountains, and lovely green surroundings. Very popular with Moroccan families and young couples as well
as tourists, it makes for a pleasant stroll between downtown and the
beachfront. ⊠ *Bd. Mohammed V* 🎫 *5 DH* ⊗ *Daily 9:30–12:30 and
2:30–6:30.*

BEACHES

AGADIR

FAMILY **Agadir Beach.** The beach here swings around a crescent from southeast to northwest. You're more likely to find a quiet spot if you wander south, although be careful to avoid the private beaches of the resorts. The most crowded areas, frequented year-round by families and locals, are to the north. Along the flanking thoroughfare, known as the Corniche (Promenade), you'll find cafés, bars, and restaurants. At the very northern end is the swanky marina development where private yachts are moored. The promenade comes alive at dusk, when families and youngsters take their evening walks, but as night falls, it can become a little sketchy. Nonetheless, from the shelter of a café terrace, it's still a good spot to stop and watch the world go by. The northern tip is also the place to rent a jet ski, catamaran, or surf equipment. **Amenities:** food and drink; water sports. **Best for:** sunset.

NORTH OF AGADIR

Taghazoute. In summer the beaches north of Agadir on the Essaouira road—especially those in the rapidly expanding Taghazoute area—are crammed with Moroccan families (who often camp there), but it empties out in winter. This is the area to visit if you want to tackle some of Morocco's best surf; a range of cafés, hostels, and rental apartments have been springing up to meet the demand. Although lots of land here had been prepared for luxury and family resorts, construction stopped during the Eurozone economic crisis and is only now recommencing. As a result, Taghazoute still has the feel of a rough-and-ready surfers' frontier town. **Amenities:** food and drink; water sports. **Best for:** surfing; swimming; sunset.

CAP RHIR

Cap Rhir. During most of the year, a few stray Western surfers seek out waves around the bend from the lighthouse at Cap Rhir, but otherwise the neighboring village of Aghroud is, like Taghazoute, quiet—a pretty detour, with empty sands and calm waters. You may come across a bald ibis, as their preserve is south of Agadir at the Souss Massa National Park and Estuary. **Amenities:** none. **Best For:** solitude; sunset.

OFF THE BEATEN PATH

Imouzzer. If you are looking for a more isolated and less developed excursion away from the beach, from Aourir (12 km [7 miles] north of Agadir), take the paved road 50 km (31 miles) up into the Ida Outanane Mountains to the waterfalls here, near Immouzer des Ida Outanane. Check with locals—the waterfalls are often dry when the region is experiencing drought. On your way you'll pass through the palm gorge of Paradise Valley, where the rocky riverbank welcomes picnicking Moroccan families and foreigners alike. The Berber souk in Immouzer on Thursday is a great place to buy local honey. The many opportunities for walking and hiking make this an ideal day excursion from Agadir.

Agadir is Morocco's top resort destination, with more all-inclusive beach resorts than any other place in the country.

WHERE TO EAT

Neon signs throughout Agadir lure you in to sample not so much the delights of Moroccan cuisine as the woes of fast food and international menus. Nevertheless, many of these restaurants have good locations along the beachfront or in the town center.

Agadir is famous for its fish and seafood, as well as its lively deep-sea fishing port (Morocco's busiest) where you can eat lunch at the stalls. Each stall offers nearly identical food, including squid, prawns, sole, lobster, and whiting, and for nearly identical prices. So walk around and pick what you'd like; the better-organized stalls have chalkboards listing the catch of the day and the price. Frequented by locals and travelers alike, it's a great bet for cheap and fun eats and now shares space with Morocco's swankiest marina, which is also becoming a culinary hot spot.

All major hotels have both Moroccan and Continental restaurants, which has led to the sad demise of many well-established local restaurants, but there are many sophisticated new eateries springing up around the marina. Downtown there is a good selection of Italian, French, Thai, and even Japanese and Indian restaurants.

$ ✕ **116.** This small but buzzy salad-and-crêpe bar was developed to fill
FAST FOOD a gap in the downtown market for great value and healthy snacks and small meals. It attracts local office workers, foreign residents, and tourists with its DIY salads, excellent Italian espresso, and fresh juices and smoothies. Salads come in three sizes, and crêpes, quiches, and panini are also available, so it's a great spot for vegetarians. Take a form and

pen and design your own salad, picking the size, base, ingredients, and dressing to suit. It's often packed by midday, but service is fast. ⓢ *Average main: 40DH* ✉ *116, av. des F.A.R.* ☎ *0528/82–03–12* ▭ *No credit cards* ☽ *Closed Sun.*

$
CAFÉ

✕ **Boulangerie Pâtisserie Yacout.** For breakfast have a buttery *pain au chocolat* (chocolate croissant) and strong coffee at the Boulangerie Pâtisserie Yacout. A full Moroccan breakfast of *m'smen* pancakes, *harira* soup, orange juice, and coffee is also available. ⓢ *Average main: 35DH* ✉ *Corner of rue de L'Entraide and bd. Mohammed VI* ☎ *0528/84–65–88* ⚐ *Reservations not accepted* ▭ *No credit cards.*

$$
STEAKHOUSE

✕ **Camel's.** On the heels of two successful U.S.-style restaurants in Denmark, the Iraq-born owner moved to Morocco in 2011 and relaunched this beachfront favorite. Like its neighbors, it caters to all audiences with candlelit tables, flat-screen TVs, live music, a wine list, and an international menu. As the name suggests, the menu includes fantastic camel tagines, plus jambalaya chicken for any homesick Americans. It's not a great option for vegetarians, but everyone will enjoy watching the evening promenade along the beach. ⓢ *Average main: 80DH* ✉ *Rue de la Plage* ☎ *0528/82–85–60.*

$$$
SEAFOOD

✕ **Chez Mimi la Brochette.** Run by Mimi and her husband since 1981, this popular seaside institution brings a little style to the strip at the northern end of the beach. Everything is grilled over a wood fire, and you can get great fish, including lobster and prawns. Don't miss the local fig-based digestif, Mahia, or the chance to have hot prawns or smoked-eel salad. The house specialty is, of course, brochettes of any kind and there's plenty of meat on the menu, too. The only downside is that you can't eat here Friday night. ⓢ *Average main: 100DH* ✉ *Rue de la Plage* ☎ *0528/84–03–87* ☽ *No dinner Fri.; no lunch Sat.*

$$
BRITISH

✕ **English Pub.** Just when you thought you couldn't get Yorkshire pudding in Morocco, you come across this streetside bar, café, and restaurant. You can also get a full English breakfast of sausage, bacon, eggs, and beans, and, of course, fish 'n' chips. British soccer games and other major sports events are broadcast on 20 television screens; there are also pool tables and nightly karaoke. British and international beers are served in pints alongside a range of wines and spirits. ⓢ *Average main: 80DH* ✉ *Bd. du 20 Août* ☎ *0528/84–73–90.*

$$$$
SEAFOOD

✕ **La Scala.** Ideally located across from the beachfront strip of resort hotels, La Scala has rapidly gained a reputation as one of Agadir's finest fish restaurants. Here you can enjoy excellent quality seafood including lobster and John Dory; there's also a tasty duck breast for those who prefer meat. A free shuttle service is available for those staying further away. ■TIP→ **The view from the terrace is decidedly uninteresting, so enjoy the atmosphere inside for a top-class dinner.** ⓢ *Average main: 300DH* ✉ *Rue de l'Oued Souss, Complexe Tamelt* ☎ *0528/84–67–73.*

$
PIZZA

✕ **La Siciliana.** With a broad menu of pizzas, homemade pasta, and Italian desserts, this Moroccan-run Italian eatery is a favorite among locals amid the string of Italian restaurants that line Avenue Hassan II. They can also deliver, should you crave a quiet night in, but they don't serve alcohol. Credits cards are accepted, but only for meals over 250

DH. $ *Average main: 70DH* ✉ *65–67, av. Hassan II, near Vallée des Oiseaux* ☎ *0528/82–09–73* ☉ *Closed during Ramadan.*

$$$$
EUROPEAN

✕ **L'Eden.** This is French owner Jean-Pierre's third restaurant in Agadir with his chef wife, Virginie, so we can assume they know how to please crowds. At the southern end of the beach ahead of the strip of resort hotels, L'Eden offers panoramic views of the beach and the sea, plus a great-value lunch menu served in a light, breezy atmosphere by the multilingual staff. In order to attract locals and repeat customers, the menu is changed regularly and new dishes are often tested at the chef's suggestion. There is also a menu of French wines and pastries. $ *Average main: 120DH* ✉ *6, Front de Mer* ☎ *0528/84–85–96.*

$$$
MOROCCAN
Fodor's Choice
★

✕ **Le P'tit Dôme.** This chic eatery towards the southern end of the beach aims to take on the more established Agadir restaurants with its menu of Moroccan specialties and local seafood, including a large Moroccan and French wine list (including champagne). A car can be sent to collect customers from their hotel. On arrival, diners are seated on the terrace or in the dining room with modern black-and-white décor. All bread is freshly baked on the premises. $ *Average main: 100DH* ✉ *20, bd. Aout* ☎ *0528/84–08–05.*

$$$$
MEDITERRANEAN

✕ **Le Quai.** Tourists and wealthy Moroccans flock to this chic corner of the Agadir marina for a Mediterranean-style menu with an emphasis on local fish, French-style meat dishes, and pasta. It's great for an alfresco dinner or a sunset cocktail. Be sure to book in advance to guarantee a table, especially on weekends. $ *Average main: 180DH* ✉ *Marina Agadir Quai Ouest* ☎ *0661/60–58–22.*

$$$$
SPANISH
Fodor's Choice
★

✕ **Les Blancs.** At the edge of Agadir's trendy Marina district and sitting right on the northern end of the beach, Les Blancs is a shiny, white, modernist retreat. There's an informal bar-cum-restaurant with boardwalk-style flooring and huge windows overlooking the bay; there is also an outdoor terrace with woven seagrass umbrellas and a contemporary indoor dining room. You can sit at the bar and snack on tapas or choose from house specialties such as colorful Spanish paellas including black squid-ink rice, green rice with veggies, and red king prawns. Reservations are recommended in high season. $ *Average main: 180DH* ✉ *Marina* ☎ *0528/82–83–68.*

$$$
AUSTRIAN

✕ **Mozartstube.** If you get sick of tagines and yearn for some hearty European dishes, head to Mozartstube in the heart of downtown Agadir. Driss and his Austrian wife guarantee a cozy, chalet-style atmosphere along with schnitzel as big as your plate. With the potato salad side, apple strudel, and ice cream, you might forget that you're even in Africa. $ *Average main: 100DH* ✉ *24, av. des F.A.R* ☎ *0528/82–45–64* ⊕ *www.mozartstube.net* ▭ *No credit cards* ☉ *Closed Sun. No lunch.*

$
CAFÉ

✕ **Pâtisserie La Fontaine.** For a light meal or coffee at any time of day, go straight to the open-air Pâtisserie La Fontaine, which serves outstanding individual pastillas and spicy shrimp rolls as an alternative to plain old toast. It's also great for a snack before or after a visit to the nearby museum. $ *Average main: 60DH* ✉ *Passage Aït Souss, Av. Hassan II* ☎ *0528/84–83–40.*

8

WHERE TO STAY

Besides a couple of boutique guesthouses, you can forget riad-style intimacy in Agadir; your choices are mainly executive-style functionality or giant beachfront complexes that cater primarily to European package tours. As a general rule the luxury (and price) increases as you move southwards down the beach, where five-star resort complexes are still being built.

The hotels along boulevard du 20 Août leading onto Chemin des Dunes have so many amenities and restaurants that you'll feel no need to leave their beachside complexes. Indeed, more and more hotels are becoming all-inclusive. Be wary of these, however, as they don't guarantee fine dining and many local experts think they will lead to a slip in standards. If you just need a bed while passing through Agadir, there are less expensive, basic hotels in the center of town, north of the beach. There's also a lively trade in "*résidences*," self-catering apartments which you can rent by the night. These even have communal hotel facilities such as swimming pools and are an affordable option for families.

$$$$
RESORT

Atlantic Palace. If you think you're entering a royal palace when approaching this place, you're not far from the truth; owned by a Moroccan royal cousin, this ornate affair is the king's choice when he's in town. **Pros:** relaxing spa and great facilities; beautiful pool. **Cons:** some rooms could do with an update. $ *Rooms from: 1500DH* ⊠ *Chemin des Dunes, Secteur Touristique* ☎ *0528/82–41–46* ⊕ *www.atlanticpalaceresort.com* ⤳ *277 rooms, 52 suites* ¶◯¶ *Multiple meal plans.*

$$$$
RESORT
ALL-INCLUSIVE
FAMILY

ClubHotel Riu Tikida Dunas. One of three Riu resorts on the beachfront, this one gives you value for your money as all-inclusive options go (drinks are also included). **Pros:** pretty pools; lovely gardens. **Cons:** very busy with package tour groups; minimum seven-night stay. $ *Rooms from: 2600DH* ⊠ *Chemin des Dunes* ☎ *0528/84–90–90* ⊕ *www.riu. com* ⤳ *400 rooms, 6 suites* ¶◯¶ *All-inclusive.*

$$$$
B&B/INN
Fodor'sChoice
★

Dar Maktoub. Set on the edge of the Souss-Massa National Park but within easy reach of Agadir, Dar Maktoub is a gorgeous boutique hotel set in a beautiful garden. **Pros:** stellar service in an intimate location; close to golf courses and nature reserve. **Cons:** a taxi journey or hired car ride into Agadir. $ *Rooms from: 1045DH* ⊠ *Piste en Bordure de l'Oued Souss, Bensergao* ☎ *0528/33–75–00* ⊕ *www.darmaktoub.com* ⤳ *3 rooms, 5 suites* ¶◯¶ *Multiple meal plans.*

$
HOTEL

Hotel el Bahia. If you're not desperate for beach views and don't mind a 20-minute walk to get there, then El Bahia is a central and good-value option. **Pros:** inexpensive rates; clean rooms. **Cons:** few amenities; no restaurant. $ *Rooms from: 320DH* ⊠ *Rue el-Mehdi ben Toumert* ☎ *0528/82–39–54* ⤳ *27 rooms* ▭ *No credit cards* ¶◯¶ *Breakfast.*

$$
HOTEL

Hotel Kamal. If you don't need to be near the beach, this is an affordable option in downtown Agadir. **Pros:** clean and neat; all rooms have a bath; parking on site. **Cons:** no restaurant, but there are plenty nearby. $ *Rooms from: 465DH* ⊠ *Av. Hassan II* ☎ *0528/84–28–17* ⤳ *128 rooms* ¶◯¶ *No meals.*

$
HOTEL

La Petite Suède. While the name is a little baffling (it means "small Sweden"), this is an inexpensive hotel, often used by local agencies.

Pros: very affordable; friendly staff; close to beach. **Cons:** the hotel itself is drab and old-fashioned; few facilities. $ *Rooms from: 350DH* ✉ *Corner of av. Hassan II and av. General Kittani* ☎ *0528/84–07–79* ⊕ *www.petitesuede.com* ⇄ *20 rooms* ⅼ⊙ⅼ *Breakfast.*

$$$
HOTEL

🖼 **Le Tivoli.** Also called "Blue Sea Le Tivoli", this is a less expensive option than many of the Agadir behemoths and it's only 500 yards from the beach. **Pros:** wide range of activities and facilities available. **Cons:** uninspiring buffet meals; noisy pool area. $ *Rooms from: 990DH* ✉ *Bd. du 20 Août, Secteur Touristique* ☎ *0528/84–76–40* ⊕ *www. hoteltivoli.com* ⇄ *256 rooms, 24 suites* ⅼ⊙ⅼ *Multiple meal plans.*

$$
RENTAL
FAMILY

🖼 **Résidence Yasmina.** Common areas at this self-catering complex have impressive hand-painted tiles and trickling fountains, but the older apartments are outdated and shabby. **Pros:** two pools; balconies with great views. **Cons:** shabby décor in old wing; lift only goes to fifth floor (of six). $ *Rooms from: 700DH* ✉ *Rue de la Jeunesse, off av. Hassan II* ☎ *0528/84–26–60* ⊕ *www.residence-yasmina.com* ⇄ *104 apartments, 12 suites* ⅼ⊙ⅼ *No meals.*

$$$$
B&B/INN
Fodor's Choice
★

🖼 **Riad Villa Blanche.** An elegant boutique hotel—the first of its kind in Agadir—Riad Villa Blanche feels as though it has been plucked from the chicest Marrakesh address and dropped at the edge of the ocean. **Pros:** beautiful décor; intimate scale; excellent service. **Cons:** beyond the garden walls are major hotel sites; far from main tourist beach or downtown. $ *Rooms from: 2000DH* ✉ *No. 50 Cité Founty, Baie des Palmiers, Sonaba* ☎ *0528/21–13–13* ⊕ *www.riadvillablanche.com* ⇄ *25 rooms, 3 suites* ⅼ⊙ⅼ *Some meals.*

$$$
HOTEL

🖼 **Ryad Mogador Al Madina.** Part of the Moroccan Ryad Mogador chain, this complex has four wonderful restaurants but does not serve alcohol. **Pros:** friendly and helpful staff; close to beach. **Cons:** overpriced; no real views. $ *Rooms from: 980DH* ✉ *Bd. du 20 Août* ☎ *0528/29–80–00* ⊕ *www.ryadmogador.com* ⇄ *180 rooms, 26 suites* ⅼ⊙ⅼ *Multiple meal plans.*

$$$$
RESORT

🖼 **Sofitel Agadir Royal Bay Resort.** Overshadowed by the newer and more glamorous sister Sofitel hotel next door, this place still manages to provide both privacy and intimacy on a grand scale. **Pros:** excellent amenities; comfortable rooms. **Cons:** starting to feel a little dated; very expensive. $ *Rooms from: 2475DH* ✉ *Cité Founty P4, Baie des Palmiers, Bensergao* ☎ *0528/82–00–88* ⊕ *www.sofitel.com* ⇄ *248 rooms, 25 suites* ⅼ⊙ⅼ *Multiple meal plans.*

$$$$
RESORT
Fodor's Choice
★

🖼 **Sofitel Agadir Thalassa Sea & Spa.** If luxury is important to you or if you're looking for total relaxation and detox, the newer Sofitel in Agadir is for you. **Pros:** heated pool; great health and fitness facilities. **Cons:** corridors are rather dark; rooms are open plan to the bathroom. $ *Rooms from: 2000DH* ✉ *Baie des Palmiers, Secteur Touristique, Cité Founty P5, Bensergao* ☎ *0528/38–80–00* ⇄ *129 rooms, 44 suites* ⅼ⊙ⅼ *Multiple meal plans.*

NIGHTLIFE

For many in Agadir, nightlife constitutes a stroll along the waterfront and a coffee with friends. But with its relaxed mores, Agadir can be a clubbing hotspot, particularly for young people looking to cut loose. Many

CLOSE UP

Western Sahara

In 1975 over 350,000 unarmed Moroccans walked south in the Green March, taking possession from the Spanish of what are now officially known as Morocco's Southern Provinces (though internationally known as the Western Sahara). Since 1975, conflict between the Polisario (Saharan separatists) and the Moroccan military has been sporadic, and a referendum to determine the province's political future has been postponed numerous times. There is currently a ceasefire, and the U.N. has a large presence in the big cities. Foreign visitors to the area are likely to be surfers or here on business, as Morocco is encouraging significant investments in the area. The main attraction for the traveler, aside from the journey to the middle of nowhere, is a chance to set foot in the Sahara, as the cities are new and charmless, food and wine scarce, and the military presence pervasive. However, there are several towns worth visiting before crossing the disputed border.

At the time of writing, tourists with Moroccan entry stamps were free to travel to the Southern Provinces. However, the situation is politically charged, so check before you head this far south and be prepared for numerous police checkpoints. These are usually amicable, but it could be worth it to prepare a form with your vital information printed in French, especially if you don't speak the language (which has replaced the Spanish of the colonial era).

THE TOWNS

Guelmim is known as the Gateway to the Sahara, and the ensuing drive south to Tan-Tan—along which the landscape turns ever more arid and desertlike—illustrates why. It's an easy trip (107 km [66 miles] south of Tiznit), shooting through empty stretches of flat *hamada* (stony desert) broken only by the occasional village or café and one gas station. Although you're likely to catch your first glimpse of large camel herds here, the town doesn't have much to entertain a tourist, and even the exotic-sounding camel market is little more than an average weekly souk.

As you approach **Tan-Tan** (125 km [78 miles] south of Guelmim), you may think you're seeing a giant mirage. Fear not, for your eyes do not deceive you: there really are two enormous kissing camels forming an archway over the road into town. Carved out of stone in the 1970s, these affectionate creatures are one of Tan-Tan's chief claims to fame and the subjects of many a Western Sahara postcard. Tan-Tan's main significance (beyond the kissing camels) is that it was the official starting point for the Green March of 1975. The southern end of Boulevard Mohammed V is Tan-Tan's main square, Place de la Marche Verte (Green March Square). This is the main transportation hub for taxis and cars headed back to Guelmim and on to Laayoune. The town makes a logical stop on a trip farther south, and is a passable choice for an overnight stay, although some tourists report unfriendly locals. The beach here, Tan-Tan Plage, is popular with surfers.

At 150 km (93 miles) south of Tan-Tan, the modest fishing village of **Akhfenir** has the first gas station, cafés, and stores on the coastal route after Tan-Tan. Footpaths down to a gorgeous beach make Akhfenir a good place for an en-route swimming stop. At 85 km (53 miles) south of Akhfenir, you'll find the largest of the few coastal towns on this route and the last before the disputed border. **Tarfaya** offers panoramic ocean views, excellent seafood, and a nice place to explore before the road turns inland.

Laayoune, the former capital of the Spanish Sahara, has thrived under Moroccan rule. A calm and easy place to navigate, Laayoune (115 km [71 miles] south of Tarfaya) makes the best base for trips around the Western Sahara. It's quite impressive to look around at surrounding dunes and landscape and contemplate the very existence of a town this size in the middle of the Sahara Desert. Moroccan investment is pouring into the town to capitalize on the benefits of deep-sea fishing, and any Moroccans one encounters are as likely to be from elsewhere, drawn here by construction work, fishing, and government subsidies.

Smara's central site has long been an important Saharan caravan stop, but most of the fun, it must be said, is in getting here. Once you *are* in Smara, however, the remains of the Palace Ma el-Ainin make a great stopping point. There is a guardian who will be happy to show you around, if you can find him.

Dakhla is the last frontier for most travelers to the Western Sahara, as those wishing to go farther south can only do so as part of a police-escorted convoy to the Mauritanian border. Dakhla's main attractions are its superb beaches and the surrounding cliff, and it's become a magnet

for kite-surfers. In recent years, the Moroccan government has invested heavily in infrastructure development in the town, and since 2006 Dakhla has celebrated the meeting of ocean and desert with the annual Dakhla Festival (⊕ *www.dakhla-festival.com*) held in February.

8

places don't get going until after midnight, but the beachfront is always busy earlier on, with diners and drinkers making the most of the beach environment. Although Agadir lacks the class of Marrakesh, a number of places, mostly based in the resort hotels, are putting up some decent competition.

Be warned: Nighttime also attracts many prostitutes, some underage, who throng the cheap bars. The authorities aren't afraid to imprison foreigners who patronize them. Hotel clubs tend to have a more exclusive patronage; in general, the more expensive the drinks, the fancier the clientele. Many bars and clubs close during the Muslim holy month of Ramadan.

BARS AND CLUBS

Actor's. Part of the Royal Atlas Hotel, Actor's attracts a young crowd with its playlist of Western dance, house, and R&B music, often with well-known Moroccan and Arab hits towards the end of the night. *Shisha* (a hookah water pipe) is also available. ⊠ *Royal Atlas Hotel, 20, av. du 20 Août* ☎ *0528/29–40–40.*

Papagayo. A long-standing favorite is Papagayo, attached to the Rui Tikida Beach resort, which attracts international DJs pumping out fairly mainstream tunes. ⊠ *Hotel Riu Tikida Beach, Chemin des Dunes* ☎ *0528/83–27–27* 🍸 *200 DH.*

So Lounge. The chicest and best nightclub is without doubt So, which charges a hefty admission price for nonguests of the Sofitel (300 DH each, including a small drink). Located on two levels, there's live music every night, a chic restaurant, and three bars, including exclusive champagne and vodka bars. It's so trendy you could scream, or simply dance the night—and morning—away. ⊠ *Sofitel Agadir Royal Bay Resort Hotel, Baie des Palmiers* ☎ *0528/82–00–88.*

Zanzibar. Those looking for post-dinner, pre-club drinks with a touch of East African colonial elegance should stop by Zanzibar at the Riu Tikida Beach Resort. ⊠ *Hotel Riu Tikida Beach, Chemin des Dunes* ☎ *0528/84–54–00.*

CASINOS

Casino Atlantic. Part of the Atlantic Palace Hotel, Casino Atlantic is the long player of the bunch, with 16 gaming tables offering blackjack, roulette, poker, and 200 slot machines going all afternoon, night, and early morning. ⊠ *Atlantic Palace Hotel, Secteur Balnéaireet Touristique* ☎ *0528/84–33–66* ⊕ *www.casinoagadir.com.*

Casino Le Mirage. This casino is part of the Hotel Valtur and has blackjack, poker, roulette, and slot machines. ⊠ *Village Valtur, Chemin des Dunes* ☎ *0528/84–87–77.*

Casino Shem's. This long-standing favorite offers poker, blackjack, and slot machines. ⊠ *Bd. Mohammed V, near McDonald's* ☎ *0528/82–11–11* ⊕ *www.shemscasino.fr.*

SHOPPING

Baz'Art Salam. This store offers a wide range of quality Moroccan-made items at fixed prices near the Lebanese mosque. The selection features modern twists on classic crafts such as Fez leather bags, glazed ceramics, oversize candles, and Sens de Marrakech cosmetics. The shop is owned by two brothers who speak excellent English and are happy to advise on purchases without being pushy. ✉ *124–126, av. des F.A.R.* ☎ *0528/82–45–53.*

La Fabrique. Established in 1989, La Fabrique sells leather goods and designer-label fashions. This is not the kind of place where a bit of haggling will halve the price for you, so be ready to pay higher prices. ✉ *91, av. Hassan II* ☎ *0528/84–61–76.*

Madd. This boutique jewelry store entices you with 18-carat gold from behind a warm wooden exterior. There's another branch in the new Marina development at the north end of Agadir beach. ✉ *38–40, av. Hassan II* ☎ *0528/84–05–92.*

Palais du Sud. For an emporium of carpets, ceramics, leather, lanterns, and ornate boxes, visit Palais du Sud. Behind the golden doors, all goods have price tags, which makes buying hassle-free. ✉ *Rue de la Foire, north of av. Hassan II* ☎ *0528/84–35–00* ⊕ *www.palaisdusud. com* ☉ *Closed Sun.*

Scarlette Idées K-do. This lovely boutique sells everything you could possibly want for the home, from candles and lanterns to mirrors, fabrics, and small chests of drawers. ✉ *Imm. I'Yazid, Av. Hassan II, next to La Fabrique* ☎ *0528/82–32–93.*

Tawarguit. The shop's name means "dream" in Amazigh and sells stylish home wares, gifts, artisanal works, and art. ✉ *Lot Faiz 1, rue 206, 1 block north of rue d'Oujda* ☎ *0528/84–82–25* ⊕ *www.tawarguit.com.*

SPAS

Diar Argan. This spa offers a range of treatments such as massages, manicures, and pedicures as well as advising on and selling argan oil products, the so-called Berber gold. An two-hour massage with argan oil costs 330 DH. ✉ *104, Immeuble Iguenouane, at bd. Mohammed V, next to Délegation du Tourisme* ☎ *0528/84–82–33* ⊕ *www.diarargan.com.*

Les Bains de la Villa Blanche. Seven kinds of exotic massages using Western and Eastern techniques and essential oils are offered in the sumptuous, candlelit spa of Riad Villa Blanche. You can choose from a Sahara hot-sand massage, an "aprés-souk" massage, or an energizing massage with argan oil and lemon. ✉ *Riad Villa Blanche, Baie des Palmiers Secteur N, Cité Founty, Sonaba* ☎ *0528/21–13–13.*

8

SPORTS AND THE OUTDOORS

GOLF

Golf Les Dunes. This golf course is an American-style course 10 km from central Agadir. The fee for 9 holes is 490 DH or 700 DH for 18 holes. ✉ *Chemin Oued Souss* ☎ *0528/83–46–90* ⊕ *www.golflesdunesagadir. com.*

Golf de L'Océan. The newest of the golf courses along Agadir's coast, the Golf de L'Océan is part of the Atlantic Palace Hotel resort and is open to both resort guests and nonresidents. Designed by Belt Collins and opened in 2009, the course has 27 holes, and the green fees start at 400 DH for 9 holes. Caddies are required and cost 100 DH for 18 holes. Regular minibus shuttles run from the Atlantic Palace Hotel. ✉ *Bensergao* ☎ *0528/27–35–42* ⊕ *www.golfdelocean.com.*

Golf du Soleil. The Golf du Soleil has two 18-hole courses. The Tikida course was designed in a classic style amid a eucalyptus forest. The American-style championship course has several challenging obstacles. The green fee for 9 holes is 470 DH, including caddie. Guests of any of the three Tikida resorts in Agadir receive a discount and shuttle bus service to and from the hotels. ✉ *Chemin des Dunes, Bensergao* ☎ *0528/33–73–30* ⊕ *www.golfdusoleil.com.*

Royal Golf Club. Established in 1952 by a Scotsman, the Royal Golf Club is Agadir's oldest. One of the smaller courses in Agadir, it is 12 km (7 miles) from Agadir on the road to Aït Melloul. It has 9 holes over 30 acres, with English-style Bermuda 419 and Cucuyo grass. Green fees are 250 DH, for 9 holes including caddie. ✉ *Km 12, rte. Aït Melloul* ☎ *0528/24–85–51* ⊕ *www.royalgolfagadir.com.*

JET-SKIING

Club Royal de Jet-Ski. At the north end of Agadir beach, next to Ecole de Nautisme, you'll find jet skis for hire. The honorary president of the Club Royal de Jet-Ski is actually Moroccon King Mohammed VI, although it's unlikely you'll find him here.

SURFING

Surf dudes the world over rate Morocco's southern Atlantic coast one of the world's best places to catch waves. There has recently been something of a surfer boom in the region. Today there are countless surf schools, many run by foreigners who came to surf and then simply couldn't tear themselves away. Many surf shops and schools are based in Taghazoute, 22 km (14 miles) north of Agadir. From there, instructors will take clients to local bays and points according to wind and tides.

Original Surf Morocco. A professional, English-speaking outfit, Original Surf Morocco is based in Tamraght, a village famous for its bananas and beaches, about 4 km (2 miles) to the north of Agadir. With over 10 years of experience, it offers surfing lessons and accommodations in a so-called surf house. ✉ *BP 263, Tamraght* ☎ *0671/92–28–69* ⊕ *www. originalsurfmorocco.com.*

Surf Town Morocco. This surf school and guesthouse is 12 km (8 miles) north of Agadir in Aourir. English-speaking instructors can take you to local surfing points like Boiler, Killer Point, and Devil's Rock. Board hire is 100 DH a day and the type of instruction depends on the experience of the surfer and the length of time chosen. Inexpensive accommodations are also available with half-board. ⊠ *BP 247, Aourir* ☎ *0664/47–81–76* ⊕ *www.surftownmorocco.com.*

ESSAOUIRA

171 km (103 miles) north of Agadir.

Once Morocco's main trading port and a stronghold of Jewish culture, Essaouira became famed as a hippie hangout for surfers and expat artists in the 20th century. These days Essaouira offers its cool breezes and relaxed atmosphere to a broader range of visitors. The windy city remains a favorite destination for its picturesque fishing harbor, medina walls, blue shutters, twisting *derbs* (alleyways), and sea, sand, and surf.

Essaouira pretty much has a nine-month high season, from mid-March until early November, with extra peaks around Christmas, New Year's, and the hugely popular Gnaoua Music Festival in June. More hotels and guesthouses have opened in recent years, including a five-star resort and golf course south of the town in Diabat, but the town remains peaceful in its laid-back bustle—an enticing blend of fishing port, historical medina, and seaside haven.

EN ROUTE The coastal stretch between Sidi Ifni and Essaouira presents the most spectacular drive anywhere in Morocco. The northern half of the trip from Agadir on the P8/N1 road to Essaouira is particularly stunning. A drive is pleasant in itself, but you can stop and relax at several turnoffs from the main road both north and south of Agadir. Unspoiled beaches lie just 10 km (6 miles) north of Sidi Ifni; the only travelers who find the unmarked dirt road come in campers during the summer months.

GETTING HERE AND AROUND

Essaouira's airport is served by only a handful of European budget airlines, so the easiest and most common way to get to Essaouira is by bus. There is no train service and little parking space for private cars, but road connections are good, and buses can get you efficiently and easily to and from Agadir, Casablanca, and Marrakesh. The drive from Marrakesh or Agadir to Essaouira takes about three hours, with bus companies Supratours and CTM operating several daily services. Grands taxis are also an option.

The medina of Essaouira is compact, pedestrian-friendly, and easily walkable. Outside the walls, the local petits taxis are blue and have a fixed price of 6.50 DH during the day and 8 DH after 8 pm. A journey to Diabat costs 30 DH to 50 DH. You can hail the taxis on the street or pick them up at taxi stands outside the main medina gates.

Several local travel agents can arrange day trips and longer tours in a minibus or 4x4.

Bus Contacts CTM Essaouira ⊠ *Gare Routière* ☎ *0524/78–47–64* ⊕ *www.ctm. ma.* **Supratours** ⊠ *South Bastion, Medina* ☎ *0524/47–53–17.*

Rental Cars **Araucaria Car** ✉ *12, av. el-Koutoubia, Lot 5* ☎ *0524/47–22–25* ⊕ *www.araucariacar.com.* **El Ghazwa Car** ✉ *501, av. Al Aqaba, Lot 4* ☎ *0524/78–48–41, 0661/66–18–41* ⊕ *www.essaouira-location-cars.com.*

TOURS

Fikra Travel. Based out of Essaouira and Ouarzazate, Fikra Travel offers personalized tours of Morocco, specializing in the south and desert regions. It will tailor tours to suit your traveling needs and often deals with small groups and families traveling by 4x4, but can also offer routes by bus, camel, or even donkey. ✉ *4 bis, Derb Agadir, Medina* ☎ *0662/82–55–46* ⊕ *www.fikratravel.com* ⊟ *From 1,000 DH.*

Morocco Made Easy. A specialist in tailor-made holidays in Morocco, Australian-born founder Jane Folliott has over 15 years' experience working and living in Morocco. Based in Essaouira, this company can arrange a broad range of trips for individuals, families, and small groups, from day excursions to longer cultural and historical journeys throughout the country. Itineraries can be designed to suit your budget, level of comfort, and sense of adventure. ✉ *Dar Mouna Mogador, rue Ibn Khaldoun, Medina* ☎ *0666/40–95–48* ⊟ *From 450 DH.*

PLANNING YOUR TIME

Weekend visitors to Essaouira often leave wishing they had more time. If you can, plan to spend several days in this relaxing seaside town. The most popular time to visit is summer, but the best time is September when both tourist numbers and winds drop. Although the temperature is tolerable year-round, this is Africa's windy city, so don't expect to swim before May or after September.

FESTIVALS

Fodor's Choice
★

Gnaoua and World Music Festival. Essaouira is always packed over the third weekend of June, as 400,000 people from all over the world come to enjoy the annual four-day Gnaoua and World Music Festival. It's one of the best times to listen to traditional Gnaoua musicians. These descendants of African slaves established brotherhoods across Morocco and are healers and mystics as well as musicians. Among their troupes of *krakab* (metal castanet) players, *gimbri* (bass lute) players, and drummers, they have mediums and clairvoyants who perform wild, spellbinding acts. ■ TIP→ **If you plan to visit the festival, make sure you reserve accommodations at least three months in advance, as hotels and guesthouses will be full.** ⊕ *www.festival-gnaoua.net.*

VISITOR INFORMATION

Contacts **Delegation Provincial de Tourisme** ✉ *10, rue du Caire, Medina* ☎ *0524/78–35–32* ☉ *Closed weekends.*

EXPLORING

Dar Souiri. Home to the active Essaouira-Mogador Association, Dar Souiri is the hub of cultural life in Essaouira. Check the notice board outside the door for information on upcoming festivals, concerts, film screenings, and other cultural events. Inside, the building is an excellent example of 18th-century Mogador architecture and now houses an art gallery and a library. Free Wi-Fi is also available. ✉ *2, rue de Caire,*

Medina ☎ 0524/47–52–68 ⊕ *www.association-essaouiramogador.org*
⊙ *Tues.–Sun. 10–12:30 and 3–6.*

Patisserie Chez Driss. This local institution off the main square dates back
to 1929. Prices are very reasonable, so you can start your day with great
coffee and breakfasts. You can also take your pick from the French and
Moroccan pastries baked fresh every day. ■ TIP→ Take away some cakes
and coffee in the late afternoon and eat them at one of the cafés on the
square—it's what the locals do. ⊠ *9, rue el-Hajjali* ☎ *0524/47-27-93* ▭ *No
credit cards.*

Medina. This isn't so much a sight as the very essence of Essaouira,
where you are most likely to stay, eat, shop, and wander. The medina
was designed by French architect Théodore Cornut in the late 18th
century, on the instructions of Sidi Mohammed Ben Abdullah, who
wanted to create a new town and port to rival Agadir and demonstrate Morocco's outward focus. Cornut built the kasbah and the Sultan
invited prominent Jewish traders to settle here. Mogador (as it was then
known) soon thrived.

The medina is now a UNESCO World Heritage Site and efforts are
underway to restore some of the key buildings of Mogador's heyday,
namely the Simon Attia synagogue and the Danish consulate. The former Portuguese consulate and church are also earmarked for restoration. All feature the colonnaded ground floor and rooms off internal
walkways on the higher levels that are typical of the era.

From the kasbah, heading northwest, pass through the Mellah Kdim
(old Mellah) before finally reaching the Mellah proper. It was in this
latter area that less affluent Jews settled. Following the end of the French
Protectorate and the creation of the state of Israel, most of Mogador's
Jews left and the area is now home to poorer urban families and squatters in the ruined shells of former Jewish townhouses. It's best avoided
after dark. ■ TIP→ As you approach the Mellah, look for the Star of
David carved in stone above doorways.

North Bastion and Medina Skala. The distinctive outlines of the medina
skala and its citadel (the North Bastion) frame the waves dramatically
at sunset. The bastion once held emergency supplies of fresh water
and the large circle of stones in the center marks what was known as a
call-point, or alarm-system, to warn of approaching invaders. Guards
would warn of danger by stomping on the resonant circle. ■ TIP→ If
you stand in the middle of the circle and stomp your foot or yell, you'll
hear the echo ring far.

Fodor'sChoice
★

Port of Essaouira. Built in 1769 in the reign of Sidi Mohammed Ben
Abdellah by an Englishman who had converted to Islam, Essaouira's
port is still going strong in the southwest corner of town, and it's the one
must-see sight for any traveler coming here. Trawlers and other boats
bob along the quay, and middlemen and independent sailors sell the
daily catch of sardines, calamari, and skate fresh from small dockside tables.
You'll be selling yourself short if you don't have a meal of the freshest
fish imaginable at one of the shoreside grill restaurants. As Moroccan

8

ports go, it's also one of the most beautiful, not to mention accessible and tourist-friendly.

Port Skala. Essaouira has two principal *skala* (fortified bastions), with fabulous cannons: the medina skala and the port skala. Each was a strategic maritime defense point. Unlike the straight-edged Moorish constructions in other Moroccan cities, the ramparts in Essaouira are triangular, so the insider looking out has a broader field of vision than the enemy peering in. Orson Welles filmed scenes of his film *Othello* from the tower of the port skala, picking up a magnificent panorama of town, port, and bay all in one that can still be seen today. ■TIP→ **The entrance fee is well worth it to get the picture-postcard view of the medina through a round opening in the wall.** ⌨ *10 DH (free for Muslims on Fri.)*

Sidi Mohammed Ben Abdellah Ethnological Museum. The stunning former French-colonial town hall holds this smartly arranged collection of items from everyday and ritual life in and around the Essaouira area. Current exhibits include items related to the China tea trade in anticipation of the construction of a tea museum. The permanent collection includes musical instruments of both Gnaoua and Sufi sects; displays of regional carpet styles and wood-carving techniques and motifs; and examples of Muslim, Jewish, and rural Ishelhin Berber rites and dress. ✉ *7, rue Laalouj, Medina* ☎ *0524/47–23–00* ⌨ *10 DH* ☾ *Wed.–Mon. 8:30–6.*

NEED A BREAK? **Gelateria Dolcefreddo. Come here for the best coffee and the best ice cream in town; its location on the main square is also great for people-watching.** ■TIP→ **Pick a shady seat on the inside of the terrace under a parasol to avoid the passing street hawkers.** ✉ *25 bis, pl. Moulay Hassan, right on the main sq.* ☎ *0663/57–19–28.*

South Bastion. The South Bastion, also known as the Bastion Bab Marrakech, is a carefully restored element of the original fortified medina walls. Managed by the local Delegation of the Culture Ministry, it is open to the public when exhibitions and events take place, like the annual Gnaoua Festival. The flat roof offers a view over the rooftops to the beach and is often the backdrop to concerts and other performances. The area in front of the bastion (now a parking lot) was the site of the town's original Muslim cemetery.

OFF THE BEATEN PATH **Val d'Argan Vineyard.** Just outside Ounagha, about 35½ km (22 miles) from Essaouira, is the Val d'Argan vineyard, which was established by Charles Melia, an experienced winemaker of the Rhône valley in France, in 1994. It covers 128 acres, 100 of which are under cultivation, and it was the first Moroccan vineyard to be run organically. The vineyard produces a selection of ranges and labels featuring red, white, rosé, and—typical in Morocco—*vin gris* (gray) wines. Many of the wines here are commonly featured on wine lists in Essaouira and Marrakesh restaurants. Tours and tastings can be arranged in French, English, or Arabic, and there is a restaurant on site with a panoramic view of the vineyard and olive trees. ✉ *Domaine du Val d'Argan, Ounagha* ☎ *0524/78–34–67* ⊕ *www.valdargan.com.*

Essaouira's medina was built by a French architect to house Jewish merchants and create the country's foremost trading port.

BEACHES

Diabat Beach. Essaouira's beach is fine for an early-morning jog or a late-afternoon game of soccer, but serious sunbathers typically head south to quiet Diabat. Walking along the beach, cross over the mouth of the river and continue past the Borj el-Baroud, a former Portuguese fortification. To your left, a few miles south of town nestled in eucalyptus fields, you'll see the ruins of the so-called "Sultan's Palace." This building is said to have inspired Jimi Hendrix to write "Castles in the Sand," although he actually released the track a couple of years before his visit to this village, which has been trading on his name ever since. On a windy day the only escape is behind the Borj at low tide. **Amenities:** none. **Best for:** solitude; sunset. ✢ *A petit taxi can take you to the rotary at the edge of town (from which point you can walk to the beach via the unpaved road) or into the village of Diabat (via the new Sofitel Golf complex).*

FAMILY **Essaouira Bay.** Essaouira's main beach is a sweep of sand along the bay that has provided shelter to seafarers from Atlantic storms since antiquity. Although temperatures are moderate all year and the sun is nearly always shining, the wind is consistently strong, making sunbathing or swimming less attractive than further south in Agadir. Nonetheless, sun-bed rentals are relatively inexpensive or even free if you eat at one of the cafés at the southern end of the beach.

The wind comes from the north and creates three main areas. The most northerly part, tucked up into the armpit of the port, has wind that comes in gusts. Just south of this the wind strengthens, with fewer gusts.

Farther south are the steady, strong trade winds the town is known for, and that make it a mecca for wind- and kite surfers. The range of areas makes the bay perfect for every level of water-sports enthusiast.

The surrounding islets, the Iles de Mogador, are home to nine bird species, including the endangered Eleanora's falcon. They are closed to visitors during breeding season (April through October), but otherwise you can get a ride from the port, on boats leaving morning and afternoon depending on weather conditions.

Since summer 2013, the seafront promenade has been under renovation. Plans are to provide more strolling, parking, and relaxation areas interspersed with palm trees and other vegetation. **Amenities:** food and drink; lifeguards (summer only); toilets; parking (10 DH); water sports. **Best for:** sunset; swimming; walking; windsurfing.

Sidi Kaouki. The tranquil beach village of Sidi Kaouki is often touted as an alternative to Essaouira's beach, but it doesn't have the amenities of its larger neighbor. It is, however, the destination of choice for younger backpackers, surfers, and windsurfers, which should give you an idea of the typical wind velocity and wave size. "Town" consists of a number of guesthouses, a couple of shops, and some small restaurants all serving the same standard tourist menus. It's easy to rent mountain bikes, quad bikes, or ponies for a jaunt along the beach towards Ouassane (the village to the north) or Sidi M'barek (with a waterfall and wide sandy beach) to the south. ■TIP➔ For the energetic, it's possible to walk along the beach and over a cliff from Essaouira to Sidi Kaouki—about 13 miles one-way. Walking in the opposite direction (against the wind) is not recommended. **Amenties:** food and drink; parking (5 DH–10 DH per day in summer); toilets; water sports. **Best for:** sunset; surfing; walking. ⊠ *Sidi Kaouki, 27 km (17 miles) southwest of Diabat* ✛ *The turnoff is 15 km (9 miles) south of Diabat on the Agadir road. The No. 2 Lima bus goes to Sidi Kaouki.*

OFF THE BEATEN PATH

Numerous paved roads jut off the road to Agadir heading toward the beaches along the coast, including the fishing and camping site at **Plage Tafadna**, 37 km (23 miles) south of the Sidi Kaouki turnoff. Farther south, **Imssouane**, a fishing village on a peninsula just inside the border between Essaouira and Agadir provinces, is a popular spot for locals and backpackers who want to find total seclusion. There are two beaches here—one for surfing and a calmer one that's perfect for families. Accessibility to the beaches and the locals' experience of foreign visitors lessen as you move south until you head beyond Cap Rhir and the increasingly developed beaches north of Agadir.

WHERE TO EAT

There are some great restaurants in Essaouira. From port catches grilled in front of you to inventive and expensive fish dishes in the swankiest restaurants, seafood tends to headline menus when the surf permits. A must-do experience is lunch or dinner in one of the seafood grills near the port: feast on charcoal-grilled sardines, calamari, red snapper, sea bass, whiting, and shrimp (crab is usually too dry) from among the array of stalls, and experience the color and bustle of the port. You choose your fish, then establish a price based on weight. The later in the day, the lower you'll be able to negotiate the price, but as Essaouira can be very windy, enjoying lunch alfresco in the sun makes much more sense than a breezy dinner. This is a great place to go if you are tiring of tagine. You could also take a stroll along Avenue L'Istiqlal (known by locals as "Haddada"), or better still Avenue Mohammed el-Quori (known by locals as "Souk Waka"). Here you'll be able to pack an exotic picnic of salty battered fish, potato patties, stuffed sardines in fresh Moroccan bread, almonds and peanuts, fruit, and sticky Maghrebian sweets.

In addition, there are also lots of traditional Moroccan options and excellent examples of French, Italian, and even Asian food.

$ ✕ **Café Rio.** If you are in Essaouira long enough to want to get out of the
CAFÉ medina, take a stroll along the beach and into what locals are calling "Guéliz on the Sea." Here you'll find a short strip of shiny new cafés, the best of which is Rio. There's a great menu featuring good-value European-style (juices, croissants, coffee) or Moroccan-style (breads, soup, omelets, tea) breakfasts. Plus, snacks and meals are served all day. ■ TIP➡ Make like a local and watch the world go by over a large nouss-nouss (it's like a latte), with pastries from the bakery around the corner. The staff doesn't mind and will even bring a plate for you. $ *Average main: 50DH* ✉ *38–39, av. Lalla Amina* ☎ *0524/47–43–69.*

$$$$ ✕ **Caravane Café.** Artist Didier Spindler invites you to join him in this
ECLECTIC renovated riad filled with his own works, various pieces he has collected from around the world, and some tasty food. The décor is an eclectic mix of Buddha statues, pop art, and palm trees. The menu is equally imaginative, featuring a fusion of Moroccan, European, and Asian flavors. There is frequently entertainment in the form of a band or fire eater as well as a great wine list; many people pop in just for a drink. The trio of desserts is the perfect sharing dish to conclude your meal (and often features more than three sweet delicacies). $ *Average main: 120DH* ✉ *2 bis, rue Cadi Ayad, Medina* ☎ *0524/78–31–11* ▭ *No credit cards* ⊘ *Closed Mon.*

$ ✕ **Chez Françoise.** There's a daily range of bites, including quiches, sal-
EUROPEAN ads, and the occasional crêpe, at this nice little lunch place that's great for vegetarians. With only two rows of four small tables set beneath the artwork of owner Françoise's husband, it makes a good stop for afternoon tea. $ *Average main: 60DH* ✉ *1, rue Houmane el-Fetouaki* ☎ *0668/16–40–87* ▭ *No credit cards* ⊘ *Closed Sun. No dinner.*

$$$ ✕ **Dar Loubane.** In this long-standing restaurant of more than 20 years,
MOROCCAN you can eat among cascading plants in the airy courtyard of an 18th-century *caravanserai* (roadside inn). There's a daily lunch menu as well as a dish of the day and you can order à la carte anytime. The menu includes *pastilla* (sweet pigeon pie), *briouates* (phyllo pastry parcels), ray with capers, grills, and tagines. Half portions are available and there's a wine list of local and Meknès wines. On Thursday there's jazz; local Gnaoua musicians play on Saturday night. $ *Average main: 100DH* ✉ *24, rue de Rif* ☎ *0524/47–62–96.*

$ ✕ **Dar Mounia.** Easy to find in the heart of the medina underneath a hotel
MOROCCAN of the same name, this unpretentious Moroccan restaurant is spacious

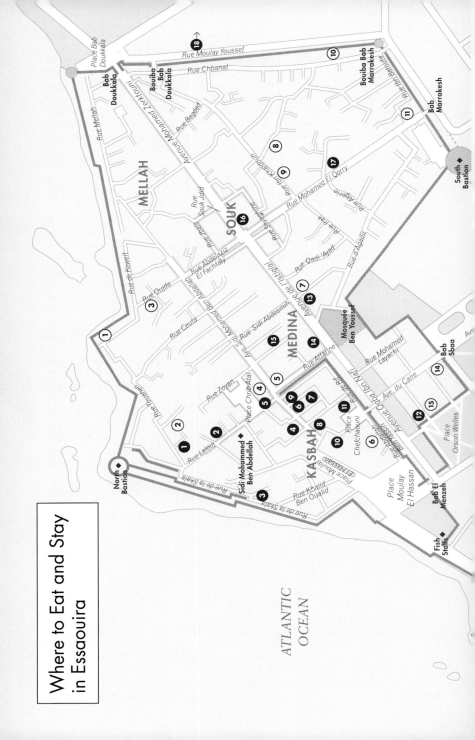

Where to Eat and Stay in Essaouira

ATLANTIC OCEAN

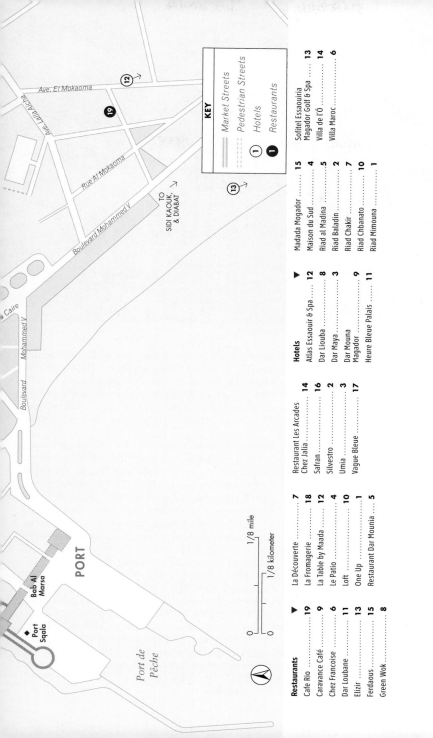

Restaurants ▶
Cafe Rio **19**
Caravance Café **9**
Chez Francoise **6**
Dar Loubane **11**
Elizir **13**
Ferdaous **15**
Green Wok **8**

La Découverte **7**
La Fromagerie **18**
La Table by Maada **12**
Le Patio **4**
Loft **10**
One Up **1**
Restaurant Dar Mounia ... **5**

Restaurant Les Arcades ... **14**
Chez Jalia **16**
Safran **2**
Silvestro **3**
Umia **3**
Vague Bleue **17**

Hotels ▶
Atlas Essaouir & Spa ... **12**
Dar Liouba **8**
Dar Maya **3**
Dar Mouna **9**
Magador **11**
Heure Bleue Palais **11**

Madada Mogador **15**
Maison du Sud **4**
Riad al Madina **5**
Riad Baladin **2**
Riad Chakir **7**
Riad Chbanato **10**
Riad Mimouna **1**

Sofitel Essaouria ......
Magador Golf & Spa **13**
Villa de l'Ô **14**
Villa Maroc **6**

KEY

━━━ *Market Streets*
- - - *Pedestrian Streets*
① *Hotels*
❶ *Restaurants*

PORT

Port de
Pêche

Port Sqala

Bab Al
Marsa

0 ————— 1/8 mile
0 ————— 1/8 kilometer

Boulevard Mohammed V

Caire

Ave. El Mokaoma
Ave. Lalla Aïcha
Rue Al Mokaoma

TO
SIDI KAOUK,
& DIABAT →

The Essaouira medina is a UNESCO World Heritage Site.

and cool. Hidden amongst the extensive menu of couscous, tagine, and pastilla variations are a few refreshing surprises. Try the grilled zucchini short-crust tart or a melt-in-the-mouth marinated fish kebab, and wash it down with a zingy, freshly squeezed lemon juice with ginger. Along with great food and decent prices, there's also a kid's menu. There's no alcohol. $ *Average main: 70DH* ⊠ *2, rue Laalouj, Medina* ☎ *0524/47–29–88.*

$$$$
MEDITERRANEAN

✕ **Elizir.** Amid a collection of retro *objets* and mismatched furniture, you can enjoy a short but fine menu of Moroccan-Italian fusion cuisine. Diners are seated in a number of small rooms with kitschy décor—if you're lucky, you might spot a visiting celebrity. This is consistently a local favorite: the menu features the best steak in town, alongside some twists on Moroccan classics such as chicken tagine with bleu cheese. Owner Abdellatif prepares the steaks himself, having spent nine years in Bologna; he claims Moroccan chefs don't do rare or medium-rare—only well-done. There is a limited wine list and the desserts are fabulous. $ *Average main: 130DH* ⊠ *1, rue Agadir, Medina* ☎ *0524/47–21–03* ⬛ *Reservations essential* ▬ *No credit cards* ☾ *No lunch.*

$$
MOROCCAN

✕ **Ferdaous.** At this favorite for authentic, homely, Moroccan cuisine, chef Madame Souad, formerly of the Villa Maroc, cooks up excellent starters and mains while the tagines bubble and boil deliciously in the kitchen downstairs. This is as close as you'll get to Moroccan home cooking in a restaurant. The specialties are meat tagines with dried fruits and nuts. Be sure to try the three-course set menu at 140 DH, but call ahead to see if there are any vegetarian options available that day. $ *Average main: 80DH* ⊠ *27, rue Abdesslam Lebadi* ☎ *0524/47–36–55* ▬ *No credit cards* ☾ *Closed Sun.*

$$ ⫻ **Green Wok.** When you've had one tagine too many and feel like some-
ASIAN thing with a bit of a chili kick, the guys from Green Wok come to
the rescue. Essaouira's only Asian restaurant is surprisingly good and
serves a range of pan-Asian staples such as *nems* (minced pork sausage),
spring rolls, *tom yam* soup (spicy and sour soup), Thai curries, and stir-
fries. They can also prepare dishes to take away. Be aware that they
are closed during Friday prayers. Ⓢ *Average main: 85DH* ⊠ *6, rue el
Hajjali, Medina* ☎ *0524/78–30–28* ▭ *No credit cards* ⊘ *Closed Mon.
and daily 3:30–7.*

$$ ⫻ **La Découverte.** Owner and chef Frederique employs only locals and
MOROCCAN uses ingredients from local farmers and co-ops to implement her slow-
food philosophy. Using traditional recipes and always with the greatest
respect for the heritage and provenance of her dishes, she and sous-chef
Khadija create a menu of authentic salads, mains, and desserts plus
daily specials. The emphasis is on avoiding waste, so customers are
encouraged to order exactly what they want—no more, no less. Try
the camel couscous on a Monday and ask for a copy of Fred's book
about the medicinal and culinary uses of Moroccan spices. Ⓢ *Average
main: 80DH* ⊠ *Rue Houmman el Fatouaki* ☎ *0524/47–31–58* ⊕ *www.
essaouira-ladecouverte.com* ▭ *No credit cards* ⊘ *Closed Sat.*

$$$$ ⫻ **La Fromagerie.** A few miles outside town on the edge of thuya and olive
MEDITERRANEAN groves, owners Abderrazak and Jawad welcome you warmly to their
Fodor's Choice artisanal cheesery and open-air restaurant. Enjoy a fixed-menu lunch
★ of salads topped with local goat-and-sheep-milk cheeses, followed by
(for nonvegetarians) a goat tagine. A *mechoui* (lamb spit roast) is also
available by prior arrangement. Wines are served. If you can still move
after the feast, bike rentals and horse or camel rides can be arranged.
Ⓢ *Average main: 170DH* ⊠ *Rte. de Safi, 1 km (½ mile) after the rotary
on the Essaouira–Marrakesh rd.* ☎ *0658/83–99–99, 0666/23–35–34*
⌧ *Reservations essential* ▭ *No credit cards* ⊘ *No dinner.*

$$ ⫻ **Le Mogadorien.** Often overlooked in favor of the smaller lounge-style
MOROCCAN restaurants further along the street, Le Mogadorien has a similar menu
but a lot more style. The décor reflects Essaouira's Berber, Arab, Jew-
ish, and Christian heritage, giving you a choice of low-slung Moroccan
salon seats or regular chairs and tables. Chef Najiba prepares a range
of Moroccan classics and local seafood. The vegetarian tagine features
no less than eight vegetables; ask for it with *tfaya* (caramelized onions
and raisins) for an authentic twist. Alcohol is not served. Ⓢ *Average
main: 70DH* ⊠ *7, pl. Chefchaouni* ☎ *0524/47–49–50.*

$$$$ ⫻ **La Table by Madada.** In a former warehouse of the sultan's Jewish
SEAFOOD traders, this is one of three Madada brand businesses in Essaouira.
Next to the Madada cooking workshop, the restaurant and bar offers
fresh seafood prepared imaginatively and according to the seasons.
Try the monkfish tagine with caramelized apples or the lobster pas-
tilla. You can also pop in to enjoy tapas and a cocktail. There is live
music on the weekends. While pricier than other establishments in the
area, Madada's enduring popularity with residents of the local upscale
hotels proves it's worth every penny. ■TIP➔ **Be sure to reserve a table
ahead of time, especially in summer.** Ⓢ *Average main: 145DH* ⊠ *7, rue*

8

Youssef el-Fassi, Medina ☎ 0524/47–55–12 🌐 www.latablemadada.com ✍ Reservations essential ⏲ No lunch.

$$$$ MOROCCAN 🍴 **Le Patio.** This French-run restaurant offers Moroccan cooking with a twist; for example, fish tagines are made with pears, apples, or prunes. The small tables are set around a large starry lantern, and the deep-red walls, white muslin, and candles create a romantic atmosphere, although it's a little too dark for gazing into each other's eyes. There is a decent list of local wines. [$] *Average main: 120DH ✉ 28 bis, rue Moulay Rachid ☎ 0524/47–41–66 ⏲ Closed Sun.*

$$ MEDITERRANEAN 🍴 **Loft.** This is a new kid on the "Tagine Alley" block. A café, restaurant, and art gallery, this little corner is a sure-fire hit with local artists and bohemians. All the art objects on display are for sale. The seasonally changing menu features mainly seafood and a few surprises such as a *mille-feuille* (stack) of eggplant and local goat cheese. After your meal, try a spiced coffee or Berber tea. [$] *Average main: 70DH ✉ 5, rue Haj-jali ☎ 0524/47–63–89 💳 No credit cards.*

$$$$ MODERN FRENCH 🍴 **One Up.** Scottish hairdresser John has created this restaurant within the former British consulate building of old Mogador and decorated it to fit in among the pages of an interior-decorating magazine. It's worth a visit for the funky décor alone, but the food is equally enticing, and the service is friendly and attentive. The menu, created by a chef from Le Zinc restaurant in Marrakesh, includes fish and meat dishes and a particularly wonderful gourmet burger. Make sure to leave space for dessert—there's an eclectic and tasty collection to choose from. [$] *Average main: 130DH ✉ 1, Derb Laalouj ☎ 0634/92–02–01 🌐 www.oneup-essaouira.com 💳 No credit cards ⏲ Closed Sun. No lunch.*

$$ MOROCCAN 🍴 **Restaurant Les Arcades Chez Jalila.** At Chez Jalila, you will find the effervescent Joelle, a Frenchwoman who has made Essaouira her home, bringing with her a love of cooking and the ability to mix her French flair with local ingredients and recipes. The restaurant is bright and airy with a surprisingly large roof terrace overlooking a main medina street. Specialties include traditional dishes such as chicken pastilla, *tagia* (a Marrakshi dish traditionally baked in a ceramic tureen), or sardines *farcies* (butterflied and sandwiched around an herbed, spicy filling). Be sure to try the homemade juices and ice creams. [$] *Average main: 70DH ✉ 3, av. de l'Istiqlal ☎ 0524/78–32–01 💳 No credit cards.*

$$ MOROCCAN 🍴 **Safran.** In a sunny spot in the cobbled old grain market, Safran offers a range of grilled fish, à la carte lunches and suppers, freshly made juices, and much more. A great location for an alfresco meal or just a coffee, if you sit here long enough you'll see plenty of Essaouira's musical and acrobatic street entertainers. It's open into the early evening, when patio heaters keep diners warm. There's also free Wi-Fi. [$] *Average main: 70DH ✉ 116, pl. Marché aux Grains ☎ 0600/60–50–31.*

$ ITALIAN 🍴 **Silvestro.** A long-standing favorite among locals, expats, and tourists, Silvestro serves the best crispy pizzas in the medina straight from a wood-fired oven. Diners eat in an eclectically decorated dining room or upstairs on the enclosed terrace. The menu also features home-cooked pasta dishes. Wines and other alcoholic drinks are available. [$] *Average main: 60DH ✉ 70, rue Laalouj ☎ 0524/47–35–55 💳 No credit cards.*

$$$$ MOROCCAN Fodor's Choice ★ 🍴 **Taros.** Taros is a restaurant, bar, boutique, art gallery, and international meeting space all in one. It's named after the wind that blows off the sea, and you can sip cocktails on a terrific rooftop terrace with views of the port. The lunch menu changes daily, and for dinner, chef Abdesamad prepares specialties such as Oualidia oysters and other dishes that blend local ingredients with modern inspiration. The goat tagine (with a delicious nutty flavor thanks to the goat's argan diet) is fantastic. For dessert, try the chocolate fondant. Dinner is served downstairs by the attentive staff while a band or DJ plays on the roof to a hip crowd. **TIP→ On chillier evenings on the terrace, ask the staff for a poncho.** [$] *Average main: 130DH* ✉ *Pl. Moulay Hassan, at rue de la Skala* ☎ *0524/47–64–07* 🌐 *www.taroscafe.com.*

$$$$ MODERN EUROPEAN Fodor's Choice ★ 🍴 **Umia.** When it first opened in 2014, Umia was the talk of Essaouira and it's not hard to see why. The daily changing menu—prepared in an open kitchen—blends seasonal and local ingredients with French *savoir faire*. The airy restaurant draws in a clientele of expats and tourists with its muted dove grays, glossy white furniture, and quirky art touches, such as a gorgeous Gnaoua mural. Be sure to try the goat cheese from a women's co-op in nearby Meskala; you also can't miss the chocolate fondant with salted caramel ice cream. [$] *Average main: 120DH* ✉ *26, rue de la Skala* ☎ *0524/78–33–95.*

$ ITALIAN 🍴 **Vague Bleue.** One of Essaouira's best-kept secrets, this little hole-in-the-wall restaurant never fails to impress. Manager Brahim offers freshly prepared Italian mains (fish, chicken, and pasta), all served with a trio of salads and two juices to start. The ray with caper butter sauce is especially incredible. The place is tiny, so if you can't get in at first, come back later. [$] *Average main: 50DH* ✉ *2, rue Sidi Ali Ben Abdullah, Medina* ☎ *0611/28–37–91* 💳 *No credit cards* ⏲ *Closed Fri.*

COOKING CLASSES

Many riads offer cookery classes or demonstrations, but the best place in Essaouira to learn about Moroccan cuisine is L'Atelier de Madada, next to the eponymous restaurant.

Fodor's Choice ★ **L'Atelier by Madada.** By far the best setup for cooking classes in town, here you'll get an authentic, step-by-step introduction to Moroccan cuisine. Chef Mouna shares the secrets of generations of Moroccan housewives with simultaneous English translation. The first to reserve each day gets to choose from a range of menus, including tagines, pastilla, couscous, and traditional cooked salads. Classes last around four hours and include a tour of the spice souk where the meal's ingredients come from. A glass of wine costs extra. ✉ *7 bis, rue Youssef el-Fassi* ☎ *0524/47–55–12* 🌐 *www.lateliermadada.com* ⏲ *From 500 DH.*

WHERE TO STAY

The riad mania spread to Essaouira just a few years ago and is still going strong, although many of the first foreign riad renovators have now built villas in the countryside where the winds and humidity are lower. Rooms are generally less opulent and less expensive than those in Marrakesh, but you'll find plenty of charm and elegance. There are also plenty of even less expensive hotels, but fewer of the seriously budget hippie hangouts of yesteryear.

For hotels with swimming pools you'll have only one expensive option within the medina: L'Heure Bleue Palais. Other beachfront hotels with pools are fine if you have a large family, and may offer shelter on windier days, but the beach is never very far away on foot.

Another option is to rent an apartment, by the night or by the week. There's a wide range of options, from spartan bedrooms with showers that don't work, to an entire superstyled riad. Renting is often a better deal than staying in a hotel, especially if you're with a group. Rooms book up quickly, especially in summer, so reserve (sometimes months) ahead. ■ TIP→ You can only take a car as far as a medina gate, so you'll have to heave your luggage to that dear little out-of-the-way spot down 10 twisting alleys yourself. The best option? Pick up a carossa (a small cart on wheels) from the parking lot outside Bab Sbâa and pay the owner and cart wheeler 20 DH for his trouble.

$$$
B&B/INN

🏨 **Dar Liouba.** This is actually two properties combined and remodeled to ensure the atrium and bedrooms are flooded with light. **Pros:** more light than most riads; warm welcome; rooftop sea views. **Cons:** tucked away in the Chbanate neighborhood, so you may need some guidance to find your way. $ *Rooms from: 792DH* ✉ *28, Impasse Moulay Ismail* ☎ *0524/47–62–97* ⊕ *www.darliouba.eu* 🛏 *8 rooms* 🍽 *Multiple meal plans.*

$$$$
B&B/INN

🏨 **Dar Maya.** With only five rooms but plenty of communal spaces, every inch of Dar Maya is designed to perfection, creating the boutique hotel Essaouira has been waiting for. **Pros:** intimate and chic; attentive English-speaking staff. **Cons:** rooms are often booked up. $ *Rooms from: 1595DH* ✉ *33, rue d'Oujda* ☎ *0524/78–56–87* ⊕ *www.riaddarmaya.com* 🛏 *2 rooms, 3 suites* 🍽 *Multiple meal plans.*

$$
B&B/INN

🏨 **Dar Mouna Mogador.** Manager Jane offers a warm welcome at this hotel in the Essaouira medina, where she is happy to help plan excursions and activities in and around the city. **Pros:** the warmest welcome in town; family rooms available. **Cons:** dark interior; no external windows in rooms. $ *Rooms from: 600DH* ✉ *44, rue Ibn Khaldoun* ☎ *0524/78–32–56* 🛏 *5 rooms* 🍽 *Multiple meal plans.*

$$$$
HOTEL
Fodor'sChoice
★

🏨 **Heure Bleue Palais.** Enjoy ample space and amenities like nowhere else in the medina at Essaouira's most prestigious lodging, a meticulously designed property with a colonial-era feel in cream, granite, and darkwood decor. **Pros:** more space than you'd think possible in the medina; the only pool inside the medina walls. **Cons:** not the typical Moroccan décor some might expect; by far the most expensive rates in the medina. $ *Rooms from: 1870DH* ✉ *2, rue Ibn Batouta* ☎ *0524/78–34–34* ⊕ *www.relaischateaux.com/heurebleue* 🛏 *19 rooms, 14 suites* 🍽 *Multiple meal plans.*

$$$$
HOTEL

🏨 **Hotel Atlas Essaouira and Spa.** The Hotel Atlas provides beachfront five-star service with all the facilities you would expect from the Moroccon brand. **Pros:** private beach; delicious restaurant. **Cons:** corporate feel; lacks charm. $ *Rooms from: 1400DH* ✉ *Bd. Mohammed V* ☎ *0524/47–99–99* ⊕ *www.hotelsatlas.com* 🛏 *149 rooms, 7 suites* 🍽 *Multiple meal plans.*

$$$$ ⬚ **Le Medina Essaouira Hotel Thalassa Sea & Spa by M Gallery Collection.**
HOTEL   The closest to the medina of the city's two beachfront five-star hotels,
FAMILY   the property formerly known as the Sofitel has a location and facilities that are second to none. **Pros:** large pool; private beach; great spa;
good access for those with reduced mobility. **Cons:** lacks Moroccan
charm beyond the lobby. $ *Rooms from: 1300DH* ⊠ *Bd. Mohammed
V* ☎ *0524/47–90–00* ⊕ *www.lemedina-essaouira.com* ⤳ *102 rooms,
15 suites* ⎢◎⎢ *Multiple meal plans.*

$$$$ ⬚ **Madada Mogador.** Stylized, elegant, and designed to perfection,
B&B/INN   Madada Mogador is perfectly poised just within the medina walls to
ensure easy access and ocean views from most rooms. **Pros:** attentive
staff; cool lounge spaces. **Cons:** confusing shared entrance with hotel
next door; two-night minimum stay. $ *Rooms from: 1485DH* ⊠ *5, rue
Youssef el-Fassi* ☎ *0524/47–55–12* ⊕ *www.madada.com* ⤳ *5 rooms, 2
suites* ⎢◎⎢ *Breakfast.*

$$$ ⬚ **Maison du Sud.** Enter through a traditional, heavy, stone arch off a
B&B/INN   busy medina street, and you'll find a cool interior made of two large
town houses and a friendly, English-speaking management team. **Pros:**
great central location in the medina; triple and quadruple rooms avail-
able. **Cons:** some rooms feel cramped; can fill up with groups. $ *Rooms
from: 720DH* ⊠ *29, av. Sidi Mohammed Ben Abdellah* ☎ *0524/47–41–
41* ⊕ *www.riad-maisondusud.com* ⤳ *18 rooms, 6 suites* ⎢◎⎢ *Multiple
meal plans.*

$$$ ⬚ **Riad Al Madina.** This beautiful 18th-century riad is wrapped around
HOTEL   a stone courtyard where you'll find a trickling fountain. **Pros:** sun-filled
rooms and patio; in-house hammam. **Cons:** can feel very crowded.
$ *Rooms from: 880DH* ⊠ *9, rue Attarine* ☎ *0524/47–59–07* ⊕ *www.
riadalmadina.com* ⤳ *39 rooms, 16 suites* ⎢◎⎢ *Multiple meal plans.*

$$$ ⬚ **Riad Baladin.** Swiss manager Nicole offers her guests a multilingual,
B&B/INN   personal service that keeps them coming back. **Pros:** larger and lighter
rooms than most riads; personalized service; quiet cul-de-sac loca-
tion. **Cons:** cash only; no meals other than breakfast. $ *Rooms from:
770DH* ⊠ *9, rue Sidi Magdoul* ☎ *0524/47–30–94* ⊕ *www.riadbaladin.
com* ⤳ *10 rooms* ⊟ *No credit cards* ⎢◎⎢ *Breakfast.*

$$ ⬚ **Riad Chakir.** This colorful and friendly budget riad is actually made
B&B/INN   up of three neighboring houses. **Pros:** great value and location; friendly,
English-speaking staff. **Cons:** some rooms cramped; more homey com-
fort than boutique chic. $ *Rooms from: 495DH* ⊠ *13, rue Malek Ben
Morhal, off av. Istiqlal* ☎ *0524/47–33–09* ⊕ *www.riadchakir.com* ⤳ *20
rooms* ⎢◎⎢ *Breakfast.*

$$$$ ⬚ **Riad Chbanate.** This former 18th-century *caid*'s (local official's) resi-
B&B/INN   dence has been transformed into a boutique hotel flooded with light.
Pros: gorgeous rooftop suite with 360-degree views of the city; beauti-
fully decorated rooms. **Cons:** some rooms have open-plan bathrooms
which are not to everyone's taste. $ *Rooms from: 1760DH* ⊠ *179, rue
Chbanate* ☎ *0524/78–33–34* ⊕ *www.eng.riadchbanate.com* ⤳ *8 rooms*
⎢◎⎢ *Multiple meal plans.*

$$$ ⬚ **Riad Mimouna.** Tight against the northern side of the medina walls,
HOTEL   this riad sits over the water's edge, letting you have the raging sea all
to yourself. **Pros:** beautiful views; central heating in winter. **Cons:** some

8

rooms too weather-beaten. [$] *Rooms from: 850DH* ✉ *62, rue d'Oujda, Sandillon* ☎ *0524/78–57–53* 🌐 *www.riad-mimouna.com* 🛏 *24 rooms, 9 suites* 🍴 *Multiple meal plans.*

$$$$ RESORT 🏨 **Sofitel Essaouira Mogador Golf & Spa.** This five-star resort with villas is set on 16 gorgeous acres about 5 km (3 miles) south of Essaouira above the village of Diabat. **Pros:** heaps of facilities including three pools, a kids' club and petting zoo, gym, hammam, four restaurants, and a nightclub. **Cons:** far from the medina and the free shuttle bus stops at 6 pm; the beach is a 20-minute walk away. [$] *Rooms from: 2054DH* ✉ *Domaine de Mogador* ☎ *0524/47–94–00* 🌐 *www.sofitel.com/7145* 🛏 *133 rooms, 7 suites, 28 villas* 🍴 *Multiple meal plans.*

$$$$ B&B/INN 🏨 **Villa de l'Ô.** The Essaouira location of this small regional chain exudes sophistication, with its wood-paneled library, colonial-style décor, and sleek roof terrace with sweeping views of the whole beach. **Pros:** a level of service and style above the rest; fabulous roof terrace. **Cons:** this kind of service gets pricey. [$] *Rooms from: 2300DH* ✉ *3, rue Mohamed Ben Messaoud* ☎ *0524/47–63–75* 🌐 *www.villadelo.com* 🛏 *12 rooms* 🍴 *Breakfast.*

$$$$ HOTEL 🏨 **Villa Maroc.** Embodying much of what international travelers seek in a Moroccan hotel, the intimate Villa Maroc is delightfully decorated to epitomize a "traditional" Moroccan style that never really was. **Pros:** great service; sizable rooms; on-site hammam. **Cons:** when busy, a minimum stay may be required. [$] *Rooms from: 1320DH* ✉ *10, rue Abdellah Ben Yassine* ☎ *0524/47–61–47* 🌐 *www.villa-maroc.com* 🛏 *21 rooms* 🍴 *Multiple meal plans.*

APARTMENT RENTAL AGENCIES

Arriving in the city's outskirts, you'll see men dangling keys by the side of the road, hoping to rent you an apartment. It's best to go through official agents, however.

Castles in the Sand. British interior designer Emma Wilson rents out two medina townhouses. Dar Beida, the "White House," is one of Essaouira's most sumptuous addresses. The villa is filled with hip furnishings and décor from the 1950s and 1960s. Cool 21st-century perks include iPod speakers and wireless Internet. The other villa, Dar Emma, has a more traditional feel. ☎ *0667/96–53–86* 🌐 *www.castlesinthesand.com.*

Jack's Apartments. Several beautiful old medina studios, apartments, riads, and penthouses are available for rent. Each is serviced daily, and all are fully equipped with towels, sheets, blankets, soap, and a hair dryer. In addition, Jack's team can provide breakfast and other meals delivered to your door. ✉ *1, pl. Moulay Hassan* ☎ *0524/47–55–38* 🌐 *www.jackapartments.com.*

NIGHTLIFE

Most Essaouira residents consider nightlife to involve simply hanging out at a café on the main square, but should you fancy partying into the night after dinner, there are a few options.

Le Chrysalis. By far the most appealing of Essaouira's nightclubs, every night at Le Chrysalis has a band playing an eclectic set of covers of popular Western tunes, as well as Moroccan and West African favorites.

The drinks aren't cheap, but the atmosphere is lively and the place pulls in a range of tourists, locals, and expats of varying ages. ✉ *Bin Laswar, Bab Sbaa* ☎ *0661/74–05–68, 0666/45–00–93.*

Loubou's. At the younger end of the scene, Loubou's is loud and smoky with a DJ pumping out dance music while customers smoke water pipes in chairs around the dance floor. Admission is typically free unless a guest DJ has been flown in for the night. ✉ *32, Lot Bin Al Aswar* ☎ *0524/78–48–72* ⊕ *www.loubouslounge.com.*

So Lounge. Modeled after its successful older sister in Agadir, the So Lounge at the Sofitel in Diabat is the height of sophistication. A cocktail bar and restaurant overlooks the main bar, stage, and dance area; live music is played every night except Monday. Admission is free, but it's recommended that diners book a table. ✉ *Sofitel Essaouira Mogador Golf & Spa, Domaine de Mogador* ☎ *0524/47–94–00* ⊕ *www.sofitel. com/7145.*

SHOPPING

Essaouira is a great shopping destination. Although the range may be more limited than in Marrakesh or Fez, the vendors are lot more relaxed and starting prices are often reasonable.

Essaouira is famed as an artisan center expert in marquetry and inlay. Boxes, platters, and picture frames made of local thuya wood make excellent gifts, and the wood-carvers' souk below the skala is a popular place to purchase them. A hard, local wood that shines up to almost plastic perfection, thuya is sculpted for both artistic and practical use. Almost-life-size statues and sculptures sit alongside boxes, bowls, and chess sets. Scan a number of stores to see whether you prefer the even-toned thuya branch inlaid with mother-of-pearl or walnut or one with swirling root designs. To get a bulk price, buy a bunch of items from a craftsman who specializes in them.

The main areas for purchasing local crafts and souvenirs are rue Sidi Mohammed Ben Abdullah, Derb Laalouj, and along the skala. Colorful, woven baskets hang from herbalists' stores in the spice souk and the place Marché aux Grains across the road. While the bazaars, tended by turbaned men of the South, will sell antique (and faux-antique) silver jewelry, locals tend to buy new items from the jewelry souk off avenue L'Istiqlal. Dive into the small, shady alleyways off the main areas to find more treasures such as carpets, cushion covers, up-cycled antiques from ruined Jewish houses, jewelry and punched metal, and goatskin lamps.

Essaouira is also home to a number of expat artists and craftspeople. Many restaurants and boutique stores sell their work in glass cabinets at fixed prices.

ANTIQUES

Galérie Aida. For tasteful used pewter platters, goblets, and ceramic teapots, as well as new and used English and French books, check the Galérie Aida, underneath the ramparts. This also a large selection of antique daggers. The gallery's owner, Joseph Sebag, one of Essaouira's

BERBER GOLD: ARGAN OIL

The Moroccan argan forest, which stretches from Essaouira down past Agadir and along the Souss Valley to the Anti-Atlas, is unique, as there is nowhere else in the world where the tree grows so well. As you travel across the region, you will see the short, spiny trees in fields and on hillsides.

In recent years, as the aesthetic properties of argan oil have been widely publicized, the Moroccan government has developed a strategy to support the creation of women's co-ops to extract and market the oil, as well as to preserve the unique biosphere and protect against overuse. As prices have rise, argan oil has become known as "Berber gold," with leading beauty brands including it in their products and famous television chefs developing recipes to include it.

The difference between cosmetic and culinary oils is that the latter is the result of grinding the almonds found inside the argan nut after toasting, while cosmetic oil is ground directly.

Without a doubt, the argan boom has brought much-needed employment opportunities to rural areas, particularly for women. However, many establishments that claim to operate on cooperative principles (especially those on main tourist thoroughfares) often do not. Also, many co-ops which tout "bio" or "organic" branding may use nuts that have not been sprayed with pesticides, but few have actually been able to secure organic certification.

When buying argan oil, try to buy from a genuine cooperative to ensure you get the real deal and that your money helps rural women. The UCFA is a union created with aid from foreign development agencies to help professionalize and support women's argan co-ops. They have a list of their members online (⊕ *www. cooperative-argane.com*).

If your concern is the oil being 100% organic, it may be that the production is less hands-on and more mechanized than in rural co-ops. The oils produced at Sidi Yassine outside Essaouira are widely exported and therefore rigorously certified. You can buy them at Histoire de Filles. ⊕ *www.sidiyassine.com*

A great souvenir is *amlou*, a paste made from toasted almonds or peanuts, argan oil, and local honey. Often called "Berber Nutella," it tastes more like a kind of nut butter.

last remaining Jewish residents, is knowledgeable about the city's Jewish history. ⊠ *2, rue de la Skala, next to Cafe Taros* ☏ *0524/47–62–90.*

Galerie Jama. Tucked away at the end of the street, Galerie Jama seems more museum than shop. You can browse among wooden doors, mosaic vases, and all sorts of wonderful odds and ends. Get ready to negotiate if you see something you like. ⊠ *22, rue Ibn Rochd* ☏ *0670/01–64–29.*

ARGAN OIL

Au Petit Bonhomme de la Chance. Habiba Ajaoui was the first female shopkeeper in the Essaouira medina and she's always happy to pass the time chatting with clients (in Arabic, French, or English) over a cup of steaming tea. She sells spices and argan and cactus-seed oils at reasonable prices and can get you everything you need for the hammam. She also has a large repertoire of henna tattoo designs which are priced according to their complexity. ✉ *30, rue Laalouj* ☎ *0666/01–45–02.*

Chez Makki. The five Makki brothers have taken over their father's herbalist business and turned it into an empire. Several of the shops on the place Marché aux Grains and in the spice souk across the road are run by them. They know their stuff and are happy to explain which spices are used in which recipes and the difference between real and fake saffron over a pot of royal tea. They also sell a range of solid perfumes, argan-oil products, and ceramics. ✉ *221, Souk Laghzal, Spice Market* ☎ *0524/47–30–90.*

ART GALLERIES

There are many galleries in the medina displaying contemporary Moroccan and expatriate mixed-media productions. These are also often exhibited at Dar Souiri or in the South Bastion at Bab Marrakech.

Espace Othello Gallerie d'Art. Named after Orson Welles's *Othello*, which was shot in town, this gallery exhibits local and international artists and antiques. Look out for Scottish artist Caroline Fulton's work, which features indigenous Moroccan animals in rural and medina settings. ✉ *9, rue Mohammed Layachi* ☎ *0524/47–50–95* ⊙ *Closed Mon.*

Galerie d'Art Damgaard. Danish collector Frederic Damgaard is credited with bringing the *naive* art of Essaouira to an international audience. His Galerie d'Art Damgaard, across from the clock tower, has well-curated displays of work by Essaouira painters and sculptors and is also a great place to pick up souvenir books on local art and culture. ✉ *Av. Oqba Ibn Nafiaa* ☎ *0524/78–44–46* ⊕ *www.galeriedamgaard.com.*

La Petite Galerie. The quirky, lunar figures in the often monochrome paintings of Slimane Drissi are a humourous delight with plenty of take-home potential. ✉ *2, rue Ibn Rochd, in the tunnel from the square* ☎ *0524/78–44–49, 0665/66–06–30* ⊕ *www.artmajeur.com/soulaiman.*

HAMMAMS AND SPAS

If you want an authentic hammam experience, collect the necessary soap, scrub mitt, and other products from a spice shop such as Au Petit Bonhomme de la Chance and prepare to get down and dirty with the locals. If you prefer something a little more refined, head to a spa; there are plenty in hotels and around the medina. The following hammams and spas are open to all (even nonguests, if in a hotel).

PUBLIC HAMMAMS

Hammam Pabst. Located in the Mellah, this is one of the oldest hammams in Essaouira. Now brightly painted, it has a plaque indicating that Orson Welles once used it as a location during the filming of *Othello.* Because of this, it's popular with tourists and the ladies who are on hand to scrub and massage clients can get a little greedy. Check the door for the most up-to-date male/female opening hours. ✉ *Rue Annasr* 🖼 *10 DH (massage or scrub extra)* ▭ *No credit cards.*

Hammam Sidi Abdelsmih. On the street of the same name, this women-only hammam is open all day until midnight. For just 50 DH, you can get a great scrub-down by one of the local ladies. If your male partner wants the same, he should head over the Hammam Bolisi in

rue Dar Dheb, near Maison du Sud. Don't forget to bring a towel and a spare pair of underwear (because you wear one pair inside). ⊠ *Rue Sidi Abdelsmih.*

HOTEL HAMMAMS

Hotel Riad Al Madina. This popular riad has a rather good hammam that nonguests can use. A 30-minute scrub with argan oil, roses, sugar, and salt costs 200 DH. ⊠ *9, rue Attarine* ☏ *0524/47–59–07* ⊕ *www. riadalmadina.com* 🛌 *Treatments 70 DH–400 DH.*

Villa Maroc. The first riad guesthouse in Essaouira has a private "Oriental Spa" hammam open to nonguests and offers a range of treatment packages, including massages for children. A traditional scrub with black soap and a scrub mitt plus a *ghassoul* (therapeutic mud) wrap and a 10-minute massage costs 600 DH per person. Forty-five-minute massages with argan oil cost upwards of 320 DH. ⊠ *10, rue Abdellah Ben Yassine* ☏ *0524/47–31–47* ⊕ *www.villa-maroc.com.*

SPAS

Bio Spa. This spa and hammam offers great value in a clean and welcoming setting in the heart of the medina. The package deals frequently include an argan-oil scrub or massage. A simple hammam scrub is 130 DH while an hour-and-a-half package that includes an argan scrub, face scrub and mask, and back massage is 300 DH. ⊠ *9, rue Irak* ☏ *0524/78–46–88.*

Heure Bleue Palais. Located at Bab Marrakech in the medina, this palatial riad hotel has a hammam plus treatment and massage rooms open to nonguests who book in advance (book either one or two days ahead). A full list of packages and treatments is on the website. ⊠ *2, rue Ibn Batouta, Bab Marrakesh* ☏ *0524/78–34–34* ⊕ *www.heure-bleue.com.*

Le Medina Essaouira Hotel Thalassa Sea & Spa by M Gallery Collection. Situated on the seafront, with ocean views from the relaxation lounge, this has to be the best-equipped spa in town. It specializes in thalassotherapy with water jet showers, hydrating baths, massages, and aqua gym workouts. There's also a gym, hammam, hair salon, heated outdoor pool, and sun deck as well as a whole menu of beauty treatments. ⊠ *Bd. Mohammed V* ☏ *0524/47–90–00* ⊕ *www.thalassa.com* ☺ *By reservation only.*

HOUSEWARES

Trésor. This shop offers a range of handmade items from all over Morocco and the Sahara, including mirrors, jewelry, leather bags, and small pieces of furniture. The kettle is always on and you'll eventually be invited to join in for a cup of sweet mint tea to seal your deal. ⊠ *86, rue Laalouj* ☏ *0662/82–55–46.*

JEWELRY

Basma. Hafida welcomes all her customers with a smile and offers a keenly curated selection of Morocco-made jewelry, leather bags, shoes, small paintings, and other decorative items. ⊠ *20 bis, rue Skala* ☏ *0524/78–34–66.*

Histoire de Filles. Essaouira's only concept store is located near Bab Sbaa and offers a range of clothing, jewelry, accessories, organic argan oil,

ESSAOUIRA'S LOCAL MARKETS

If you don't mind getting up early to catch the action, your hotel or a local tour operator will be happy to arrange a visit to a local market (although all are also accessible by local bus or grand taxi). The highlight is Had Draa on a Sunday, where the earliest risers are rewarded with a view of camel trading. Cattle, donkeys, horses, sheep, and goats are also traded, the latter often taking a direct route to the on-site abattoir. This is a farmers' market in the true sense; it's unlikely you'll find many souvenirs to buy between the animal feed, fresh vegetables, cobblers, and vendors of plastic sheeting, but it is a fascinating insight into rural Moroccan life. Other smaller markets are on Wednesday (Ida Ougourd), Thursday (Meskala), Saturday (Akermoud), and Sunday (Smimou). Rural Moroccans are often conservative, so please dress accordingly and cover thighs and shoulders to avoid unwanted attention. The markets are very picturesque, but local people may be offended if you photograph them without asking and may say no if you do.

and small decorative items. Products are designed locally by Moroccan and international designers. This is the closest you'll get in Essaouira to the modern design stores of Marrakesh. ⊠ *1, rue Mohamed Ben Messaoud* ☎ *0524/78–51–93.*

La Fibule Berbère. Amid dozens of other Ali Baba–cave-style shops in the Essaouira medina, La Fibule Berbère is one of the oldest and one of the few that accepts credit cards. The shop displays stunning ethnic jewelry, such as huge silver pendants, *fibules* (clasps for attaching pendants and closing shawls), and bulky necklaces made in the Berber and Toureg styles. ⊠ *51–53, rue Attarine* ☎ *0524/47–62–55, 0661/06–97–74.*

Mashi Mushki. Shopping at the Mashi Mushki store in Essaouira gives you the chance to support locals, as a percentage of the profits goes to the Project 91 charity, which helps young Souiris (natives of Essaouira) to improve their lives through job training and other activities. Some of the items are made in the neighborhood or by co-ops, which also benefits locals. Pick up craft items with a conscience. While you're there, leave your unwanted clothes at the thrift shop across the street. ⊠ *91, rue Chbanat* ⊕ *www.dar91.com.*

Othman Shop. Owner Othman might be the funkiest guy in town and can often be seen outside his shop at the foot of rue Laalouj, just around the corner from where his father crochets wool hats on the skala. Inside the shop, you can spot beautiful examples of silver jewelry and a few of Othman's own designs alongside brightly colored bread and sugar baskets and examples of tribal art. ⊠ *86, rue Laalouj* ☎ *0666/09–05–28.*

WOODWORK

Thuya furniture is as unavoidable on the streets of Essaouira as in-line skaters in Malibu Beach, and just as painful if you bump into it. Try to buy from the artisans, as this is the only way they can make a decent return on their ancient craft. The cheap boxes you see in the tourist shops have passed through so many middlemen that the craftsman ends up with nearly nothing. If you want to find nontouristy workshops off the main streets, take a right onto rue Khalid Ibn el-Walid, just off place Moulay Hassan to seek out the thuya cooperative called Coopérative Artisanale des Marqueteurs.

Coopérative Artisanale des Marqueteurs. Walk through a nondescript passageway into a classic 19th-century riad and you'll find the Coopérative Artisanale des Marqueteurs, whose members have been turning out finely decorated boxes, ornaments, tables, and other furniture since 1948. Everything has a tag with the artisan's code number and reasonable, fixed prices. At the end of the month, the craftsmen collect their income, and a small portion goes to the upkeep of the building and the running of the co-op. You won't find tour groups here as there is no commission for guides, making it a tranquil place to stop and admire decades of craftsmanship. ⊠ *6, rue Khalid Ibn el-Walid, off pl. Moulay Hassan* ☎ *0524/47–56–76.*

SPORTS AND THE OUTDOORS

CYCLING
Velo Mogador Chez Youssef. You can hire bikes from Velo Mogador Chez Youssef. Their bicycles go for 50 DH for a half day, 80 DH for a full day, or 120 DH with a guide who can point out good local trails depending on interest, distance, and time. ⊠ *Hotel Arboussas, 24, rue Laalouj* ☎ *0668/25–46–02, 0626/95–77–43.*

FOUR-WHEELING
Sahara Quad. This company organizes quad-bike excursions including pickup from your hotel to their starting point. Rentals are offered for as little as one hour to as long as three days; a popular circuit takes in Diabat and Cap Sim, south of Essaouira, returning through the thuya cedar forests. A two-hour circuit for two riders costs approximately 660 DH. ⊠ *355, Lot Eraounak* ☎ *0673/44–95–41* ⊕ *www.saharaquad.net.*

GOLF
Golf de Mogador. The 18-hole golf course at Diabat is an integral part of the same resort that includes the Sofitel hotel. Surrounded by sand dunes, the course rolls down towards the sea and sits among forests of eucalyptus and thuya. Lessons are available, and daily green fees are 750 DH; a week of unlimited use will run you 3,500 DH, with discounts for Sofitel guests. ⊠ *Domaine de Mogador* ☎ *0524/47–43–46.*

HIKING
Ecotourisme et Randonnées. Owner Edouard is a former forester from France and is fanatical about sustainable tourism. His colleague, Ottman, can take you on a number of walking circuits around the local countryside, where he will explain flora, fauna, and local culture and customs in English. You can also eat with a local family during the tour. They will organize trips to the local vineyard as well as to a Berber market. Make your reservation at La Découverte restaurant in the medina. ⊠ *8 bis, rue Houmman el-Fatouaki* ☎ *0615/76–21–31* ⊕ *www. essaouira-randonnees.com.*

HORSEBACK AND CAMEL RIDING

Ranch de Diabat. This is a long-standing family-run business that can organize horse-riding and camel trips from a ranch in Diabat. A camel trip costs from 180 DH per hour; one hour on horseback is 150 DH. Horseback riding lessons and trail rides of several days can be organized for groups. ⊠ *Ranch Diabat* ☎ *0524/47–63–82* ⊕ *www.ranchdediabat.com.*

Zouina Cheval. This company organizes horseback riding excursions on Diabat beach and in the countryside around Essaouira, with treks from one hour to a full day for beginners and experienced riders alike. Longer multiday treks with camping for groups and camel trips are also possible. Prices start from around 160 DH per hour and 600 DH for a full day with a picnic lunch. ⊠ *Diabat* ☎ *0669/80–71–01* ⊕ *www.zouina-cheval.com.*

WATER SPORTS

If you are a water-sports enthusiast, it is important to understand where the wind and wave conditions are best for each sport. In Essaouira Bay and further south to Sidi Kaouki, you will most often find kite-surfing. When the wind gets going, windsurfers come out in Essaouira and to the north at Moulay Bouzerktoun. Only beginner surfers attempt anything around Essaouira; the best breaks for experienced surfers are much further south, between Imssouane and Agadir.

Club Mistral. This joint venture with Ocean Vagabond is the biggest outfit in town. It prides itself on the quality of its equipment and its multidisciplinary and multilingual instruction. Factor this into the cost of courses, which are pricier than elsewhere along the bay: two hours of kite-surfing instruction cost 825 DH in a group, while a private lesson is double that price. The more experienced can rent everything they need to explore the coast: boards, a kit, and even roof racks. ⊠ *Plage, at the southern end of the beach, Quartier des Dunes* ☎ *0524/78–39–34* ⊕ *www.oceanvagabond.com/essaouira-en.html* ☉ *Daily 9–6.*

FAMILY
Fodor's Choice
★

Explora. A professional Moroccan-English company offers a wide range of water sports with qualified instruction at prices considerably cheaper than the nearest competition. The company can also arrange your accommodations and many other outdoor activities such as horseback riding, quad-biking, camel-treks, and mountain-biking. Kite-surfing lessons start at 660 DH for two hours. The company has its activity base at the southern end of the beach (on the beach at avenue Mohammed V near junction with route d'Agadir) and also a supplies shop in the medina. ⊠ *12, av. Istiqlal* ☎ *0611/47–51–88* ⊕ *www.exploramorocco.com.*

Magic Fun. After 10 years on the Essaouira seafront, Magic Fun has moved to a base farther north at Moulay Bouzerktoun. Here, the multilingual owner specializes in windsurfing and paddleboarding while his wife runs a café with sheltered views of the sea. Because of the wind conditions here, they don't cater to beginners, but concentrate instead on improving skills. They can pick you up for no extra charge from Essaouira, and offer a lounge area and basic rooms for those who don't want to travel back the same day. ⊠ *Moulay Bouzerktoun* ☎ *0661/10–37–77* ⊕ *www.magicfunafrika.com.*

8

The beaches south of Essaouira are among Morocco's top surfing spots.

THE SOUSS VALLEY AND ANTI-ATLAS

Few venture this far south in Morocco, but those who do are rewarded with a real insight into the life and culture of at the edge of the great Sahara. The Moroccan southwest combines glorious beaches, arid mountains flanked by lush palm groves, hillsides scattered with spiny argan and Barbary fig cactus, and olive, almond, and orange orchards. The region's character is strongly flavored by its Tashelhit-speaking Berbers, who inhabited these mountains and plains before Arabs ever set foot in Morocco, giving the region a distinctively rural feel.

East and south of Agadir you leave the world of beach vacations and enter Berber country. Scenic drives take you past hills covered with barley and almond trees, palm groves, kasbahs, and the Anti-Atlas Mountains themselves. In town, poke around the monuments and souks of Taroudant or shop for Morocco's finest silver in Tiznit. Keep in mind the towns are not the attraction in the region; people come here to commune with nature, admire the vistas, and get away from it all.

TAROUDANT

85 km (51 miles) east of Agadir, 223 km (138 miles) southwest of Marrakesh.

Known as the "Grandmother of Marrakesh," Taroudant is often promoted as an alternative destination to that other former Saadian capital, but these labels are misleading and deny Taroudant its essence. The Taroudant medina walls were built in the 16th century to defend the capital and are almost entirely complete. Today, they encircle a spacious, fully functional Moroccan market town serving a large rural hinterland where tourism plays only a limited role in the local economy. People in Taroudant are less jaded than in more tourist-focused areas and are happy to chat with visitors as they go about their daily business. You're more likely to see an artisan at one of the cities' markets up-cycling something for use on a farm than creating a trinket for a tourist.

People, customs, and the Arabic and Tashelhit Berber languages mix in this town of around 60,000 inhabitants. The town's relaxed feel, the easy interaction with locals, inexpensive dining, and a couple of guesthouse gems make Taroudant an ideal base for exploring the Souss Valley and the western High Atlas.

GETTING HERE AND AROUND

The principal road routes to Taroudant are easily navigable and well signposted. The N10 runs east from Agadir and leads eventually to Taliouine, Tazenakht, and Ouarzazate. There are also scheduled buses from Agadir (1½ hours), Ouarzazate (5 hours), Casablanca (10 hours), Rabat (13 hours), and Marrakesh (6½ hours). Efficient and comfortable CTM buses leave from the gare routière outside Bab Zorgane on the southern side of the medina.

Once you arrive in the city, everything is within walking distance.

Bus Contact CTM ✉ *Gare Routière, Bab Zorgane, just inside city walls* ☎ *0528/85–38–58* ⊕ *www.ctm.ma.*

Rental Cars Malja Cars ✉ *Bab Targhount, Mbarek Oussalem* ☎ *0528/55–17–42* ⊕ *www.maljacars.com.*

GUIDES AND TOURS

Moulay Brahim Bouchra. For a guided tour of the city, Moulay Brahim Bouchra has encyclopedic knowledge of Taroudant and speaks English very well. ☎ *0662/19–24–63* 🎫 *From 125 DH.*

TIMING AND PRECAUTIONS

Taroudant attracts visitors all year round thanks to its favorable climate, although it can get very hot in summer. Most visitors stay a night or two to explore the local region while en route to another destination such as Tafraoute or Ouarzazate.

EXPLORING

Whatever you do in the late afternoon, don't miss the sight of colorfully dressed Roudani (Taroudant native) women lined up against the ramparts near the hospital like birds on a ledge, socializing in the cool hours before sunset. Sunset tours of the ramparts aboard a *calèche* (horse-drawn carriage) are available; the driver may expect you to haggle for your fare—around 50 DH per hour is about right.

City Walls. The city walls of Taroudant are unique in their completeness and for the fact that the new city has not yet encroached upon them, making them not only easily visible but also approachable. There are five main entry points (from the northwest, going clockwise): Bab el-Kasbah, Bab Zorgan, Bab Targhount, Bab Ouled Bounouna, and Bab el-Khemis. A walk around them is a good 5 km (3 miles). The best way to see the ramparts is at sunset in a calèche as the setting sun casts a

Some of Taroudant's fortified walls are 900 years old.

golden glow over the walls and local women come out in their bright costumes to chat in the cooler air.

Dar Baroud. Diagonally across from Bab Sedra, across the avenue Moulay Rachid and with the hospital on your right, is the Dar Baroud, once a French ammunition-storage facility. This high-walled building is closed to the public—and is locally rumored to be haunted—but stand back on the sidewalk opposite and you can admire its delicately carved stone walls from the exterior.

Kasbah. In the northeast side of the city, you'll find the kasbah, or the former king's quarter. It was built by Alouite leader Moulay Ismail in the 17th century—some of the pasha's palace remains intact and has been converted into a hotel (which you can visit for a drink or meal). On avenue Moulay Rachid, with the main gate (Bab el-Kasbah) behind you, you'll see a smaller gate (Bab Sedra) on the right, which is the old entrance into the kasbah quarter. Inside the walls is a typical medina residential area. The area in front of the hotel is now a public park and a great place for watching the evening promenade.

Place Assareg. This plaza sits between the two main souks (the so-called Arab and Berber markets) and serves as the center of life in Taroudant. Although not as lively as Marrakesh's Place Djemâa el-Fna, you still may be able to see performers on the square. Be sure to join the locals in taking a mint tea on a café terrace and watching the scene unfold.

Souks. In the city itself, the municipal market (also referred to as the Berber souk) sells spices, dried fruits, and other household essentials. In an open-air area to the east, you'll find men up-cycling plastics and tires into saddles, water troughs, and panniers for donkeys. The older, so-called Arab market is the better one for souvenirs, and here you can pick up local terra-cotta, brass, and copper items, along with leather sandals, rugs, jewelry, and the standard attire of the Moroccan house-wife: fleece pajamas.

Tanneries. Just outside Bab Taghrount, you'll find the gifted artisans of Taroudant's tanneries. You can see them working the leather first-hand (not always a pleasant olfactory experience) and can then pur-chase locally made leather goods such as bags, poufs, sandals, and decorations.

WHERE TO EAT

$$ ✕**Chez Nada.** If you want to stick within the city walls for some no-
MOROCCAN hassle Moroccan food, you can't go wrong at this father-and-son joint established in 1950. While the décor is nothing special, the views over the medina are great, and the menu features standards such as cous-cous, harira, and pigeon pastilla (order in advance). $ *Average main: 90DH* ✉ *Rue Moulay el-Rachid, near Trek Lahbab* ☎ *0528/85–17–26* ▭ *No credit cards.*

$$$ ✕**Dar Zitoune.** Set among gorgeous gardens and featuring a menu of
MEDITERRANEAN local produce, Dar Zitoune is worth the visit from Taroudant. Serving
Fodor'sChoice a more refined menu than the standard tagine and couscous, it's no
★ wonder that this is a favorite with locals as well as with passing tour groups. Sit outside under citrus trees or inside in the large dining room and make the most of the opportunity to eat steak tartare or a Roque-fort cheese–and-endive salad. The staff are courteous and speak English well. ■TIP➔ Reserve in advance, especially for special dishes such as couscous, mechoui (spit-roast lamb), or pastilla. $ *Average main: 100DH* ✉ *Boutarialt el-Barrania, 2 km (1 mile) south of Taroudant* ☎ *0528/55–11–41* ⊕ *www.darzitoune.com* ⚿ *Reservations essential.*

$ ✕**L'Agence.** An addition to Taroudant's rather sketchy restaurant scene,
MOROCCAN L'Agence shares street-level premises with a real-estate office under the same ownership. Both businesses are run by French-Moroccan couple Maria and Yann, and they have created a charming and eclectic rustic eatery. With only six tables, whitewashed walls, hand-painted wooden beams, Berber textiles, and quirky metal-sculptures, it has plenty of character. The food is distinctly Moroccan—salads, tagines, and cous-cous—but the menu is constantly changing to offer variety. Try the *safa,* couscous with minced chicken and sprinkled with almonds and cinna-mon. It's fine to bring your own wine and beer (discreetly). $ *Average main: 50DH* ✉ *Bd. Prince Heritier Sidi Mohamed* ☎ *0528/55–02–70* ▭ *No credit cards* ⊗ *Closed Sun. and during Ramadan.*

$$ ✕**Restaurant Jnane Soussia.** This outdoor restaurant is a long-standing
MOROCCAN favorite for Moroccan families, offering great food and lots of space.
FAMILY Traditional cuisine is served under a *caidal* (white canvas) tent around two small swimming pools, in a garden full of orange, fig, and papaya trees and flowers. Weekending Moroccan families are drawn to the excellent specialties of the house, such as the *briouates* (filo pastry par-cels) and *mechoui* (roasted shoulder of lamb, best ordered in advance). No alcohol is served. ■TIP➔ Non-Moroccan families with children should be advised that only girls under 12 are allowed to enjoy the

swimming pool with the boys. $ *Average main: 80DH* ✉ *Just outside Bab Zorgan, on right side of road as you head west* ☎ *0528/85–49–80.*

$$$$
MOROCCAN
Fodor'sChoice
★

✕ **Riad Maryam.** Taroudant's oldest family-run riad prides itself on its restaurant for good reason. While Habib greets the guests, his wife Latifa works wonders in the kitchen. Book in advance for a spread of salads, pastilla, tagines, or couscous fit for a king, and the best *pastilla du lait* (a dessert of fine, crispy phyllo pastry layered with pastry creme) in town. $ *Average main: 200DH* ✉ *140, Derb Maalem Mohamed* ☎ *0666/12–72–85* ⊕ *www.riadmaryam.com* ⚭ *Reservations essential* ▬ *No credit cards.*

WHERE TO STAY

$$
B&B/INN

🛏 **Dar Dzahra.** Tucked away south of the main square, Dar Dzahra is full of surprises. **Pros:** very central; great pool; triple and family rooms offered. **Cons:** easy to get lost on the way there. $ *Rooms from: 605DH* ✉ *73, Derb Akka* ☎ *0528/85–10–85* ⊕ *www.dzahra.com* ⛵ *10 rooms* ⋓ *Multiple meal plans.*

$$$$
HOTEL
Fodor'sChoice
★

🛏 **Dar Zitoune.** Rooms at this countryside retreat are spaced out in a fragrant garden of roses and orange trees, with outdoor patios ideal for breakfast. A "Berber village" of eight luxury tented rooms with full en-suites and WiFi has been added around one of the pools. **Pros:** beautiful gardens with pools; English-speaking staff. **Cons:** 2 km from old city. $ *Rooms from: 1320DH* ✉ *Boutarialt el-Barrania, on road to Agadir Airport, 2 km (1 mile) from town* ☎ *0528/55–11–41* ⊕ *www.darzitoune.com* ⛵ *12 bungalows, 14 suites, 8 tented rooms* ⋓ *Multiple meal plans.*

$$$
HOTEL

🛏 **Hôtel Palais Salam.** Having previously welcomed world ambassadors and aristocracy, the management at the Salam are seeking to regain the former glory of the pasha's court that this hotel once was. **Pros:** lovely gardens and terraces; easy access by car. **Cons:** building up to its former reputation after a rocky patch. $ *Rooms from: 850DH* ✉ *Av. Moulay Ismail, outside the ramparts* ☎ *0528/85–25–01* ⊕ *www.palaissalam-taroudant.com* ⛵ *102 rooms, 18 suites* ⋓ *Breakfast.*

$$$$
RESORT

🛏 **La Gazelle d'Or.** One of the most exclusive and expensive hotels in Morocco, the Gazelle d'Or has secluded bungalows with airy, exquisitely tasteful rooms and terraces. **Pros:** exclusive feel; first-rate service. **Cons:** very expensive. $ *Rooms from: 6400DH* ✉ *2 km (1 mile) outside Taroudant on Amskroud–Agadir rd.* ☎ *0528/85–20–39* ⊕ *www.gazelledor.com* ⛵ *29 suites* ⊗ *Closed mid-July–mid-Sept.* ⋓ *Multiple meal plans.*

$$$
B&B/INN
Fodor'sChoice
★

🛏 **Le Palais Oumensour.** Opened in 2008 and extended in 2013 with the addition of a bar, gym, Jacuzzi, and more guest rooms, this luxurious boutique hotel in the heart of Taroudant's medina has been beautifully renovated from an old riad. **Pros:** great location; good value; beautiful architecture. **Cons:** often fully booked; no credit cards accepted. $ *Rooms from: 990DH* ✉ *Al Mansour, Borj Oumensour* ☎ *0528/55–02–15* ⊕ *www.hotel-taroudant-maisondhotes-maroc-hotes.com* ⛵ *4 rooms, 6 suites* ▬ *No credit cards* ⋓ *Multiple meal plans.*

$$
B&B/INN
FAMILY

🛏 **Naturally Morocco Guest House.** Also known as "La Maison Anglaise," this English-speaking, family-friendly guesthouse doubles as a cultural center with rooms arranged over four floors. **Pros:** very eco-friendly; great activity program. **Cons:** not all rooms have air-conditioning or

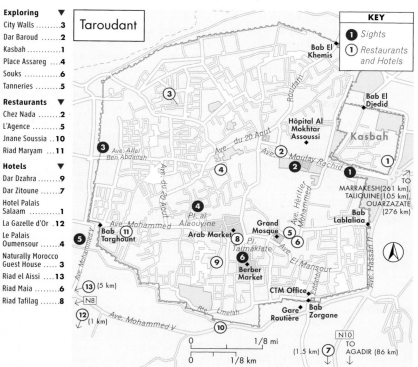

an en-suite bathroom; often booked up in advance. $ *Rooms from: 600DH* ✉ *422, Derb Aferdou* ☎ *1239/65–42–67 in the U.K., 0528/55–16–28 in Morocco* ⊕ *www.naturallymorocco.co.uk* ⤶ *9 rooms* 🚫 *No credit cards* ⦿ *Multiple meal plans.*

$$ 🍴 **Riad El-Aissi.** On the other road out of town towards Agadir, Riad El-Aissi is considered Dar Zitoune's country cousin. **Pros:** huge rooms; local kitchen; great value. **Cons:** décor is a little faded; a bit outside Taroudant. $ *Rooms from: 580DH* ✉ *Village Nouayl, 3 km (2 miles) from Taroudant off N8 (Amskroud–Agadir rd.)* ☎ *0528/55–02–25* ⊕ *www.riadelaissi.com* ⤶ *3 suites, 6 rooms, 1 bungalow* 🚫 *No credit cards* ⦿ *Multiple meal plans.*

B&B/INN
FAMILY

$$ 🍴 **Riad Maïa.** You immediately get a warm welcome at this small but perfectly renovated historical townhouse. **Pros:** in the heart of the medina; spacious bedrooms all with windows. **Cons:** no twin rooms, only doubles. $ *Rooms from: 500DH* ✉ *12, Tassoukt Ighezifen* ☎ *0641/03–79–89* ⊕ *www.riad-maia-taroudant.com* ⤶ *4 rooms* ⦿ *Breakfast.*

B&B/INN

$$$ 🍴 **Riad Tafilag.** In a typical Moroccan neighborhood, Riad Tafilag is the kind of place you could stay for a week. **Pros:** complete relaxation in boutique style at B&B prices. **Cons:** slightly off the beaten track. $ *Rooms from: 715DH* ✉ *31, Derb Taffellagt* ☎ *0528/85–06–07* ⊕ *www.riad-tafilag.com* ⤶ *6 rooms, 2 suites* 🚫 *No credit cards* ⦿ *Multiple meal plans.*

B&B/INN
FAMILY

8

SHOPPING

Taroudant is famous for leather: there are 200 shops in Taroudant dedicated to sandals alone. A walk down even the quietest of streets will feature the incessant tap-tapping of cordwainers at work. Other local products include saffron and lavender, sold by the ounce in herbal stores. The locally pressed olive and argan oils are nationally renowned; ask the herbalists if they can get you a liter. You can also pick up antique jewelry in Taroudant from local Muslim and Jewish Berber tribes.

Antiquaire Haut Atlas. For serious collectors, Antiquaire Haut Atlas has one of the best collections of Berber jewelry in southern Morocco, some of it dating from the 17th and 18th centuries. Even if you're not in the market for a trinket, wandering around the dusty rooms of carpets, candlesticks, and charms makes for a diverting half hour. And if you *are* in the market, Mr. Houssaine accepts all major credit cards and is open every day. ⊠ *61, Souk el-Kabir* ☎ *0528/85–21–45.*

Sculpteur De Pierre. Here's the best place to go for sculpture, both for quality and range of workmanship. Craftsman Larbi El Hare uses marble, limestone, and alabaster. Small stone masks start at 60 DH. He also makes some of the best mint tea in town, brewed by his erstwhile team of draftsmen polishers. He's been here a while, so ask in the Grande Marché if you can't find his shop. ⊠ *Fondouk el-Hare, 29, Rahba Kedima, near soap souk* ☎ *0668/80–78–35.*

EN ROUTE
A loop drive east of Taroudant will take you through the agriculturally rich Souss Valley plains and on a tour of colonial-era *caids'* (local dignitaries') former homes. From the main circle outside Taroudant's Bab Kasbah, take the road toward Tata/Ouarzazate to Aït Iazza; then turn right toward Igherm/Tata, crossing the Souss River (provided it's not flooded, as it sometimes is in winter) into Freija. Look on your right for a decorated mud house, the **Kasbah de Freija.** It's now largely deserted, but you can usually find someone to show you around. Continue on until a sign marks the turnoff to Tioute. The **Tioute palmery,** about a 45-minute drive from Taroudant, was the base used by merciless colonial caid El Tiouti, whose French-armed forces broke some of the last pockets of mountain resistance to French rule. From the kasbah or a short hike up the hillside, you have superb views over the palmery and verdant fields of mint.

From here you can continue the scenic loop northeast to Aouluz, then turn back west toward the Tizi-n-Test until argan trees give way to olive groves and you reach **Ouled Berhil,** which houses the unique and delightful hotel Riad Hida. As an alternative, if you're pressed for time, simply return to Aït Iazza and take the Ouarzazate road straight to Ouled Berhil.

TAFRAOUTE

152 km (94 miles) southeast of Agadir.

Tafraoute is a pretty and quiet regional market and administrative center, nestled at the bottom of a valley. Usually overlooked by groups, it's a great base for exploring an area rich in natural beauty and overflowing with walks, many of which can be undertaken without bumping into another tourist. It is also a base for those wishing to experience some of Morocco's best rock climbing. Although the dizzying mountains around Tafraoute may prove forbidding to cyclists or light hikers, half-day excursions can take you to prehistoric rock carvings, the Ammeln Valley, or the villages off the main road to Tiznit. It's also worth planning a day's excursion to the Aït Mansour gorges to the south of town, where you'll find a lush, verdant palm grove. The region around Tafraoute is a great place to visit some spectacular *agadirs*—hilltop granaries perched at the top of sheer cliffs. They include those at Amtoudi, Tasguint, and Ikouka.

GETTING HERE AND AROUND

The R105 is a spectacular road running over mountains from Agadir to Tafraoute via Aït Baha. You can pick up this road coming from Taroudant to Tafraoute or travel via the alternative Igherm road. There are buses to Tafraoute from Aït Baha (2 hours), Agadir via Tiznit (5 hours), Marrakesh (10 hours), and Casablanca (14 hours). There are also grand taxis from Tiznit. Once in Tafraoute, if you don't have a rental car, your best bet is to travel on foot or by bicycle.

TIMING AND PRECAUTIONS

This region can get extremely hot in summer. Climbers prefer to come in winter and spring, when almond blossoms cover the hillsides. Walkers and trekkers following less obvious routes should hire a local guide, or if you want to include Tafraoute as part of a longer Souss Valley tour, then it's worth going through one of the many agencies based in Agadir.

EXPLORING

Ammeln Valley. The Ammeln Valley is becoming a magnet not only for climbers, but also for nature-lovers and hikers. A walk in the valley might start at the village of Oumesmat, where the **Maison Traditionelle** is well worth a visit. ■TIP→ **Wear sturdy shoes for the short walk from the car park.** At the museum in a traditional Berber house, the caretakers will happily explain the old ways of the Anti-Atlas, introducing you to domestic implements, the tea ceremony, and the local women's embroidered black wrap, the *tamelheft*. Express your appreciation for the tour by tipping generously. From Oumesmat you can follow paths to the neighboring villages. **Taghdicte** makes a good base for ambitious Anti-Atlas climbers.

Fodor's Choice
★

Gazelle Rock Carving. The prehistoric gazelle rock carving just 2 km (1 mile) south of Tafraoute is an easy walk or bike ride from town. The sparse etching has been retouched, but it's still interesting and gives you an idea about how long these desolate mountains have sustained human cultures. To get here, follow signs to "Tazka" from behind Hôtel Les Amandiers; go through the village to the palm and argan fields beyond. You may find offers to guide you from local children: if you accept, then be sure to thank them with a small gift, such as a pen or toy, but avoid giving money. Although everyone calls it a gazelle, locals in the know will tell you that the celebrated rock carving just out of town is in fact of a *mouflon* (wild sheep). Those energetic enough can visit more

8

cave paintings at Ukas, south of the town of Souk Had Issi, 50 km (31 miles) southeast of Tafraoute.

Painted Rocks. A slightly bizarre tourist attraction, the Painted Rocks outside Tafraoute (follow signs) is most dramatically experienced in late afternoon, when the hillsides stacked with massive round boulders turn a rich mustard hue before sunset. Belgian artist Jean Veran painted a cluster of these natural curiosities in varying shades of blue in 1984 and they have been retouched ever since. Checking out amateur copies is as much fun as looking at the originals. On quieter days, it's also a great place to spot local geckos, lizards, and squirrels. The route to the rocks is now paved, making access easier than ever.

Palm Groves of Aït Mansour. The palm groves of the Aït Mansour Gorge southeast of Tafraoute deserve a full day's excursion, although you could take the road as a scenic (and longer) route to Tiznit.

About 2 km (1 mile) southwest out of town, you'll see the so-called "Napoleon's hat" of massive boulders on your right. Occasionally, you'll see foreign climbers here, with their incongruously high-tech rock-climbing gear. Follow signs toward Aguerd Oudad. When the road forks, the right one going to the Painted Rocks, take the left branch. A winding paved road takes you higher into the Anti-Atlas Mountains. The views are spectacular and the scenery changes as the road rises and then descends again, crossing a river bed which—even when dry—betrays the presence of underground water by the cactus and oleander growing in them. Twenty km (12 miles) out of Tafraoute, turn right toward Aït Mansour. You are now heading counter-clockwise around the circuit of Afella Ighir.

After another 14 km (9 miles) of winding descent, you reach the palm groves. Suddenly, water, shade, and greenery are abundant, and you may find an open shop happy to serve you a sweet mint tea or soda. The lone goatherds of the peaks are replaced here by shrouded women, either transporting on their backs palm-frond baskets of dates supported by ropes around their foreheads or walking to Timguilcht to visit its important saint's shrine. Continue on the piste to Souk Had Issi, whose busy market is held on Sunday. From there the piste loops back to Tafraoute, or you can take a lower road to connect to Tiznit over the dramatic Col de Kerdous.

WHERE TO EAT

$ ✕ **La Kasbah.** This is a well-priced restaurant filling a clear gap in the
MOROCCAN   Tafraoute market. The menu is classic tourist fare (omelets, tagines, soups, and salads), but the quality is excellent. Try the vegetarian tagines featuring prunes, nuts, and plenty of veggies. Beer and wine are also available. $ *Average main: 65DH* ⊠ *Rte. Imiane (R107), on the right as you leave town* ☎ *0660/95–42–69* ▭ *No credit cards.*

$ ✕ **Restaurant L'Etoile du Sud.** Since 1968 the "Star of the South" has been
MOROCCAN   serving delicious couscous and tagines in a red-velvet dining room or under a huge red-and-green velvet caidal tent. The harira is hearty and satisfying after a long day's drive, and there is plenty of parking. The staff is friendly, and the atmosphere is cheery, with many tour agencies choosing this spot for their groups. The restaurant also serves

Tafraoute, in a quiet valley, is often overlooked by the larger tour groups, but offers beautiful walks in the surrounding countryside.

alcohol. $ *Average main: 70DH* ⊠ *Av. Hassan II, next to the post office* ☎ *0528/80–00–38* ▭ *No credit cards.*

$ ✗ **Restaurant Marrakech.** This is a basic spot, frequented by locals, hence
MOROCCAN tagines here are fresh and cheap. Haute cuisine it isn't, but cool, fresh-squeezed juices make this a nice spot to catch your breath and get out of the sun. $ *Average main: 50DH* ⊠ *Av. Hassan II, in the center of town* ☎ *0663/22–92–50* ▭ *No credit cards.*

WHERE TO STAY

$$ ⚏ **Auberge Kasbah Chez Amaliya.** Nestled among the mountains and
B&B/INN occasional almond blossoms of the Ammeln Valley, Chez Amaliya is
FAMILY a great base for hikers, climbers, and the less active. **Pros:** vivacious host will make you feel right at home; great views. **Cons:** outside the city center. $ *Rooms from: 500DH* ⊠ *Valley d'Ammeln, signposted off the R105 as you approach from Aït Baha* ☎ *0528/80–00–65* ⊕ *www. chezamaliya.com* ⌇ *14 rooms* ⦿ *Multiple meal plans.*

$$ ⚏ **Hôtel Les Amandiers.** This former officers' mess of the French Protec-
HOTEL torate is a piece of Moroccan postcolonial history as well as a hotel that dominates the town, providing panoramic views of the mountains that surround it. **Pros:** great views; very clean; pretty pool. **Cons:** parts of the hotel still have a slightly institutional feel. $ *Rooms from: 510DH* ⊠ *Town center* ☎ *0528/80–00–88* ⊕ *www.hotel-lesamandiers. com* ⌇ *51 rooms, 7 suites* ⦿ *Multiple meal plans.*

$ ⚏ **Hotel Salama.** A favorite with groups and right in the center of town,
HOTEL the Salama overlooks the busy area around the market, where old men sell dates and local women bring their homemade argan oil. **Pros:** central location; nice views. **Cons:** décor is rather dated; rooms overlooking

the market can be noisy. [$] *Rooms from: 256DH* ☎ *0528/80–00–26* ⊕ *www.hotelsalama.com* ⇩ *33 rooms, 4 suites* ⊟ *No credit cards* ¡⃝ *Multiple meal plans.*

SHOPPING

Tafraoute's market is held on Tuesday and Wednesday and often has a good selection of woven palm-frond baskets, argan oil, and *amalou* (almond and argan paste). Tafraoute is the place to come for mountain *babouches* (slippers). These are different from the slip-on varieties found in the souks of Marrakesh and Fez, as they are specially made with a heel covering to aid mountain walking. Take note of Berber babouche color-coding: yellow for men, red for women, pompoms for unmarried girls, and spangled designs only for special occasions. The traditional local woman's dress is a large black piece of fabric with braiding or embroidery at the edges. These can easily be converted into soft furnishings such as table cloths or curtains.

Maison du Troc. With a great range of carpets and other artisanal goods, this place is worth a visit if you feel the need for souvenirs. Although the area isn't well known for carpet making, Mohammed and his team are happy to explain the different types of rugs from various regions. ✉ *Rte. Imiane* ☎ *0528/80–00–35.*

Maison Touareg. Not to be confused with the excellent Maison Traditionelle museum, the Maison Touareg is a bazaar, carrying a nice selection of regional Berber carpets. ✉ *Rte. de l'Hotel Les Amandiers, av. Mohammed V* ☎ *0528/80–02–10* ⊕ *www.maisontouareg.com.*

EN ROUTE The newer road from Tafraoute to Tiznit (follow signs out the back of Tafraoute, beyond the post office) is flat and bike-accessible for about the first 15 km (9 miles), after which it begins an incline into the mountains.

Col du Kerdous. As the road from Tafraoute to Tiznit winds over the Anti-Atlas peaks and through the valleys, you'll enjoy many panoramic views. The former Kasbah site at Col du Kerdous (1,203 in altitude) is almost exactly halfway between Tafraoute and Tiznit (54 km [34 miles] and 53 km [33 miles] respectively), and is now the Hotel Kerdous. If you stop, don't expect anything more than tea unless you call well in advance. The sound of the call to prayer as it echoes from village to village around the valleys is quite incredible. ⊕ *www.hotel-kerdous.com/site.*

TIZNIT

100 km (62 miles) west of Tafraoute, 98 km (61 miles) south of Agadir.

Typically a lunch stop en route to somewhere else, Tiznit is not a popular destination for tourists. But it is a great base for exploring the surrounding area and for those who dislike the high-rise, beach-resort feel of Agadir. The restaurant scene isn't great, but a couple of smaller guesthouses have emerged in recent years that serve excellent home-made cuisine. The big draw of Tiznit is its reputation as Morocco's silver center. Otherwise it has few sights, and even the ones it does have are currently under restoration as of this writing.

GETTING HERE AND AROUND

Tiznit is well signposted if traveling by road, with the N1 bringing you from Agadir, or the R104 from Tafraoute. Several daily buses arrive from Sidi Ifni (1½ hours), Agadir (2 hours), and Tafraoute (2 hours). The bus station is a 15-minute walk along avenue Hassan II from the medina entrance at Bab Jdid. The CTM office is located inside the medina at the end of avenue du 20 Août. There are also grand taxis from Agadir.

Tiznit is a compact city and everything within the medina walls is within walking distance. Bikes can be hired on the Méchouar Square or from certain riads.

TIMING AND PRECAUTIONS

Tiznit makes for an easy day trip from Agadir or for a break in an exploration of the Anti-Atlas and southern Morocco region. In summer it gets extremely hot and it may be more pleasant to stay on the coast at Aglou Plage or Agadir.

EXPLORING

Grande Mosquée (*Great Mosque*). The minaret of the Grande Mosquée is the oldest example of a Saharan-style minaret in Morocco, an architectural feature more commonly seen in Niger and Mali. Perches poke out from all sides, making it look like someone forgot to take out the scaffolding after it was completed. These perches are said to assist the dead in their ascent to paradise.

Lalla Zninia Spring. Near the Grand Mosque, the Lalla Zninia Spring (also known as the Source Bleue) is touted as Tiznit's main sight. Until recently this did not bode well for Tiznit's tourism industry, as it was pretty much dried up and certainly not blue. The Tiznit authorities have plans to turn around the fortunes of the spring and major renovation works were underway in 2014. The spring honors the saint after whom Tiznit is named. There are several legends relating to this woman. One has it that she was a shepherd girl who brought her flocks to this spot and smelled the then-undiscovered spring below; her sheep dug (if you can imagine sheep digging) until they found the water, and the town was born. Another story talks of a repentant prostitute who later became a saint. In any case, to catch a glimpse of her tomb on afternoons when devotees visit, follow the prison wall and turn left on the first narrow neighborhood street; the tomb is behind a green-painted door on your left.

Méchouar. The main square, the Méchouar, is the heart of town and was once a military parade ground. Nowadays it has become a car park with a clutch of cheap hotels and cafés around it. Down a side street off the main square (heading in the direction of the ramparts) you'll find a smaller square lined with orange trees, where locals buy from the mint, date, and dried-thyme vendors whose carts are parked between the rows of clothing and housewares. Off the square, you'll find the town's main souks. ⊠ *Pl. el-Méchouar.*

WHERE TO EAT AND STAY

$$
MOROCCAN
✕ **Riad Le Lieu.** Popular among the guests of local riads and hotels, Riad Le Lieu fills a gap in the dismal dining market in Tiznit. In a part of the former palace next door, chef Jihad prepares a range of Moroccan

8

specialties which are served on the patio and terraces. The rabbit and camel tagines are always great choices. The riad also runs a B&B, so don't be surprised to see guests making their way to the shared bathroom. [$] *Average main: 75DH* ✉ *23, Impasse Issaoui, rue Imzilen, pl. el-Méchouar* ☎ *0528/60–00–19* 🌐 *www.riadlelieu-tiznit.com* 💳 *No credit cards.*

$$$$ HOTEL 🏨 **Hotel Idou Tiznit.** It may cater primarily to the business market, but this hotel is the best in town. **Pros:** full range of services available, including a pool; helpful staff. **Cons:** can get busy with large groups. [$] *Rooms from: 1100DH* ✉ *Av. Hassan II* ☎ *0528/60–03–33* 🌐 *www.idoutiznit.com* 🛏 *87 rooms, 6 suites* 🍴 *Multiple meal plans.*

$$ B&B/INN 🏨 **Maison du Soleil.** One of a number of newer and smaller establishments catering to the independent traveler, this townhouse combines traditional and modern elements in both its form and function. **Pros:** more authentic feel than larger hotels; good for groups. **Cons:** only a couple of rooms are en suite. [$] *Rooms from: 484DH* ✉ *470, rue Tafoukt* ☎ *0667/55–09–92* 🌐 *www.maisondu-soleil.com* 🛏 *5 rooms* 🍴 *Multiple meal plans.*

SHOPPING

Tiznit has earned a reputation as *the* place to buy silver jewelry in Morocco, and the local market has responded accordingly. The silver markets of Tiznit sell more—and better—silver per square foot than any other market in Morocco. Some vendors also sell handwoven cream-color blankets, traded by local women for a few pieces of new silver. Merchants cater increasingly to Western tastes and wallets. Many shops around the main square are really wholesalers, trading their silver all over Morocco and abroad, so don't expect any encounters with the artisans. Most items are produced in the home, so tourists are unlikely to see any actual production and the shops advertising it are unlikely to be manufacturing real silver jewelry.

Bijouterie Aziz. This low-pressure jewelry store sells Saharan and Berber silver jewelry. ✉ *5, Souk Joutia* ☎ *0668/69–77–47.*

Trésor du Sud. Away from the souk, Trésor du Sud has an enormous showroom of high-quality, hand-crafted Berber jewelry. In addition, the workshops allow you to see the silversmiths in action. This is not the cheapest jewelry showroom in town, but you can pay with credit card. ✉ *Bab al-Khemis* ☎ *0528/86–47–89* 🌐 *www.tresordusud.com.*

MOROCCAN ARABIC VOCABULARY

Most Moroccans are multilingual. The country's official languages are modern standard Arabic and French; most Moroccans speak Moroccan Arabic dialect, with many city dwellers also speaking French. Since the time of the French protectorate, French has been taught to schoolchildren (not all children) starting in the first grade, resulting in several French-language newspapers, magazines, and TV shows. Spanish enters the mix in northern Morocco, and several Berber tongues are spoken in the south as well as the north. In the medinas and souks of big cities, you may find merchants who can bargain in just about any language, including English, German, Japanese, and Swedish.

A rudimentary knowledge of French and, especially, Arabic will get you far in Morocco. If you're more comfortable with French, by all means use it in the major cities; in smaller cities, villages, and the mountains, it's best to attempt some Moroccan Arabic. Arabic is always a good choice, as Moroccans will go out of their way to accommodate the foreigner who attempts to learn their national language. Some letters in Arabic do not have English equivalents. When you see "gh" at the start of a word in this vocabulary, pronounce it like a French "r," lightly gargled at the back of the throat. If unsure, stick to a "g" sound.

MOROCCAN ARABIC

English	Arabic Transliteration	Pronunciation
GREETINGS & BASICS		
Hello/Peace upon you.	Salaam ou alaikum.	sa-**lahm** oo allah-ee-**koom**
(Reply:)		
Hello/And peace upon you.	Wa alaikum salaam.	wa allay-koom sa-**lahm**
Goodbye	Bislamma.	bess-**lah**-ma
Mr./Sir	Si	see
Mrs./Madam/Miss	Lalla	lah-la
How are you? Fine, thank you.	Labass, alhamdul'Illah	la-**bahs,** al-**hahm**-doo-lee-**lah**
(No harm?) (No harm, praise be to God.)	Labass	la-**bahs**
Pleased to meet you.	Mitsharafin.	mitsh-arra-**fayn**
Yes/No	Namm/La	nahm/lah
Please	Afek	**ah**-feck
Thank you	Baraka Allahu fik	**ba**-ra-kah **la**-hoo **feek**
You're welcome.	Allah yubarak fik.	ahl-lah yoo-**bah**-rak feek

MOROCCAN ARABIC

God willing	insh'Allah	in-**shah**-ahl-lah
Excuse me./I'm sorry (masc.).	Smahali.	**sma**-hah-li
Excuse me./I'm sorry (fem.).	Smahailia.	sma-high-**lee**-ah

DAYS

Today	el yum	el yom
Yesterday	imbarah	im-ber-ah
Tomorrow	ghadaa	gha-dah
Sunday	el had	el had
Monday	tneen	t'neen
Tuesday	thlat	tlet
Wednesday	larbaa	lar-bah
Thursday	el khamis	el kha-mees
Friday	el jemaa	el j'mah
Saturday	sebt	es-sebt

NUMBERS

1	wahad	**wa**-hed
2	jouj	jewj
3	thlata	**tlet**-ta
4	rbaa	ar-**bah**
5	khamsa	**khem**-sah
6	sta	stah
7	sbaa	se-**bah**
8	taminia	ta-**min**-ee-ya
9	tseud	tsood
10	aachra	**ah**-she-ra
11	hadash	ha-**dahsh**
12	tanash	ta-**nahsh**
20	aacherine	ah-**chreen**
50	khamsine	khum-**seen**

MOROCCAN ARABIC

100	milla	**mee**-yah
200	millatein	mee-ya **tayn**

USEFUL PHRASES

Do you speak English?	Ouesh tat tkelem belinglisia?	**wesh** tet te-**kel**-lem **blin**-gliz-**ee**-yah?
I don't understand.	Ma fahemtsh.	ma-**f'emtch**.
I don't know.	Ma naarf.	ma-**nahr**-ef.
I'm lost.	Ana tilift.	ahna t'-lift.
I am American (masc.).	Ana amriqui.	ahna am-ree-kee.
I am American (fem.).	Ana amriqiya.	ahna am-**ree**-kee-yah.
I am British.	Ana inglisi.	anna in-ge-**lee**-zee.
What is this?	Shnou hada?	**shnoo** ha-da?
Where is . . . ?	Fein . . . ?	fayn . . . ?
the train station	mahatat el tren	ma-ha-**tat** eh-tren
the city bus station	mahatat tobis	**ma-ha**-tat **toh**-beese
the intracity bus station	mahatat al cairan	**ma**-ha-tat al-kah-ee-rahn
the airport	el l'aéroport	el lehr-oh-por
the hotel	el l'hôtel	el l'oh-**teel**
the café	l'khaoua	al-kah-**hou**-wah
the restaurant	el restaurant	el rest-oh-**rahn**
the telephone	tilifoon	**til-lee**-foon
the hospital	el l'hôpital	el l'oh-bee-tahl
the post office	l'bosta	**al**-bost-**a**
the restroom	w.c.	**vay**-say
the pharmacy	pharmacien	far-**ma-cienn**
the bank	l'banca	**al** bann-**ka**
the embassy	sifara	**see**-far-**ra**
I would like a room.	Bghit bit.	**bgheet**-beet.
I would like to buy . . .	Bghit nechri . . .	bgheet-nesh-**ree** . . .

MOROCCAN ARABIC

cigarettes	garro	**gahr**-oh
a city map	kharretta del medina	kha-**ray**-ta del m'**dee**-nah
a road map	kharretta del bled	kha-**ray**-ta del blad
How much is it?	Bi sha hal hada?	**bshal hah**-da?
It's expensive.	Ghaliya.	**gha**-lee-ya.
A little	Shwiya	**shwee**-ya
A lot	Bizzaf	bzzef
Enough	Baraka	**ba**-rah-ka
I am ill. (masc.)	Ana marid.	ah-na ma-**reed**.
I am ill. (fem.)	Ana marida.	**ah**-na ma-**reed**-ah.
I need a doctor.	Bghit doctor.	bgheet dok-**tohr**.
I have a problem.	Aandi mouchkila.	**ahn**-dee moosh-**kee**-la.
left	lessar	**lis**-sar
right	leemen	**lee**-men
Help!	Awni!	**aow**-nee!
Fire!	Laafiya!	**lah**-fee-ya!
Caution!/Look out!	Aindek!	**aann**-deck!

DINING

I would like . . .	bghit . . .	bgheet . . .
water	l'ma	l'mah
bread	l'khobz	l'khobz
vegetables	khoudra	**khu**-dra
meat	l'hamm	l'hahm
fruits	l'fawakeh	el fah-**weh**-kee
cakes	l'haloua	el **hahl**-oo-wa
tea	atay	**ah**-tay
coffee	kahoua	**kah**-wa
a fork	forchette	for-**shet**
a spoon	maalka	**mahl**-ka
a knife	mousse	moose

TRAVEL SMART
MOROCCO

GETTING HERE AND AROUND

■ BY AIR

Morocco is served by major airlines from North America and Europe. Consider flying if traveling long distances within Morocco. To concentrate on the southern oasis valleys, land in Casablanca, fly directly to Ouarzazate, and rent a car. Domestic carriers may require reconfirmation to hold your seat, so remember to place this call ahead of time, or ask your hotel to do it for you. A call to the airline also suffices. The national airline, Royal Air Maroc, flies to more than 80 destinations worldwide and within Morocco. Look for special offers and last-minute promotions on the airline's website, especially every Thursday under "Booking & Promotions" in the drop-down menu.

Airline Security Issues Transportation Security Administration. ⊕ *www.tsa.gov.*

AIRPORTS

Although Rabat is the capital, it is Casablanca's Mohammed V Airport (CMN) that serves as the main entry point for nonstop flights from the United States. From here, U.S. travelers can easily connect to other destinations throughout the country on frequent domestic flights. They can also reach Morocco easily through European hubs like London, Paris, Amsterdam, Madrid, and Frankfurt. A number of airlines offer regularly scheduled direct flights to major destinations like Marrakesh (RAK), Agadir (AGA), Fez (FEZ), Ouarzazate (OZZ), Rabat (RBA), and Tangier (TNG). Other airports with regularly scheduled domestic or international service include Al Hoceima (AHU), Dakhla (VIL), Essaouira (ESU), Fez Ifrane (GMFI), Laayoune (EUN), Oujda (OUD), Nador (NDR), and Tetouan (TTU).

Airport Information Casablanca Mohammed V Airport ⊠ *Office National des Aéroports* ☎ *0522/53–90–40* ⊕ *www.onda.ma.* **Moroccan Airport Authority** ☎ *0522/53–90–40* ⊕ *www.onda.ma.*

GROUND TRANSPORTATION

Office National des Chemins de Fer, the national rail company, has a station directly under Casablanca's Mohammed V Airport. Trains come and go between 6:30 am and 11 pm and make travel to and from the airport easy and hassle-free. The ride to the city takes 30 minutes. Taxis are always available outside arrivals at the Casablanca airport; fares to the city are approximately 300 DH. Many hotels run shuttle buses into central Casablanca as well.

Contacts Office National des Chemins de Fer ☎ *0890/20–30–40* ⊕ *www.oncf.ma.*

FLIGHTS

Royal Air Maroc and other major airlines offer daily direct or one-stop flights to Agadir, Casablanca, Fez, Marrakesh, Rabat, and Tangier from nearly all western European countries. Consult RAM's website for their popular Thursday deals. In addition, discount airlines such as Air Arabia, EasyJet and Ryanair fly to some but not all of the major cities. Destinations and timetables are subject to sudden change, so be sure to consult a flight-comparison website prior to booking to confirm which routes are available at which time of year.

■ BY BOAT

If traveling from Spain, take a ferry across the Strait of Gibraltar. The most popular crossing is from Algeciras to Tangier. Algeciras to Ceuta (Spanish territory inside mainland Morocco) is a popular and shorter route. High-speed ferries make the trip in 30 to 40 minutes. Unfortunately, disembarking in Tangier can be a traumatic way to enter Morocco. You're likely to be greeted by unpleasant characters, who won't cease to harass you until you've parted company with some money, or at best suffered some verbal abuse. If you do find yourself hassled by bogus peddlers or officials asking for a bribe, rest assured, there is no need to hand over any extra cash if you have a boat ticket, no matter what you are told. Always buy a ticket from an official source as there are many tricksters at the ports.

Information Southern Ferries Ltd ☎ 0844/815–7785 in the U.K. ⊕ www. southernferries.co.uk. **Trasmediterrá-nia** ☎ 902/45–46–45 in Spain ⊕ www. trasmediterranea.es.

■ BY BUS

For cities not served by trains (mainly those in the south), buses are a good alternative. They're relatively frequent, and seats are usually available.

Compagnie de Transports Marocains (CTM), the national bus company, runs trips to most areas in the country and guarantees your seat and luggage service. No-smoking rules are enforced (the exception is the driver who sometimes smokes out his side window). These buses stop occasionally for bathroom and smoking breaks, but be sure to stay near the bus, as they have been known to leave quickly, stranding people without their luggage in unfamiliar places.

Another major bus company, Supratours, is connected to Morocco's national rail service. It offers comfortable service to major cities. Supratours has ticket counters at each train station and allows travelers to extend their trip past places where the train service ends. Departure times are coordinated with the arrival of trains.

There are a number of smaller bus companies, called "souk buses." They're the only way to get to really rural areas not served by larger companies. They are neither comfortable nor clean. You're much better off shelling out a few extra dirhams for the punctual and pleasant CTM or Supratours buses unless you're going to out-of-the-way places only served by small companies.

In each city the bus station—known as the *gare routière*—is generally near the edge of town. Some larger cities have separate CTM stations. Ignore the posted departure times on the walls—they're never up to date. Ask at the ticket booth when the next bus leaves to your chosen destination. There's nothing wrong with checking out a bus before you buy your ticket, as some are dilapidated and uncomfortable. The *greeson* will sell you a ticket, take you to the bus, and put your luggage underneath (you should tip a few dirhams for this).

Buy tickets at the bus station prior to departure (ideally a day ahead of time); payment is by cash only. Tickets are only sold for the seats available, so once you have a ticket you have a seat. Other than tickets, there are no reservations. Often, tickets only go on sale an hour before departure. Inquire at the bus station for departure times; there are no printed schedules and the displayed schedules are not accurate. Children up to age four travel free. Car seats and bassinets are not usually available for children.

FARES

Fares are very cheap (currently around 20 DH for a one-hour journey to 250 DH for daylong trips). Luggage is usually charged by weight. Expect to pay no more than 10 DH per piece. Additionally, most CTM stations have inexpensive luggage storage facilities.

Bus Information CTM (*Compagnie de Transports Marocains*). ✉ Km 13.5, rte. de Casa-Rabat, Sidi Bernoussi, Casablanca ☎ 0522/54–10–10 ⊕ www.ctm.ma. **Supra-tours** ☎ 0537/73–10–61, 0537/73–10–64 ⊕ www.supratourstravel.com.

■ BY CAR

A car is not necessary if your trip is confined to major cities, but sometimes it's the best and only way to explore Morocco's mountainous areas, small coastal towns, and rural areas such as the Middle or High Atlas.

Driving in Morocco is relatively easy and a fantastic way to see the country. Roads are generally in good shape, and mile markers and road signs are easy to read (they're always written in Arabic and French). Remember that small mountain villages are still only reached by *piste* (gravel path), and that these rough roads can damage a smaller car. Bear in mind that traffic becomes more erratic during the holy month of Ramadan and no matter what time of year, you are likely to be approached at red lights or even on village roads with pleas to buy tissues, chewing gum, and souvenirs, or simply for any loose change.

If traveling with young children, you may have trouble finding child seats for rental cars, which are nearly always stick shift.

Hiring a car and driver is an excellent but expensive way to really get into the crevices of the country. Drivers also serve as protectors from potential faux guides and tourist scams. Be warned, however, that they themselves are often looking for commissions and might steer you toward particular carpet sellers and tourist shops. Be sure to negotiate an acceptable price before you take off. Expect to pay at minimum between 1,500 DH to 2,000 DH for a private tour, with prices higher depending on itinerary. Drivers must be licensed and official, so be sure to ask for credentials to avoid any unpleasantness down the road.

BOOKING YOUR TRIP

The cars most commonly available in Morocco are small European sedans, such as Renaults, Peugeots, and Fiats. Expect to pay at least 450 DH a day for these. Many companies also rent four-wheel-drive vehicles, a boon for touring the Atlas Mountains and oasis valleys; expect to pay around 2,800 DH per day for a new Land Cruiser. A 20% VAT (value-added tax) is levied on rental rates. Companies will often let you rent for the day or by the kilometer.

Note that you can negotiate the rental of a taxi with a driver just about anywhere in Morocco for no more than the cost of a rental car from a major agency. Normally you negotiate an inclusive price for a given itinerary. The advantage is that you don't have to navigate; the disadvantage is that the driver may have his own ideas about where you should go and will probably not speak English. For less haggling, local tour operators can furnish vehicles with multilingual drivers at a fairly high daily package rate.

The best place to rent a car is Casablanca's airport, as the rental market is very competitive here—most of the cars are new, and discounts are often negotiable. Local companies give a lower price for the same car than the international agencies (even after the latter's "discounts"). Most recommended agencies have offices at Casablanca's airport and branches in the city itself, as well in Rabat, Marrakesh, and Fez. To get the best deal, book through a travel agent, who will shop around.

Rental Agencies Europ Car ☎ *0522/53–91–61 at Casablanca at Mohammed V Airport, 0535/62–65–45 at Fez Saiss Airport, 0524/43–77–18 at Marrakesh Menara Airport, 0537/72–41–41 at Rabat Sale Airport, 0539/94–19–38 at Tangier Ibn Battouta Airport, 0539/93–01–08 at Tangier Maritime Port* ⊕ *www.europcar.com.* **National Car Rental** ☎ *0522/53–91–61 at Casablanca airport, 0524/43–77–18 at Marrakech airport, 0535/62–65–45 at Fez airport, 0528/84–03–37 at Agadir airport* ⊕ *www.nationalcar.com.* **Sixt Car** ☎ *0522/53–80–99 at Casablanca Mohammed V Airport, 0522/53–66–15 at Marrakesh Menara Airport, 0528/83–90–13 at Agadir Airport, 0522/53–66–15 at Rabat Sale Airport, 0522/53–66–15 at Ibn Battouta Airport Tangier, 0522/53–66–15 at Fez Saiss Airport* ⊕ *www.sixt.com.* **Thrifty Car** ☎ *0522/54–00–22 at Casablanca airport, 0528/83–90–54 at Agadir Airport, 0522/54–00–22 at Rabat Sale Airport, 0522/54–00–22 at Ibn Battouta Airport Tangier, 0522/54–00–22 at Marrakesh Menara Airport, 0661/84–36–38 at Fes Saiss Airport* ⊕ *www.thrifty.com.*

GASOLINE

Gas is readily available, if relatively expensive. The gas that most cars use is known as *super,* the lower-octane variety as *essence.* Unleaded fuel (*sans plomb*) is widely available but not currently necessary for local cars; it costs around 11 DH a liter.

Diesel fuel (*diesel* or *gasoil*) is significantly cheaper. Most gas stations provide full service; tipping is optional, but if you do, the standard amount is 2 DH. Only a few stations take credit cards. Most gas stations have restrooms and some have cafés, with Afriquia stations being generally regarded as the best.

PARKING

When parking in the city, make sure that you're in a parking zone or the authorities will put a locking device on one of your wheels. If you are unlucky enough to have your wheel clamped, look out for the clamper, who will most likely be lurking nearby. A payment of 50 dirhams is usually all it takes for him to remove the locking device.

In parking lots, give the *gardien* a small tip (2 DH) upon leaving (this increases to 5 DH outside fancier establishments such as high-end restaurants). Some cities have introduced the European system of pre-paid tickets from a machine, valid for a certain duration.

ROAD CONDITIONS

Road conditions are generally very good. A network of toll highways (*autoroutes*) runs from Casablanca to Larache (near Tangier) and east from Rabat to Meknès and Fez, and from Casablanca to Settat (south toward Marrakesh). These autoroutes are much safer than the lesser roads. There are periodic tollbooths charging from 5 DH to 20 DH. Make sure that you carry loose change in coins as booths generally do not accept credit cards.

On rural roads expect the occasional flock of sheep or herd of goats to cross the road at inopportune times. In the south you'll see road signs warning of periodic camel crossings as well. In the mountains, side-pointing arrows designate curves in the road. However, be aware that some dangerous curves come unannounced. In the countryside you're more likely to encounter potholes, narrow roads, and speeding taxi drivers.

Night driving outside city centers requires extreme caution. Many roads are not lit. Beware of inadequate or unfamiliar lighting at night, particularly on trucks—it's not uncommon for trucks to have red lights in the front or white lights in the rear. Ubiquitous ancient mopeds rarely have working lights or reflectors. Many drivers think nothing of driving on the opposite side of the road or reversing at high speed along busy roads. Taxis pull up without notice to the side of the road.

ROADSIDE EMERGENCIES

In case of an accident on the road, dial 177 outside cities and 19 in urban areas for police. For firemen and emergency medical services, dial 15. As emergency numbers in Morocco may not be answered quickly, it's wise to hail help from street police if possible. When available, it's also more effective to summon a taxi to reach medical help instead of relying on ambulance service.

RULES OF THE ROAD

Traffic moves on the right side of the road, as in the United States and Europe. There are two main rules in Morocco: the first is, "priority to the right," an old French rule meaning that in traffic circles you must yield to traffic entering from the right; the second is, "every man for himself." Any car that is ahead of you—even by an inch—considers itself to have priority.

You must carry your car registration and insurance certificate at all times (these documents are always supplied with rental cars). Morocco's speed limits, enforced by radar, are 120 kph (75 mph) on autoroutes and from 40 or 60 kph (25 or 37 mph) in towns. The penalty for speeding is a 400 DH fine, payable to the issuing officer, or confiscation of your driver's license. Always ask for the fine "ticket" as this reduces the risk of corruption.

It is mandatory to wear seat belts for both drivers and passengers. Failure to do so will result in a hefty fine. Talking on cell phones while driving is also illegal.

▍ BY TAXI

Moroccan taxis take two forms: *petits taxis,* small taxis that travel within city limits, and *grands taxis,* large taxis that travel between cities. Drivers usually wait until the taxi is full before departing.

Petits taxis are color-coded according to city—in Casablanca and Fez they're red, in Rabat they're blue, in Marrakesh they're beige, and so on. These can be hailed anywhere and take a maximum of three passengers. The fare is metered and not expensive: usually 5 DH to 30 DH for a short or medium-length trip. Taxis often pick up additional passengers en route, so if you can't find an empty cab, try hailing a taxi with one or two passengers already.

Grands taxis travel fixed routes between cities and in the country. One person can sit in front with the driver, and four sit, very cramped, in the back. Don't expect air-conditioning, a luxurious interior, or even fully functioning windows. Fares for these shared rides are inexpensive, sometimes as little as 5 DH per person for a short trip. You can also charter a grand taxi for trips between cities, but you need to negotiate a price in advance.

▍ BY TRAIN

If sticking mainly to the four imperial cities—Fez, Meknès, Rabat, and Marrakesh—you're best off taking the train and using petits taxis. Morocco's punctual rail system, Office National des Chemins de Fer, mostly serves the north. From Casablanca and Rabat the network runs east via Meknès and Fez to Oujda, north to Tangier, and south to Marrakesh. Buses link trains with Tetouan, Nador, and Agadir, and you can buy through tickets covering both segments before departing.

Trains are divided into first class (*première classe*) and second class (*deuxième classe*). First class is a very good buy compared to its counterpart in Europe, but second class is comfortable, too. Long-distance trains seat six people to a compartment in first class, eight to a compartment in second class.

Fares are relatively inexpensive compared to Europe. A first-class ticket from Casablanca to Fez costs 160 DH. You can buy train tickets at any station up to six days in advance. Purchasing your ticket on the train is pricier and can only be done in cash. Kids travel at half price on Moroccan trains.

Smoking is prohibited by law on public transport, but in practice people smoke in corridors and areas between coaches.

Information Office National des Chemins de Fer ☎ *0890/20–30–40* ⊕ *www.oncf.ma.*

▍ BY TRAM

Both Casablanca and Rabat now have sparkling-new tram services, which have taken the burden off the urban buses and lessened some of the traffic crush. Tickets are easy to purchase on platforms, and announcements and destinations are provided in French and English. Take great care on the tram route while driving, as accidents are common, despite tram stoplights and on-street ushers.

ESSENTIALS

■ ACCOMMODATIONS

Accommodations in Morocco range from opulent to extremely spare, with everything in between. Hotels can be on a par with those of Europe and the United States, but five-star comforts begin to disappear the farther off the beaten path you venture. Particularly in smaller towns and villages, hotels lack amenities. Take a closer look, though—these hotels often make up for a lack of luxury with genuine charm, character, and, most of all, location.

RIADS

Book a room in or rent an entire well-furnished *riad* (a traditional house) in the medinas of the most visited cities, such as Fez, Marrakesh, and Essaouira, as well as in smaller seaside towns such as Asilah and Oualidia. This is a unique opportunity to experience traditional Moroccan architecture and live like royalty of old.

Riad Rentals Marrakech Medina ✉ *102, rue Dar el Bacha, Souika sidi abd al Aziz, Medina, Marrakesh* ☎ *0526/10–04–93* ⊕ *www.marrakech-medina.com* ⊘ *8-22:00 daily.* **South France Villas** ☎ *0871/711–33–72 in the U.K. only, 0033/467–360–554 outside the U.K.* ⊕ *www.southfrancevillas.com/other-destinations/morocco* ⊘ *9 am Mon.–Fri.* ⊘ *6 pm Mon.–Fri..* **Riad Selection** ☎ *(39) 340/60–840-14 in Italy* ⊕ *www.riadselection.com.* **Splendia** ☎ *786/216–1602* ⊕ *www.splendia.com.*

HOTELS

Hotels are classified by the Moroccan government with one to five stars, plus an added category for five-star luxury hotels. In hotels with three or more stars, all rooms have private bathrooms, and there is an on-site bar. Air-conditioning is common in three-star hotels in Fez and Marrakesh and in all five-star hotels. Standards do vary, though; it's possible to find a nice two-star hotel or, occasionally, a four-star hotel without hot water.

In the same vein, hotels that are outside the star system altogether ("unclassified") can be satisfactory.

High season in Morocco is generally from mid-December to mid-January and mid-March to mid-April. Early June, before the intense summer heat settles in, is also considered high season. In the Atlas region, January and February attract many visitors for winter sports. In the Sahara, September through November are the most popular months. Many properties charge peak-season rates for your entire stay even if travel dates straddle peak and nonpeak seasons. As with everything in Morocco, hotel rates may be negotiable; always ask if there are specials.

Most hotels in Morocco now accept email requests for reservations. A few smaller establishments and family-owned riads still require a fax confirmation. Check with your hotel directly upon booking to verify which method is accepted.

■ COMMUNICATIONS

INTERNET

Internet use has exploded in Morocco, and cybercafés are everywhere, even in the smaller towns. On average they charge 10 DH to 20 DH an hour. Wi-Fi is becoming increasingly available in hotels and upscale cafés, so it's easy to keep in touch with friends and family with a laptop, tablet computer, or smartphone.

Take the same security precautions you would anywhere with your electronics, and always use a surge protector.

PHONES

The country code for Morocco is 212. The area codes are as follows: Agadir, 0528; Casablanca, 0522; Settat and El Jadida, 0523; Marrakesh, 0524; Fez and Meknès, 0535; Oujda, 0536; Rabat, 0537; Tangier, 0539; Taroudant, 0528; Tetouan, 0539. When dialing a Moroccan number from overseas, drop the initial 0 from the area code. To call locally, within the area code, just dial the number (local numbers are six digits).

For international calls from Morocco, dial 00 followed by the country code. Country codes: United States and Canada, 1; United Kingdom, 44; Australia, 61; New Zealand, 64. There are nine digits in local numbers, starting with "0." Note that when calling from out-of-country into Morocco you always drop the "0," and the number becomes nine digits. After the zero there is a two-number area code. Numbers that start with 01, 04, 05, 06 or 07 are mobile phones.

CALLING WITHIN MOROCCO
Public phones are located on the street, and you must purchase a telecarte, or phone card, to use them. They come in denominations from 10 DH to 100 DH. You insert the card and then place your local or international call.

Téléboutiques are everywhere in Morocco. These little shops have individual coin-operated phones. You feed the machine with dirhams to make local calls. You can also make international calls by calling directory assistance or calling directly.

Access directory assistance by dialing 160 from anywhere in the country. Many operators speak English, and all speak French.

CALLING OUTSIDE MOROCCO
To call the United States directly from Morocco, dial 001, then the area code and phone number. Calls from Morocco are expensive, but rates are cut by 20% if you call after midnight. The cheapest option in direct international dialing is from a public phone, using a telecarte.

Both AT&T and MCI have local access numbers for making international calls. These are especially useful if you already have calling cards with these companies.

Contacts **AT&T Direct Access** ☎ 00/211–0011 in Morocco. **MCI** ☎ 00/211–0012 in Morocco.

CALLING CARDS
Phone cards for use in public phones can be purchased at any téléboutique, librarie, photocopy shop, tobacco shop, or small convenience store. Maroc Telecom and Meditel phone cards, to be used with mobile phones, can also be purchased in these places in denominations of 20, 30, 50, 100, 200, and 600 DH.

MOBILE PHONES
GSM mobile phones with international roaming capability work well in the cities and along major communication routes. Roaming fees can be steep, however: $0.99 a minute is considered reasonable. It's almost always cheaper to send a text message than to make a call, since text messages have a very low set fee (often less than $0.25).

Alternatively, if you just want to make local calls, you can buy a new SIM card in Morocco with a prepaid service plan (note that your provider will have to unlock your phone to use a different SIM card). You'll have a local number and can make local calls at local rates. Morocco currently has two major mobile-phone companies, Maroc Telecom and Meditel. Both offer prepaid calling cards and phone sales. A simple phone costs as little as 100 DH. If spending more than a few weeks in the country or traveling in remote spots, these are indispensable.

Contacts **Cellular Abroad**. Cellular Abroad rents and sells GMS phones and sells SIM cards that work in individual or multiple countries. ☎ 800/287–5072 within the U.S., 310/862–7100 outside the U.S. ⊕ www.cellularabroad.com. **Mobal**. Mobal rents mobiles and sells GSM phones (starting at $29) that will operate in 190 countries. Per-call rates vary throughout the world. ☎ 888/888–9162 for sales ⊕ www.mobalrental.com ⊘ 24/7. **Planet Fone**. Planet Fone rents cell phones and international mobile broadband data keys, but it has expensive per-minute rates for usage. ☎ 888/988–4777 ⊕ www.planetfone.com.

■ CUSTOMS AND DUTIES

Customs duties are very high in Morocco, and many items are subject to taxes that can total 80%. The following may be imported without duty: 5 grams of perfume, 1 liter of wine, 200 cigarettes or 50 cigars or 400 grams of tobacco. Large electronic items will be taxed. (It's possible to import large electronics—such as laptop computers—temporarily without tax, but this will be marked in your passport, and the next time you leave the country you must take the equipment with you.) It's always easier to take things in person instead of having them sent and cleared through customs at the post office, where even the smallest items will be taxed.

The importation and exportation of Moroccan dirhams is strictly forbidden. There is no limit for how much foreign currency you import; however, when leaving Morocco, you are limited to changing back only 50% of the amount you exchanged at the beginning of your vacation. This transaction will be questioned at the Bureau de Change in airports, hotels, and banks, often with the specific demand to see verification of any currency transactions made during your stay. Keep all currency exchange receipts on hand, or you may bring home more dirhams than you would like as an unwanted souvenir.

Information Government of Morocco Customs ☎ *080/100–7000* ⊕ *www.douane. gov.ma* ⊗ *Mon.–Thurs. 8:30–4:30.* **U.S. Customs and Border Protection** ☎ *877/227– 5511 for general inquiries, 202/325–8000 for international callers* ⊕ *www.cbp.gov.*

■ EATING OUT

Moroccan cuisine is delectable. Dining establishments range from outdoor food stalls to elegant and disproportionately expensive restaurants, with prices approaching those of Europe. Simpler, cheaper restaurants abound. Between cities, roadside restaurants commonly offer delicious tagines, couscous, or grilled kebabs with bread and salad; on the coast, fried fish is an excellent buy, and you can often choose your meal from the daily catch. Marrakesh and Fez are the places for wonderful Moroccan feasts in fairytale surroundings, and Casablanca has a lively and diverse dining scene. The listed restaurants represent the best in each price range and cuisine type.

MEALS AND MEALTIMES

Moroccan hotels normally serve a Continental breakfast (*petit déjeuner continental*), often included in the room rate. If not, you can buy an equivalent meal at any of numerous cafés at a much lower price. The more expensive hotels have elaborate buffets. Hotel breakfasts are usually served from 7 to 10 or 10:30. Lunch, typically the most leisurely meal of the day, is served between noon and 2:30. Hotels and restaurants begin dinner service at 7:30, though crowds are on the thin side until 8:30 or 9. In a Moroccan home you probably won't sit down to eat until 9 or 10 pm. Restaurants stay open later in the more cosmopolitan city centers.

Lunch (*déjeuner*) in Morocco tends to be a large meal, as in France. A typical lunch menu consists of salad, a main course with meat and vegetables, and fruit. In restaurants this is generally available à la carte. On Friday the traditional lunch meal is a heaping bowl of couscous topped with meats and vegetables.

At home, people tend to have afternoon mint tea, then a light supper, often with soup. Dinner (*diner*) in French and international restaurants is generally à la carte; you may select as light or heavy a meal as you like. Many of the fancier Moroccan restaurants serve prix-fixe feasts, with at least three courses and sometimes upwards of five. If you're a vegetarian or have other dietary concerns, state this when you make a reservation; many restaurants will prepare special dishes with advance notice.

Lunch and dinner are served communal-style, on one big platter. Moroccans use their right hands to sop up the juices in these dishes with bread. Bread is used as an all-purpose utensil to pull up little pieces of vegetables and meat. In restaurants bread will always be offered in a basket. Utensils will be offered to foreigners. All restaurants, no matter how basic, have sinks for washing hands before and after your meal.

Unless otherwise noted, the restaurants listed *in this guide* are open daily for lunch and dinner.

Sunday is the most common day for restaurant closings.

During Ramadan, everything changes. All cafés and nearly all restaurants are closed during the day; the *ftir*, or "break fast," is served precisely at sunset, and most people take their main meal of the night, the *souk hour*, at about 2 am. The main hotels, however, continue to serve meals to non-Muslim guests as usual.

PAYING

For price charts deciphering the price categories of restaurants and hotels, see "Planning" at the beginning of each chapter. Only the pricier restaurants take credit cards; MasterCard and Visa are the most widely accepted. Outside the largest cities you'll rarely be able to use your credit card.

RESERVATIONS AND DRESS

Reservations are always a good idea: we mention them only when they're essential or not accepted. Book as far ahead as possible, and reconfirm as soon as you arrive. Jacket and tie are never required.

WINES, BEER, AND SPIRITS

Although alcohol is forbidden by Islam, it is produced in this country. The more expensive restaurants and hotels are licensed to serve alcohol. Morocco produces some red wines in the vicinity of Meknès, and the national beer is Flag Special. Heineken is produced under license in Casablanca. Apart from restaurants, drinks are available at the bars of hotels and lounges classified by the government with three stars or more. Supermarkets like Marjane, Label Vie, and Acima sell alcohol to foreigners with proper identification (except during Ramadan, when liquor shelves are restocked with tasteful displays of chocolates and dates). Little shops in small towns also sell beer and spirits.

▐ ELECTRICITY

To use electric-powered equipment purchased in the United States or Canada, bring a converter and adapter, though many electronics these days are dual-voltage; check your AC adapter to see if yours is. The electrical current in Morocco is 220 volts, 50 cycles alternating current (AC); wall outlets take the two-pin plug found in Continental Europe. Power surges do occur.

Contacts Global Electric & Phone Directory. A comprehensive website for global electrical and phone information. ⊕ *www.kropla.com.* **Walkabout Travel Gear.** Walkabout Travel Gear has a good coverage of electricity under "adapters." ☎ *800/852–7085* ⊕ *www.walkabouttravelgear.com.*

▐ EMERGENCIES

Although pharmacies maintain normal hours, a system is in place that ensures that one is always open. You'll find a schedule of late-closing pharmacies posted on the pharmacy door or the adjacent wall. Pharmacies are easy to spot, just look for the neon-green crescent-moon symbol.

▐ HEALTH

Although Moroccan water is generally safe to drink (in cities at least), it's better to drink only bottled water and canned or bottled soft drinks to be on the safe side. Look for the blue-and-white labels of Morocco's most popular bottled mineral water, called Sidi Ali. Try to resist the temptation to add ice to room-temperature beverages. Use reasonable precautions and eat only fully cooked foods, but if you have problems, mild cases of diarrhea may respond to Imodium (known generically as Loperamide) or Pepto-Bismol. Be sure to drink plenty of fluids; if you can't keep fluids down, seek medical help immediately.

In summer, heatstroke and dehydration are big risks to travelers and Moroccans alike. Be sure to drink plenty of water and rest in the shade any chance you get. If you do get dehydrated, pharmacies sell rehydration salts called Biosel. ■TIP→ Sunscreen is widely available in pharmacies and specialty cosmetic stores but is outrageously expensive. Pack your own.

Note that scorpions, snakes, and biting insects live in the desert regions. These rarely pose a problem, but it wouldn't hurt to shake out your shoes in the morning. Dog bites pose the risk of rabies; always get a rabies vaccination at the earliest possible opportunity if you are bitten. Fez has seen an inordinate amount of stray cats within the medina. Avoid petting these cute critters that weave in and out of narrow passageways, feeding on refuse.

Medical care is available but varies in quality. The larger cities have excellent private clinics. The rest of the country depends on government-run smaller clinics and dispensaires. The cost of medical care is low—an office consultation and exam will cost 250 DH. Seeing a specialist can cost up to 500 DH. While medical facilities can be quite adequate in urban areas, English-speaking medical help is rare.

OVER-THE-COUNTER REMEDIES
Nearly all medicines, including antibiotics and painkillers, are available over the counter at Moroccan pharmacies. Aspirin is sold as Aspro; ibuprofen is sold as Analgyl, Algantyl, or Tabalon. Acetaminophen, the generic equivalent of Tylenol, is sold as Doliprane and is widely available.

■ HOURS OF OPERATION
Moroccan banks are open Monday to Thursday 8:30 to noon and 2 to 4. On Friday, the day of prayer, they close slightly earlier in the morning and open a little later in the afternoon. Post offices are open Monday to Thursday 8:30 to noon and 2:30 to 6:30, Friday from 8:30 to 11:30 and 3 to 6:30. Government offices have similar schedules.

Museums are generally open 9 to noon and 2:30 to 6. Standard pharmacy hours are 8:30 to 12:30 and 3 to 9:30. Your hotel can help you locate which pharmacies are open around the clock. Shops are open every day except Sunday from about 9 to 1 and from 3 or 4 to 7.

Remember that during Ramadan the above schedules change, often with the midday closing omitted. On Friday many businesses close down for the day or for the noon prayer.

HOLIDAYS
The two most important religious holidays in Morocco are Aïd el-Fitr, which marks the end of the monthlong Ramadan fast, and Aïd el-Adha or Aïd el-Kebir, the sheep-sacrifice feast commemorating the prophet Ibrahim's absolution from the obligation to sacrifice his son. Both are two-day festivals during which all offices, banks, and museums are closed. The other religious holiday is the one-day Aïd el-Mouloud, commemorating the birthday of the prophet Mohammed. The dates change each year, so check ahead.

Ramadan (which lasts 30 days and becomes progressively earlier in the year as the decade passes) is not a holiday per se, but it does change the pace of life. Because the Muslim calendar is lunar, the dates for Ramadan and other religious holidays shift each year.

The most important political holiday is Aïd el-Arch, or Throne Day (July 30), which commemorates the coronation of King Mohammed VI. Morocco's other holidays are as follows: January 1, New

Year's Day; January 11, anniversary of the proclamation of Moroccan independence; May 1, Labor Day; May 23, National Day; August 14, Oued ed-Dahab, otherwise known as Allegiance Day; August 20, anniversary of the revolution of the king and the people (against the French); August 21, Youth Day; November 6, commemoration of the Green March, Morocco's claim on the Western Sahara in 1975; November 18, Independence Day.

▌ MAIL

Post offices are available everywhere and visible by their yellow signs. Outgoing airmail is reliable. Note that if you mail letters at the main sorting office of any city (usually situated on Avenue Mohammed V), they will arrive several days sooner than if you mail them from elsewhere, sometimes in as little as three days to Europe. Airmail letters to North America take between 5 and 14 days; to Europe between 3 and 10 days; and to Australasia about two weeks.

For a 20-gram airmail letter or postcard, rates are 12 DH to the United States, and 15 DH to Australia or New Zealand.

SHIPPING PACKAGES

Within Morocco, the Express Mail Service (EMS, or Poste Rapide) offers overnight delivery from main post offices to major cities. There is also same-day service between Rabat and Casablanca. The international EMS takes three to five days from Morocco to Europe. DHL is quicker but more than double the price. UPS operates only in Casablanca. FedEx has locations in Agadir, Casablanca, Fez, Marrakesh, Rabat, and Tangier.

Sending packages out of the country is easy enough. Go to the Colis Postaux (parcel post office; one in each town), where you can also buy boxes. You'll need to fill in some forms and show the package to customs officials before wrapping it. Airmail parcels reach North America in about two weeks, Europe in about 10 days. DHL offers a special rate for

handicraft items shipped overseas, and some carpet stores can arrange shipping, though some scams have been reported whereby a substandard carpet is shipped to your home, so proceed with caution.

Express Services DHL ✉ *40, av. de France, Rabat* ☎ *0537/77–99–34, 0537/77–99–35* ⊕ *www.dhl.com* ✉ *52, bd. Abdelmoumen, Casablanca* ☎ *0522/23–15–23 for DHL Express Service Center* ⊕ *www.dhl-ma.com.* **FedEx** ✉ *298, bd. Mohammed V, Casablanca* ☎ *0522/45–80–41 for branch* ⊕ *www. fedex.com/ma.* **UPS** ✉ *210, bd. Mohammed Zerktouni, Casablanca* ☎ *0522/48–36–36* 🖷 *0520/33–49–50* ⊕ *www.ups.com.*

▌ MONEY

Most costs in Morocco are low compared to both North America and Europe. Fruit and vegetables, public transportation, and labor are very cheap. (Cars, gasoline, and electronic goods, on the other hand, are relatively pricey.) Sample costs are in U.S. dollars:

Meal in cheap restaurants, $8–$12; meal in expensive restaurant, $25–$60; liter of bottled water, $0.85; cup of coffee, $0.90; museum admission, $1.50; liter of gasoline, $1.20; short taxi ride, $1–$3. Prices here are given for adults; reduced fees are usually available for children and large groups, but not students or senior citizens.

Because the dirham's value fluctuates, some upscale hotels, tour operators, and activity specialists geared towards tourists publish their prices in euros, pounds, and sometimes dollars, but accept dirhams (these places also usually take credit cards).

ATMS AND BANKS

You'll usually get a better rate of exchange at an ATM than you will at a currency-exchange office, hotel, or even international bank, even accounting for the fees your bank may charge. Reliable ATMs are attached to banks in major cities, and there's one in the arrivals hall at Casablanca's airport. BMCE and Wafabank belong to the Cirrus and Plus networks.

CREDIT CARDS

Inform your credit-card company before you travel, especially if you're going abroad and don't travel internationally very often. Otherwise, the credit-card company might put a hold on your card, owing to unusual activity—not a fun thing halfway through your trip. Record all your credit card numbers and keep them in a safe place in case something goes wrong.

Although it's usually cheaper (and safer) to use a credit card for large purchases (so you can cancel payments or be reimbursed if there's a problem), note that some credit card companies and the banks that issue them add substantial percentages to foreign transactions, whether in foreign currency or not.

Credit cards are accepted at the pricier hotels, restaurants, and souvenir shops. In all but the top hotels, however, the vendor occasionally has problems obtaining authorization or forms, so it's prudent to have an alternative form of payment available at all times.

CURRENCY AND EXCHANGE

The national currency is the dirham (DH), which is divided into 100 centimes. There are bills for 20, 50, 100, and 200 DH, and coins for 1, 5, and 10 DH and 5, 10, and 20 centimes. You might hear some people refer to centimes as francs; others count money in rials, which are equivalent to 5 centimes each. A million is a million centimes, or 10,000 DH. There is usually more than one style of banknote in circulation at any time.

The exchange rate for the U.S. dollar is the same at all banks, including those at the airport; wait until you get to Morocco to get your dirhams as they are not widely available anywhere else. You can change dirhams back into U.S. dollars or euros at the airport upon departure, as long as you've kept the exchange receipts from your time of entry. The limit for this transaction is 50% of what you converted over the duration of your stay.

Currency Conversion Google ⊕ *www. google.com.* **XE.com** ⊕ *www.xe.com.*

▮ PACKING

The average temperature in Morocco is 63°F (17°C), with minimums around 45°F (7°C) in winter to above 80°F (27°C) in summer (and significantly hotter in the desert). Unless you visit in the sweltering heat of August or the biting cold snap in January, you will most likely need to pack for a range of temperatures. It's especially important not to underestimate how incredibly cold it gets in the mountains, where indoor heating is scarce. If you expect to hike and camp, pack all your gear, including a 0°F sleeping bag. The Atlantic coast is cooled by fresh breezes, even during the summer months.

Crucial items to bring to Morocco include sunscreen, walking shoes, and for women, a large shawl or scarf (to be wrapped around your head or arms for respect or your shoulders for warmth), a French and/or Moroccan Arabic phrase book (in the countryside many people will not speak French).

Don't expect to find soap, washcloths, or towels in budget hotels, nor toilet paper in most bathrooms; it's smart to pack your own, including tissues, hand sanitizer, and pocket-sized baby wipes for convenient hygiene. Tampons are rarely found in Morocco, so it is best to pack those, too.

Casual clothes are fine in Morocco; there's no need to bring formal apparel. Everywhere but the beach, however, you'll need to wear trousers or long skirts rather than shorts; tank tops, short skirts, and midriff-baring shirts should not be worn.

▮ PASSPORTS

U.S. citizens with a valid passport can enter Morocco and stay up to 90 days without a visa.

RESTROOMS

It's customary to tip the attendant in a public toilet 1 DH. Be warned that many public toilets are Turkish-style squatters. It's prudent to carry hand sanitizer, a small bar of soap, and a cotton bandana for drying your hands when traveling around the country. ■TIP→ Always carry your own toilet paper or tissues—while easy to find in stores, only hotels can be relied on to have well-maintained bathrooms.

SAFETY

Morocco is a relatively safe destination. Violent crime is rare. People who pester you to hire them as guides in places like Marrakesh and Fez are a nuisance but not a threat to your safety. Pickpocketing, however, can be a problem. In souks, open markets, and other crowded areas, carry your backpacks and purses in front of you. Cell phones, cameras, and other portable electronics are big sellers on the black market and should be kept out of sight whenever possible. Bags and valuables can be snatched by thieves on mopeds. Keep an eye on your belongings at crowded beaches, as it is not unheard of for roving gangs to make off with your stuff while you are swimming.

Female travelers—and especially single female travelers—sometimes worry about treatment on the streets of Morocco. There really isn't anything to worry about; you'll most likely be leered at, spoken to, and sometimes followed for a block. Women walking alone are targeted by vendors hoping to make a sale. This attention, however, while irritating, isn't threatening. Don't take it personally; Moroccan women endure it, as well. The best way to handle it is to walk purposefully, avoid eye contact, and completely ignore men pestering you. If they don't let up, a firm reprimand with the Arabic "*hashuma*" ("shame"), or the French "*Laissez-moi tranquille*" ("Leave me alone") should do the trick. If this still

THE FODORS.COM CONNECTION

Before your trip, be sure to check out what other travelers are saying in travel talk forums at ⊕ www.fodors.com.

doesn't work, look for a local police officer or head into a restaurant or museum.

Contacts U.S. Consulate. Check for travel alerts and other important current events direct from the U.S. Department of State. ⊠ 2, av. de Mohamed El Fassi, Rabat ☏ 0537/76–22–65 in Rabat, 0537/76–96–39 in Rabat (after hours), 0522/26–45–50 in Casablanca ⊕ morocco.usembassy.gov ⊙ Weekdays 8–5. **U.S. Department of State** ☏ 888/407–4747 in the U.S., 202/501–4444 outside the U.S. ⊕ www.travel.state.gov. **U.S. Transportation Security Administration** (*TSA*). ☏ 866/289–9673 ⊕ www.tsa.gov.

TAXES

City, local, government, and tourism taxes range between 10 DH and 40 DH at all lodgings. There are no airport taxes above those originally levied on the ticket price. The VAT (called TVA in Morocco) is generally 20% and not refundable.

TIME

Morocco observes Greenwich Mean Time year-round (five hours ahead of Eastern Standard Time), so for most of the year it's on the same clock as the United Kingdom: five hours ahead of New York and one hour behind Continental Europe. During Daylight Saving Time, Morocco is four hours ahead of New York, and two hours behind Continental Europe.

TIPPING

Tipping in Morocco is not as common as in the United States. There are no hard-and-fast rules concerning how much and when to do it. Waiters in proper

restaurants are always tipped up to 10%
of the bill. In taxis, round up to the nearest 5 DH (for example, if the meter says
12 DH, pay 15 DH). At informal cafés
the tip is normally 1 DH or 2 DH per
person in the dining party. Porters, hotel
or otherwise, will appreciate 5 DH or 10
DH. It's customary to give small tips of
1 DH or 2 DH to people such as parking
and restroom attendants. When in doubt,
you can't go wrong by tipping. It is considered normal to give money to beggars
should they ask for it. Most, but not all,
are deserving of a small coin or two.

∎ VISITOR INFORMATION

The Moroccan National Tourist Office
maintains a website in eight languages,
including English.

**Contacts Moroccan National Tourist
Office** ✉ *Angle Rue Oued Al Makhazine/ Rue
Zalaga-BP, Agdal, Rabat* ☎ *0537/27–83–00 in
Morocco, 212/221–1583 in New York* ✉ *info@
mnto-usa.org* ⊕ *www.visitmorocco.com.*
Weather Morocco ⊕ *www.morocco-weather.
com.*

INDEX

PHOTO CREDITS

About Our Writers: All photos are courtesy of the writer except for the following: Sarah Gilbert, courtesy of Ruth Cohen.

NOTES

NOTES

NOTES

NOTES

NOTES

ABOUT OUR WRITERS

Rachel Blech is a travel writer and former broadcaster for Irish radio and RTÉ Radio based in Marrakesh. While making a radio documentary for Essaouira's Gnawa Music Festival in 2006, she met Saharoui nomads from southern Morocco who invited her to visit their local festival and experience their way of life. Since then, she has juggled projects between Ireland and Morocco and now lives mainly in Marrakesh, organizing cultural tours to the southern oases and desert regions. Her company, SheherazadVentures, is run in partnership with the nomadic family she met on that first visit. Rachel also writes for *Footprint* and *Time Out* and has been published in *EasyJet* inflight magazine and *Travelspeak* magazine. She updated the Marrakesh and Great Oasis Valleys chapters in this edition.

Over a decade ago, **Olivia Gunning Bennani** left London's journalism world and headed to Morocco for a six-month trip. Since then she's been writing about her expeditions through the country and beyond, covering everything from family treks through the Atlas peaks atop a mule to the prolific verdure of the Honey Route and Paradise Valley. She lives in Casablanca with her husband and two young children. For this edition, she updated the Rabat and Casablanca and High Atlas chapters.

Fez and the Middle Atlas updater **Sarah Gilbert** is a freelance writer and photographer who calls London home when she's not traveling for numerous magazines, newspapers, and websites such as *Condé Nast Traveller* (UK), *Wanderlust*, *The Guardian*, and *The Independent*. She fell in love with Morocco in 2002 and has returned many times. A former resident of Fez and honorary Fassi, Sarah finds its history, culture, and people endlessly fascinating.

Safia Shah is a writer of Anglo/Afghan/Indian/Scottish ancestry who splits her time between Casablanca and the United Kingdom. Before settling in Morocco, Safia worked with Afghan refugees in Pakistan, almost starved to death in Germany, and spent a considerable time pretending to perfect her French in Paris. Safia updated the Experience and Travel Smart chapters this edition.

In 2012, **Lynn Sheppard** left a career in government and diplomacy to pursue her dream of living in Morocco. She has lived in the U.K., Belgium, Germany, and Japan, worked across Europe, Asia, and Africa, and speaks six languages, but it was Essaouira, on Morocco's Atlantic coast, that captured her heart when she first visited in 2001. She's now lived there for over two years, supporting local nonprofits on project management, fundraising, and social media, as well as writing for her ⊕ *www.maroc-o-phile.com* blog. Lynn updated the Agadir and the Southern Atlantic Coast chapter in this edition.

Joe Worthington updated the Tangier and the Mediterranean chapter in this edition while studying for an International Politics degree and writing for the likes of *National Geographic Traveller* and Garuda Indonesia's *Colours* magazine. Since the age of 15, Joe has been traveling far and wide, discovering places both on the beaten path and off it, where the politics of the destination is just as important as its people and culture. Morocco (especially Tangier) has left a lasting impression on Joe.